NATIONAL UNITY
AND REGIONALISM IN
EIGHT AFRICAN STATES

Africa. (Adapted from a Department of State map of November 1, 1962.)

National Unity and Regionalism

in Eight African States

NIGERIA ＊ NIGER ＊ THE CONGO
GABON ＊ CENTRAL AFRICAN REPUBLIC
CHAD ＊ UGANDA ＊ ETHIOPIA

EDITED BY

GWENDOLEN M. CARTER

CONTRIBUTORS

Richard L. Sklar, C. S. Whitaker, Jr.,
Virginia Thompson, John A. Ballard,
Donald Rothchild, Michael Rogin,
and Robert L. Hess

Cornell University Press

ITHACA, NEW YORK

Copyright © 1966 by Cornell University

CORNELL UNIVERSITY PRESS

First published 1966

Library of Congress Catalog Card Number: 66-12113

PRINTED IN THE UNITED STATES OF AMERICA
BY VAIL-BALLOU PRESS, INC.

PREFACE

National Unity and Regionalism in Eight African States is the third
and final volume of essays on individual African states prepared under the same editorship and published by Cornell University Press.
The two earlier volumes, *African One-Party States* and *Five African
States: Responses to Diversity*, appeared in 1962 and 1963 respectively.
In 1964, *African One-Party States* was reissued in an expanded and
updated form. Although the three volumes do not constitute a series
in any formal sense, the essays in each book follow the same general
outline, designed to provide a broad coverage of historical, economic,
and political information and a basic understanding of the sources of
action and distinctive features of the particular countries considered.

Together, the three volumes describe and analyze nineteen countries: one North African state, Tunisia; seven West African states,
Nigeria, Niger, Dahomey, Ivory Coast, Senegal, Guinea, and Liberia;
three East African states, Tanganyika (now merged with Zanzibar
to form Tanzania), Uganda, and Ethiopia; six Central and Equatorial
African states, the Republic of the Congo (Léopoldville), the Cameroun Federal Republic, the Congo Republic (Brazzaville), Gabon,
the Central African Republic, and Chad, the last four treated together;
and two Southern African states, the Republic of South Africa and
the Rhodesias and Nyasaland, the latter a single federated entity at
the time the study was made, but now divided into three countries.

The choice of states for inclusion in these volumes was based in
most instances on the lack of easily accessible published studies, but

v

in two cases in this present work on the belief that it was time for a
new appraisal. Thus the section on Nigeria considers the most populous African country after it has experienced several years of independence, thereby complementing the masterly basic study presented
by James S. Coleman in *Nigeria: Background to Nationalism* (University of California Press, 1958). Similarly, the section on Uganda
by Donald Rothchild and Michael Rogin, written after that country
achieved its independence in 1962, complements the stimulating and
perceptive work by David E. Apter, *The Political Kingdom in Uganda*
(Princeton University Press, 1961).

The general rationale behind this enterprise is the belief that what
is most needed at the present time for an understanding of Africa is
basic information. The singleness of aim that pervaded political activity during the rapid achievement of independence by so many
African countries has been succeeded by a natural but complicated
variety of political pressures within individual states. Until these
pressures and their effects are identified, described, and analyzed,
it is not possible to secure a broad perspective view of current developments. Hopefully the essays in these three volumes provide not
only an understanding of the formative years of a large number of
new states (and the present situation in three older ones: Ethiopia,
Liberia, and South Africa) but also essential material for the broad
comparative studies that remain the goal of social scientists.

In each of the first two volumes the editor wrote only an introduction as background and to point out factors common to or contrasting
among the states described. She left it to the individual studies and
the common outline to provide both comprehensive information and
whatever broader view and comparison was desired. In this volume,
an additional general synthesis or interpretation suggested by the
individual sections has been included. This conclusion is intended to
be suggestive rather than didactic, for three reasons: the mobility of
African political life; the difficulty of knowing what in fact is the
impact of and reaction to political and other pressures on the population outside the small urbanized and organized sectors; and the fear of
popularizing stereotyped views that may reflect only temporary or
limited phenomena rather than generally valid judgments. These circumstances must be especially respected because the countries considered in this volume encompass a wide spectrum of national experiences and of geographic and economic conditions.

Although the same general outline was used to prepare the essays for this book as for the two earlier ones, there has been reason to modify it in particular cases. Ethiopia's long history and the reflection of ethnic diversity in political organization both in Nigeria and in Uganda have required a certain variation in treatment. At the same time, all the authors have been punctilious about including the wide range of information requested in the detailed outline. Although the sections on Nigeria and Uganda have each been prepared by two authors, the smooth cooperation of the contributors has produced essays as integrated as those by a single person.

The contributors include six political scientists and one historian. The editor is also a political scientist. All have done extensive field research in Africa, and several wrote their essays while they were still in the countries they describe. It is perhaps a reflection of the primacy of politics in current African development that this field has attracted the attention of so many American specialists in the subject.

Richard L. Sklar has taught at the University of Ibadan in Nigeria and is now Assistant Professor of Political Science at Brandeis University. He is the author of *Nigerian Political Parties: Power in an Emergent African Nation* (Princeton University Press, 1963). C. S. Whitaker, Jr., is Assistant Professor at the University of California at Los Angeles and is preparing a book entitled *The Politics of Tradition: A Study of Continuity and Change in Northern Nigeria.*

Virginia Thompson is the coauthor with her husband, Richard Adloff, of two basic books on French Africa: *French West Africa* (Stanford University Press, 1958) and *The Emerging States of French Equatorial Africa* (Stanford University Press, 1960). She is Lecturer at the University of California at Berkeley.

John A. Ballard has taught at the University of Ife at Ibadan, Nigeria, and is now at the University of Ibadan. He was a Ford Foundation Fellow in French Equatorial Africa for two years.

Donald Rothchild has been Associate Professor of Government at Colby College and is now Associate Professor at the University of California at Davis. For two years he taught at Makerere College in Uganda. He is the author of *Toward Unity in Africa: A Study of Federalism in British Africa* (Public Affairs Press, 1960). Michael Rogin is Assistant Professor of Political Science at the University of California at Berkeley and has also taught at Makerere College.

Robert L. Hess has been Assistant Professor of History at Mount Holyoke College and at Northwestern University and is now Associate Professor at the University of Illinois at Chicago. He has done research in Ethiopia and Somalia and is the author of *Italian Colonialism in Somalia* (University of Chicago Press, 1965).

The editor, Gwendolen M. Carter, formerly Professor of Government at Smith College, is Director of the Program of African Studies at Northwestern University and Melville J. Herskovits Professor of African Affairs. She is the author of *The Politics of Inequality: South Africa since 1948* (Praeger, 1958, 1959) and *Independence for Africa* (Praeger, 1960) as well as the editor of several books on Africa in addition to those in this series.

In conclusion, the editor would like to acknowledge the interest, patience, and help of the staff of Cornell University Press in the preparation of these volumes and particularly of this book.

GWENDOLEN M. CARTER

Evanston, Illinois
December, 1965

CONTENTS

Contents

MAPS

NATIONAL UNITY
AND REGIONALISM IN
EIGHT AFRICAN STATES

I

INTRODUCTION

By GWENDOLEN M. CARTER

Northwestern University

THE title of this book, *National Unity and Regionalism in Eight African States,* reflects the common problems faced by all these countries in developing and maintaining their national unity against internal regional divisions and supranational regionalism. Each must seek answers to its own ethnic diversity. Most either have confronted or now confront constitutional divisions of power, either ethnically based, as in Nigeria and Uganda, or administratively imposed, as in former French Equatorial Africa. Although each study focuses on the distinctive ways in which the national leaders in each of these states attempt to maintain political stability within the framework provided by history and economic potentialities, their experience has general relevance, for many if not most African countries are subject to relatively similar strains.

The regionalism affecting national unity in Africa is of two types: intranational regionalism and supranational regionalism. Intranational regionalism refers to those divisions within a state that are sufficiently self-conscious to command local loyalty whether or not they have a defined constitutional base. Supranational regionalism refers to units embracing more than one state, such as the proposed East African Federation, or even wider pan-African plans, that may receive the support of individuals and groups within a state because they offer opportunities for improved economic growth or a stronger international position. Both types of regionalism may—although not necessarily do—vie with the national unit for the allegiance of its citizens. Moreover, both kinds of regionalism may exert pressures against each other, as when some Baganda leaders opposed the union of Uganda, Kenya, and Tanganyika in the East African Federation because they feared Buganda would lose its privileged strong position within Uganda if that country were incorporated in a larger union.

Like much else in the current African situation, the impact of intranational and supranational regionalism on individual states tends to reflect colonial experiences. Intranational regionalism is relatively weak in the former French territories mainly because centralizing French administrators subordinated the power and prestige of the traditional chiefs and largely replaced them as local agents with appointed functionaries, the canton chiefs. Supranational regionalism, in contrast, was strongly fostered by the two federations of French West Africa and French Equatorial Africa, the first of which was formed as early as 1904. Each of these federations, centered respectively at Dakar and Brazzaville, had an integrated administrative structure that embraced even the local areas of the individual territories. Moreover, when several levels of representation were provided in French Africa after World War II, the most significant political experience French African leaders received was not in their own particular areas but in the French Parliament in Paris. In the latter they developed both personal and party links of a transterritorial character, in particular through the RDA (Rassemblement Démocratique Africain), founded in October, 1946, by Félix Houphouët-Boigny of the Ivory Coast. Moreover, participation in the French National Assembly was the most effective way for Africans to exert political influence on French colonial policy until June, 1956. Thereafter the *loi-cadre* opened the way for African-controlled executive councils in each territory to share power with the local French administrators, and shortly thereafter to exercise sole control.

The personal and political links forged in Paris and in electoral activity within the federations were supplemented through the Grand Council of each federation, in which territorial representatives periodically met at the federation capital to consider a limited number of matters of common regional concern. The locus of political power and concern soon shifted to the territories themselves, a move consolidated by the transition to the Fifth French Republic, which replaced the two federations by the short-lived Franco-African Community. Nonetheless, these older regional links were strong enough to provide the underpinning for the UAM (Union Africaine et Malgache or Afro-Malagasy Union), sometimes called the Brazzaville Group, which was created in 1961 after all the former French African territories had become independent, and for its weaker successor, OCAM (Organisation Commune Africaine et Malgache) which includes the same members except for Mauretania and the Congo (Brazzaville).

Although the experience acquired in Paris and in the federal institutions had less impact in French Equatorial Africa than in French West Africa, particular difficulties in securing adequate communications and developing economic viability have led the four equatorial states, as we will see, to maintain constant although sometimes fragile links of cooperation. Similarly Niger—dependent for its outlet to the sea on either a route across its huge neighbor, Nigeria, or on the longer but more traditional route through Dahomey—builds its communications on the links established in the earlier federation period.

The former British territories of West Africa were geographically too far from one another to be linked by any plan of federation. Moreover, British empiricism and response to local African pressures helped to increase their political differences. Thus in British West Africa there was no supranational regionalism comparable to that of the French territories. Ghana's postindependence pan-African drive arises from President Kwame Nkrumah's early association with the pan-African movement rather than from any particular political experience. In British East Africa, in contrast to British West Africa, contiguous territories, held together by long-established links, seemed to provide ideal conditions for federation. Had it not been for the African fear that domination by white settlers in Kenya in the days before responsible government would be extended to all three territories, the British plans for federation might well have succeeded. As it was, East African federation did not secure the support of influential African leaders until close to the achievement of national independence in each territory, a fact that weighted the scales against a decision for closer union. Despite continued affirmations of support from groups in all three countries— Uganda, Kenya, and Tanganyika, now Tanzania—for a federation that economically could be most useful to its members, the decisive political move has not been made.

In contrast to French policy, the British both in West and East Africa had encouraged internal division by perpetuating and sometimes even in effect increasing the authority and prestige of traditional rulers. In Northern Nigeria, birthplace of the concept of indirect rule, and in Buganda, intranational regionalism has its strongest holds because it is related to local structures of authority. Intranational region-. alism in Nigeria has not only an ethnic and, to varying degrees, a local power base, but to an extent not found elsewhere in independent Africa it also has a constitutional framework which specifically divides the spheres of authority between regional and national jurisdictions. Uganda possesses only a quasi-federal structure but the degree of ethnic self-consciousness in its regions provides strong—although not necessarily permanent—restraints on national integration. Both Ghana and Kenya, it may be noted, had regional legislatures and protected regional powers at the time of independence but in neither were regional institutions able to maintain their existence.

The Ethiopian situation seems to fall somewhere between the experiences of former French and British colonies. Whereas in theory the central government has striven to undercut the role of traditional regional elements, in practice the Ethiopian government has had to recognize the existence of these strong regional pulls. Although the Emperor attempts to concentrate all power in his hands within a political framework that is highly centralized and permits only those open expressions of sentiment that reflect political unity, regionalism in fact cannot be ignored, even if it is at present unable to voice its ambitions. The Ethiopian government, moreover, has chosen to become involved in supranational regional movements with a pan-African character whose support may ultimately encourage divisive tendencies within the empire

However significant intranational or supranational regionalisms may have been at particular stages in the development of individual African states, their current importance is conditioned by the degree of cohesion possessed by national administrations and/or political party structures. The unified character of administrative or party control is one of the most common features of the newly independent African states. This strong trend toward unified control has many causes. In the period before independence the overriding objective of transferring political power from the imperial nation to local hands held together many disparate groups; so did the insistence of the colonial power, particularly of the British, that it would not transfer political control unless one national leader or group held a pre-eminent position throughout the country. Once independence was achieved the goal that dominated all others was economic development, a fact that also worked in the interests of unified control.

To maintain strong regional organizations in the face of these pressures has not been easy. The role of political opposition is a sophisticated one, much more difficult to perform than that of governing. All too often in African states opposition groups representing a particular region, ethnic group, or interest have used tactics that the government could label treasonable and thus condemn—along with those who used them. From the other side, the increasing consolidation of power in national administrations or party hands has driven some opposition groups to feel that only through force would they be able to change the policies and leaders of the country. The Western Region crisis in Nigeria, described in the first section in this book, illustrates how difficult it is for new developing countries to maintain a balance among regionally organized political parties.

In countries in which there is little intranational regional sentiment (as in Niger), or where the latter lacks political expression (as in Ethiopia), political parties may play little or no role. Mr. Hess considers that Ethiopia has a "no-party" regime, and indeed the fact that that country had no need to engage in a struggle for independence removed the customary spur to party organization. At the opposite end of the political spectrum are the "mobilizing" political party regimes like those of Mali and Guinea. Apart from Ethiopia, the countries considered in this volume belong on the continuum between these extremes, rather closer to the administrative states than to the highly politicized ones.

The interplay of the counterdemands of national unity and of intranational and supranational regionalism forms the theme that runs through the accounts of individual states in this volume. Only after they have been considered and analyzed in detail will it be possible to see how far the uniformities induced by colonial regimes are still present and how promising are the prospects for continued national unity of these eight African states.

II

THE FEDERAL REPUBLIC OF NIGERIA

By RICHARD L. SKLAR

Brandeis University

AND C. S. WHITAKER, JR.

University of California, Los Angeles

Introduction

THE Federal Republic of Nigeria is by far the largest single political aggregation in all Africa. Its population, now officially estimated to exceed 55 million, is greater than the combined populations of all other West African states.

For the student of society, Nigeria is an exciting country. Its cultural and linguistic make-up is exceedingly heterogeneous. Its potential for self-sustained economic growth is relatively great. And its political future is anybody's guess.

At the present time, Nigerians operate a constitutionally established federation of four regions. These perform vital functions and nurture powerful political parties that compete in elections for mastery over the organs of government. Thus far, political competition has been rough-and-tumble, tending, at times, to menace the very constitutional framework within which it occurs. In a way, Nigeria is Africa's India. Both countries are multilingual and both experience the political effects of a major cultural divide between their northern and southern regions.

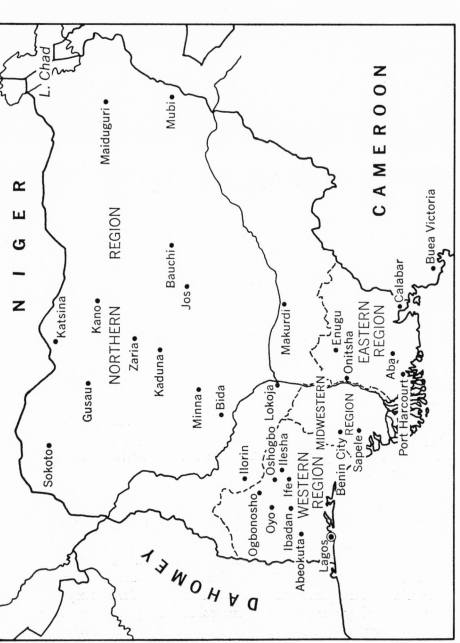

Map 1. The Federal Republic of Nigeria. From *Politics in Africa: 7 Cases*, edited by Gwendolen M. Carter; © 1966 by Harcourt, Brace & World, Inc ; reproduced by permission of the publishers.

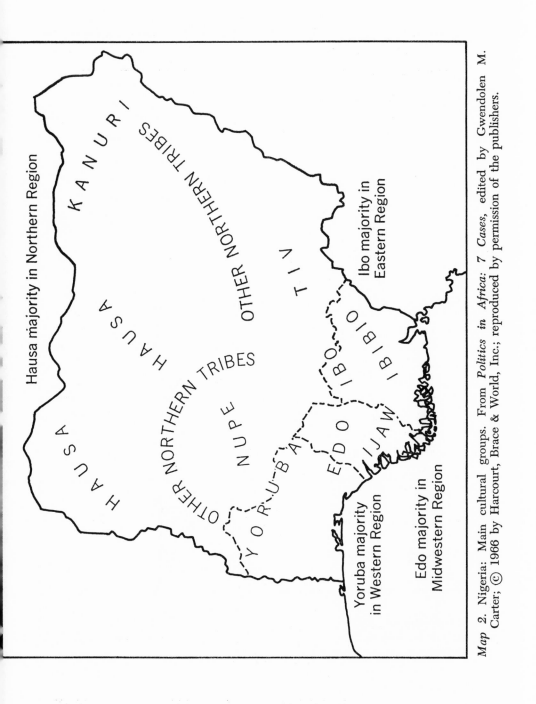

Map 2. Nigeria: Main cultural groups. From *Politics in Africa: 7 Cases*, edited by Gwendolen M. Carter; © 1966 by Harcourt, Brace & World, Inc.; reproduced by permission of the publishers.

On many counts—size, economic promise, and the sophistication of its leadership, to remark a few—India is thought to be the crucial test for constitutional democracy in Asia. For similar reasons, on a smaller scale, Nigeria presents a comparable test for democracy in Africa.

The Land

Nigeria comprises a territory of 356,000 square miles at the eastern end of the Gulf of Guinea between the fourth and fourteenth parallels north of the Equator. Its name is derived from its main inland water-way, the river Niger, which flows from the distant hills of Sierra Leone into the enormous fluvial complex of the Niger Delta. The country is trisected by the Niger and Benue rivers which join in the vicinity of its geographical center.

Geographers distinguish at least three primary vegetation zones: a coastal belt of swamp forests intersected by innumerable rivers and creeks, an inland zone of high tropical rain forests, and a northerly sector of relatively open savanna land which covers most of the country before turning, in the far north, into thorn-bush and semidesert. There is a central plateau with an average elevation of about 4,000 feet, rising at one point to nearly 6,000 feet. Here tin, columbite, and granite are plentiful. Coal is found in eastern Nigeria, limestone is widely distributed, and large deposits of crude oil have been discovered and are being profitably extracted in the Niger Delta. The distribution of complementary natural economic resources, including raw materials, water resources, and ports, is sufficiently wide to foster a desire on the part of leaders in every section of the country to preserve Nigeria as one nation.

The Political Culture of a Plural Society

Nigeria exemplifies the proverbial plural society. Within the country's boundaries, nearly 250 distinct languages have been identified, ten of them, according to the 1953 census, being spoken by groups then thought to number more than 350,000.[1] At that time, some 9.5 million people in the north were classified as Hausa-speaking; Ibo- and Yoruba-speaking peoples, inhabitants mainly of southern Nigeria, numbered more than 5 million each. These major linguistic groupings correspond to basic variations in culture generally—family and social customs, religious affiliations, and above all political organization.

Nigeria's political culture (to use the term by which political scien-

[1] Linguistic group tabulations based on the 1963 census would show marked increases, but they had not been published when this study went to press.

tists recently have come to refer to prevalent beliefs, values, and attitudes regarding politics in any given society) is actually pluralistic in two respects: it incorporates several major and divergent indigenous political traditions, and superimposed on these, it operates a set of institutions derived from modern Western society, particularly British. In a succinct discussion of the character of traditional African political systems generally, James S. Coleman distinguishes four types of traditional political systems "in terms of scale and the degree to which political authority is centralized and operates continuously through explicit institutions of government: (1) large-scale states, (2) centralized chiefdoms, (3) dispersed tribal societies, (4) small autonomous local communities." [2] All four types are indigenous to Nigeria. Thus, understanding the course of political development in Nigeria requires attention both to the autochthonous and borrowed elements of its political culture and to the particular results of this admixture in the case of each major indigenous subculture.

TRADITIONAL POLITICAL CULTURES

Peoples of Northern Nigeria

The vast Northern Region of Nigeria, extending along its interior border from 150 to 600 miles from the sea, is the largest unit of the Federation in population as well as in territory. Here the large-scale state is the predominant form of traditional political organization, although it is concentrated in the upper savanna-land portion of the region, where some thirty-odd such units, called emirates, widely varying in size, are found. Although the emirate system in fact encompasses a number of nationality groups—including such large ones as the Kanuri people of Bornu Emirate, the Nupe of Bida, and the Yoruba of Ilorin—it is identified mainly with the Hausa.

Strictly understood, "Hausa" is a linguistic term; the so-called Hausa people in fact derive from two broad subcultural components: a more ancient indigenous and sedentary conglomeration of ethnic groups whose distant ancestors' tongue was Hausa, and the "settled" segment of the originally nomadic and lighter-skinned Fulani people, whose acquisition of Hausa as a first language is relatively recent. (Reference to that first component as *Habe*—a Fulani word meaning non-Fulani—is analytically convenient so long as it is detached from its originally pejorative connotation and provided it is understood that the two com-

[2] James S. Coleman, "The Politics of Sub-Saharan Africa," in Gabriel Almond and James Coleman, eds., *The Politics of the Developing Areas* (Princeton: Princeton University Press, 1960), p. 254.

ponents are no longer readily distinguishable physically or linguistically.) Most of the existing traditional emirates were founded early in the nineteenth century in the wake of an Islamic *jihad,* or holy war, led by a learned and devout Fulani clan head, Shehu (Sheik) Usuman dan Fodio. His followers, who were mostly but not exclusively Fulani, conquered the ancient Habe states. These, together with a few newly created kingdoms, thus made up the so-called "Fulani Empire." Upon conclusion of the jihad, Dan Fodio, renowned for his code of personal humility, relinquished his temporal authority and divided the empire between his son, Bello, who became the first Sultan of Sokoto, and his brother, Abdullahi, afterward Emir of Gwandu. Each functioned as overlord of an extensive network of vassal states ruled locally by virtually autonomous emirs.

Each of the political systems of the emirates has distinctive features, but certain principles of emirate rule are general in their application. First, emirate rule is theocratic in the sense that an emir is thought to personify the Islamic fusion of political and religious authority. Second, it is dynastic: emirs are chosen from the membership of royal dynasties by traditional electors, subject to the special customary procedures of particular states. Third, emirs govern their domains through ranks of titled officials. Some traditional offices are restricted to men of royal birth and some to men of noble birth; others are within the emir's unrestricted power of appointment. Among those eligible for office, competition is keen, and its intensity is reinforced by the participation of those who stand to gain by the advancement of a prospectively more powerful patron. This implies a fourth important principle of emirate rule, namely, clientage, defined by M. G. Smith as "an exclusive relation of mutual benefit which holds between two persons defined as socially and politically unequal, which stresses their solidarity." [3]

In precolonial days clientage pervaded the system of territorial organization. Fief-holders residing at the capital of an emirate were clients of the emir; they were in turn, patrons of subordinate agents through whom they administered and exploited the subject communities within their jurisdictions. The concentration of *de jure* power and authority in the hands of the emir tended to inhibit any opposition to him, even from within the ranks of the ruling stratum. From the standpoint of the commoner emirate rule was despotic in form; his personal security depended wholly upon the uncertain benevolence of his overlords.

Elsewhere in the Northern Region traditional patterns of govern-

[3] *Government in Zazzau* (London: Oxford University Press, 1960), p. 8.

ment vary widely. The Kanuri of Bornu Emirate actually repulsed the Fulani jihad, but their own political system substantially resembles that of Hausaland. In the large lower section of the Northern Region, known familiarly as the middle belt, indigenous systems of authority range from "plural emirates" (that is, those having mostly non-Hausa pagan and Christian subjects and Muslim rulers) to the divine kingships of the Igala and Jukun and to the egalitarian, fragmented power-system of the populous Tiv. This area also contains many small autonomous communities in which "political structure and kinship organization are completely fused." [4]

Peoples of Southwestern Nigeria

The Yoruba people are believed to have settled in their present homeland about a thousand years ago. Their unity has been essentially cultural rather than political, although the city-state of Oyo does have a tradition of imperial power. Tribal legend attributes the origin of the Yoruba to a deity, Oduduwa, who is said to have reigned at Ife. The royal dynasties or lineages of the principal Yoruba states are purported to have been founded by the deified grandsons of Oduduwa. Other royal lineages stem from the major branches of the family, so that numerous kings, great and petty, reign in Yorubaland. *Oba* is the Yoruba term for king, but most kings have titles unique to their chiefdoms. Unlike the theocratic Northern emirs, whose religious sanctions in theory derive from divine delegation, obas are regarded as innately sacred because of their putative descent from Oduduwa and their identification with the mystical essences of their states.

The basic element of the Yoruba political system is the patrilineage, an exogamous descent group whose members venerate a founding ancestor. As Lloyd remarks, "the Yoruba descent group is a gerontocratic institution." [5] Its head is the oldest male member. A basic characteristic of the Yoruba lineages is their tendency to cluster, forming politically unified towns. Accordingly, the degree of traditional urbanization in Yorubaland is exceptionally high: some 30 per cent of the Yoruba people live in cities exceeding 25,000; in the densely populated administrative divisions of Ibadan and Oshun, "60 per cent of the population live in towns exceeding 20,000 inhabitants." [6]

[4] M. Fortes and E. E. Evans-Pritchard, *African Political Systems* (London: Oxford University Press, 1940), p. 7.

[5] P. C. Lloyd, *Yoruba Land Law* (London: Oxford University Press, 1962), p. 37. This section is based largely on Lloyd's discussion of the Yoruba political system.

[6] *Ibid.,* p. 50.

A key to the Yoruba political system is the distinction between the lineage head and the chief. "The head of the descent group is concerned primarily with matters affecting the group; the chief is concerned with the government of the town." [7] In many cases, specific titles of chieftaincy are vested in particular lineages. When a vacancy occurs, every adult male member is eligible for election by the members at large, with due regard for the principle of rotation among the several segments or kinship divisions of the lineage. As Busia has observed with respect to another African people, the controlling principles of appointment to office are "kin-right and popular selection," [8] subject to ratification by the king and his council of senior chiefs. In effect, the chiefs represent their lineages in the king's government or in the government of a subordinate town.

Similarly, candidates for the office of oba are nominated by the royal descent group for selection by the "kingmakers," or council of senior chiefs. Rarely is the oba regarded as the head of his own descent group. His person, sanctified in the process of his accession, and such wealth as may accrue to him by virtue of his office belong to the state. Although the personal influence of an able oba may be enormous, state policies are subject nonetheless to control by the senior chiefs who represent the major segmentary lineages. "There has always been a delicate balance of power between the chiefs who make . . . policy, and the oba whose sacred status commands such authority as will ensure obedience. If the oba misused his powers he might be deposed by his chiefs who would 'ask him to die.' " [9] In a real sense, the Yoruba states were constitutional monarchies, which effectively enforced *de jure* limitations on the exercise of power.

Pronounced cultural contrasts exist between the Yoruba and the other nationality groups of southwestern Nigeria. In the Edo-speaking kingdom of Benin lineage organization plays a relatively minor part in political structure, the primary political unit being the village. Certain chieftaincies, including the sacred kingship of Benin, are inherited by primogeniture; other titles are bestowed by the king irrespective of lineage considerations. According to tradition, the entire territory of Benin is vested in the king by virtue of his office, whereas the characteristic landholding unit in Yorubaland is the lineage. Everything con-

---

[7] *Ibid.*, p. 40.

[8] K. A. Busia, *The Position of the Chief in the Modern Political System of Ashanti* (London: Oxford University Press, 1951), p. 21.

[9] Lloyd, *op. cit.*, p. 46.

sidered, the structure of society in Benin is more unitary than pluralistic, and the traditional powers of the King of Benin are more absolute than those of a Yoruba oba. Still elsewhere in southwestern Nigeria, among Edo, Ibo, and Ijaw language groups, traditional forms of government are conciliar, with age grades and title associations playing an important part.

Peoples of Southeastern Nigeria

Southeastern Nigeria is both thickly forested and densely populated. In the Ibo heartland population densities average about 450 persons to the square mile. Ibo political institutions exemplify the pattern of dispersed tribal authority. As a rule, authority, extending to matters of land tenure, is based on patrilineal kinship groups. Typically, the Ibo village chief is the head of a specified lineage; the chief of a senior village in a group may "preside" at meetings of the village group. In some cases village-group heads enjoy great prestige, but their authority never reaches beyond the village group. Indeed, there are parts of Iboland where chieftaincy is virtually unknown, and "tribal government is thought of as the collective rule of the senior age grades." [10]

Yoruba institutions may be said to resemble constitutional monarchies; the characteristic features of traditional government in Iboland may be termed republican and, by virtue of a high degree of popular participation in the actual making of decisions, parademocratic. Prior to the European conquest, Ibo communities were continuously linked together by strong cultural bonds and intermittently linked by specific challenges to common interests. But the Ibo people, "for environmental and historical reasons," never developed permanent large-scale systems comparable to those of the Hausa or the Yoruba.[11]

The second largest linguistic group of southeastern Nigeria, including the Ibibio-Annang nationality, is Efik-speaking. In the southeast traditional governments are based mainly on small landholding villages, intervillage clan associations, and societies of titled men. A multiplicity of small, autonomous tribes, speaking many different languages, inhabit the Cross River Basin, while peoples of the coastal creeks, including the Ijaw, have monarchical traditions, stemming from

[10] G. I. Jones, *Report of the Position, Status, and Influence of Chiefs and Natural Rulers in the Eastern Region of Nigeria* (Enugu: Government Printer, 1957), p. 44.

[11] See James S. Coleman, *Nigeria: Background to Nationalism* (Berkeley and Los Angeles: University of California Press, 1958), pp. 337–338.

the once powerful states of the Niger Delta, which flourished during the era of the slave trade.

Some Political Implications of Traditional Culture

In many African societies machinery for the making and enforcing of decisions is based on the kinship structure of the extended family, the lineage, and the clan. In other African societies kinship structure is subsidiary to modes of social organization which cut across groups based on descent. Morphologically, a broad distinction may be drawn between political systems based primarily on principles of segmentation and those based primarily on principles of stratification. In these terms every society is structured along both horizontal and vertical lines, but the degree to which one structural principle or the other predominates is an aspect of political culture that profoundly influences conceptions of authority.

The traditional systems of both the Yoruba and the Ibo nationalities rest primarily on principles of segmentation. One is also a state system; the other is not. In both societies the idea of limited power, especially the refinement of constitutional restraints on executive authority, is deeply ingrained in traditional culture and may be expected to influence popular attitudes toward modern representative government accordingly. Furthermore, the traditions of both societies, particularly that of the Ibo, lay great stress on the value of individual initiative and achievement.[12] Among the Yoruba merit or achievement has always been an important factor, particularly in the selection of chiefs. Thus, the rebirth of Yoruba chieftaincy as a symbol of achieved status in the era of modern representative government suggests a process of mutual reinforcement of similar tendencies in the autochthonous and borrowed political cultures.

The political systems of Benin and Hausaland rest primarily on principles of stratification. Among both peoples the idea of a centralized state is well established. Beyond this, the two societies differ profoundly. In the Benin Kingdom age grades and title associations stratify a cohesive social order. In the Hausa emirates a sharp social division between the nobility and the commonality conditions modern political development. We shall see that the emirate system of government proved an ideal vehicle for the implementation of colonial rule. Insofar as the emirate system was adapted to modern require-

---

[12] See Simon Ottenberg, "Ibo Receptivity to Change," in W. R. Bascom and M. J. Herskovits, eds., *Continuity and Change in African Cultures* (Chicago: University of Chicago Press, 1959), pp. 130–143.

ments, high status in the traditional order and high status in the new order went hand in hand, with one result that the hereditary emphasis of traditional Hausa society persists still

A second variable of traditional culture, one that is even more difficult to analyze than social morphology, is the texture of the spiritual domain of society. The broadest distinction between texture types [13] is suggested by Howard Becker's well-known distinction between the conceptions of a sacred society and those of a secular society. Briefly, a sacred society is characterized by emphatic resistance to cultural change, whereas a secular society is highly receptive to innovation.

Insofar as the entire social system, including political authority, is sanctioned spiritually and blends with religious institutions, social change necessarily involves a profound psychological reorientation. With the development of a cash economy, the spread of literacy, and the growth of communications, new interests are perceived and differentiated from the integrated value systems of traditional society. In the process the gyroscopic tribal community is absorbed into a new and wider network of social relationships.

All African societies have experienced traumas of secularization, but these vary in the extent to which social disorganization is induced by the absorption of modern values. Most worthy of note in this context is yet another contrast between Yoruba and Hausa societies. While the presumptively sacred authority of the Yoruba oba is in the process of succumbing to new secular structures of power and authority, the principal occupants of these structures in Northern Nigeria strive to convey the impression that a religious mantle envelops them and emirs alike. Thus, there has been little popular dissociation of political and religious legitimacy in the society of the emirates.

SECULARIZATION: THE COLONIAL CONTRIBUTION

Background to British Nigeria

Throughout the eighteenth century native states in the Niger Delta and contiguous coastal areas funneled African slaves to European merchants for shipment across the Atlantic. This trade was dominated by British nationals until 1807, when it was declared illegal by an Act of Parliament. The traffic in human cargoes persisted, however, for some

[13] Rudolf Heberle has also differentiated between structure types and socio-psychological texture types in a commentary on the sociology of political parties. See "Ferdinand Tonnies' Contribution to the Sociology of Political Parties," *American Journal of Sociology*, LXI (November, 1955), 213–220.

40 to 50 years thereafter, despite energetic police action by the British navy. During this period mercantile interests shifted rapidly to the enormously lucrative trade in palm oil, ivory, and other items of so-called legitimate commerce. At first, relations of European merchants with the primary producers were mediated by the African middlemen of the coastal states. When it was discovered that a natural artery of trade, the Niger River, flowed into the Atlantic, and that the dreaded malarial fever could be prevented by the use of quinine, British companies established permanent stations in the interior. This spelled an end to the ascendancy of the coastal kingdoms. At length, Britain succumbed to the logic of territorial acquisition. A first step was taken in Yorubaland, at the coastal island of Lagos, named by Portuguese traders, for whom it had been a principal depot in the slave trade.

Yorubaland in the mid-nineteenth century was an arena of intermittent warfare between tribal states, owing in part to Fulani pressures from the north, and in part to the activities of die-hard slave-raiding chieftains. Lagos was the focal point of British policy in this area. Responding to an appeal from British missionaries in the neighboring city of Abeokuta, British authorities deposed the slave-trading ruler of Lagos. Subsequently, in 1861, Britain annexed that island and a portion of the coastal strip, hoping thereby to secure the abolition of the lingering slave trade and to promote the growth of inland commerce.

Free trade was the spirit of the age. Its strict apostles were imbued with a principled aversion to imperial adventures and the costs of colonial administration. But commercial enterprise in West Africa was impeded by the absence of political order. Undoubtedly, the time was ripe for a commercial statesman to proclaim the indivisibility of commercial and political interests.

In 1879, George Goldie Taubman (later Sir George Goldie) accomplished the amalgamation of all British trading companies then operating in the Niger Basin into a single company that was strong enough to exclude French competition. As a consequence of this maneuver, British claims to the Niger Basin were conceded by other European powers at the Berlin Conference of 1885. Goldie's enterprise was then granted a royal charter to administer all territories in the Niger Basin, exclusive of the crown colony of Lagos and the Niger Delta itself, where Britain established a protectorate.[14] In this way, it came to pass that "three separate, independent, and uncoordinated forces, centered respectively

---

[14] The Oil Rivers Protectorate, reorganized in 1893 as the Niger Coast Protectorate.

at Lagos (under a colonial governor), Old Calabar (under a Foreign Office consul), and Lokoja (under a chartered trading company), spread out from their bases and ultimately acquired control over an immense block of tropical Africa endowed with the name of Nigeria." [15]

Colonial rule was instituted by decree throughout most of the territory of modern Nigeria at the turn of the century. Goldie's charter was then revoked and separate protectorates were proclaimed in Northern and Southern Nigeria. From 1900 to 1906, Sir Frederick Lugard, a former army officer and agent of the Royal Niger Company, served as High Commissioner of the Protectorate of Northern Nigeria. There he established a form of administration through emirs and chiefs known as indirect rule, or the Native Authority System.

The Impact of Colonial Rule on Traditional Patterns of Authority

NORTHERN NIGERIA

Indirect rule in Northern Nigeria was the offspring of expediency and parsimony. The tiny administrative force and the minimal revenues at Lugard's disposal made necessary his decision to govern the vast northern protectorate through existing systems of authority. His fame derives from his remarkable refinement of that necessity into a virtue of such strong appeal that it became the sublime conception of British colonial thought. From the viewpoint of the northern emirs Lugard imposed a settlement of conquest without dishonor. In each northern province the mainstay of British authority was a senior official known as the Resident, deliberately so styled in token of his capacity as a quasi-diplomatic representative to the local emir.

In principle, however, Lugard's delimitation of spheres between supreme and dependent rulers did not detract from British sovereignty, which possessed, as he declared, "the ultimate title to all land, the right to appoint Emirs and all officers of state, the right of legislation and taxation." [16] He determined that emirs would still be nominated by the traditional electors of their states, but legally they would be appointed by the British, by whom they could also be deposed. Their powers of control over the subordinate officials of their kingdoms were restricted by law and subject to British administrative supervision. The territorial fiefs of noblemen were abolished and members of the nobility were

[15] Coleman, *Nigeria*, p. 42.

[16] Margery Perham, *Lugard: The Years of Authority* (London: Collins, 1960), p. 148.

employed as salaried officials in the newly constituted native administrations. By proclamation, in 1901, all newborn infants were declared to
be free persons and slaves were authorized to claim their freedom in
the native courts. Finally, the native courts were required to enforce
laws and regulations promulgated by the Protectorate Government, in
addition to customary laws and the edicts of traditional authorities.

These, to be sure, were far-reaching reforms. Nonetheless, pursuit of
administrative reform had to be counterbalanced against the need of so-
licitude for the prerogatives of the traditional rulers. Lugard's policy
was to preserve the emirate system and make it, in the words of his
biographer, "an integral part of the machinery of the administration." [17]

In political terms his object was the limitation and enlightenment of
autocracy, not its overthrow. It was asserted above that traditional
emirate rule was in form despotic, which is not to say that in practice
no constraints operated upon it. In this regard the crucial point that
divides the Hausa system and constitutional systems is extralegitimate
as against legitimate means of possible resistance to authority. The
difficulty in the emirates with Lugard's approach was that the very *Pax
Britannica* he imposed ineluctably removed those extralegitimate
means of resistance—intrigue and subversion, assassination, civil war,
desertion, sabotage; the result was that the British alone were in a position to influence the emir. (This development later furnished northern
reformers with the convenient argument that colonialism had deflected
the institution of emirship in an autocratic direction—an argument
which paralleled that of southern nationalists in regard to their systems
of chieftaincy, although its import was necessarily different, as we shall
see.) Lugard's approach also implied that insistence on piecemeal and
gradual political reform from above which the colonial regime's successors have observed to such faithful effect that until now the local councils of the emirs virtually have advanced no farther than the distance
between autocracy and oligarchy

Lugard's personal commitment to the centralization of power in
Northern Nigeria set him apart from those of his contemporaries who
interpreted the concept of indirect rule so romantically and doctri-
nairely as to visualize the evolution of the larger emirates into
relatively autonomous native states. Lugard declined to indulge in this
vision; he even viewed with particular disfavor the creation, during his
absence from Nigeria, of separate native treasuries at the emirate level.

[17] *Ibid.*, p. 149.

But he could not destroy the influence of an entire school of administrative thought that believed in the self-governing native state as an article of faith. Contrary to Lugard's personal intention,[18] a pattern of decentralized power, based on the principle of strong native authority, was established in the north; this too constitutes a crucial aspect of the profound political contrast between northern and southern Nigeria.

SOUTHERN NIGERIA

The northern and southern protectorates were amalgamated in 1914 as the Colony (Lagos) and Protectorate of Nigeria, with Lugard as governor-general. Firm in his belief that correct principles of indirect rule were consonant with the requirements of every African society, Lugard undertook to reproduce his northern achievements in the south. The inconclusive results of his attempt and the subsequent record of administrative failures in the southern provinces suggest that a certain kind of chieftaincy institution, on the pattern of the autocratic Fulani emir, is a precondition for the successful application of indirect rule. We have seen that the divine obas of the Yoruba states in southwestern Nigeria do not possess rule-making and enforcement powers comparable to those of the northern emirs; that rather they are subject to traditional controls by the senior chiefs who represent the constituent lineages of their states. This fundamental difference between northern and southwestern systems of chieftaincy was not immediately appreciated by the British. In keeping with northern practice, they designated the leading obas of Yorubaland as Sole Native Authorities. By this witless innovation, obas were converted into autocratic agents of the colonial administration, while the lineage chiefs were deprived of their accustomed political powers. Inevitably, deep currents of resentment were engendered among the people. These were given expression in the form of agitation for the deposition of unpopular obas and protests against policies of the government. A fairly common form of protest was antitax agitation, which illustrates another and related precondition for the successful operation of Lugard's system. In the emirates systematic tax collection had been a feature of the precolonial order. When the British seized power in the north, they merely modernized an already accepted political institution. In the south, however, taxation was introduced to support a new order, which the people were prone to regard as tyrannical and antithetical to revered traditions. It was not until the 1930's, when steps were taken to reform the

[18] *Ibid.*, pp. 480–488.

system of administration in accordance with the character of Yoruba society, that genuine progress in local administration was accomplished in southwestern Nigeria. One by one, the Sole Native Authorities were replaced by Native Authorities-in-Council, meaning that the obas were required to act once again in consultation with their senior chiefs. By the time it had been put into effect, however, the reform was too late to relieve the general atmosphere of grievance against native administration and too weak to satisfy the demands of the new and educated elite

Indirect rule, as practiced by the British, was even less suited to the character of society in southeastern Nigeria, where its successful application would have required considerably more knowledge of the indigenous system of dispersed authority than the colonial administration ever possessed. Lugard, to be sure, was noted for his pragmatic and imaginative approach to problems of local administration; but "he could not escape from the association of his system with its recurring central figure of the chief." [19] Those who followed in his footsteps were similarly handicapped. Wherever the colonial administration failed to perceive the existence of real traditional rulers at effective levels of local authority, it was inclined to create the desired chiefs by administrative fiat. These so-called "warrant chiefs" were often despised by the people. As in the southwest, deep-seated currents of discontent were prone to eruption in the form of agitation against government policies. A notorious demonstration of protest occurred at Aba in 1929, when Ibo women gave vent to their resentment against a new and widely misunderstood method of taxation. Only then did the government concede its failure and embark upon an intensive program of investigation into the social and political institutions of the region, hoping vainly to reinstate the prestige of native administration in the eyes of the people.

Nowhere did this form of administration encounter more determined hostility than among the Ibo and Ibibio peoples of the southeast. In 1948, the system was condemned by a select committee of the Eastern House of Assembly as inefficient, incompatible with the spirit of the people, and inconsistent with the nature of indigenous institutions. Even the term "native administration" was rejected as being offensive to peoples who were naturally inclined to substantially democratic forms of local government. Furthermore, a system of authority based on tribal structure was resented for its failure to give scope to the value

[19] *Ibid.,* p. 466.

of individual achievement so fundamental to the cultural tradition of the eastern peoples.

The breakdown of indirect rule in southern Nigeria was manifest in the dissonance between administrative policies and traditional political expectations and in the failure of the system to accommodate the emergent intelligentsia. Educated and progressive elements bridled at the unpopular system of Native Authorities and its incapacity to meet the changing needs of the times. Specific failings of the system and some particular objections to which it was liable have been summarized by L. Gray Cowan:

The emergence of a middle class in the postwar years brought for the first time demands for local social services far in excess of anything previously required of the Native Authorities. While these bodies had been reasonably successful in maintaining law and order and in carrying out such simple tasks as the regulation of road construction, they were totally incapable of operating the new and complex services called for in the postwar urban and rural development plans. They were unable to manage (or often even to understand) the detailed budgets necessary for the capital construction which was to be financed from local funds and governmental grants. Nor were they capable of overseeing the technical staff required to operate the new services. Many of these schemes could not be carried out without the cooperation of the people, and the Native Authorities were clearly unprepared to offer the leadership necessary to enlist popular support. Essentially the difficulty proceeded from the fact that the rate of social development outpaced a system which was designed for gradual change. Given time, the Native Authorities might have been able eventually to adjust to modern administration requirements, but the press of events made this adaptation impossible. In addition to lacking respect in the eyes of the educated minority, the Native Authorities began to lose popular support as well since they were all too evidently unsuited to the new requirements of local government.[20]

During the immediate postwar period British officials in southern Nigeria were obliged to assume increasing burdens of initiative and responsibility in the sphere of local administration in order to compensate for the growing inadequacy of the Native Authorities. "As a result, the system of indirect rule in which the district officer was supposed to be no more than a guide became more and more one of direct rule." [21] Under these circumstances, the intellectual justification for the system

[20] *Local Government in West Africa* (New York: Columbia University Press, 1958), p. 29.
[21] *Ibid.*, p. 30.

of Native Authorities collapsed. Only when that occurred, with the rise of nationalism, did it become possible for the traditional authorities of southern Nigeria to attain a new stature, one which constituted a regeneration of African society within a democratized system of local government.

Agencies of Social Change

Thus far we have been concerned with initial factors in the wide divergence between northern and southern paths of modern political development. Northern societies, meaning especially the great emirates, were culturally predisposed and historically conditioned to absorb the shocks of European conquest and tutelage without social disintegration. Cultural and historical factors also account for the greater vulnerability of most southern societies to the intrusive forces of change, a circumstance which favored the rise of relatively new and socially creative elites. Brief consideration must be given to variant responses in such social and economic spheres of continuing development as education, mass communications, urbanization, and commercial growth.

THE INTELLECTUAL AWAKENING

In 1937, a Nigerian journalist, Nnamdi Azikiwe, published a highly influential, nationalistic book, entitled *Renascent Africa*. In it he excoriated the character and consequences of the colonial-style education then available to African students, alleging that it propagated "false values which are based on the veneer of a decadent civilization"; that it enabled "the un-fits and mis-fits to thrive," and facilitated "the claims of Uncle Toms to leadership"; that it failed to engender "the moral courage which is the basis of dynamic leadership"; and that it encouraged "the existence of a privileged class of alphabetists." In short, he argued, "Africans have been mis-educated. They need mental emancipation so as to be re-educated to the real needs of Renascent Africa." [22]

Miseducation: here indeed was a telling criticism of the educated minority, especially the top echelon of university graduates and members of the learned professions, for their failure to acquire through study such pride in themselves as would stir them to desire the political emancipation of their people. For all their academic qualifications, these natural leaders of Nigerian society were nonetheless political ciphers in the colonial regime. Doubtless because of the concrete benefits to be gained, they were prone to accept political and (perhaps

[22] *Renascent Africa* (Accra: [privately printed,] 1937), pp. 134–135.

racially founded) social inequities. Eventually they were made all the more acutely sensitive about their marginality in the colonial system by nationalists, who in the end induced them to join in the fight for African political participation. Beginning in the early 1930's, leaders of the Lagos intelligentsia actively opposed the proposed institution in Nigeria of higher vocational education for medical and technical students. In the eyes of Nigerian intellectuals the proposal represented a diversion of precious talent into limited, subprofessional channels to service the need for subordinate administrative functionaries, who themselves would never be able to rise to the top within the existing system. Grievances such as this, lodging in the minds of the educated few, helped spark the political awakening in prewar Nigeria.

The extent to which a relatively small number of intellectuals, concentrated in a few urban areas, were able to disseminate political ideas among the masses of their countrymen depended largely upon the spread of literacy and the development of media of communications. These, in turn, depended upon the provision of elementary schooling. James S. Coleman has amply documented the generally inauspicious colonial record in education.[23] In southern Nigeria the actual conduct of education was almost entirely in the hands of Christian missions, to which Nigerian parishioners made substantial monetary contributions.[24] In keeping with Lugard's pledge to the emirs, Christian schools were excluded from Muslim sectors of the north, except in those rare instances when an emir specifically requested the establishment of a mission school in his jurisdiction. In lieu of mission schools the northern administration sponsored a very modest educational program of its own, tailored carefully to the needs and values of the Native Authorities. Of necessity, "thousands of southerners" were imported "into the north as clerks and artisans. . . . These small groups of educated southerners, concentrated in the sabon garis [new towns] of the northern townships, became centers of intensive secondary acculturation and the foci of the northern awakening."[25]

In 1947, there were approximately 538,000 pupils in the primary schools of southern Nigeria, compared with 71,000 in the more populous north. At the secondary level, southern enrollment was about 9,600, compared with 251 in the north. "As late as 1951 the 16 million people

[23] *Nigeria*, pp. 125–130.

[24] "As late as 1942 [missionaries] controlled 99 per cent of the schools, and more than 97 per cent of the students in Nigeria were enrolled in mission schools." *Ibid.*, p. 113.

[25] *Ibid.*, p. 140.

of the north could point to only one of their number who had obtained a full university degree—and he was a . . . convert to Christianity." [26] It is instructive to compare school attendance figures in 1947, given above, with similar figures for 1957, five years after elected Nigerian leaders were first accorded the opportunity to implement nationalistic policies of mass education. By then, some 2,343,000 pupils were attending primary schools in the south, and 28,000 were enrolled in secondary schools; in the north, primary-school enrollment had reached 185,000, and 3,600 pupils were at the secondary level. This achievement represents an investment in education proportionate to other public expenditures that few nations have matched in recent history.

MASS COMMUNICATIONS

Nigerian journalism is not less than one hundred years old, the first English-language weekly newspaper having made its debut in Lagos in 1863. From 1891 to 1931, the nationalistic *Lagos Weekly Record,* published by a Liberian, John Payne Jackson, and his son, Thomas Horatio Jackson, was a thorn in the side of British officialdom. Other pioneers of the press helped shape an informed public opinion before World War II. In 1947, a well-financed and technically superior British-owned newspaper entered into competition for the limited reading public and the services of talented local personnel. To survive, Nigerian-owned newspapers had to secure financial support beyond the proceeds of their sales and advertising revenues. At present, only one of the four English-language national daily newspapers published in Lagos is a Nigerian-owned private enterprise. Significantly, it has been supported by a Nigerian commercial bank since 1947.[27] Far and away the greatest daily circulation (over 100,000) is enjoyed by a newspaper belonging to the London *Daily Mirror* chain.

In 1959, all English-language daily newspapers (national, regional, and local) had a combined circulation in excess of 250,000, mainly in southern Nigeria, where 17 per cent of the population over seven years of age was found by the census of 1952 to be literate in roman script. Newspapers circulate much less widely in northern Nigeria, where a mere 2 per cent of English-language literacy was recorded. (It should be noted, however, that 5.4 per cent of the northern people was reported as being literate in Arabic script.) Among northern people, the rate of literacy in Hausa is increasingly high, now approximating in urban areas 20 per cent of the adult male population, primarily as a result

---

[26] *Ibid.,* p. 139.   [27] See below, p. 87.

of intensive efforts by the regional government in the field of adult education. African-language newspapers circulate in northern and southwestern Nigeria, mainly in the Hausa and Yoruba languages. In appraising the actual rates of circulation of all newspapers, their publication statistics should be taken together with estimates of the rate at which papers are "passed on" after purchase. It is thought that for every newspaper sold, there are no less than five regular readers.

Other mass media, including radio, television, and film production enterprises, are publicly owned (by the federal and regional governments). The ratio of people to radios in Nigeria is about 130:1. Telecommunication is an exclusive responsibility of the federal government; at present, there are some 50,000 telephones in use, mainly in Lagos and the larger regional cities.

URBANIZATION AND THE EMERGENCE OF MODERN ELITES

The progress of modern Nigeria is also rooted in the development of its cities. "From the broadest possible point of view the towns of Nigeria fall into two generic groups: those that are largely European-created, and those in which the urban nucleus is basically indigenous." [28] Of the great northern traditional towns, Kano City, over 1,000 years old, is both typical and pre-eminent. Situated in the heart of the groundnut belt, Kano is the leading commercial entrepôt of the north. It is also the capital of the largest area of native administration, Kano Emirate, the population of which exceeds 3 million. Each of the largest traditional towns of the north, Kano, Zaria, Katsina, and Sokoto in Hausaland, Yerwa-Maiduguri in Bornu, and the Fulani-Yoruba metropolis of Ilorin, has its traditional nucleus, its modern commercial sector, and its cosmopolitan *sabon gari,* or new town, inhabited mainly by immigrants from the south. Nontraditional northern towns, such as Kaduna, Jos, Gusau, and Minna, are commercial and administrative in origin. Their diverse populations tend to live in residential sectors based on cultural and linguistic affinities. As these towns are not entirely subsumed within the authority structures of traditional kingdoms, political impulses in them are relatively self-generated. Insofar as uncompromisingly antitraditionalist thought and activity have at all made headway in the upper north, these towns have been their depot.

The highest percentage of urban dwellers in Nigeria live in the

---

[28] K. M. Buchanan and J. C. Pugh, *Land and People in Nigeria* (London: University of London Press, 1955), p. 65.

Yoruba towns of the southwest. We have noted previously that 30 per cent of the Yoruba people inhabit traditional towns of 25,000 or more. As a result, social change in Yorubaland has involved a relatively low rate of urban growth as compared with regions to which urban life is not traditional. Similarly, the impact of secular forces which tend to produce social disorganization has been cushioned by the traditional pattern of urban society. "Yoruba city dwellers could absorb the characteristic aspects of urbanization without being physically uprooted. In short, the new economic forces resulted in the commercialization and adaptation of a relatively homogeneous and structured community, with minimal changes in social stratification, political authority, and place of domicile." [29] Yet the two principal cities of Yorubaland, which are indeed the largest cities in Nigeria—Lagos, the federal capital, and Ibadan, capital of the Western Region—have not escaped the shocks of modern urbanization; in both cities large cosmopolitan communities, populated mainly by Nigerians who are not sons of the soil, have arisen beside the traditional settlements. As might be expected, the juxtaposition has been a constant source of political friction.

The highest rate of urban growth has been experienced by the densely populated Ibo sector of southeastern Nigeria. Largely as a result of population pressures on the land, many Ibo people have migrated to urban areas in all parts of the country. The Ibo account for one-fourth of the population of Lagos and approximately one-third of the nonindigenous population of urban centers outside the southeast.[30] Of the five major urban centers in Iboland itself, only the Niger River metropolis of Onitsha has a traditional nucleus of any political importance. Port Harcourt, the second seaport and petroleum capital of Nigeria, Enugu, capital of the Eastern Region and coal-mining center, Aba, and Umuahia are boom towns which display the attitudes, values, and occupational concerns of newly emergent classes.

In all the new urban centers members of the learned professions—including lawyers, doctors, leaders in the fields of education and religion, and senior members of the civil service—rank high in the scale of political influence and social prestige. The eminence of the professional elite remains far greater in southern societies, which are predisposed to value such forms of individual achievement, than in the north, where Western criteria for prestige continue to compete with those of the established traditional order. This is apparent in the occupational backgrounds of legislators from southern Nigeria as compared with those

[29] Coleman, *Nigeria*, p. 75.   [30] *Ibid.*, p. 76.

from northern Nigeria. Coleman tabulated, for the years between 1952 and 1957, that approximately 49 per cent of the southerners were professional men or headmasters or principals of schools, while 6 per cent of the northerners were so employed, the vast majority of the latter being functionaries of native administrations.[31] Similarly, businessmen engaged in the produce trade, the sale of imported merchandise, motor transport, construction, finance, and new industries are far more prominent in the south than in the north. They comprised nearly 25 per cent of the previously mentioned group of southern legislators, compared with 6 per cent of the counterpart northern group.

After World War II, a significantly large and affluent group of independent businessmen emerged in southwestern Nigeria, where private enterprise flourished in consequence of a sustained boom in the world price of that region's principal export crop, cocoa.[32] P. C. Lloyd has vividly described the effects of the cocoa boom on people:

There seem to be few cases where all the members of a family have become wealthy; rather does one see the fine house of the prosperous man standing next to the poor structures of his brothers. Since cocoa growing is so recent most of the wealthy men of today have reached prosperity by their own efforts. The richest man in Ado-Ekiti today has an estate of approximately £50,000; he owns a shop, several lorries, two cars, many houses including the one in which he lives which has probably cost £3,000 to build. He is a cocoa buyer. Twenty years ago he was very poor, too poor, it is said, to take a wife even though he was thirty years old. He was unschooled although he now speaks passable English. His success is due to his own hard work; his story could be paralleled in many other towns.[33]

It is upon foundations of agricultural prosperity and aggressive entrepreneurship like this that a new class of wealth and intellect has arisen to seize power in southern Nigeria. Partly for reasons already suggested, a similar path of social development has not been followed in the north. Further, it is not simply that governmental and native authorities in the north were conservative in their approach to Western education. At an early stage, British authorities realized that the new functions they had introduced into the traditional bureaucracies implied trained cadres. To this end they established the famous Teacher Training College at Katsina and, in 1921, a skeleton school system in

[31] *Ibid.*, p. 380.

[32] In 1952–1953, the per capita regional products were reported as £34 in the West, £21 in the East, and £21 in the North.

[33] P. C. Lloyd, "Cocoa, Politics, and the Yoruba Middle Class," *West Africa*, January 17, 1953, p. 39.

the several northern provinces. But most of the educated minority was at first recruited consciously from the traditional aristocracy. Other recruits belonged to the class of the aristocracy's retainers, clients, and former slaves. Such men, including notably the first Prime Minister of Nigeria, later contributed to the survival of the system of native administration through incisive but fundamentally sympathetic criticism that led to constructive reforms.

From a Western standpoint, the position of the northern businessman might be regarded as equally anomalous. Merchants are mostly men of commoner origin, whose cordial but deferential relation to the bureaucratic elite has possibly been fostered by long experience with the mutual advantages of division of function. It is in any case significant that as in the new age of parties and ballots the need to have more serviceable communicative links with the masses has become apparent to the old ruling stratum, it has been quick to enlist the merchant's political participation—as a junior partner. The structure of this relationship is no doubt reinforced by the discovery of the northern businessman, as of the educated and aspiring northern young man, that conformity to the mores of the emirate system facilitates access to the portals of patronage and other avenues of advancement.

Economic Development

Recent estimates of the distribution of occupations in Nigeria indicate that some three-fourths of the labor force is engaged in agriculture, forestry, animal husbandry, fishing, and hunting. Workers in these fields produce for subsistence consumption, for the internal market, and for export. Village markets form the basis of the internal exchange system. An official profile of the Nigerian economy tells us that "almost every village has its own market and most towns are served by a ring of several. These markets, the more busy of which function daily, range from the small village type, comprising a dozen or so temporary stalls, to permanent concrete constructions extending over as much as 200 acres and having a daily attendance in the region of 15,000, such as at Onitsha, Kano and Ibadan." In southern Nigeria "women traders predominate in the market-places" but in the Muslim sectors of northern Nigeria "trading is mainly confined to men."

Agriculture alone is reported to account for some 56 per cent of Nigeria's national income and 85 per cent of the country's export trade. The principal export crops are palm produce, mainly from the southeast, cocoa and rubber from the southwest, and groundnuts, cotton, benniseed, and soya beans from the north. Nigeria is the world's largest exporter of palm produce and of groundnuts; it ranks second, after Ghana, among producers of cocoa. Most agricultural exports are handled by government marketing boards which prescribe minimum prices for the purchase of the crops from producers. In practice, these boards appoint qualified firms as licensed buying agents which are authorized to purchase specified crops either directly or through middlemen. Prior to 1954, British firms, notably the United Africa Company, took the lion's share of this lucrative trade. Since then, the boards have come under African control, and it has been their policy to license Nigerian firms (including cooperative societies) as their buying agents. As a result, Nigerians have taken over most of the trade.

The marketing-board system was established after World War II, mainly to insulate primary producers from the harmful effects of price fluctuation. A second economic function performed by these boards is the accumulation of capital. Briefly, they earn profits which correspond roughly to the difference between prices in the world market and the fixed prices paid to the licensed buying agents. Funds accruing to the boards are used not only to improve cultivation, but also to finance nonagricultural projects and, inevitably under existing conditions, to promote the commercial interests of Nigerian businessmen. What is more, the fortunes of politicians and political parties have often turned on their control (or loss of control) of these economic mechanisms, as will be amplified elsewhere in this chapter.[34]

Public investment plays a major role in the developing economy: according to current calculations Nigerian governmental bodies are expected to provide nearly one-third of the total amount of capital (£1,183.3 million) that will be invested during the 1962–1968 national planning period; close to another third is anticipated in the form of foreign aid; while private investors, foreign and domestic, are expected to provide the remainder. Such large-scale projects as the multipurpose Niger Dam, now under construction, and the proposed iron and steel industry depend entirely upon public finance. But public investment, however large, is mainly directed toward providing the infrastructure (underpinning) of the modern economy, while the task of developing its "directly productive sector" is assigned primarily to private enterprise.

Public authorities are largely responsible for the conduct of infrastructural enterprises, such as electric power production, rail transport,

[34] See below, pp. 111–117.

and the airlines. These services and the management of the port system are entrusted to federal government corporations which are expected to pay their own way. While they are subject to ministerial (and parliamentary) control in matters of policy, they operate on a relatively autonomous basis and their employees are not civil servants. There is also a federal corporation for overseas shipping; at present, however, it can handle only a small fraction of Nigeria's exports. In the field of finance, commercial banking services are provided mainly by foreign-owned (mostly British) banks, but there are also banking institutions owned wholly or in part by the regional governments. Nigerian private banks figured prominently in the nationalist movement of the 1950's, but the major ones have since been "socialized." Finally, there are several government-owned "development banks" (capital lending agencies) for the promotion of private enterprise. One such institution, the Nigerian Industrial Development Bank, is financed by the federal government in partnership with an international lending agency and private investors, mainly non-Nigerians.

Industrial production is still in an incipient state; it accounts for some 3 per cent of the gross domestic product. Extractive industries exploit minerals which belong to the state. Some minerals, notably coal, are reserved for public enterprise. Tin, on the other hand, is mined mainly by British firms, while the oil resources of southeastern Nigeria are being exploited by several international companies, notably Shell-BP, a British-Dutch enterprise. Most manufacturing and processing enterprises are privately owned, although joint state-private ventures are increasingly common. Foreign investors are encouraged by tax incentives and other inducements to form partnerships with domestic investors, both private and public.

Nigeria's total national product of more than £1,000 million ranks second, after the Republic of South Africa, in the African continent. But its rate of per capita income of less than £30 per annum is dangerously low. Average incomes vary from place to place, and long-term imbalances in the distribution of wealth between regions of the country have been politically significant. Some economic aspects of Nigeria's federal system of government are considered below.[35] No less significant a disparity in the distribution of wealth is that between high-income and low-income groups in the population. Most families hover near the so-called "poverty datum line," defined by D. G. Bettison as an income which "allows no margin for anything other than the essen-

[35] See below, pp. 48, 63–64.

tials of existence," while the privileged few live in comparative luxury on incomes of several thousand pounds a year. In the absence of compensatory taxation and social insurance, this unequal distribution of wealth is a salient cause of social and political instability.

Nationalism and Constitutional Development

Nationalism is sometimes not so much an ideology as a response to certain changing social and economic conditions. It is conceived by one discerning author as "a collective demand motivated by personal predispositions which are the results of environment." [36] In colonial dependencies nationalism is endemic to the new urban environment, where secular forces, such as education, mass communication, and commercial growth, have their greatest impact. Thus did the new Nigerian towns nurture that sense of national identity which transcends traditional perspectives. On the expanded urban social horizons, personal destinies became bound up with perceptions of a national destiny, and personal frustrations were politicized through their imputation to alien rule or foreign economic domination.

The new urban environment in Nigeria fostered nationalism for yet another reason. We have seen that cosmopolitan towns of commercial origin were unsuited to the system of indirect rule, even in areas like Northern Nigeria, where native institutions were insulated from disruptive Western influences. Insofar as the urban life of a colonial territory could not be regulated by native law and custom, European law was extended to it under the aegis of European courts. The application of British law in colonial Nigeria had its greatest effect in the crown colony of Lagos, where the inhabitants were classified as British subjects rather than British protected persons. Invariably, the possession of legal rights renders the deprivation of social and political "rights" all the more intolerable to an awakened people. The new urban dwellers of Nigeria, especially those in Lagos, came to resent deeply both the existence of a color bar to their social and economic advancement and the restrictions to which they were subject in the political sphere.

THE RISE OF POLITICAL PARTIES

Shortly after World War I, African intellectuals in the several territories of British West Africa petitioned London for the introduction of

[36] Khosrow Mostofi, *Aspects of Nationalism: A Sociology of Colonial Revolt* (University of Utah Institute of Government, Research Monograph No. 3; Salt Lake City: University of Utah Press, 1959), p. 15.

representative government and other democratic reforms. Subsequently, in 1923, a restricted number of taxpayers in Lagos and Calabar were granted the right to elect representatives, three and one respectively, to the Nigerian Legislative Council. This concession scarcely affected the power structure of the dependency, since an overwhelming majority of the Council's membership consisted of officials of the administration and other persons appointed by the governor. But it did motivate the "father of Nigerian nationalism," Herbert Macaulay, a civil engineer, surveyor, and journalist, to inaugurate a political party, called the Nigerian National Democratic Party (NNDP), in Lagos.

The NNDP did not fulfill its early promise as a vehicle of militant nationalism. Its performance in this respect was hampered by its political orientations, which were at once very broad and very parochial. On one hand, its leadership was genuinely cosmopolitan, including able men of non-Nigerian birth, who were strongly committed to an interterritorial program of nationalist action. On the other hand, Macaulay's party was constantly preoccupied with burning issues of an essentially local nature, particularly with the fluctuating fortunes of the royal House of Docemo. Unlike traditional authorities in areas of indirect rule, the descendants of King Docemo were extraneous "blue bloods" under the system of direct rule in effect at Lagos, which had been ceded to Britain in 1861. Initially astute though it may have been for Macaulay to champion the cause of this prestigious dynasty, the end product of his policy was little more than a certain popularity for the leaders and electoral standard-bearers of the NNDP. As a result, he forfeited the support of youthful nationalists who were prepared to follow more widely purposeful leadership in quest of self-government.

In point here is the bitter opposition in the early 1930's on the part of the leaders of the Lagos intelligentsia, many of whom were hostile to Macaulay's machine and to the introduction of a program of subprofessional, vocational training, which did not appear to contemplate the promotion of Africans to high-level jobs. One consequence of this protest was the organization in 1934 of an association called the Lagos Youth Movement, devoted to the propagation of nationalist ideas on educational policy. Two years later, this association's name was changed to the Nigerian Youth Movement (NYM). In keeping with its national orientation, the NYM established branches in urban centers throughout the country to become the first truly national party in Nigerian history.

But in prewar Nigeria, indeed until 1951, the organizational diffusion of a political party mattered less than its performance in Lagos, the only significant electoral arena in the entire dependency. The bedrock of the NYM in Lagos—the African intelligentsia—was a politically conscious, educated minority, prominently represented in the professions and in the business world, preponderantly Christian, and largely composed of first- and second-generation settlers, mainly from the Yoruba hinterland. Since the indigenous people of Lagos, most of whom were Muslims, were loyal to the NNDP, the NYM was obliged to recruit its mass support from the nonindigenous working class of both Yoruba and non-Yoruba descent. Among the latter, Ibo-speaking people from Eastern Nigeria comprised the largest cultural group. Their devotion to the NYM was secured by their most prominent compatriot, Nnamdi Azikiwe.

Nnamdi Azikiwe (born in 1904) had returned to Nigeria in 1937, after twelve eventful years abroad. Thanks to his father, a clerk in the Nigerian Regiment, young Azikiwe had been educated in a few of the finest schools of his day in various parts of Nigeria. As a student in the burgeoning towns of Nigeria and, subsequently, as a junior clerk in the civil service, Azikiwe experienced the indignation common among his racially sensitive, anticolonial peers. Ambitiously, he resolved to seek higher education in the United States. During his first years in America he underwent poverty and other hardships; eventually he earned an M.A. at Lincoln University in Pennsylvania, where he was employed as an instructor in political science, an M.Sc. in anthropology at the University of Pennsylvania, and a certificate in journalism at Teachers College, Columbia University. In 1934, he became editor of a daily newspaper in Accra, now the capital of Ghana, and in 1937, he was prosecuted by the Gold Coast government for the publication of an allegedly seditious article. Following the reversal of his conviction on appeal, Azikiwe returned to Nigeria to inaugurate in Lagos his famous daily newspaper, *West African Pilot;* its masthead featured the motto: "Show the light and the people will find the way."

Rapidly he became "the most important and celebrated nationalist leader on the West Coast of Africa, if not in all tropical Africa." [37] He joined the NYM but clashed with its leaders; probably their decision to publish a rival newspaper had a divisive effect. Azikiwe's resignation from the NYM in 1941 cost that party dearly in mass support as it set the stage for political cooperation between the indigenous and nonindigenous masses of Lagos.

[37] Coleman, *Nigeria*, p. 220.

Radical Nationalism: The National Council of Nigeria and the Cameroons

In 1944, nationalistic youth associated with the Nigerian Union of Students persuaded Nnamdi Azikiwe to join with Herbert Macaulay in the formation of a national front, which became the National Council of Nigeria and the Cameroons (NCNC). Macaulay was elected president, Azikiwe became general secretary. All existing nationalistic associations (which included trade unions, professional groups, associations based on ethnic affinity, and political parties) were invited to affiliate with the National Council, but the NYM, sensing that affiliation implied subordination to its antagonists, declined. Soon its authority within the nationalist movement was eclipsed by the more aggressive and broadly representative NCNC.

Within a year of its inauguration, the NCNC had embarked upon a campaign to compel the revision of a postwar constitution which fell far short of nationalist demands for democratic representation and responsible government. Repugnant though it may have been to nationalist opinion, the "Richards Constitution" (so-called for Sir Arthur Richards, then Governor of Nigeria) marked the beginning of a new era. It created semilegislative bodies in each of three governmental regions, the North, the East, and the West, based on elections from the local native administrations. In turn, the regional legislatures were empowered to choose from among their members representatives to the central Legislative Council, which would include northern members for the first time. The heart of this constitution was its contemplation of a link between newly created parliamentary institutions and previously existing native authority councils, in which traditional rulers were dominant. In support of this plan, official spokesmen argued in the idiom of Lugard that the new constitution was rooted in the indigenous institutions of the country and that it gave expression to the "real" interests of historic African communities.

This notion was tied up with the belief that a culturally plural dependency like Nigeria should not be regarded as an authentic nation. From this it followed that the nationalistic minority, centered in a few towns, could not pretend to represent interests other than its own, the only true representatives of the people being those chosen by and from traditional communities "in accordance with custom."

In rebuttal to this colonial doctrine, nationalists invoked the principle of popular sovereignty, demanding democratic elections based on universal suffrage. The NCNC, in particular, also condemned the constitution's prescription of regionalization, or the creation of separate regional governments in the southeast and the southwest in addition to a government in the north. Although the NCNC favored the creation of eight or more states in Nigeria, based on the principle of cultural and linguistic affinity, it viewed the triregional setup as a British attempt to perpetuate powerful artificial divisions inimical to the nationalist cause.

In 1946, leaders of the NCNC toured Nigeria to obtain a popular mandate for a delegation that would present the nationalist case to the Colonial Office in London. At the conclusion of this highly successful tour, the NCNC took advantage of the long-standing electoral privileges of taxpayers in Lagos to demonstrate the extent of its popular support in the national capital. Fortified by the resounding majorities that elected Azikiwe and two of his lieutenants to the Nigerian Legislative Council, the NCNC delegation proceeded to London. On the eve of its departure, Azikiwe was elected to the presidency of the NCNC, succeeding the "grand old man," Herbert Macaulay, who had died during the tour across Nigeria.

Although the NCNC delegation failed to win an immediate concession from the Secretary of State for the Colonies, its exertions were instrumental in persuading British officials to initiate a policy of reform, leading to the constitution of 1951. Starting in 1948, conferences on constitutional reform were organized by administrative officials at village, provincial, and regional levels, culminating in a General Conference at Ibadan in 1950. As James S. Coleman has observed, "There can be little doubt that the method of constitutional revision did in fact give heavy weight to rural and traditional elements and minimized the influence of urban, educated, and nationalist elements." [38] Predictably, this method of revision was objectionable to most radical nationalists, who wanted an elected constituent assembly. But it was a popular method in the country at large; it absorbed the political energies of the nation and appears to have been responsible for the temporary decline of the NCNC.

Hoping to rejuvenate the NCNC and to impel it on a new course of militant, even revolutionary action, youthful followers of Azikiwe banded together in the Zikist Movement, an autonomous youth wing of the party.[39] Zikists shrewdly saw in the regionalization of Nigeria the

[38] *Ibid.*, p. 312.
[39] Zikism was the conception of A. A. Nwafor Orizu, a Nigerian student in the

prospect of ethnic rivalries, engendered by the alignment of each regional government with one of the major cultural nationalities. Overtly repudiating British rule in Nigeria, Zikist spokesmen instead affirmed loyalty to the NCNC as virtually a rival government under the headship of Azikiwe. The specific tactics of "positive action" adopted by the Zikist Movement, however, were not always endorsed by Azikiwe himself, who at this time eschewed revolutionary action. Consequently, the Zikist Movement adopted an increasingly independent course of action. In 1950, it was banned by the government for pursuing allegedly seditious aims by unlawful means. But its name and its distinctive radical spirit have survived in succeeding youth wings of the NCNC.

Cultural Nationalism: The Action Group

After its affiliation with the NCNC in 1944, the NNDP regained electoral supremacy in Lagos. This development was distressing to a great many leaders of social, economic, and intellectual life in Lagos, especially men of Yoruba descent who were loyal to the NYM. Unless they could devise some way to recapture the political initiative, it appeared virtually certain that the NCNC, under Azikiwe, would come to power in Western Nigeria. For the purposes of these NCNC opponents, a useful focus of activity was a pan-Yoruba cultural organization, called the *Egbe Omo Oduduwa* ("Society of the Descendants of Oduduwa"—the mythical progenitor and culture-hero of the Yoruba people).

This society had been organized by students in London in 1945. Its moving spirit was an able law student of humble birth, Obafemi Awolowo (born in 1909), previously a leader of the NYM at Ibadan. In London Awolowo wrote an influential book, entitled *Path To Nigerian Freedom,* the theme of which appealed strongly to many of his Yoruba compatriots and others of similar persuasion. His basic observation was that each one of the cultural nationalities of Nigeria possesses its own indigenous constitution, conforming to the cultural traditions of the people concerned. These African "constitutions," he explained, had been distorted or corrupted by alien rule, as evidenced by the despotization of the Yoruba monarchies. Properly speaking, he argued, the constitution of each cultural nationality should be its own "domestic concern." Every such nationality is entitled to and should be

United States during World War II. His book, *Without Bitterness, Western Nations in Post-War Africa* (New York: Creative Age Press, 1944), called for the social, economic, and political redemption of Africa in the spirit of Azikiwe's earlier work, *Renascent Africa.*

encouraged to develop its own political institutions within the framework of a Nigerian federation. Furthermore, he insisted on the "natural right" of the educated minority of each cultural group "to lead their fellow nationals into higher political development." [40]

The sum of Awolowo's ideas was political reform at the local level, political unity at the cultural level, federalism at the national level, and the assumption of leadership within each cultural group by its educated minority; these provided an intellectual program for political action by the Yoruba elite. In theory, the program was inconsistent with a constitution like that of 1946, which left the major nationalities in a position to dominate smaller cultural groups. In reality, however, as members of a major nationality group, Yoruba leaders sought to reconcile the principles enunciated by Awolowo with that constitution. For they perceived that regionalism would enable their group to secure its own political interests pending the institution of an ideal federation of culturally homogeneous states at some future time. In years to come, the supporters of Awolowo's political program in Western Nigeria were to be haunted by their unresolved ambivalence on the question of regional power.

In 1948, a conference attended by eminent Yoruba personalities inaugurated the *Egbe Omo Oduduwa* in Nigeria. Throughout Yorubaland important obas and other prominent chiefs were persuaded to become patrons and members of this society, which gained prestige as a mediator of disputes among chiefs and between chiefs and their communities. As a center of cooperation on the part of the natural leaders of Yorubaland—the intellectuals, the businessmen, and the chiefs—the Society might have developed as a fully political organ. But its more youthful and militant nationalist wing considered that the membership of the Society was too conservative and too closely identified with social and official respectability to formulate and put into effect a proper political program. Under the leadership of Obafemi Awolowo, now general secretary of the Society and a barrister in Ibadan, this wing organized a political party which they called the Action Group (AG).

Undoubtedly the AG was at first the political wing of the Society of the Descendants of Oduduwa. AG leaders have always regarded the Society, in its political aspects, as an instrumentality of the party, subject to party control. Inasmuch as the AG had been organized expressly to achieve power in the Western Region, its operational sphere ex-

[40] *Path to Nigerian Freedom* (London: Faber, 1947), pp. 53–54, 64.

tended beyond Yorubaland to the non-Yoruba provinces of the midwest. At an early stage, steps were taken to organize a midwest section
of the party, which could then represent itself as a Western regional
organization, pledged to cooperate with all associations founded on
ethnic affinity in that region.

Regional Nationalism: The Northern Peoples' Congress and the
Northern Elements Progressive Union

At the General Conference on Review of the Constitution, held at
Ibadan in early 1950, Northern delegates disagreed sharply with their
Eastern and Western counterparts on several important issues. For
one, the southerners were determined to demand ministerial responsibility in the regional and central governments, an advance toward self-
government that the northerners, with more than an eye toward the
sensibilities of the influential emirs, were not as yet prepared to make.
Secondly, with respect to fiscal policy, northern delegates pressed for
the distribution of central revenues to the regions on a per capita basis,
while southerners preferred other principles, more beneficial to themselves, such as regional need or volume of trade. And, in the most
crucial area of disagreement, northerners invoked the population principle to demand, and eventually to win, 50 per cent representation in
the proposed central legislature. During the course of these debates
and negotiations, northern leaders recognized the need for a permanent political organization to protect their constitutional and parliamentary interests.

Before 1950, independent political activity was relatively inconse-
quential in the northern provinces. Educational backwardness in
comparison with southern Nigeria and the authoritarian political tradition in areas of emirate rule operated to inhibit assertive nationalism.
Protopolitical groups in the North were first organized by educated
youth in the employ of both government and native administration
public services. Most of these young men were either born into the ruling class or were closely associated with it; nearly all of them had been
exposed to nationalist thought from southern Nigeria and abroad. The
earliest potential political interest group in the North was the College
Old Boys Association, organized in 1939–1940 by graduates of the only
secondary school in the entire region, Kaduna College, and its predecessor, the famed Teacher Training College at Katsina. Although the
"old boys" were at most moderate reformers, their organization incurred the disapproval of certain emirs and British officials, and as a

result it was disbanded within two years of its inauguration. Subsequent groups, such as the General Improvement Union at Bauchi, the Youth Social Circle at Sokoto, and the Friendly Society at Zaria, were also subjected to crippling official surveillance on the plausible ground that any association of educated men for the purpose of serious discussion was potentially subversive to the northern political system. Then, in 1948, a group of civil servants and educated employees of native administrations, resident in Zaria and Kaduna, resolved to form a society to promote the modernization of northern institutions. In 1949, a conference attended by delegates from several provinces inaugurated "a social and cultural organization," called in Hausa the *Jam'iyyar Mutanen Arewa*, "The Northern Peoples' Congress." The commitment of this society to political reform was implicit in its declaration of intention: to war against ignorance, idleness, and oppression.

The composition of the Congress' membership meant that an open declaration of the organization as a political party was neither prudent nor, in fact, feasible. Regulations prohibiting political activity by civil servants were then in force, and the employees of native administrations were similarly vulnerable to pressures exerted by traditional authorities. Yet members of the Congress were motivated by at least one purpose which aroused no objection from traditional or governmental authorities: they were determined to exclude southerners from political leadership in the north, and to ensure that the inevitable movement for self-government in the Northern Region would proceed with an appreciation for northern institutions and traditions

Organized radicalism in the Northern Region appeared first at Kano in 1946, in the form of the Northern Elements Progressive Association (NEPA). Unlike the founders of the College Old Boys Association and of its derivative, the Northern Peoples' Congress (NPC), the NEPA members were, with few exceptions, men of low traditional status, employed as junior functionaries (mostly clerks) by the government or commercial firms. The sector of the Northern Region not under emirate rule was conspicuously represented in the group. Furthermore, a few leaders of the NEPA were closely associated with the southern-based NCNC; indeed the general secretary of the NEPA was also president of the Zikist Movement.

In time the NEPA was undermined by official hostility, as manifested in the discharge or transfer of key leaders from their government jobs in Kano. But its spirit was reborn at Kano with the inauguration of the first avowed political party in Northern Nigeria—the Northern Elements Progressive Union (NEPU), organized in 1950 by youthful radicals of commoner origin. A "Declaration of Principles" issued by the NEPU bluntly proclaimed the existence of a "class struggle" between those who controlled the native administrations and the "ordinary *Talakawa*" (commoner class).

Ostensibly, the NEPU had been organized to function as a political vanguard within the broader, more conservative NPC. By 1950, however, moderate northern leaders looked forward to readapting the NPC as a political party. At the second annual convention of the NPC in December, 1950, moderate aims were promoted by the passage of a resolution that forbade members of the NPC to hold membership in the NEPU as well. Furthermore, persons identified with the NEPU, including Aminu Kano, were excluded from membership in the central executive committee of the NPC.

Alhaji Aminu Kano (born in 1921) belongs to a prominent Kano Fulani family, noted for its juristic and scholarly traditions. He attended Kaduna College and began his career in teaching at the Bauchi Middle School. There he made his reputation as a nationalist and a critic of the system of native administration. In 1946, he was awarded a government scholarship to attend the University of London Institute of Education. Upon his return to Nigeria in 1948, he organized the highly influential Northern Teachers' Association and participated in the founding of the NPC. He was appointed headmaster of a teacher training college in Sokoto, but his increasingly overt commitment to political radicalism seemed inconsistent with his professional career. In 1950, he resigned from the education service and plunged into the political ferment at Kano.

The constitution of 1951 provided for indirect elections to the regional houses of assembly. Elections in the North were initiated by open voting in some 20,000 villages and ward areas at the primary stage. To the dismay of conservatives, prominent officials of certain native administrations, whose candidatures were supported by emirs, suffered defeat at the hands of NEPU candidates at the primary and intermediate stages. Ultimately, all the NEPU candidates were defeated, since the electoral regulations in force empowered emirs and other Native Authorities to "inject" into the final electoral colleges at provincial levels additional members equal to 10 per cent of the elected membership. This device augmented the susceptibility of these relatively small groups of electors to the influence of their traditional rulers and produced some curious results. In Kano, for example, not one of the twenty persons elected to the Northern House of Assembly by the final college had been chosen by the voters at lower stages; in fact, ten of them had actually been defeated in balloting prior to their "injection" into the provincial college by the Emir of Kano.

This experience finally persuaded moderately conservative northern leaders to convert the NPC immediately into a political party. In keeping with governmental regulations, members of the civil service were required to resign from the Congress, but spokesmen for and officials of the native administrations joined it in greater numbers. Among these new members were the two most prominent political personalities in the North, Ahmadu Bello and Abubakar Tafawa Balewa.

Alhaji Sir Ahmadu Bello, the Sardauna of Sokoto (born in 1910), is a lineal descendant of Shehu Usuman dan Fodio, founder of the Fulani empire, and his son, the first Sultan of Sokoto. Sir Ahmadu's grandfather was a Sultan of Sokoto, and it is widely known that he aspires to succeed his elder cousin, the incumbent Sultan. It is to be noted that the Sultan is the pre-eminent spiritual leader of Hausaland as well as the executive head of the Sokoto Native Authority.

In his youth, Sir Ahmadu attended the Teacher Training College at Katsina. Subsequently, he taught English and mathematics at the Sokoto Middle School until his appointment as District Head of Rabah, the office formerly held by his father. In 1938, Ahmadu was a candidate for the sultancy. Following the selection of his cousin, Ahmadu was appointed to the Sultan's Council with the title of Sardauna (literally, "Commander of the Bodyguard"). In time he became one of the most influential administrative councilors in Sokoto, and in 1949, he was chosen to represent his province in the regional legislature. When the newly-elected Northern House of Assembly met in 1952, an overwhelming majority of its members, elected with the support of traditional authorities, acknowledged the Sardauna's leadership and declared for the NPC.

In 1950, the outstanding political figure in Northern Nigeria was undoubtedly Abubakar Tafawa Balewa, then representative for Bauchi Province in the Northern House of Asembly. The future Prime Minister of Nigeria was born in 1912 into a very humble Muslim family in the village of Tafawa Balewa, from which he takes his name. Bauchi legend has it that Abubakar, like several other prominent northerners, was enrolled in primary school as the son of a district head who preferred not to expose his own blood issue to European education. Eventually, Abubakar attended the Teacher Training College at Katsina,

where he met the future Sardauna of Sokoto. Shortly after his graduation, he became headmaster of the Bauchi Middle School; Aminu
Kano, the future leader of the NEPU, was a member of his staff. In
1945, Abubakar was chosen to study for a teacher's professional certificate at the London University Institute of Education. Returning to
teach in Bauchi, he was also appointed to the council of the emir. He
was chosen to represent Bauchi in the Northern House of Assembly,
and elected by that body in turn as a northern member of the Nigerian
Legislative Council. At a meeting of the Legislative Council in 1947, he
disputed the claim of the NCNC London delegation to speak for all
Nigeria, expressing his own view that independence would not be
feasible until a significantly greater measure of national unity had been
achieved.

In August, 1950, Abubakar delivered an historic speech in the Northern House of Assembly, condemning the archaic, autocratic, and exploitative aspects of native administration, and calling for the appointment of a commission to study the system with a view to its reform.
Specifically, he urged the abolition of the office of Sole Native Authority, which permitted its holder, normally an emir, to exercise power
without consulting the Native Authority Council. All but one of the
African members of the Northern House of Assembly voted for
Abubakar's motion, which passed by a single vote over the disapproval
of the official block to usher in a period of reform. Yet Sir Abubakar
appears to have been singled out as a target of resentment by conservative emirs, some of whom tried without success to prevent his
election to the Northern House of Assembly in 1951.

THE NEW NATION

The Breakdown of Unitary Government

While the Nigerian constitution of 1951 did have a few federal
features, these did not obscure its essentially unitary character. Like its
predecessor, this constitution required the regional houses of assembly
to elect a specified number of their members to a central House of
Representatives. Though demarcating a broad area for regional legislative initiative, it gave unlimited legislative authority to the central
legislature and provided further that regional laws could not be enacted without the approval of the central Council of Ministers. In other
words, the constitutionality of regional legislation was subject to
determination by the central executive. These arrangements were

resented by Nigerian leaders who entered the regional governments in 1952.

Under this constitution Nigerians were appointed to ministerial office in the regional and central governments for the first time. These ministers, however, were not collectively responsible to their respective legislatures; their appointments were revokable only on an individual basis by a two-thirds vote of the legislature concerned. All executive councils included official, that is, British members, headed by a governor at the center and lieutenant governors in the regions.

We have seen that in 1952 an overwhelming majority of the elected members of the Northern House of Assembly acknowledged the leadership of the Sardauna of Sokoto and declared for the NPC. Similarly, in Eastern Nigeria, all but a few of the elected members of the House of Assembly accepted invitations from Dr. Azikiwe to join the NCNC Eastern Parliamentary Party. Azikiwe himself stood for the Western House of Assembly from Lagos, where the electoral position of the NCNC/NNDP had been strengthened by the introduction of universal adult suffrage for direct elections. Resigned to the probability of an NCNC victory in Lagos, the newly formed Action Group decided to outmaneuver Azikiwe in the provincial constituencies, where the electoral-college system still obtained. To implement this strategy, prominent members of the AG, normally resident in Lagos or Ibadan, returned to their native towns and villages to solicit the support of chiefs and other local dignitaries. By and large, the Yoruba chiefs reconciled themselves to the march of democratic reforms. Having endorsed a program of cultural unity sponsored by the Society of the Descendants of Oduduwa, the chiefs were on the whole responsive to the appeal of its political offspring, the AG. In return for political support, the AG assured the chiefs that it would dignify and preserve the institution of chieftaincy under African rule.

When the Western House of Assembly met in January, 1952, it was apparent that the AG maneuver had been successful. A decisive majority of the elected assemblymen declared for that party, enabling its leader, Obafemi Awolowo, to organize the Western regional government. Moreover, the AG majority capitalized on a flagrant breach of party discipline among NCNC assemblymen elected from Lagos to bypass Azikiwe in choosing the requisite numbers to sit in the central House of Representatives. NCNC leaders had been prepared for an AG victory in the West, but they had not foreseen the exclusion of their national president from the central government. Utterly exasperated, militant members of the party resolved with greater determination than ever to overthrow the constitution, which they had condemned in any case for its failure to provide for democratic representation and responsible government.

In the Eastern Region, however, members of the NCNC government displayed a more conservative mood. Nearly all the Eastern regional ministers, supported by NCNC ministers in the central government, were inclined to give the constitution of 1951 a "fair trial," despite the determination of extraparliamentary leaders of their party to "break" it as rapidly as possible. At stake was the authority of the national president vis-à-vis the parliamentary leaders of the party. At length, several ministers in the regional and central governments were expelled for failing to "toe the party line." But the expelled Eastern ministers decided to abide by the letter of the constitution, and refused to resign from office when the Eastern House of Assembly passed a simple vote of no confidence in the Eastern government. Thereupon, a majority of the NCNC assemblymen, supporting the national leadership of their party, paralyzed the Eastern government by voting to defeat or defer every bill before the House of Assembly. Since the constitution provided that dissolutions of the central and regional legislatures had to occur simultaneously, the Eastern deadlock could not be resolved by means of a normal dissolution, and the lieutenant governor of the East was compelled to use his reserve power of legislation to enact the bill for regional appropriations

Prior to the elections of 1951, the NCNC had revised its constitutional goal from federalism to unitary government, in order to offset the regional separatist tendencies of the other parties and safeguard the ideal of "One Nigeria." During the Eastern crisis the AG and the NPC, both of which were regionally based and receptive to proposals for regional autonomy, explored the possibility of collaboration in the regions and at the center. But the AG, a more overtly nationalistic party than the NPC, was engaged in a bitter dispute with the colonial administration on matters of policy in the Western Region. As a result, its hostility to the constitution matched that of its rival, the NCNC. In March, 1953, an AG member of the House of Representatives filed a motion which called for the attainment of national self-government in 1956. Both the AG and the NCNC supported this motion fully, but the northern representatives, comprising 50 per cent of the membership of the House, were unwilling to set a specific date until preparations for self-government were considerably more advanced in the Northern Region. In the face of a northern attempt to postpone debate on the motion for self-government, the AG and the NCNC members walked out of the House of Representatives. On a subsequent motion to adjourn, the Sardauna of Sokoto observed: "The mistake of 1914 has come to light and I should like to go no further." This, of course, was an allusion to the amalgamation of Northern and Southern Nigeria under Lugard

Subsequently, the Northern regional legislature adopted a resolution which called for the abolition of the central legislature and the reorganization of Nigeria as a loose association of autonomous regions. In these bleak circumstances, with the unity of Nigeria in question, representatives of the political parties met with colonial officials in London to frame a new constitution.

The Federal Solution

The constitution of 1954 established a genuinely federal form of government. It assigned exclusive responsibility for the discharge of certain functions to the federal government; other functions were included in a concurrent (federal-regional) legislative list, subject to the proviso that in cases of conflict federal law would prevail; residual functions were reserved to the regions. Provision was made for the establishment of regional judiciaries and regional public services alongside their federal counterparts. Delegates to the all-party conference which framed this charter agreed that the majority party leader in each regional legislature would be appointed to the office of Premier; that separate elections would be held for the federal legislature, although uniformity of electoral procedures among the regions would not be required; that the North would continue to have 50 per cent membership in the central (henceforth "federal") House of Representatives; and that federal ministers would still be appointed in equal number from the regions. It was further decided that a conference to review the constitution would be convened within three years, and that internal self-government would be granted to any region requesting it in 1956.

These agreements, which preserved the unity of Nigeria, were reached in a spirit of compromise. The NCNC retracted its demand for unitary government, agreeing to an American or Australian type of federal constitution, which would provide for the reservation of residual powers to the regions. The NPC gave up its demand for extreme regional autonomy, without conceding anything, however, on the pace of advance toward self-government. The AG, which had consistently favored a federal solution, gained most from the fiscal arrangements which were devised to buttress the new federal structure. These provided for the allocation of revenue to the regions mainly in accordance with the principle of derivation; that is, insofar as possible, revenues were returned to the region of origin. Given the relatively great revenue derived from the export of cocoa, grown mainly in the Western Region, the AG reaped an immediate financial benefit relative to the other major parties. But the AG was, with difficulty, persuaded to accept the separation of Lagos from the Western Region and its designation as a federal territory, in accordance with the views of other parties.

SUBREGIONAL SEPARATISM

Ever since 1943, when Azikiwe published his *Political Blueprint for Nigeria,* nationalists generally have supported the reorganization of Nigeria into a larger number of states based on the criteria of cultural and linguistic affinities; and, as previously observed, the AG convictions on territorial organization were at odds with the existing triregional set up. On the other hand, leaders of the NPC were, for important reasons, determined to preserve the political unity of the Northern Region. Plainly stated, the NPC could not expect to retain political control of minority areas which might secede from the North. This would entail a considerable reduction of NPC strength in the central legislature, in which case it would be very difficult to allay northern fears of southern domination.

Separatism in the North has been a factor of political importance in the so-called "middle belt" or southerly provinces of the region, an area inhabited by multifarious ethnic and linguistic groups totaling some one-third of the region's population. Together, these numerous groups constitute a cultural and social minority vis-à-vis the people of the emirate state systems of the upper North in that they are predominantly non-Muslim (animist and Christian) and natively not Hausa-speaking peoples, most of whom have histories and traditions which favor small-scale or highly decentralized, parademocratic forms of political organization. It is not surprising that the gradual devolution of constitutional powers to the Northern regional government stimulated the rise of a political movement among the peoples of the middle belt to secure a separate state in which they would not be numerically or culturally dominated by the people of the upper North.

In 1949, a small group of prominent Christians organized the Northern Nigerian non-Muslim League to defend the interests of their churches in the North. Subsequently, in 1950, the name of this organization was changed to the Middle Zone League, in order to emphasize the goal of a separate region and at the same time to disclaim any intention of fostering religio-political conflict. In point of fact, however, the middle-belt separatist movement has always derived most of its support from persons associated with Christian missions, which are numerous in the lower North. But the popularity of middle-belt separatism, even among Christians, has varied among ethnic groups, with the more than 800,000 Tiv of Benue Province in the forefront. Clearly, a large majority of the inhabitants of the lower North have not favored separatism as a remedy to their grievances, and the movement for a middle-belt state has been debilitated further by ethnic particularism and chronic internal strife.

In the upper North itself an ostensibly separatist movement was organized in 1954 among the Kanuri of Bornu. The Kanuri are a Muslim people, however, with indigenous traditions of political organization similar to those of the Fulani-Hausa. The Bornu Youth Movement was actually more akin to the NEPU, with which it was allied, than to the separatist movement in the middle belt, for the BYM's advocacy of a separate North East State was less pronounced than its interest in reform of the emirate system.

Subregionalism in the midwest was sustained primarily by the Edo-speaking people of Benin and Delta provinces, all of whom are linked traditionally to the Kingdom of Benin. The overwhelming desire of the midwestern peoples for a separate state was never in serious doubt, as it was shared by the two largest non-Edo groups, the Western Ibo and the Western Ijaw.

The earliest and most powerful movement for separation from the Eastern Region arose in the Southern Cameroons, a United Nations Trust Territory of some 750,000, which had been attached to the Eastern administration. During the constitutional and political crises of 1953, Cameroonian representatives adopted an attitude of neutrality with respect to Nigerian party politics, demanding for themselves separation from the Eastern Region. Under the constitution of 1954, the Southern Cameroons was designated a quasi-federal territory with a government of its own. Thereupon, political leaders in other non-Ibo areas of the East inaugurated a movement, called the Calabar-Ogoja-Rivers State Movement, for separation from the Ibo majority. In this case, as in the lower North, the minority zone is a loose belt of culturally diverse peoples who are united only, if at all, by feelings of hostility to the cultural majority. Consequently, the C-O-R State demand has been firmly opposed by the NCNC.

These ethnosectional reactions to regionalism have undoubtedly been responsible for the widespread use of ethnic prejudice in political campaigns. As a result, minority leaders have been vehemently criticized for having sown seeds of dissension to the detriment of national unity. In rebuttal, leaders and supporters of minority movements have contended that a division of the existing regions into smaller units, such as they propose, would strengthen the federal government and render it less vulnerable to divisive regional pressures.

The Timetable of Independence

In December, 1953, Dr. Azikiwe led the NCNC to a landslide electoral victory in the Eastern Region. Subsequently, under the constitution of 1954, he became Premier of the Eastern Region, Obafemi Awolowo became Premier of the West, and the Sardauna of Sokoto was designated Premier of the North. Federal elections were held for the first time in 1954. To the framers of the constitution of 1954 it seemed probable that the dominant regional parties would win the majority of federal seats in their respective regional strongholds. Once again, it was anticipated that the NPC and the AG would form a parliamentary coalition at the center. Contrary to expectation, the NCNC won a majority of the seats in the East *and* the West, giving it the right to designate a majority of the federal ministers—three from each region. Consequently, a coalition of expedience was formed between the NCNC and the NPC, which controlled the largest single block of representatives. The major parties then settled down to consolidate their power in the regions. By 1956, it began to look as though the regional power systems would become virtually impregnable as the AG won a decisive majority in the Western House of Assembly and the NPC scored an even more impressive victory in the Northern regional election, including a majority of the urban seats, which were subject to direct election for the first time in the North.

The methods employed by regional government parties to consolidate their powers were given dramatic attention in the Eastern Region, where public funds were invested in a private banking institution, the controlling shares of which belonged to the Premier, Dr. Azikiwe. This was done in keeping with two settled NCNC policies: to provide for the extension of credit to African businessmen and to break the financial monopoly held by British banks in Nigeria. Nonetheless, the Secretary of State for the Colonies saw fit to appoint a Tribunal of Inquiry, necessitating a postponement of the impending constitutional conference. Certain findings of the Tribunal were clearly unfavorable to the Eastern Premier. But the NCNC presented the issue as a conflict between indigenous and foreign banking. On that issue, the Eastern government resigned and won its vindication at the polls.

The constitutional conference of 1957 provided for regional self-government with safeguards to protect the unity and paramount interests of the Federation. Both the Eastern and Western regions requested immediate self-government; the North declared that it would take that step in 1959. Meanwhile, full regional status was granted to the Southern Cameroons. Agreement was reached to enlarge the federal House of Representatives on a strict population basis—approximately one representative per 100,000 people—with the result that 174 of 320 seats were allocated to the North. Furthermore, provision was made for a Prime Minister of the Federation, empowered to choose his cabinet without regard to regional representation. All parties agreed to the appointment of Alhaji Sir Abubakar Tafawa Balewa, leader of the NPC in the House of Representatives, as Prime Minister of the Federation. Shortly after his appointment, Alhaji Abubakar formed a national government with ministers from the AG and the Kamerun National Congress [41] as well as the NCNC and the NPC.

On the question of independence for the Federation, the Secretary of State for the Colonies refused to set a date until regional self-government had been tested and other problems, especially the related questions of minority fears and the demand for new states, had been resolved. In quest of a solution to the minorities issue, the conference authorized the Secretary of State to appoint a commission of inquiry "to ascertain the facts about the fears of minorities" and to submit recommendations for allaying them to a resumed conference. After an intensive investigation in Nigeria, the commission advised against the creation of new states, on the ground that they would not allay minor-

[41] Victor T. Le Vine, "The Cameroun Federal Republic," in Gwendolen M. Carter, ed., *Five African States: Responses to Diversity* (Ithaca: Cornell University Press, 1963), pp. 263, 277–281, 315–320.

ity fears, while new minority problems might well result from them. This recommendation was promptly endorsed by the NPC and the national leadership of the NCNC, but deplored as unrealistic by the AG and by spokesmen for the principal new state movements.

The resumed constitutional conference of 1958 set October 1, 1960, as the date for Nigerian independence. A procedure for the creation of additional regions was added to the constitution, but the Secretary of State for the Colonies declared that "the early creation of new states was not for practical reasons compatible with the request for independence in 1960." This view was rejected by the AG, which had developed into a party of truly national scope through its championship of minority movements in the East and the North. Thus, in the federal election of 1959, the AG campaigned for the creation of a new state in the minority sector of each region prior to independence. The NPC reiterated its refusal to part with "an inch" of northern territory, while the NCNC declared that in the interest of the overriding national goal, the question of new states should be deferred.

The federal election of 1959 demonstrated again the decisive supremacy of each regional government party in the section of each region inhabited by the majority ethnic group. The NCNC won all 50 seats in the Ibo constituencies of the East; the NPC won 104 of 110 seats in the upper North; and the AG won 32 of 47 seats in the Yoruba sector of the West. The AG also won 14 seats of a total of 23 in the minority sector of the East, and, in alliance with the United Middle Belt Congress, 25 of 74 seats in the lower North. Similarly, the NCNC won 14 of 15 seats in the midwest. All told, the NPC emerged from the election with a strong plurality—142 seats of a total of 312; the NCNC/NEPU alliance ran second with 89, and the AG trailed with 73. Eight seats, allocated to the Southern Cameroons, were not contested pending clarification of the future disposition of that region, then under United Nations Trusteeship.

For several years, especially since 1957, the relationship between the NPC and the AG had been bitterly antagonistic, mainly as a result of the latter's determined campaign to create a middle-belt state and its demand for a revision of the North-West boundary so as to transfer some 500,000 Northern Yoruba to the Western Region. Meanwhile, the NCNC had established a notably cordial relationship with the NPC, notwithstanding its traditional alliance with the North's radical NEPU. After the election, the NPC and the NCNC once again formed a coalition federal government with Alhaji Sir Abubakar Tafawa Balewa as

Prime Minister. Dr. Azikiwe, who had been elected to the House of Representatives, resigned his seat to assume the essentially honorific office of president of the newly created Nigerian Senate; Chief Awolowo became leader of the federal Opposition, while the Sardauna of Sokoto, the only major leader who had not stood for the federal Parliament, remained in office as Premier of the North. When Nigeria attained independence, the Cameroons Trust Territory was separated from it pending the outcome of a plebiscite under United Nations auspices. In 1961, the people of the Northern Cameroons chose to rejoin the Northern Region of Nigeria, while the Southern Cameroons, having previously attained full regional status in Nigeria, voted to federate with the neighboring Cameroun Republic instead.

Table 1. Elections, 1951–1965
(*: Figures not available)

Election	Number & percentage of registered persons voting	Party	Percentage of votes	Seats
1951				
Eastern Regional	*	National Council of Nigeria and the Cameroons (NCNC) United National Party	* *	65 4
Western Regional	*	Action Group NCNC	* *	45 30–35
Northern Regional	*	Northern Peoples' Congress	*	Indefinite; over-whelming majority
1953				
Eastern Regional	*	NCNC National Independence Party United National Party	* * *	72 9 3
1954				
Eastern Federal	1,039,551	NCNC United National Independence Party Action Group Independent Candidates	* * * *	32 4 3 3
Western Federal	*	NCNC Action Group Others	* * *	23 18 1

Table 1. (cont.)

Election	Number & percentage of registered persons voting	Party	Percentage of votes	Seats
Northern		Northern Peoples' Congress	°	79
Federal		Action Group	°	1
		Small Parties and Independents	°	10
Southern		Kamerun National		
Cameroons		Congress	°	5
Federal	°			
Lagos		NCNC	°	1
Federal	°	Action Group	°	1
1956				
Western		Action Group	48.3	48
Regional	1,291,174	NCNC	45.3	32
	68.	Northern Peoples' Congress		
Northern		and Allies	°	107
Regional	°			
		NEPU and allies	°	9
		Action Group and allies	°	4
		Others	°	11
1957				
Eastern		NCNC	63.26	64
Regional	°	Action Group	10.75	13
	46.78	United National Independence Party	6.32	5
		Independents	19.67	2
1959				
Federal totals	7,185,555	Northern Peoples' Congress	28.2	134
	79.8	NCNC/NEPU Alliance	35.1	89
		Action Group	27.6	73
		Others	8.1	16
Eastern		NCNC/NEPU	64.6	58
Federal	1,929,754	Action Group	23.1	14
	75.3	Others	12.3	1
Western		Action Group	49.5	33
Federal	1,887,209	NCNC/NEPU	40.2	21
	71.2	Northern Peoples' Congress	1.7	—
		Small Parties and Independents	8.6	8
Northern		Northern Peoples' Congress	61.2	134
Federal	3,258,520	Action Group	17.2	25
	89.4	NCNC/NEPU	16.1	8

Table 1. (*cont.*)

Election	Number & percentage of registered persons voting	Party	Percentage of votes	Seats
		Small Parties and Independents	5.5	7
Lagos		NCNC/NEPU	55.9	2
Federal	110,072	Action Group	43.8	1
	76.2	Northern Peoples' Congress and others	0.3	—
1960				
Western		Action Group	✿	79
Regional	✿	NCNC	✿	33
		Others	✿	10
1961				
Northern		Northern Peoples' Congress		
Regional	✿	and allies	✿	156
		Action Group/UMBC	✿	9
		NCNC/NEPU	✿	1
Eastern		NCNC	58.0	106
Regional	1,554,420	Action Group	14.4	15
	57.3	Others	27.5	25
1963				
Midwestern		NCNC	59.0	53
Regional	✿	Midwestern Democratic		
		Front	37.0	11
		Action Group	1.5	—
		Independents	1.5	—
1964–1965				
Federal totals	✿	NNA	✿	198
		UPGA	✿	108
		Independents	✿	5
				(One seat still to be recontested)
Eastern		NNA	✿	—
Federal	✿	UPGA	✿	68
		Independents	✿	2
Western		NNA	✿	36
Federal	✿	UPGA	✿	20
		Independents	✿	1
Northern		NNA	✿	162

Table 1. (*cont.*)

Election	Number & percentage of registered persons voting	Party	Percentage of votes	Seats
Federal	°	UPGA	°	4
		Independents	°	1
Midwestern		NNA	°	—
Federal	°	UPGA	°	13
		Independents	°	—
Lagos		NNA	°	—
Federal	°	Independents	°	1
		UPGA	°	3

Political Structures and Processes

THE CONSTITUTIONAL SYSTEM

The Nigerian constitution embodies the federal solution of 1954, augmented and modified by the decisions of three constitutional conferences before independence and various amendments thereafter. This document actually comprises five separate constitutions, namely, that of the Federal Republic and the four regional constitutions. They nonetheless comprise a single comprehensive constitution; indeed, the procedures to be followed in amending the regional constitutions are stipulated in the federal constitution. The whole document is exceedingly detailed; as originally published in a Supplement to the Official Gazette, it covered 165 pages.

Any consideration of the constitutional system must include the structure of the Federal Republic, the structure of the several parliamentary governments, and the process of constitutional amendment. A tentative appraisal of the strengths and weaknesses of the federal government vis-à-vis the regional governments also is in order.

The Federal Structure

The Federal Republic of Nigeria consists of regions and a federal territory. At the time of independence in 1960 there were three regions, the Northern, Western, and Eastern; in 1963, a fourth region—the Midwestern—was created. Since 1954, a "Schedule" consisting of two "Legislative Lists" has been appended to the federal constitution. Subjects which lie within the exclusive competence of the federal Parliament are enumerated in "The Exclusive Legislative List"; these include external affairs, defense, citizenship, immigration, external trade, monetary exchange control, customs and excise duties, currency, mining, maritime shipping, and the principal modes of communication and transportation. Others are enumerated in "The Concurrent Legislative List"; among them are public order, prisons, labor relations, welfare, higher education, and industrial development. Residual subjects, reserved to the regions in accordance with the federal compromise of 1954, include the regulation of local government, land tenure, chieftaincy, the customary courts, and major aspects of the agricultural export economy. These powers have a crucial bearing on the consolidation of party rule in the regions, as will be shown below.

The constitution of the Federation asserts its supremacy over the constitutions of the regions [42] as well as the supremacy of federal law over regional law in all cases of concurrent jurisdiction.[43] Furthermore, it empowers the federal Supreme Court to interpret the regional constitutions as well as the constitution of the Federation.[44] Since independence, the Supreme Court has exercised its power to declare regional legislation unconstitutional in only one case of relatively minor significance.[45] In 1962, however, the Supreme Court did nullify an action taken by the constitutional Governor of the Western Region. But the Court's decision in this case was reversed by the British Judicial Committee of the Privy Council. Subsequently, the constitution was amended, in accordance with the examples of India, Pakistan, Cyprus, and Ghana, to abolish the right of appeal to this traditional "supreme Court of the Commonwealth," thereby confirming the federal Supreme Court as the highest tribunal of constitutional interpretation.

The Parliamentary Structure

The Parliament of the Federation is bicameral, consisting of a House of Representatives and a Senate, in addition to the constitutional Head of State. Until October 1, 1963, the Head of State was the representative of the Queen, styled "Governor-General." It was characteristic of the new Commonwealth that this office was held by Nigeria's foremost nationalist, Dr. Nnamdi Azikiwe, who withdrew from active politics in order to qualify for the appointment. Upon the proclamation of the Republic, Dr. Azikiwe became its first President. The constitution now provides for the election of the President to a five-year term of office by

[42] *The Constitution of the Federal Republic of Nigeria*, Sec. 1.
[43] *Ibid.*, Sec. 69 (4).   [44] *Ibid.*, Sec. 115.
[45] See Taylor Cole, "Emergent Federalism in Nigeria," in Robert O. Tilman and Taylor Cole, eds., *The Nigerian Political Scene* (Durham: Duke University Press, 1962), p. 48, n. 12.

an electoral college consisting of the members of the Senate and the
House of Representatives.

The federal Senate consists of twelve senators from each region, supplemented by four senators from the Federal Territory of Lagos and
four additional senators selected by the President on the advice of the
Prime Minister. Senators representing the regions are chosen by their
regional governments subject to confirmation by the regional legislatures. Apart from its moral authority, the Senate has little power over
legislation; it is empowered to delay the enactment of nonmonetary
bills for six months and money bills for one month only. Constitutional
amendments, however, require the assent of the Senate as do alterations of the boundaries of parliamentary constituencies.[46]

The House of Representatives consists of 312 members elected from
single-member constituencies based on distribution of population. No
person can sit in this House, or in the Senate, if he is also a member of
a regional legislature. By and large, the procedures of the House of
Representatives are derived from the example of the British House of
Commons: Question Time is observed; bills are read three times before
being sent to the Senate; the presiding officer of the House is an
elected Speaker, who need not, however, be an otherwise duly elected
member of the House.[47]

The executive authority of the Federation is vested in the President
and exercised in his name by a Council of Ministers, collectively responsible to Parliament. The President appoints to the office of Prime
Minister "a member of the House of Representatives who appears to
him likely to command the support of the majority of the members of
the House." [48] Other ministers of the government are appointed by the
President on the advice of the Prime Minister. Apart from the Attorney

----

[46] *Constitution,* Sec. 51 (4).

[47] In actual practice, Nigerian parliamentary procedures do not attain the West-
minster standard in affording the Opposition chance to influence the conduct of
parliamentary work. The House of Representatives is in session for about fifty
days a year. "There is no equivalent to the twenty-six Supply days when the
Opposition in the British House of Commons can choose the subject for debate or
can put down a motion of censure." Tuesday meetings are set aside for debating
motions by private members; but the crucial regulatory function of listing such
motions on the Order Paper is discharged by the government-controlled Business
Committee of the House. (John P. Mackintosh, "The Nigerian Federal Parliament," *Public Law* (Autumn, 1963), pp. 339–341.) These observations were
pertinent to the restricted role of the federal opposition even before its precipitous
decline in 1962.

[48] *Constitution,* Sec. 87 (2).

General, no person who is neither a senator nor a member of the House of Representatives can hold an office of ministerial rank in the federal government for more than four months. In 1962, there were 23 members of the Council of Ministers, three of whom were chosen from the Senate.

Each of the regional legislatures is also bicameral, consisting of a popularly elected House of Assembly, based on single-member constituencies, and an upper chamber called the House of Chiefs. All parliamentary business is conducted in English, save in Northern Nigeria, where Hausa is accorded recognition as a second official language. Similar consideration has been suggested for predominant local languages in other regions, in particular, for Yoruba in the Western Region.

In Nigeria "Chief" is a legal title for which provision is made in the constitutions of the regional governments. A person is legally a chief if he is recognized as such by the government of a region; regional laws regulate the appointment, grading, and deposition of chiefs. In all regions the most prestigious among the traditional rulers are designated First Class or Head Chiefs and *ex-officio* or permanent members of the upper legislative chamber, while the qualifications, modes of selection, and tenure of ordinary members of these houses are variously prescribed by regional laws.

Nigeria's multiple traditional political culture influences the regulation of chieftaincy, the constitution of the House of Chiefs, and the power it wields in each region. In the Northern Region, where hierarchical traditions are deeply rooted, the House of Chiefs, established in 1946, is, like the United States Senate, a coordinate legislative chamber, subject to the sole proviso that money bills are required to originate in the House of Assembly. In the event of a disagreement between the two legislative chambers of the North, the constitution provides that each house shall elect twenty representatives to a joint sitting, which shall be competent to take final action on the measure in question.[49] Since the president of the House of Chiefs is to preside over any joint sitting and vote in the event of a tie, it is technically possible that the Northern House of Chiefs may assert a decisive role in the legislative process of that region.

At the very least, the Northern chiefs are constitutionally protected against the inroads of total democracy. The ordinary, or nonpermanent members of the House of Chiefs are selected by meetings of chiefs in every province. And the power to regulate chieftaincy by means of

[49] *The Constitution of Northern Nigeria,* Sec. 28.

appointment, recognition, grading, deposition, or banishment is vested in a Council of Chiefs, composed as follows: the Premier of the region, those ministers of the government of the region who are members of the House of Chiefs, and four additional members of the House of Chiefs coopted by the Premier for the consideration of specific cases. Obviously, in any given case, the will of the Premier is virtually certain to prevail. But formal authority is vested in the chiefs themselves, for the government is required to act in accordance with the advice of the Council.[50]

Until 1959, the Western House of Chiefs, established by the constitution of 1951, was also a coordinate legislative chamber. But the institution of chieftaincy in Western Nigeria has been subject to increasingly stringent control by the regional government party. Although the Western regional government has established a Council of Obas and Chiefs to advise it on chieftaincy matters, including questions of discipline, the power of decision lies with the government and not with the Council of Chiefs, as it does in the North. Furthermore, until 1960, the temporary members of the Western House of Chiefs were chosen under conditions which permitted direct party control. They were elected at divisional meetings attended by representatives of local government councils. Chiefs constituted a minority at such meetings, which were dominated by commoners who were likely to vote in accordance with party direction. In light of all this, it is not surprising that the powers of the upper chamber were reduced without public protest on the part of chiefs. Today the Western House of Chiefs, like the federal Senate, is empowered to delay the passage of money bills for one month and other bills for six months. Temporary members of the House are now chosen by local electoral colleges composed of chiefs only.

In the Eastern Region, a House of Chiefs was created in 1959, mainly in response to the demands of minority ethnic groups, among whom the traditional political role of chieftancy is greater than it is among the "republican" Ibo. It seems probable that the Eastern government party also perceived a partisan advantage in obtaining control of a legalized system of chieftaincy. At present, ordinary members of the Eastern House of Chiefs are chosen for specified terms by the recognized subordinate chiefs in every administrative division from among themselves. The Eastern House of Chiefs is a subordinate chamber with powers of delay similar to those of the Western House of Chiefs and the federal Senate.

In each region executive authority is vested in a constitutional Gov-

[50] *Ibid.*, Sec. 75.

ernor. The regional cabinet is styled the Executive Council; it is headed by a Premier, who must be a member of the House of Assembly in the Eastern, Western, and Midwestern regions, but may be chosen from the House of Chiefs in the North. Although the regional executive councils are responsible to their respective legislatures, the regional constitutions of 1960, following a similar provision in the constitution of the Federation, empowered the Governor to remove the Premier of the region when "it appears to him that the Premier no longer commands the support of a majority of the members of the House of Assembly." In 1962, the Governor of Western Nigeria removed the Premier from his office upon receipt of a statement signed by a majority of the members of the Western House of Assembly to the effect that they no longer supported the incumbent Premier. This action was held unconstitutional by the federal Supreme Court on the ground that it contravened those conventions of the British constitution upon which the relevant provisions of the Nigerian constitution had been patterned.[51] The decision of the Supreme Court was reversed by the Judicial Committee of the Privy Council on appeal, whereupon immediate steps were taken to amend the constitution of Western Nigeria with retrospective effect to provide that a Premier may be removed from office only in consequence of a resolution of no confidence passed by the House of Assembly. This principle was later embodied in the republican constitution of 1963. The President of the Republic is not empowered to remove the Prime Minister from office except in consequence of a vote of no confidence in the government by the House of Representatives. In such event, moreover, the President is explicitly required to dissolve Parliament (Section 68, 5, a). Members of Parliament know that a vote of no confidence in the government will automatically send them back to their constituencies to incur the expense, trouble, and possibly adverse verdict of an election. These provisions do, therefore, appreciably strengthen the hand of the government vis-à-vis the legislature.

The Amending Process

For purposes of amendment, the provisions of the constitution are classified as "ordinary" and "entrenched." [52] An amendment to an ordinary provision of the federal constitution requires a two-thirds majority

---

[51] See Oluwole Idowu Odumosu, *The Nigerian Constitution: History and Development* (London: Sweet and Maxwell, 1963), pp. 290–298.

[52] This terminology appears in the *Report by the Resumed Nigeria Constitutional Conference held in London in September and October, 1958* (Lagos: Federal Government Printer, 1958), pp. 24–26. The amending procedure is set forth in the Constitution of the Federation, Sec. 4 and 5.

of all the members of each federal House; similarly, amendments to the ordinary provisions of a regional constitution require the assent of two-thirds of all the members of each legislative house of the region concerned. The entrenched provisions of the federal constitution, comprising some 100 out of 166 sections, are amendable by a two-thirds majority of all the members in each federal House followed by the concurrence, by simple majority, of each House of the Legislatures of a majority (now three) of the regions. Finally, amendments of the entrenched provisions of the regional constitutions require "a two-thirds majority of all the members of each House of the Legislature of the Region concerned, with the concurrence of a two-thirds majority of all members of each House of the Federal Legislature." [53]

The entrenched provisions of the federal and regional constitutions are those "of general concern," including provisions governing the establishment and dissolution of the various legislative houses, the contents of the Exclusive and Concurrent Legislative Lists, the basis of representation in Parliament, the allocation of federal revenues, the organization of the federal Supreme Court, the High Courts of the regions, the public services, and the Nigerian Police, the emergency powers, fundamental rights, rights of appeal, and the amending procedure itself. Provisions designating the units of the Federation and their boundaries are also entrenched, and precise procedures are laid down to effect changes in regional boundaries and to create new regions. The final step in the creation of a new region, after the law providing for a constitutional amendment has been passed by the federal Parliament and approved by the legislative houses of a majority of the regions, is a referendum in the area of the proposed new region. For the region to be created, it must be supported by at least 60 per cent of its registered electorate, that is, all those *entitled* to vote.[54] In 1963, the Midwest State Movement attained its objective when 89 per cent of the midwestern electorate voted for the establishment of Nigeria's fourth region.

Federal Government: Powers and Limitations

Constitutional and political developments during the first five years of Nigerian independence attest to the vitality of centripetal forces which strengthen the federal government vis-à-vis the governments of the regions. At the same time there is an even more pronounced tendency, perhaps generic to parliamentary democracies, for the elective

[53] *Report by the Resumed Nigeria Constitutional Conference*, p. 25.
[54] Federal Republic of Nigeria, *Constitution*, Sec. 4 (5).

branch of government to assert its supremacy over the courts in matters of constitutional construction. It should not be forgotten, however, that the Nigerian constitution is designed to accommodate major social groups, including cultural nationalities and socioeconomic interest groups, which have common interests in limited government. A brief assessment of constitutional limitations ventured here on the basis of a few years' performance will not, of course, purport to gauge their long-term effectiveness.

The overriding authority of the federal government is guaranteed by the supremacy clause, the wide powers of constitutional interpretation vested in the federal Supreme Court, and provisions of the constitution which pertain to specific circumstances or objects. The power of Parliament to declare the existence of a state of public emergency in any part of Nigeria [55] was exercised in 1962 in the Western Region under circumstances described subsequently in this chapter. Parliament is also empowered to legislate for a region in the event that two-thirds of all the members of each federal house declare that the exercise of executive authority in the region concerned threatens either the existence of federal government in Nigeria or the exercise of executive authority by the federal government.[56] Federal supremacy is fortified by the constitutional provision for a national police force under federal control.[57] Although the regional governments are permitted to maintain local police forces, region-wide forces are proscribed.

Among the most important sources of federal strength are the constitutional provisions on finance. These retain the principle of derivation adopted in 1954: the proceeds of most import and excise duties, collected by the federal government, are distributed to the regions of their origin. Mining revenues, however, are divided between the regional government of origin and the federal government on a 50–50 basis; 30 per cent of all federal mining revenues and import duties (other than those levied on fuel oil, tobacco, and intoxicating beverages) are contributed to a "Distributable Pool," intended to foster a balanced program of economic development for the Federal Republic.[58] It is reported that "well over three-fifths of the regional revenue is . . . derived from federal 'grants and allocations' to the Regions." [59] The federal government has exclusive jurisdiction in respect of sales taxes and taxes on the incomes and profits of companies, while the regional

[55] *Constitution*, Sec. 70.   [56] *Ibid.*, Sec. 71, 86.   [57] *Ibid.*, Sec. 106–110.
[58] *Ibid.*, Sec. 136, 141. See also *Nigeria. Report of the Fiscal Commission*, Cmd. 481 (London: H.M.S.O., 1958), pp. 30–32.
[59] Cole, *loc. cit.*, pp. 51–52.

governments have basic jurisdiction over personal income taxes. Finally, the power to borrow from external sources is included in the Exclusive Legislative List, with the proviso that regional governments may borrow abroad on the security of their external assets only, for terms which do not exceed one year.

Probably the most important limitation on the centralization of power through constitutional development is the special amending procedure for the so-called entrenched provisions of the federal and regional constitutions. In effect, the boundaries and territories of the existing regions are indeed entrenched. With the size of the Northern Region—167 of 312 parliamentary constituencies lie in the North—and the electoral predominance of the Northern government party in that region, the likelihood of two-thirds of all the members of the House of Representatives voting for a resolution aiming to reduce the size of the North is very remote. Since 1963 the NPC, joined by former members of the opposition, has commanded an absolute majority in the federal House of Representatives. Therefore, what may seem to be a shift of power from the regional capitals to Lagos during the first few years of independence, may actually mask the growing influence of Northern regional leaders in federal affairs. Weaknesses of the federal government under these conditions were recently reflected in the maintenance of a coalition government at the center; the alternative would have been for the regionally oriented NPC to adopt the necessarily precarious policy of attempting to "go it alone." The mechanical shortcomings of government by coalition were magnified by the ideological disparities that separated the federal coalition partners. It is too soon to discern the impact of the assumption of power by one of the two national alliances of parties that formed to contest the federal election in December, 1964.

LIMITATIONS ON PARLIAMENTARY SUPREMACY

One might suppose that the intrinsic weakness of party-parliamentary government at the federal level in Nigeria would enable the federal Supreme Court to assert itself as a powerful defender of the constitution by construing it boldly as a veritable declaration of rights against government. In 1961, the Supreme Court declared unconstitutional certain sections of an Act of Parliament empowering the Prime Minister to appoint commissions of inquiry. The case was politically very sensitive in that it involved a federal investigation into the affairs of a bank owned by the Western regional government. Since then, the court has exercised caution in disposing of questions involving acts of Parliament.

POLITICAL DYNAMICS

Patterns of Leadership

In all societies leadership is partly a function of the development of intellectual skills. In "developing" societies such leadership skills derive mainly from Western education. Furthermore, the median level of such necessary skill varies with the rate and nature of social development.

THE SOCIAL BACKGROUND OF POLITICAL LEADERS

Given the disparities in social development between northern and southern Nigeria, one might anticipate that dissimilar educational requirements for leadership would obtain in these two sectors of the country. In the case of southern leaders we find that educational qualifications essential to the operation of modern economic and legal institutions are increasingly common. The leaders of the north have also determined to acquire modern skills. But that region's deep attachment to its reformed and rejuvenated tradition of emirate rule reduces the potential significance of educational qualifications for leadership. Armed with a favorable set of hereditary or personal connections, most of the present generation of northern leaders are in a position to sustain political eminence without the added impetus of higher education.

The differential impact of Western education is revealed by James S. Coleman in his tabulations on the educational backgrounds of the elected members of the central and regional legislatures from 1952 to 1957.[60] Thus, about two-thirds of all southern legislators (in the Eastern and Western Houses of Assembly and the House of Representatives) had received secondary education, and about one-third had received university education. By contrast, only 49 per cent of the northern members of the House of Representatives were educated up to the secondary level and only 8 per cent of them had reached the university level. In the Northern House of Assembly, the secondary level had been attained by only 17 per cent and the university level by 2 per cent of the members. What is more, in 1959, there were no university graduates in either the Northern House of Assembly or among the Northern members of the House of Representatives. An analysis of Northern assemblymen by one of the present writers in 1959 revealed that the average number of years of completed Western-type education

[60] *Nigeria*, pp. 378–383.

for all members was 7.5; the Northern ministers, regional and federal, had completed 10.6 and 11.5 years respectively. Still another author's survey of the educational backgrounds of candidates in the federal election of 1959 revealed that 63 of 164 candidates sampled in the south (44 per cent of the total number of persons nominated) had university backgrounds, while 69 of them had secondary-school backgrounds. Among the 183 northern candidates sampled (32 per cent of the total), there was none with a university background and only 51 who had attended a secondary school.[61]

This north-south contrast is equally sharp in relation to the primary occupational backgrounds of the major party leaders. The present writers have determined that, in 1958, the leadership cores of the three major parties were composed preponderantly of persons with elite occupational backgrounds. Thus, some 27 per cent of the 71 members of the top executive bodies of the NCNC were members of the learned professions, principally law and medicine; some 28 per cent were engaged in entrepreneurship or finance, while close to 20 per cent were educators. Similarly, the 66 members of the federal executive council of the AG included 33 per cent professionals, 21 per cent prominent businessmen, and 18 per cent educators. By contrast again, some 62 per cent of the 74 members of the national executive committee of the NPC were native administration functionaries and 26 per cent were independent businessmen. Coleman has presented data of a similar import with respect to the primary occupational backgrounds of the legislative group noted above. He found that "educators and barristers are heavily represented" among the southern legislators, whereas, among the northerners, "there is an extremely heavy representation from the native authorities, ranging from 75 to 95 per cent," [62] K. W. J. Post's findings on the occupational backgrounds of 183 southern candidates in the federal election of 1959 (49 per cent of the total) includes 55 businessmen, 50 "educationalists," and 31 lawyers. Only three were listed as trade-union officials. Of 161 NPC candidates (out of a total of 170), 135 were either Native Administration Councillors, officials, and

[61] K. W. J. Post, *The Nigerian Federal Election of 1959* (London: Oxford University Press, 1963), p. 280. These samples were "heavily weighted" with candidates who were actually elected.

[62] *Nigeria*, p. 379. In "The Politics of Sub-Saharan Africa," Almond and Coleman, eds., *op. cit.*, p. 342, Professor Coleman has observed that 30 per cent of the combined memberships of the Eastern and Western Houses of Assembly for the period 1952–1957 consisted of teachers and headmasters, that 20 per cent consisted of professional persons, and 27 per cent were engaged in private enterprise.

employees, or district and village heads. Over half of the NEPU candidates and nearly half of the AG candidates in the North were merchants, traders, and farmers.[63] Furthermore, a recent survey has disclosed that 9 of the 12 Northern members of the federal Senate were employed in the central offices of Native Administrations.[64] Although the role of the Senate as a legislative chamber is relatively minor, many of the individual senators are either influential members of their respective parties or persons of independent political stature.

Most Nigerian leaders are accountable to organized political movements based on distinctive combinations of group interest. Naturally, the leadership of each major political party tends to reflect the proportionate participation in that party of groups based on ethnic and religious affinity as well as on socioeconomic status. Of the 74 members of the NPC national executive committee, cited above, approximately 32 per cent were Fulani, 19 per cent Habe, 9 per cent Nupe, 7 per cent Kanuri, and 7 per cent Yoruba. In this case, the prominence of leaders who belong to the traditional Fulani ruling class in the emirate sector is noteworthy. Some 86 per cent of this group was Muslim, but it should be remarked that the NPC diligently recruits leaders who are Christian, mainly from the various ethnic groups of the middle belt.

Yoruba members predominate among leaders of the AG, having comprised 68 per cent of its federal executive council in 1958. Despite the fact that Islam is as widespread among the Yoruba people as Christianity, the overwhelming majority of high-level AG leaders have been Christian, owing undoubtedly to the historic contribution of the mission schools to the education of the nationalist elite. The AG has also been keen, however, to establish its nonsectarian character. In response to the formation of a Muslim opposition party in the Western Region in 1957, AG leaders organized a United Muslim Council and intensified their efforts to recruit Muslim members. It is noteworthy that a Muslim, Alhaji D. S. Adegbenro, was chosen by the party executive to succeed to the premiership of the West during the AG party crisis of 1962.

In terms of its ethnic distribution the NCNC is the most cosmopolitan of the Nigerian parties. Forty-nine per cent of the leadership group noted above was Ibo, reflecting the regularity with which Ibo-speaking constituencies support NCNC candidates, but 10 per cent of the

[63] Post, *op. cit.*, pp. 278–279.
[64] Billy J. Dudley, "Focus on the Nigerian Senate," *West Africa,* July 21, 1962, p. 787.

leaders were drawn from other Eastern groups and 27 per cent were Yoruba. Furthermore, the NCNC is the dominant party in the newly created Midwestern Region, in which the preponderant cultural group is Edo-speaking. Over 90 per cent of the NCNC leaders were Christians, the remainder being Muslims, mainly from Yorubaland. Muslim participation in the NCNC, however, is enhanced by that party's firm alliance with the NEPU. Alhaji Aminu Kano, Life-President of the NEPU, also holds the office of first vice-president of the NCNC, and many Muslims of northern origin who reside in the urban areas of southern Nigeria regularly support the NCNC.

SOME REPRESENTATIVE LEADERS

Among the major political leaders, it would be difficult to distinguish a more nationally representative figure than Nigeria's first President, Dr. Nnamdi Azikiwe. He was born in the northern town of Zunguru, and his ethnic heritage is Onitsha Ibo. The Niger River port of Onitsha is one of the principal centers of Ibo culture, but the original inhabitants of the town, including Azikiwe's family, nevertheless trace their roots to the Edo city of Benin, capital of the Midwest. In his youth, Azikiwe studied in the southeastern city of Calabar, home of the Efik people, and in Lagos, where, after twelve years abroad, he established the *West African Pilot* and a group of related commercial companies. He is the only major leader to have acquired a working knowledge of the three great languages of Nigeria, Yoruba and Hausa in addition to his native Ibo. He has been a journalist, businessman, and banker, a radical nationalist, respected statesman, and the founder of a university. His ideological inclinations are socialistic, but in consequence of the conditions of nationalist action in Nigeria, and in furtherance of the economic development of the country, he has, in practice, adopted a pragmatic, welfare capitalist point of view. Above all, he is a democrat, and it has been reported that his recent opposition to the enactment of a preventive detention law in Nigeria was crucial to, and perhaps decisive for its defeat.

His successor as national president of the NCNC and Premier of the East is Dr. Michael I. Okpara, a medical doctor, and a personification of the Ibo intelligentsia. Known for his ability to conciliate conflicting viewpoints, Dr. Okpara is less prone than his predecessor to alienate influential sectors of middle-class opinion. Like Azikiwe, he is a pragmatic socialist, who also believes in the promotion of private enterprise.

A more forceful proponent of Nigerian capitalism is the powerful federal Minister of Finance, Chief F. S. Okotie-Eboh, who is also the national treasurer of the NCNC and its parliamentary leader in the House of Representatives. Chief Okotie-Eboh is from the Midwestern division of Warri, of Itsekeri-Urhobo descent. He is a rubber-export dealer and school proprietor. He studied business administration in Prague, where he witnessed the Communist coup of 1948, an event which is said to have left a lasting negative impression. His fellow Midwesterner, Chief D. C. Osadebay, is a talented intellectual, barrister, and poet, noted for the esteem his opponents have for him. Leader of the Midwest State Movement, he was chosen as first Premier of the new region, despite the fact that he belongs to a minority ethnic group in that region, the Western Ibo. Previously he had been leader of the Opposition in the Western House of Assembly and, in succession to Dr. Azikiwe, president of the federal Senate. A socialist and democrat, he has nonetheless decried the effects of party competition in Nigeria, in particular its tendency to foment ethnic antagonisms.

Dr. K. O. Mbadiwe, former leader of the NCNC federal parliamentary party, has recently regained the federal cabinet rank that he lost in 1958 in the course of an unsuccessful attempt to force Azikiwe's resignation from politics. Educated in the United States, Dr. Mbadiwe upholds the proud leadership tradition of the Aro Ibo people of Eastern Nigeria. An avowed socialist, he is also a successful businessman, and his strategic political connections lie in the business community. His cabinet colleague, barrister Jaja A. Wachuku, is the favorite son of the largest Ibo subgroup, the Ngwa. As Minister of Foreign Affairs, he has become an international personality, having served as chairman of the UN Conciliation Committee for the Congo.

Finally, Alhaji Aminu Kano carries the NCNC/NEPU banner in the North. In the top leadership his equalitarian views are most clearly enunciated. As the one northerner of stature who commands the respect of rank and file NCNC members in the south, he has perhaps the most intriguing political future of all.

The two most prominent leaders of the NPC, Sir Ahmadu Bello, the Sardauna of Sokoto, and Sir Abubakar Tafawa Balewa, clearly overshadow the field.[65] The Northern Premier is an avowed conservative,

---

[65] For an analysis of fundamental ideological differences between Bello, Balewa, and Aminu Kano, see C. S. Whitaker, Jr., "Three Perspectives on Hierarchy: Political Thought and Leadership in Northern Nigeria," *Journal of Commonwealth Political Studies*, III, No. 1 (1965), 1–19.

dedicated to the development of the North within the framework of traditional authority and values. Sir Abubakar is more the reformer and spokesman for the northern intelligentsia. Since 1954, these two have been president-general and first vice-president, respectively, of the NPC. The carefully kept delimitation of their respective spheres of authority is a remarkable achievement in light of the Sardauna's forcefulness as a political leader. To be sure, the leader of the NPC is a national power; his personal power clearly exceeds that of any party leader in the Federation. Yet Sir Abubakar is, by all odds, the most experienced parliamentary leader in Nigeria and, by all accounts, master of his ministry.

Until 1965 Sir Abubakar's principal deputy in the federal government was the second vice-president of the NPC and federal Minister of Defence, the late Alhaji Muhammadu Ribadu, an aristocrat of Fulani descent. In Kaduna Sir Ahmadu relies principally on two of his trusted colleagues, the Northern Minister of Finance, Alhaji Aliyu, *Makaman Bida* (Nupe), who alone of the members of the executive council is senior in age to the Sardauna, and Alhaji Isa Kaita, *Madawakin Katsina* (Habe), Minister of Education. Only one Northern minister, Alhaji Ibrahim Musa Gashash (Arab-Hausa) of Kano, has an occupational background in commercial enterprise rather than native administration. This is a circumstance that reflects the point of our previous remarks on the subject of the political role of northern men of this background generally.

Prior to independence, the top leaders of the AG constituted a closely knit directorate, with Obafemi Awolowo as the first among equals. As a rule, party policies were formulated by regular procedures, involving extensive consultations among party leaders, important chiefs, and influential supporters in the professional and business communities of the Western Region. Most party policies were debated well in advance of their adoption at informal "Leaders' Meetings" convened by Awolowo in his home town of Ikenne. A majority of those in the top directorate of the party had been prominent in the movement for Yoruba unity, and their cohesion was buttressed by membership in the cultural Society of the Descendants of Oduduwa. Their common interests in the development of the West, in the establishment of a federal form of government, and in such specific policies as the restoration of Lagos to the Western Region, the regionalization of the Nigerian police force, and the creation of new states, overrode the ideological disparities among them.

Factional forces within the directorate intensified in the aftermath of the federal election of 1959. Despite its vigorous, well-financed campaign in all parts of the country, the AG ran third, and its hope for federal power was dashed by the resumption of an NPC/NCNC coalition government. In keeping with party policy, Chief Awolowo had relinquished his premiership of the West; in the Independence Parliament he became leader of the Opposition. His policy, fully endorsed by his more militant supporters, was to develop the AG into a nationwide people's party, which would seek power by democratic means, involving, particularly, the overthrow of the ruling element in the North. Under these conditions of opposition to the federal government coalition, Awolowo's explicit ideology developed from welfare statism to equalitarian socialism. In matters of international policy he abandoned his previously affirmed pro-Western orientation for the policy of positive neutralism and alliance with the Ghana-Guinea-Mali Union.

The argument for radical opposition to the federal government was difficult for the conservative, business-oriented wing of the party to accept. The latter preferred to safeguard the political and economic benefits of regional power and work out a settlement with the federal government coalition based on the principle of regional security. This, of course, would have been a "class settlement," consonant with the interests of the dominant social group in each region. It would have been guaranteed by the withdrawal of AG support for opposition elements in the Northern and Eastern Regions, and cemented by the formation of a national government that would have included all the regional government parties. It was unacceptable to the radical wing of the party, and an ideological storm gathered around the conflict between two strong personalities, Chief Awolowo and his deputy party leader, Chief Akintola, who had succeeded to the premiership of the West. At issue was the control and use of Western regional resources, involving appointments to key positions in the West, as well as the ideological complexion of the party. In 1962, their differences became flagrant. A party congress repudiated the Akintola wing and a subsequent meeting of the executive council directed him to resign as Premier. When he refused to do so, the constitutional governor, a long-time associate of Awolowo, removed him from office. This action precipitated a crisis in the West, which in turn led to the downfall of the AG government.

In the course of these events many of the original leaders of the AG fell by the wayside. The towering leader still is Chief Awolowo, once the resourceful proponent of Yoruba unity and federal government, now an avowed democratic socialist to whom the appellation "revolutionary socialist" is given with increasing frequency. In 1963, he was convicted of treasonable felony by the High Court of Lagos and sentenced to ten years imprisonment for having allegedly conspired to seize power by means of a *coup d'état*. Nonetheless, his political stature among the radical youth and supporters of the AG, in Yorubaland especially, has, if anything, been enhanced by these adversities; and he is said to have maintained a remarkably strong hand in the direction of party affairs through officials who visit him regularly in prison.

Awolowo's close associate, sentenced to serve a prison term of fifteen years for the same offense, is Chief Anthony Enahoro, formerly Western Minister of Home Affairs and shadow foreign minister in the House of Representatives. Chief Enahoro was born into the royal family of Ishan, an Edo-speaking, Midwestern people. In his youth he had been imprisoned on three different occasions by the colonial government for nationalist activities. The parliamentary leader of the party in Western Nigeria, as noted above, is Awolowo's devoted lieutenant, Alhaji D. S. Adegbenro.

Chief S. L. Akintola, restored to his premiership in 1963, now leads the newly organized Nigerian National Democratic Party. Once editor of the *Daily Service* (official organ of the Nigerian Youth Movement), Chief Akintola, a barrister, has been the foremost leader of the most populous Yoruba division, Oshun. He is noted for his wit, his talent as a phrasemaker, and his political acumen.

Finally, the contribution of certain sectional movements and parties to the national leadership of the AG should be noted. Ibrahim Imam, one-time leader of the Bornu Youth Movement and of the Opposition in the Northern House of Assembly, later became a federal vice-president of the AG, as did J. S. Tarka, president-general of the United Middle Belt Congress (UMBC). Tarka, youthful leader of Nigeria's largest minority, the Tiv, was returned to the House of Representatives with the highest individual vote in the federal election of 1959. Indeed, the adhesion of the Tiv electorate to Tarka's branch of the AG was so firm that, in 1961, Ibrahim Imam, whose position in Bornu had become untenable, actually stood for and won election to the Northern House of Assembly from a Tivland constituency. Still later, Imam quit the opposition altogether. In the Eastern Region, several AG leaders sprang up with the movement to create a non-Ibo state in the former provinces of Calabar, Ogoja, and Rivers, the most prominent among them being S. G. Ikoku (Aro Calabar), leader of the Opposition in the

Eastern House of Assembly. As an outspoken socialist, Ikoku was elected federal secretary of the party during the crisis of 1962. Subsequently, he went into political exile in Ghana.

POLITICAL STYLE

Analysis of leadership recruitment requires concepts that probe the relationship between politics and personality with more subtlety than is found in the impersonal categories of educational background, socioeconomic status, ethnic identification, and religious affiliation. With a need for the added dimension of political style in mind the present writers have ventured a shorthand classification of Nigerian political leaders as "organizational intelligentsia," "cosmopolitan celebrities," "communal heroes," and "traditional notables"—in roughly that order of importance.[66] The "organizational intelligentsia" are typically educators, professionals, and businessmen who devote their talents and high social prestige to the service of a political party and generally control its machinery. Many of them are not widely known in the country. Among the more promising such persons at present are the youthful intellectuals who have risen to prominence within the AG during the postindependence party crisis. The new generation of leaders, currently supporting Awolowo, is more seriously concerned about the specific ideologies of development than were its eclectically nationalistic predecessors. Their counterparts in other parties include a few of the younger federal ministers, such as Maitama Sule, Waziri Ibrahim, and Shehu Shagari of the NPC and C. Olu Akinfosile of the NCNC. Certain leaders of the NCNC youth wing belong to this category, as do a few trade unionists and the leaders of the minor socialist and radical parties, such as the Lagos physician, Dr. Tunji Otegbeye.

"Cosmopolitan celebrities" are popular professionals and businessmen who appeal to the multitribal electorates of the cosmopolitan towns. A good example is the first mayor of Enugu, Malam Umaru Altine, a cattle dealer of Fulani descent who rose to high municipal office with the backing of a preponderantly Ibo electorate in the capital city of the Eastern Region. Since independence, the trend has turned away from the celebrity. Persons of this type were more likely to rise to power during the nationalist era, when strong vote-getters of sufficient affluence to bear the costs of campaigning were in greater demand than at present. Those who presently remain at the top have secured

[66] R. L. Sklar and C. S. Whitaker, Jr., "Nigeria," in J. S. Coleman and C. G. Rosberg, eds., *Political Parties and National Integration in Tropical Africa* (Berkeley and Los Angeles: University of California Press 1964), pp. 597–654.

key positions in their parties, the government, or the national economy.

"Communal heroes" are the leaders of homogeneous cultural sub-groups in areas of traditional habitation—typically, traditional towns with their rural peripheries. Typically, the "communal hero" is an astute politician who acts consciously as the crucial political link between traditionalists who resist change at the local level and modernists who foster change at the national level. This type is most likely to arise in a cohesive community which finds itself in opposition to a regional government party. The prototypes are the late Alhaji Adegoke Adelabu of Ibadan and Chief Humphrey Omo-Osagie of Benin. Ibadan, the greatest Yoruba city and capital of the West, is traditionally antagonistic to the AG. The explanation lies partly in the hostility of the Ibadan people to other Yoruba settlers, especially those from the neighboring province of Ijebu. Obafemi Awolowo, himself an Ijebu who practiced law in Ibadan, was prominent among those who promoted settler interests in the name of Yoruba unity during the late 1940's. Consequently, the Ibadan people regarded Awolowo's party with hostility, despite the fact that many enlightened citizens of Ibadan joined the AG and with it attained regional power in 1952. The mass of the Ibadan people rallied to Adelabu and his communal party, the *Mabolaje*, which means literally, "Do not lower the dignity of chiefs," or more loosely, "Bring back the old glories." Adelabu, truly a man of the people, had become first vice-president of the NCNC and leader of the Opposition in the Western House of Assembly prior to his accidendal death in 1958.

Similarly, in Benin, the Edo-speaking community resented the predominantly Yoruba regional government at Ibadan and gave a cold reception to the local branch of the AG, which was centered in an elite social and political club called the Reformed *Ogboni* Fraternity. Chief Omo-Osagie and his associates organized the Benin masses into the *Otu Edo* (Edo Community), which, like the Mabolaje of Ibadan, the People's Party of Oyo, and the mass party of *Ilesha*, affiliated with the NCNC. For a time, in the late 1950's, Chief Omo-Osagie campaigned with vigor against the sacred Oba of Benin, who had, in the manner of nearly all Western chiefs, thrown his lot in with the regional government party. Unable to sway public opinion, the Oba changed his allegiance in 1960 and resigned from his office as Minister without Portfolio in the regional cabinet. In 1964, he became the first president of the Midwestern House of Chiefs. His former antagonist, Chief Omo-Osagie, now virtually master of Benin with the traditional title of *Iyasse*, became Minister of Local Government and Chieftaincy Affairs in the new region. By and large, however, "communal heros" today loom much less large than in the 1950's, since power has gravitated to the organization men, who are more concerned with national planning and rational-institutional control than with mass popularity.

It may not be amiss at this point to note the unique case of a working-class hero, Michael A. O. Imoudu, who has been president of the Railway Workers' Union since 1940 and is called "the father of Nigerian trade unionism." Imoudu earned his reputation as a labor agitator during the war when the government deported him from Lagos and placed him under restriction in his rural home district for two years. He was released in time to play a leading part in the general strike of public employees for higher wages in 1945. The following year, he joined with the leaders of the NCNC, Macaulay and Azikiwe, in their tour of Nigeria to obtain a popular mandate for revision of the constitution. Subsequently he drifted away from the NCNC to more radical and explicitly socialistic alternatives. While there is a world of difference between the populist working-class leader and the "communal hero," they do display some similar characteristics. Both types "belong to the people," with whom they establish a somewhat mystical identity as the larger-than-life image of themselves. Imoudu is Nigeria's "labor leader number one" because his devotion to the working man is so transparently genuine. Unlike many trade-union leaders of his stature who live in relative comfort, he chooses to live an apparently humble life in a slum area of Lagos. When recently Imoudu, dressed in an all-red costume, ate a meal of garri (diluted casava) and stockfish in the presence of an official commission on wages— deliberately to spotlight the poor quality of the working-class diet—the prolonged laughter he provoked in the public gallery was neither disdainful of him nor lighthearted.

Finally, "traditional notables" are leaders who derive their authority mainly from their stature in the traditional order. Few such men retain great political influence in southern Nigeria, where regional government parties have gained virtually absolute control over traditional institutions. Those who have held important positions in recent years are modern men as well as "traditional notables." Sir Adesoji Aderemi II, the *Oni* of Ife, for example, the pre-eminent traditional spiritual ruler of Yorubaland, and first constitutional Governor of the West, is a long-time associate of Chief Awolowo, at first in the latter's publishing enterprise at Ibadan and subsequently in politics. The Oni lost his gover-

norship during the crisis of 1962. Most of those in high positions in the
West who are addressed as "chief" hold "courtesy titles," rather than
titles of traditional rulership. Such honors are bestowed upon eminent
men and women by the traditional chiefs of Yoruba communities in
token of their personal achievements and contributions to community
welfare. In this way chieftaincy has meshed with the modern social
and political development of Yorubaland to become the supreme symbol of achieved social status. Chief Awolowo, for example, received his
title after his appointment as Premier of the West. Less political significance attaches to title-taking in the East than in the West, but many
political leaders, among them Dr. Azikiwe and Dr. Okpara, have been
so honored by Eastern communities.

In Northern Nigeria nobility of birth matters enormously. An ex-
haustive survey of the parentage and personal positions of members of
the Northern House of Assembly in 1959 revealed that no less than 82
per cent were drawn from various segments of the class of traditional
rulers.[67] The most illustrious of the "traditional notables" are the great
emirs, the Sultan of Sokoto, the Emir of Kano, the Shehu of Bornu, and
the Emir of Katsina. Normally, emirs and chiefs are patrons rather
than members of the NPC, but their influence on the party within their
respective jurisdictions, especially with respect to parliamentary nominations, is prodigious, and collectively they exert considerable influence
on the NPC central executive. Recently, the Northern Premier, in reluctantly forcing the abdication of Sanusi, Emir of Kano, demonstrated
his resolve and ability to bend even the most powerful emir to his and
the party's will if necessary. It must be remembered, however, that the
Sardauna is not only a traditional notable in his own right; as a practical politician he is naturally concerned to promote the conditions of
viable traditional legitimacy with which the mass roots of his own regime are deeply entwined.

Political Parties

The major Nigerian parties have unrestricted membership: any Nigerian may join the NCNC [68] or the AG; any person of northern origin
is eligible for membership in the NPC or the NEPU while any person of

[67] C. S. Whitaker, Jr., "The Politics of Tradition: A Study of Continuity and
Change in Northern Nigeria" (unpublished Ph.D. thesis, Princeton University,
1964), pp. 389–391.
[68] When in 1961, the people of the Southern Cameroons voted to federate with
the Cameroun Republic rather than Nigeria, the NCNC changed its name from
National Council of Nigeria and the Cameroons to National Convention of Nigerian Citizens, retaining the old, popular initials

middle-belt origin may belong to the UMBC, although membership in the latter tends to be mediated through local affiliates. Unquestionably, the actual distribution of party strength is affected decisively by ethnic solidarity. Thus, the NCNC enjoys the overwhelming support of Ibo-speaking peoples: in the 1959 federal election it made a clean sweep of the fifty constituencies in the Ibo sector of the Eastern Region; in the regional election of 1961, it garnered 77 of 103 "Ibo seats" in the Eastern House of Assembly. It is also the predominant party among non-Ibos in the East, among the Edo- and Ibo-speaking peoples of the Midwest, and in certain Yoruba communities, notably in Ibadan, Ilesha, and Oyo township. In the North it operates mainly through the NEPU, which has evinced continued strength mainly in urban centers.

Historically dominant in the West, the AG appears, since the party crisis of 1962, to have declined in those sectors of the Eastern and Northern Regions where it had made its greatest headway prior to independence, namely, the Calabar-Ogoja-Rivers section of the East, and the Yoruba-speaking districts of Ilorin Province, the middle belt, and Bornu in the North. In 1962, the AG secured control of the Lagos Town Council, which achievement has been widely interpreted as an expression of Yoruba solidarity with the embattled Chief Awolowo.

Of all parties, the NPC most fully controls its sphere of operations, having lately gained firm electoral control of the Yoruba-speaking districts of Ilorin and most sectors of the middle belt, with the exception of Tivland, which remains an opposition stronghold on which the NPC has recently exerted considerable pressure to change allegiance. Local parties of consequence in the North, are, like the Igbirra Tribal Union and the Idoma State Union, aligned with the NPC or, like the Habe Tribal Union of Bauchi, with the NEPU. The Dynamic Party, identified with social criticism and its self-proclaimed "Kemalist" leader, Dr. Chike Obi, has adherents mainly in the East, where it won five seats in the last regional election.

Prior to the federal election of 1965, small socialist parties, such as the defunct Nigerian Labour Party (based on the left wing of the trade-union movement) remained outside the arena of electoral contests. In 1963, left-wing socialists, including radical trade-union leaders and members of the Nigerian Youth Congress, organized the Socialist Workers and Farmers Party to hasten the occurrence of "national democratic revolution" and "build socialism in Nigeria." Dr. Tunji Otegbeye, president of the Nigerian Youth Congress, became secretary-general of the SWAFP. Subsequently, a serious division developed within the socialist movement. Alleging that SWAFP had succumbed to "bourgeois" and "revisionist" tendencies, certain members of the Nigerian Youth Congress, led by Mr. Eskor Toyo, a teacher and publicist, formed an autonomous group, called the Revolutionary Council of the Nigerian Youth Congress, which teamed up with like-minded trade unionists to inaugurate a new Nigerian Labour Party under the leadership of Michael Imoudu. But this party too has been factious.

PARTY ORGANIZATION

The major parties observe procedures for "direct" individual membership, based on branches formed at the local government or regional constituency level. Generally, in the case of the NCNC and of the AG, ancillary associations, including tribal unions, affiliate with local party branches on a de facto basis. In rural districts of the Northern Region the local leadership of the NPC usually coincides with the traditional-administrative authority group. Thus, it was found that of 68 rural district branches of the NPC investigated in 1959, 60 had chairmen who were also district heads, or traditional subchiefs in the emirates. Indeed, the apparatus of native administration as a whole—from the central councilors and heads of departments to the district and village heads and subordinate technical agents whose work places them in constant contact with the rural masses—in effect doubles as the political machinery of the party. This helps to explain why the party as such has never required, despite its much more populous clientele and far vaster territorial scope, anything like the strength in personnel and financial resources typical of its southern counterparts.

The National Convention of Nigerian Citizens. Supreme authority in the NCNC is vested in its national convention, held annually and for special purposes. The right of participation is extended to members of the national executive committee, all the party's parliamentarians, and four representatives of every regional constituency, including representatives of the constituency Women's Association, the Zikist Movement, and the recently recognized Okpara Youth Brigade. These militant auxiliaries, in particular the Zikist Movement, perpetuate the heritage of radical nationalism and socialism handed down from the old Zikist Movement (banned in 1950) and succeeding youth wings of the party.

NCNC conventions are noted for the freewheeling spontaneity of their proceedings. The action of the Jos convention of 1952, for example, expelling the NCNC central ministers from the party for their failure to "toe the line," was a severer one than Dr. Azikiwe had contemplated; the "trial" and expulsion of radical members of the NCNC Youth Association for insubordination at the Ibadan convention of 1955 had not been predicted beforehand; and the motion empowering the national president to appoint national officers (adopted by the Aba convention of 1957) was made from the floor as an alternative to more drastic measures proposed by Dr. Azikiwe. Currently, eleven national officers are subject to annual re-election by the convention. These, in addition to an appointed national political adviser, chairmen of the regional working committees, and the chairman of the Lagos branch, comprise the central working committee, an inner core of the broadly representative national executive committee. The latter, which includes some 82 members, meets semiannually and as required; some famous meetings of the national executive committee have been, in effect, "little conventions," distinguished by a presidential address, the presence of many observers, and an air of controversy.

Regional affairs of the party are conducted by regional working committees including ministers of government and members of the national executive committee, in addition to members elected by regional conferences. The regional working committees are strictly subordinate to central party organs, specifically the Central Working Committee, national executive committee and the convention. These bodies, responsible for the enforcement of party discipline, are also empowered to control the various parliamentary wings of the NCNC. Furthermore, approval of the central working committee must be obtained for parliamentary nominations made by the regional working committees or constituency nomination committees. In practice, central party authorities have rarely vetoed the local choice.

The Action Group. Supreme authority in the AG is vested in its annual federal congress, comprising two representatives of every federal constituency, two representatives of the party in the Lagos City Council, all the party's federal parliamentarians, all regional ministers and members of the regional shadow cabinets, and all members of the federal executive council.

The federal executive council consists of all federal officers, the chairman and secretary of each regional conference, the leaders of the several parliamentary councils, the speaker of any legislature controlled by the AG, and twelve members from each region annually elected by the federal congress. It is the principal decision-making unit of the party. The powers of the executive council, which meets quarterly, are delegated to a working committee, authorized to direct the administrative and financial affairs of the party at both federal and regional levels. All officers of the party, save the federal president, are subject to annual re-election. In 1963, the imprisoned Chief Awolowo was made Life-President of the party. Before the 1962 crisis, regional organizations were set up in accordance with the party's position on the creation of new states. A high degree of centralization within the party was ensured by strict central control of finances and the employment of party workers.

While the origins of the AG, like those of other parties, were extra-parliamentary, the primary object of the founders of the AG (and of the NPC) was the attainment of power in a single region under a colonial constitution. It is only since independence that radical nonparliamentarians have asserted their views vigorously within party councils, thereby creating a potential for conflict between parliamentary and "organizational" elements. The party constitution provides for the election of regional parliamentary leaders by joint meetings of the regional parliamentary council and the executive committee of the regional conference. Chief Awolowo, federal president and federal parliamentary leader, is also styled "Leader of the Party"—he was elected to the latter office by a joint meeting of the federal executive council and all parliamentary councils. Until 1962, there was also a deputy leader of the party, elected in the same way. The leader and, formerly, the deputy leader have had indefinite tenure of office. In 1962, a joint meeting of the federal executive council and all parliamentary councils dismissed Chief Akintola as deputy leader of the party. Previously, a joint meeting of the Western and Midwestern regional executive committees (large, representative bodies) had directed him to resign his premiership of the West. A majority of the AG members of the Western House of Assembly, consisting of a slim majority of the total membership of that chamber, acted to implement these directives by signifying, in a letter to the Governor, their lack of confidence in the Akintola Ministry. This resulted in the Governor's controversial decision to dismiss him from office and the ensuing constitutional crisis.

All AG candidates to elective local and legislative office are supposed to be chosen in accordance with strict procedures of nomination. In those areas where AG organization had been established prior to its preparation for the federal election of 1959, as in Western Nigeria and the "C-O-R State" area of the East, AG candidates for that election were selected by constituency committees representing local government electoral wards. The typical selection committee comprised a few hundred party members, and all nominations were made by secret ballot, subject to formal approval by the federal executive council.

The Northern Peoples' Congress. Since 1952, when a convention of the NPC ratified its leaders' decision to proclaim a political party, the Congress has been ruled by its parliamentary caucuses. In consequence, there is little correspondence between the constitution of the NPC, adopted in 1948, and its effective power structure. Thus, the constitution provides for the annual election of party officers; in 1955, however, the party convention voted to "freeze" for five years the selected slate of officers. As it happened, these years coincided with the crucial period during which terms for the transfer of colonial power to the federal and NPC regional governments were negotiated. As of early 1965, another convention had not yet been called. The present extent of parliamentary control over the extraparliamentary organization of the NPC was first demonstrated in 1959, when the parliamentarians of the party met at Kaduna to adopt the party's election manifesto, which no other body even considered prior to its publication. This remarkable degree of parliamentary ascendancy has never been formally sanctioned, but seems rather to reflect the hierarchical relationships and expectations vis-à-vis authority which prevail in the predominant cultural sector of the North.

Owing to its primary dependence upon the institutions of native administration, the NPC, alone of the major parties, adheres to the principle of extreme decentralization. This principle carries over to the organization of the regional and federal parliamentary parties, which choose executive subcommittees comprising representatives of the several provincial "delegations." Harmony between the federal and regional parliamentary wings is sought after in joint (federal-regional) parliamentary committee meetings and consultations between leaders, which normally ensures it. In one case only since 1954 have the parliamentary bodies of the NPC openly disagreed—in the decision of Sir Abubakar's government to accept a proferred loan from Israel, despite the fact that the NPC majority in the regional House of Assembly under Sir Ahmadu, the Sardauna, actually passed a resolution voicing its opposition to the proposal.

By contrast with proceedings at annual conventions of the NPC, the atmosphere of parliamentary party meetings is one of free give-and-take. At the regional level, where the party holds all but a few of the 166 seats, discipline is enforced on motions of importance to the government, but the principle of decentralization is honored in the right of representatives to assert the views and interests of their constituents. The relative social homogeneity of the parliamentary party facilitates a process of discussion and compromise, which in turn reflects the influence of the emirate hierarchies in the nomination of NPC candidates.

The Northern Elements Progressive Union and the United Middle Belt Congress. Closely tied to the NCNC, upon which it depends for financial assistance, the NEPU nonetheless maintains its organizational autonomy. Its alienation from the institutions of native administration is manifest in its membership, which is drawn primarily from the urban petty trading class rather than from the traditionalist peasantry or the functionary and laboring classes employed by local authorities. In marked contrast to the NPC, the NEPU is a highly centralized party. Formerly, the president-general was subject to annual re-election, but the annual conference of 1959 elevated Alhaji Aminu Kano to the position of Life-President. Four of the national officers are selected by the president; the others are chosen by a committee consisting of one representative of each of the thirteen northern provinces plus Kano City, over which Alhaji Aminu presides. The Life-President also submits a list of candidates for membership in the national executive committee to the annual conference for its approval. Local branches of the party are supervised by paid provincial organizers, all of whom hold positions in the national executive committee.

In 1960, NEPU, as an ally of the NCNC, became a partner in the federal government coalition. Inevitably, militant members of the party resented the implication of NEPU/NPC collaboration ostensibly underlying this move. For the first time, Aminu Kano was subject to sharp criticism from his most ardent and principled admirers, including some members of the militant Freedom Youth Wing. Splits in the party, accompanied in significant instances by declarations of support for the AG, ensued. Thus weakened by the disillusionment of its cadres, NEPU managed to win only one seat in the regional election of 1961. In token of its national orientation, NEPU has since changed its name from Northern to Nigerian Elements Progressive Union.

Unlike NEPU, the UMBC at one point actually merged with the organization of a major southern party—the AG—upon which it had come to depend almost completely for financial and technical support. This somewhat amorphous and fragile alliance of dispersed tribal components was shattered, however, by defections to the NPC during the AG crisis of 1962. A remnant, based mainly in Tiv Division, resumed its autonomy and in 1963 joined the NEPU in a new alliance of northern opposition parties called the Northern Progressive Front (with Alhaji Aminu Kano as chairman and J. S. Tarka as general secretary).

PARTY FINANCE

The principal "fixed" source of party revenue is the levy that all parties make on the salaries of their parliamentary members and of the recipients of patronage appointments to statutory bodies. The levy embodies a principle of the nationalist movement: those who are elected to office must not forget that their perquisites are incidental to the cause. Both the NCNC and the NPC impose a 10 per cent levy on parliamentary and patronage emoluments, but the AG exempts ministerial salaries on the ground that these are professional rather than political stipends. Ministers and junior ministers, however, in the AG and the NPC especially are expected to defray substantial portions of the expenses of their constituency organizations. In addition, all parties collect enrollment fees (one shilling for the NCNC/NEPU and the AG; two shillings for the NPC) and monthly dues (sixpence for the NCNC/NEPU; one shilling for the AG and the NPC) in addition to affiliation fees from their member-associations. Other sources of revenue include the sale of party literature, emblems, and other material, income from public and social functions, and donations from supporters. In the case of the AG, substantial private "donations" have been coordinated with the diversion of loan capital on the part of agencies of the Western regional government.[69] Finally, all parties have utilized the loan facilities of allied banking institutions as indicated below.

Interest Groups

ETHNIC AND RELIGIOUS INTEREST GROUPS

Organized interest groups function in many spheres of Nigerian life with varying degrees of attachment to political parties. A widespread form of social organization is the voluntary association based on kinship or territorial affinity, such as occur within the clan, village group, district, or tribe. Many such associations in new urban areas are affiliated with parent bodies in the home towns and villages of their members. It is only to be expected that political parties tend to seek members and organizational support from the urban and rural branches of these associations. Compared with southern Nigeria, however, ethnic group associations in the North play a comparatively minor role in politics. Their absence among the historic Muslim communities

---

[69] See below, pp. 100–101.

may be attributed both to the integrative force of religion and to the multitribal span of the Fulani empire. Ethnic group associations affiliated with the NPC represent mainly peoples indigenous to the middle belt.

The highest level of ethnic group organization is the nationality association, which unifies ethnic groups on the basis of their widest cultural and linguistic affinities. Two such "peak associations," the Ibo State Union and the Society of the Descendants of Oduduwa, have alter-ego relationships with the NCNC and AG respectively. This has tended to create an exaggerated impression of the purely ethnic impact on party policies and the internal distribution of party power. Within the major parties ethnic factions have not been more conspicuous than factions based on other principles. Nor have the leading nationality associations been able to mediate all serious disputes between party colleagues of the same ethnic nationality. The Ibo State Union achieved only partial success in its mediation of the Eastern crisis of 1952–1953; its executive committee remained neutral during the Azikiwe-Mbadiwe row of 1958–1959, after failing to effect a reconciliation. Similarly, the Society of the Descendants of Oduduwa failed utterly in its attempt to heal the disastrous Awolowo-Akintola breach in 1962. In the aftermath of that conflict, prominent Yoruba personalities, among them the Chief Justice of the Federation, other high judicial officers, the emergency Administrator of the Western Region, traditional rulers, and supporters of the Akintola government, formed a new pan-Yoruba cultural organization, called the Society of the Descendants of Olofin (alleged to be the proper name of the legendary Oduduwa). But this society was scorned by AG loyalists as a political device; it thus failed to reconcile the warring factions.

In a few cases, associations based on religious affinity are closely related to the major parties. We have seen that leaders of the AG in the Western Region formed a United Muslim Council in 1957 to counter the influence of the National Muslim League (later the National Emancipation League, an ally of the Northern Peoples' Congress). Occasionally, leaders of Islamic congregations in southwestern Nigeria have been highly partisan to one party or another, particularly in Lagos and Ibadan. Interdenominational conflict in the Eastern Region over the issue of public support for parochial schools has ranged the Eastern Nigeria Catholic Council against the Convention of Protestant Citizens, although both associations are subject to dominant NCNC influence. In Northern Nigeria leaders of the separatist UMBC are typically members of Christian mission congregations.

Throughout the North Muslim *mallamai* (plural of malam—here the term refers specifically to teachers or learned men) are the main vehicles for the interpretation of religious doctrine to the masses and therefore have enormous influence. Probably the largest number and certainly the most influential mallamai identify and are identified with the NPC and they tend to be extremely conservative, possibly reactionary, in their outlook on the modern world. To propagate the party's "religious" dicta, NPC must cultivate the mallamai, whose counsel usually reinforces the predilections of its more tradition-minded members and supporters.

In contrast to the role of these mallamai, the religio-political tendencies of the Tijaniyya *turuq* (Arabic, plural: *tariqa*), or mystic brotherhood, tend to link it to NEPU. Probably the majority of Tijaniyya adherents in Northern Nigeria vote for the NPC and are politically quiescent. What may be called a "left wing" of the Tijaniyya in Northern Nigeria—known as *Yan Wazifa* (those who practice the litany of *Wazifa*)—is a radical influence, however, in both religion and politics. Religiously, the Tijaniyya, and especially the "Yan Wazifa," is a reformist, puritanical, mission-minded group which rivals the Khadiriyya—the other major turuq in Northern Nigeria—which is identified with the ruling house of Sokoto. Politically, it has been suggested that in Northern Nigeria the Tijaniyya stands in relation to the Khadiriyya and orthodox Islam as a nonconformist sect to an established church. Where the head of an emirate follows the Khadiriyya but Tijaniyya is strong, as in Sokoto, the latter is regarded as a threat to existing authority and treated accordingly. More orthodox Tijani emirs look on the "Yan Wazifa" in much the same way. Such hostility merely intensifies friction between the traditional ruling class and members of the Tijaniyya, the greatest number of whom are Habe commoners. The net result is a natural alliance between the *turuq* and NEPU in certain parts of the "holy North."

SOCIOECONOMIC INTEREST GROUPS

Nigerian trade unions represent some 250,000 employed workers, roughly one-half of all wage earners but less than 1 per cent of the total population. In general, their commitments to political parties are few; the prudent exception to this rule is the organization of northern tin miners on the Jos plateau (Northern Mine Workers Union), which, for cultural and political reasons, is affiliated with the NPC. For over a decade, the role of organized labor in national politics was surprisingly minor.[70] A few leading trade unionists have been included in executive bodies of the NCNC and the AG, but many others shied away from party identification, owing perhaps to the tactical requirements of collective bargaining with government as the largest employer of labor. A small number of radical unionists, repelled by the bourgeois orientations of the major parties, sporadically supported the small socialistic parties. In June, 1964, organized and unorganized workers, mostly public employees, engaged in a thirteen-day general strike to protest the federal government's rejection of recommendations made by a commission it had appointed to examine the national wage structure and related matters. By the time a compromise agreement to negotiate had been reached, the trade union leaders had effectively challenged government authority for the first time. A few of them have since become more active politically.

At present, there are three central labor bodies—the United Labour Congress, which is affiliated with the International Confederation of Free Trade Unions, the left-leaning Nigerian Trades Union Congress, and the Nigerian Workers Council, an affiliate of the International Federation of Christian Trade Unions. There is also an informal alliance of large, unaffiliated trade unions, under the leadership of Mr. Imoudu, called the Labour Unity Front. During the general strike, solidarity was achieved through the agency of a nonpartisan Joint Action Committee.

By contrast, business interest groups—traders and merchants, produce-buyers and motor-transport owners, builders, and bankers—are deeply involved in party politics. Most firms concentrate their activities in a single region, and those company directors who support the regional government party are most likely to obtain the trading licenses, contracts, and loans which spell prosperity. Of course, they are expected, in turn, to give moral and material backing to their patron parties.

Of particular significance among business interest groups are the newspaper publishers. Most of the mass circulation newspapers have been allied with political parties. An exception is the British-owned *Daily Times* and *Sunday Times*. The *Morning Post* and *Sunday Post* are owned by the federal government and support its leadership. News-

---

[70] A recent study by Eliot J. Berg and Jeffrey Butler substantiates this conclusion and finds it typical of trade-union experience in most of the new African states. "Trade Unions and Politics in Tropical Africa," in J. S. Coleman and C. G. Rosberg, eds., *op. cit.*, pp. 340–381.

papers owned by the regional governments, including the *Nigerian Outlook* (Eastern Region daily), and the *Nigerian Citizen* and *Gaskiya Ta Fi Kwabo* (Northern Region biweeklies), vigorously support the regional parties in power. In addition, the NCNC is supported by the Zik group of newspapers, which includes the *West African Pilot* and a chain of provincial newspapers managed by associates of Dr. Azikiwe. The rival Amalgamated Press of Nigeria, publisher of the *Daily Express*, and an allied chain of provincial newspapers, have espoused the cause of the AG.

Each of these two publishing groups has in the past been financed by a private banking institutions, the Zik group by the African Continental Bank, and Amalgamated Press by the National Bank of Nigeria. With the nationalization of these banks by the Eastern and Western regional governments respectively, the principal means of party propaganda were placed virtually in direct dependence upon regional government officials. Only the intervention of foreign capital (from a Canadian-British publishing firm) saved the *Daily Express* for the AG, when the federal government seized all the Western regional statutory corporations during the 1962 emergency. The provincial newspapers of the AG chain were less fortunate. Ultimately, the *Daily Express*, under complete foreign ownership, severed its tie with the AG.

No survey of interest groups would be complete without mention of the foreign corporations—export-import houses, petroleum companies, mining interests, and investors of various kinds—that operate in Nigeria under favorable conditions, often in partnership with Nigerian firms or government agencies. Undoubtedly, they play an important part in the political process; but their influence has yet to be studied.

Elections

EVOLUTION OF THE ELECTORAL SYSTEM

The federalist compromise of 1954 provided for separate elections to the regional and federal legislatures, but left the responsibility for determination of electoral procedures and for qualifications of electors and candidates to the several governments. Consequently, a different system obtained in each of five electoral areas for the first election to the House of Representatives. Once again, representatives from the Northern Region were elected indirectly through the medium of electoral colleges, culminating in final colleges into which candidates could be injected, this time by the vote of 10 elected members of the college. In Kano Division 16 of the 18 ultimately successful candi-

dates, known to have enjoyed the backing of the emir, were so nominated. As a result of such electoral manipulations, no members of the
NEPU were elected to the House of Representatives. Electoral colleges were also employed in the Southern Cameroons, but the Eastern
Region adopted a system of universal adult suffrage in both single-
member and double-member constituencies. In Lagos and the West
single-member constituencies were created; the franchise was universal
in Lagos, but restricted to taxpayers in the West.

In 1955, Dr. Azikiwe expressed his view that the absence of a uniform electoral system for the entire federation seriously hampered the
evolution of stable national parties, based on programmatic principles
rather than communal interests. This observation was particularly
germane to the plight of the NEPU in the North. Other factors, however, notably and hostility of the Northern authorities to political opposition, and partisan applications of Islamic law by Native Court judges,
were also pertinent. In 1956, the North experimented with direct elections in 19 urban districts. Despite its generally weak organization, resulting in the diversion of votes to independent candidates who were
disappointed in their bids for party nomination, the NPC won 11 of
these contests, including all four in Kano. Western regional electoral
regulations were also liberalized in 1956, virually to the point of introducing universal suffrage, but the Eastern Region retained plural voting in multimember constituencies for the election which redeemed
Dr. Azikiwe's government in 1957.

The federal elections of 1959 and 1964 were conducted on the basis
of universal adult suffrage from single-member constituencies in the
Eastern Region, the Western Region, and Lagos, but adult male
suffrage was adopted in the Northern Region. While the NCNC, the
AG, and the NEPU were committed in principle to female suffrage in
the North, the NPC, pleading religious precept, refused to modify its
stand on this issue. Since the female population of the North counts in
the delimitation of parliamentary constituencies, the southern-based
parties logically criticized the "overrepresentation" of the northern
male electorate. Otherwise, the franchise was extended to all British
subjects or British protected persons (subsequently to Nigerian citizens) of twenty-one years of age who were "ordinarily resident" in
Nigeria. The federal constitution now provides that a qualified voter
may be nominated as a candidate for Parliament from any constituency
in the federation, although male persons only are eligible to stand in
the North. It is accepted that the qualifications for voters in regional

elections shall be the same as in federal elections, and the regional constitutions provide that members of the Houses of Assembly shall be elected directly from single-member constituencies.[71]

OBSERVATIONS ON THE ELECTORAL PROCESS. HOW FREE AND FAIR?

The organization and conduct of a democratic election in a developing country of such internal complexity as Nigeria is an administrative undertaking of immense proportions. Problems of the most intricate difficulty, requiring the highest degree of administrative effort and ingenuity, have to be faced in the course of preparing a satisfactory register of electors, certifying nominations, regulating political campaigns, conducting the poll, and, finally, tabulating the results. Mismanagement of any of these phases of the operation may undermine civic loyalties and threaten the unity of the country. Thus far, there have been two general elections to the House of Representatives. The federal election of 1959 was a highly successful undertaking; that of 1964 was a failure of nearly disastrous proportions. Responsibility for the organization and conduct of the 1959 election devolved mainly upon British administrative officers. At the conclusion of his penetrating study of that election, K. W. J. Post observed that it had been "in a sense . . . the last great act of the British *Raj*. Nigeria still has to face the test of a federal election not only fought but administered by Nigerians."[72]

In theory, a democratic election gives expression to the "will of the people." The extent to which theory and practice correspond depends upon the degree to which electoral procedures are free from corruption by fraud, violence, and abuses of authority. The method of voting must be suitable for use by a largely nonliterate electorate. (Only some 15 per cent of the Nigerian population was literate in 1959.) In Nigeria votes are cast by the insertion of a ballot paper in a box that is marked with the name of the candidate, an optional photograph, and the all-important symbol of his party, or special symbol, if he is an independent candidate.[73] Officials have to guard against forged ballot papers, defective ballot boxes, and such offenses as impersonation,

[71] The first "ethnic" qualification for candidates to a regional House of Assembly was stipulated in the constitution of Midwestern Nigeria. It provides that members of the legislature from four special minority group areas have to belong to the ethnic groups associated with those areas.

[72] *The Nigerian Federal Election of 1959*, p. 439.

[73] The symbols of the major parties are: NCNC, cock; AG, palm tree; NPC, hoe; and NEPU, star. Other symbols used in the 1964 election were: NNDP, hand; Midwest Democratic Front, umbrella; and Niger Delta Congress, fish.

double voting, and illegal possession of ballots. Moreover, the recruitment of the thousands of persons needed to serve as registration and
polling officers is complicated by the widespread feeling that local government officials in all regions, especially Northern native administration staff members, are incorrigibly partial to the regional government
party.

In the Eastern and Western Regions and Lagos local government
elections are conducted on the basis of universal adult suffrage. But in
the North electoral registers are made up with the help of tax lists.
Therefore, there is a tendency in the North, which also lingers even in
the other regions, for voters to associate their right to vote, even in
parliamentary elections, with their obligation to pay regional taxes or
local government rates. "If," as K. W. J. Post inquires, "tax lists were
used in the North to help find out potential electors, and if the administration made every effort to get people to register, how far could registration there be regarded as voluntary?" [74] At any rate, more than 9
million Nigerians—some 88 per cent of the estimated eligible population—registered to vote in 1959.

Nigerian political campaigns have normally been conducted under
conditions of substantial freedom, always subject, however, to the variable applications of regional law. Thus, in 1959, two members of the
AG were indicted by the Eastern regional government for having
published documents charging official discrimination against supporters of their party, which were alleged by the government to contain seditious statements. One of these cases resulted in a conviction
and the imposition of a £100 fine (or two years imprisonment).[75]
Throughout the campaign, allegations were made that certain of the
"customary courts" in Western Nigeria were being used by the regional
government party to "victimize and intimidate" supporters of the
opposition.[76]

In Northern Nigeria opposition party members have been subjected
at various times to multiple and pervasive restrictions on their freedom
of action and expression. Prior to 1960, these were effected principally
by judges in native courts, who enforced both statutory and customary
law (customary law in the area of the emirate system being defined as
Islamic law, of the Maliki school), as well as the ordinances of Native
Authorities. Under the new Penal Code enacted in 1960, customary law

---

[74] *Op. cit.*, p. 177. Post reports instances of persons in all regions having been
approached by tax collectors when they went to register.
[75] *Ibid.*, p. 287.   [76] *Ibid.*, pp. 289–290.

as such is no longer a category of criminal law. This new code, however, represents an attempt to reconcile Nigerian (in effect British)
criminal law and constitutionally protected civil liberties with doctrines
derived from the Maliki texts, with the result that certain of its provisions seem by Western standards highly restrictive of political liberty.[77] Furthermore, in the emirate sector judges are still appointees of
the emirs and frequently members of the ruling hierarchies. In rural
districts especially, the district head, who is also appointed by the emir,
and the native court judge wield virtually absolute power over the
peasantry. Collusive action on their part renders activity by the opposition party exceedingly difficult in many parts of the North.

Among the offenses of a political nature most frequently tried before
native court judges are utterances deemed potentially provocative of
public disorder. Many such utterances are also actionable as slanders
against individuals—a prescription influenced by Maliki concepts. On
occasion, prohibitions of slander or defamation of character have been
stretched by certain Native Authorities into virtual proscriptions of any
derogatory mention of the names of individuals in political addresses.
Thus, during the local election campaign at Sokoto in November, 1957,
it was declared illegal to mention the names of the Sultan and the
Sardauna, despite the fact that the former is the executive head of
Sokoto Division and the latter is Premier of the Region and president
of the NPC. Native administration officials purport to observe a distinction between criticisms of political institutions, which are permissi-
ble, and personal attacks, which are not, but this thin line is easily
blurred in practice, especially in the heat of an election campaign.

Northern law prohibits the wearing of any kind of party uniform.
Other forms of expressive symbolism have also been proscribed. (During the course of his 1954 campaign in Kano City, Aminu Kano,
president-general of the NEPU, was sentenced to three days in prison
by a Native Court judge for flying the NEPU flag on his car, thereby, it
is said, comparing himelf to the Emir of Kano, who alone, with the exception of the British Resident, had the prerogative of flying a flag on
his car.) In reaction to the enthusiasm of many children for the NEPU

[77] See especially Sections 136, 137, 138, and 393. Likewise in approximation of
Maliki precepts, Sections 381, 387, 388, and 403 deal with matters (breach of
contract, drunkenness, drinking of any alcohol by a Muslim, adultery) which
under prevailing Western law are not regarded as criminal offenses at all. For
a heated debate on this and other controversial aspects of the Northern Penal
and Criminal Procedure Codes, see the symposium: "Criminal Law Reform in
Northern Nigeria," *Modern Law Review*, XXIV, No. 5 (September, 1961).

candidates, the Emir of Kano issued a proclamation forbidding them to shout NEPU slogans, sing NEPU songs, or write the word NEPU on their caps or the doors of their houses. In 1959, this prohibition was generalized by a regional statute which "made it an offence for anyone under the age of sixteen to belong to a political party, attend political meetings, wear party badges, carry banners, shout slogans or distribute party literature. It also forbade adults to incite children to do any of these things." [78]

Finally, it should be noted that permits to hold political meetings, required by law in all regions, give rise to special problems in the North, since the power to issue them is vested in the Native Authorities and lies largely in the hands of district heads, who are themselves active politicians. Reviewing the experience of the last federal election campaign in the North, Post observed that "throughout 1959 members of the Action Group and NEPU were sentenced to be jailed, fined or caned for addressing public meetings without a permit, abusing the Sardauna or the NPC, shouting the name of the Opposition leader at a chief, and similar offences. At various times in the last few months of the campaign Action Group and NEPU candidates were jailed in constituencies in Bornu, Kano, and Sokoto Provinces, usually for holding illegal meetings. It is easy to see why lawyers loomed so large in the Action Group's organization in the North. NEPU was less well provided for in this respect." [79]

In 1959, after an intensively fought campaign marked by "distressingly frequent" acts of violence, there was nevertheless an "almost complete absence of outbreaks of violence on polling day." [80] More than 7 million people, nearly 80 per cent of those registered, went to the polls. Despite technical problems arising from the method of voting, secrecy of the ballot was on the whole preserved, [81] and there is no reason to doubt that the tallies, counted by hand, were substantially correct. [82] Post concluded that "a high poll of high registration figures could be held to represent 'the will of the people,' therefore, though it must be remembered that in the North women were not regarded as 'people' in this respect." [83] According to opposition allegations, the Northern campaign atmosphere of 1959 as described by Post was re-

---

[78] Post, *op. cit.*, pp. 290–291.   [79] *Ibid.*, p. 292.   [80] *Ibid.*, pp. 299, 345.

[81] The exceptions were mainly in the North. *Ibid.*, pp. 343–344.

[82] One of the present writers experienced the arduous and somewhat harrowing task of counting ballots throughout an entire night, in the presence of anxious candidates and their agents, during a local government election in 1958.

[83] Post, *op. cit.*, p. 350.

produced or intensified prior to the federal election of December 30, 1964, except that in the second instance opposition frustrations produced a national crisis.

MONEY IN ELECTIONS

Most observers agree that the electoral college system for parliamentary elections, which lingered in the North until 1956 (for local elections, it lingers still), was particularly liable to various forms of "fixing," not least of all to bribery. Final colleges were composed of relatively small groups of several hundred persons or less, and the members were vulnerable to the temptations of a "dash." Bribery, however, was an expensive practice for those who sought to buy the votes of an elector. For, in the words of one member of a final college in the Eastern Region during the 1953 election, a bribe given at "the last minute . . . usually carried more weight than thousands of pounds already spent." [84]

With the introduction of direct elections, the significance of the "dash" to members of electoral colleges generally declined, although support of candidates by local traditional sovereigns is widely held to come at a price in the North, and similar arrangements are not unheard of in the south. The "natural" costs of campaigning have remained steep, however, especially in highly competitive constituencies, where campaign expenses totaling £2,000 to £4,000 are not unusual. These include the costs of transportation, publicity, and remuneration for agents, as well as "treats" and gifts to villagers. In the past, party contributions to candidates have rarely been sufficient to defray these costs; candidates have frequently contracted heavy debts, and successful ones have, for this reason, often resented having to pay party levies on a portion of their emoluments. Under these conditions, and in the absence of legal limitations on campaign expenditures, most candidates in competitive constituencies have been men who can either afford to stand on their own or manage to enlist the financial support of their "friends" or of partisan ethnic group welfare associations. [85]

[84] Quoted in Richard L. Sklar, *Nigerian Political Parties* (Princeton: Princeton University Press, 1963), p. 29.

[85] K. W. J. Post reports that in Warri Division (Midwest), "an area where creeks and mangrove swamps made travel particularly difficult," the NCNC candidate in 1959 met "the major part of all expenses from his personal fortune, and some of the Field Secretaries seemed to regard themselves as serving him rather than the party." *Op. cit.*, pp. 143–144. Post also relates the story of a candidate in the Eastern regional election of 1957, whose campaign was financed by several local businessmen. "He understood their contributions to be a gift, but

To relieve the burden on individual candidates, to ensure their dependence upon the party and subservience to it, and incidentally to open the parliamentary gate to men of modest means, the political parties have assumed increasing responsibilities for electoral finance. In 1959, for example, it was reported that the annual convention of the NCNC "decided to give each candidate £500 from party funds for campaign purposes. If this decision was in fact implemented, it meant an expenditure of about £75,000." [86] The costs of electioneering appear, however, to have risen beyond the normal capacity of the parties to defray from routine sources, including donations from their wealthy supporters. The AG, for example, is reported to have spent an astonishing sum, in excess of £1 million, on the 1959 campaign alone. The strain of this effort was followed by a set of difficult and expensive election campaigns in all three regions during 1960–1961. To meet these expenses and other costs of maintaining an effective opposition to the federal government coalition, the AG has relied upon the credit facilities of the National Bank of Nigeria and, more recently, upon more dubious means of party finance. Finally, it has been suggested that regional government parties may be tempted to seek donations from foreign business interests in return for promises of government contracts. This practice, too, has been publicly attributed mainly to the AG.[87]

THE CAMPAIGN AND THE VOTER

In the present state of our knowledge of Nigerian voting behavior, to assess the influence of political campaigns on the electorate is to enter the realm of conjecture. Clearly, the several major parties command large and devoted followings, as do certain of their leaders personally, notably Nnamdi Azikiwe, who has withdrawn from "party politics" to serve as Head of State. Nonetheless, most observers seem to agree that elections usually turn on local issues and matters which affect the everyday lives of the voters. To cite but one example: in 1957, the NCNC Eastern regional government "went to the country" in order to demonstrate public confidence in the integrity of its leader and the

---

when he lost the election they informed him that the money had only been a loan, and that now he must pay it back." *Ibid.,* p. 49, n. 1. Nor should we overlook the occasional role of money in securing party nominations, explicit formal procedures notwithstanding. Post has noted that "current rates for securing a hotly disputed nomination in the East were quoted at between £1,500 and £2,000." *Ibid.,* p. 254.

[86] *Ibid.,* p. 151.   [87] *Ibid.,* pp. 155–156.

wisdom of its financial policy, following the adverse report of the Tribunal of Inquiry appointed by the Secretary of State for the Colonies. In most constituencies, however, other issues, such as the demand by minority ethnic groups for greater local autonomy, and the vexed question of public support for Catholic schools, occupied the electorate. It would be unwarranted to conclude that the population did not respond at all to the national issue, especially since the NCNC, contesting in its strong region, was virtually certain to win a resounding victory. Neither can it be denied that a majority of the people *apparently* were most concerned about local problems and interests, and disposed to vote accordingly.[88]

Post observed that in most federal constituencies, which were delimited to conform mainly (but not solely) with the population principle of 100,000, it was impossible to discern a cohesive community of interest. For "a man's sense of community was bounded by his family, his village, his clan, or at most in the North and West by his town or emirate." [89] It is largely to this circumstance, and to the drag of deeply ingrained ethnic sensibilities, that he would seem to attribute the failure of the AG in 1959, then undoubtedly the best-organized and best-financed party, waging the most systematic national campaign, to overtake either of its two major rivals.

In Nigeria, then, the political campaign would appear to have a "reinforcement effect" on voters with strong initial political predispositions, much the same as it does in the United States. Nigerian leaders themselves seem to sense as much in marshaling their forces to bring out the maximum vote. At the same time, we must recognize that social pressures productive of new political attitudes multiply rapidly in a developing society, so that studies of its electoral behavior, however soundly conceived, are liable to accelerated obsolescence.

PUBLIC ADMINISTRATION

A colonial regime typifies the pristine administrative state, wherein officials who are not responsible to representatives of the local population exercise all the legislative, executive, and judicial functions of government. In the event of planned political advance toward democratic

---

[88] The Eastern regional election of 1961 provides further evidence of the persistence of localism, as candidates other than those sponsored by the NCNC and the AG obtained some 22 per cent of the vote, returning 25 of 135 members to House of Assembly.

[89] Post, *op. cit.*, p. 254.

self-government, the formal role of administration mutates gradually from master to servant of the state. Its actual function then becomes partly a matter of the extent to which government assumes responsibility for economic development and social welfare. In Nigeria government is the principal instrument of development and modernization. Most opportunities for nonagricultural employment lie in the public sector. In 1958, for example, 63.2 per cent of the 478,300 persons employed in the nonagricultural sector of the economy were public employees, including salaried employees of the federal and regional governments, local government councils, and public corporations, in addition to wage laborers.[90]

Organization and Composition of the Public Services

Until 1954, the Nigerian civil service was unified and country-wide. With the adoption of a federal constitution, four separate establishments were created, serving the federal government and the three regions. In composition the federal service only is a national corps. Interservice transfers between the regional and federal services are not uncommon, and relatively uniform standards of administrative practice are promoted by a National Council on Establishments.

In British administrative theory the value of bureaucratic subordination to democratic authority is balanced against the value of administrative freedom from excessive political interference. Thus coordinate systems of control are implied. Similarly, at the federal level in Nigeria, political responsibility for civil service is vested in the Prime Minister, whose Permanent Secretary (a top-level civil servant) is the service's "unofficial head." Specific political responsibilities in regard to the service are assigned to the federal ministries of Establishments and Finance. The constitution delegates responsibility for appointments, promotions, and discipline to a nonpolitical Public Service Commission of five members, appointed by the President on the advice of the Prime Minister. "On paper," Professor Cole has observed, "the Federal Establishment Office of the Ministry of Establishments approves the need for the establishment of a new post; the Permanent Secretary of the Ministry of Finance, acting for the Minister, decides whether funds are available for the post; and the Public Service Commission recommends the person for appointment after the Nigerianization Officer of the Ministry of Establishments has determined whether a qualified Ni-

[90] Taylor Cole, "Bureaucracy in Transition," in Tilman and Cole, eds., *op. cit.*, p. 90.

gerian is available." In practice, however, many decisions concerning personnel "are the product of informal handling . . . and defy formal explanation." [91]

At the regional level each civil service establishment is supervised by a Permanent Secretary in the office of the Premier or Minister of Finance, and appointments to the service are made by the regional Governor upon recommendation of the regional Public Service Commission.

FROM HOURGLASS TO PYRAMID

In the mid-1950's, Nigeria's public service was likened to "an hourglass, broad at the bottom, narrow in the middle, and broad again at the top." Its chief defect was identified as "the lack of an adequate middle part." [92] Subsequently, all governments of the Federation abolished the twofold division of their civil services into "junior" and "senior" staffs in favor of a five-tiered structure for the clerical-administrative and technical-professional branches of service. Between the high-ranking administrative-professional grades and the low-ranking clerical-technical grades an intermediate grade of executives and higher technicians was created to strengthen the middle part. In general, admission to the two highest grades of service (superscale and administrative-professional) is open to holders of university degrees, while the requirement of post-secondary education is normal for direct appointment to the executive class. In the North, however, special training courses are usually accepted in lieu of higher education.

NIGERIANIZATION

"One of the fundamental rights and privileges of a self-governing country is that it must have control of its public service." This declaration of administrative independence by the government of Malaya was reiterated in 1959 by a special committee of the Nigerian federal Parliament on the Nigerianization of the federal public service. To reflect on Nigeria's reliance upon British administrative personnel during the federal election of 1959 is to appreciate the force of the argument for rapid replacement of expatriate officials by trained Nigerians.

Few issues illustrate so clearly the intricacies of cooperative decolonization. Both sides, Nigerian and British, seek to reconcile their

[91] *Ibid.*, pp. 92–93.
[92] Federation of Nigeria, *Report of the Commission on the Public Services of the Governments in the Federation of Nigeria, 1954–1955* (Lagos: Government Printer, 1955), pp. 35–36.

commitments to competing values. On the Nigerian side there is a strong interest in the maintenance of an efficient, adequately staffed civil service, equal to the exacting administrative tasks imposed by independence and an ambitious program of development. To this end, the Nigerian government resolved to head off a mass exodus of British civil servants. On the other hand, Nigerians naturally resent their dependence upon expatriate officials, particularly the inevitable influence of such officials on national policy, and the real or imagined obstruction they present to the professional advancement of qualified Nigerians.

On the British side there is a sense of responsibility to a new member of the Commonwealth for its administrative viability at the culminating point of British political tutelage. At the same time, the Colonial Office has a moral obligation to members of the overseas service whose careers are affected adversely by the termination of colonial rule. The story of Britain's attempts to balance these commitments has been lucidly told by Kenneth Younger.[93]

With the approach of independence in British Africa and Malaya, the government of the United Kingdom decreed that each of the governments concerned would be required to pay compensation to officials who chose to retire before the end of their normal terms of service or were compelled to do so. This obligation has been called, sardonically, "the price of independence." Eventually, the amount of compensation to be paid by the Nigerian government was computed to reach a maximum of £9,000 per officer, when he reached the age of 41 or 42, on the ground that loss of career at that age would entail the greatest sacrifice for a successful officer. Since the amount of compensation declined steadily thereafter, the scheme proved to be an incentive to retire early with the largest possible lump sum. To offset this incentive, the several Nigerian governments were persuaded to "freeze" the compensation of needed officials at its most favorable point for a period of three years or more. When this did not produce the desired effect, an arrangement was made to pay expatriate officers in advance up to 90 per cent of the maximum compensation to which they were entitled, in the hope that they would decide to stay on during the critical period of political transition. Since the officers were under no obligation to remain at their posts, they were viewed with suspicion by Nigerian critics of the scheme and alleged to be "passengers" who would probably abandon the ship of state as soon as the colonial pilot was dropped. Further-

[93] *The Public Service in New States* (London: Oxford University Press, 1960).

more, it was considered unfair for officers who had taken compensation to be allowed to remain in the service indefinitely, thus enjoying the same privileges and opportunities for promotion as others who had received nothing. In these circumstances the inducements to stay have never been strong. By the end of 1963, 75 per cent of all pensionable expatriate officers who were in the federal service in 1960 had resigned, and the vast majority of higher posts, including all the permanent secretaryships, had been Nigerianized.[94] Similarly, in the Eastern and Western Regions, Nigerianization of the administrative and superscale grades had been virtually accomplished by the end of 1963. No such claim, however, could be made with respect to the Northern Region.

NORTHERNIZATION

Although a preponderant majority of the Nigerian members of every regional civil service consists of persons who are indigenous to the particular region, this norm of recruitment has special significance in the North. The Northern aristocracy is intensely proud of its tradition of administrative competence. Yet the relative retardation of Western education in the North has resulted in a scarce supply of qualified candidates for high-level posts in the civil service. To the North, therefore, Nigerianization implied the uncongenial consequence of an administrative service dominated by Nigerians of non-Northern origin. Defensively, Northern leaders proclaimed their policy of Northernization, interpreted by the Public Service Commission of the Northern Region as follows: "If a qualified Northerner is available, he is given priority in recruitment; if no Northerner is available, an Expatriate may be recruited or a non-Northerner on contract terms." [95] The extent to which this policy has been implemented to exclude southern Nigerians is indicated by the regional and national origins of 221 members of the Northern regional administrative class in 1959: 161 were expatriate officers, 59 were Northern Nigerians, and one was a non-Northern Nigerian.[96]

Northernization has become a political issue in Nigeria less on account of its object, which is not exceptional, than on account of the vigor with which it has been proclaimed and pursued, even at the expense of national values. Hence, the policy has entailed periodic dismissals of southern Nigerians from their jobs in the North. Further, it

[94] Federation of Nigeria, *Sixth Report on the Federal Public Service Commission for the period 1st January to 31st December, 1962* (Lagos: Government Printer, 1963), pp. 7–8.

[95] Cole, "Bureaucracy," *op. cit.*, p. 108.   [96] Younger, *op. cit.*, p. 5.

has been alleged that the commitment of Northerners to the process of Nigerianization of the federal civil service is qualified as a consequence of the unavailability of Northern candidates for federal employment. In 1961, Northerners held fewer than 1 per cent of the higher posts in the federal service,[97] although Northern applicants are aggressively encouraged, at the special behest of Northern federal ministers.

Politics and Administration

It is too early to discount the ability of the Nigerian public service to preserve its professional integrity from partisan exploitation. Its performance thus far appears to augur well. The Western regional service, for example, has experienced a constitutional crisis, involving an irregular overthrow of the regional government party after ten years in power, without apparent serious damage to its own efficiency or morale. Nor has it been subject to a politically inspired purge of its ranks despite the probable sympathy of a great many civil servants for Chief Awolowo and his embattled AG. If members of the public services of Nigeria generally display steadfastness in political storms, they may be expected to develop a professional camaraderie of no small importance to the unity of the country.

The formal position of the Northern civil service in relation to the ruling party is no less British-inspired than its southern counterparts, but this formal similarity belies the unusual intimacy that actually characterizes the northern relationship. This may be in part a reflex of traditional patterns, and doubtless it is also partly attributable to the original circumstances of modern Northern political development, in which government and native administration officials were virtually the sole source of political activism and leadership. Although their proportion of the entire service is slowly decreasing, nearly all of the top appointees in the initial phase of northernization had a background of NPC membership or partisanship; several were close political associates of the men who, later chosen to be government ministers, are now the servants' bosses. Whatever the origin, it is important to note that Northern ministers, most notably the Premier, appear deliberately to cultivate the quality of personal loyalty in civil servants and to welcome openly their identification with the causes of the party, as instanced in the Northern Premier's statement, in the wake of the 1964–1965 constitutional crisis, expressing satisfaction that the crisis had shown that the "goal of the politician and the civil servant in Northern Nigeria is the same."

[97] Cole, "Bureaucracy," *op. cit.*, p. 109.

Some observers believe that the new civil service has more to fear from the debilitating effects of pecuniary corruption than from the threat of political interference. Cases of bribery and corruption are not uncommon, and the Western regional government has, to its credit, appointed an officer to combat corruption. Influence-peddling is an occupational peculiarity of all democratic politicians, however, and a recent author has suggested that Nigerian administrative functionaries have actually encouraged their political superiors to engage in corrupt practices in order to keep them "preoccupied with nonadministrative matters in the interest of efficiency." [98] This may be an exaggerated view, but it does serve to remind us of the experience of countries where relatively upright civil servants and military officers, despairing of political reform, have seized power in the name of efficiency and progress. Thus far antidemocratic tendencies have not been evident among top-level Nigerian bureaucrats. At most it has been suggested that the civil servants and politicians together constitute a "power elite" and "an economically privileged class." [99] But this social characteristic may of itself detract from the ability of the Nigerian civil service to follow a thoroughly nonpolitical path.

LOCAL GOVERNMENT

Under the Nigerian constitution the power to regulate local government is residual and therefore reserved to the regions. It has been exercised by them mainly in accordance with principles determined by the historical experiences of their major cultural groups. In the Northern Region, therefore, modern local government has developed in the matrix of traditional institutions, formal and informal. Elsewhere in Nigeria traditional institutions and values have merely somewhat qualified full adoption of imported British forms.

The Northern Region

The principal units of local government in Northern Nigeria are still styled Native Authorities. In recent years these venerable corporate entities have been modified in the direction of modern democratic norms and practices without eradicating many of the traditional assumptions, objects, relationships, and popular expectations toward them in accordance with which they had previously operated. Until re-

[98] Henry L. Bretton, *Power and Stability in Nigeria* (New York: Praeger, 1962), p. 79.

[99] J. Donald Kingsley, "Bureaucracy and Political Development, with Particular Reference to Nigeria," in Joseph LaPalombara, ed., *Bureaucracy and Political Development* (Princeton: Princeton University Press, 1963), p. 315.

cently the most important emirs governed their domains through councils which they were legally obliged to consult but which they could override, subject to the intervention of a higher authority. Their legal capacity has since been restricted in this regard to that of casting a deciding vote in the event of a tie. These councils currently comprise "traditional" members, others nominated (coopted) by the council itself, and elected members. Principally in lesser chiefdoms, which include most Native Authorities not historically part of the emirate system, the trend has been toward elected majorities, some 50 per cent of all Native Authorities in the region now falling in this category.

Most central councils of the great emirates, however, do not contain popularly elected majorities. Even in those councils where elected members do predominate, the usual indirect method of electing them and their limited participation hardly permit the central councils to be characterized as democratically controlled. The councils rarely meet more than three times a year in plenary session, when elected members would be present. The election procedure to the central councils makes use of the membership of other councils, which in official nomenclature as well as in practice are considered "subordinate" bodies of the central councils, and which include all village, district, and urban councils. The central councils invariably impose combinations of restrictions on the finances, permitted functions, and general decision-making discretion of the subordinate councils. These restrictions seriously qualify the extent to which even the subordinate councils may be considered democratic—notwithstanding the legal requirement that they contain elected majorities.

All told, there are in Northern Nigeria some seventy Native Authorities, grouped into thirteen provinces. Until recently, each province was administered by a senior functionary, styled the "resident," whose quasi-diplomatic relation to the major emirs in the colonial era we have already noted. This relationship had every appearance of incompatibility with the postcolonial age, which required the conversion of the administrative service into an instrument of representative government. Accordingly, the title "resident" was abolished in favor of "provincial secretary" initially, and shortly thereafter a new post of provincial commissioner was created and filled in each case with an elected regional legislator, who thereafter assumed ministerial rank in the regional government.

The relationship of a provincial secretary to a provincial commissioner is in essence equivalent to that of a permanent secretary to a

Minister of Government with portfolio. The net effect of the innovations has been widely interpreted as a decisive move in the direction of political centralization, and there is no doubt that the policy in fact reinforces the principle of the regional government's ultimate authority over that of the Native Authorities and gives the regional government a degree of visibility in the provinces not attained previously. As suggested before, however, sight should not be lost of the mutually beneficial relationship of traditional and modern representative centers of political power and authority in contemporary Northern Nigeria. Indeed, on the basis of pertinent testimony it may be reliably ventured that the new provincial commissioners, most of whom are politically the products of established systems of emirate rule, themselves most certainly have not lost sight of this relationship.

The Eastern Region

The problem of local government in Eastern Nigeria has always been to reconcile a multitude of traditionally cohesive communities with the necessity of centralization at levels which would be relatively self-supporting and effectively able to provide services. In 1958, a two-tier system was adopted: directly elected local councils form county councils; at each level provision is made for the inclusion of chiefs or "traditional" members, not to exceed one-fifth of the total. The county councils are grouped into twelve provinces, and provincial assemblies, limited to functions of deliberation and consultation, are constituted by representatives of the local councils. As in the North, each province is administered by a political agent of the regional government, called the provincial commissioner. All provincial commissioners are government party stalwarts; most of them are members of the House of Assembly. The efficiency of the Eastern system of local government is buttressed by civil service officials, called district officers, who supervise local government councils

The Western Region

In contrast with the East, Western Nigerian societies are traditionally cohesive at sufficiently high administrative levels to sustain effective local government. As in the East, a two-tier structure obtains: local or district councils are elected directly; divisional councils are elected by and from the members of the lower-tier councils. Invariably, the party in control of a lower-tier council will elect the specified number of its members to represent that council in the divisional council. At both levels instruments establishing the councils may prescribe the in-

clusion of a stipulated number of "traditional" members, either specified by title or elected for stated terms of office by specified colleges of
chiefs. Normally, councils have a traditional president and an elected
chairman. If there is no single pre-eminent traditional chief in the
council area, the presidency will rotate among the leading chiefs.
Wherever possible, divisional council areas correspond to the spheres
of authority of the paramount traditional kings, who are also permanent members of the regional House of Chiefs.

Since the introduction of this system in 1952, the AG has dominated
the triennial local elections. In 1958, for example, the AG won elected
majorities in 123 of 165 lower-tier councils in the West. Nowhere in
Nigeria have local government councils under the control of opponents
of a regional government party functioned smoothly for sustained intervals of time. In Western Nigeria, "opposition" councils have been
commonplace targets of criticism for their alleged obstructionist tendencies, including failures to collect local rates. In 1956, for example, the
NCNC-controlled Ibadan District Council, representing the largest
electorate of any council in the region, was dissolved by the regional
government following the adverse report of a commission of inquiry
into its management. In 1963, following the restoration of Chief
Akintola as regional premier, heading a United People's Party-NCNC
coalition government, the tables were turned on the AG. By the end of
that year, the regional government had dissolved virtually all the local
government councils, substituting appointed committees of management or provisional authorities under the direction of civil servants
called Local Government Advisors.

At the time of writing, local government in Western Nigeria is subject to a degree of central control far in excess of the formally centralized systems of the Northern and Eastern Regions. In 1964, the
regional legislature did, in fact, provide for the institution of a system
of provincial administration similar to the systems in effect in other
regions. The imperatives of provincial administration in the North
and East, however, are absent from the West. Unlike the Northern
emirs, chiefs in the Western Region have all but lost their capacity to
muster an effective opposition to policies of the regional government
party. Nor do the Western regional councils suffer from the innate organizational defects which have hampered the functioning of fragmentary units in the East. We should not be surprised, therefore, if
strong local self-government is restored when political normalcy finally
returns to the Western Region.

Some Observations

Strictly speaking, local government councils are creatures of the regional governments. They are established by statutory instruments, issued by the regional ministers of local government, which specify their functions, compositions, and procedures. Their functions encompass the health, welfare, safety, and morals of the people. The effectiveness with which they serve the needs of their communities depends upon the adequacy of their financial resources. This, in turn, is a matter of regional government policy respecting the size and taxing power of councils.

In the Northern Region Native Authority bodies are sufficiently large and strong to accept a portion of responsibility for implementation of that region's current development plan. They collect taxes levied under regional law, amounting to a significant portion of the Northern Region's total revenue. In the Eastern Region, the county council is the focal point of local government authority; tax collection is mainly a function of regional government and local councils have only limited powers to levy rates. By contrast, local councils in the West and North have comparatively wide taxing powers; in addition to local rates, they actually collect the regional income tax levied on individuals, and they retain most of this revenue to finance services, including education. Personal incomes are assessed by special committees appointed by the councils. This procedure is liable to political exploitation. Frankly acknowledging the problem, several councils have tried to strike a fair balance by appointing their assessment committees on a strictly partisan basis in proportion to demonstrated electoral strength. There is, however, widespread agreement on the impropriety of "political" tax assessment, and the trend since 1960 is toward more stringent supervision by regional tax boards.

In sum, the pattern of local government organization has developed distinctively in each region. Western practice exemplifies the introduction of a wholly modern form in a cultural setting of traditional constitutional monarchy. The "traditional" members of local government councils in the Western Region lend continuity and dignity to these bodies without detracting unduly from their democratic character.[100]

[100] A caveat may be in order: the "traditional" members of councils commonly "toe the line" of the regional government party. On occasion, the regional authorities have tipped the balance of closely divided councils in their favor by securing the "injection" of traditional members who could be relied upon to vote with the regional government party

Moreover, traditional authorities have also been appointed to act as public trustees in respect of communal rights in land. In the Northern Region local government reflects both the resiliency of the Native Authority system and, in respect of taxation and expenditure, the extent to which regional authorities still rely upon these units to implement governmental policies. Stable and reciprocally advantageous relations between local and regional governments have been facilitated by the recently instituted system of provincial administration. Finally, Eastern Nigeria, having pioneered an entirely modern and democratic system of local self-government in 1950, has borrowed in turn from the Northern idea of provincial administration and the Western practice of appointing "traditional" members to local government councils. These fluctuating patterns blend conceptions of European and African origin, thereby exhibiting potential contributions to the general science of government.

THE ADMINISTRATION OF JUSTICE

Courts and the Law

The Nigerian constitution admits of a dual system of federal and regional courts.[101] Thus far, however, Parliament has not created federal courts of the first instance in the regions. In other words, federal offenses may be tried in the magistrates' courts of the regions, subject to appeal to the regional high courts before reaching the Supreme Court of Nigeria.

The Chief Justice of Nigeria is appointed by the President on the advice of the Prime Minister. Parliament has provided for the appointment of eight additional Justices of the Supreme Court by the President. Each of four of them must be appointed in accordance with the advice of the Premier of a different region; the others are appointed on the advice of the Prime Minister. Justices serve until the age of retirement; they are subject to removal by the President on petition of two-thirds of all the members of each house of Parliament.

Below the Supreme Court there are regional high courts and a High Court of Lagos, over each of which a chief justice presides. Judges of the regional high courts are appointed by the regional Governor upon the advice of the regional Premier; they are subject to removal upon a two-thirds vote of all the members of each house of the regional legislature. Two systems of lower courts exist in each region: magistrates' courts and customary courts. Magistrates are appointed by the regional

[101] Nigeria, *Constitution*, Sec. 126.

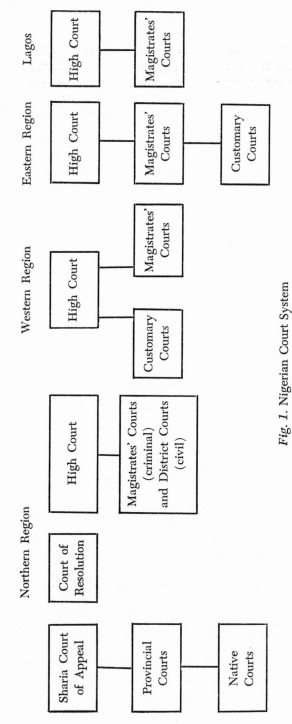

Fig. 1. Nigerian Court System

governors or, in the case of Lagos, by the President of the Federal Republic, in accordance with the recommendations of the respective Public Service Commissions. They administer Nigerian statutory laws in addition to the English common law and doctrines of equity. Many cases, however, including most land and matrimonial cases, are governed by the principles of local customary law. Indeed, the vast majority of court cases in Nigeria are tried in customary courts applying native law and custom insofar as "it is not repugnant to natural justice, equity, and good conscience," nor incompatible with any written law in force. Within limits, customary courts are also empowered to enforce the criminal codes of the several regions.

Just as Northern local government is called "native administration," customary courts in the Northern Region are still called native courts. The predominant type of Northern native court is the Muslim court, over which an *alkali,* or judge schooled in Muslim law, presides. In the emirate sectors of the region emirs, who are the highest executive officials of their native administrations, also preside over the highest native courts. Prior to the reforms of 1960, criminal cases, including cases of a political nature, were tried in native courts, where judges often applied vague doctrines in a spirit of hostility to opponents of the regional government party. Since then, native courts have been required to try all criminal cases in accordance with new regional statutory codes. Furthermore, provincial courts have been set up to hear appeals from the lower native courts. This innovation helps to curb the tendency toward abuse of judicial power by providing a right of appeal beyond the native authority (or emir) who had appointed the lower court judge. Appeals from the decisions of the higher native courts, such as the emir's courts and the courts of the senior *alkalis,* and from the provincial courts lie to the regional High Court. Appeals involving Muslim personal law lie to the Sharia Court of Appeal, over which a Grand Kadi presides. Jurisdictional conflicts between the High Court and the Sharia Court of Appeal are resolved by a Court of Resolution, comprising members of both.

It must be noted that in addition to applying Muslim personal law and allotting Muslim jurists a special role in civil cases, where political implications are likely to be minimal, the Northern legal system features concessions to traditional norms and practices in the emirates that seem far from being politically innocuous. Several provisions of the Northern penal code approximate the relatively severe traditional restrictions on the liberties of individuals vis-à-vis officially constituted authority.[102] Judicial and executive authority coalesce in the person of the emir, whose extent of jurisdiction is defined largely on the basis of his traditional ranking. The criminal procedure code bars professional lawyers from native courts (where the great bulk of all litigation in the North still originates and terminates) and makes provision for those courts to be guided (rather than bound) by that code, thus excusing them from strict observance of prescriptions observed in noncustomary courts. Perhaps most important of all, *alkalis,* who, by virtue of patronage and or family relationship almost always are personally intimate with often politically embattled native authorities, inevitably continue to confront powerful informal sources of resistance to the exercise of disinterested and even-handed justice.

In the Eastern and Western Regions the members and assessors of customary courts are appointed by the regional Ministers of Justice upon the advice of the regional Public Service Commissions. The Western regional system provides for the appointment of experienced lawyers as presidents of the higher customary courts. When the judge is a lawyer, lawyers may appear before him to represent litigants. Despite these legalistic reforms, customary courts in the Western Region have been sharply criticized for discriminating politically against opponents of the regional government party. A general reorganization was initiated by the federal administration during the 1962 state of emergency.

Fundamental Rights

The constitution of the federation includes a comprehensive declaration of fundamental rights based largely on the UN Declaration and on the European Convention for the Protection of Human Rights and Fundamental Freedoms. The framers of the constitution were explicit in their intention to ensure a right of appeal to the Supreme Court in all cases regarding the infringement or enforcement of fundamental rights.[103] Since independence, three cases involving political speech have been decided by the Supreme Court. The technical charge in each of these cases was criminal sedition arising from the publication of a newspaper article or pamphlet. In each ruling the Supreme Court upheld the validity of the Act of Parliament in question, in consequence

---

[102] See note 77, above.

[103] Federation of Nigeria, *Report by the Resumed Constitutional Conference, September and October, 1958* (Lagos: Government Printer, 1958), p. 28.

of which a conviction was affirmed in the High Court and a fine levied.[104]

A "political trial" of some notoriety was commenced in 1962. Chief Awolowo, leader of the federal Opposition, and thirty other members of his AG party were alleged to have plotted overthrow of the federal government by means of a *coup d'état*. After an eight-month trial, Awolowo and sixteen of his codefendants were found guilty of treasonable felony, not a capital crime. Awolowo was sentenced to ten years imprisonment; his principal associate, Chief Anthony Enahoro, drew a fifteen-year sentence.[105] In fairness, the facts of these cases do not permit a clear test of the Supreme Court's resolve to uphold the fundamental rights of opponents of the regime. Official Nigeria takes pride in the independence of its judiciary. Nonetheless, the convictions of political dissenters cannot but create an impression of "political justice": [106] the use of courts to accomplish political ends.

Power in Nigerian Society

THE SOURCES OF POWER

The structure of power in a developing country is built around its pyramid of intellectual skills. From an ever-widening base of elementary education, this pyramid tapers sharply to its narrow apex of persons who are qualified to hold high-level administrative, managerial, professional, educational, scientific, and technical positions. In 1960, there were about 30,000 such persons in Nigeria—less than 0.1 per cent of the population—and one-third of them were non-Nigerians.[107] At that time, the output of Nigerian university graduates from domestic and foreign institutions was estimated to be about 1,000 per year. This, on a conservative estimate, was only 50 per cent of the minimum number of graduates thought necessary to sustain the rate of economic

[104] Director of Public Prosecutions v. Chike Obi (1961) 1 *All N.L.R.*, Part II, 186–98 (Federal Supreme Court); Queen v. Amalgamated Press (of Nigeria) Ltd. and Fatogun (1961) 1 *All N.L.R.*, Part II, 199–202 (Federal Supreme Court). A third case—actually two cases—decided in 1963, involved publications by two university lecturers criticizing the report of a federal commission of inquiry into the affairs of the Western regional government.

[105] Chief Enahoro's case attracted wide notice when he was denied asylum in the United Kingdom and extradited to Nigeria.

[106] The term is Otto Kirchheimer's in *Political Justice* (Princeton: Princeton University Press, 1961).

[107] Frederick Harbison, "Human Resources and Economic Development in Nigeria," in Tilman and Cole, eds., *op. cit.*, pp. 204–210.

growth of approximately 4 per cent per annum which had been achieved during the decade prior to independence.

Since 1960, all regions have intensified their efforts to promote education at every level, and the number of Nigerian universities has been increased from one to five. With a reasonable rate of economic growth, those who acquire intellectual and technical skills may expect to reap rich rewards of income, prestige, and influence in addition to personal satisfaction. But a sluggish pace of economic development due to deficiencies of capital, faulty planning, or defective political organization may result in failure to provide adequate opportunities, even for the relatively small number of technically and professionally trained people. What is more, the existing laissez-faire policy in higher education and the relatively high cost of facilities for technological training may soon give Nigeria a "surplus" of graduates in law and the liberal arts, while engineering, agriculture, medicine, and the sciences languish for lack of attention. Such an imbalance would doubtless add to the grievances of many among those who are most qualified to assume positions of leadership.

To be sure, every society fails in some measure to provide scope for the ambitions of its talented members. Highly organized industrial societies are relatively safe from the resentments bred by personal disappointment. The energies and capacities of their natural leaders are channeled by established institutions into ready-made occupational slots, while surplus enthusiasm is either drained off into socially harmless entertainment or projected vicariously upon social and political celebrities who support the existing order. In developing countries, however, the institutional pattern is fluid and political action often results in a transformation of the existing institutional framework. With talent at a premium, ambition is relatively free to aim for the highest berth. Today's graduate is tomorrow's minister. Opportunities abound for the man of ambition who is adept at manipulating the symbols of political thought. It is characteristic of politics in a new nation that every aspirant for power must be taken seriously. Ambition itself is a primary source of power and the incumbent rulers ignore the pretensions of insurgent newcomers only at their peril.

Political and Economic Power

In developing societies political power is the primary force that creates economic opportunity and determines the pattern of social stratification. One manifestation of this principle in Nigeria is the immense income gap between the "political" man and the common man. The take-home pay of an ordinary laborer in the employ of government is less than 6 shillings per day, or less, often much less, than £100 per year. By contrast, the salary of an elected member of a regional legislative house in Nigeria is about £720 per annum while members of the federal Parliament receive £900 per annum. Parliamentary sessions, it might be added, have rarely occupied more than fifty days each year. The pay of a junior minister is about £1,350; that of a full minister, £2,700. This salary scale has already been adjusted for the 10 per cent pay cut recently voted by the several legislatures in response to demands for austerity in government. Legislators still draw generous allowances to cover their expenses, including the purchase and operation of private cars. It may be said that the financial liabilities and losses incurred by the members of Parliament in the course of their campaigns for nomination and election are generally recouped many times over in office. Parliamentary emoluments alone (not to mention other, extra-legal sources of income) are sufficient to boost the Honorable Members into the ranks of the privileged class. Similarly, high-ranking civil servants, who earn more than £3,000 per annum, are subsidized by car allowances, allowances for their children, and low-rent deluxe housing, all of which magnifies the income gap between the privileged class and the poor, deepening the latter's resentment against social distance.

The political basis of economic power, rooted in the ownership and control of business enterprise, is as clear as the political basis of social stratification. We have seen that Nigeria's economy depends mainly on the export of tropical produce. Shortly after World War II, the government of Nigeria created statutory agents known as commodity marketing boards to purchase the main export crops from producers at fixed prices for sale abroad. These boards accumulated surpluses, or profits, corresponding to the difference between world market prices and the prices paid to the producers. In 1954, the commodity marketing boards were dissolved; in conformity with the requirements of the new federal constitution, their assets were distributed among newly created multi-commodity regional marketing boards in accordance with the principle of derivation. Therefore, £34 million was allocated to the Western Region, which had earned the largest regional revenue as a result of the postwar cocoa boom; £24 million was allocated to the Northern Region, and £15 million to the Eastern Region.

In support of economic development the regional marketing boards provide investment and loan capital to statutory corporations, including regional development corporations, which undertake agricultural and industrial projects independently and in partnership with other governments or with private interests. The development corporations include subsidiary loan boards and finance corporations, which make grants to local government authorities, private firms, and individuals. These institutions and facilities have given rise to extensive networks of administrative and commercial patronage under the control of the leaders of the major political parties. Top politicians reward their followers with jobs and money. They appoint their lieutenants to manage the marketing boards and development corporations which control the allocation of trading licenses, contracts, and loans to hopeful businessmen, whose interests are thereby linked to the parties in power.

In short, class formation is precipitated or, as in the case of Northern Nigeria, confirmed by the wielders of new political power. To this extent we may speak of a political class of persons who control the dominant institutions of society. The composition of this class may be specified in terms of such objective criteria as high status occupation, high income, superior education, and the ownership and control of business enterprise. In southern Nigeria a new political class reigns supreme, having imposed a wholly secular system of values on society. In Northern Nigeria, however, class privilege based on a traditional system of values persists and aristocratic birth is still to be reckoned with as a primary source of power.

THE USES OF POWER

". . . come to the aid of the party"

A succinct observation on the reciprocal relationship between political and economic power is attributed to Julius Caesar. He is reported by Dio Chrysostom to have said, in effect, that men are needed to get money and money is required to control men.[108] The experiences of Dr. Azikiwe, Chief Awolowo, and Sir Ahmadu Bello, Sardauna of Sokoto, illustrate that principle.

In 1955, the Eastern regional government, under the premiership of Azikiwe, made an investment of more than £750,000 in the African Continental Bank. This money was obtained from the Eastern Region

---

[108] Francis D. Wormuth, *Class Struggle* (Indiana University Publications, Social Science Series No. 4; Bloomington, Indiana: University of Indiana Press, 1946), p. 49.

Marketing Board, which granted £2 million to the Eastern Region Finance Corporation for investment and deposit in the bank. This enabled the bank to avert a threat of liquidation for failure to meet statutory requirements, remain in competition with established British banks, and extend an increasing volume of credit to Nigerian businessmen. The transaction, however, was not without political significance. For the bank made loans to the NCNC; it also provided working capital to a number of companies related to the *West African Pilot* and a chain of provincial newspapers, all of which support the NCNC. Dr. Azikiwe, it will be recalled, is the founder and principal owner of the *West African Pilot*. He is also the principal shareholder in the related Zik Group of companies, and he is reported to have founded the African Continental Bank primarily to finance the activities of these companies. Therefore, Azikiwe's political-journalistic enterprise depended upon his multipurpose banking enterprise, which, in turn, was financed by a government of which he was premier. We see in this situation the entanglement of political and economic strands in the nationalist movement.

Azikiwe's strength—his effective combination of economic and political power—nearly proved to be his undoing. In 1956 the Secretary of State for the Colonies appointed a Tribunal of Inquiry to investigate the propriety of the transaction involving the Eastern regional government, its Premier, and his bank. Although the Tribunal did not return a verdict of guilty, Azikiwe's conduct was heavily criticized. He was able to survive this criticism and go on to greater political glory because his party could represent the issue as a nationalist struggle against an expatriate banking monopoly in the interest of Nigerian economic development. Eventually the Eastern regional government acquired full ownership of the African Continental Bank.

Just as the NCNC and the Eastern regional government are closely aligned with the African Continental Bank, the AG and the Western regional government are linked with the National Bank of Nigeria. The Western regional government has supported this bank by means of investments and deposits for over a decade. In 1960, the National Bank was the major shareholder in the Amalgamated Press of Nigeria Limited, publisher of a newspaper chain supporting the AG. The principal directors and many of the shareholders of the National Bank were identified with the AG and its cultural ally in Yorubaland, the Society of the Descendants of Oduduwa. In 1961, the Western regional government increased its investment in the National Bank, thereby acquiring total ownership. By then, however, the AG had become financially dependent on another company, which came to light, as we shall see, during the "public emergency" of 1962.

In the case of the Sardauna of Sokoto, the effectiveness of Caesar's gambit perhaps owes less to styles of manipulation sophisticated in the West than to mastery of techniques hallowed by indigenous custom, but they have served him no less well for that. For generations, gift-giving, in cash and kind, has served in the emirates as the cement for mutually binding political relations between persons of unequal status and position. As a prominent hereditary member of the imperial house of Sokoto, the Sardauna was thus able, upon his entry into the realm of modern representative institutions, to exploit his superior traditional status over colleagues and supporters alike. With the help of prece-dented customary presentations like a horse and such modern elabora-tions thereon as the Cadillac automobile, he has created a network of personal allegiance not remotely approximated by any of his govern-ment and party associates, much less by the relatively impecunious antagonists who comprise the leadership of the opposition parties. This traditional mode of expressing political solidarity is also known to have entered into his relations with prominent traditional rulers. About the financial estate which makes all this possible there is little public knowledge, except that it includes extensive private farming lands.

Public Emergency

The events leading up to the 1962 emergency in the Western Re-gion, noted previously in this chapter, may be summarized briefly. Chief Awolowo, leader of the federal Opposition, clashed repeatedly with Chief Akintola, his deputy and successor as Premier of the West, over matters of party policy and control of the regional government. Awolowo advocated an unremitting political struggle against the Northern Peoples' Congress under the banner of antiregional socialism. Akintola favored a political settlement with the NPC based on recipro-cal recognition of existing spheres of regional power. Concretely, he advocated AG participation in an all-party National Government. Akintola was repudiated by a meeting of the AG party congress; sub-sequently, he was directed by the party executive council to resign his position as Premier. He refused to do so and asked the Governor to dissolve the House of Assembly instead. But the Governor invoked a provision of the regional constitution, since amended, to remove Akintola as Premier upon receipt of a letter declaring nonsupport of the Premier signed by a majority of the members of the House of Assembly. He then designated a new Premier known to command the support of a majority of the members of the House. When the House met, a determined minority, supporting Akintola, caused a disturbance in the assembly chamber. Federal police intervened to restore order, and the Prime Minister summoned a meeting of the federal Parliament, which declared a state of public emergency in the Western Region. Federal statutes were enacted providing for the suspension of the regional government, the detention of persons deemed likely to provoke breaches of the peace, and the temporary appointment of a federal administrator to govern the region.

The federal administration of Western Nigeria lasted for seven months, from May to December 1962. That it would produce far-reaching political consequences became evident when the federal government appointed a commission of inquiry into the post-1954 administrative and financial practices of the regional government. This commission disclosed that between 1958 and 1962 the Western Region Marketing Board made loans in excess of £6 million to a private company, the National Investment and Properties Company Limited, owned in its entirety by four leading members of the AG. Over £2 million more, allocated by the Western Region Marketing Board to the Western Nigeria Development Corporation, was also diverted to the NIPC. Between 1959 and 1961, a period of intense electoral activity, the NIPC contributed more than £4 million to the AG. Three of the four directors of the NIPC were prominent businessmen holding high office in the party; the fourth was the director of the Western Nigeria Development Corporation and political secretary to Chief Awolowo. The shares held by all four directors of the NIPC were purchased with funds diverted from the company itself. The commission concluded that the company had been formed mainly to finance the AG, that Awolowo had chosen all four directors, and that he had full knowledge of the surreptitious means whereby public funds were diverted to the party. Akintola was absolved as "a veritable deputy" who had not been privy to the clandestine scheme. In 1963, he was restored to the Western regional premiership, heading a coalition of his new party, the United People's Party, and the NCNC. Meanwhile, Awolowo was prosecuted by the federal government for conspiring to seize power illegally, convicted of treasonable felony, and imprisoned.

Certain parallels may be drawn between Azikiwe's predicament in 1956 and Awolowo's ordeal (apart from his criminal prosecution) in

1962. In both cases the principal actors operated through the agency of trusted lieutenants: Azikiwe disclaimed responsibility for the decision of his government to invest in the African Continental Bank; Awolowo was not a director of the NIPC. In neither case had the regional executive council, or cabinet, been informed of the transfer of public funds to private companies before the determinative steps were taken. In other respects, however, the two cases differ. Although the Eastern regional government's investment in the African Continental Bank did serve to strengthen the financial position of a newspaper business owned by Azikiwe, there is no evidence in that case of an exceptional relationship between the bank and the NCNC. In the case of the AG and the NIPC, however, the overriding purpose of the transaction was political party finance. It may perhaps be suggested, in partial exculpation of this deed, that the AG was sorely pressed by its assumed burden of political opposition in all parts of the federation. (AG organizational and publicity expenses, exclusive of special election expenses, had risen to a rate of £300,000 per annum.) Finally, the earlier case posed a real question of conflict between indigenous and expatriate banking. Azikiwe survived by invoking the principle of economic nationalism in the court of public opinion. Awolowo's best hope in the hour of his ordeal is the prospect that public opinion will ultimately identify his cause with another valued principle—social justice.

Planning for What?

In Nigeria, as in all developing countries, the rising tide of social discontent is a matter of concern to national leaders. The sources of such discontent are familiar to students of the developing areas; they include poverty, disease, malnutrition, unemployment, corruption, ostentatious high living on the part of the political-economic elite, and the belief, widespread among intellectuals, that exploitative foreign interests still retard local economic development. Perhaps the most acute social problem at present is posed by the flood of school-leavers on the labor market. Some 200,000–300,000 students per year graduate from, or simply leave, Nigerian primary schools, mainly in the south. The vast majority of them are loath to return to rural life and flock to the cities in quest of nonexistent jobs. Urban poverty and unemployment plague the cities of Nigeria, giving rise to demands for radical political solutions.

The present government's answer to this challenge is contained in its six-year development plan (1962–1968), comprising plans for the regional and federal governments. This plan aims to maintain a rate of growth of 4 per cent per annum, roughly equal to that which had been achieved in the decade before independence. It relies on foreign sources (public and private) to provide nearly one-half of the projected capital investment. Although the public sector (domestic and foreign) is expected to account for some two-thirds of total capital formation, private enterprise (domestic and foreign) is given pride of place among the economic and ideological values of the planners. Critics have questioned this "capitalistic" orientation, suggesting in addition that the planned rate of capital investment may be too "conservative" to cope with the problem of unemployment and the effects of a rapidly growing population.

In the decade before independence the Nigerian political elite acted with acumen and ingenuity to mobilize the resources of the country in order to achieve nationalist goals. Often such goals were consistent with the pursuit of purely personal interests. In its economic aspect the nationalist movement was promoted mainly by the initiative of persons who were motivated by the lure of private gain. An economic elite, indistinguishable from the political elite, emerged within the ranks of the nationalist movement. We have termed this social formation, whose members control the dominant institutions of society, the political class. At independence, this class inherited both the power of the colonial regime and its responsibility for the well-being of the country. The new rulers, defining their responsibilities in conformity with nationalistic ideals, are committed to the principle of social reconstruction. They seek through comprehensive national planning to mobilize the economic resources of the country on a scale of far greater magnitude than ever before. It remains to be seen whether the incumbent political class will be equal to the challenge of this historic task.

THE BALANCE OF POWER

The Governmental Balance

The federal constitution of 1954 was intended to promote responsible self-government at the regional level by extending regional autonomy and curtailing the power of the central government to intervene in regional affairs. This concession to regional sentiment checked the secessionist tendencies of leaders in the North and West short of the loose confederation then in contemplation. At bottom, however, the new

constitution was a majority group settlement; it confirmed the dominance of the Fulani-Hausa in the North, the Ibo in the East, and the
Yoruba in the West. Although no group has been forced to remain in
the Federation against its will,[109]it is nonetheless true that the minority ethnic groups have often appeared to resent their inclusion within
one or another of the original regions. In most cases such minorities
have demanded the creation of new regions by constitutional means.
The regional governments are sensitive to minority grievances and
seek, so far as is possible, to alleviate them within the existing political
framework. But the desire for home rule is deeply seated; its stubborn
persistence in minority group areas is a compensating counterforce to
the centrifugal tendencies of the entrenched regional power groups.

In 1957, the pendulum of power appeared to swing away from the
regions to the government of the Federation; the latter was immensely
strengthened by the creation of the offices of Prime Minister of the
Federation and federal Minister of Finance. Subsequently, federal
supremacy in the field of finance was asserted through the constitution; as noted above, the power of the federal government to raise
money abroad is practically exclusive. The federal government is solely
responsible for defense and the conduct of foreign affairs; its authority
in respect of the administration of justice is overriding. Finally, the
importance of federal control of the Nigerian police can hardly be exaggerated. Nor has this power been devoid of purely political significance. In May, 1962, for example, Alhaji D. S. Adegbenro, Premier-
designate of the Western Region, fearing that parliamentary supporters
of his opponent, Chief Akintola, would resort to violence in an attempt
to disrupt the proceedings of the Western House of Assembly, asked
the Nigerian police to stand by in the chamber and, if need be, maintain order. Adegbenro's request was referred to the Prime Minister,
who declared that the federal government would not accept the validity of any decision taken by the House of Assembly in the presence of
the police. A previous meeting of the House of Assembly had already
been disrupted by members of the Akintola group; in the event of a
second outburst of violence, the Prime Minister instructed the police to
"clear the chamber and lock it up." When this actually occurred, the
Prime Minister summoned the federal Parliament to declare a state of
public emergency in the Western Region.

[109] It will be recalled that the people of the Cameroons Trust Territory were
allowed to choose between membership in the Nigerian Federation and in the
Cameroun Republic.

As a constitutional precedent, this incident and its aftermath might be held to foreshadow the twilight of regional power in Nigeria. Political realities, however, suggest that a more cautious interpretation would be nearer the mark. Indeed we may even here, detect the strong hand of the Northern government party, acting through the federal government to destroy the regional power base of a redoubtable opponent.[110]

At bottom it is the sheer size of the Northern Region that prevents a decisive shift of power to the federal center. So long as the North holds its population edge over all the rest of Nigeria, implying a majority of Northern seats in the House of Representatives, the incumbent Northern leaders will bid fair to dominate the federation. In the Northern Region itself the electoral hegemony of the Northern government party has become increasingly absolute; at the time of writing, the NPC held 156 of 166 seats in the Northern House of Assembly; when Parliament was dissolved in December, 1964, the NPC held about 168 of 174 Northern seats in the House of Representatives. A serious threat to the incumbent Northern leadership may be expected to arise from the persistent agitation for more states in the federation. The creation of the

[110] It may be of interest to note here that, before 1962, the AG was actively pursuing a political strategy that *in theory* might eventually have produced a national majority in place of that now enjoyed by the NPC. The NPC's majority in the 1960–1964 federal House of Representatives was the result of victories only in constituencies lying wholly within one region, which it governs, with all the advantages to a party that entails. None of the other regions contains enough constituencies to allow its governing party to win a national majority within its boundaries. Indeed, not even control of all the constituencies of all the southern regions put together would of itself provide any party with a national majority. One might be formed, however, through a combination of victories in all the constituencies of one region plus all those lying within the cultural minority areas of the others. Thus, for example, had a party in 1959 won all the Western constituencies (62) plus the minority constituencies in the North (74) and East (23), the total of 159 would have allowed it to form the government of the Federation. To be sure, the AG in fact fell far short of achieving this, but its strategy of championship of the minority sectors of all regions together with that of hegemony in Yorubaland (itself not achieved) pointed precisely toward that possible end. Also, it is not inconceivable, of course, that in time a certain number of setbacks within such an otherwise successful grand strategy might have been offset with equivalent inroads into the Ibo and Hausa-Fulani "heartlands" of the East and North, which the AG in fact tried hard but failed to penetrate in 1959

The same reasoning from the threat to the NPC that the AG potentially represented up until its precipitous decline in 1962 may help explain the NPC's preference in the period for coalition with the NCNC, which then made only feeble organizational efforts in the North. With the AG decline, by the same token, the NPC was in a position to engage in turn in the kind of direct and bitter confrontation with the NCNC that in fact has characterized the period since 1962.

Midwestern Region in 1963, supported by the NPC, stimulated a renewal of demands among other minority groups for home rule. The NPC does not object to the division of the southern regions; it does, indeed, seek to enlist political support among the traditional opponents of the regional government parties of southern Nigeria. The Northern leaders remain, however, adamant in their opposition to any partition of the North, fearful perhaps that the momentous precedent of federal intervention at Ibadan in the West would then cast its shadow over the government at Kaduna.

The Party Balance and the Crisis of 1964–1965

After the constitutional settlement of 1954, each of the regional government parties, having gained control of such wealth-producing agencies as marketing boards, development corporations, and banks, proceeded to entrench itself in its house of power. Gradually, party control was extended into the spheres of chieftaincy, local government, and the administration of justice by customary courts. In no region has the movement for centralization of power been so subtly yet effectively executed as in the North. Sworn to uphold the Northern emirate tradition, the Sardauna's government has nonetheless transformed that decentralized system of dual authority (regional administrative and native) into a stable and more centralized political order. Under the new regime of provincial administration, provincial commissioners, who are political appointees of the Premier, supervise the administrations of the leading emirs. By assuring political conformity on the part of powerful emirs and chiefs, the NPC reduces the vulnerability of the Northern Region to external political forces.[111]

Persistent opposition to the multipartite regional power system has emanated from three principal sources: minority ethnic groups, economically deprived classes in urban areas, and intellectuals who are dissatisfied with the progress of the country and the performances of the several governments. After the federal election of 1959, the criticisms of all these groups were echoed by the AG opposition to the federal government.

The subsequent prosecution and imprisonment of Awolowo, the de-

[111] Shortly after independence, the political authority of the Premier of the North was increasingly defied by the Emir of Kano, one of the most powerful of the Northern traditional rulers. In 1963, the administration of the Kano Native Authority was investigated by the regional government and the Emir was compelled to abdicate. Meanwhile it was reported that AG strategies for penetration of the North had contemplated cooperation with the former Emir of Kano.

fection of many influential persons, including members of Parliament, from the AG to Akintola's party, and the destruction of the party's system of patronage in the West reduced the AG to a low ebb of effective power. By December 1962, AG strength in the House of Representatives "had fallen from its original seventy-five to twenty-one members and the Prime Minister, Sir Abubakar Tafawa Balewa, announced that he did not recognize anyone as leader of the Opposition: 'The whole idea of an Opposition, I think, is that the Opposition should provide an alternative Government. . . . A handful of 20 people here cannot provide an alternative Government and thus officially the Opposition in the Federal House of Representatives has ceased to exist.' " [112]

While the Action Group was reduced to a hard core of loyalists, mainly in the Western Region, the NCNC joined with Premier Akintola's new United People's Party to form a coalition government in the Western Region. Radical elements within the NCNC, however, favored the formation of a "progressive alliance" with the AG, as advocated by Awolowo prior to his imprisonment. Frequent criticisms of the federal government in general and the NPC in particular were expressed by the NCNC members of the Eastern House of Assembly, the Zikist Movement (an NCNC auxiliary), the *West African Pilot*, and spokesmen for the NCNC national headquarters. In turn, the NPC gave impetus to the formation of a Midwestern Democratic Front to challenge the NCNC's predominance in the newly created Midwestern Region. Tension between the federal coalition partners almost reached a breaking point in 1964 over the results of the decennial census. At issue was the population of the North in relation to the rest of the country. A census taken in 1962 had been annulled by the federal government as unreliable, and a costly recount of the population was made in 1963. Early in 1964, the federal government released preliminary statistics; 55.4 million people were enumerated, distributed thus: Northern Nigeria, 29.7 million; Eastern Nigeria, 12.3 million; Western Nigeria, 10.2 million; Midwestern Nigeria, 2.5 million; the Federal Territory of Lagos, 675,000.[113]

[112] See John P. Mackintosh, "The Nigerian Federal Parliament," *Public Law* (Autumn, 1963), p. 348.

[113] The announced total indicates an annual population rise of 5.5 per cent. Two factors could qualify this statistically startling rate of increase: the 1952 census may have erred grossly on the side of underenumeration; the 1963 figures, which are subject to verification by demographic tests, may prove to have been

The NCNC-controlled governments of the Eastern and Midwestern Regions immediately challenged the accuracy of these figures, which preserved the Northern Region's population edge over the rest of the country and, consequently, its numerical supremacy in the House of Representatives. The Northern and Western regional governments accepted them. In a display of solidarity with Akintola, all but a few of the NCNC members of the Western House of Assembly bolted their party and rallied to the Premier's standard in the formation of a new regional party, called (after the historic party of Herbert Macaulay) the Nigerian National Democratic Party.[114] Thereupon, NCNC loyalists in the Western Region formed an alliance with the AG, which still appeared to be the most popular party in the region, despite the erosion of its strength in the House of Assembly. Previously, opposition parties in the Northern Region, principally the NEPU and the UMBC, had combined to form a Northern Progressive Front. Only die-hard opponents of the AG, mainly in the Midwestern Region, still resisted the formation of a nationwide "progressive" alliance.

As a result of the disputed census (challenged unsuccessfully in the Supreme Court by the Eastern regional government), the North was allotted 167 parliamentary seats out of a total of 312 (a reduction of 7), the East was allotted 70 (a reduction of 3), the West received 57 (an increase of 10), the Midwest 14 (a reduction of 1), and Lagos 4 (an increase of 1). In August, 1964, the NPC in alliance with the NNDP, the MDF, and the separatist Niger Delta Congress of Eastern Nigeria inaugurated the Nigerian National Alliance, to which other small parties in the Eastern Region, including the unpredictable Dynamic Party, also adhered. In accordance with the terms of the alliance, the Prime Minister added two NNDP members of Parliament to his federal cabinet. Soon thereafter, the NCNC-AG-Northern Progressive Front alliance was launched formally as the United Progressive Grand Alliance (UPGA), setting the stage for a two-party battle on election day. The Socialist Workers and Farmers Party opted for affiliation with the UPGA; but that alliance would not share its candidatures

inflated. While the results of the abortive 1962 census were never officially released, they are said to have been less favorable to the Northern Region than the 1963 results.

[114] See above, pp. 33–34. The new NNDP also absorbed a recently formed ally of the NPC, called the Southern People's Congress, and the adherents of various parties in Lagos.

in the urban centers of southern Nigeria with a minor party, and the SWAFP decided to field a slate of its own.[115]

Election Crisis

Before the election, UPGA leaders calculated that they would have to win some 20–30 seats out of 167 in the Northern Region to win an over-all majority of the 312 parliamentary seats at stake. Their hopes dimmed with the increasingly frequent complaints of harassment (including mass arrest and malicious prosecution) by their supporters in the North. They were shattered some ten days before the election by the announcement that 68 NPC candidates had been returned unopposed. At first, UPGA demanded a postponement of the election, pending clarification of the disputed "unopposed" returns. Ultimately, the UPGA leaders, professing to despair of a free and fair election, decided upon a boycott. President Azikiwe urged the Prime Minister to postpone the election for six months, but Sir Abubakar rejected that advice and the election was held as scheduled on December 30 in the face of an UPGA boycott. In accordance with the instruction of Dr. Okpara (Premier of Eastern Nigeria and national president of the NCNC), no voting took place in the 70 Eastern constituencies, although NCNC candidates were returned unopposed in 19 of them, which were in any case safe. In the Midwestern Region, leaders of the NCNC disagreed and vacillated with the result that voting there was light as the NCNC won all 14 seats. In the Western Region, NNDP candidates were declared elected in 36 constituencies to UPGA's 18 (13 AG and 5 NCNC). In the Federal Territory of Lagos, an independent candidate who received less than 600 votes was declared elected in the one constituency (out of four) where any voting took place. The Northern Region, true to form, gave the NPC 162 out of 167 seats, boosting the NNA total to the comfortable figure of 198. All told, only 4 million voters went to the polls, compared with more than 7 million in 1959. The percentage of the eligible electorate actually voting dropped from nearly 80 per cent in 1959 to something on the order of 20 per cent in 1964.

For six days, the peace and unity of the nation appeared to hang in the balance while intensive negotiations were conducted involving the

[115] The SWAFP operates mainly in southern Nigeria in opposition to the NCNC, the AG, and other "bourgeois" parties. It is hostile to the NCNC doctrine of pragmatic African socialism and the AG doctrine of democratic socialism. SWAFP has demonstrated, however, that it will support these parties in a showdown with the NPC.

President, the Prime Minister, leaders of the regional governments, and other influential persons. At length, it was agreed that the President should ask Sir Abubakar to form a government that would be "broadly based." Most of his new cabinet choices were northerners who had been members of his previous cabinet, but it was understood that additional appointments would be made from the Eastern and Western Regions after the conduct of elections in those constituencies which had been successfully boycotted. In this follow-up election of March, 1965, no additional seats were won by the NNA, while 53 seats were won by the UPGA. The Prime Minister then enlarged his cabinet to include 7 members of the UPGA (all NCNC) in addition to 22 members of the NNA (15 NPC and 7 NNDP).

In the wake of this crisis the veil of presidential detachment was lifted to record for the world Azikiwe's own analysis and prescription. In an article written for the American journal, *Foreign Affairs*,[116] he specified the "immediate" and "remote" causes of the crisis. Mentioned in the first category were faulty electoral procedures, campaign violence and lawlessness, the election boycott by his own former party, and the alleged (but disputed and disavowed) threat of secession by the Eastern Region. A host of alleged ills were listed under the second heading, including the population predominance of the Northern Region, combined with the inequity whereby Northern constituency delimitation is in accordance with total adult population while voting is by male suffrage only, in contrast to universal adult franchise in the southern regions. Other serious faults to which he alluded were as follows: inadequate opportunity for debate in Parliament; the "immoral practice" of parliamentary carpet-crossing; political featherbedding,[117] inordinate ambition, opportunism, and dereliction on the part of politicians; discrimination on the basis of regional origin; and the lack of checks and balances with respect to governmental powers. His proposed remedies included strengthening of the Senate through elected membership and increased powers; judicial and legal reforms, ranging from the transformation of regional high courts into federal courts of appeal and the unification of laws; elimination of exceptions and pro-

---

[116] "Essentials for Nigerian Survival," *Foreign Affairs*, XLIII, No. 3 (April, 1965), pp. 447–461.

[117] Azikiwe observed that of a total of 54 NNDP members of the Western House of Assembly, 53 held offices (49 Ministers and Parliamentary Secretaries, the Speaker, Deputy Speaker, Chief Whip, and Party Whip) and the 55th had recently resigned from the party. *Ibid.*, p. 450. The NNDP retorted that a few of its members in the House of Assembly did not actually hold office.

visos in the constitution which permit the impairment of fundamental rights; extension of federal responsibility for development and welfare programs; the creation of new states in the territories of existing regions; the consolidation or modification of executive authority in favor of a strong Head of State; and the establishment of a Federal Privy Council with sole responsibility to advise the President on matters relating to the military use of the armed forces and police for internal security, and matters of war and peace. Whatever the diagnostic or remedial merits of these specific items, much of what Azikiwe has written in this article serves to show that the civil freedoms enshrined in Nigeria's constitution are not merely ideals for that nation to savor but staples of its political life.

In October, 1965 a tensely awaited election was held in the Western Region. The party in power—NNDP—had yet to win a fully contested election. The opposition parties—AG and NCNC—campaigned as one party under the banner of UPGA, aiming to eliminate its rival— NNA (which includes NNDP)—from serious contention in southern Nigeria. Once again the election was misconducted. With 94 seats at stake, 16 NNDP candidates were returned unopposed. UPGA protested vehemently that its candidates had been fraudulently excluded. On election day, policemen found thousands of ballot papers in the illegal possession of electoral officials who were appointed by the regional government. Many ballot boxes were stuffed; it was the consensus of impartial observers that the election had been rigged to give the NNDP a three-to-one victory. UPGA leaders refused to accept that result. Many violent and rebellious acts occurred in the West as the national crisis continued.

Nigerian Foreign Policy

Nigeria affords no exception to the general proposition that a country's foreign policies are in large part the outcome of salient internal conditions and aspirations. It has been shown that the Nigerian federal system derives from an effort to accommodate deep social, economic, religious, and ideological cleavages that are potentially total, by leaders who envision a greater destiny for their people in national unity and industrially based prosperity. To reach these ends, a distinctive and complicated set of political institutions, viable if shifting national political coalitions and alliances, and a certain strategy of economic development have been carefully devised. These means and constraints above all have inspired Nigeria's choice of foreign policies among the limited range of alternatives which its own resources and the geopolitical situations in Africa and the larger world have presented.

Limited relations between the great constituent communities of Nigeria and the outside world, of course, existed in the precolonial era: Hausa-Fulani with North Africa and the Middle East, and later Ibo, Yoruba, and Benin with the traveler-explorers, missionaries, slavers, and traders of Europe. As a national entity, Nigeria's external experience commenced with the terminal phase of colonialism, in which Britain retained ultimate control while permitting Nigerians such tutelary excursions into foreign affairs as a Liaison Office in Washington to deal with Nigerian students and official visitors, and similar arrangements for such problems as Nigerians on pilgrimage to Mecca, and Nigerian workers in the Spanish territory of Fernando Po and in French-ruled Gabon and Cameroun. They also made representations to the Trusteeship Council and other UN agencies. In London the most important of the quasi-diplomatic establishments, in addition to the sort of functions carried on by the Washington Office, worked to stimulate foreign trade, investment, and recruitment of British civil servants. Significantly, in this period, the London Nigeria Office included three regional commissioners each of whom sought advantages in trade, investment, scholarships, and expatriate personnel recruitment for his respective government.

The crux of the final stage in the transfer of power was complete Nigerian control of foreign affairs; this devolved principally upon the federal government. The first serious public debate on foreign policy occurred during the federal ("independence") election campaign of 1959. That campaign revealed significant differences at the time in the foreign policy orientations of the major parties, especially on two critical subjects: relations with the Eastern and Western blocs and the pan-African idea.

EVOLUTION OF NIGERIA'S NONALIGNMENT POLICY

The first statement of any detail came from Azikiwe, who at a press conference in August, 1959, associated himself and his party with the neutralist position on cold war issues; at the same time, he endorsed the widely held assumption that upon independence Nigeria should join the Commonwealth, and he vowed vigorous support of the UN. A neutralist approach appeared consistent with the NCNC's desire to promote economic links with any amenable country and with the relatively assertive role which the party evidently envisaged for the government in the domestic economy. A month later, Awolowo seized the occasion of the annual national conference of the Action Group to deliver an extensive and explicit repudiation of neutralism as "an unmitigated disservice to humanity" which in the economic sphere called for tactics that were "double-dealing," "disreputable," and "dangerous." [118] Ensuing exchanges in party newspapers and later the election manifestoes revealed, however, that the AG wanted Nigeria to identify with the West short of entering into military alliance, while the NCNC thought that Eastern bloc relations based strictly on Nigerian national interest were compatible not only with Commonwealth membership but with an "intimate and cordial" relationship with the United States.[119]

Balewa had given advance indication of the NPC's view in a press conference in London in October, 1958, when he remarked that "however tempting it may be to adopt a neutralist position in world affairs, I myself doubt whether Nigeria will be wise even to contemplate such a course." [120] The NPC manifesto now strongly confirmed and elaborated Balewa's initial reaction, declaring that the party's political beliefs "rule out completely any idea of adopting a policy of neutrality in international affairs" in favor of "the closest relationship" with Britain and "increasing friendship with the United States of America," countries it regarded as "animated by the same beliefs." [121]

Within a year after independence, each party's original stand in this controversy changed perceptibly and in one case, drastically. Having begun farthest apart, the two partners in the postindependence coalition government arrived at a mutually acceptable ground they called nonalignment. The term was meant to suggest an attitude of selective judgment and response with regard to East-West conflicts, in contrast to a fixed posture of impartiality, aloofness, or indifference sometimes conveyed by the word neutral. For the NPC-NCNC coalition, the beauty of this concept was that it left room, in principle, for the seemingly divergent international programs of the two parties without having immediately to reconcile them. Meanwhile, in his new role as parliamentary opposition leader, Awolowo proceeded to move his

---

[118] See Claude S. Phillips, Jr., *The Development of Nigeria's Foreign Policy* (Evanston: Northwestern University Press, 1964), pp. 15–20.

[119] *Ibid.*

[120] Quoted in J. S. Coleman, "The Foreign Policy of Nigeria," in Joseph E. Black and Kenneth Thompson, eds., *Foreign Policies in a World of Change* (New York: Harper and Row, 1963), p. 395.

[121] Phillips, *op. cit.*, p. 18.

party all the way from decidedly pro-Western inclinations to aggressive criticism of any ostensible bias in that direction on the part of the government. That the Nigerian government has indeed kept the Eastern bloc at more than arm's length is obvious from merely a cursory examination of its behavior. More careful consideration is necessary, however, to determine whether that behavior has been truly characterized by nonalignment or by attachment to the West.

Those who interpret Nigeria's foreign policy as attachment to the West typically posit that the realities of its economy must lead to such a policy. The extreme reliance on Western sources of capital formation reflected in the 1962–1968 Development Plan has been pointed out; to this circumstance may be added Nigeria's patterns of trade, featuring (in 1962) 70 per cent of imports and 90 per cent of exports from and to the Western bloc as against the Eastern countries' 4 per cent share of Nigeria's imports and 1 per cent of its exports. Moreover, Nigeria is the recipient of the largest single U.S. aid contribution to date to any African nation ($225 million), while aid from the Eastern bloc has been minimal. One summary of Nigerian foreign policy actions which have been alleged to be the result of these realities lists the following:

delaying the establishment of diplomatic relations with the Soviet Union; imposing restrictions on the size of the Soviet mission in Lagos, on travel to the Soviet bloc especially for study, and on the importation of Communist literature; discouraging Soviet-bloc aid and trade; proposing a "two-China" policy and supporting India in her dispute with China; concluding a defense pact with Britain, permitting the establishment of a "secret N.A.T.O. radio station" in the country, and co-operating with the American Mercury Project; refusing to attend the Belgrade conference of non-aligned nations; adopting a policy of silence—or worse—on Cuba, Berlin, and the resumption of U.S. nuclear tests; collaboration with neo-colonialists in the Congo and Welensky in Central Africa; and opposing the creation of a union of African states.[122]

Perhaps the cardinal example of a Nigerian policy susceptible of this interpretation was Nigeria's outspoken approval, contrary to the bitter condemnation voiced by most African nations, China, the Soviet bloc, and others, of the Belgian-led and American-aided armed intercession in the Congo, in hopes of freeing white hostages of antigovernment forces, in November, 1964. The Nigerian view of this poignant episode extended to a denunciation in the UN of any support of Congolese

[122] Douglas G. Anglin, "Nigeria: political non-alignment and economic alignment," *The Journal of Modern African Studies*, Vol. 2, No. 2 (July, 1964), p. 248.

insurrectionists as "interference in the Congo's internal affairs," despite the fact that those rendering such assistance included several African states. The Congo Premier Moise Tshombe's reputation in nearly all parts of the continent as the archtraitor to African interests failed to deter Nigeria from taking this stand, alone among all the African states.

In support of the government's official claim to be nonaligned in international affairs with any bloc, including that of nonaligned nations,[123] we may, in the first instance, cite the care and apparent determination with which the Prime Minister has often articulated this claim.[124] Most relevant, of course, is the record of deeds. On this score, it may be pointed out that the government, in response to pressure or not, reversed itself on several of the important items in the "pro-West" list cited above: it entered into formal diplomatic relations with the Soviet Union and other Communist countries, abrogated the Anglo-Nigerian Defense Pact, lifted the ban on importation of Communist literature, liberalized regulations on Soviet scholarships, and sent a trade delegation to China and one to eastern Communist countries resulting in a loan of $15 million from Poland and another for an undisclosed amount from the Soviet Union.[125] A trade agreement signed in July, 1963, called for the sale to Russia of Nigerian columbite, although none appears to have been actually shipped as yet. The significance of this gesture in the present context is the existence of a law providing for abrupt termination of U.S. assistance to any country which supplies strategic material to a Communist-bloc member, and

[123] Balewa is quoted as having said that "when a neutral country joins a neutral bloc it ceases to be neutral. We want to pursue an independent view, which is not the same as neutralism" in Coleman, "Nigeria's Foreign Policy," *op. cit.*, p. 399.

[124] In his first parliamentary statement on foreign affairs the Prime Minister asserted that his government "shall not blindly follow the lead of anyone; so far as it is possible, the policy on each occasion will be selected with proper independent objectivity in Nigeria's national interest. We consider it wrong for the Federal Government to associate itself as a matter of routine with any of the power blocs. This freedom of action will be an essential feature of our policy and will ensure that full attention is paid the opinions expressed by our representatives." *House of Representatives Debates*, August 20, 1960, col. 2670. In the same place in November of that year, the Prime Minister elaborated on the meaning of his phrase "as a matter of routine," saying it implied that "Nigeria will follow an independent line no matter from where the truth comes whether it be from the East or the West, Nigeria will go to the path of truth." (October, 1962), 131–140, also expounds on this theme.

[125] Anglin, *op. cit.*, p. 248.

columbite is an essential alloy in certain metals used in connection with nuclear weapons and space instruments.[126]

The two actions that undoubtedly most deserve to be cited as evidence of the integrity of Nigeria's proclaimed nonalignment principles, however, are the severance of diplomatic relations with France (resumed in the fall of 1965) because of its nuclear testing activities in the Sahara and Nigeria's prolonged refusal to participate as an associate member in the European Economic Community. Breaking relations with France was accomplished at no little inconvenience to Nigeria (and at considerable cost to its friendly French Community neighbors, Dahomey and Niger, which have used Nigeria's port as an outlet for commerce with France). It achieved for Nigeria the thankless distinction of having been the only African state to have invoked this severe sanction against a Western power. Nigeria's refusal in 1962 to seek association with the EEC was at variance with Britain's effort to become a full EEC member; had Britain succeeded, the economic basis of Nigeria's Commonwealth association could have been undercut. Nigeria was also obviously impervious in this matter to American advice. In 1965, however, Nigeria, acting on the basis of economic self-interest, shifted its position and negotiated a separate free trade area agreement with the EEC, giving some trading concessions to the Common Market to which the British government has taken exception.

A fair conclusion would appear to be a slightly modified version of an observation made by the author of the first book on Nigerian foreign policy: "While Nigeria's dominant values appeared to be those of the West [a desire for] independence of action seemed to be stronger than such identification." [127] Taken as a whole, Nigeria's positions to date on major international issues certainly have failed to conform to any external conception of correctness in international behavior, as its role within the African scene will make clearer.

NIGERIA AND PAN-AFRICAN COOPERATION

Black leaders the world over have been inspired by the vision of pan-African unity. Its historic currency assured that the emergence of a large group of independent African states would precipitate an issue that is basic to African interstate relations: not *whether* such relations should be close, but *how* intimate they should be. As in the case of its interpretation of nonalignment, Nigeria's position on this issue has

[126] *Ibid.*, p. 251.   [127] Phillips, *op. cit.*, p. 51.

been greatly regretted by left-wing radicals within Nigeria and abroad. Here again, however, the Nigerian government has maintained certain fundamental principles of action with a degree of consistency that may command general respect. These principles have been summarized by Coleman as follows: "non-intervention, functional integration, and non-violent resolution of Africa's remaining colonial and racial problems." [128] In contrast, those who find these orientations disappointing tend to conceive pan-African unity in terms of some kind of political union in the near future between presently sovereign African states. To that end, they sanction political action across existing national boundaries and believe in the use of force to liberate African majorities from repressive white rule.

In Nigeria during the first period after independence (1960–1964), the latter views were voiced in whole or in part by the official opposition, quasi-official bodies like the all-Nigeria People's Conference of 1961 (convened, incidentally, by the Prime Minister's personal adviser on foreign affairs), "radical" minor parties and individuals, including prominent members of both government coalition parties.[129] Again, as in the case of nonalignment policy, however, shifting positions have marked the course of the Nigerian debate on pan-African issues. Most conspicuous in this regard was Awolowo's *volte-face* from utter disdain of any notion of feasible political union to vociferous condemnation of the Nigerian government for failure to embrace such ventures as the Union of African States (which tentatively linked Ghana, Guinea, and Mali).

Outside Nigeria, unofficial and imbalanced delegations attended nongovernmental All-African Peoples Conferences (Accra, 1958; Tunis, 1960; Cairo, 1961) where supranationalism prevailed. On the diplomatic plane, the debate was conducted through a parallel series of high-level interstate conferences composed respectively of two blocs of countries that more or less agreed with one or the other of the two syndromes of policies. In the conferences of Brazzaville (December, 1960), Monrovia (May, 1961), and Lagos (January, 1962), the principles advocated by Nigeria were also embraced by the far larger group of African states; indeed, Nigeria, perhaps inevitably given its pre-eminent size, assumed leadership status among these countries. At Conakry (May, 1959) and Casablanca (January, 1961) the alternative

---

[128] *Op. cit.*, p. 402.
[129] Notably Alhaji Muhtari, *Sarkin Bai*, NPC Chief Whip, and Dr. Kalu Ezera, NCNC backbencher in the House of Representatives.

set of principles enjoyed currency among a much smaller group of states. By the same token, the latter group came to regard Nigeria as something of a conservative ringleader. On issues not strictly relevant to the fundamental controversy, such as the UN role in the Congo and Morocco's claim to suzerainty over Mauretania, Nigeria was similarly active in opposition to the stand taken by the minority bloc.

In these situations, Nigeria was strategically placed to exercise a mediating influence between the burgeoning African blocs. Thus, Nigeria received much of the credit for the success of the African "Summit" meeting in May, 1963, at Addis Ababa, at which the members of both groups subscribed to a Charter that represented virtually a triumph of the Nigerian principles. Though Nigeria's role has earned its leaders a reputation for moderation on continental issues, it is well to keep in mind that in rejecting EEC affiliation largely on grounds that it would impede African economic integration, challenging France's use of the Sahara for nuclear testing, and confronting South African apartheid policies with hostility on nearly every possible occasion, these leaders have demonstrated a willingness to take maximum steps consistent with their self-imposed standards of international conduct.

SPECIAL PROBLEMS AND RELATIONS

In addition to broad controversies involving the cold war or pan-African unity, certain specific considerations and circumstances inevitably influence the conduct of Nigeria's foreign affairs. These include, notably, the country's former colonial relationship with Britain, the bonds of faith and history between Nigeria's all-important upper Northern area and Muslim nations to the north and east, the existence on all three Nigerian inland borders of states whose principal extra-African connection is with France, and perhaps most important, exigencies arising out of Nigeria's particular kind of federal constitution.

The relationship of an ex-colony to its former ruler invariably involves factors that are psychological as well as geopolitical in nature. One aspect of Nigeria's colonial legacy is a continued disproportionate reliance on Britain in such matters as trade, private capital formation, education, technical personnel, and the organization of defense. Doubtless this circumstance continues because Nigeria's policy-makers dispassionately deem it to be in the country's interest; national language affinity in itself is a major factor favoring continued close association with the United Kingdom. Understandably, the cordiality and good faith that evidently have characterized Anglo-Nigerian relations after independence are a mutual achievement much admired in the West. Yet, just as understandably, the passions aroused by a heritage of alien subjugation persist and sometimes erupt even in the midst of this concord; indeed, their incidence may be in direct proportion to the very realism that secures the partnership. The Nigerian government rejected a British offer to subsidize expatriate civil servants, notwithstanding Nigeria's quest for development assistance. Bitter nonofficial attacks on the Anglo-Nigerian Defense Pact led to its abrogation despite the fact that its provisions were sufficiently unobtrusive to be sustained afterward without benefit of that document. These incidents underscore the delicacy that inevitably will inhere for some time in the relations of these two countries especially.

Nigeria has faithfully observed its nonintervention principle with respect to the affairs of its neighbors, all of them much weaker. Its equanimity in losing territory through the UN Plebescite that resulted in transferring the former region of the Southern Camerouns of Nigeria to the domain of the former French-administered Cameroun Republic presents an obvious contrast to the sentiments of revanche manifested by other states in comparable circumstances. In this regard, inadequate awareness of its neighbors seems the only score on which Nigeria might reasonably be faulted, and here too its colonial legacy is extenuating. The mere fact that Nigeria apparently had not anticipated the impact on Dahomey and Niger of its diplomatic break with France, however, was indicative of the need for wider horizons in the making of Nigerian foreign policy.

An apparently less easily attainable but more urgent necessity is that of striking a balance between legitimate desires on the part of Nigerian Muslims for solidarity with foreign co-religionists and the crucial necessity of speaking in foreign affairs with one voice, in this case out of a chorus that includes other faiths. That balance would seem to be jeopardized by incidents such as the Northern Government's disassociation from the Israeli loan initially negotiated by the federal government and by verbal initiatives on the part of the Northern Premier toward some form of interstate affiliation between Muslim countries.

Regional misconception of the foreign policy function's proper location is related to certain potentially troublesome features of the Nigerian constitution. In that instrument, regional governments are invested with concurrent jurisdiction in respect of industrial development, and, under Section 74, with the remarkable power to nullify or prevent the operation within their spheres of any federal government international undertaking touching any matter not exclusively or concurrently delegated to it. The first provision accounts for the existence of influential regional Agents General in the U.K., each handling economic, educational, and other important affairs for his own government, as well as Nigeria's Hydra-headed efforts in soliciting aid and investment funds in various parts of the world. The full implications of the second constitutional compromise are yet to be manifested, but its existence seems, if nothing else, an invitation to regional stress in deliberations on foreign issues.

Finally, it is worth drawing attention to one other highly probable regional influence on Nigeria's foreign policy, which is difficult to measure: the attempt to reconcile traditional institutions and values with modernity in Northern Nigeria, which may have some bearing on the country's choice of foreign associates. In the last analysis, leaders who seek to preserve the existing order may be expected to prefer allies who value continuity and stability above revolutionary changes.

Conclusion

Whatever the future may hold for Nigeria, the story of its debut as a sovereign state cannot fail to make a strong impression on the world. Like other newly independent nations, Nigeria has to make its way under the most trying conditions: extreme cultural and social diversity, great poverty, pervasive illiteracy, tenacious traditionalism, socially debilitating nepotism, widespread corruption in public life—and the strains of political discontent, disaffection, and demoralization that such conditions inevitably breed. Elsewhere in Africa, Asia, and Latin America, these conditions and their consequences have resulted in the "erosion" of constitutional democracy.[130]

Nigeria, like India, is still trying to solve the problems that are inherent in the condition of industrial underdevelopment within a framework of constitutional democracy. On the whole, Nigerians enjoy fundamental political freedoms, including freedom of political association and the right to engage in organized political competition. It might be observed, in the light of this study, that limited government is a virtual dictate of necessity for Nigeria to survive as one nation on the basis of consent rather than force. But the logic of limited government,

[130] See the perceptive statement of this problem in Rupert Emerson, *From Empire to Nation* (Cambridge: Harvard University Press, 1960), pp. 172–292.

especially with regard to freedom of political association, leads to the formation of political and quasi-political groups based on loyalties which tend to undermine loyalty to the nation. India has its "caste-ism" and "provincialism"; Nigeria has rampant "tribalism" and "regionalism." Will these potentially disruptive forces be contained by democratic means?

In a large and culturally heterogeneous democracy, security against destructive sectional conflict may be sought in the formation of broadly based political parties. In Nigeria, the two new major political formations—the Nigerian National Alliance and the United Progressive Grand Alliance—are in fact broadly based. With a little leniency, each could be fairly described as a national party. Clearly, however, a threat to Nigerian unity could arise anew were either of these two formations to indulge in identification with its primary geographical base (north and south respectively) above loyalty to the nation. In that event, future electoral defeat might well be taken by the majority faction of the defeated grouping to mean an intolerable prelude to permanent political domination by agents of an alien political culture.

Pat generalizations rarely hit their mark. But many of the observations here seem to imply acid tests for constitutional democracy in the developing nations: Is it compatible with the effective pursuit of economic development, social justice, and lasting national unity?

Postscript

In January, 1966, a military government took over in Nigeria in the wake of a shattering plot which involved the assassination of several of the country's most eminent politicians, including the Prime Minister, Sir Abubakar Tafawa Balewa, and the northern and western regional premiers, Sir Ahmadu Bello and Chief S. L. Akintola. This was the fifth military government installed south of the Sahara within two months. Major General Johnson T. U. Aguiyi-Ironsi announced that he was asked by members of the former cabinet to assume power until the formation of a new civilian government. These grave developments followed widespread bloodshed in Nigeria's Western Region, arising out of public outrage at the conduct of the October, 1965, elections there; but the beginnings of the constitutional breakdown go back to the very foundations of Nigeria itself.

The new military government was given a truly delicate task. As this passage is written, secession, civil war, or prolonged martial rule remain grim alternatives to the restoration of constitutional government in a united republic. Certainly the present authors did not anticipate the specific events of January, 1966; but we have found no cause to alter our essay, which seems to us to identify the principal conditions that led to them. Indeed this new turn of events gives the essay an unexpected historical significance, since it treats an entire era of Nigerian political history which is now concluded.

Richard L. Sklar
C. S. Whitaker, Jr.

January, 1966

Bibliography

Scholarly publications that treat a wide range of subjects concerning Nigerian government and politics are now readily available. The authors of this study have attempted to synthesize what many students of Nigerian government have previously written. This bibliography therefore represents a compilation of our sources. But official documents have been listed only if they appear to be standard items of reference. In addition to the studies listed, a recently published work, Eme O. Awa's *Federal Government in Nigeria* (Berkeley and Los Angeles: University of California Press, 1964), deserves special mention. Continuing students will also wish to consult the *Journal of the Nigerian Society of Economic and Social Studies,* published quarterly at the University of Ibadan, *Nigerian Opinion,* a new (January, 1965) monthly magazine of the Nigerian Current Affairs Society, and the informative London weekly magazine, *West Africa.*

THE POLITICAL CULTURE OF A PLURAL SOCIETY

On the concept of political culture see

Almond, Gabriel A. "Comparative Political Systems," *The Journal of Politics,* XVIII (August, 1956), 391–409.

————. "A Functional Approach to Comparative Politics," in Gabriel A. Almond and James S. Coleman, eds., *The Politics of the Developing Areas.* Princeton: Princeton University Press, 1960, pp. 3–64.

————., and Verba, Sidney. *The Civic Culture.* Princeton: Princeton University Press, 1963.

Beer, Samuel H. "The Four Variables of a Political System: Political Culture," in Samuel H. Beer and Adam B. Ulam, eds., *Patterns of Government.* 2d revised ed. New York: Random House, 1962, pp. 32–45.

Pye, Lucian W., and Verba, Sidney, eds., *Comparative Political Culture.* Princeton: Princeton University Press, 1965.

Two relevant general analyses of African political systems are

Coleman, James S. "The Politics of Sub-Saharan Africa," in Gabriel A. Almond and James S. Coleman, eds., *The Politics of the Developing Areas.* Princeton: Princeton University Press, 1960, pp. 247–368.

Fortes, M., and Evans-Pritchard, E. E., eds., *African Political Systems.* London: Oxford University Press, 1940, pp. 1–23.

There is a vast literature on the traditional cultures of Nigerian peoples; the following items have been especially useful in the preparation of this chapter:

Biobaku, Saburi O. *The Egba and Their Neighbors, 1842–1872*. Oxford: The Clarendon Press, 1957.

Bohannan, Laura and Paul. *The Tiv of Central Nigeria*. London: International Africa Institute, 1953.

Bradbury, R. E. *The Benin Kingdom and the Edo-Speaking Peoples of Southwestern Nigeria*. London: International Africa Institute, 1957.

Cohen, Ronald. "The Analysis of Conflict in Hierarchical Systems: An Example from Kanuri Political Organization," *Anthropologica*, IV, No. 1 (1962), 87–120.

Dike, K. Onwuka. *Trade and Politics in the Niger Delta, 1830–1885*. Oxford: Clarendon Press, 1956.

Hodgkin, Thomas. *Nigerian Perspectives, An Historical Anthology*. London: Oxford University Press, 1960.

Jones, G. I. *Report on the Position, Status, and Influence of Chiefs and Natural Rulers in the Eastern Region of Nigeria*. Enugu: Government Printer, 1957.

————. *The Trading States of the Oil Rivers*. London: Oxford University Press, 1963.

Lloyd, P. C. *Yoruba Land Law*. London: Oxford University Press, 1962.

Nadel, S. F. *A Black Byzantium*. London: Oxford University Press, 1942.

Ottenberg, Simon. "Ibo Oracles and Intergroup Relations," *Southwestern Journal of Anthropology*, XIV, No. 3 (Autumn, 1958), 295–317.

————. "Ibo Receptivity to Change," in William R. Bascom and Melville J. Herskovits, eds., *Continuity and Change in African Cultures*. Chicago: University of Chicago Press, 1959, pp. 130–143.

Smith, M. G. *Government in Zazzau*. London: Oxford University Press, 1942.

Trimingham, J. Spencer. *Islam in West Africa*. Oxford: Clarendon Press, 1959.

Whitaker, C. S., Jr. "Three Perspectives on Hierarchy: Political Thought and Leadership in Northern Nigeria," *Journal of Commonwealth Political Studies*, II, No. 4 (March, 1965), 1–19.

On the background to British Nigeria see

Biobaku, Saburi O. *The Egba and Their Neighbors, 1842–1872*. Oxford: The Clarendon Press, 1957.

Burns, Alan. *History of Nigeria*. 5th ed. London: Allen and Unwin, 1953.

Coleman, James S. *Nigeria: Background to Nationalism*. Berkeley and Los Angeles: University of California Press, 1958. Chapter 2.

Crowder, Michael. *A Short History of Nigeria.* New York: Praeger, 1962.

Dike, K. Onwuka. *Trade and Politics in the Niger Delta, 1830–1885.* Oxford: Clarendon Press, 1956.

Flint, J. E. *Sir George Goldie and the Making of Nigeria.* London: Oxford University Press, 1960.

Hamilton, W. B. "The Evolution of British Policy Toward Nigeria," in Robert O. Tilman and Taylor Cole, eds., *The Nigerian Political Scene.* Durham, N.C.: Duke University Press, 1962. Chapter 2.

Newbury, C. W. *The Western Slave Coast and its Rulers.* Oxford: The Clarendon Press, 1962.

For the impact of colonial rule on traditional patterns of authority see

Akpan, Ntieyong U. *Epitaph to Indirect Rule.* London: Cassell and Co., 1956, pp. 13–45.

Cowan, L. Gray. *Local Government in West Africa.* New York: Columbia University Press, 1958. Chapter 1.

Crocker, W. R. *Nigeria: A Critique of British Colonial Administration.* London: Allen and Unwin, 1936, pp. 213–227.

Hailey, Lord. *Native Administration in the British African Territories.* Part III. London: H.M.S.O., 1951.

Lloyd, P. C. "The Changing Role of the Yoruba Traditional Ruler," *Proceedings of the Third Annual Conference of the West Africa Institute of Social and Economic Research.* Ibadan: University College, 1956, pp. 57–65.

Lugard, Sir Frederick. *The Dual Mandate in British Tropical Africa.* 4th ed. London: William Blackwood, 1929.

Meek, C. K. *Law and Authority in a Nigerian Tribe.* London: Oxford University Press, 1937, pp. ix-xvi, 325–355.

Perham, Margery. *Native Administration in Nigeria.* London: Oxford University Press, 1937.

———. *Lugard: The Years of Authority, 1898–1945.* London: Collins, 1960.

Smith, M. G. *Government in Zazzau, 1800–1950.* London: Oxford University Press, 1960.

On education and the intellectual awakening see

Ashby, Sir Eric, *et al. Investment in Education. The Report of the Commission on Post-School Certificate and Higher Education in Nigeria.* Lagos: Federal Ministry of Education, 1960.

Azikiwe, Nnamdi. *Renascent Africa.* Accra: [privately printed,] 1937.

Bunting, Reginald. "Nigeria," in Helen Kitchen, ed., *The Educated African.* New York: Praeger, 1962, pp. 364–386.

Coker, Increase. "The Nigerian Press, 1929–1959," in Ayo Ogunsheye, ed.,

Report on the Press in West Africa. Ibadan: (mimeographed) 1961, pp. 73–133.

Coleman, James S. *Nigeria: Background to Nationalism.* Berkeley and Los Angeles: University of California Press, 1958. Chapter 5.

Cowan, L. Gray, O'Connell, James, and Scanlon, David G., *Education and Nation-Building in Africa,* New York: Praeger, 1965.

Ikejiani, Okachukwu, ed. *Nigerian Education.* Ikeja: Longmans of Nigeria, 1964.

Kirk-Greene, Anthony H. M. "Bureaucratic Cadres in a Traditional Milieu," in James S. Coleman, ed., *Education and Political Development.* Princeton: Princeton University Press, 1965, pp. 372–407.

Nduka, Otonti. *Western Education and the Nigerian Cultural Background.* Ibadan: Oxford University Press, 1964.

Ogunsheye, Ayo. "Nigeria," in James S. Coleman, ed., *Education and Political Development.* Princeton: Princeton University Press, 1965, pp. 123–143.

Weiler, Hans., ed. *Education and Politics in Nigeria.* Published in German and English. Freiburg im Breisgau: Verlag Rombach, 1964.

On ubanization and social structure see

Bascom, William R. "Urbanization Among the Yoruba," *American Journal of Sociology,* LX, No. 5 (March, 1955), 446–454.

Buchanan, K. M., and Pugh, J. C. *Land and People in Nigeria.* London: University of London Press, 1955.

Coleman, James S. "The Development of Urban Centers," in *Nigeria: Background to Nationalism.* Berkeley and Los Angeles: University of California Press, 1958, pp. 72–79.

"Leopoldville and Lagos: Comparative Study of Urban Conditions in 1960," *United Nations Economic Bulletin for Africa,* I, No. 2 (June, 1961), 50–65.

Marris, Peter. *Family and Social Change in an African City.* Evanston: Northwestern University Press, 1962.

Smith, M. G. "The Hausa System of Social Status," *Africa,* XXIX, No. 3 (July, 1959), 239–252.

Smythe, Hugh H., and Smythe, Mable M. *The New Nigerian Elite.* Stanford: Stanford University Press, 1960.

Two essays of general interest are

Little, Kenneth. "The Role of Voluntary Associations in West African Urbanization," *American Anthropologist,* LIX, No. 4 (August, 1957), 579–596.

Wallerstein, I. "Ethnicity and National Integration in West Africa," *Cahiers D'Etudes Africaines,* No. 3 (October, 1960), pp. 131–139.

Among the many works on Nigerian economic development, see in summary.

Callaway, Archibald. "School Leavers in the Developing Economy of Nigeria," in Robert O. Tilman and Taylor Cole, eds., *The Nigerian Political Scene*. Durham, N.C.: Duke University Press, 1962, pp. 198–219.

Carney, David E. *Government and Economy in British West Africa*. New York: Bookman's, 1961.

Coleman, James S. "Western Economic Forces," in *Nigeria: Background to Nationalism*. Berkeley and Los Angeles: University of California Press, 1958. Chapter 3.

Federation of Nigeria. *National Development Plan, 1962–68*. Lagos: Government Printer, 1962.

Harbison, Frederick. "Human Resources and Economic Development in Nigeria," in Robert O. Tilman and Taylor Cole, eds., *The Nigerian Political Scene*. Durham, N.C.: Duke University Press, 1962, pp. 198–219.

International Bank for Reconstruction and Development. *The Economic Development of Nigeria*. Baltimore: The Johns Hopkins Press, 1955.

National Economic Council. *Economic Survey of Nigeria, 1959*. Lagos: Government Printer, 1959.

Perham, Margery F., ed. *The Economics of a Tropical Dependency*. 2 vols. London: Faber, 1946–1948.

Schatz, Sayre P. *Development Bank Lending in Nigeria: The Federal Loans Board*. Ibadan: Oxford University Press, 1964.

––––––. "Nigeria's First National Development Plan (1962–68), An Appraisal," *The Nigerian Journal of Economic and Social Studies*, V, No. 2 (July, 1963), 221–235.

Sokolski, Alan. *The Establishment of Manufacturing in Nigeria*. New York: Praeger, 1965.

Stewart, Ian G. "Nigeria's Economic Prospects," *The Three Banks Review*, No. 49 (March, 1961), pp. 16–28.

"Symposium on the New Nigerian Development Plan," *The Nigerian Journal of Economic and Social Studies*, IV, No. 2 (July, 1962), 85–146.

NATIONALISM AND CONSTITUTIONAL DEVELOPMENT

The basic official documents relating to the development of the Nigerian Constitution until independence are as follows:

Colonial Office. *Report by the Conference on the Nigerian Constitution held in London in July and August, 1953*. Cmnd. 8934. London: H.M.S.O., 1953.

––––––. *Report by the Resumed Conference on the Nigerian Constitution held in Lagos in January and February, 1954*. Cmnd. 9050. London: H.M.S.O., 1954.

Colonial Office. *Report by the Nigeria Constitutional Conference held in London in May and June, 1957.* Cmnd. 207. London: H.M.S.O., 1957.

———. *Report of the Fiscal Commissioner on the Financial Effects of the Proposed New Constitutional Arrangements.* Cmnd. 9026. London: H.M.S.O., 1953.

———. *Report of the Fiscal Commission for Nigeria.* Cmnd. 481. London: H.M.S.O., 1958.

———. *Report of the Commission Appointed to Enquire into the Fears of Minorities and the Means of Allaying them.* Cmnd. 505. London: H.M.S.O., 1958.

Federation of Nigeria. *Report by the Resumed Nigeria Constitutional Conference held in London in September and October, 1958.* Lagos: Government Printer, 1958.

The Nigeria (Constitution) Order in Council, 1960. Published in the Supplement to the Official Gazette Extraordinary No. 62, Vol. 47, 30 September 1960—Part B, including the Constitution of the Federation of Nigeria and the Constitutions of the Northern, Western, and Eastern Regions.

Other sources, including commentaries, are

Ahmadu, Bello, The Sardauna of Sokoto. *My Life.* Cambridge: Cambridge University Press, 1962.

Anyiam, Fred. U. *Men and Matters in Nigerian Politics (1934–1958).* Lagos: 1959.

Awolowo, Obafemi. *Path to Nigerian Freedom.* London: Faber, 1947.

———. *Awo: The Autobiography of Chief Obafemi Awolowo.* Cambridge: Cambridge University Press, 1960.

Azikiwe, Nnamdi. *The Development of Political Parties in Nigeria.* London: Office of the Commissioner in the United Kingdom for the Eastern Region of Nigeria, 1957.

———. *Economic Reconstruction of Nigeria.* Lagos: 1942.

———. *Political Blueprint of Nigeria.* Lagos: African Book Co., 1943.

———. *Renascent Africa.* Accra: [privately printed,] 1937.

———. *Zik: A Selection from the Speeches of Nnamdi Azikiwe.* Philip Harris, ed. Cambridge: Cambridge University Press, 1961.

Coleman, James S. "Nationalism in Tropical Africa," *American Political Science Review,* XLVIII (June, 1954), 404–426.

———. *Nigeria: Background to Nationalism.* Berkeley and Los Angeles: University of California Press, 1958.

Elias, T. Olawole. *Government and Politics in Africa.* 2d ed. rev. and enlarged. New York: Asia Publishing House, 1963.

Emerson, Rupert. *From Empire to Nation.* Cambridge: Harvard University Press, 1960.

Ezera, Kalu. *Constitutional Developments in Nigeria.* Rev. ed. Cambridge: Cambridge University Press, 1964.

Hazelwood, Arthur. *The Finances of Nigerian Federation.* Oxford University Institute of Colonial Studies, Reprint Series No. 14, London: Oxford University Press, 1955.

Hodgkin, Thomas. *Nationalism in Colonial Africa.* London: Frederick Muller, 1956.

Ikeotuonye, U. C. *Zik of New Africa.* London: P. R. Macmillan, 1961.

Odumosu, Oluwole I. *The Nigerian Constitution: History and Development.* London: Sweet and Maxwell, 1963.

Rothchild, Donald. *Toward Unity in Africa: A Study of Federalism in British Africa.* Washington, D.C.: Public Affairs Press, 1960.

———. "Safeguarding Nigeria's Minorities," *Duquesne Review,* VIII, No. 2 (Spring, 1963), 35–51.

Sklar, Richard L. *Nigerian Political Parties: Power in an Emergent African Nation.* Princeton: Princeton University Press, 1963.

———. "The Contribution of Tribalism to Nationalism in Western Nigeria," *Journal of Human Relations,* VIII (Spring and Summer, 1960), 407–418.

———. "Le Nationalisme au Nigeria et les Droits de l'Homme," *Etudes Congolaises,* VI, 1 (January, 1964), 31–47.

Sklar, Richard L., and Whitaker, C. S., Jr. "Nigeria," in J. S. Coleman and C. G. Rosberg, eds., *Political Parties and National Integration in Tropical Africa.* Berkeley and Los Angeles: University of California Press, 1964, pp. 597–654.

Wheare, Joan. *The Nigerian Legislative Council.* London: Faber, 1950.

Whitaker, C. S., Jr. "The Politics of Tradition: A Study of Continuity and Change in Northern Nigeria." Unpublished Ph.D. thesis, Princeton University, 1964.

POLITICAL STRUCTURES AND PROCESSES

On the Nigerian constitutional system see

Brett, Lionel. "Digest of Decisions on the Nigerian Constitution," *Journal of African Law,* VIII, No. 3 (Autumn, 1964), 185–194.

Cole, Taylor. "Emergent Federalism in Nigeria," and "The Independence Constitution of Federal Nigeria," in Robert O. Tilman and Taylor Cole, eds., *The Nigerian Political Scene.* Durham, N.C.: Duke University Press, 1962, pp. 45–88.

De Smith, S. A. *The New Commonwealth and its Constitutions.* London: Stevens, 1964.

Federal Republic of Nigeria. *The Constitution of the Federal Republic of Nigeria.* Lagos: Government Printer, 1963. This contains the Constitution of the Federation and the Constitutions of Northern, Eastern, and Western Nigeria. The constitution of Midwestern Nigeria is published in the *Supplement* to the *Official Gazette Extraordinary*, No. 99, Vol. 50, 16 December 1963—Part C.

Federation of Nigeria. *Proposals for the Constitution of the Federal Republic of Nigeria adopted by the All Party Constitutional Conference held in Lagos on July 25 and 26, 1963*. Sessional Paper No. 3 of 1963. Lagos: Government Printer, 1963.

Mackintosh, John P. "The Nigerian Federal Parliament," *Public Law* (Autumn, 1963), pp. 333–361.

Nwabueze, B. O. *Constitutional Law of the Nigerian Republic*. London: Butterworths, 1964.

Odumosu, Oluwole I. *The Nigerian Constitution: History and Development*. London: Sweet and Maxwell, 1963.

On leadership, political parties, interest groups, and elections see

Awa, Eme O. "Roads to Socialism in Nigeria," *Conference Proceedings of the Nigerian Institute of Social and Economic Research, March 1962*. Ibadan: N.I.S.E.R., 1963, pp. 16–30.

Coleman, James S. "The Emergence of African Political Parties," in C. Grove Haines, ed., *Africa Today*. Baltimore: The Johns Hopkins Press, 1955, pp. 225–255.

———. *Nigeria: Background to Nationalism*. Berkeley and Los Angeles: University of California Press, 1958. Chapter 5.

Dudley, B. J. "The Nomination of Parliamentary Candidates in Northern Nigeria: An Analysis of Political Change," *Journal of Commonwealth Political Studies*, II, No. 1 (November, 1963), 45–58.

Hodgkin, Thomas. *African Political Parties*. Harmondsworth: Penguin Books, 1961.

———. *Nationalism in Colonial Africa*. London: Frederick Muller, 1956. Chapter 5.

Lloyd, Peter C. "The Development of Political Parties in Western Nigeria," *American Political Science Review*, XLIX, No. 3 (September, 1955), 693–707.

Post, K. W. J. *The Nigerian Federal Election of 1959*. London: Oxford University Press, 1963.

Sklar, Richard L. *Nigerian Political Parties: Power in an Emergent African Nation*. Princeton: Princeton University Press, 1963.

Sklar, Richard L., and Whitaker, C. S., Jr. "Nigeria," in J. S. Coleman and C. G. Rosberg, eds., *Political Parties and National Integration in Tropical Africa*. Berkeley and Los Angeles: University of California Press, 1964, pp. 597–654.

Whitaker, C. S., Jr. "The Politics of Tradition: A Study of Continuity and Change in Northern Nigeria." Unpublished Ph.D. thesis, Princeton University, 1964.

Other election studies and commentaries include

Abernethy, David B. "Nigeria Creates a New Region," *Africa Report*, IX, No. 3 (March, 1964), 8–10.

Awa, Eme O. "The Federal Elections in Nigeria, 1959," *Ibadan*, No. 8 (March, 1960), pp. 4–7.

Dent, M. J. "Elections in Northern Nigeria," *Journal of Local Administration Overseas*, I, No. 4 (October, 1962), 213–224.

Harris, Richard. "Nigeria: Crisis and Compromise," *Africa Report*, X, No. 3 (March, 1965), 25–31.

Lloyd, Peter C. "Some Comments on the Election in Nigeria," *Journal of African Administration*, IV (July, 1952), 82–92.

Lloyd, P. C., and Post, K. W. J. "Where Should One Vote," *Journal of African Administration*, XII (April, 1960), 95–106.

Post, K. W. J. "Some Pre-election Public Opinion Polls in Eastern Nigeria," *Nigerian Institute of Social and Economic Research, Conference Proceedings, December 1960*. Ibadan: N.I.S.E.R., n.d., pp. 186–197.

———. "The Federal Election: An Outside View," *Ibadan*, No. 8 (March, 1960), 7–9.

Price, J. H. "The Eastern Region of Nigeria, March, 1957," in W. J. M. Mackenzie and Kenneth Robinson, eds., *Five Elections in Africa*. Oxford: Clarendon Press, 1960, pp. 106–167.

Wallace, J. G. "The Tiv System of Election," *Journal of African Administration*, X (April, 1958), 63–70.

Whitaker, Philip. "The Preparation of the Register of Electors in the Western Region of Nigeria, 1955–56," *Journal of African Administration*, IX (January, 1957), 23–29.

———. "The Western Region of Nigeria, May, 1956," in W. J. M. Mackenzie and Kenneth Robinson, eds., *Five Elections in Africa*. Oxford: Clarendon Press, 1960, pp. 106–167.

For Nigerian public administration, the basic official documents, in addition to various reports of constitutional conferences, are

Federation of Nigeria. *Final Report of the Parliamentary Committee on the Nigerianisation of the Federal Public Service*. Sessional Paper No. 6 of 1959. Lagos: Government Printer, 1959.

———. *Matters Arising from Final Report of the Parliamentary Committee on the Nigerianisation of the Federal Public Service. Statement of Policy by the Government of the Federation*. Sessional Paper No. 2 of 1960. Lagos: Government Printer, 1960.

———. *Report of the Commission on the Public Services of the Governments in the Federation of Nigeria, 1954–55*. Lagos: Government Printer, 1955. (Gorsuch Commission.)

Federation of Nigeria. *Views of the Government of the Federation on the Interim Report of the Committee on Nigerianisation.* Sessional Paper No. 7 of 1958. Lagos: Government Printer, 1958.

Phillipson, Sir Sydney, and Adebo, S. O. *The Nigerianisation of the Civil Service: A Review of Policy and Machinery.* Lagos: Government Printer, 1954.

See also the Annual Reports of the Public Service Commissions of the Federal and Regional Governments.

Among the commentaries, see in particular

Cole, Taylor. "Bureaucracy in Transition," in Robert O. Tilman and Taylor Cole, eds., *The Nigerian Political Scene.* Durham, N.C.: Duke University Press, 1962, pp. 89–114.

Hanson, A. H. "Public Enterprise in Nigeria: I, Federal Public Utilities," *Public Administration,* XXXVI (Winter, 1958), 366–384.

Kingsley, J. Donald. "Bureaucracy and Political Development with Particular Reference to Nigeria," in Joseph La Palombara, ed., *Bureaucracy and Political Development.* Princeton: Princeton University Press, 1963, pp. 301–317.

Wraith, Ronald, and Simpkins, Edgar. *Corruption in Developing Countries.* London: Allen and Unwin, 1963.

Younger, Kenneth. *The Public Service in New States.* London: Oxford University Press, 1960.

For local government and politics see

Akpan, Ntieyong U. *Epitaph to Indirect Rule.* London: Cassell and Co., 1956, pp. 13–45.

Campbell, M. J. *Law and Practice of Local Government in Northern Nigeria.* London: Sweet and Maxwell, 1963.

———. *Principles of Local Government in Northern Nigeria.* London: Oxford University Press, 1963.

Coleman, James S. *Nigeria: Background to Nationalism.* Berkeley and Los Angeles: University of California Press, 1958. Chapter 2.

Cowan, L. Gray. *Local Government in West Africa.* New York: Columbia University Press, 1958. Takes the story through 1956.

———. "Local Politics and Democracy in Nigeria," in G. M. Carter and W. O. Brown, eds., *Transition in Africa: Studies in Political Adaptation.* Boston: Boston University Press, 1958, pp. 44–61.

Whitaker, C. S., Jr. "The Politics of Tradition: A Study of Continuity and Change in Northern Nigeria." Unpublished Ph.D. thesis, Princeton University, 1964.

Wraith, Ronald E. *Local Government in West Africa.* London: Allen and Unwin, 1964.

Other sources and commentaries include

Awa, Eme O. "Local Government Problems in Nigeria," in H. Passin and K. A. B. Jones-Quarterly, eds., *Africa: The Dynamics of Change.* Ibadan: Ibadan University Press, 1963.

Cameron, I. D., and Cooper, B. K. *The West African Councillor.* London: Oxford University Press, 1961.

Eastern Region of Nigeria. *Self-Government in the Eastern Region, Part I: Policy Statements.* Sessional Paper No. 2 of 1957. Enugu: Government Printer, 1957.

Harris, Philip J. *Local Government in Southern Nigeria.* Cambridge: Cambridge University Press, 1957.

Holland, S. W. C. "Recent Developments in Local Government in Eastern Nigeria," *Journal of Local Administration Overseas,* II (January, 1963), 3–15.

Hudson, R. S. *Provincial Authorities, Report by the Commissioner.* Kaduna: Government Printer, 1957.

Kirk-Greene, A. H. M. "A Redefinition of Provincial Administration: The Northern Nigerian Approach," *Journal of Local Administration Overseas,* IV (January, 1965), 5–26.

Nicholson, E. W. J. *Report of the Commission of Inquiry into the Administration of the Ibadan District Council.* Abington, England: The Abbey Press and Burgess for the Western Region of Nigeria, 1965.

Orewa, G. Oka. *Taxation in Western Nigeria.* Nigerian Social and Economic Studies, No. 4. London: Oxford University Press, 1962.

Ottenberg, Simon. "The Development of Local Government in a Nigerian Township," *Anthropologica,* N.S., LV, No. 1 (1962), 121–161.

Scarritt, James R. *Political Change in a Traditional African Clan: A Structural-Functional Analysis of the Nsit of Nigeria.* Social Science Foundation and Graduate School of International Studies. Denver: University of Denver, 1965.

Tugbiyele, E. A. "Local Government in Nigeria: Some Suggestions for Solving Some Problems of Structure and Finance," *Journal of Local Administration Overseas,* I (October, 1962), 225–230.

Western Nigeria. *Local Government Manual* (incorporating The Local Government Law, The Chiefs Law, and Local Government Staff Regulations). Ibadan: Government Printer, n.d.

On the administration of justice see

Daniels, W. C. "Federation of Nigeria," in A. N. Allott, ed., *Judicial and Legal Systems in Africa.* London: Butterworths, 1962.

Elias, T. O. *The Nigerian Legal System.* 2d rev. ed. London: Routledge and Kegan Paul, 1963.

Lloyd, Peter. *Yoruba Land Law.* London: Oxford University Press, 1962.
Nwabueze, B. O. *The Machinery of Justice in Nigeria.* London: Butterworths, 1963.
Park, Andrew. *Sources of Nigerian Law.* London: Sweet and Maxwell, 1964.

Nigerian fundamental rights are considered in

De Smith, S. A. *The New Commonwealth and its Constitutions.* London: Stevens, 1964, pp. 183–193.
Grove, David La Van. "The 'Sentinels' of Liberty? The Nigerian Judiciary and Fundamental Rights," *Journal of African Law,* VII, No. 3 (Autumn, 1963), 152–171.
Holland, D. C. "Human Rights in Nigeria," *Current Legal Problems,* XV (1962), 145–158.
Nwabueze, B. O. *Constitutional Law of the Nigerian Republic.* London: Butterworths, 1964. Chapters 10–11.

Legal limitations on political liberties in Northern Nigeria during the period before independence are discussed in R. L. Sklar, *Nigerian Political Parties: Power in an Emergent African Nation.* Princeton: Princeton University Press, 1963, pp. 355–365.

Also see

Anderson, J. N. D. "Conflict of Laws in Northern Nigeria: A New Start," *International and Comparative Law Quarterly,* VIII, Part 3, 1959.
————. "Islamic Law in Africa: Problems of Today and Tomorrow," in Anderson, ed., *Changing Law in Developing Countries.* London: Allen and Unwin, 1963, pp. 164–183.
Elias, T. Olawole. *Nigerian Land Law and Custom.* 3d ed. rev. London: Routledge and Kegan Paul, 1962.

On the customary courts in Western Nigeria see

Keuning, J. "Some Aspects of the Administration of Justice in Yorubaland," *Conference Proceedings of the Nigerian Institute of Social and Economic Reform, March, 1962.* Ibadan: N.I.S.E.R., 1963, pp. 31–40.

POWER IN NIGERIAN SOCIETY

Most of the items listed under Leadership, Political Parties, and Interest Groups above are pertinent here, as are items on the Nigerian economy. In addition to R. L. Sklar, *Nigerian Political Parties: Power in an Emergent African Nation,* and C. S. Whitaker, Jr., "The Politics of Tradition: A Study of Continuity and Change in Northern Nigeria," see

Anglin, Douglas G. "Brinksmanship in Nigeria," *International Journal,* XX, No. 2 (Spring, 1965), 173–188.

Azikiwe, Nnamdi. "Essentials for Nigerian Survival," *Foreign Affairs*, XLIII, No. 3 (April, 1965), 447–461.

Bretton, Henry L. *Power and Stability in Nigeria*. New York: Praeger, 1962.

Diamond, Stanley. "The Trial of Awolowo," *Africa Today*, X, No. 9 (November, 1963), 22–28.

Mackintosh, J. P. "Electoral Trends and the Tendency to a One Party System in Nigeria," *Journal of Commonwealth Political Studies*, I, No. 3 (November, 1962), 194–210.

————. "Federalism in Nigeria," *Political Studies*, X, No. 3 (October, 1962), 223–247.

————. "Politics in Nigeria: The Action Group Crisis of 1962," *Political Studies*, XI, No. 2 (June, 1963), 126–155.

Post, K. W. J. *The New States of West Africa*. Harmondsworth: Penguin Books, 1964.

————. "Nigeria Two Years After Independence," *The World Today*, XVIII, No. 11 (November, 1962), 468–478, No. 12 (December, 1962), 523–532.

Sklar, Richard L. "Contradictions in the Nigerian Political System," *The Journal of Modern African Studies*, III, No. 2 (1965), 201–213.

————. "The Ordeal of Chief Awolowo: Nigerian Politics, 1960–65," in Gwendolen M. Carter and Alan F. Westin, eds., *Politics in Africa*. New York: Harcourt, Brace and World, 1966.

NIGERIAN FOREIGN POLICY

Anglin, Douglas. "Nigeria and Political Non-Alignment," *The Journal of Modern African Studies*, II, No. 2 (July, 1964), 247–263.

Coleman, James S. "The Foreign Policy of Nigeria," in Joseph E. Black and Kenneth W. Thompson, eds., *Foreign Policies in a World of Change*. New York: Harper and Row, 1963, pp. 379–405.

Cowan, L. Gray. "Nigerian Foreign Policy," in Robert O. Tilman and Taylor Cole, eds., *The Nigerian Political Scene*. Durham, N.C.: Duke University Press, 1962, pp. 115–143.

Mackintosh, J. P. "Nigeria's External Relations," *Journal of Commonwealth Political Studies*, II, No. 3 (November, 1964), 207–218.

Phillips, Claude S. *The Development of Nigerian Foreign Policy*. Evanston, Ill.: Northwestern University Press, 1964.

————. "Nigeria and Pan-Africanism," *Ibadan*, October, 1962, pp. 7–11.

On Nigeria in world affairs see

Hovet, Thomas. *Africa in the United Nations*. Evanston, Ill.: Northwestern University Press, 1963.

Rivkin, Arnold. *African Presence in World Affairs*. Glencoe, Ill.: The Free Press, 1964.

Nigerian statements on foreign policy include

Azikiwe, Nnamdi. "The Future of Pan-Africanism," *Présence Africaine,*
XII, No. 40 (1962), 7–29.
———. "Nigeria in World Politics," *Présence Africaine,* IV and V, Nos.
32 and 33 (1960), 19–30.
Balewa, Sir Abubakar Tafawa. "Nigeria Looks Ahead," *Foreign Affairs,*
XLI (October, 1962), 131–140.
Davies, H. O. *Nigeria: Prospects for Democracy.* London: Weidenfeld and
Nicolson, 1961, pp. 109–125.

III

NIGER

By VIRGINIA THOMPSON

University of California, Berkeley

Introduction

NIGER is the least well-known nation of former French West Africa because it lies off the beaten track of travel and has few recognized attractions. Of all the members of the Council of the Entente Niger is the largest and poorest, and among the Saharan borderlands it is the least favored. Landlocked like Mali and Chad, it does not have their manpower resources. With as disproportionately large an area covered by desert as Mauritania has, its known mineral resources are not so outstanding. It is sometimes said that Niger is merely a geographical expression, a fluke or historical accident, and an unjustifiable by-product of European imperialism.

Yet this relatively inaccessible, harsh, and poor country has certain physical attractions and a political situation that merits more study than it has received. Niger covers a huge area in the heart of West Africa, and in Aïr it has a unique geographical phenomenon—a surprisingly verdant mountain mass rising sharply out of the surrounding desert, and one that may yet be found to contain considerable mineral resources. Politically, too, Niger's situation presents some unusual features. It has a single party which has come to control the government and has grown in strength almost wholly through the skillful manipulations of two Western-educated commoners, Diori Hamani and Boubou Hama, who belong to a minority tribe. They have forced into pro-

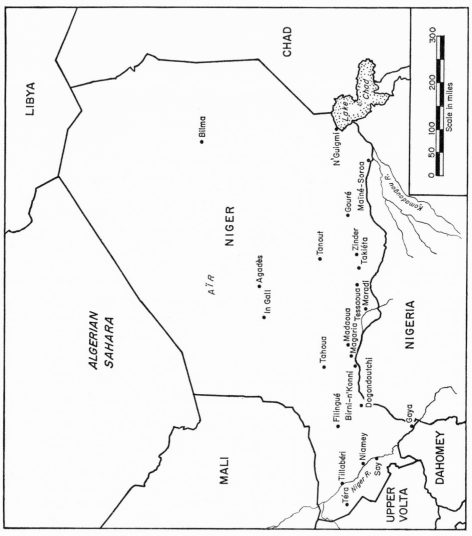

Map 3. Niger

longed exile the only popular leader and determined Marxist that Niger has yet produced, and they have succeeded in cutting down both his internal and external support as an opponent of their government. Moreover, Niger's present leaders rose to power largely through the aid of still powerful traditional chiefs, whose influence they are now gradually and successfully sapping.

Although it cannot be said yet that Niger's current leaders have created a nation out of their scattered and divergent tribes, they have been able to maintain their country's territorial integrity against the pull of strong centrifugal tendencies. Despite Niger's poverty they have attracted outside aid to develop its backward economy, and they have neutralized the external forces to the north and south that have been encouraging secessionist movements inside the country. Niger exists at the sufferance of stronger powers: it has been allowed to survive and to improve its economy because it has nuisance value as a potential source of disorder in central West Africa. But should its present government fail to maintain control, or should rich mineral deposits be discovered in the country, Niger might disintegrate and be absorbed by its neighbors.

Historical Background

THE PRECOLONIAL PERIOD

Of all the regions of Niger only that of mountainous Aïr in the north has thus far yielded evidence of prehistoric occupation. During the neolithic period a population of hunters lived there. About 2500 B.C., they were apparently succeeded by peoples who practiced cattle husbandry. For the historical period the first reference to this region dates back to Roman times, when Ptolemy reported that several military expeditions had penetrated it.

For the history of Niger as a whole there are few written documents, and the local oral traditions are patently unreliable.[1] The most accurate data have been provided by a handful of travelers, first Arab and then European, who described the successive and competitive empires that occupied all or portions of the region now comprised in the Republic of Niger. Its scarcely accessible location and vast spaces devoid of human habitation kept Niger *terra incognita* until the sixteenth century. At that time all western Niger belonged to the Songhai empire, which had been founded in the seventh century and which was based

[1] E. Séré de Rivières, *Le Niger* (Paris: 1952), pp. 34–35.

at Gao, while the eastern zone was divided between the Hausa states of Dawa and Katsena and the empire of Bornu.[2] Aïr alternated between dependency under the Songhai empire of Gao and under Mali, only to fall under the domination of Bornu late in the sixteenth century. From then until the French conquest Niger continued to be a turbulent and amorphous region, subject to successive migrations and conquerors.

From the north came the Djerma, who early in the seventeenth century settled in large numbers on the banks of the middle Niger River.[3] At about the same time the Hausa states underwent a revival, and the nomadic Touareg tribes formed large confederations in Aïr. For a short time late in the eighteenth century, the Touareg were able to impose their rule on the Songhai living in the Niger valley. The riverine populations had been weakened by their long struggles against the Peul (Fulani), who had begun infiltrating in the fifteenth century and who came in ever larger numbers during the next two hundred years. By the end of the eighteenth century, the Peul warrior Usuman dan Fodio had carved out the great kingdom of Sokoto at the expense of the Negro states that stretched from Liptako to the Adamaoua. His successors, however, could not hold his conquests against the resurgence of the Hausa states and of Bornu. The wars between these states lasted throughout the nineteenth century with fluctuating fortunes for each, the Touareg intervening first on one side and then on the other. This century also saw the advent to this region of European travelers, the most renowned of whom were Mungo Park and Heinrich Barth. Both of these men found the territory in a state of anarchy, the empires crumbling, and small isolated groups unable to defend themselves against aggressive warrior chiefs.

THE FRENCH PENETRATION AND CONQUEST

The French were relative late-comers to the scene. Their conquest of the region was somewhat delayed by an agreement reached with Great Britain on August 5, 1890, which established the northern frontier of Nigeria along a line that ran from Say to Baroua. During the next decade, however, French military expeditions began entering the region, using the Niger River valley as the channel of penetration, along which they set up posts. A new agreement, negotiated with the British on

[2] See Jean Rouch, *Les Songhay* (Paris: 1954).

[3] Ambassade de France, Service de Presse et d'Information, *The Republic of Niger*, October, 1960, p. 6.

June 14, 1898, opened to France the left bank of the river and enabled it to organize three missions designed to gain control of the Lake Chad area. These were small-scale expeditions whose progress toward their goal was delayed by frequent combats and murders. By 1900, however, the expeditions were united under a single command, and that year they managed to defeat the sultan of Bornu. In 1901, they organized the military territory of the Middle Niger, and the following year Commandant (later General) H. J. E. Gouraud set up his headquarters at Zinder and his supply base at Niamey. The first task assigned to his command was that of conquering the populations in the Aïr and Tibesti mountains, from which the Touareg and Toubou nomads were raiding those Negro populations to the south which had accepted French rule. Military columns moving up from the Niger River in 1904 occupied Agadès with the consent of its sultan, who also facilitated the French occupation of N'Guigmi. By joining forces with other French troops marching south from the Algerian Sahara in 1906, they succeeded in setting up a post in the key oasis of Bilma and from this won control of Aïr.

These successes marked only the beginning of the pacification of eastern Niger, which was not accomplished until after another agreement with Great Britain in 1906 gave the French a more advantageous frontier in the south. In the northeast the continuation of nomad raids finally convinced France that it must conquer all Tibesti. When military posts were established on that massif's western slope in 1914, Niger was "officially" conquered, but peace did not reign permanently throughout the territory until the early 1920's. Although western Niger was quieter than the eastern region, it was not wholly free from disorders. In the Djerma country south of Dosso a short-lived revolt broke out in 1905, and the following year there was another outbreak along the river. An unusual aspect of these rebellions was that Djerma partisans aided the French in putting them down. Also in 1905, a plot reportedly hatched by the sultan of Zinder was discovered only in the nick of time. It led to his removal from office, and it was not until 1923 that his successor was named.[4]

French reverses during the early years of World War I led to fresh trouble in Niger, mainly from the Touareg.[5] After smoldering for two years, the Oullimiden tribe revolted and raided Filingué in April, 1916. Here again the French were able to quell the revolt with the help

[4] See M. Abadie, *La Colonie du Niger* (Paris: 1927), pp. 99 *et seq.*
[5] F. J. R. Rodd, *People of the Veil* (London: 1926), pp. 84, 194, 360.

of local partisans. In December of that year more serious trouble arose. Koassen, head of another dissident tribe (the Kel Gress), captured Agadès. After receiving support from the Senussi based in Libya, he persuaded many of the Aïr Touareg to join him. In time it was learned that this uprising had been part of a larger scheme planned by pro-German elements in the Fezzan and Tripolitania provinces of Libya to cause difficulties for the French and British in their West African empires. From Nigeria the British sent troops to help the French cope with this joint menace. In February, 1917, Agadès was recaptured and the next month In Gall reoccupied. For the next two years French forces tracked down Koassen's followers in the Aïr mountains, but it was not until 1919 that they were driven out of Tibesti and back into the Fezzan. Although this defeat marked the end of serious aggression from that quarter, raids from the north continued to be made as far south as Tahoua *cercle,* and it was not until 1922 that peace finally prevailed throughout Niger.

THE COLONIAL PERIOD

Even before Niger officially became a colony in 1922, the territory had undergone the numerous administrative transformations characteristic of French rule in West Africa. In 1900, Niger was styled a Military Territory and attached to a larger unit known as Haut Sénégal-Niger. A decade later it was enlarged by the addition of Gao *cercle,* but in 1911 Gao was handed back to Soudan (Mali) and Niger itself placed under the government-general based at Dakar. In 1920, it underwent still another metamorphosis, and finally two years later it settled down as a colony largely administered by civilians. Niger's capital was shunted back and forth between Zinder and Niamey until 1927, when it was ultimately established in the latter town. For some years thereafter fluidity and change continued to characterize internal administrative divisions and territorial boundaries. In 1929, Niger lost some of its eastern areas to Chad colony, but two years later, when Upper Volta was dismembered, Niger acquired, to the southwest, 27,200 additional square miles and 268,239 more inhabitants.[6] These gains were canceled out again by the reconstitution of Upper Volta in 1947. In consequence, Niger's area shrank, the number of its *cercles* was reduced to nine, and the first of the three remaining military zones was handed over to civilian administration. Bilma *cercle* in 1949 was made into a

---

[6] *L'Afrique Française,* December, 1932.

subdivision of Agadès, and this move placed the territory for the first time wholly under the control of civilians.[7]

Niger's geography and the composition of its population greatly help to explain the unusually high number of administrative alterations to which it was subject during the colonial period. In the north belligerent and sizable nomad tribes wandered in a terrain particularly difficult to patrol. To the south and east lay territories belonging to two foreign powers: Great Britain and Italy. Although the 1906 boundary with Nigeria remained unchanged, the Libyan boundary led to disagreements with the Italians even before World War II broke out. In the north so much trouble arose from the turbulence of the desert tribes and the incessant migrations of their vast herds that it required long and arduous negotiations before the authorities in Niger, Soudan, French Equatorial Africa, and Algeria could work out a satisfactory way of administering the huge region in which all of them had responsibilties.

Although the administration of Niger had many features common to French rule in other Saharan borderlands, it was characterized by more stability in its personnel and a better adaptation to native institutions than elsewhere. As in Mauritania and Soudan, the French had to combine within a single framework the administration of "white" nomads and Negro sedentary peoples, but in Niger the administrative divisions were less artificial, more chiefs were consecrated by tradition, and the handful of French officials who governed Niger remained longer at their posts. Few French administrators cared to shoulder the ungrateful task of administering this complex, harsh territory, and the decade-long incumbency of Governor Jean Toby during the postwar period set a record for professional longevity among the territorial heads of the Federation of West Africa. Above all, the nature and strength of the nomad component of the indigenous population were responsible for the perpetuation of military rule in the most northerly *cercles* and for greater recourse on the part of France to methods of indirect rule throughout Niger.

Among the Touareg nomads, the most stable chieftaincies were those of the tribes living in the regions of Tillabéri, Filingué, and Madaoua, which had become partly sedentary.[8] Far harder to control were the Touareg of Tahoua, who were organized into seven distinct groups, lacked a paramount chief, and engaged in continual intertribal in-

[7] Séré de Rivières, *op. cit.*, p. 48.　　[8] Rodd, *op. cit.*, pp. 136, 145 *et seq.*

trigue. Some of the tribes in the Agadès region owed loyalty to the
sultan who ruled the Hausa town bearing that name, but the majority
recognized as their overlord the Anastafidet (paramount chief) of the
Kel Oui. Moreover, the authority of those potentates was not solidly
established among their local tribes, and neither of them was wholly
trusted by the French government. The status of the nomadic Toubou,[9]
only some of whose tribes inhabited Niger's easternmost *cercles*, was
even more confused. The one point of common endeavor among all the
nomadic chiefs seemed to be their determined, albeit covert, resistance
to French control. Despite their severe defeat during World War I and
an enhanced prosperity due to their ever-growing herds, the Touareg
nobles in particular could not forgive the French either for depriving
them of their anarchic independence and the booty they had acquired
formerly through raids, or especially for progressively and legally
emancipating their serfs.

On the eve of World War II the huge colony of Niger was divided
into only thirteen *cercles*, but it had a comparatively large number of
chiefs—3 paramount chiefs, 5 heads of large tribal groups, 183 chiefs of
smaller tribes and cantons, and 6,585 village chiefs.[10] Despite the
chronic strife and anarchy that led to the untimely death of many
tribal leaders, and despite some French appointments of chiefs to head
the new cantons and subdivisions created particularly in the western
cercles, France tampered as little with the established Negro emirates
as it did with the nomad chieftaincies. Even where cantons and subdivisions were created, notably in the Djerma country, many of the traditional chiefs were retained in positions of command and left in almost
complete control of their rigidly ranked subjects. Indeed, French support so reinforced the authority of some that they enjoyed a power and
stability which their predecessors had never known. In such cases the
canton chiefs—French appointees—became primarily servitors of the
local sultan and only secondarily functionaries of the Third Republic.

This preservation of the established social order probably accounted
largely for the long period of internal peace that Niger enjoyed from
1922 to 1946. World War II, unlike its predecessor, touched Niger only
lightly. The Senussi chiefs' hostility to the Italians, Niger's proximity to
Free French territory, its small population, and its underdeveloped
economy were responsible for the tranquillity that prevailed and the

---

[9] Jean Chappelle, *Nomades Noirs du Sahara* (Paris: 1958).
[10] Ministère des Colonies, Paris, *Bulletin Quotidien*, August 3, 1939 (mimeographed).

minimal demands made by the authorities on its inhabitants. Only a little more intensively than before did Niger have to live from its own resources, and its contributions to the war effort were almost nil.

POLITICAL DEVELOPMENTS AFTER WORLD WAR II

The postwar reforms of 1946 entitled Niger to send two deputies, two senators, and two representatives respectively to the National Assembly, the Council of the Republic, and the Assembly of the French Union in France. That same year in Niger, the Parti Progressiste Nigérien (PPN) was founded as a territorial branch of the interterritorial movement called the Rassemblement Démocratique Africain (RDA). Three of the PPN's founders—Diori Hamani, Boubou Hama, and Djibo Bakary—have continued to be the dominant political figures of their territory. Diori Hamani was elected to the French National Assembly; Boubou Hama was elected to the Assembly of the French Union; and Djibo Bakary became a territorial assemblyman, the party's secretary-general, and the organizer of Niamey's confederation of labor unions, which were affiliated with the French Confédération Générale du Travail (CGT). All three men were Muslims and schoolteachers, graduates of the Ponty school at Dakar—which trained many of West Africa's prominent politicians—and they worked closely together during the RDA's radical period. But in 1950, when the RDA's president, Félix Houphouët-Boigny of the Ivory Coast, altered that movement's policy to one of cooperation with the French administration, the PPN leadership was split asunder, with Djibo Bakary following a course of his own.

By late 1958, Diori's political astuteness and his relationship of mutual support with Houphouët had made him the dominant figure in Niger. Born in 1916, Diori had been a teacher in Niger and Paris. Closely associated with the RDA from its inception in 1946, he has faithfully followed Houphouët in his various and drastic changes of policy. No less faithful to Diori than Diori to Houphouët has been Boubou Hama, who is now regarded as the number two man in the government of Niger. Although he is a Songhai and Diori is a Djerma (a closely related tribe), and although he is not only Diori's senior by ten years but also his former teacher, Boubou Hama has been willing to follow wherever Diori has led. Earlier than Diori, Boubou Hama left the teaching profession, and he became a staff member of the Niamey branch of the Institut Français d'Afrique Noire. Elected on the RDA ticket to the Assembly of the French Union, he distinguished himself there as a forceful orator. But he did not rise to prominence in the PPN until after the defection from its ranks of the third member of the party's original leadership, Djibo Bakary.

The Rise and Fall of Djibo Bakary

Certainly the most dynamic and interesting of Niger's politicians and the only one who can be called a mass leader is Djibo Bakary, whose political fortunes have gone from one extreme to the other. A member of the Hausa tribe on his mother's side, he is five years younger than Diori and thus junior to Boubou Hama by fifteen years. He was the PPN's first secretary-general and a regular contributor to the RDA organ, *Réveil*. Djibo was not only a militant politician and journalist but also a main organizer of Niger's Communist-oriented trade unions as well as of RDA resistance to the French administration in the Ivory Coast during 1948–1949. His loyalty to Marxist doctrines in general and to the CGT in particular prevented him from accepting the change in RDA policy made by Houphouët in 1950. So in that year he gave up teaching, broke away from the PPN, and formed his own party, the Union Démocratique Nigérienne (UDN). This move endeared him to the French Communist Party, but it led to his expulsion from the RDA and to the local administration's active hostility to him. Moreover, Djibo's defection so weakened the PPN that the French authorities in Niger were able to bring about Diori's defeat for re-election to the National Assembly in 1951 and to sponsor some purely regional parties, of which the most important was the Union Nigérienne des Indépendants. That party, under the leadership of a member of the Touareg tribe, Zodi Ikhia, and of a French doctor, Francis Borrey, affiliated itself with the Indépendants d'Outre-Mer (IOM), the RDA's rival in the French parliamentary bodies. Moreover, in the 1952 elections to the Territorial Assembly it won 34 of the 60 seats at stake.

From 1951 to 1956, Niger seemed to be as much a political as an economic backwater. The territory produced no leaders who shone in the French assemblies. In the Grand Council of French West Africa at Dakar its delegates did little but complain that their territory was neglected and ignored. In the meetings of the Territorial Assembly there was a conspicuous lack of the spirited discussion, personal wangling, and heckling of the French administration that characterized such bodies in most of the rest of French West Africa. But beneath this tranquil surface, changes were taking place that came suddenly and surprisingly to the fore in the legislative elections of January 2, 1956.

In Niger, as elsewhere in French West Africa, the RDA staged a comeback at that time, and consequently Diori was returned to the National Assembly in Paris. But the surprise provided by this election was that he was almost defeated by Djibo, largely as a result of Hausa support. In the years since 1950, Djibo had been studying and touring in eastern Europe under the sponsorship of the French CGT. His near-victory in the 1956 elections was the only instance in French West Africa at that time of large-scale electoral support for a leader of Marxist inclinations. This was not the only surprise that Djibo gave observers of the French African political scene. In mid-1956, he wrote an article for the Niamey newspaper, *Le Démocrate*, in which he expressed approval of the *loi-cadre* of June 23 of that year, which permitted decentralization of political power to the individual territories, and of continued ties with France. Moreover, he went so far as to urge Houphouët and L. S. Senghor of Senegal to unite all African political parties in order to create a genuine French Union.[11] Djibo's change of front gave rise to considerable speculation. His detractors were inclined to interpret it as his ultimate bid for readmission to the RDA. If this was indeed his motive Djibo failed, probably because he posed conditions that were unacceptable to Houphouët.[12]

Perhaps his failure to be readmitted to the RDA, along with the advent to power in France of the Socialist Party, accounted for Djibo's next surprise move: he joined the African Socialists led by Lamine Guèye of Senegal. Djibo then absorbed into his UDN the small Socialist Bloc Nigérien d'Action, led by Djerma chief Issoufou Seydou Djermakoye, and gained sufficient support to be elected mayor of Niamey in November, 1956. Two months later the new party became a territorial section of the Mouvement Socialiste Africain (MSA); in March, 1957, it won the territorial elections and Djibo became the vice-president of Niger's new government council.

Djibo's triumphs in 1957 were not confined to Niger. In January of that year he was elected to the executive committee of the newly founded, radical African trade union federation, Union Générale des Travailleurs d'Afrique Noire (UGTAN), and he was named deputy secretary-general of the MSA. At the constituent congress of the Parti du Regroupement Africain (PRA), held at Cotonou, Dahomey, in July, 1958, Djibo was among the most vociferous and effective advocates of

[11] E. Milcent, *L'A.O.F. Entre en Scène* (Paris: 1958), p. 106.

[12] Governor D. J. Colombani, in a talk with the writer at Niamey, December 1, 1958.

an African-inspired federation for French West Africa and of immediate independence from France. Not surprisingly he was forthwith elected secretary-general of that interterritorial movement.[13] Returning to Niamey from the conference, he changed the name of his party on August 29 from Union Démocratique Nigérienne to Sawaba (Freedom) and made it a territorial section of the PRA. He then announced that he would campaign for a negative vote in the referendum on the constitution of the Fifth French Republic to be held on September 28, 1958. This decision to vote against Niger's membership in the French Community proposed by General de Gaulle was announced one day before Sékou Touré reached a similar decision, and Djibo's stand may well have been the decisive influence in determining Guinea's policy.[14]

In the referendum Niger officially voted in favor of the Community, but with little enthusiasm. Of the country's 1,300,000 or so registered electors, only some 500,000 went to the polls: of these, 102,000 cast negative votes.[15] The only *cercle* to register a majority of negative votes, however, was Tessaoua, the fief of Georges Condat, president of Niger's Territorial Assembly and Djibo's principal collaborator. In Maradi *cercle* the electorate was about equally divided, but in all the other *cercles* a majority voted in favor of the new French constitution.[16]

Inevitably the stand taken by Djibo and the Sawaba on this issue was opposed by the French government and by the PPN, which followed Houphouët in favoring Niger's membership in the Community. More than any other French West African territory, Niger was subject to external pressures in this vote, though to what degree, by whom they were exerted, and how far they affected the outcome are matters of conjecture. Unverified rumors circulated in Niamey [17] to the effect that Djibo had received financial support from Prime Minister Kwame Nkrumah of Ghana, who was eager at this time to encourage all elements seeking independence from France. On the other side Houphouët sent one of his ablest collaborators, Gabriel d'Arboussier, to help Diori campaign, and Djibo charged that Governor D. J. Colombani

[13] *Marchés Tropicaux,* July 26, 1958, p. 1820.

[14] See I. Wallerstein, "How Seven States were born in former French West Africa," *Africa Report,* March, 1961, p. 7.

[15] La Documentation Française, *La République du Niger* (Paris), February 26, 1960, p. 9.

[16] G. Dugué, *Vers les Etats-Unis d'Afrique* (Dakar: 1960), p. 151.

[17] Information gathered by the writer during a stay at Niamey, November–December, 1958.

used French money and troops to exert pressure on voters. Colombani was, to say the least, less neutral in his attitude during the referendum campaign than were his colleagues in the rest of French Negro Africa. On the eve of the referendum he rescinded the powers of Djibo's ministers on the ground that they had been illicitly using public funds and vehicles belonging to the administration to promote the Sawaba's propaganda. But even such highhanded action on the part of the local French administration could not wholly account for Djibo's defeat, since such pressure normally would be expected to produce a popular reaction favorable to the victimized party and its leader.

Indeed there is no simple, single explanation for the sharp fluctuations in fortune that have characterized Djibo's whole career. As a charismatic mass leader he has attracted the type of African partisans that would not be alienated by his frequent changes in tactics and in party alignments. Nor can either the strength of his rivals or outside intervention, in his favor or against him, account for his sudden rise and equally rapid falls from power. Rather, it seems that his intransigence and impatience led him to commit serious errors, of which his vigilant opponents have been able to take advantage. He continued to advocate Marxist doctrines long after the tide of radical extremism in French West Africa had ebbed, and when he apparently switched to a more moderate course other African leaders were not fully convinced of his sincerity. Unlike D'Arboussier, who had also been expelled for clinging to Marxist doctrines, he was not conciliatory enough to be taken back into the RDA fold, and he remained too far to the Left ever to be whole-heartedly accepted by the African Socialists.

On the issue of constituting a West African federation, Djibo saw eye to eye with Senghor, but ideologically (though not personally) he was closer to Sékou Touré than to any other French African politician. In exact contradiction to the course followed by the Guinean leader, however, Djibo came to power in 1957 by forming an alliance with the local chiefs who had become estranged from the PPN during the latter's radical period. Just as he had joined the MSA for purely practical purposes, so Djibo utilized the chiefs' animosity toward the PPN to win the votes that gave him control of Niger's first government council. At heart, however, he remained a confirmed Marxist, as fundamentally opposed to the moderate socialist creed of Lamine Guèye as he was to the feudal social order on which the Nigérien chieftaincy rested.[18]

[18] The French form *Nigérien* is used throughout to distinguish the inhabitants of Niger from those of Nigeria.

Without waiting to build up party machinery comparable in strength to that of the Parti Démocratique de Guinée (PDG), Djibo then made a frontal attack in 1957 on the chiefs by brusquely removing seven of them from their posts.[19] At almost the same time he alienated an important segment of his left-wing support by clamping down on a strike by Niamey's teachers in November of that year. Virtually the only organized group that remained consistently loyal to Djibo was the CGT trade unions, but their membership was so small and so restricted to Niger's main towns that they could not tip the balance in his favor.

From its unpromising position early in 1957, the PPN began to make headway against Djibo's government mainly by profiting from the tactical mistakes he was making. The chiefs were becoming frightened by Djibo's undermining of their authority but not yet to the point that they were ready to change party allegiance. Then Niger's teachers became resentful when Djibo denounced their strike as political after they had said it was called purely in protest against the "arbitrary" way in which his Minister of Education had reassigned many of them to new posts. In an official communiqué Djibo charged that their strike was simply a maneuver instigated by the PPN for the purpose of discrediting the government.[20] Boubou Hama then took up the cudgels and in his party's organ, *Le Niger,* described Djibo's regime as worse than the worst colonialist government and as the "dregs of Negro imperialism." The next month Djibo barely averted a schism in the UDN which would have put his party in a minority position in the Assembly. But the conflict did not long remain confined to rifts among his supporters and to the exchange of journalistic pleasantries between the opposing parties. In April, 1958, violence broke out in Niamey between the partisans of Djibo and Diori. The troops intervened after two persons were killed and fifty wounded.[21] But neither verbal nor physical sniping by his opponents would probably have led to Djibo's downfall. It was his decision to vote "no" in the September, 1958, referendum that caused his most powerful supporters to desert the newly constituted Sawaba and join the ranks of the PPN.

In opting for independence from France, Niger had nothing to fear, Djibo told his compatriots.[22] Since 80 per cent of the funds which France had been giving to its African dependencies returned to French

[19] *Le Monde,* December 17, 1958.

[20] *Marchés Tropicaux,* November 23, 1957, p. 2840, and André Blanchet, *L'Itinéraire des Partis Africains depuis Bamako* (Paris: 1958), pp. 65–66.

[21] *Marchés Tropicaux,* May 10, 1958, p. 1253.

[22] *Ibid.,* September 20, 1958, p. 2312.

nationals in one form or another, Niger could easily dispense with such aid if General de Gaulle actually carried out his threat to cut off assistance from those countries that voted against his constitution.[23] In fact, Djibo said he had already received assurances of adequate aid from other quarters, notably from Ghana and Nigeria.[24] Earlier in the year Djibo had visited Accra and probably had received encouragement from Nkrumah. But it was with Nigeria, slated to become independent in 1960, that Djibo envisaged new and beneficial ties. The prospect of obliterating the southern frontier was pleasing to many Nigérien Hausa, commoners like himself; but it appealed less to their chiefs, who did not relish being subordinated to the emirs of Northern Nigeria, an autonomous region in Nigeria's federation. The nomads of northern Niger were anything but eager for a union with Nigeria, which would vastly increase the Negro component of the population. They openly favored joining the Organisation Commune des Régions Sahariennes (OCRS, founded by the French to give a common administration to France's Saharan regions), which Djibo had rejected.[25] As for the Djerma chiefs in western Niger, they actively opposed any step that would place them under Hausa rule. In brief, the chiefs in Niger regarded continued close ties with France as the best guaranty for maintaining their privileged status. And since the PPN wanted Niger to join the Community, they reacted favorably to Diori's advances and united with his party to overthrow Djibo, whom they had initially raised to power. The move in this direction that was initiated by Senator Djermakoye and Zodi Ikhia in mid-September, 1958, soon gathered momentum.[26] On the eve of the referendum, eight outstanding members of the Sawaba abandoned Djibo, among them the key figures Adamou Mayaki (Minister of the Interior), Marcel Fourier (former Councilor of the Republic), Pierre Vidal (Minister of Health), Robert Frémien (Minister of Education), and the canton chief of Tahoua, Mouddour Zakara.

Desertion by his principal supporters proved to be the decisive factor leading to Djibo's defeat in the referendum. As soon as the results were announced, the defectors from the Sawaba and the leadership of the PPN formed a new party called the Union pour la Communauté Franco-Africaine (UCFA). (Within two years the UCFA had gradually reverted to using the name of Parti Progressiste Nigérien.) Its leaders

---

[23] *Le Monde,* August 13, 1958; G. Dugué, *op. cit.,* p. 95.
[24] *Marchés Tropicaux,* September 20, 1958, p. 2312.
[25] *Le Monde,* May 8, 1959.   [26] *Ibid.,* September 17, 19, 1958.

insisted that Djibo resign as head of the government, but he refused because he still controlled a majority in the Assembly. A deadlock ensued, and to find a way out of the impasse in Niger the high command of the PRA went into action in Paris, Dakar (still the seat of the French West African Federation), and Niamey. They came up with a compromise whereby Djibo was to resign and then try to form a government of national union.[27] Not only did Djibo refuse to accept this proposal but he made the serious mistake of trying to call a general strike in Niger on October 9. The failure of the strike led to another mass exodus from the Sawaba, which by mid-October had been deserted by 32 assemblymen—among them many chiefs who had been Djibo's erstwhile supporters. This left Djibo with no alternative but to resign, which he finally did on October 20.

Djibo's resignation opened the way for Governor Colombani to assert his authority once again in the political field. On November 14, he dissolved the Assembly and called for new elections. At the same time he instituted judicial proceedings against Djibo and his ministers, charging them with abuse of their authority during the referendum campaign. His moves elicited strong protests from the PRA leaders, Senghor and Lamine Guèye of Senegal, and Emile Zinsou of Dahomey.[28] Five days later these men held a press conference in Paris at which they denounced Colombani for his "suspension of democratic practices" and appealed to General de Gaulle to assure free and fair elections in Niger for the new territorial assembly.[29] This intervention by the PRA leaders was apparently motivated more by their resentment of Colombani's authoritarianism than by any spontaneous support for Djibo, who had always acted more as a political free lance than as a wholly loyal member of either the MSA or the PRA.

The Election of 1958

As might have been expected, the election campaign for Niger's new assembly proved to be a tumultuous one. In a telegram to Senghor, Djibo claimed that the UCFA candidates had perpetrated "aggressions" against their PRA rivals at Maradi, and that he himself had been the target of an attack at Doukoulou on December 10. Senghor obligingly responded by describing Niger's elections of December 14 as a "new masquerade," [30] although they had been supervised by a magistrate sent by the French government to Niger from the Cotonou Court

[27] *Ibid.*, November 16–17, 1958.   [28] *Ibid.*, November 21, 1958.
[29] *Ibid.*, November 22, 1958.   [30] *Ibid.*, December 27, 1958.

of Appeals. Even though the local French administration naturally supported the UCFA, once again the support given to that party by the great Djerma chiefs was mainly responsible for its resounding victory. In all the electoral circumscriptions except Tessaoua and Zinder, the UCFA candidates—among whom were many chiefs—won decisively. Of the 60 assembly seats contested, the UCFA took 54 as compared with the 19 held previously by the PPN, and the Sawaba was reduced to 6, whereas it had won 41 in the preceding body.[31]

This election proved beyond a doubt that the balance of power in Niger was still held by chiefs whenever they cared to exercise their influence. Nevertheless, it may be reasonably questioned whether this election, or any election in Niger for that matter, reflected public opinion. In Niger large-scale abstentions have been the order of the day. In the March, 1957 elections, 73 per cent of the electorate failed to vote; in the referendum, 62 per cent; and in the elections of December 14, 1958, over 70 per cent. To a large extent, the nomadic character of the northern tribes, the coincidence of certain elections with the peanut harvest in the east, and the frequency of elections within a comparatively short span of time, accounted for the apparent indifference of Nigériens to the exercise of their franchise. One facet of the December 14 vote, however, deserves special mention—that is, the personal defeat of both major political leaders, Diori and Djibo. Yet as the head of the victorious party Diori was named Niger's premier, and Djerma-koye, as the chief mainly responsible for the UCFA victory, became the vice-premier. On December 20, the new assembly, which had immediately transformed itself into a constituent body, made Niger an autonomous republic and member state of the Community. Only its six Sawaba members abstained in this vote.[32]

Diori Consolidates his Power

Diori, now in the saddle, lost no time before consolidating his power and linking Niger with the other RDA states that still accepted Houphouët's leadership. Niger successively became a member of the OCRS, the Council of the Entente—with the Ivory Coast, Dahomey, and Upper Volta—and the West African Customs Union. The Assembly, on January 21, 1959, voted Diori full powers for six months to set up an administration appropriate to Niger's new status, and the following August it renewed this special grant for another six months. The constitution, which the Assembly accepted on February 25, 1959, made

[31] *Nice-Matin,* December 17, 1958.   [32] *Le Monde,* December 20, 1958.

the overthrow of Diori's government legally impossible until 1962. More solicitous of local nationalist sentiments than Djibo had been, Diori gave all his cabinet posts to native Nigériens, but at the same time he was careful not to exclude resident Europeans from all share in the conduct of public affairs. (Eight assemblymen, one Economic Councilor, and nine Nigérien Senators of the Community were Frenchmen.) All Diori's ministers belonged to the UCFA and three of them—Issoufou Djermakoye, Yansambou Maiga Diamballa, and Mouddour Zakara—were influential chiefs. Among his other appointments were those of Courma Bourcogne as Minister of Finance; Léopold Kaziendé, Public Works; Maida Mahoudou, Agriculture; Harou Touka, Labor; Diallo Boubakar, Health; Malzoumbou Sama, Animal Husbandry; Zodi Ikhia, Education; and Adamou Mayaki, Economic Affairs. Boubou Hama, though not a chief, was rewarded for his perennial fidelity to Diori with the presidency of the Assembly, a post which he has subsequently retained. On four occasions (January 17, 1959, October 31, 1959, December 31, 1960, and June 26, 1963) Diori has reshuffled his cabinet, mainly through a redistribution of portfolios. The only two important changes he has made were the dismissal of Zodi Ikhia in December, 1963, and of Diallo Boubakar in October, 1964.

As soon as he had constituted his first government, Diori began a series of moves designed to liquidate the Sawaba and its supporting organizations. Two successive elections had reduced Djibo and his followers to political impotency but not to silence, and they continued to oppose Niger's membership in the OCRS and the Entente and to urge its adherence to the Mali Federation, composed of Senegal and Soudan. On January 22, 1959, in retaliation, Diori dissolved Niamey's municipal council, of which Djibo was the mayor, and replaced it with a nominated committee. Then a decree of February 22 forbade all political meetings in the capital, while another on March 1 made illegal any public gatherings organized by the UGTAN, of whose territorial branch Djibo was still the head. In March, also, Traoré Saloum, who had been the Sawaba government's labor minister, was expelled from Niger to his native Soudan. On April 30, at Diori's behest, the Assembly annulled the elections of its Sawaba members who represented the constituencies of Tessaoua and Zinder. Those who had been elected from Tessaoua were simply replaced by the UCFA candidates whom they had defeated on December 14, 1958, but at Zinder new elections were slated for June 27. Since the Sawaba refused to participate in this election on the ground that the government's candidates would in any case be declared victors, Niger's Assembly acquired a solid UCFA membership. In July, Diori used his special powers to dissolve the Nigérien branch of the UGTAN, and that same month his Minister of Education refused to allow the Nigérien students who had voiced their sympathy with the Sawaba to hold a meeting in Niamey.[33]

It had proved so easy to eliminate the legal channels through which the Sawaba supporters might express their views that the UCFA leadership was tempted to go farther. When Diori announced that he would bring Djibo and his ministers to trial on the old charges made against them by Governor Colombani at the time of the referendum, he went too far. In France the announcement stirred up a hornets' nest: the League for the Rights of Man registered a formal protest, and a French lawyer was engaged to defend Djibo and his colleagues.[34] In Africa, too, the adverse reaction was so strong that the Niger government, fearing a revival of Sawaba strength, prudently drew in its horns. Though Diori continued to complain about foreign support for Djibo, particularly from neighboring countries, the date for his trial was repeatedly postponed.[35]

While the UCFA leaders recoiled before the risk involved in formally condemning Djibo and his confreres on trivial charges, in other respects they proceeded to follow the pattern set by other single-party governments in French-speaking Africa. On October 12, 1959, Diori dissolved the Sawaba party "for collusion with alien powers."[36] Then in November, he announced the discovery of a plot said to have been hatched by the Sawaba with support from outside the country. This enabled the Minister of the Interior to denounce the Sawaba as a Communist party, authorize a police search of the houses of suspects, and seize firearms from those allegedly holding them without permits.[37] These measures, perhaps because of their Draconian character, were obviously not completely effective. A mission sent to the provinces by the government in February, 1960, to explain and promote official policies and also to take political soundings reported that the Sawaba was far from moribund in the Zinder, Maradi, and Manga regions.[38] This report, instead of impelling the government to compromise and clemency, seems to have hardened its determination to extirpate the Sawaba die-hards. After the arrest of six of his faithful

[33] *Afrique Nouvelle,* July 10, 24, 1959.   [34] *Le Monde,* August 4, 1959.
[35] *Afrique Nouvelle,* September 4, 1959.
[36] *Marchés Tropicaux,* October 24, 1959, p. 2357.
[37] *Afrique Nouvelle,* November 20, 1959.   [38] *Ibid.,* February 10, 1960.

followers on June 30, 1960, Djibo fled the country with a handful of loyal companions. Now that he was safely out of Niger, the government dared to proceed with his trial. In September, Djibo and his fellow exiles were tried in absentia on the charge of having attempted to revive a banned political party, and he was sentenced to two years in prison and a fine of 500,000 CFA francs.[39]

Djibo's departure came only a month before Niger gained its independence from France. On August 3, 1960, Niger was proclaimed a sovereign state; on September 20, it was admitted to the United Nations under France's sponsorship; and in the spring of 1961 it left the Community in company with other member states of the Entente. These developments robbed the Sawaba in Niger of its outstanding leader and also of most of its propaganda appeal. Nevertheless, Djibo continued to denounce Niger's independence as fictitious, speaking and writing from Bamako (capital of Mali), Conakry (Guinea), or Accra (Ghana), where he found sympathetic audiences and financial support. Diori, however, now felt strong enough to emulate his political mentor, Houphouët, and to conciliate those of his opponents who publicly recanted and rallied to his government. Many former members of the Sawaba decided it was high time to abandon a lost cause, and after almost all political offenders were released from prison in November, there was a big rush to join the UCFA bandwagon.[40] By the end of 1960, the opposition to the government seemed, at least as an organized force, to have melted away. Among those officially rehabilitated and promoted was Georges Condat, formerly Djibo's close associate, who was named Niger's envoy to Dahomey and then to Brussels.[41]

To Djibo, Diori held out an olive branch on several occasions, reportedly against the wishes of his less conciliatory colleagues, Boubou Hama and Diamballa Maiga.[42] Djibo responded by expressing his desire for a "pacific and fraternal solution to the problem of Niger," but he refused to accept the condition laid down by the UCFA that he return to Niger, where a warrant was still out for his arrest. Diori, at a press conference on December 17, 1961, complained that Djibo had given himself a martyr's halo as an exile, though he had left Niger of his own volition.[43] If he returned to his own country and agreed to settle his quarrel with the government *en famille*, it would be up to the courts of

---

[39] *Le Monde*, September 8, 1960.   [40] *Ibid.*, November 29, 1960.

[41] *Afrique Nouvelle*, February 8, 1961.

[42] André Blanchet, in *Nice-Matin*, January 27, 1961.

[43] *Afrique Nouvelle*, January 3, 1962.

justice either to acquit him or to send him to prison. "A condemnation by the court does not eliminate the possibility of amnesty," Diori went on. "But Niger's problems must be settled on its soil, and though we are deeply attached to African unity and fraternity, we cannot permit any outside state to intervene as mediator in our problems." Djibo was clearly unwilling to take his chances at the hands of a Nigérien court, and he and his "politburo" remained in voluntary exile, mainly in Bamako and Accra.

Like other governments-in-exile, that of Djibo has not been free of internecine strife. In May, 1962, one of Djibo's closest collaborators was murdered under circumstances that remain shrouded in mystery. Arlaly Daoua, Djibo's "Minister of External Affairs," was killed by a fellow Sawaba militant, who was himself later shot by the Malian police. Although observers were inclined to believe that this had been simply a settling of private accounts, Djibo exploited it politically to the hilt and accused the UCFA government of responsibility. To this charge Niger's Minister of the Interior, Diamballa Maiga, replied with more humor than anger. "In Niger we do not commit murder for political reasons. We may kill for a woman or for possession of some land, but never for a political party." [44]

Wherever the truth lay in the charges and countercharges, this murder created great disturbance in Niger, resuscitated old quarrels, and again put off the day when Djibo might return to his native land. In September, 1962, he announced at Accra that he was organizing a group of Freedom Fighters, whose dual objective was to assist all anticolonial movements in Africa and to defend Kwame Nkrumah from attack.[45] At the time it was thought that perhaps Djibo had now come to realize that time had run out for him in Niger, and therefore he was turning to other fields where he could utilize his undeniable talents in a cause congenial to his convictions. Two years later it became clear that Djibo had not given up his hope of returning to power in Niger.

During 1963, the situation in Niger began to evolve in a way favorable to Djibo's cause. The assassination of President Olympio of Togo in mid-January was followed by reports of a plot foiled at Niamey the next month. On the night of February 6, armed guards stopped all motor vehicles entering and leaving Niamey and checked the identity of their occupants. This led to the circulation of rumors in the capital that written propaganda emanating from the Sawaba had been found in the home of El Hadj Gabriel, former administrative secretary of

[44] *Ibid.*, June 5, 1962.   [45] Radio Ouagadougou, September 10, 1962.

Djibo's party, that fifteen persons had been arrested, and that *cercle* commandants had been ordered to root out subversion in their respective regions.[46] The government refused to clarify the situation, blandly insisting that the identity check had been merely a preventive measure. In November, there occurred a short-lived mutiny in the new national army, thought to have been stimulated by the successful *coups d'état* that had recently taken place in the Congo (Brazzaville) and Dahomey. Signs of unrest multiplied during the summer and fall of 1964.[47] In June, trouble occurred in the Maradi region during a tour made there by Boubou Hama, and 24 of the 27 persons arrested at the time died soon after of suffocation in the local jail. More arrests followed, mainly in east-central Niger, almost all involving former members of the Sawaba party. Early in September, Diallo Boubakar, Minister of Civil Service, was suddenly dismissed from his post without any explanation by the authorities.

The first official admission of serious trouble came with the announcement on October 13 that Diori had canceled an official visit to Bonn and a private one to Paris. His presence was needed in Niger, it was said, because of "attempted subversion by armed groups whose bases are outside the country." The next day it was announced that armed rebels had made unsuccessful attacks on administrative posts in east, central, and west Niger, and that four of those captured had been executed at Niamey before a crowd estimated at 10,000 persons. Since then the attacks have continued, and, reportedly with the cooperation of the population, more rebels have been caught, including two of Djibo's principal lieutenants. On October 26, 1964, Boubou Hama convened a special session of the Assembly to secure its authorization to set up a court martial to try all captured rebels. At the same time he announced that the Niger government had sent notes to neighboring governments, notably to those of Ghana and Dahomey, protesting the support they had allegedly given to Djibo and intimating that Niger might carry its complaints against them to the Organization of African Unity in the event that it did not find their replies satisfactory. Concurrently, Niger's ambassador to Paris denied the report that such a protest had also been sent to the government of Algeria, but skeptics continued to link the troubles in Niger with the alleged training of Nigérien terrorists on Algerian soil and with unrest among the Touareg

[46] *Ibid.*, February 15, 1963.
[47] See *Le Monde*, October 13, 14, 1964; *The New York Times*, October 15, 1964; *Le Figaro*, October 29, 1964.

of Niger. Late in October, reports of the movements by Malian troops along Niger's western frontier added still another complication to a situation that is still far from clear.

The Land and the People

GEOGRAPHY

Niger occupies an almost central position in the African continent, and it covers an area about twice the size of France (1,189,900 square kilometers or nearly 460,000 square miles). Its capital, Niamey, in the extreme west of the country, is some 1,200 miles east of Dakar, and 1,080 miles north of the Guinea Gulf. Essentially a borderland of the Sahara desert, Niger is bounded to the north by Algeria and Libya, to the east by Chad, to the west by Mali, and to the south by Upper Volta, Dahomey, and Nigeria.

Most of Niger is an immense plateau, 600 to 1,500 feet in altitude, from which arise some mountainous areas, of which the most noteworthy is the northern massif of Aïr. Niger is divided into two main vegetation zones of unequal size. North of the 16th parallel lies the far larger area made up of desert and semidesert land; to the south is steppe and savanna-type country, which extends from the Niger River to Lake Chad over a width of about 90 miles. This is Niger's most productive zone and therefore the most heavily populated. The Niger River is the main artery for the far western region, and the country's only other river in which water flows throughout the year is the Komandougou, which flows into Lake Chad in the extreme northeastern corner.

THE SOCIAL STRUCTURE: DEMOGRAPHY AND URBANIZATION

On January 1, 1964, Niger's population was said to number 3,175,-565, of whom only 6,000 were Europeans.[48] The population density works out to about 2.3 persons to the square kilometer—the lowest of any French-speaking West African country except Mauritania. Regionally, the variations in population are striking, ranging from 0.07 persons to the square kilometer in Agadès *cercle* to 16.3 in that of Tessaoua. Generally, the lowest density is found in the north, where the great empty spaces are traversed by scattered nomad tribes, and the highest occurs in the south. This latter area is the granary of Niger, which is peopled by sedentary Negro farmers. Three-fourths of the total population are Negroes, less than 1 per cent are non-Africans, and

[48] *Afrique Nouvelle,* March 12, 1964.

the balance is composed of three nomad groups who call themselves "white" but who are strongly crossbred with Negroes.

Niger's racial composition is the subject of widely varying estimates and nomenclatures, as well as definitions.[49] Of its two major Negro tribes, the Hausa is by far the more numerous, being variously estimated at 905,000 and 1,350,000 members. It is made up of seven main groups, almost all of which are themselves divided into subtribes. The second major group of Negro tribes is called collectively the Djerma-Songhai, variously estimated at 200,000 and 540,000 members, who live in the regions of Niamey, Dosso, Filingué, and Tillabéri. Greater numbers of Hausa and Djerma-Songhai live in neighboring countries—respectively, in Nigeria and the Mali Republic.

The situation of the nomads is similar. A little under half of all the Berber Touareg have their habitat in Niger (from 291,000 to 330,000), in the north-central and western part of the territory, but a larger number of their fellow tribesmen are to be found in the Mali Republic and in Upper Volta. Some of Niger's Touareg are partially sedentary, and all of them have a strictly hierarchical social structure composed of nobles (*imaggeren*), tributary vassals (*imrad*), and Negro servitors (*bellah*). Far more nomadic and anarchic are the Toubou, whose main home is in the Tibesti mountains of Chad. In Niger they number perhaps 5,000, in the areas of Djado, Kouar, and N'Guigmi. Niger's third "white" group is that of the Peul (Fulani) cattle-herders, who are spread all over West Africa from Cape Verde to Chad. In Niger they form an intermediate element between the true nomads and the Negro sedentary peoples by virtue of their geographical location, numbers, and way of life. The great majority of them live in the sahl zone, where they are becoming increasingly sedentary. Of Niger's total population it is believed that more than 20 per cent are nomadic or seminomadic.[50]

Well over 90 percent of the Nigérien people are rural, although in recent years the number of urban dwellers has been rapidly increasing. Yet even now only 2.3 per cent of the total population live in the four main towns, Niamey, Tahoua, Zinder, and Maradi. Of these towns, Niamey is by far the most populous, and between 1955 and 1963 the number of its inhabitants rose from less than 19,000 to over 40,000.[51] None of Niger's secondary centers—Agadès, Dosso, N'Guigmi, Tillabéri, and Gouré—has as many as 10,000 inhabitants. Although infant

[49] For an authoritative description of the tribes and their numerical importance, see *La République du Niger*, February 26, 1960, p. 9.

[50] *Afrique*, September, 1961.   [51] *Afrique Nouvelle*, March 12, 1964.

mortality remains high, the population in recent years has been growing at the rate of 2.9 per cent annually.[52] This means that the Nigériens of today are a predominantly young people, and about 54 per
cent of them are under twenty years of age. For a country as economically underdeveloped as Niger this recent rapid growth of the population, as well as the trend toward urbanization—albeit on a comparatively modest scale—has created problems of unemployment and lack
of housing, particularly in Niamey and Maradi.[53] Of Niger's many
population problems, those posed by the wage-earning class in both
the political and economic domains are a cause of considerable concern
to the government.

Wage-earners and Civil Servants

So contradictory are the figures given in official and semiofficial publications that it is difficult for the student of Niger's labor problems to
reach accurate conclusions, even about the size of the country's working
population or about the number and distribution of its wage-earners.
In 1958, Niger's population of working age was estimated at 865,000
persons, of whom 13,500 were said to be wage-earners. Among the latter, 6,357 were employed in the public sector, one-third of them as civil
servants. Only a little over half (7,850) of those then described as
wage-earners were native Nigériens, the balance being 4,318 alien
Africans and 1,100 Frenchmen.[54] Another analysis, made four years
later by the Niger Labor Service, listed 9,351 wage-earners in the private sector, of whom 5,320 were Nigériens, 3,506 were alien Africans,
and 525 were Europeans. Of those employed in this sector, 6,139
worked in Niamey, 1,390 in Maradi, and 1,822 in Zinder.[55] A still more
recent study lists 18,350 wage-earners in a working-age population
numbering 1,110,000, of whom 7,500 were in public services, 1,500 in
commerce, 4,000 in industry, building, and transport, and 2,350 in domestic service.[56]

From these fragmentary data it appears that there has been an appreciable growth in the number of persons working for wages in Niger
and a concurrent decline in its alien component. Yet the total of
wage-earners is still very small compared with the size of the whole

[52] *Marchés Tropicaux*, April 27, 1963, p. 992; *L'Afrique d'Expression Française*, no. 409, p. 171.
[53] *Afrique Nouvelle*, August 1, 1963.
[54] *Marchés Tropicaux*, August 2, 1958, p. 1871.
[55] *Ibid.*, August 25, 1962, p. 1798.
[56] *L'Afrique d'Expression Française, op. cit.*, p. 178.

population and with the total of those self-employed or working in non-remunerated family enterprises. A very large majority of Niger's wage-earners remain localized in the main towns, particularly in Niamey, and are employed mainly in the public services, domestic service, trade, and the building and transport industries. A far larger group is made up of unskilled seasonal laborers, variously estimated at 100,000 and 160,000, who go each year principally from the Niger River region to work in Ghana and the Ivory Coast. This migration is believed to be motivated mainly by the social prestige it confers and by a spirit of adventure. The length of the emigrants' stay abroad ranges between five months and five years.[57]

If the foregoing can be taken as a realistic picture of Niger's wage-earning class, it is easy to see why labor has been very slow to organize and why the few unions that exist are localized in the main towns. The CGT civil service unions were the first in the field, but it was not until August, 1958, that Djibo Bakary, the secretary-general, transformed them into a territorial section of UGTAN, which had been founded one and a half years before at Cotonou. Characteristically, a resolution passed at the constituent congress in Niamey denounced the *loi-cadre* as a failure and urged that Africa take the "revolutionary" path to national liberation. But concerning Niger itself, the congress was suprisingly conservative. It simply urged that a territorial plan be drawn up and that foreign capital investments be attracted to stimulate the country's economy.[58]

A few months after this congress was held Djibo Bakary fell from power. In March, 1959, the far more conservative government that succeeded his severed the ties which bound the local UGTAN to the main Conakry organization; six months later it was transformed into an autonomous territorial union called the UGTAN-Autonome. This union retained its press organ, *Le Travailleur Nigérien,* through which it expressed views on a wide range of subjects. In some issues, the autonomous UGTAN asked for an improvement of wage-earners' living and working conditions through collective labor agreements on a national scale, a revision of the labor code to guarantee full employment, and the establishment of schools of administration and trade. In other issues it urged a reappraisal of the customary laws governing marriage, called for suppression of the state-run Orphanage for Mulattoes to eliminate racial discrimination, and denounced the "cult of political

[57] *Ibid.,* p. 178; *Marchés Tropicaux,* March 11, 1961, p. 2637.
[58] *Marchés Tropicaux,* August 9, 1958, p. 1915.

personalities." The habit of passing political resolutions and of advocating policies more radical than those of the government was clearly a
hold-over from its practice of harassing the colonial administration.

In September, 1960, the PPN government replaced the autonomous
UGTAN by the Union Générale des Travailleurs Nigériens (UNTN),
on the ground that Niger's recently acquired independence required a
single national *centrale,* or federation, whose mission would be the implementation of the party's development plan. Since its formation, successive congresses of the UNTN have echoed official foreign policy, as
in their denunciation of colonialism in Angola and Southern Rhodesia
and of apartheid in South Africa. They also advocated a negotiated
peace in Algeria and cooperation with other labor *centrales* in the
countries belonging to the Union Africaine et Malgache (UAM). But
other resolutions passed by these congresses show a continuing concern
with local social problems, such as improvement of the status of
women and sumptuary controls. In the economic domain, too, the
UNTN has retained a residue of the radicalism which characterized its
previous incarnations. Not only has it denounced retention of French
personnel and military bases in Niger, but it has deviated in other ways
from the PPN position. It has attacked the transport monopoly exercised by the French Compagnie Transafricaine, demanded nationalization of the Société Africaine d'Electricité (also French-owned), criticized the government's management of the family allowance fund and
of agricultural cooperatives, and asked that the official loan organization (Crédit du Niger) be transformed into a national development
bank. More recently the government has shown itself favorably disposed to the UNTN's request to be associated more closely with policy
decisions, especially on economic matters.[59]

Wages in Niger have risen proportionately much faster than in any
other French-speaking West African country except Upper Volta, but
both states still have the lowest wage scales in that group. In 1959, the
minimum wage for the highest-paid category of Nigérien workers was
increased from 10.75 CFA francs an hour to 24 CFA francs, but it remained frozen at that rate until July 1, 1962. (Since October, 1948, the
CFA franc has had twice the value of the metropolitan franc.) Thereafter, the minimum wage was calculated on a different basis and was
raised to 4,680 francs monthly. Also in July, 1962, family allowances
were increased from 260 CFA francs a month per laborer's child to 700
CFA francs in both the public and private sectors. In the field of labor

[59] *Ibid.,* October 7, 1961, p. 2438; *Afrique Nouvelle,* September 12, 1963.

legislation Niger has also moved slowly. Not until two years after independence was a national labor code drawn up to supersede the overseas code passed by the French parliament a decade earlier.[60]

Niger's poverty and its small wage-earning class largely explain the PPN's delays in improving the living and working conditions of Nigérien laborers. In any case, it is another aspect of the labor question that has chiefly preoccupied the government: the shortage of agricultural labor and the plethora of unskilled and unemployed urban youths —problems which Niger, on a smaller scale, shares with many neighboring countries. Like them it has sought the answer in "human investment" as the best means available for carrying out its development plans and for checking urban parasitism and juvenile delinquency. In particular, to implement Niger's three-year plan, the government aims to keep in the country the young men who have been going every year as seasonal laborers to Nigeria, Ghana, and the Ivory Coast.

Work on projects of public utility is part of the obligatory service required of recruits for the national army formed in August, 1961. Under a law passed on May 13, 1962, similar service must be performed by all unemployed urban youths who refuse to return to work in their native villages. Apparently this measure was ineffectually enforced, for in April, 1963, it was reported that the police had rounded up all such youths in Niamey and shipped them back to the rural regions from which they had come. Again in June, 1964, the government ordered all unemployed men to take up agricultural work on pain of being prosecuted as vagabonds.[61] Even before the authorities resorted to such measures, they were hurt and indignant to learn that in 1962 the International Labor Organization had classified Niger among the African countries which was practicing a disguised form of forced labor. With considerable fanfare the UNTN leadership invited many foreign observers to its congress in September, 1962, at which secretary-general René Delanne protested against the ILO report. Nigériens, he claimed, were spontaneously offering their services to the government, and organized labor through its work in nation-building was promoting African development and unity.[62]

Generally, the PPN's labor policy has been much the same as that of

---

[60] *Marchés Tropicaux*, August 25, 1962, pp. 1798–1799; December 12, 1962, p. 2618.

[61] *Afrique Nouvelle*, April 26, 1963; June 4, 1964.

[62] *Ibid.*, September 21, 1962.

other French-speaking African governments. When organized labor has asked for improvements in living and working conditions, the government has been sympathetic and acceded insofar as its meager resources permitted. But when the UNTN has tried to assert itself as an independent political force and has made demands that moved too far ahead of official policy, the government has clamped down. The PPN is determined that the UNTN will not serve the radical forces in the country that are eager to overthrow or transform the government, and that it be molded into a docile instrument which would help to achieve party objectives. The UNTN has had little alternative to submission, for Djibo's self-imposed exile has deprived Niger's unions of competent radical leadership, and their membership is too small for them to exercise effective pressure on employer groups, including the government. Thus far, the only important strike that Niger has experienced was organized by civil servants in November, 1957, and it was a failure. Organized labor's current acceptance of PPN controls and guidance is based on the assumption that the government will satisfy the workers' legitimate grievances and assure their physical well-being. The government's fulfillment of its side of the bargain depends, however, as do many other things in Niger, on a marked improvement in the economy.

In French-speaking Negro Africa the civil service includes salaried professional persons, such as doctors and teachers. Because they comprise the great majority of educated Africans, the civil servants' unions are among the oldest and strongest in French West Africa. This is true in Niger, but compared with those in countries like Senegal and the Ivory Coast, the unions of Niger are weak. The lack of indigenous cadres, which has been frequently lamented since Niger attained independence, is of course related to the country's low literacy rate. For many years the French made considerable use of the better-educated Dahomeans and Togolese to staff Niger's civil service in the echelons not occupied by Europeans. This was common practice throughout French Negro Africa, but wherever independence has stimulated the development of territorial nationalism this practice has been increasingly resented. When Niger achieved its sovereignty, about 25,000 alien Africans occupied posts in the administration or were active in commerce. Among them it was the Dahomeans holding conspicuous posts who were especially unpopular for several reasons. They were Christians, had supported the Sawaba party and, in 1954, some Dahomean civil servants had been caught pilfering Nigérien public funds. In any case, the Dahomeans and to a lesser extent Togolese were the main targets of an attack by Nigérien youths at Niamey in January, 1961.[63] About fifty persons were wounded, and approximately the same number were arrested by the police. Although this outbreak was on a much smaller scale than similar riots at Abidjan in October, 1958, it was sufficiently serious for the Maga government of Dahomey to send a minister to Niger to conduct an investigation.

This manifestation of Nigérien nationalist feeling, coupled with the protests of the UNTN against the government's continued employment of aliens in the civil service, led to a more rapid Nigérienization of the local cadres. Although the government refused to dismiss French technicians, who were irreplaceable and whose salaries, moreover, were paid by France, in 1961 it did promote fifteen Nigériens who had been trained in Paris to posts of command in the general administration.[64] But the number of qualified Nigériens was too small and the civil servants' unions were too weak to force the government's pace in this matter. As of January 1, 1964, Niger still employed 348 Frenchmen; of these 122 were teachers, 111 were technicians, 41 were in the health service, 25 were in the judiciary, 5 were army officers, but only 44 remained in the general administration.[65] The force of African opinion, both local and in neighboring countries, has put the PPN on the defensive, as was shown by an editorial in the party organ, *Le Niger,* on October 15, 1962. The author asserted that Niger's government was as "revolutionary" as any in Africa, but in order to assure competence and efficiency in its services it was proceeding slowly as well as surely toward the total Nigérienization of its cadres.

The inability of Nigériens, both numerically and professionally, to supersede foreigners is by no means the only reason that the government continues to employ many Frenchmen. Like other dominant single parties in Africa, the PPN distrusts its own national civil servants because they want to maintain the position of a highly privileged minority that they enjoyed under the colonial regime. Furthermore, it has been among the Nigérien functionaries that the Sawaba found its strongest sympathizers. The PPN high command therefore regards the civil servants with a distrustful eye, and has even made them a target of discriminatory measures. In the guise of austerity in January, 1962, it cut down functionaries' perquisites in the dispensation of free housing

[63] *Ibid.,* January 25, 1961.

[64] Diori Hamani, "Le Plan Triennal, 1961–1963," *Afrique Nouvelle,* December 13, 1961.

[65] *L'Afrique d'Expression Française, op. cit.,* p. 177.

and the use of official motorcars. A year later, in January, 1963, after the assassination of President Olympio of Togo and the discovery of a plot in the Ivory Coast, the government made any civil servant who had resigned from his post and attempted to leave the country liable to criminal prosecution. In April, 1963, the government decided neither to promote civil servants nor to recruit new personnel for a two-year period.[66] More recently, the pressure exercised by the PPN leaders on civil servants to contribute to the national loan had the dual objective of saving the government money and of cutting the income of functionaries.

In August, 1963, the government transformed the Center for Administrative Training, founded in 1960, into a National School of Administration with seven specialized sections. The enlargement of training facilities, however, was too recent to enable Niger to meet the need for more local administrators that suddenly arose four months later as a result of Diori's expulsion from Niger of all Dahomean civil servants (see below). This drastic measure wrought havoc in the handling of public business, but it also forced the government to satisfy the demand of the civil servants' unions to fill more administrative posts with native-born Nigériens. Nevertheless, despite repeated protests from those unions, the government continued to employ almost as many Frenchmen as before.

Religion

Islam is clearly the dominant religious faith in Niger among both the nomadic and sedentary populations. In a total population estimated at 2,695,000 in 1961, there were 1,975,000 Muslims and 713,000 animists,[67] only the small remainder being Christians. From the northwest Islam was brought to Niger by the Songhai of Gao and from the east by the Peul conquerors, but today its main source of inspiration in Niger comes from the Muslim emirates of Northern Nigeria.

Although the two major West African Islamic brotherhoods, Tidjaniya and Qadriya, have members throughout Niger, and even the Senussi have followers among the Touareg and in the southeast, the practice of Islam differs markedly from one region and from one group to another. In the west and center, the Djerma-Songhai, Maouri, Béribéri, and rural Hausa practice magical and animist rites and at the same time consider themselves good Muslims because they observe the

[66] *Marchés Tropicaux,* June 1, 1963, p. 1231.
[67] J. C. Froelich, *Les Musulmans d'Afrique Noire* (Paris: 1962), p. 360.

fast of Ramadan and perform the five daily prayers. As a rule their Marabouts (Muslim religious leaders) are uneducated men, mainly concerned to sell amulets and charms profitably to their credulous followers. Among these tribes Islam appears to be a social veneer comfortably superimposed on basic animist concepts. Very different is the kind of Islam practiced by the Touareg, Peul, Kanouri, and urban Hausa. Theirs is an austere, intolerant, and archaic form of that religion, seemingly little influenced by reformist trends in the Arab world. The extremist element is represented by a Peul group called Yan Koblé who number some 5,000 in Zinder and Gouré *cercles*. The Yan Koblé are puritanical fundamentalists who keep their women strictly cloistered and who live apart from their coreligionists. Although the caliber of Islam is undoubtedly higher in the center and east of Niger, it has produced no exceptional Marabouts or scholars comparable to those of Mauritania, who are outstanding in French West Africa. Many small elementary Koranic schools dot the Nigérien countryside, and in a few of the towns there are institutions of higher Islamic learning. But even in the latter the curriculum is rudimentary and the attendance small. None of them has more than fifty pupils and some have no more than ten. Probably the best is the *medersa* at Say, which is slated to be transformed into an institute of Franco-Arabic education modeled after similar schools in Boutilimit (Mauritania) and Abéché (Chad).[68]

The dominance of Islam and the isolation of Niger account for both the long delay in establishing Christian missions and the small scale of their operations. Estimates of the number of Christian converts in Niger, some of them non-Nigérien Africans, range from 7,000 to 13,000, of whom the great majority are Catholics. Everywhere the Christianization of Muslim peoples is an uphill struggle, and in Niger the effort was not made until 1931, when the Catholic Mission of Lyon started work in Niamey. During the following sixteen years it expanded its operations to include Zinder and Dogondoutchi, but in 1948 its missionaries were replaced by members of another order. During the first postwar decade French and Canadian nuns joined the missionary-priests, and the Catholic mission of Niger was promoted to the rank of apostolic prefecture. Catholic missionaries do some medical and social work, but their main stress has been on primary education, especially for girls. As of 1963, the Catholic Church of Niger was

[68] *Ibid.*, see pp. 209, 177. In 1964, 49 Nigériens were studying Islamic doctrines and Arabic in foreign countries, chiefly Egypt, Nigeria, and Tunisia.

staffed by twenty missionaries and thirty nuns, and its primary schools were attended by 2,600 pupils.[69]

Protestantism in Niger is represented by two American organizations. The Sudan Interior Mission, whose main field of activity is in Nigeria, has its Niger headquarters at Tibiri near Maradi, and stations at Zinder, Madaoua, Dogondoutchi, and Gamli. The Africa Christian Mission is concentrated in the Niamey, Gaya, and Dosso regions, where it strives to make converts among the Djerma and Gourmantché populations. While the Protestant missions include some teachers and doctors, they are mainly concerned with evangelical work among the comparatively lax Muslims of western Niger.

Although the government leaders of Niger are solidly Muslim, the very great majority of them are western Nigériens, which probably accounts for their lack of fanaticism and their acceptance of Christian missionaries. To be sure, Diori made the pilgrimage to Mecca in May, 1962, but probably a main object of this journey was to establish closer political and economic relations with the Near Eastern countries. In any case, the Nigérien Christians are too few in number to be regarded as a menace, and the mission schools and hospitals receive official subsidies for their contribution to the country's development. In 1961, such subsidies amounted to 13 million CFA francs. Although the government has sometimes been reproached with the relatively generous scale of such subsidies they have not been discontinued, and some PPN ministers have even sent their children to Catholic schools.[70]

Indeed, not Christian but certain Islamic practices in Niger have aroused the government's ire and even its fears. The superstitions cultivated by the amulet-selling Marabouts in the west, and the hostility to secular education and the emancipation of women on the part of the ultra-conservative Muslims of the north and east, are regarded by PPN leaders as serious obstacles to their plans for modernizing the country. Even more dangerous in their eyes is the religious attraction exercised upon all southern Niger's Muslims by the sultans of Northern Nigeria. These potentates are regarded by the Nigériens as the authentic representatives of the Prophet, and whenever they celebrate religious holidays Nigérien Muslims flock by the thousands to attend them.[71]

Nevertheless, religion of any persuasion—so long as it is unaccompanied by fanaticism or political coloration—is welcomed by the PPN

[69] *Afrique Nouvelle*, September 12, 1963.   [70] *Nice-Matin*, January 27, 1961.
[71] Simon Kiba, "Problèmes Nigériens," *Afrique*, January, 1962.

government as a stabilizing influence that helps to maintain public order. Diori regards the continued religious authority of the chiefs over the populations still subject to them as an important reason for not suppressing the chieftaincies, and he told André Blanchet that the fundamentally religious character of the Nigériens is an obstacle to the spread of Communism among them.[72]

Education and the Youth Movement

All the government's plans to transform Niger into a modern country depend upon a rapid and large-scale expansion of its educational system. Niger has long had the sorry distinction of having the lowest literacy rate of all French West African countries. This remains true, although there has been a great improvement since the end of World War II. Then only 1 per cent of its school-age children actually attended school, but the proportion rose to 8 per cent in 1963. On August 2, 1962, Diori could proudly announce that in the two years since independence the number of children attending school had doubled. As of early 1964, there were 32,806 boys and 13,694 girls studying in state primary schools, and 2,040 boys and 1,808 girls attending Catholic and Protestant primary schools.[73] Over 2,100 pupils were receiving instruction in state and mission secondary schools and technical institutions. Since Niger still lacks schools above the secondary level, it has to send students abroad for higher learning. In 1964, there were 57 state scholarship-holders studying in France, 17 at Dakar, and 5 in Abidjan, as well as 14 other students in West Germany and 5 in Poland. Many of the causes of Niger's economic underdevelopment are the same as those that account for its backwardness in education. Many teachers have been reluctant to serve in Niger not only because the harsh climate, inaccessibility, and lack of communications and amenities made it unattractive, but because certain elements of the Muslim population have been hostile toward their work.

Niger's nomads, like those in other Saharan borderlands, have had little or no interest in modern secular education, and have treated contemptuously the few Negro teachers willing to share with them the hardships of their nomadic life. It was not until 1944 that the French set up the first schools for nomads, initially among the semisedentary Kel Gress Touareg of Madaoua, Tanout, and Dakoro. Since they employed a Marabout to teach the nomad children Arabic, the tribal chiefs offered no objections. But when the French tried to introduce

[72] *Nice-Matin*, January 27, 1961.   [73] *Afrique Nouvelle*, May 28, 1964.

such schools among the more nomadic Touareg of Agadès and Tahoua they ran into trouble, and it was only in April, 1950, that the consent of these chiefs was reluctantly given.[74] So that parents might see their offspring frequently, the sites of all nomad schools were carefully chosen along the main trek routes. Pupils were left as free as was compatible with school routine, and an effort was made to reproduce—with some improvements—the conditions of their tribal life.[75] School attendance continued to be irregular, however, and before Niger became independent there were never more than 1,000 nomad children at school in any one year. Since the PPN has taken over the government, its leaders have realized that a much greater effort must be made if the nomads are ever going to produce an educated elite. In 1959, more schools were opened in the nomad zones, and in 1962, a decisive forward step was taken with the inauguration of the first secondary school for nomads at Agadès.[76] Yet only 2 per cent of the population in the nomad subdivision of Tahoua attended school.

A far larger group of Nigérien Muslims, the Hausa, were also opposed to sending their children to French lay or mission schools. Since they expected their sons to become traders or farmers like themselves, they saw no reason for an education beyond the elementary religious instruction given in Koranic schools.[77] As was the case with the nomads, the French made little headway against such opposition until 1950. Among the western Muslims, however, the French found a much better response, not only because they were less orthodox but because the Nigériens of that area had more contacts with French-educated Africans from Upper Volta, Dahomey, and the Ivory Coast. Inevitably, therefore, Niger's elite was formed in the west, and this elite group has now come to control the country's government to the virtual exclusion of their more numerous but less educated compatriots in the east.

Because Niger has had so few educational facilities, the country still has to rely heavily on foreign teachers to staff its schools, and there are not enough schools or teachers.[78] When Niger became independent, it had only about four hundred qualified teachers, approximately one-fourth of whom were French. Most of the teaching in its schools has been done by inadequately trained monitors—a situation which the

[74] Journal Officiel de la République Française, *Débats de l'Assemblée de l'Union Française,* July 21, 1950.

[75] Y. Allainmat, "Ecoles Nomades du Niger," *Encyclopédie Mensuelle d'Outre-Mer,* October, 1954, pp. 272–275.

[76] *Afrique Nouvelle,* July 3, 1962.   [77] Kiba, *op. cit.*

[78] H. Kitchen, ed., *The Educated African* (London: 1962), p. 479.

government is trying hard to remedy. Many of its ministers are former teachers, and in a policy declaration of June 18, 1960, PPN leaders stated that the expansion of education was a major aim of the government.[79] In 1959, centers for the rapid training of auxiliary monitors were opened at Niamey, Maradi, Zinder, and Tahoua, and in October of the following year two more were inaugurated at Agadès and Maïne-Soroa as was a normal school at Zinder. At the end of 1961, 340 young men and 171 young women were undergoing teacher-training at various levels in Niger, and a few Nigérien teachers were taking refresher courses in France. During that year, the government sent a mission to France to recruit additional personnel by offering qualified French teachers exceptionally high salaries if they would go to Niger.

Virtually all the 122 professors of French origin serving in Niger during the 1962–1963 school year were concentrated in the country's eleven secondary and technical schools, which were attended by a total of 1,983 pupils. (The balance were in mission schools which did not go beyond the primary level.) Niamey's old classical and modern college had been transformed by then into the national *lycée*, and it was attended by about six hundred students, of whom the great majority held scholarships. For the time being this *lycée* seems able to accommodate all the students in Niger who are qualified for admission, and the only expansion currently planned at the secondary-school level is in technical training. Maradi's Apprenticeship Center, the only one of its kind in the country, became a technical college in 1963. It is hoped that this center, which now has about one hundred pupils, will soon be able to turn out many of the masons, electricians, and mechanics that Niger sorely needs.

The government's present major objective is to achieve mass literacy through the diffusion of primary education, first of all in the towns and with special emphasis on the teaching of girls. In the face of Muslim hostility, the French government did little to promote women's education in Niger. It was mainly due to the Christian missions that as many as 1,500 Nigérien girls received primary instruction during the colonial period. In 1958, there were actually more girls (325) than boys (227) studying in mission schools, while in state schools the proportion was reversed. The PPN leaders realize that to make any appreciable progress in educating girls the number of women teachers must be in-

[79] See article by the Minister of Education, Mamadou Maiga, in *Afrique Nouvelle,* December 13, 1961.

creased, and for that reason they encouraged the Canadian nuns who in 1962 opened the Mariama college for women.[80]

The funds required to carry out the PPN's education program cannot be provided wholly from local resources, especially in view of Diori's assertion that the per capita cost of schooling in Niger is the highest in the world.[81] It is the more creditable, therefore, that by early 1963, the number of Nigériens attending school had more than doubled since 1961, and teachers' salaries had also been appreciably raised. Niger has been spending from 9 to 12 per cent of its own small revenues on education; most of the funds allotted to it have come from France. To finance the expansion now planned for its school system, the Niger government is soliciting additional money from foreign countries and UNESCO.

Niger's need for cadres is so urgent that the PPN is pushing ahead with its educational program despite the obstructionism it has encountered among radical teachers and students. The teachers' unions in particular have been so recalcitrant to authority that even Djibo Bakary, himself a teacher and left-wing labor leader, felt compelled to deal severely with them when they went on strike. Inevitably, the far more conservative PPN government has met with stiffer opposition from both teachers and secondary-school students. At their Niamey congress in July, 1959, the teachers' unions attacked the government for subsidizing mission schools (whose teachers had refused to join their 1957 strike) and for maintaining close ties with France. That year, the students in Niamey's college went on strike, voicing a wide range of grievances that were never clearly formulated. After analyzing their complaints, the French journalist Ernest Milcent concluded that Niger's students simply felt they were not receiving their "just due." [82] Because a modern education is based on principles alien to Niger's conservative Muslim traditions, the youths who receive advanced training react strongly against both customary authority and any form of constraint. Naturally they have been attracted by radical doctrines, and it was admittedly their support for the Sawaba party that motivated the PPN's refusal to permit students to hold a congress at Niamey in

[80] *Marchés Tropicaux*, October 6, 1962, p. 2113. It had 65 pupils in 1964.

[81] Speech to pupils of the Niamey *lycée*, quoted in *Afrique Nouvelle*, August 6, 1964. The figures Diori cited were: 19,800 CFA francs per primary school student, and from 175,000 CFA francs to 275,000 CFA francs for a secondary-school student.

[82] *Le Monde*, May 8, 1959.

mid-1959.[83] Since higher education is very rare in Niger, it is not surprising that Nigérien university students in Dakar and Paris have been
outspoken critics of the French and PPN governments and also of the
traditional chiefs. The latter are scorned for their illiteracy and hated
for their abuse of power, and the former are attacked for having allied
themselves with the chieftaincy and other "reactionary" elements.

In Niger, as in other French-speaking African countries, students
lead the youth movement. In fact, in Niger students *are* the youth
movement, if "movement" can be applied to so small and so poorly
organized a segment of the population. Antagonistic as some of their
leaders are to the present government, the students do not yet constitute a danger to it or even form an effective pressure group. Because
they have acquired higher living standards and feelings of superiority
as a result of their schooling, Nigérien students in the higher schools
have lost touch with the masses whom they expect to lead and in
whose name they claim to speak. Boubou Hama, the PPN disciplinar-
ian, told a party congress in May, 1960, that he knew how to keep the
country's students in line, but that he was also aware of the dangers of
ignoring their demands. Niger already has four *agrégés* and today's
handful of university students will be tomorrow's leaders there.

Recognizing the country's need for a larger and better-educated
elite, the PPN—anti-Communist as it is—has adopted a tolerant and
flexible attitude toward Nigérien youths who have gone to the Soviet
Union for study without obtaining official permission.[84] When asked
by a journalist how he would treat the Nigériens who had accepted the
Soviet invitations (channeled through the Sawaba government-in-
exile), Diori replied with remarkable humor and understanding. To
begin with, he said, they are not real students but impulsive youths
who have gone to the USSR in a spirit of adventure rather than from
ideological convictions.[85]Because in Niger there is nothing to do during the rainy season, a Nigérien youth will go any place to which a
ticket is offered him. "The Pravda comrades must be under no illusion
that (our) students are drawn to the USSR for love of the Soviet
Union. . . . If they return with medical diplomas they will be given
posts in Niger because we need doctors. But if they return to plant a

[83] *Afrique Nouvelle,* July 24, 1959.
[84] An outstanding Nigérien student now in Moscow, Abdou Moumouni, published a book in 1964 on African education.
[85] *Afrique Nouvelle,* January 3, 1962.

flag here and to tell the people that the government is not moving fast enough, we have laws which forbid them to make speeches and which will require them to labor on works of public utility. After they have done that, they can then plead their causes."

Diori has already taken into his administration many of the educated youths who have been radicals, and his Minister of the Interior has asserted that Niger has the youngest cadres of any country in Africa.[86] In accepting them, Diori has emulated his mentor, Houphouët, and has also acted out of sheer necessity. Higher education for Nigériens is such a recent phenomenon that only the very young have been able to profit by the chance to acquire it. Perforce Diori has had to utilize youths who continue to express more revolutionary views than do their counterparts in Abidjan. In Niger, far more than in the Ivory Coast, the government relies on the support of strong and conservative traditional chiefs, and this alliance has made the younger generation of Nigériens particularly receptive to indoctrination by Djibo Bakary. Perhaps Diori, like other conservatives before him, is counting on the moderating influence of responsibility when he assigns posts of command to such youths. But there is little doubt that if the newly educated elite were to take over the government of Niger now, they would pursue a policy very different from that of the PPN.

Press and Communications Media

Even though the number of literate Nigériens has increased since the end of World War II, the reading public is still so limited that a genuine press has yet to be born in the country. Niger's few newspapers are mimeographed and highly partisan sheets. The Information Service publishes a daily news bulletin called *Le Temps du Niger* and a weekly entitled *Le Niger*. Both are edited by Boubou Hama, president of the PPN and of the Assembly, and so reflect the PPN viewpoint. *Le Niger*, more interesting of the two, first appeared on November 27, 1961. It was followed by an eight-page monthly, called *Labari*, of which the first issue appeared in July, 1963. *Le Travailleur Nigérien*, organ of the UNTN, sometimes expresses views more advanced than those of the PPN. Far more radical is the Sawaba party publication, *Gaskya* (Truth), which is more alarming to the authorities in that it is published clandestinely, although irregularly, "somewhere in Niger." Its dissemination, despite official vigilance, probably accounts for the press

[86] *Ibid.*, April 4, 1962.

censorship imposed by the government in July, 1959, whereby all newspaper articles touching on political subjects are required to have official approval prior to publication.

The Fourth Estate has little honor or audience in Niger; quite the contrary is true of radio broadcasting. In view of the large percentage of illiterates, the government regards radio as the ideal medium for guiding and communicating with the masses. On March 3, 1963, there was inaugurated a 30-kw. transmitter, built with French aid, which can be heard within a 300-mile radius of Niamey. This new transmitter already enables Radio Niger to broadcast programs for one hundred hours weekly, and expansion is planned.

As early as July, 1961, the government prepared for this development of broadcasting by organizing an Association des Radio-Clubs, a unique venture in French-speaking Africa. Officially, this is a private association, but it has been launched, guided, and controlled by the government with the threefold purpose of "informing, educating, and diverting the population." [87] Since at the time of its organization there was only one radio set for every three hundred Nigériens and since the distribution of free receiving sets was beyond the country's resources, the authorities decided to organize collective listening posts. In July, 1962, a communal center was built by "human investment" at Tahoua, as the first of a series of fifteen posts for group auditors. At about the same time the government selected 68 candidates for training as radio-club leaders. After being taught the elementary principles of broadcasting and the technique of leading group discussions, these young men were equipped with tape recorders and sent out to specific regions. They were to study the daily life and psychology of the population, guide groups listening to and discussing broadcasts, and then report back to the government. It was on the basis of such reports that Radio Niger revised and drew up its programs. Broadcasting them on an experimental basis was begun in December, 1962. These radio clubs are so highly regarded as a two-way channel of communication with the population that to get them into operation Diori donated a million CFA francs and the French ambassador provided the technical equipment.

Diori has announced his government's intention of utilizing mobile cinema units "to tour the country and educate the people through pictures." As the size of the literate population increases, the government

[87] J. E. Kouawo, "Les Radio-Clubs à Travers le Niger," *Afrique Nouvelle,* July 4, 1963.

plans to lean more heavily on the press and to make books available at low cost. This, it is hoped, will fulfill the same function for the elite that the radio is now performing for the masses.[88]

THE ECONOMY

Agriculture

Although 94 per cent of Niger's population is rural, agriculture plays a less important role in the country's economy than in that of any other French-speaking African state except Mauritania. This is because Niger's exceptionally unfavorable climatic conditions have reduced two-thirds of the whole area to desert or semidesert land. Farming is confined to the extreme southern region bordering on Nigeria and Dahomey, and even there great seasonal variations in rainfall cause marked differences in harvests from one year to another. North of this relatively productive belt lies sandy and lateritic soil, which sharply restricts cultivation both in area and yield. Beyond this zone agricultural output is negligible, being limited to the very small-scale production of dates and wheat in a few scattered oases.

The famines which decimated Niger's population twice during the first half of the twentieth century are now a phenomenon of the past. This danger has been averted by the establishment of millet granaries and better communications, and by the introduction of a few new crops and technical improvements by the Sociétés de Prévoyance under the colonial regime. The unpopularity of the latter institutions, caused by their compulsory nature and defective and arbitrary management, led to their gradual elimination in the postwar years. Various formulas were tried out to replace them, but none proved to be wholly satisfactory. The government of independent Niger is feeling its way along generally orthodox lines—creating cooperative societies, enlarging credit facilities, modernizing farming methods, encouraging agronomic research, and improving the water supply.

Food crops are by far the most important of Niger's agricultural output, both for the population's sustenance and for its income. Although peanut exports provide the government with its largest revenues, they bring their growers a cash income of only 1.8 to 2.5 billion CFA francs, compared with the 14 billions which the sedentary population realizes in most years from cultivating food crops.[89] Among the latter, millet

[88] See *Afrique Nouvelle*, December 13, 1961; November 16, 1962; and *Afrique*, May, 1963.

[89] *Marchés Tropicaux*, September 17, 1960, p. 2035.

and sorghum account for 11.5 billion CFA francs and provide the great majority of Nigériens with their basic food. Many varieties of millet are grown in Niger, but it is the slow-growing type that furnishes most of the harvest, which during the first postwar years averaged some 500,000 tons. Since insufficient rainfall can dangerously reduce the size of a crop on which the population is so dependent, Niger's successive governments have encouraged its production. Between 1954 and 1958, the area planted to millet increased from 988,000 to 1,505,000 hectares.[90] Since then millet farming has continued to spread, and in 1962 Niger harvested 934,000 tons.[91] The production of sorghum, Niger's second most important cereal crop, amounts to only about one-third that of millet, but it can be grown so widely on clayey soils that in an average year the country has been able to export some 40,000 tons. It is largely as a result of the increased output of millet and sorghum that Niger can now provide its population with a fairly adequate food supply. Harvests are still at the mercy of climatic conditions, however, and when the rains fail the role played by secondary crops becomes vital.

Niger's supplementary food crops are rice, manioc, corn, beans, and wheat. Rice production, concentrated in Tillabéri *cercle,* came to only 4,727 tons in 1958, and additional quantities had to be imported. In 1962, Niger's harvest of over 11,000 tons of paddy was exceptionally abundant, and only insignificant quantities of rice had to be imported. Because Niger's agricultural economy is so precariously balanced and because paddy-growing does not cut into the land planted to millet and sorghum, the government would like to expand the production and milling of that nutritious food crop. But any marked increase in the area now planted to paddy would require costly hydraulic works to regulate the Niger River's inundations on which that crop is now dependent. If the money were found to build more dams and canals, southern Nigériens could produce annually—in addition to millet— two series of food crops: rice from irrigation in the dry season and corn, sorghum, and manioc during the rains.

When the rainy season begins and the Niger River's waters recede, manioc is planted on some 15,000 hectares in the valley bottoms and along the edges of ponds. Manioc production has risen spectacularly from 25,000 tons a year in the mid-1950's to 117,000 tons in 1962. Corn, although it exhausts the soil and is produced in only small quantities

[90] *La République du Niger, op. cit.,* p. 11.
[91] *L'Afrique d'Expression Française, op. cit.,* p. 175.

(3,200 tons in 1962), can be grown throughout the year and is cherished as a supplementary food. Wheat is produced in even smaller quantities, ranging between 1,000 and 1,800 tons a year, but it is a vital source of nourishment for the oasis-dwellers of the north whose only other food is dates (3,500 tons in 1960). In the south, beans are a supplementary food, whose output grew rapidly from 15,000 tons in 1954 to 73,000 tons eight years later. This is a popular crop because it requires little care and can be intersown with millet.

Of Niger's two industrial crops, peanuts are far more important than cotton. To provide Nigérien farmers with a cash income the French introduced peanut culture in 1930, and within about 25 years peanuts came to provide from 80 to 90 per cent of the country's exports. Production in central Niger, particularly in Magaria *cercle,* is far greater than in the western zone, but peanut culture has spread rapidly throughout the southern region. In 1945, Niger harvested only 8,980 tons, exclusively in the south-central area: today peanuts are cultivated from Gouré to Tillabéri and are spreading north to Tahoua *cercle.* The production of 205,370 tons of nuts in shell in 1962 marked Niger's peak output. Of this total, 92,340 tons of nuts in shell were sold. Some 5,000 tons a year are kept by the farmers for seed, and about three times that amount is crushed for oil by Niger's three mills. In dollar terms, peanuts annually provide an income of $8 million in cash to their growers and $810,000 to millers, middlemen, and transporters, and the duties paid on peanut exports account for one-tenth of the country's revenues. A drastic redistribution of the income derived from peanut sales should soon occur as the result of a complete reorganization of the peanut market in May, 1963, which was aimed at eliminating the middlemen.

The rapidity with which peanuts have assumed so important a place in Niger's economy has alarmed the authorities. Production has increased not through higher yields but through geographical expansion which has exhausted the soil and, in the east, been effected at the expense of traditional food crops. Transporting Niger's rapidly increasing tonnages to either Lagos or Cotonou for export has been onerous and expensive, and shipping costs have added appreciably to the difficulties of marketing so "poor" a commodity as peanuts. France has been taking a very large if variable proportion of Niger's annual peanut exports and paying higher than world prices for them, but this will end when Niger's agreement with the European Economic Community enters into force. Even now the country is left each year with some thousands of tons of unsalable stocks. Moreover, despite establishment of a Stabilization Fund for Peanuts in 1957, the peanut farmers have been earning proportionately little money for their labors compared with the sums that go into the pockets of middlemen and truckers in return for considerably less effort. For all these reasons the government is reorganizing the local peanut market, discouraging expansion of that crop, and favoring substitute or supplementary agricultural sources of cash income.

Cotton is regarded as the most promising of the new industrial crops and with official encouragement has made remarkable progress. It was introduced on a commercial basis in Niger as recently as 1955, and its success has been largely due to the activity of the French Compagnie pour le Développement des Fibres Textiles (CFDT) in distributing selected seed, training farmers, ginning, baling, and marketing the crop. The production of raw cotton rose from 218 tons in 1956 to 5,400 tons in 1963–1964. According to a six-year agreement made in 1960, the CFDT buys almost all the crop sold in Niger, but a considerable tonnage is smuggled into Nigeria, where the price paid for cotton is higher. Naturally the government is trying to check such fraudulent sales and also to keep in the country enough cotton to supply the textile mill which it plans to set up in the Maradi-Madaoua producing region.

Among the noncultivated sources of agricultural income in Niger should be mentioned kapok (40–125 tons a year) and gum arabic (70–480 tons annually). The amount of these commodities that is actually gathered and sold is known only approximately and it varies widely according to the current price and the monetary needs of the pickers. Much of the output, especially of gum arabic, is sold illicitly in Nigerian markets, and much the same can be said of the south's surplus production of cereals, fruits, and vegetables. Nor are more accurate data available in regard to the legitimate trade in agricultural items between Niger and nearby coastal territories. It is believed that many thousands of tons of millet, beans, and so forth are shipped to the south each year in return for yams, flour, fruit, and colas.[92]

The government of independent Niger has carried on and even intensified the efforts made by the colonial regime to increase, diversify, and process the country's agricultural output. To teach the rural populations modern cultivation techniques, monitors trained at the Kolo Agricultural Station have been assigned to every canton. To promote specific crops, experimental farms have been established, such as that

[92] *Marchés Tropicaux*, September 17, 1960, pp. 2035–2036.

for peanuts at Téra and for cotton at Gabi-Maradi. Various credit institutions and funds have been set up to aid farmers, the most important being the Union Nigérienne du Crédit et de Coopération and the Fonds National pour le Développement Economique et Social. The havoc caused by locusts in 1958 induced the authorities to reorganize and improve their antilocust campaigns. The only setback thus far recorded is the agricultural service's failure to persuade Nigérien farmers to make a greater use of draft animals for ploughing.

Animal Husbandry [93]

Niger's animal resources are broadly estimated at 3.5 million head of cattle, 7 million sheep and goats, 350,000 camels, 300,000 donkeys, and 115,000 horses. The size of Niger's herds is comparable to the size of those of Mali or of Upper Volta, but Niger has more horses than any other French-speaking West African country. Its herds represent a capital estimated at 40 billion CFA francs, and the income realized from the sale of its animals and animal products amounts roughly to 34 per cent (10 billion CFA francs) of the total gross revenues from all rural activities. About one-third of that income derives from the export trade, and it could be considerably increased if Niger's animals were better cared for and the market reorganized.

The vast uninhabited stretches lying between the 13th and 16th parallels, which constitute 58 per cent of Niger's total surface, would be ideally suited to animal husbandry if more water were available. Niger's rainy season is so short that for seven to eight months of the year its pastures provide only mediocre grass, and the animals have to be watered from wells. In late May, when the first rains permit farming to begin in the south, the animals are moved north. Then in October, after the rains have ceased and the crops are harvested, they are returned south. Chronically underfed and irregularly watered, they have little resistance to disease, and their mortality rate is particularly high whenever the rains are delayed.

To some extent these natural drawbacks are offset by the devotion Niger's Peul and Touareg herders give to their animals. They concentrate on rearing sheep, camels, and goats, among which the red goat of Maradi is highly valued. Although the milk, meat, and leather supplied by their herds are vital to the Touareg, these people are more inclined to sell their animals than are the Peul. To the Peul cattle-herders the

[93] For most of the data in this section, the writer is indebted to *La République du Niger, op. cit.,* pp. 16–19.

number of head they own is of primary importance as a status symbol. Their cattle are slaughtered for meat on rare occasions only, and they are not sold unless their owners badly need money. The sedentary peoples, whose herds are much smaller and of poorer quality than those of the nomads, have no such inhibitions about selling or slaughtering their animals.

All Niger's administrations have tried to instill in the herders more modern concepts and methods of animal husbandry, but the present government is the first to have given the project top priority in its program for developing the country's resources. Each circumscription in the pastoral zone now has a veterinarian, serums are produced in a specialized laboratory in Niamey, and herds must now be inoculated against major diseases. The stud at the Filingué-Tokounous station has so improved the local stock by crossbreeding and by scientific feeding that it receives requests for selected animals from a number of neighboring countries. A large program of well-digging is under way, especially in the sahl zone, supported mainly by funds supplied by the OCRS and the European Economic Community. In September, 1962, a company was set up with Israeli aid to determine the best ways of utilizing Niger's water resources, and in May, 1963, a special government bureau was created to supervise the digging and upkeep of wells. Laws have been passed regulating slaughtering and enforcing inspection of abattoirs; a meat industry is being encouraged; and a few refrigerated warehouses have been built at the airports. The government seems determined to make Niger the leading meat-exporter of all West Africa.

At present, Niger's animal exports consist mainly of livestock, for which Nigeria is by far the most important client. Of the 160,000 cattle on the hoof exported from Niger in 1958, Nigeria took 125,000, and in the same year also bought 400,000 of the 470,000 sheep and goats sold outside the country. These official figures do not include Niger's considerable contraband trade in livestock with Nigeria, just as those for slaughtering concern only the controlled operations at Niger's eight urban abattoirs. It is estimated that from all sources 19,700 tons of meat are available annually for local consumption. Although this works out to about eighteen and a half pounds of meat consumed annually per inhabitant, which is high for a West African country, the amount is much smaller than in the other most sparsely inhabited country, Mauritania (over 46 pounds). The government would like to increase domestic consumption to improve the population's health, but it is even more eager to increase Niger's meat exports. In 1952, the French began encouraging air shipment of refrigerated meat from Niger's abattoirs to towns on the Guinea Gulf. This venture was slow in getting under way both because it took time and much money to build the necessary facilities and because until 1955 this export was in the hands of a group of butchers who practiced a paralyzing policy of small sales for high prices. In 1959, the government stepped in to establish a monopoly over meat exports. As of 1962, Niger was able to freeze 1,500 tons of fresh meat and to export 415 tons, mainly to the Ivory Coast, Dahomey, and Togo.[94] Another related activity that has recently been made subject to official controls is the production of leather and hides. By 1962, the output of such commodities, especially sheepskins, had risen to 1,445 tons, of which about two-thirds were exported and one-third made by artisans into leather objects for local use.

In the case of Niger's meat industry, the government can exert effective controls on both production and sales, for the demand in coastal towns is such that Niger could find buyers there for twice the volume of its present shipments. But in regard to hides and livestock exports, the government can only try to improve their quality and quantity. World market conditions determine the price paid for Niger's hides, and the Nigérien herders who drive their animals to the livestock markets of Ghana and Nigeria for sale have no alternative to accepting the prices offered them by local middlemen. Thus the outlook for capitalizing on Niger's vast animal resources seems most promising with respect to the export of frozen fresh meat, and here the government faces real though not insuperable obstacles. It must persuade the herders to take a more commercial view of their animals, standardize the quality of meat exports, and increase their sales by bringing down production and shipping costs. As an incentive for expanding animal husbandry, the authorities plan to set up a corned-beef factory and a tannery whose output will be destined for domestic consumption.

Mining

The hopes placed in Niger's meat industry seem to have a reasonable foundation, but those for the country's mineral resources—despite optimistic reports [95]—have not yet been justified by the discovery of commercially significant deposits. Aside from the small-scale rudimentary extraction of salt and iron by a few families of artisans, the only real mining operations in Niger have been carried on in the Aïr massif,

[94] *Marchés Tropicaux,* January 19, 1963, p. 152.
[95] See *The New York Times,* June 3, 1962.

under extremely adverse conditions, by the French-owned Société Minière du Dahomey-Niger (SMDN).[96] Between 1949 and 1962, when it abruptly ceased operating, that company exported annually from 70 to 90 tons of tin and tungsten from known reserves amounting to some 1,500 tons. Only the exceptionally high grade of these ores enabled the SMDN for thirteen years to meet the cost of developing a concentration technique that required little water, to build almost 600 miles of track in mountainous desert terrain, and to maintain and train a labor force of some hundred Touareg. To prevent the dismissal of the laborers, which might have caused difficulties in the sensitive Agadès area, and pending a reorganization of the SMDN, the government in 1962 resumed mining operations for its own account. It was able to export only 59.3 tons. Its Mines Service, in mid-1962, was reported to have found nearby a far larger tungsten deposit, but this was promptly denied either because the report was erroneous or because such a discovery might have had political repercussions.[97]

If mineral deposits are not found in northern Niger it will not be for the lack of trying. Prospecting is being actively carried on there not only by the Mines Service but by the OCRS, the French Atomic Energy Commission, Canadian geologists, and three petroleum companies.[98] Because their efforts are dispersed over a huge and scarcely accessible area little is known about them even in Niamey, but the scale of such operations is said to be larger than in any other West African country.[99] Traces of numerous minerals have been cited, but thus far the only significant finds that have been reported are of uranium in Aïr and of copper and iron near Say. Few details are known about the uranium and copper deposits, but the readily extractable iron deposits are said to amount to 100 million tons with possible reserves of several billion more. French experts are studying the best ways of handling Niger's iron and are believed to favor creating a small iron-metal industry producing only for the domestic market. Since no petroleum has yet been found in Niger and since imported fuel is very expensive, the country cannot hope to establish a large-scale metal industry. Nor would the export of iron ore be economical, given Niger's distance from world markets and the inadequate development of its means of communication. Optimistically, the gov-

[96] *La République du Niger, op. cit.,* p. 20.

[97] See pp. 223–225; also *Le Monde,* August 1, 1962.

[98] *Europe-France-Outre-Mer,* no. 408, 1er trimestre, 1964.

[99] *Nice-Matin,* January 27, 1961.

ernment drafted laws in 1961 to regulate mining and petroleum development.

Transportation

Niger has no railroad, a road system largely confined to the extreme south, a scattering of airfields only one of which can handle jet planes, and a river that is navigable between Niamey and Gaya only from October to March. Most of Niger's efforts to improve its means of communication have been concentrated on its road links with railheads in Nigeria and Dahomey, which provide access to their seaports of Lagos and Cotonou. The leaders of this landlocked country feel that they must have faster, easier, and less costly routes for their foreign trade than now exist. It is this determination that lies behind their requests for funds from the Western powers to build roads and bridges, behind the establishment of an interstate transportation commission with Nigeria, and behind the calling of an international conference to improve the navigability of the Niger River.

Niger's road system has an impressive length of 4,260 miles, but of this total 1,080 miles are mere tracks leading to the northern settlements and oases from the southern towns. Even the principal east-west highway, 780 miles long, linking Niger with Chad and Mali, is in poor condition because of the difficulties and expense of road building and upkeep. (All of the country's budgetary expenditures for roads are now absorbed by their upkeep.) In all Niger, as of January, 1962, there were only 4,302 motor vehicles. Even so modest a number represented a substantial increase over the 3,834 registered in 1958, which was probably a result of the road improvements effected in the last few years. In 1958, France financed the construction of a bridge over the Niger at Malanville, which has speeded up road traffic with Dahomey. Then the roads linking Maradi and Zinder to Nigeria were tarred. In 1964, the World Bank granted Niger a loan for $1.5 million to improve roads in the southeast with a view to facilitating the transportation of peanuts to the Nigerian frontier.[100] Late in 1962, the European Economic Community agreed to spend 3 billion CFA francs on improving Niger's roads, including the road between Dosso and Gaya, which should improve communications between Niamey and Cotonou, especially if the same source also agrees to finance the extension of the Dahomean railroad from Parakou to the Nigérien frontier. Trade with the Mali Republic should be increased by the bridge to be built with

[100] *Afrique Nouvelle,* July 9, 1964.

American financial aid connecting Niamey with the west bank of the Niger River.[101]

Not surprisingly, all these road and bridge projects—past, present, and future—are concentrated in the extreme south, Niger's most productive region. Neither the population density nor the terrain would justify or permit building more than tracks in Niger's sahl and desert zones, except as part of a far larger project to connect north and central west Africa. (In the spring of 1964, the Economic Commission for Africa recommended an itinerary for a trans-Saharan route that included a branch from Tamanrasset in southern Algeria to Agadès.) Camel caravans still ply between the Algerian oases and Agadès and Bilma, carrying dates and salt to be exchanged for millet and cloth. Obviously, rapid transport must depend on the airplane, and Niger has already become a sizable center for aviation.[102] Niamey now holds fourth place among the airports of former French West Africa in passenger and freight traffic. Secondary airfields have been built at Tahoua, Agadès, Zinder, and Maradi, and elsewhere there are eleven emergency landing strips. The official plan for promoting meat exports calls for enlarging such facilities in the pastoral zone.

Of the four airlines operating in Niger, only one—Air Afrique—is not French but was created by the UAM. Similarly, among the road-transport firms, Nigériens own only a few trucks, and the big French exporting and trucking companies handle the most remunerative traffic. The most important of these firms is the Compagnie Transafricaine, which holds the concession for carrying passengers and merchandise over 2,070 miles of road and is the only one that provides regular service between Niamey and Zinder. It can be expected that this monopoly will again be attacked by Niger's young radicals, but so far they have been unable to propose any indigenous substitute.

Fisheries

Another target for nationalistic resentment is the dominant role played by Nigerian fishermen and merchants in Niger's fish export trade.[103] Fishing provides food and a little income for the Nigériens living along the Niger and Koumandougou rivers and on the banks of Lake Chad, but almost all the professional fishermen are immigrants from Nigeria. Most of the catch, which totals over 6,000 tons a year, is

[101] *Marchés Tropicaux,* June 20, 1964.
[102] *La République du Niger, op. cit.,* pp. 21–25.
[103] *Marchés Tropicaux,* April 20, 1963, p. 944.

smoked and dried for export to Nigeria and Ghana.[104] In the markets of those countries the Nigérien who tries to sell his catch is as much at the mercy of the local middlemen as is his compatriot who drives his livestock there for sale. French experts who have studied Niger's fish resources believe that the catch could be doubled if professional fishermen were brought in from Nigeria and Mali to teach the Nigériens improved methods. Since such a move would heighten local nationalist feeling against foreign fishermen, however, and since some Nigérien tribes have taboos against handling fish, the government has not followed through on this suggestion. Niger's development plan simply calls for the construction of a warehouse to stock smoked fish to be sold when prices are favorable, and for the organization of a cooperative to enable Nigérien fishermen to purchase better equipment.

Industries

Because Niger is predominantly a producer of primary materials and lacks capital, fuel, and a skilled labor force, its industries are few in number and restricted to the processing of some local produce.[105] The oldest industry is the extraction of oil from peanuts. Oil mills were built at Maradi, Magaria, and Matamaye in 1954. They operate far below their crushing capacity (26,000 tons of peanuts a year) because difficulties are encountered in getting regular supplies and in marketing the output. The companies that own the mills are controlled by the big export firms, and it is principally the price factor that makes their operations irregular. In 1961, the government refused to grant them the subsidy they requested to modernize their mills, pending an investigation by experts as to whether it would be more economical for Niger to export shelled nuts than to crush them locally. No report on this question has yet been published, and in the meantime the government has been busy reorganizing the whole peanut industry.

Aside from Niger's other small industries, which manufacture bricks, ice, and furniture, distill perfume, grind millet, and gin cotton, the only ones of any importance are the refrigerated meat plant and the building enterprises at Niamey. In 1963, the industrial sector represented only 2.8 per cent of the gross national product and employed fewer than 3,000 persons.

Finances

The meagerness of Niger's known resources and its economic underdevelopment are inevitably reflected in its financial situation. Although

[104] *La République du Niger, op. cit.,* p. 19.   [105] *Ibid.,* p. 21.

the national budget doubled between 1958 and 1962, it is still one of the smallest in all French-speaking Africa, and in 1964 came to only 6,522 million CFA francs. Public expenses, particularly for personnel and the social services, have increased since independence. Through increased taxation and a more effective collection of taxes, revenues have been growing but more slowly and irregularly than have expenditures. In 1963, Niger was able to devote only a small sum for equipment, and even to meet one-fourth of its recurrent expenditures still depended upon outside aid, notably subsidies from France. To hasten the slow process of attaining national economic independence, the government instituted austerity measures, launched a successful national development loan, and drew up two development plans. At the same time it sent out numerous missions to solicit technical and financial aid from foreign sources, and initiated or participated in international conferences with the aim of developing jointly those natural resources which Niger shares with neighboring countries.

In August, 1964, the government took the courageous step of renouncing all subsidies from France and the Entente theretofore granted to help it balance its operating budget, intensified its policy of austerity, and increased the rates of many of its taxes. Although its expenditures for economic and social development are continuing to increase and the only exceptional revenue it has received is 50 million CFA francs as Niger's share from the liquidation of the holdings belonging to the French West African Federation, the government expects to balance its 1965 budget wholly from local revenues.[106]

Planning

The goals of Niger's three-year plan were announced in January, 1961, by President Diori, who said that it was but the forerunner of a more ambitious ten-year plan. Like those of other French-speaking African states, these plans are aimed at creating national unity, raising the population's living and cultural standards, and achieving economic independence.[107] Priority has been given to counteracting Niger's isolation by developing its means of communication, internally and externally: this objective was allotted one-quarter of the first plan's total amount of 15 billion CFA francs. The school system is to be rapidly expanded so that trained Nigériens can replace the foreign experts now employed by the government. To raise local living standards, the

[106] *Marchés Tropicaux*, September 5, 1964, p. 2140.
[107] See J. E. Kouawo, "Le Nouveau Plan Décennal du Niger," *Afrique Nouvelle*, May 28, 1964.

planners have begun to set up various organizations to develop agriculture, especially animal husbandry. Modest industrialization is also envisaged, but before any major projects are launched the authors of the plan are trying to determine more precisely Niger's resources and needs. Thus most of the funds for the interim plan were earmarked for studies and inventories and for propaganda to win the population's cooperation in carrying out the program. The French expert in charge of Niger's planning has persuaded PPN leaders to avoid spectacular schemes and to concentrate on spadework. Diori seems to realize that in terms of concrete improvements he cannot expect too much too soon.[108]

Foreign Trade

The domain in which the government has thus far moved most resolutely is foreign trade, and its action has already had a revolutionary effect on Niger's economy. Customs duties, particularly on peanut and livestock exports, have been the backbone of local revenues. The government is trying to increase their yield by stopping the contraband trade with Nigeria, eliminating the large profits being made by foreign middlemen, and increasing production both for export and for domestic consumption. Nigeria is officially cooperating, but the practical problems involved in policing so long a frontier are difficult to overcome. The increase of taxation in Nigeria early in 1964, however, is expected to curtail smuggling. Preferential trade agreements with France have long enabled Niger to market almost all its peanuts advantageously, but they have also permitted France to supply Niger with at least half its high-priced imports. French subsidies until 1964 were regarded as indispensable to balancing Niger's budget, and still are to financing its development projects. Consequently, the PPN leaders have been eager to retain the advantages of this arrangement and for some time after independence they moved cautiously within the existing framework.

Nigérien leaders still prefer not to apply radical policies.[109] Only the inability or unwillingness of local French businessmen to adapt themselves to competition and official controls, and the prospect of a drastically altered trade situation—especially as regards peanut sales—arising from Niger's association with the European Common Market have induced Niger's government to tighten its grip on the local economy. In fact, Diori and his colleagues were deeply disappointed when

[108] *Afrique Nouvelle,* June 21, 1961; *West Africa,* March 3, 1962.

[109] Diori's Independence Day speech, broadcast over Radio Niamey, August 3, 1962.

the resident French firms showed no enthusiasm for their first moderate proposals. Despite a new code guaranteeing the security of foreign investments, the Niamey Chamber of Commerce (composed almost exclusively of vested French interests) did no more than voice empty pledges of cooperation with the government. Its members continued to impose arbitrarily high prices on the goods they imported and refused to invest locally more than a small percentage of their profits. In 1960, when they repatriated 3 billion CFA francs and invested only 700 million in Niger, they were able to plead that the government's instability and its failure to negotiate new agreements with France after independence gave them insufficient security.[110] The next year, however, when such excuses were groundless, they remained intransigent, and the government reluctantly adopted a more aggressive policy to bring the economy more under its own control.

In some domains like the export of live animals and the retail trade in isolated areas, the government's new controls did not affect the established French firms. But they felt their very foundations undermined when, in 1961–1962, the government established a national development bank, a monopoly over the export and crushing of peanuts (Sonara), two building companies (Les Batisseurs Nigériens and Sonuci), and a chain of retail stores in the main towns (Coproniger). The government promised in vain that it would leave to the private sector the wholesale trade and large blocks of stock in the new companies and would entrust technical management of the latter to private business. Not only did the French firms refuse to help set up the new organizations but two of the largest among them—the Banque Nationale du Commerce et de l'Industrie and the Compagnie Française du Niger—pulled out of the country in 1962. The few French firms operating in Niger were simply branches of companies based elsewhere, and the volume of local business probably seemed negligible to their directors. In any case, their withdrawal enabled the government to substitute other companies and give two African countries the opportunity to win Niger's gratitude by their cooperation. The experienced cooperative society of Upper Volta helped with the technical aspects of setting up Coproniger, and a Tunisian bank took 15 per cent of its stock.

Diori has repeatedly said that his economic policy is pragmatic and that he rejects both *dirigisme* and laisser-faire. The withdrawal of the established French firms has forced him, however, to expand state controls. Diori continues to insist that his primary motive in founding

[110] *Nice-Matin,* January 27, 1961.

Coproniger was to stimulate production by enabling Niger's most isolated populations to buy cheap essential consumer goods as a result of increased output. His government has, nevertheless, become increasingly involved in the retail trade. Five stores have already been opened at Niamey, Zinder, Maradi, Madaoua, and Tahoua, and more are projected for the nomad zones. As a consequence of direct measures and of Coproniger's operations, consumer goods are now cheaper and more abundant in Niger, and this success has encouraged the trend toward a state-controlled economy. Coproniger is already planning to expand its trading operations and the government intends to establish factories to make plastics, cement, perfumes, and so forth. In the absence of sufficient local private enterprise and capital, it is inevitable that the government should play the dominant role in their creation and control, but to enable them to come into existence at all the cooperation of foreign countries is indispensable.

Foreign Aid and International Cooperation

Between 1949 and 1960, France granted Niger a total of 6,218 billion CFA francs, and since independence Niger has continued to receive French subsidies on an even more generous scale. In 1963, France invested 1,400 million CFA francs to promote Niger's economic and social development. Moreover, the Diori government has obtained substantial aid by negotiating agreements with twelve other countries. In 1962 alone, funds from various French sources amounted to 4,350 milion CFA francs, the Common Market countries provided 4,500 million, American monetary aid came to 500 million, and technical assistance came from Israel and the United Nations. Diori is naturally encouraged by such an increase of foreign-aid investments in Niger, as well as by the success of his national development loan, but much more money must be found if he is to carry out even the three-year interim plan.

In other directions, too, Diori has sought to enlist international cooperation, particularly to develop the Niger River and the Chad basin. Agadès has been made the headquarters of a recently organized African Institute for Arid Zones, and Dr. Francis Borrey, former French Union Assemblyman from Niger, is in charge of a vast project to develop the Chad basin for the benefit of the populations living there. François Tombalbaye, president of the Republic of Chad, is as enthusiastic about the potential of this institute as Diori, but it took time to convince President Ahidjo of Cameroun and even more the Prime Minister of Nigeria of its importance.[111] Eventually, in May, 1964, these four men signed an agreement for the development of the Chad basin which also respected the sovereign rights of each state in that area.

What is to Diori a far more important program is the development of the resources of the Niger River to stimulate the economies of all the countries through which it flows. Diori first started working on the Niger project in August, 1960, but it was not until February, 1963, that he managed to convene a conference at Niamey that brought together representatives of seven riverine countries, only Mali and Cameroun being absent. The agreement drafted at this conference aimed to supersede as an all-African project the Act of Berlin of 1885 drafted by the European imperialist powers, while retaining that Act's provisions guaranteeing freedom of navigation on the Niger River. It went much farther than the 1885 agreement by providing for the signatories' joint development of the river's resources, specifically of navigation, fishing, and hydroelectric energy. In October, 1963, representatives of all nine countries signed the agreement at a second meeting in Niamey. If this agreement is ratified by all the countries concerned, it may provide the framework for the realization of two of Diori's fondest desires: opening the Niger River to navigation between Niamey and Lagos and utilizing the river's energy as the basis for coordinating Niger's industrial projects with those of Nigeria.

The Political Process

FORMAL STRUCTURE

Within two years after it had become a republic, Niger had successively adopted two constitutions, both approved by the assembly elected on December 14, 1958. The first constitution, that of February 25, 1959, made Niger an indivisible, secular, democratic republic, which would collaborate closely with other member states of the French Community and would guarantee to its population civil liberties as defined in the 1789 Declaration of the Rights of Man. National sovereignty, it stated, belonged to the people, who could exercise it either through their elected representatives or by means of a referendum. All citizens of both sexes who had come of age were entitled to vote. The Republic's official language was to be French.

According to this first constitution, the Republic's basic structure rested on four main organs: the premiership, the National Assembly,

[111] *Le Monde Diplomatique,* February, 1963.

the State court, and the Economic and Social Council. The Premier was to be named by the unicameral legislative assembly and invested by an absolute majority of its sixty members. Assemblymen were to be elected by direct universal suffrage for a five-year term. The State court was to have three sections: one to judge the constitutionality of laws, another to deal with civil cases, and the third to audit official accounts. Provision was also made for a High Court of Justice, to be composed of assemblymen elected to it by their peers. Should the Premier or any of his ministers be indicted by the Assembly for crimes or misdemeanors committed in the performance of their duties, this court was empowered to try them. Finally, there was to be an Economic and Social Council to advise the Premier on economic and social laws which he submitted to it.

This constitution instituted a parliamentary regime in Niger, for the Premier was made responsible to the Assembly. But after his investiture three years had to elapse before he might pose a question of confidence or the Assembly pass a motion censuring the government. Then, if a simple majority of the assemblymen refused their confidence, or if two-thirds of them voted a motion of censure, the government had to resign and the Assembly would be dissolved. The time-lag required before governmental responsibility could be challenged, followed, if successful, by the automatic dissolution of the Assembly, was obviously designed to promote stability. The executive branch was certainly preponderant, for the Assembly could only initiate and pass legislation in specific spheres, and under certain circumstances the Premier was able to legislate by decree.

The independence that Niger acquired on August 3, 1960, made it necessary to adopt a new constitution, which was done on November 8 of that year. At the same time Niger acquired its own flag, a national anthem ("La Nigérienne"), and a motto, "Fraternity, Work, and Progress." The official language, State court, and Economic and Social Council remained as before. The main change made by the new constitution was to give Niger a presidential regime, like those adopted by its Entente partners at the same time. The President of the Republic now not only wields full executive powers but is no longer responsible to the Assembly, and he can be judged by the High Court only if he is charged with high treason. He is elected directly by all qualified voters, and he may be re-elected upon completion of his five-year term. The President names and dismisses his ministers, who cannot at the same time be members of the Assembly. He is commander-in-chief of the armed forces and head of the civil administration, is charged with negotiating treaties, and is empowered to pardon criminals. With the consent of the Assembly's executive committee, he may consult the population on any issue by means of a referendum.

At the same time, by the same electorate, and for the same term, Niger's assemblymen are chosen from a single national slate of candidates. The Assembly votes the budget and also the draft laws submitted to it either by the President or by one of its members. If he approves of a bill rejected by the Assembly, or if he disapproves of one the Assembly has accepted, the President can ask for reconsideration, but to become law under such circumstances the bill has to be passed by two-thirds of the assemblymen.

On November 9, 1960, Diori Hamani was the sole candidate for the presidency of the Niger Republic, and he was elected unanimously.

THE ROLE OF THE JUDICIARY

Niger's judicial system has been reorganized several times since the French West African Federation was dissolved in 1959. A court of appeals was then established at Niamey, which eliminated Niger's previous dependence on that of Cotonou in Dahomey. To replace justices of the peace, courts of first instance were set up at Zinder (with sections at Maïne-Soroa and N'Guigmi) and at Niamey (with sections at Agadès and Birni N'Konni). In criminal cases the courts applied the French penal code; in commercial and civil cases between Nigériens, courts at all levels applied customary law. At that time there were seventeen career magistrates in Niger, almost all of them French.

After Niger became independent in August, 1960, more changes were made in this system. On July 1, 1961, a high court of justice was created, but it was not until March 1, 1962, that the whole system was overhauled. At that time the courts applying customary law were suppressed, though the traditional chiefs and *cadis* retained their authority in the conciliation of disputes. Concurrently, labor courts were instituted, a third court of first instance was created at Maradi, and justices of the peace with varying degrees of jurisdiction were posted to areas where no tribunals had previously existed. The importance of this reinforcement of the judicial structure was overshadowed, however, by that of the legal reforms undertaken at the same time. Niger was the first French-speaking African country to draft and adopt its own penal code and to begin work on a civil code. On the second anniversary of his country's independence, Diori was able to state that Niger had a judicial code, a nationality law, and courts "adapted to our particular conditions and the diversity of our traditions." [112]

On many occasions, PPN leaders have stressed the independence of their country's judiciary. Nonetheless, they have not hesitated to revise the penal code and to strengthen the hand of the executive by extralegal devices when they believed their party's authority was being challenged. Opening the 1962–1963 session of Niamey's Court of Appeal, Diori revealed his conception of the "independence" of the judiciary:

Independence does not mean opposition to the executive, nor does it entitle the judiciary to ignore the will of Parliament. True independence consists in being able to remain unmoved in the face of pressures and solicitations to which judges are sometimes subject. . . . The independence which has been sanctioned by the constitution and guaranteed by the president of the republic is not granted to judges (who are named by the government) for their own personal interests but for those of the accused.[113]

LOCAL GOVERNMENT

As in other newly independent countries of French-speaking Africa, in Niger more local governmental institutions have been set up and more administrative units have been created since the country became a republic. Progress in this respect, however, has been impeded by the vast area and meager population and by the government's preoccupation with other matters.

Only three weeks before the referendum of September 28, 1958, the Sawaba government had passed a law creating circumscription councils. According to its provisions, each circumscription was to have its own budget and elected council, but there is no evidence that the authors of this law seriously intended to decentralize the administration. Control over the new councils was vested in the Minister of the Interior, whose appointees—the circumscription officials—were to be present at all council meetings and to represent the central administration. This project was shelved after the defeat of its Sawaba sponsors, and for a long time the PPN was too absorbed in its own struggle with Djibo and in its foreign relations to revive the plan. In fact, no elections were held even to replace the Niamey municipal council which was dissolved in February, 1959, in order to oust Djibo and his Sawaba

---

[112] Radio Niamey, August 3, 1962. [113] *Ibid.*, November 6, 1962.

followers. In the whole country, Niamey is still the only full commune —that is, it has an elected mayor and council. Zinder has a mayor appointed by the government, and at Maradi some councilors and the mayor are appointees of the administration.

It was not until October, 1959, that the government made any moves to encourage local governmental institutions, and then it simply created five new circumscriptions in order to break up a few overlarge *cercles.* As of 1963, Niamey and Tahoua *cercles* each had three circumscriptions; Agadès, Birni N'Konni, Dosso, Gouré, Madaoua, Magaria, Maradi, Tessamou, Tillabéri, and Zinder, two each; and the remaining ones—Dogondoutchi, Filingué, N'Guigmi, and Téra—were still administered as units. After independence was attained, the government began to favor the creation of circumscription councils as a handy means of indirectly undermining the powers of the traditional chieftaincy. Late in 1960, Diori sent out an official mission which was to tour the country and determine where and when elections for such local councils should be held. Still another year passed before a law creating elected circumscription councils was passed on December 31, 1961. Nothing more was heard of this project until the following March, when it was announced that the government was drawing up, "without passion or prejudice," lists of candidates for the new councils.[114] The aim of such councils, Diori said in his Independence Day speech on August 3, 1962, was to "achieve better results in the remotest regions" through a decentralization of the administration.[115]

At long last, on December 2 and 3, 1962, elections took place and, as expected, resulted in a great success for the PPN. The only surprising element in this event was the large turnout of voters. Massive abstentions have characterized other elections in Niger, but on this occasion 86 per cent of the registered electorate (then numbering 1,387,053) reportedly went to the polls.[116] Officials hailed this large-scale participation as evidence of the growth of civic spirit among the Nigériens. A more likely explanation is that the government party machine had become more effective and that its leaders were anxious to revitalize the PPN by winning wider support from the rural population. In May, 1963, elaborate ceremonies marked the inauguration of the circumscription councils. Budgets for these new councils in 1964 totaled 564,503,950 CFA francs—a sum equal to about one-twelfth of the whole Nigérien budget.

[114] *Afrique Nouvelle,* April 4, 1962.   [115] Radio Niamey, August 3, 1962.
[116] *Afrique Nouvelle,* December 14, 1962.

Contemporary Issues

The goals of Niger's present government are the same as those of other French-speaking Negro governments; national unity and economic independence. In trying to realize these goals, Niger faces to a greater degree the same handicaps that they do. These handicaps consist of a poor, uneducated, and disease-ridden population scattered over a vast and largely unproductive area; cleavages between tribes, regions, and generations; a very small elite; and the lack of internal and external communications and of developed natural resources.

The PPN is trying to give Niger a genuine *raison d'être* against great odds. But the outcome of this uphill struggle depends very largely on outside forces. Niger's present government is politically and economically weak because it is not based on wide popular support but, even more, because it depends heavily on foreign aid. To some extent, however, the hope for Niger's survival as a national entity is that its liabilities may also be assets. It is to the interest of other countries that so huge and centrally located a land mass not be torn by strife which would invite outside intervention. And if its resources do not spontaneously attract foreign capital on a large scale, they have the advantage of not arousing the covetousness of Niger's more powerful neighbors.

Niger's lack of natural boundaries and its political frontiers with seven other countries are not the only reasons that its foreign relations are so vitally important to the achievement of national unity and to the maintenance of its territorial integrity. Because all tribal groups in its population are members of larger tribal units living outside Niger's borders, centrifugal tendencies are strong and have deeply influenced Niger's political evolution. In the north of Niger, the perennially anarchic and restless Touareg are more attracted to independent Algeria, which is governed by Arabs, than to the administration at Niamey, which is controlled by Negroes. In the south the Hausa, numerically the largest tribal group in Niger, are drawn to their fellow tribesmen in Nigeria, in part because they are politically dominated by a government run by the better-educated Djerma-Songhai.

The threat of secession in the south has seemed until very recently more alarming to the PPN leaders than that in the north, for in the late 1950's it looked as if the Nigérien Hausa might move to join Northern Nigeria. Djibo Bakary championed such a union, but his sponsorship proved fatal to it in 1958 because he alienated the chiefs in both Niger and Nigeria. Sovereign Nigeria now seems to be quite indifferent to the

Hausa secessionist movement in Niger. Since the two countries became independent and after Djibo had fled from Niger, the Nigerian government established good relations with Djibo's opponent and successor, Diori.

In many ways the personality and career of Djibo Bakary illustrate the major obstacles which Niger faces on its road to national unity. He is the only leader Niger has produced so far who might have welded its peoples together. Unlike Diori and Boubou Hama, Djibo was able to rally mass support with his dynamism and magnetism and to attract the youthful elite with his radical program. At the same time he lacked the flexibility and sense of timing of the PPN leaders. To his miscalculation in underestimating the power of the traditional chiefs and his persistence in advocating Marxist doctrines in Niger after the tide had turned against such extremism, he added more serious errors. He voluntarily left his native land; he sought support from foreign countries; and he refused to compromise with the PPN and return home. In 1962, his host countries began to withdraw their support for his cause and to make peace with Diori in the interests of African unity. This picture of Djibo as a lone figure whose voice was crying in the African wilderness changed abruptly in late 1964.

As yet too little is known about the scope and origin of the outbreaks that occurred in Niger during the fall of 1964 to assess the degree to which they were given support by outside forces. Certainly they would never have been instigated or would have taken place at so many wisely dispersed places had Djibo not felt assured and received support from a considerable following inside the country. What is mainly uncertain is the degree to which this uprising—if such it can be called —stemmed from sentiments of personal loyalty to Djibo and devotion to the principles enunciated by the Sawaba party or derived from a widespread discontent with the PPN government. This discontent has its origin in the antagonisms between regions and tribes and between the younger and older members of Niger's elite, which have been heightened by the authoritarian and conservative character of the PPN government and the nepotism practiced by its leaders. Not only have the PPN leaders not come to grips with the problems created by these basic antagonisms but they have consistently denied their very existence.

The Diori regime has never had secure foundations because it lacks broadly based support. It came to power largely for negative reasons. When the traditional chiefs recognized that Djibo was their enemy they deserted him and threw their considerable weight behind Diori, whose party offered the only politically organized alternative to the Sawaba. But the feudal lords have never given their wholehearted support to Diori and Boubou Hama because the two did not belong to the chieftaincy and because they had been associated with the RDA during its radical period. Nor have Diori and Boubou Hama ever fully trusted the chiefs, except perhaps a few of the more progressive ones. In fact, they have been moving steadily, though cautiously, to reduce the powers of the chieftaincy.

Prudence has been the keynote of their policy, for in 1957 and again in 1958 the chiefs demonstrated that they could still deliver the vote that unseated and made governments in Niger. A frontal attack on their position by a political party would cause them to close ranks effectively against it. Moreover, Diori and Boubou Hama are grateful to the chiefs whose support enabled them to come to power, and they realize that the chiefs still represent the cement that holds the country's social structure together. On the other hand, being Western-educated politicians, they cannot approve of chieftaincy as an institution, and they know that their alliance with the chiefs is antagonizing the youthful intelligentsia which will govern Niger in the future. In principle and in practice, the young Nigérien elite is hostile to the chiefs because they are vestiges of an obsolete feudalism and because they abuse their power. Since there is no common ideological ground on which all Nigériens can agree, Diori and Boubou Hama have tried to steer a middle course between the conservative and radical elements—without pleasing either. To provide the framework and cohesion needed to keep themselves in power and to carry out their program, they have resorted to the single-party system that is so widespread in French-speaking Africa. In this system the PPN has made room for some of the youthful elite and for several handpicked traditional chiefs, but it never apparently tried to associate the Hausa and Touareg tribes closely with a government that has remained under the control of Djerma-Songhai commoners.

Like the leaders of similar African governments, Diori and Boubou Hama have insisted that Niger has no need of an organized opposition. There is an Alice-in-Wonderland quality to their assertions that no opposition exists in the country because none should exist. Yet from the outset it was obvious that the government had tribal and political opponents, on both the right and extreme left. As time went on, it became increasingly evident that the PPN had not succeeded in eliminating by repressive measures all opposition to the single-party system it had instituted. Even the solid PPN Assembly showed some resistance, as on February 22, 1962, when its members rejected the government's request for an eighteen-month extension of its special powers. In particular, they refused to permit the government to make changes in the budget by simple decree, and to make the wives of civil servants, military officers, and traders liable to head tax.[117] Increasingly, the chiefs resented the government's attempts to transform them into agents of the central administration.

To the casual observer, however, the government of Niger appeared to be stable and to control the country through the steady expansion of the PPN organization. Moreover, Diori seemed to have been remarkably successful in persuading neighboring countries to refrain from encouraging secessionist movements that could break Niger asunder and in inducing the wealthy Western nations to finance his economic development program. Djibo's attempt to overthrow the PPN government and stage a comeback in late 1964 showed up the basic weaknesses in Diori's position, and forced him to abandon his ostrich-like attitude toward their existence. As of the present writing it seems unlikely that Djibo, who has long been away from his country, can effectively rally the Nigérien malcontents to his banner and return to the leadership of Niger. Nor is it at all certain that he can persuade his external supporters—all of them officially committed to a policy of noninterference in the internal affairs of other African nations—to intervene more actively in his behalf. Yet he will at least have succeeded in gravely weakening the PPN government if he has unleashed the centrifugal forces inside Niger so that it cannot maintain order.

All the newly independent countries of West Africa require time, peaceful conditions, and technical and financial help for their development, but Diori's government is particularly dependent on the forbearance and generosity of outside forces. Niger has little to offer in terms of either weighty political support or opportunities for economic gain, and it seems likely to remain indefinitely on the receiving end of any international agreements it makes. In soliciting support from as wide a range of sources as possible, Diori has been perhaps—consciously or unconsciously—counting upon Niger's nuisance value as his trump card. But if his government does not prove strong enough to keep order in Niger, his neighbors and the overseas powers may no longer find it worth their while to pay the price he has been asking for

[117] *Ibid.*, February 28, 1962.

support of his leadership and the maintenance of Niger's present frontiers.

External Relations

Houphouët and the Council of the Entente

For some time after he came to power in December, 1958, Diori Hamani pursued a foreign policy that seemed merely a pale reflection of that of Houphouët-Boigny. From the inception of the RDA, he had been one of Houphouët's closest and most faithful followers, and even after he became president of an independent republic he never flagged in his loyalty to the Ivory Coast leader. In the spring of 1959, when Houphouët proposed forming a Council of the Entente, Diori at once welcomed the idea and even helped persuade Dahomey to join it. A few weeks later he again followed Houphouët's lead by joining the West African Customs Union.

Gradually Diori came to succeed Ouezzin Coulibaly (former senator of the Ivory Coast who died in 1958) as Houphouët's most trusted lieutenant and emissary. To this task he brought the valuable experience he had gained as a deputy and then as a vice-president of the French National Assembly (June, 1957–December, 1958) and as a member of the French delegation to the Assembly of Europe at Strasbourg (March, 1958). So loyal and competent was Diori that Houphouët used him increasingly not only to settle differences within the Entente but to prepare the ground for the successive groups that he organized among the new African states. In April, 1960, Diori was sent to the four countries of French Equatorial Africa, whose leaders he helped induce to join (in December, 1960) the Brazzaville bloc of twelve moderate French-speaking African countries which formed the Union Africaine et Malgache (UAM) in March, 1961. This success caused Houphouët to use Diori as his intermediary in improving relations between the UAM and the Guinea-Ghana-Mali Union. Though there were other cogent reasons that led to the reorientation of "revolutionary" Africa's policies, Diori's successive visits to Mali, Ghana, and Guinea certainly contributed to their leaders' *rapprochement* with "reformist" Africa in 1962–1963.

Because Diori undertook so many delicate missions on behalf of the RDA president, it was not always realized that he might have valid reasons of his own for supporting Houphouët's foreign policy. If Diori had not sincerely believed in the cause of African unity, he would certainly not have consented to visit Mali, Guinea, and Ghana—the very countries that had harbored and encouraged his bitterest enemy, Djibo Bakary. But there was more to his policies than this. Like Houphouët, although for very different reasons, Diori had resented the French government-general at Dakar, which he accused of having neglected Niger grievously in both the economic and cultural spheres. He believed that any attempt to form a primary federation in West Africa would simply restore the government-general. Therefore he refused to be represented at the federalist congress held at Bamako late in December, 1958. Then when Djibo urged that Niger join the Mali Federation, formed early in 1959, Diori had an additional reason to follow Houphouët's lead in opposing it. Diori realized, too, that because of its geographical location and poverty Niger could not afford to remain isolated in Africa. This became urgent particularly after the dissolution of the government-general in March, 1959, had eliminated the rebates (virtually subsidies) which his country had been receiving from the federal budget. So for both ideological and practical reasons Diori was glad to join the Entente on May 29, 1959, and thus have Niger benefit from the subsidies which the rich Ivory Coast channeled to its junior partners—Niger, Dahomey, and Upper Volta—through that council's solidarity fund. In 1960, Niamey was made the headquarters of the Entente's permanent secretariat and Diori himself became president of the council for that year.

Primarily it is the political and personal ties between Diori and Houphouët that bind their two countries together, although the Ivory Coast has the additional attraction of providing seasonal employment for thousands of Nigérien laborers. It must be noted, however, that an equally large number of Nigériens annually go to work in Ghana, with which government Diori has generally been on chilly terms.

Between Niger and Upper Volta there is a striking lack of political contact outside their joint membership in the Entente. Despite their common frontier and some recent coordination in their trading policies, the leaders of these two countries did not exchange visits until 1963, when they met several times mainly to discuss frontier problems, though they encountered each other frequently at conferences of the Entente. To be sure, in February, 1960, Diori rushed to Ouagadougou to help patch up the quarrel that had developed between Upper Volta's premier, Maurice Yaméogo, and Houphouët. At that time, however, Diori seemed far less concerned with the validity of Yaméogo's grievances against Houphouët than he was lest Upper Volta withdraw from the Entente and thereby isolate Niger physically from the Ivory Coast.

It is with Dahomey that Niger is linked most directly. Under the French administration Niger was encouraged to use Cotonou as its seaport; and after independence, from both political and economic motives, Dahomey and Niger reinforced the ties between them. Although both Diori and Premier Hubert Maga took the initiative in improving their relations with Nigeria and continued to use Lagos as a supplementary port, each leader was drawn to the other by fear of being swallowed up by their powerful neighbor. Therefore they perpetuated and expanded Opération Hirondelle; [118] Dahomey associated Niger with the management of its raiload; and Niger planned to make greater use of Cotonou after that city's deepwater port is completed. In January, 1963, Maga and Diori went to Brussels together to plead with the European Economic Community for aid in financing the extension of the railroad from Parakou to Dosso and the surfacing of a road from Niamey to Zinder. That same month, Diori was the first Entente leader to proffer aid to Maga in fighting any subversive movement that might have arisen in Dahomey as a result of the assassination of Olympio in neighboring Togo.[119]

Relations between Dahomey and Niger changed profoundly and adversely after October, 1963, when the "revolution" in Dahomey overthrew the administration of Maga, a lifelong friend of Diori, and supplanted it with an army-backed government headed by Maga's two rivals, S. M. Apithy and Justin Ahomadegbé. In the course of this self-styled revolution three Nigériens living in Dahomey were killed and several others wounded. This might have been overlooked as an incidental, although tragic, by-product of the Dahomean coup had subsequent developments not caused relations between Niger and the new Dahomean leaders to deteriorate rapidly. Early in December, a company of the Niger army mutinied briefly in protest against the transfer of its commanding officer, a brother-in-law of Yacouba Diallo, Minister of Defense. It was widely believed in Niamey at the time that the mutiny had been stirred up either by some locally stationed French technical aides or by the Dahomean residents in Niger, or both. Although no precise information was given by the Nigérien authorities, this conviction was certainly not unrelated to the violent speeches made by Boubou Hama against interference from French "reactionary"

[118] See below, pp. 220–221.   [119] Radio Cotonou, January 17, 1963.

elements or to the dismissal and arrest of Zodi Ikhia, Minister for African Affairs, on vague charges of plotting. At about the same time an
old quarrel was revived between Dahomey and Niger over ownership
of Lété Island in the Niger River. Late in December, after accusing
Dahomey of preparing to take the island by force, the Niger government suddenly ordered all the Dahomeans employed in the administration [120] to leave the country within twenty days.

Obviously, a small island—about 5 miles by .5 mile, submerged for
eight months of the year and only fitfully occupied by herders—was
not the basic cause of the tension between the two countries. Rather, it
was the Nigérien fear that the local Dahomeans might try to carry out
in Niger a revolution analogous to the one in their own country. This
rekindled the alarm over subversion that had been felt ever since the
assassination of Sylvanus Olympio. It also reawakened the old grievances against the resident Dahomeans and against Niger's chronic
dependence on the port at Cotonou. As to the Dahomean leaders, they
were first irked by the aspersions openly cast on their "revolution" by
Diori (and by Houphouët); then, after they were forced to cope with
the problem of absorbing their compatriots deported from Niger, they
became hostile toward all the other members of the Council of the
Entente. Soon the conflict was transposed to a larger domain, and the
frontier between Niger and Dahomey was closed, with detrimental
effects on the economies of both states.

Leaders of neighboring nations hastily offered their services as medi-
ators, but early in 1964, charging Niger with maltreatment of the
deportees, Dahomey referred the dispute to the United Nations. Gradually, however, wiser counsel prevailed, conciliatory gestures were
made by both sides, and the frontier was eventually reopened. The
Niger government offered compensation to its former Dahomean employees, and both parties agreed to negotiate their claims to Lété Island. Although these negotiations broke down in early July, Apithy at
once held out an olive branch. In a speech made a few days later near
the Nigérien frontier, he spoke warmly of the many bonds between the
two countries and even expressed the hope that one day they might
form a single nation.[121] Obviously both sides would like to restore
good relations, but without losing too much face. The entire episode
might be dismissed as a tempest in a teapot if it did not have serious

[120] Radio Cotonou in a broadcast on December 27, 1963, claimed that 16,000
Dahomeans had been dismissed by the Niger government.

[121] *Afrique Nouvelle,* July 23, 1964.

implications for the future of all African minorities and for Dahomey's future relations with other members of the Entente.

To parry common dangers and to achieve mutually advantageous economic objectives, Diori has always advocated collaboration with like-minded African leaders. Nevertheless, he still shies away from any political unions that might deprive him of the freedom of maneuver which he now enjoys within the Entente and deflect him from his task of devising a foreign policy adapted to Niger's particular needs. The issues which he regards as the most important for Niger's immediate future are its relations with Nigeria and its relations with the other Saharan countries. No major conflict has developed between these issues and his assistance to Houphouët in promoting African unity.

Diori consistently supported a negotiated peace between France and the Provisional Government of Algeria, which would place the Algerian Sahara under the sovereignty of an independent regime based at Algiers, and which would also leave a large place in the development of the great desert's resources for France and the African countries that have territory in the Sahara. The closer relations with Nigeria which Diori has taken pains to knit fell happily within the pattern of cooperation between French- and English-speaking Africa established by the charter of the Monrovia group. (This was composed of the twelve Brazzaville-bloc nations and Nigeria, Sierra Leone, Tunisia, Togo, Somalia, Ethiopia, Libya, and Liberia, whose representatives held their first meeting at Monrovia in 1961.) In his dealings with Algeria and Nigeria since their independence, however, Diori has been moved by considerations peculiarly Nigérien and irrelevant to the wider issue of African unity.

Relations with Nigeria

Diori's policy in regard to Nigeria has been molded not only by Niger's geographical and ethnic situation but also by his own struggle with Djibo Bakary during the campaign on the referendum of September, 1958. At that time Djibo adroitly capitalized on the desire of his fellow Nigériens in the southern and central regions for closer ties with British Nigeria. Technically, the Hausa of central Niger and the Peul of the eastern zone are separated from their kinsmen to the south by a frontier over 720 miles long, although that boundary had been so porous that in practice contraband and individuals flowed freely across it. Nigériens could readily sell their food crops and animals for sterling in Nigerian markets, where they were able to buy rice and manufactured goods at prices lower than those prevailing in Niger. Zinder, the political capital of the Nigérien Hausa, was the distribution center for goods imported from Nigeria for the eastern zone of N'Guigmi, Maïne-Soroa, and Gouré. The Peul and Manga of that vast, poorly administered region were dependent on Nigeria for even their basic food, and for trading they used Nigerian pounds to the virtual exclusion of the CFA franc. For western Niger Maradi played a similar role, and it was also the commercial crossroads through which most of Niger's peanut crop was channeled to the Nigerian railroad for export via Lagos.

In part because that railroad's carrying capacity was too limited to handle all Niger's growing peanut exports, and in part to save foreign currency, the French launched Opération Hirondelle in the mid-1950's, hoping to deflect some of these exports to the Dahomean port of Cotonou. The basis of this operation was a fleet of some twenty heavy-duty trucks. After the peanut harvest, trucks left the Dahomean railhead at Parakou each day on an extraordinary triangular circuit that covered about 1,500 miles. The trucks transported to Niamey imported goods brought by the railroad to Parakou, then continued empty to Birni N'Konni, where they loaded peanuts, after which they returned to Parakou via Dosso. Although this operation was speeded up by road improvements and the construction of a bridge across the Niger River at Gaya, it has been longer and more costly than the Maradi-Nigeria route. Yet for both the French and the present Nigérien government, the route has had the dual advantage of lying wholly in the CFA franc zone and of keeping Niger from complete economic dependence on Nigeria.

Realizing that Opération Hirondelle did nothing to diminish the ethnic and commercial attraction of Nigeria for Niger's Hausa and Peul, Djibo had sought their support for his policy of voting against the French Community in the 1958 referendum. He argued that a sovereign Niger could form some sort of union with Nigeria, which was itself soon to become independent. Not only would this reunite the Hausa and Peul who were kept apart by frontier barriers and formalities, but in addition, he claimed, aid from rich Nigeria could readily replace that which Niger had been receiving from France. Consequently, he argued, Nigérien living standards would rise to the higher level prevailing across the southern border. Such a prospect naturally pleased the rank and file of Niger's southern peoples but it alienated their chiefs, above all those of the Djerma-Songhai, who feared domination by Nigeria's powerful Hausa emirs. They therefore banded together against

Djibo's Sawaba and, with the support of the French administration, succeeded as we have seen in making Niger a member of the Community. The PPN government which succeeded that of Djibo was almost wholly a Djerma-Songhai combine that excluded the Hausa from any effective share in political power.

Although the PPN was able to consolidate political power in its own hands, its leaders realized that they could never reduce Nigeria's economic influence upon Niger as long as the latter did not produce enough food and clothing for its own population. Yet any appreciable increase in Niger's food crops and industrialization would require many years, and in the meantime the danger of secession in southeastern and central Niger grew stronger as the two neighboring countries neared independence. Retention of the southern zone was imperative if Niger was to survive as a sovereign state, for it contained 60 per cent of the entire population, 92 per cent of Niger's peanut production, and 70 per cent of its herds. Therefore, while aligning Niger with the Council of the Entente, Diori at the same time laid the foundations for friendlier relations with Nigeria. At first, Diori's expression of confidence in the "wisdom of Northern Nigeria in dispelling certain threats concerning creation of the Hausa-land" [122] seemed misplaced, for the Sardauna of Sokoto said in October, 1960, that Niger had once been a part of his ancestors' empire and "belonged to us." The Sardauna's irredentism remained vague, however, and was offset by the support that Diori's enemy, Djibo, had given to Mallam Aminu Kano, founder of the Northern Elements Progressive Union, which was hostile to the Sardauna and his fellow chiefs. Moreover, Ghana's pan-African propaganda was at this time inciting Nigeria to draw closer to the conservative elements in French-speaking Africa. For all these reasons the Northern Nigerians became responsive to Diori's advances. In December, 1960, Northern Nigeria's prime minister went to Niger to attend a session of its National Assembly. He expressed fraternal sentiments and remained four days at Niamey to discuss common problems and future plans with local leaders. In November, 1961, Diori made a state visit to Nigeria, and this exchange of official courtesy calls has continued.

Relations between the two countries have become still closer and more cooperative despite a few setbacks. After Nigeria broke off diplomatic relations with France in January, 1961, because the latter continued its nuclear testing in the Sahara, Nigérien interests were left temporarily without any official representative at Lagos to support

[122] *West Africa,* November 12, 1960; *Nice-Matin,* January 27, 1961.

them. Also there were a few frontier "incidents," but these were perpetrated by individuals for whom such boundaries were incomprehensi-
ble and hence had no political significance.[123] Since Niger's national
government has found it just as impossible as the French administration did to patrol the long southern frontier effectively, Diori has not
only accepted the economic *status quo* but has also taken steps to improve road and river communications between the two countries. It
was the Nigérien president who proposed setting up an interstate road
commission and who initiated conferences on improving the navigability and utilization of the Niger River. After considerable delays, he also
reached a judicial agreement with Nigeria in September, 1962, the first
of its kind between countries in French- and English-speaking Africa.
It dealt with the summoning of witnesses in criminal cases, and, most
significant of all, with the extradition of criminals and cooperation between the police forces of the two countries.

It was hard to reach agreement on these issues not only because
differences in concept as well as in organization exist between the two
judicial systems, but also because the Nigerians proved apathetic.
When their delegation finally went to Niamey its leader apologized for
its small size and for Nigeria's procrastination in the matter.[124] Indeed,
Niger is far more eager than Nigeria to develop technical cooperation
between their peoples. Niger has little to offer Nigeria that the latter
really wants: a few million more people and vast stretches of unproductive land. Theoretically, Nigeria agrees that cooperation with its northern neighbor is desirable, and a suitable framework for this was
provided by their common membership in the Monrovia group. In
practice, however, Nigeria has not been much concerned with what goes
on in Niger. Diori, on the other hand, cannot afford to be indifferent to
events south of Niger's border. Although the dangers of annexation or
secession seem to be conjured away for the moment and current relations between the two governments are good, the desire for union still
exists in certain circles on both sides of the frontier and might at any
time create a burning issue.

Relations with Arab Countries

Niger's relations with the Arabs to the north and northeast have been
complicated by the Algerian war and by its own nomad problem. The
latter, although not as acute as in Mali, Mauritania, and Chad, was

[123] Kiba, "Problèmes Nigériens," *op. cit.*
[124] Radio Niamey, September 24, 1962.

brought to the fore by Algeria's attainment of independence in 1962. It was to acquire the funds necessary to improve living conditions among Niger's nomads and thus to counter the northern attraction that Diori reversed Djibo's policy and made Niger a member of the Organisation Commune des Régions Sahariennes on May 8, 1959. Moreover, Diori did not share Djibo's conviction that France was using the OCRS as a device to divide Niger and to bring its nomads under French control. In fact, Diori went so far as to urge that OCRS operations in prospecting for minerals and water include all of Niger and not simply its Saharan zone.[125] Such a receptive attitude induced Jacques Soustelle, the OCRS delegate, to go to Niger to tour its isolated regions, which no French minister had ever before visited. Niamey's Chamber of Commerce warmly supported Diori's policy in this respect, even urging that OCRS funds be utilized to develop the whole southeast as well as the Saharan zone in order to prevent that region from gravitating into Nigeria's orbit.[126]

The OCRS has been generous with Niger—in 1961 alone it spent 14 million new francs, mainly on hydraulic projects in the Saharan zone —but political developments, particularly in the Arab world, have modified Diori's attitude toward that organization. Niger was increasingly criticized, mainly by the radical Negro and Arab countries that formed the Casablanca group, for letting itself become a "pawn in France's imperialistic designs on the Sahara" through adherence to the OCRS. Diori began to advocate a drastic reform of the latter's membership and management. He urged the French to internationalize the OCRS, make it more flexible, and withdraw their nationals from its directorate to the less conspicuous position of technical advisers. On June 9, 1961, Diori gave the first concrete indication of his new views on the future evolution of the OCRS. "The Sahara," he said, "should be placed under an international organization composed of representatives of all the bordering states." Such an organization, he went on, might resemble a cross between the technically oriented Coal and Steel Community and a loose economic group such as the Council of the Entente, and it could develop the wealth of the great desert first for the countries that bordered on it and then for all Africa. France, he felt, should have its place in this organization, at least in the technical sphere, because of the effort and money it had already invested in the Sahara.[127] To those Africans who wanted to eliminate France wholly from any further

[125] Dugué, *op. cit.*, p. 157.   [126] *Afrique Nouvelle*, January 27, 1960.
[127] *Marchés Tropicaux*, June 17, 1961.

share in the Sahara's development he gave a colorful warning: "Rather than mount a young and fiery horse and then be thrown to the ground, it is better to ride an old steed and reach our destination." [128]

For some time Diori merely embroidered this theme, but later he proposed that the Saharan countries surrender some of their sovereignty to the international technical organization he envisages. He has also urged that the desert's gas and oil no longer be shipped to Europe but be retained for the use of African countries. In April, 1963, he again pleaded for a conference of all the Saharan countries to lay the bases for their joint exploitation of the desert's wealth in collaboration with France, and urged that Algeria, "which holds the richest portion of the Sahara," be the host nation.[129] Not surprisingly, Algeria failed to respond to this plea, for it was already disputing some Saharan oases with Morocco. Its leaders could hardly relish the idea of sharing the proceeds of their known petroleum resources with the rest of Africa, or willingly agree to a perpetuation of the desert's present political frontiers. Neither in Paris nor in Africa did Diori arouse enthusiasm for his "Saharan Economic Community," though he may yet win over Chad, the only other Negro Saharan state that had joined the OCRS.

Indeed, Diori's proposals have awakened widespread African suspicions about his real motives, and to some degree he has been placed on the defensive. As early as September, 1961, he felt impelled to deny that he had ever opposed Algerian independence because he feared Algerian claims to the Nigérien Sahara. In August, 1962, rumors—promptly denied by Diori—circulated in Paris and in Yaoundé, capital of Cameroun, that he had asked the French government for increased military aid to protect from covetous Algerians some newly discovered tungsten deposits in Aïr. Although Diori was probably sincere in saying that he had "learned of Algeria's independence with the greatest satisfaction," [130] there is little doubt that he also fears Algerian intrigues among Niger's restless nomads. Even if such fears are currently unfounded—and it should be noted that the Algerian authorities have apparently been cooperating with the Mali government in suppressing a Touareg revolt in Malian territory—an independent Algeria automatically serves as a magnet for the "white" populations of Agadès and Tahoua *cercles*.

Anticipating the possibility of such repercussions as long ago as December, 1960, Diori had created a new ministry of nomad and Saharan

[128] *Afrique Nouvelle*, October 4, 1961.   [129] *Le Monde*, April 24, 1963.
[130] Radio Niamey, August 3, 1962.

affairs with headquarters at Agadès and entrusted this post to the progressive chief of the Oulimidden Touareg, Mouddour Zakara. The next month Diori toured the nomad regions of northeast Niger and asked France to transfer members of the nomad tribes serving in the French armed forces to Niger's new national army.[131] After Ben Bella assumed control of the Algerian government, Diori felt that such precautionary measures were insufficient, and he made a special effort to establish good relations with Algiers and to win its cooperation in his plans for the Sahara. This policy was given further impetus early in 1963, when the murder of Olympio reawakened fears of Sawaba subversion among PPN leaders. Rumors circulated in Niamey that Djibo Bakary was trying to induce Ben Bella to let the Sawaba create a permanent base in Algiers under arrangements similar to Ben Bella's encouragement of the Angolan rebels.[132] Even if this were not true, PPN leaders realized that pressure could easily be exerted by Ben Bella not only on Nigérien nomads in general but on the hundreds of Touareg who had gone to work as laborers in the Algerian Sahara, mainly at Tamanrasset. Diori, therefore, lost no time in touring the northern region to sound out the nomads and to try to rally them to his government. Upon his return to Niamey, Diori reported that the nomads' dearest wish was to be "more intimately integrated with the rest of the republic."[133] He also announced that Coproniger would soon help this integration by bringing cheap consumer goods to the nomad zones.

Thus far the Niger government has had less trouble with its nomads than any other Saharan borderland country, although it was certainly an exaggeration for it to proclaim officially in 1963 that "no nomad problem exists in Niger."[134] If it has had only minimal difficulties, this has been because Diori has shrewdly left the nomad chiefs alone, and not forced upon them the rapid emancipation of their Negro servitors. The withdrawal of all French garrisons from Bilma and Agadès by the end of 1964 may change the situation markedly—but this depends in part upon the attitude adopted by the Algerian authorities. On June 3, 1964, Diori took the precautionary step of signing an agreement for cooperation and friendship with Algeria.

Niger's relations with other Arab countries have been less affected by Diori's projects for the Sahara than by other phases of his foreign policy. It is curious that Diori seems to have made little effort to enlist

<hr/>

[131] *Le Monde,* February 8, 1961. [132] *Ibid.,* February 8, 1963.
[133] Radio Cotonou, March 26, 1963.
[134] *Le Monde Diplomatique,* December, 1963.

the cooperation of Mauritania for his Saharan designs, although both
he and President Mokhtar ould Daddah have the same concept of their
respective countries as links or bridges between black and white
Africa. It was not until October, 1962, that he sent any mission to
Nouakchott, capital of Mauritania, and then Mauritania was but the
first leg on a long journey that included countries of the Western hemi-
sphere and the Far East. Diori's political contacts with Tunisia have
been almost as slight, but far more tinged with emotion. In November,
1960, he accompanied Ahmadou Ahidjo, President of Cameroun, and
Mamadou Dia, Premier of Senegal, to Tunis to discuss the Algerian
problem, and on this occasion Diori praised Bourguiba's "spirit of comprehension." [135] But less than a year later the Tunisian President's spirit
of comprehension was tried and found wanting in respect to Niger
when that country (along with the Ivory Coast) refused to vote for the
Afro-Asian resolution in the United Nations condemning the French
aggression during the dispute between France and Tunisia over the
naval base at Bizerte. The Tunisian Neo-Destour party organ, *Afrique
Action,* published an article on September 2, 1961, in which Diori and
all his works were violently attacked. Among other misdeeds, Diori was
accused of having falsified the results of the 1958 referendum and of
permitting France to utilize bases in Niger for military aggression. This
article caused quite a stir in Niamey, but the hard feelings it engendered soon passed away. Early in 1962, Niger and Tunisia signed a
three-year trade agreement, and Tunisia has been helpful in launching
Coproniger.

Inevitably Niger's consistently pro-French attitude has adversely
affected its relations with other Arab countries. Diori's all-Muslim government and his pilgrimage to Mecca seem not to have softened their
feelings toward him. Diori is eager to live at peace with the Arab world,
and he has refused several invitations to visit Tel-Aviv officially. But
the goodwill missions he sent in 1961–1962 to many of the Arab countries did not produce the desired effect because at the same time he
sent other missions to Saudi Arabia and to Israel. With Egypt, Diori's
relations have been embittered by the support Nasser has given to
Djibo Bakary. In April, 1962, about two weeks after an economic
agreement between Egypt and Niger had been initialed, an article appeared in the Sawaba organ, *Gaskya,* entitled "Diori in the Service of
Israel." It contained the remarkable assertion that it was upon orders
received from Tel-Aviv that the PPN government had been giving sub-

[135] *Le Monde,* November 20, 1960.

sidies to Catholic missions in Niger.[136] If Djibo's purpose in sponsoring that article was to maintain Egypt's aid to his cause, he was doomed to disappointment. Although sixteen months passed before Niger ratified the agreement made with Egypt on March 15, 1962, and although Diori's official visit to Cairo was postponed for over a year, Niger eventually succeeded in establishing diplomatic and economic relations with both Egypt and Israel, and also in terminating Nasser's support for Djibo.

RELATIONS WITH THE WESTERN AND EASTERN BLOCS

Beyond the coasts of Africa, too, Diori's persistence in pursuing a policy of genuine neutrality has been relatively successful. Like the Ivory Coast, Niger has remained on exceptionally friendly terms with France, and when it left the Community early in 1961 it did so as a consequence of the joint decision taken by all the Entente states and not because its own leaders were eager to sever those ties. Since then it has received some aid from Western countries other than, and in addition to, France. Nevertheless, Diori, unlike Houphouët, has recently sought the cooperation of Communist nations. Probably he is as basically anti-Communist as the Ivory Coast President, but Diori cannot afford, as Houphouët can, to indulge his ideological inclinations. Diori is subject to stronger pressures from the radical wing of his party, and his country's needs are far greater than those of the Ivory Coast. He therefore has sent out many missions to solicit aid from all sources and has readily entered into negotiations with any nation willing to sign agreements with Niger. Treaties of economic and cultural cooperation with Western-bloc countries include those with France (April 24, 1961, and May 28, 1962), West Germany (June 14, 1961), the National Republic of China (November 10, 1962), the United States (March 10 and July 5, 1962), Israel (January 11, 1963), Japan (November 5, 1962), and Switzerland (March 28, 1962). In the Communist bloc, Niger has signed agreements with Poland (November 9, 1961), Czechoslovakia (January 16 and October 2, 1962), the USSR (April 25 and September 29, 1962), and Yugoslavia (October 2, 1962). Only the Ivory Coast, the United States, the European Economic Community (of which Niger is an associate member), and above all France have been financially helpful to Niger, although Canada plans to invest some 850 million CFA francs in prospecting for minerals in the country.

[136] *Afrique Nouvelle*, April 11, 1962.

Increasingly, Diori has made Niger a center for international conferences. During the last three months of 1963, Niamey was the site of the second conference on the Niger River and of meetings of special committees of the Commission for African Technical Cooperation, and it was chosen headquarters for one of the regional offices of the Economic Commission on Africa.

France, far more than any other country, has aided Niger not only by paying the salaries of the nearly four hundred Frenchmen employed by the Niger government but also by meeting most of Niger's budget deficits, equipping its new army, and paying higher than world prices for Nigérien peanut exports. For this considerable aid France receives only very slight economic benefits but significant returns in the form of Nigérien good will. Concretely this has been shown in Niger's support for France in the United Nations during the Algerian and Tunisian conflicts and by French use of military bases in Niger. In February, 1964, Diori publicly approved of France's military intervention in Gabon.

Diori's dependence on and friendly relations with France, in particular, and his lack of fanaticism in general have been a handicap in his dealings with the "revolutionary" countries of Africa—that is, with the Casablanca group: Ghana, Guinea, Mali, Morocco, and the UAR—and with the left wing of his own party. On several occasions he has had to deny that he asked France for increased military assistance, and recently he took pains to dissociate himself from France's attitude toward the United Nations' operations in the Congo (Léopoldville).[137] Diori wants to be on good terms with the Arab states, but to achieve this he will neither sacrifice Niger's territorial integrity nor be drawn into their conflict with Israel, whose aid for Niger's agricultural and hydraulic projects he has gratefully accepted. In principle he is not against admitting the People's Republic of China to membership in the United Nations, but he has diplomatic relations with the National Republic of China and South Vietnam. Diori does not approve of Communism or of Nigérien students who go to the Soviet Union, but he will not prevent them or others of his political opponents from returning to Niger if they agree to help him build up the country. The three basic aims of Diori's foreign policy are to obtain the maximum aid for Niger's development, to keep its territory intact, and to prevent foreign nations from helping his enemies overthrow the government.

Diori's approach to these goals is pragmatic and flexible. In an inter-

[137] *Ibid.,* August 10, 1962; *Le Monde,* April 24, 1963.

view he gave to *Afrique Nouvelle* on January 3, 1962, he obliquely praised the Negro African for his dislike of violence, his adaptability, and his gift for compromise. Diori was thus perhaps unconsciously drawing his own portrait. "You mustn't think," he told his interlocutor, "that Africans are as credulous as many believe them to be. They know when they meet a Russian that they must denounce colonialism, trusts, and reactionaries in order to be applauded. And when they are in the West, they know that they must say that in Communist countries man has become a robot and that there is no freedom there."

Bibliography

Written documents on Niger are very meager and difficult to find, even in Niamey and Paris. The only books written specifically about Niger are in French: those by Abadie and Séré de Rivières are outdated and that by Bonardi contains largely personal reminiscences and impressions. More fruitful are the tribal studies by Chapelle, Rodd, and Rouch, but they deal with tribes which overflow the borders of Niger. In English, the pamphlet published by the French Embassy's Information Service in New York is summary and generally restricted to economic developments. Current material must be sought in periodicals specializing in African questions and in such newspapers as *Le Monde* and *Afrique Nouvelle*. The best economic analysis of Niger has been produced by La Documentation Française in Paris, but it is now more than four years old. More up-to-date general data can be found in *L'Afrique d'Expression Française et Madagascar*, no. 409, 1964.

OFFICIAL PUBLICATIONS

Government Information Service, Niamey.
    Journal Officiel de la République du Niger, monthly
    Labari, monthly
    Le Niger, weekly
    Le Temps du Niger, mimeographed daily
La Documentation Française: Notes et Etudes Documentaires. *La République du Niger*, no. 2638, February 26, 1960.
Ambassade de France, Service de Presse et d'Information. *The Republic of Niger*. New York: October, 1960.

BOOKS

Abadie, Maurice. *Afrique Centrale: La Colonie du Niger*. Paris: Société d'Editions Géographiques, Maritimes, et Coloniales, 1927.
Bonardi, Pierre. *La République du Niger, Naissance d'un Etat*. Paris: Ed. A. P. D., 1960.
Chapelle, J. *Nomades Noirs du Sahara*. Paris: Plon, 1957.

Rodd, F. J. R. *People of the Veil.* London: Macmillan, 1926.

Rouch, Jean. *Les Songhay.* Paris: Presses Universitaires de France, 1954.

Séré de Rivières, Edmond. *Le Niger.* Paris: Société d'Editions Géographiques, Maritimes, et Coloniales, 1952.

ARTICLES AND PAMPHLETS

L'Afrique d'Expression Française et Madagascar. Paris: *Europe-France-Outre-Mer,* no. 409, 1964.

Allainmat, Yves. "Ecoles Nomades du Niger," *Encyclopédie Mensuelle d'Outre-Mer,* October, 1964, pp. 272–275.

Clair, Andrée. "Pages Nouvelles du Niger," *Afrique,* December, 1961, pp. 28–31.

———. "Au Niger: Les Touareg à l'Ombre des Transistors," *Afrique,* October, 1962, pp. 30–33.

Clifford, R. L. "Renseignements Economiques sur la République du Niger," Niamey: n.d. (pamphlet).

Diori, Hamani. "Le Plan Triennal, 1961–1963," *Afrique Nouvelle,* December 13, 1961.

Flechet, Pierre. "La Prospection Petrolière de Petropar dans le Nord-Est du Niger," *Europe-France-Outre-Mer,* no. 408, 1964, pp. 37–39.

"Has Niger a Future?" *West Africa,* March 3, 1962, pp. 230–231.

Kiba, Simon. "Problèmes Nigériens," *Afrique,* January, 1962, pp. 30–32.

Kouawo, J. E. "Le Nouveau Plan Décennal du Niger," *Afrique Nouvelle,* May 28, 1964.

———. "Les Radio-Clubs à Travers le Niger," *Afrique Nouvelle,* July 4, 1964.

Maida, Mamadou, "Il n'y a pas de Développement Economique sans Développement de l'Education," *Afrique Nouvelle,* December 13, 1961.

Mayaki, Adamou. "L'Economie du Niger et ses Problèmes," *Marchés Tropicaux,* September 17, 1960, pp. 2035–2036.

Mendy, Justin. "Au Pays du Soif," *Afrique Nouvelle,* September 5, 12, 1963.

Pageard, R. "La Réforme des Juridictions Coutumières et Musulmans dans les Nouveaux Etats de l'Ouest-Africain," *Recueil Penant,* October-November-December, 1963, pp. 462–494.

"Vain Journey," *West Africa,* February 22, 1964, pp. 230–231.

IV

FOUR EQUATORIAL STATES

By JOHN A. BALLARD

University of Ibadan

Introduction

THE political systems which have prevailed in the four states of Chad, the Central African Republic, the Congo (Brazzaville), and Gabon since their independence reflect not only sixty years of colonial rule when the states composed the Federation of French Equatorial Africa, but also the distinctive content—geographical, economic, and social—of each individual state. Their common colonial experience and the maintenance of economic ties since independence justify joint treatment in a study of their present governments and politics. At the same time, variations in the problems of attaining national unity are reflected in certain comparable but distinctive features in the political system of each state.

What distinguish the states of French Equatorial Africa (AEF) from most others in Africa are their lack of strong traditional political systems, their very sparse population, their lack of important resources (except for the minerals and timber of Gabon), their limited economic and social development, and the almost total absence of unifying geographical, social, and economic forces within each state. During the colonial period political unity on the territorial level was imposed by the drawing of colonial frontiers and the establishment of a hierarchic administration within those frontiers. The French administration, how-

231

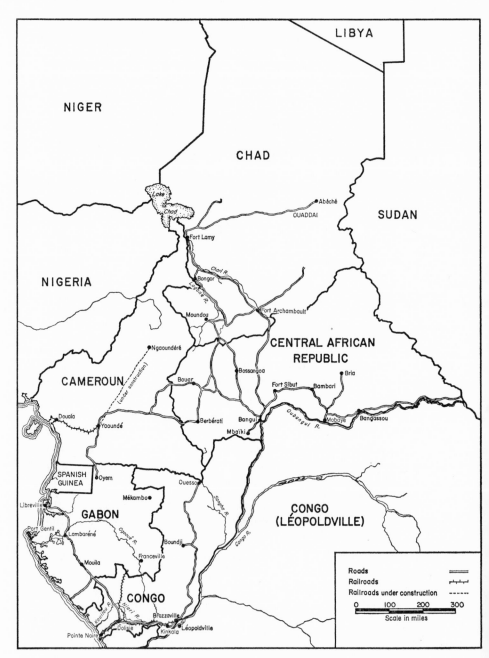

Map 4. The Congo, Chad, Gabon, and Central African Republic

ever, was not above exploiting ethnic and regional rivalries in its efforts to maintain a political balance and to defeat movements toward nationalism. Partisans of French and African political parties were also fully alert to opportunities to utilize these rivalries to their own advantage. As a result, the first and continuing preoccupation of the autonomous African governments which took office in early 1959 has been to preserve and extend whatever degree of political unity had been imposed by the colonial administration.

Few resources have been available to the equatorial governments in their efforts to mold nations within their artificial boundaries. There is no strong popular appeal based on unified nationalist movements from the colonial period, with the exception of the fragile unity obtained in the Central African Republic (RCA) in the name of its late leader, Barthélémy Boganda. The beginnings of national markets and national economies are postcolonial phenomena, and except in Gabon their expansion is made almost impossible by the absence of important resources. As a result, the standard response of the governments to political challenge has been an arbitrarily imposed maintenance of the *status quo.* In each of the four states this response has led to the rise of the executive branch, especially of the presidency, to absolute dominance over all other institutions.

To maintain power and office, however, has required deft balancing by the executive of regional and ethnic interests at each level of government and, most important, in the distribution of development projects and social facilities. At the same time, the regimes have depended in large measure on continued financial, technical, and military support from France. But with so few forces tending toward national unity it is not surprising that the imposition of strong executive rule has failed in itself to create political stability. The 1963 and 1964 revolutions in the Congo and Gabon are only the most violent forms of readjustment made in the search for new means of obtaining genuine unity with stability.

The Historical Background

THE PRECOLONIAL PERIOD

The portion of Africa administered by France as French Equatorial Africa was, even more than other African colonies, a European creation altogether lacking a basis in traditional African society. The boundaries of the Federation enclosed no large traditional state systems, though in the south they contained the northern periphery of the old kingdom of Kongo and in the far north the declining sultanates of Ouaddai and Baguirmi and several lesser sultanates. Between these groups, in the forests of Gabon and Middle Congo and the savannas of Oubangui-Chari and southern Chad, were small tribal groups whose traditional social organization had in many cases been upset by migrations and invasions coincident with the spread of the coastal slave trade and Muslim slave-raiding in the north. Hence, during the period of intensive penetration, from 1880 to 1900, the French encountered little serious organized resistance save that of Rabah, a Sudanese soldier and slave-raider who had conquered the area from eastern Oubangui-Chari to Bornu, but who fell before the French near Fort Lamy in 1900.

COLONIAL RULE

French colonial policy as applied in AEF was in many ways a parody of the methods of economic imperialism. After having participated with other European nations in the slave traffic and other trade along the coast of Gabon and Loango (Middle Congo), the French installed an antislavery naval station near the site of Libreville in 1849 and for several decades maintained trading and missionary posts there and at the mouth of the Ogooué River. Then, after Savorgnan de Brazza's peaceful exploration of the upper Ogooué and the route to the Congo River, France was caught up in the scramble for territory which led to expansion in the north, the humiliation at Fashoda, the defeat of Rabah, and establishment of the territorial limits of AEF.

Once the major outlines of the territory had been defined, the next step was the exploitation of its wealth. Following the example set by the Congo Free State under Léopold II, the French government in 1898–1900 claimed for itself all unoccupied land in the colony and granted immense concessions to companies eager to extract the rubber and ivory reportedly available in large quantity. In the absence of a firmly established colonial administration, company agents took command in most of the forest area in Gabon and Middle Congo, as well as in the southeast and southwest of Oubangui-Chari. They imposed an exceptionally brutal regime of forced labor, which was even more effective than the slave trade had been in disrupting traditional society and reducing the sparse population. The rapid exhaustion of rubber and ivory in AEF led to financial failure for most of the companies; after public exposure of the methods of exploitation, the French government exacted minor reforms reducing the extent of company control in AEF. The colonial administration, however, was financially dependent on company exports, and it continued to give full support to forced recruitment of labor for plantations, mines, and timber camps. Indeed the administration itself depended on forced labor for long-range portage and later for construction of a federal trade route based on the Oubangui-Chari road system, on the Oubangui and Congo rivers, and on the railroad linking Brazzaville with the Atlantic Ocean. Not until after World War II was forced labor for both public and private projects abandoned, and then only on orders from Paris.

The difficulties of exploiting AEF during the first phases of the concessionary regime continued to plague the administration throughout the colonial period. Known natural resources were limited to Gabon's hardwood forests and a few small gold mines. Although cotton was introduced to the savanna country of Oubangui-Chari and southern Chad in the 1920's and rapidly became the leading agricultural export, further efforts to diversify production yielded very limited returns. The administration was constantly preoccupied with the problem of finding and developing resources with which to balance its budget. Although grants-in-aid from Paris were continued in AEF long after they had been abandoned in other colonies, AEF gained a reputation as the Cinderella of the French empire.

The Legacy of Colonialism

For the four independent states which succeeded the colonial federation in 1960, the economic, social, administrative, and political legacies of the colonial period were marked by the high degree of centralization common to French administration and by its preoccupation with finance. The economic structure of the federation had been shaped to supply the government-general at Brazzaville with the funds necessary for maintaining intact the federation and a balanced budget. The easily exploited timber of Gabon was used to finance the construction and maintenance of the federal route of the other three territories, allowing the cotton of Chad and Oubangui-Chari to be exported by way of Brazzaville and Pointe Noire instead of through Cameroun or Nigeria. Preferential tariffs were precluded by the Congo Basin treaties, but government controls on imports and exports and contracts for official supply and transport were utilized to keep the economic life of AEF under French control. At the same time, the capital necessary for plantations, trade, and transport tended to concentrate economic activity in the hands of a few large companies and a few local European entrepreneurs.

Apart from officially sponsored local cooperatives, African enterprise was not encouraged. Thus the only Africans native to AEF who were able to accumulate even a modest amount of capital were a few lumbermen in Gabon and the Congo and the cocoa farmers of the Woleu-N'Tem in Gabon. Even petty trade in the cities was almost entirely monopolized by Muslims from French West Africa and by Portuguese. In Chad, where trade and transport was less fully controlled by Europeans than elsewhere, the leading African entrepreneurs were from the Sudan, Libya, and Nigeria.

When independence was achieved in 1960, there was thus no African middle class of any importance, and the economy was dependent on the activity of a few banks and trading companies, the lumbering companies of Gabon, the cotton-purchasing monopolies, and the leading transporters along the federal route. Foreign investment was almost exclusively limited to the exploitation of oil and the mineral deposits of Gabon, and manufacturing was almost nonexistent. Budget receipts were largely composed of customs duties, and while government salaries consumed a very large percentage of expenditures, social programs and major capital development were almost entirely dependent on French subsidies.

Another legacy of the colonial period was an administrative structure which, after years of understaffing, blossomed after World War II into a highly articulated bureaucracy heavily centralized at the federal and territorial capitals, though never strongly manned in the field. Since the expenses of a top-heavy administration were borne by local and federal budgets, there was a long history of complaint by Africans. When they later obtained positions of authority themselves, however, they showed no signs of eliminating posts in the higher and better paid echelons. In addition, the colonial salary structure—with its great disparity between political-administrative salaries and other salaries—was inherited intact during the period of transfer of power and gradual Africanization. Despite the size of the administrative structure, no effort was made to begin training Africans for posts of responsibility until 1955, and even then very few Africans were sent to Paris for administrative training or assigned to positions of executive apprenticeship. Hence at independence the new governments found it necessary to rely heavily on the continued services of French administrators and technicians in the capitals and regional posts.

In terms of social structure, the colonial period dissolved the few remaining traditional bonds of authority linking together more than a few villages. Except among the sultans of Chad, several of whom were maintained in authority as agents of the administration, traditional chiefs either were removed and replaced by Africans serving with the army or the administration or lost much of their authority when the unpopular duties of labor recruitment and tax collection were imposed upon them. The growth of the major cities further detracted from the strength of the traditional social structure by providing economic and social activities beyond the control of traditional society. The cities were the centers for absorption into modern economic activity of the only class to rise above the level of traditional society, i.e., the educated employees of the administration and the companies. This class was heavily concentrated in the cities, and in the absence of strong traditional groups it provided the only contenders for political succession to the colonial administration.

The attitudes of both the colonial administration and the French entrepreneurs of AEF toward Africans varied widely according to place and time, but the tradition of forced labor and exploitation outweighed the nineteenth-century tradition of cultural assimilation. The Mpongwé at Libreville in Gabon had been the early beneficiaries of several decades of education in Catholic mission schools and produced several priests and high-ranking government agents before World War I, but on the whole the assumptions implicit in the concessionary regime and the alienation of African land left little room for the principles of assimilation, and the example of Libreville was not extended elsewhere. Indeed, the colonial administration discouraged the missions from offering advanced education to Africans, and when the first official secondary school was organized in 1935 entry was limited to the numbers of students necessary to fill auxiliary posts in the administration. Even after World War II, when primary education in AEF reached exceptionally large numbers as a result of cooperation between the missions and the administration, secondary education remained restrictive and scholarships for university study in France were so limited that by 1960 there were only five university graduates in AEF.

Another important effect of the tradition of exploitation was the restriction placed on relations between Europeans and Africans. In Libreville a modicum of social and economic intercourse between the two groups was maintained and they were never segregated into strictly defined European and African quarters, but elsewhere relations were strictly those of master and servant. Urban segregation was developed to the extent of removing entire African quarters to urban peripheries in order to lay out modern European centers. In rural areas complaints against the brutality of French officials were the common currency of postwar politics. European distrust of the growing African elite extended to the ostracism of those Europeans who cooperated with African politicians. Unofficial segregation of most public facilities and all private establishments and discrimination in employment and service was such that, as late as 1956, the government-general found it necessary to issue a circular that warned against the consequences of existing practices in race relations. Despite thinly veiled hostility on the part of Europeans, however, the gradual transfer of power allowed the establishment of mutually profitable ties between Europeans and African leaders to a degree which prevented the outbreak of anti-European riots similar to those that occurred in the Belgian Congo.

ACHIEVEMENT OF INDEPENDENCE

The legacy of the colonial period in the social, economic, and administrative structures reflects in some measure the fact that AEF was less favored than other French colonies. In the development of political institutions, however, the strong tendency to uniformity and central control from Paris held AEF to the pace of institutional change taking place in French West Africa and other African colonies. As a result, representative institutions and independence itself were accorded to AEF on the basis of events external to the area, and local conditions had very little effect in determining the shape and the timing of political change.

Prior to the adoption of the constitution of the Fourth French Republic in October, 1946, sporadic efforts had been made to create local representative institutions adapted to conditions in French-speaking Equatorial Africa. A few of the experiments in administration-sponsored cooperatives and local councils which had been tried in West Africa were imported by Governor-General François-Joseph Reste in 1936–1937. During World War II, when the administration in AEF severed its ties with Vichy France, Governor-General Félix Eboué attempted to return authority to traditional chiefs in rural areas and to establish a measure of self-government among the elite in African urban quarters. Neither of these efforts, however, bore significant results. The program of limited autonomy proposed by the conference of governors at Brazzaville in January, 1943, though it found an echo in the abortive constitution of May, 1946, was overruled by provisions for a centralized unitary French Union in the constitution of October, 1946. Thereafter, until the fall of the Fourth Republic in 1958, effective control over political change continued to emanate from Paris, where French political conditions and administrative traditions tended to equate Equatorial Africa with West Africa, and hence to treat the former as a weak carbon copy of the larger and more important federation. In effect, political conditions in Indochina and North Africa—the primary colonial preoccupations of France—determined the general shape of colonial policy throughout the French Union, and political conditions in the important territories of Senegal and the Ivory Coast were frequently assumed to pertain to all of West and Equatorial Africa.

With other colonies, the territories of AEF elected representatives to the French Constituent Assemblies of 1945 and 1946 and were allotted a small number of seats in each of the parliamentary bodies of the Fourth Republic: the National Assembly, the Council of the Republic, and the ineffectual Assembly of the French Union. In addition, each territory elected a Territorial Assembly with limited powers, and these assemblies in turn elected delegates to a federal Grand Council for AEF. With very minor changes this system of representative institutions, set up in 1946 and 1947, remained in effect until 1957. Then, after the failure of French policy in Indochina and North Africa, the constitution of 1946 was stretched to permit a greater degree of autonomy. The *loi-cadre* of 1956 and subsequent decrees created territorial Councils of Government with considerable executive authority, elected by territorial assemblies which themselves gained extended powers. At the same time, the government-general of the Federation lost to the territories much of its power and responsibility.

The year of experience with the new councils of government was filled with continuing confusion and rivalry between the Governor of each territory and his administrators on one hand and the elected ministers of the Council of Government on the other. Only with the fall of the Fourth Republic did the design of a constitution for its successor offer a possibility for resolving contradictions in the existing system. De Gaulle's concept of a Community linking the African territories with France by free choice permitted each territory, through the referendum of September 28, 1958, to accept or reject the constitution of the Fifth Republic and to determine, through its Territorial Assembly, its role within the Community. The four territories of AEF, along with all those of West Africa except Guinea, approved the constitution and chose the status of autonomous republics within the Community. Each republic then drew up its own constitution for internal political institutions. Foreign affairs, control of the army and police, and certain common affairs remained the responsibility of the Community. Elaborate institutions for the Community were of little importance, with the exception of an executive council composed of the premiers of all the republics, which became the new focus for further evolution.

The achievement of independence in 1960, like each of the preceding changes, was largely the result of pressures from other areas. The government of the Mali Federation at the executive council meeting of December, 1959, forced the issue of permitting independence within the Community and obtained the essential promise from de Gaulle that French aid would not be withdrawn in retaliation against states which chose independence. Up to this time there had been no request from the four republics of the former equatorial Federation for independence, and even after the December meeting there was no clear indication from their leaders that independence was either necessary or desirable. Nonetheless, as a trend in favor of independence developed among other republics in the Community, as neighboring Cameroun became independent, and the independence of the Belgian Congo was nearing, the AEF governments were swept along.

The Question of Federation

By 1960, the question of retaining the Federation of Equatorial Africa had been settled by default. While the *loi-cadre* decrees were under consideration, Governor-General Paul Chauvet of AEF had recommended that his federation be kept fully intact, but the arguments against maintaining a strong federal administration in French West Africa were dominant. As usual, no distinction was made between the two federations in the decrees that distributed most of the federal powers among the territories. Among African leaders in AEF the question had not been openly discussed except in Gabon, where the use of its territorial earnings for expenditures in the other three territories had created a long-standing animosity toward federation. During late 1957 and 1958, while federation became the leading political issue in French West Africa, it became in AEF the shibboleth of the president of the Grand Council, Barthélémy Boganda of Oubangui-Chari, the only leader with sufficient political security in his own territory to launch a federalist movement. During the two months between the referendum of September, 1958, and the meeting of the territorial assemblies in November to choose a new constitutional status, Boganda and a few allies in Middle Congo campaigned for a federal executive and assembly, but unstable internal political conditions kept the other territories from joining with Boganda's proposed Central African Republic.

Shortly after the creation of four separate republics in November, 1958, the Federation of French Equatorial Africa was officially terminated, and the government-general and Grand Council were dismantled. Coordination among the republics remained, however, in the essentially federal services of customs duties, communications, and currency. Boganda's concept of a United States of Latin Africa, which would have included Cameroun, the Belgian Congo, and Angola, died with him in March, 1959, and for a year there was no further effort to create a stronger union. Three of the four premiers were new and inexperienced, and each government was preoccupied with the establishment of its own political and administrative controls. Thus, although the remaining federal services continued to operate under new names, the coordination of policy that was expected to evolve from regular meetings among the premiers was almost nonexistent. Indeed, apart from informal encounters at sessions of the Community executive council, they met only twice during 1959.

When the question of independence arose in December, 1959, it forced a definite answer to the question of federation. It was the opinion of the French government and of most African leaders in AEF that as independent states the four republics would not prove economically viable. With encouragement from Paris the presidents and other leaders from the four states held a series of meetings early in 1960 to determine the extent to which they were willing to commit themselves to further federation. The governments of Chad and RCA, dependent on the old federal route for their contact with the sea, were strong proponents of continued close coordination based on federal institutions. The government of the Congo, while anxiously awaiting the outcome of political maneuverings across the river at Léopoldville, in the former Belgian Congo, was also eager to retain ties which would ensure the continued flow of northern commerce through Brazzaville and Pointe Noire. The government of Gabon, however, had no interest in reviving institutions which might divert revenue from its rapidly developing resources to three states with which it had no productive economic connection.

Pressures from Paris and a desire to maintain the existing system of coordination led Gabon temporarily to agree to a limited federation, but when the charter for a Union of Republics of Central Africa (URAC) was drawn up Gabon declined to participate. The other three states, which signed the charter at Fort Lamy on May 17, 1960, agreed thereby to the creation of a federal legislature and a federal executive, with control over foreign policy, defense, and a large share of economic affairs. The three national assemblies duly ratified the accord, but in July, when the four presidents arrived in Paris to sign with France the conventions transferring the powers retained by the Community to Gabon and URAC, President Youlou of the Congo announced that his state must have separate diplomatic representation and membership in the United Nations, equivalent to that of Patrice Lumumba's rival Republic of the Congo at Léopoldville. On this point URAC foundered. Chad and the Central African Republic were left with no incentive for a two-state federation and the four republics became independent at separate, two-day intervals in August, 1960. At the same time the coordinating institutions that had been developed in 1959 and 1960 remained intact and served as the basis for gradually increasing economic cooperation.

THE DEVELOPMENT OF POLITICAL MOVEMENTS

In the absence of significant economic, social, and educational development, the institution of political reforms was often premature in AEF in the sense that no African political movements had evolved that were capable of formulating demands for reform. Indeed, political reforms of French origin, especially elections, themselves provided the impetus for the formation of political groups. This situation gave exceptional opportunities to the colonial administration and interested local Frenchmen for political maneuvering and intervention, and they exploited ethnic rivalries, poor communications between the cities and interior regions, and European control of African employment to prevent the growth of African political militancy.

Early Political Activity

Political activity in AEF before World War II was confined primarily to small groups of the educated elite at Libreville in Gabon and at Brazzaville and Pointe Noire in the Congo which protested against discriminatory regulations and demanded the rights and privileges that were associated with the policy of assimilation as practiced in Senegal. The longest-lived and most active of these groups was the branch of the French League for the Defense of the Rights of Man which had been founded at Libreville in 1918 by a group of educated young men and which was sporadically active until 1930. Education in mission schools and employment in French West Africa or France had given a few of its members considerable political sophistication. Through the League they kept up a barrage of complaints against the usurpation of African lands, the imposition of the *indigénat* (a system of administrative penalties for minor political offenses), and the decline of the easygoing assimilationist regime which had developed at Libreville in the nineteenth century. The League and other elite protest groups suffered, however, from internal ethnic and personal rivalries, and although some of the groups obtained partial redress of grievances, none developed a tradition of militant activity. Administration favor, such as was accorded mulattoes organized in an Amicale des Métis, divided the elite, and administrative suppression easily cut short the activities of the very few elite groups showing revolutionary tendencies.

A few groups, each of them primarily tribal, sought to reintegrate weakened tribal structures in new systems so as to resist colonial domination or eliminate it altogether. These were the groups which came closest to being mass movements. Farthest removed from urban elite efforts were a few tribal revolts, the most serious being that of the Baya of western Oubangui-Chari, who had been subjected to heavy recruitment of forced labor and who, under a religious leader, Karinou, held off French military forces during 1928–1930. More difficult to define are the messianic religious movements and cults in which the elite took leading roles. At Libreville, young Léon Mba, chief of the Fang tribe in the city and now President of Gabon, helped spread the reintegrative cult of *bwiti* among the Fang of the Estuary of the Gabon River until his deportation by the colonial administration in 1933. Among the Bacongo, south of Brazzaville, the messianic cult around Simon Kimbangou of the neighboring area in the Belgian Congo was spread by Protestant mission catechists during the 1920's.

The most important of the messianic movements was the Amicale des Originaires de l'Afrique Equatoriale Française, which began in 1927 among a few AEF laborers and former military men in Paris under André Matsoua, and which spread among Balali tribesmen around Brazzaville as a movement to obtain French citizenship and the rights and privileges assumed to flow therefrom. After Matsoua's arrest and exile to Chad in 1930, the Amicale became a movement of passive resistance to the administration orchestrated by an elite at Paris and Brazzaville and led in the Balali districts by traditional local chiefs. Despite administration attempts to suppress or to capture the movement, by 1940 the Amicale was capable of mobilizing the entire Balali population. Only after the recapture and death of Matsoua and a brutal military suppression were the Balali quelled and subjugated. After the war, however, the Amicale blossomed as a messianic cult around the name of Matsoua, and its leaders at Brazzaville refused to participate in the new political institutions, ordering instead that the Balali vote for Matsoua in each election. The result was massive abstention or votes for Matsoua in every election from 1946 to 1956, when Abbé Fulbert Youlou captured Matsouanist support for his candidacy and brought the Balali into political life.

During World War II, a similar elite-directed tribal movement developed among the M'Bochi at Brazzaville under Jacques Opangault. This movement aimed at the expulsion of the colonial administration and the Catholic missions from the Congo, but after Opangault called a general strike of civil servants in 1943 to protest favoritism in promotions, he was arrested and exiled to Bangui.

Few of these associations and movements prepared the way for participation in the political institutions set up after the war. When the first elections were proposed in 1945, the only active organizations were a few small urban elite groups, most of them sponsored or organized by the administration or other Europeans. With a limited electorate and with news of the elections largely confined to this urban elite, initiative in proposing candidates lay entirely with these associations.

Political Activity since 1945

THE CONGO

The Pattern of Politics, 1946–1956

Brazzaville, as the federal capital, was much more sensitive than other centers in AEF to political developments in France, and its large European population reflected French political divisions more accurately and fully than did the small contingents elsewhere in the territory. As a result, each major French political party had active supporters in Brazzaville who began in 1947 to appeal for the support of the educated African elite in the hope of winning additional votes in the National Assembly in Paris and in the Territorial Assembly. In the first elections of 1945, the National Assembly candidate of the Vili elite of Pointe Noire, Jean Félix-Tchicaya, outmaneuvered a large number of candidates representing other ethnic groups by purchasing the support of lesser candidates from the lower Congo against those of the upper Congo and Gabon. After his election, Tchicaya joined a radical group of African deputies in France who were associated with the

Communist Party, while his supporters at home joined the Groupes d'Etudes Communistes (GEC) at Brazzaville and Pointe Noire. These moves induced the French Socialists at Brazzaville to encourage the candidacy of Jacques Opangault of the upper Congo.

The result of this geographic division was a pattern of politics which persisted for ten years. The north, and particularly Opangault's M'Bochi tribe, opposed a southern coalition organized by Tchicaya, while the Balali, formerly the most dynamic group in Brazzaville, remained withdrawn from political participation in their new form of passive resistance. The larger population in the south gave Tchicaya and his party the advantage in all elections, but the division between these two African groups gave the balance of power in the Territorial Assembly to the conservative European minority.

Tchicaya's Parti Progressiste Congolais (PPC), affiliated to the interterritorial Rassemblement Démocratique Africain (RDA) organized in French West Africa, was essentially a coalition of the educated elites at Brazzaville and at Pointe Noire. It followed the RDA in its militant opposition to the French administration during 1947–1950, but for lack of experience and funds it failed to organize a widespread nationalist movement outside the cities. During its first years it received close counsel from French Communists in the Brazzaville Groupe d'Etudes Communistes, but these were weeded out of the administration by 1949. Thereafter the only continuing Communist contact lay in sporadic support to local labor unions from the Communist-dominated French Confédération Générale du Travail. After 1950, when the RDA deputies in Paris broke their affiliation with the Communists and sought a *rapprochement* with the French government parties, Tchicaya came to terms with the government-general in AEF and thereafter received administration support in exchange for moderation on the part of the PPC.

The Middle Congo branch of the French Socialist Party remained an alliance between a small group of ardent Socialists and freemasons among the lower European ranks of the administration and Opangault's following among the M'Bochi and other northern tribes. The two groups were united in their bitter opposition to the Catholic missions and to the government-general which, unlike that of the French West African Federation, was not under the control of Socialists in the Ministry of Overseas France. As a result of Opangault's undisguised tribalism and his continued association with a party that had sabotaged overseas reform in 1946, the local Socialists alienated the educated elite and found no base of support outside the north, whose small population doomed the party to be a minority in all elections.

All attempts to form third parties, and particularly to mobilize the latent electoral power of the Balali, failed to attract support away from the PPC, the Socialists, and the nonpolitical Matsouanists. The most serious effort was that undertaken by the ultraconservative Rassemblement du Peuple Français (RPF), which relied on de Gaulle's wartime reputation in AEF to rally the support of the great majority of Europeans after 1947. Its African subsidiaries lacked convincing African leadership, and after failing to win Balali support for an avowed Matsouanist candidate in 1951, the RPF limited itself to control of European representation at the National and Territorial assemblies.

The Rise of Youlou

In January, 1956, elections for the National Assembly sharply changed the political pattern in the Congo. Tchicaya's PPC majority in the Territorial Assembly had dissolved in the wake of personal and regional rivalries and of his own long absences in Paris. The party itself was demoralized after the loss of its earlier militant character. More important was the decision of a young Balali priest, Abbé Fulbert Youlou, to challenge the Matsouanist voting tradition. By claiming Matsoua's spiritual heritage and exploiting the attempted suppression of his candidacy by the Catholic Bishop of Brazzaville, Youlou succeeded in organizing the support of the Balali at Brazzaville and, through them, the support of their cousins in the villages of the surrounding region. Though he and Opangault narrowly lost the election to Tchicaya, allegedly because the administration intervened against them, Youlou emerged as an important new leader and attracted the support of dissidents from both the older parties for his new party, the Union Démocratique pour la Défense des Intérêts Africains (UDDIA). In the first municipal elections, held in November, 1956, Youlou's party captured control of the Brazzaville city council by a large majority, while his ally, Stéphane Tchitchellé, upset Tchicaya at Pointe Noire.

The stage was then set for the important Territorial Assembly elections of March, 1957. The disintegration of the PPC had left Youlou leader of the south in opposition to Opangault's north, and the election was fought along this renewed rivalry. Opangault's alliance with Simon-Pierre Kikhounga-N'Got, one of the dissident PPC leaders in the populous southern region of Niari, and open support from the Socialist governor gave him a very tenuous and unstable majority of 23 seats in the Territorial Assembly over the 22 won by Youlou's UDDIA. Long negotiations, embittered by the intrusion of the governor, of local European supporters of the two parties, and even of envoys from France, resulted for a time in a Council of Government headed by Opangault and containing five ministers from each party.

The support of Brazzaville voters for Youlou's first candidacy had nevertheless attracted the financial and advisory support of a small group of Frenchmen who were eager to control the city administration. Moreover, the strength shown by his party in the municipal and territorial elections and the decline of the PPC led the RDA leaders in Paris to transfer their patronage to Youlou. The move enlisted Governor-General Chauvet's RDA sympathies. This development, in the face of Socialist control of both the Ministry of Overseas France and the territorial administration, meant that political power in the Congo was the object of continual struggle in France. Both local Europeans and the interested French political parties opposed any possible accommodation between Opangault and Youlou, and their persistent exploitation of ethnic and other rivalries defeated all attempts to maintain stability in the Territorial Assembly and in the Council of Government.

After a year and a half of recurrent crisis, spurred by UDDIA purchase of a Socialist deputy in the National Assembly and the refusal of the Socialist governor to convoke the Territorial Assembly, Opangault sought unsuccessfully to avoid losing control of the Council of Government by supporting Boganda's proposals for a federal executive superseding the territorial Councils. Both parties supported de Gaulle's constitution in the referendum of September, 1958, but the meeting of the Territorial Assembly on November 28, 1958, called to decide on a new status for the Congo, provided an opportunity for the UDDIA with its new majority of one, to vote itself into power in a new Republic of the Congo. Amid riots by supporters of Opangault and Tchicaya at Pointe Noire, Youlou's new UDDIA government moved the territorial capital back to Brazzaville. There, the issues of constitutional design and new elections kept tension high, and when the Assembly convened at Brazzaville on February 17, 1959, Opangault's M'Bochi and other northerners in the city engaged Youlou's Balali in a three-day pitched battle which left over one hundred dead before French troops restored order. Opangault, Kikhounga-N'Got, and other Socialist leaders were arrested, constitutional legislation providing strong executive powers was pushed through the Assembly, and within another three months the UDDIA had won over enough Socialist support to call for elections for a new Assembly. In June, 1959, after careful gerrymandering and the appointment of UDDIA officials throughout the country, the UDDIA won the seats of all regions except Opangault's stronghold in the north.

Youlou in Power and the Revolution of 1963

Youlou himself, since the founding of the UDDIA, had pursued a policy of broad entente in order to obtain support outside his Balali base. His assiduous courting of potential leaders in other regions had won for the UDDIA a considerable following, which included many former PPC leaders and Socialist dissidents who were given responsibility for party organization in their native regions. Once firmly in power, Youlou continued this policy by bringing a few loyal Socialists into the Council of Ministers and by seeking reconciliation with Opangault, who was released from prison shortly after the elections. By December, 1959, when Youlou decided to promote himself from the premiership to the presidency of the Republic, he was able to secure Opangault's support and was elected without opposition. At independence in August, 1960, Opangault was taken into the Council of Ministers and shortly thereafter became a vice-president along with Tchitchellé.

The one group which stood apart and refused to be absorbed into the national consensus being negotiated or imposed by Youlou was the radical labor and youth movement which derived from the militant wing of the old PPC and from the Communist-affiliated CGT. In 1960, Kikhounga-N'Got, who had earlier been associated with this group, planned with several Brazzaville labor leaders the creation of a new political party. When, in May, 1960, it appeared that this group might ally itself with Premier Patrice Lumumba of the Congo (Léopoldville), most of its leaders were arrested on charges of subversive activity. By November, 1960, however, with the imprisoned Lumumba no longer a threat, and Opangault safely within the government, Youlou extended his efforts to obtain a national government by taking Kikhounga-N'Got from prison into the Council of Ministers and releasing the other labor leaders. Two months later he added Tchicaya's former lieutenant, Germain Bikoumat, as a link to the unreconciled members of the PPC.

Radical groups opposed his opportunistic alliance with Tshombé's Katanga and his dependence on European advisers notorious for their connections with the extreme right in French politics. Nevertheless, Youlou managed to maintain a balance both within and outside his government through distribution of rewards and privileges to all groups. Economic planning was undercut by the attempt to satisfy the immediate demands of each regional and ethnic group and its representatives, and the increasingly serious proportions of unemployment at Brazzaville were met by a token plan of youth training for agriculture and repeated promises of jobs for all when finances could be found for the construction of the Kouilou Dam near Pointe Noire. This arrangement was feasible as long as aid from Katanga and elsewhere was sufficient to provide the necessary subsidies. After the fall of Tshombé, however, a revision of the system was necessary, and to ensure that political control remained firmly in hand, Youlou began maneuvers to replace his coalition of parties and interests with a single party.

In preparation for the creation of a single party, Youlou began to remove his strongest opponents from the government. He retired Opangault from a vice-presidency in December, 1962 (although retaining him as a minister), and in May, 1963, he removed the two radical spokesmen in the cabinet, Alphonse Massamba-Débat and Germain Bikoumat. The latter removals merely added fuel to a campaign of increasing criticism by the labor unions and others against government incompetence in meeting the developing economic crisis. A few weeks later, after the 1963 Addis Ababa conference on African unity, Youlou invited President Sékou Touré of Guinea to visit the Congo to advertise the benefits of a single party. The attempt backfired when Touré openly criticized the Congolese government, and labor leaders used the occasion to demonstrate their opposition.

In July, 1963, the labor unions, grouped in a Fusion Committee, presented to Youlou's round table on constitutional and political reform detailed proposals that demanded a radical revision of the government before the creation of a single party. When Youlou rejected the proposals, the union leaders, anticipating that a single party would mean preservation of the existing political system, called a general strike for August 13. On the night of August 12, two union leaders were arrested. The next morning, when police attempted to disperse a mass meeting in the center of Brazzaville, crowds stormed and burned the prison, as well as several ministers' houses. Youlou, claiming a foreign plot aimed to oust him, imposed martial law and requested French military aid. But the next day, faced by menacing crowds, he was forced to accept the principle of political reform and he dismissed all his ministers except Opangault, Tchitchellé, and his own cousin, Dominique N'Zalakanda.

With the general strike continuing for a third day, crowds again formed on August 15, Independence Day, at the Presidential Palace to demand Youlou's resignation.. At this point, Congolese military officers intervened to prevent bloodshed, obtained Youlou's resignation, and took political control. Youlou and his ministers were arrested, the National Assembly was dissolved and the military supported the labor leaders in their choice of a provisional government composed of young technicians and headed by Massamba-Débat. Under the guidance of an anonymous National Revolutionary Council (CNR), formed by labor and youth leaders, the provisional government proclaimed a regime of financial austerity with drastically reduced official salaries and an end to special privilege. During its four months in office the government attempted to reorganize the financial shambles and nepotistic system left by the Youlou regime and reshaped the plan for economic development while trying to restore the confidence of local French entrepreneurs and foreign investors.

On December 8, 1963, the country's voters approved a new constitution, modeled on that of the Fifth French Republic, protecting the powers of the Assembly and judiciary while dividing the executive. At the same time the voters elected the unopposed slate of National Assembly candidates proposed by the CNR, almost all of them new to political activity. A few days later Massamba-Débat was elected President by a limited electoral college and, on the advice of the CNR, he chose a government composed largely of the young technicians who had participated in the provisional government. The labor leaders broke their tradition of refusing political office as they accepted places in the Assembly and the new Council of Ministers, but the most important change from the provisional government was the nomination of Pascal Lissouba, the most aggressive and radical of the young technician-ministers, as premier. Lissouba's nomination and the election of a labor union official, Léon Angor, as president of the National Assembly, were the first clear evidence of a trend in favor of the radical Marxist element in the revolutionary coalition.

During the period of confusion after the August revolution, the Catholic and Communist union leaders owed their dominant position to their role in provoking the revolution and to their command of small but relatively disciplined organizations. They were, however, traditional rivals with very different ideas concerning the direction of social and economic change and the orientation of the Congo in foreign affairs. The revolution had brought other groups into political life at Brazzaville, including the university students and various youth groups who tended to demand radical solutions. Even more important were the large numbers of unemployed youth who had contributed to the overthrow of Youlou, who were available for frequent political rallies, and who took over police functions as a popular militia. The Communist union leaders and Lissouba were better prepared to mobilize support among the youth groups than was the Catholic faction, which was increasingly isolated as a moderate group and painted as "counterrevolutionary" by its rivals. In addition, during the provisional government's period in office, Brazzaville became a haven for radical opponents of the Adoula regime at Léopoldville who formed a National Liberation Committee and attracted the support and active presence of radical African and Communist governments.

The new government had to weather a series of crises in its first weeks in office: accusations of subversion by Adoula, local French economic fears over policies of nationalization, and evidence of continuing dissidence among supporters of Youlou. Early in February, municipal elections in Brazzaville, Pointe Noire, and Dolisie were annulled when a large percentage of abstentions and void ballots showed increasing discontent, and on February 7 an uprising of Balali partisans of Youlou in the Brazzaville quarter of Bacongo required military action involving several deaths. This led to several days of anarchy as revolutionary youth groups, organized as a popular militia, arrested suspected Youlou sympathizers within the administration and halted all traffic while accusing the Catholics and Western embassies of encouraging the uprising. Lissouba publicly denied these charges and seized an issue of the Marxist *Dipanda*, which attacked moderates in the government, but Massamba-Débat found it expedient to appoint the radical leader of the National Youth Council as Secretary of State for Youth and Sports. Another serious challenge came from the National Assembly, which met in March in special session on the initiative of the deputies themselves and passed resolutions calling for a single national party, a special court for political crimes and withdrawal of the Congo from the African and Malagasy Union.

Meanwhile, the government had begun to take new directions in foreign affairs. The radical young Foreign Minister, Charles Ganao, toured states of the former Casablanca group in January and February and arranged in Ghana for diplomatic relations between the Congo and Peking. In March, he traveled throughout the Communist bloc establishing diplomatic ties, while the Finance Minister journeyed more quietly among Western capitals. Later, Massamba-Débat himself went to Ghana, to Algeria, to the Conference of Non-Aligned States at Cairo and, in September, 1964, to Peking, which had granted the Congo a large credit and begun sending technical assistance.

The most important foreign problem, however, remained relations with Léopoldville. In May, Adoula closed traffic between the two capitals and Brazzaville anticipated a military attack. Tshombé's succession to power in July led to a short détente, but when he failed to attract support from the Brazzaville-based CNL, a new and more serious crisis developed. On August 15, the first anniversary of the revolution at Brazzaville, Massamba-Débat announced the discovery of American arms smuggled from Léopoldville by Youlou supporters. Tshombé replied immediately that, if need be, he could take Brazzaville in two hours, and two days later he accused Brazzaville of subversion and began expelling Congo (Brazzaville) residents from Léopoldville. By mid-September, 18,000 people had been deported to Brazzaville, increasing the economic strain in the city. Brazzaville and Burundi demanded an OAU inquiry and the focus of crisis shifted elsewhere.

Meanwhile each of these developments at home and abroad tended to separate farther the radical and moderate factions at Brazzaville. Trade union unity, the original basis of the revolutionary coalition, was the issue on which they most clearly split. Gilbert Pongault, the longtime leader of Catholic union activity in AEF and president of the Union Panafricaine des Travailleurs Croyants (UPTC), was one of the leading African exponents of the position that labor must be independent of government and party, and the local CATC made this a condition of unification with the other unions. When in March a Confédération Syndicale Congolaise (CSC) was organized by all other unions, the CATC refused on this grounds to participate.

The pattern of division deepened thereafter. At the National Assembly session in May, Angor was re-elected president over a CATC leader by 43 votes to 6. At the end of June, when the first congress of the Mouvement National de la Révolution (MNR) was held to establish the institutions of the national party, Massamba-Débat was unanimously elected secretary-general, but CSC candidates were elected over those from the CATC by 35 votes to 28 for other offices in the political bureau. This assured the radicals of a controlling majority in all future political and government decisions, and the elimination of the moderate faction began.

In August, when the National Assembly met to discuss arms plots and relations with Léopoldville, Angor threatened the government with a motion of censure if "corrupt" and "counterrevolutionary" ministers and administrators were not dismissed. A few days later, a CATC congress which confirmed the union's refusal to join the CSC was broken up by the Jeunesse MNR, which Catholic youth groups had refused to join. At the end of October, Massamba-Débat, "in response to popular demand," dismissed the two outstanding moderate ministers, named two radical youth leaders to the government, and increased Premier Lissouba's powers. Finally, in November, when the handful of moderates at the Assembly put forward a motion of censure accusing the government of suppressing political liberties, Angor refused to entertain the motion and the moderates were instead stripped of their parliamentary immunity from prosecution. At the same time the CATC president was arrested on charges of distributing subversive tracts.

GABON

Politics, 1946–1956

The educated elite in Libreville, with its long tradition of semipolitical activity, was divided among the Mpongwé tribe, the Fang tribe, and people from the south and interior who were resident in the city. The coastal Mpongwé, who had received the benefit of several decades of education from the Catholic mission at Libreville, held an elite status which was limited by their small numbers. The more industrious Fang, on the other hand, had migrated in large numbers from the Woleu-N'Tem down into the Estuary, threatening the Mpongwé hegemony over privileges and land rights. Among the many small tribes of the south and the interior, only the coastal Vili had considerable numbers of educated men at Libreville. Rivalry between the Mpongwé and the Fang had developed during the period between the world wars, but the Mpongwé's education and position within the civil service had easily overridden relatively inchoate attempts by the Fang to assert a claim to equality, especially after the exile of the young Libreville Fang chief, Léon Mba, in 1933.

In the first elections for the Constituent Assembly in 1945, the vote in Libreville and in all Gabon was divided among the Mpongwé, Fang, and Vili candidates. With Gabon and Middle Congo forming a single constituency, Jean Félix-Tchicaya, the Vili candidate from Mid-

dle Congo, was elected, but the election exacerbated relations between
the Fang and the Mpongwé and almost provoked open warfare. The
Fang candidate, Jean-Hilaire Aubame, was a protégé of the government-
general, having aided Governor-General Eboué to spread Gaullist
propaganda at Vichyist Libreville during the war and to establish elite
cultural associations. His close ties with both the administration and
the missions alienated the Libreville leaders of other tribes during the
increasingly hard-fought battle for political rights at Paris in 1946.
These leaders, led by young Vili and Mpongwé tribesmen and by
Léon Mba, newly returned from exile, worked together under the
aegis of a few Frenchmen in a Groupe d'Etudes Communistes and followed Tchicaya in developing ties with the RDA. As happened to other
groups throughout AEF, however, their delegates named to the RDA
conference in Bamako in Soudan (Mali) in October, 1946, were prevented by the government-general from attending.

In the territorial elections for the French National Assembly in
November, 1946, the Libreville elite proved ineffective, since poor
communications between the city and the rest of the territory prevented the spread of propaganda, and administration support for the
candidacy of Aubame ensured his election over the Mpongwé candidate supported by the GEC. In the elections to the Territorial Assembly, too, the elitist candidates were uniformly defeated by candidates
supported by regional administrators. Isolated from political position,
the radicals among the Libreville elite were easily dispersed by the
administration, and only a small nucleus of men around Mba maintained a militant stance in opposition to Aubame, who joined the moderate Indépendants d'Outre-Mer in the National Assembly at Paris.

Gabon itself was largely isolated from the main trends in French
African politics during the years after this election. The administration
and the European lumbermen, themselves divided on personal and
business grounds, agreed to stifle party politics within the territory.
Thus, except for the short-lived GEC and a weak European-sponsored
branch of the RPF, which was enfeebled by the lack of a Gaullist tradition in the territory, French parties were successfully excluded. Isolation was further aided by Gabon's traditional particularism and the
opposition of all European and African groups to exploitation of the
territory's resources for use elsewhere in AEF. In addition, easy social
relations between most Europeans and Africans, reflecting the
nineteenth-century tradition at Libreville, stood in sharp contrast to
the social discrimination in force elsewhere.

Competition among African leaders and ethnic groups, though it did not appear in the form of rival political parties, was nonetheless heated. Among the Fang, the division between Aubame and Mba was accentuated by differences between Aubame's supporters in the north and the followers of Mba in the Estuary. Mba attempted without success to gain control of a pan-tribal movement at the Pahouin (Fang) Congress of 1947, and relied on the spread of the *bwiti* cult for much of his political support in the Estuary. Aubame, on the other hand, depended on his influence with the administration to obtain social reforms in the Woleu-N'Tem and during the late 1940's sought to capture control of movements of clan regroupment active in that region. Meanwhile a clear rivalry developed within the Territorial Assembly between Aubame's Fang supporters and Paul Gondjout, the only Mpongwé elected to the Assembly and the most able of the African parliamentarians. Aided by Mpongwé mulatto lumberman Joseph Walker-Deemin, who with European support became permanent president of the Territorial Assembly, Gondjout obtained election as senator and began an effort to mobilize southern and interior support against the danger of Fang domination.

By 1951, Gondjout had joined forces with Mba, who dropped his radicalism at the time of the RDA break with the Communists. Although they had no success against Aubame in the elections of 1951 and 1952, they began to organize support within the Territorial Assembly, and in 1954 Gondjout began to build a political party, the Bloc Démocratique Gabonais (BDG). Its official program featured opposition to tribalism, and Gondjout took pains to give prominence to Mba and to southerners within the party. Aubame, who had organized a purely nominal party, the Union Démocratique et Sociale Gabonaise (UDSG), in 1947, replied by making his first efforts at organization and propaganda in the territory. Poor communications in the interior, however, kept both parties from serious efforts at organizing outside the main centers. Aubame, relying on his usual sources of support, had no difficulty winning re-election to the French National Assembly over Mba in January, 1956.

The BDG in Office

The rival African parties aligned themselves rapidly with rival European economic groups, forming alliances that were strengthened by institutional reforms which made African political groups potentially significant in the shaping of economic policy. The municipal elections of

November, 1956, provided Mba with an opportunity to display the heavy majority support he had developed in Libreville among all tribal groups and thus set the stage for the crucial elections to the Territorial Assembly in March, 1957. With financial support from Roland Bru, the leading independent lumberman in Gabon, Gondjout organized a BDG campaign for support in each region. Aubame, in contrast, continued to rely on his support from the administration and from local leaders who had been associated with him in the past. The election results placed the balance of power in the hands of independent regional leaders, but Gondjout's aggressive efforts to enlist their votes, when set against Aubame's easygoing assumption of broad support, gave Gondjout a majority of 20 to 19 for the presidency of the Assembly. Refusing the compromise favored by Mba, Gondjout pushed his advantage and obtained a Council of Government composed of eight BDG members and four UDSG members, headed by Mba.

The narrow BDG majority in the Assembly made for continuing instability as Aubame sought occasions to upset the Council of Government. After several crises Aubame withdrew his UDSG ministers from the Council, and the BDG, using the government powers at its command, in January, 1958, succeeded in prying a few UDSG assembly members away from their party by offering them ministries.

During 1958, party competition continued outside the Assembly over policy concerning de Gaulle's Community and the appropriate status for Gabon. The BDG government, allied with the interterritorial RDA, decided early in favor of the Community and against federation. Aubame's UDSG, a non-RDA party, was affiliated with the Parti du Regroupement Africain (PRA) of French West Africa, which resolved in July, 1958, in favor of federation and the right to independence. After considerable hesitation, the UDSG met in congress to agree on support for the Community and separate republican status. At this point, however, an ambitious southern politician, Rémy-Paul Sousatte, organized a Parti de l'Unité Nationale Gabonaise (PUNGA), based on regional and labor grievances against the BDG regime, and seized on opposition to de Gaulle's constitution as a means of making his mark. Thus while the other AEF territories were turning in majorities of 98 to 99 per cent in favor of the constitution in the referendum of September, 1958, 7 per cent of Gabon's voters, most of them concentrated in neglected districts in the southwest, voted against it.

To avoid further evidence of division, the government called a round table of all parties and interest groups to decide upon the status Gabon should take within the Community and succeeded in obtaining broad agreement for a separate republic. Boganda's plans for federation, described above, received no support in the territory, where all groups insisted on utilizing Gabon's resources for its own economic development. Thus, on November 28, 1958, the Territorial Assembly voted unanimously in favor of republican status within the Community. An all-party committee drew up a constitution similar to those being adopted in other French African states, with the government well protected against overthrow. When the constitution was passed on February 19, 1959, however, the BDG majority overrode the objections of the other parties to prolonging the life of the existing Assembly, and thus avoided the elections which were called in each of the other new republics at this time. Despite threats of violence by the UDSG and PUNGA, the BDG held its ground and the French government refused to intervene.

Assured of continuing Assembly support, the BDG leaders made full use of government powers during 1959 to implant their party in the administration. UDSG support was gradually confined to the party's Fang bastion, the Woleu-N'Tem. Toward the end of the year, when Sousatte began proposing independence and UDSG radicals spoke of transferring the Woleu-N'Tem to independent Cameroun, the government pushed through the Assembly a number of restrictive security measures and promptly arrested Sousatte and other opponents of the regime.

Early in 1960, questions of independence and federation found the UDSG agreeing with the BDG to refuse any federation which would commit Gabon's funds to a federal authority. Thereafter Aubame joined government delegations at interstate conferences. But once separate independence was achieved in August, the problem of drawing up a new constitution led to serious differences between Mba and Gondjout which threatened to wreck their long and successful partnership. The constitution of February, 1959, had been a compromise between the Assembly and the presidency, which gave each considerable initiative. In the eighteen months of operation under that constitution friction had developed between the executive and legislature. At the same time, Fang and southern members of the BDG objected to the important public role taken by Gondjout as spokesman for the country, while Mba's European counselors objected to the increasing nationalism of Gondjout and other Assembly leaders. Extended constitutional discussions found Gondjout and a majority of the BDG executive committee joined by the UDSG in favor of strong parliamentary powers and a weak presidency. As a result, Mba and his Council of Ministers, after obtaining a few concessions to their views, were forced to accept an essentially parliamentary constitution, which was passed by the Assembly on November 3, 1960.

Immediately after passage of the constitution, Mba attempted to divide the developing radical coalition in the Assembly by inviting the UDSG to join a national government, but although two leading UDSG moderates who were opposed to Gondjout accepted the invitation, Aubame and the UDSG executive refused Mba's terms. At the same time, despite several meetings of conciliation sponsored by the BDG, Mba and Gondjout failed to agree on an interpretation of the constitution that allowed greater executive prerogative. Finally, on November 29, after Mba had discovered a motion of censure circulating among UDSG and BDG deputies, Gondjout and five other BDG leaders, all but one of them Mpongwé, were arrested and confined to isolated posts in the interior. Mba quickly called a BDG party congress and took Gondjout's post as secretary-general. In January, 1961, he dissolved the Assembly and called for new elections. Aubame, faced with the alternative of imprisonment, agreed to join a single slate of candidates selected by Mba, and he and two UDSG moderates were given seats in the Assembly elected on February 12. Five days later, the Assembly met to pass by acclamation a new constitution vesting effective powers in the President. Louis Bigmann, an older Mpongwé who had sided with Mba, was elected to succeed Gondjout as Assembly president.

Thereafter Mba pursued a program of national unity aimed at bringing all elements into cooperation with the government. Aubame and three other UDSG leaders were given ministerial portfolios and a year later even Sousatte was admitted to cabinet rank. University students, who had provided a vocal opposition to the conservative policies pursued by the President, were absorbed into the government and given responsible posts with perquisites. Even Gondjout and his collaborators were released and accepted back into responsible positions. Then, early in 1963, with BDG control secure, a party congress demanded that all ministers declare themselves in favor of the party. When the UDSG leaders and Sousatte refused, Mba removed them from the Council of Ministers but persuaded them to accept other posts. Holding all effective political authority himself, he neatly pigeonholed his two former rivals for leadership in nonpolitical offices: Aubame as president of the Supreme Court, and Gondjout as president of the Economic and Social Council.

The Mba Regime under Pressure

After the overthrow of Youlou in the Congo, ostensibly because he tried to impose single-party rule, Mba quietly dropped plans for a single party in Gabon, but began forcefully to recruit long-term UDSG supporters to the BDG and to arrest intransigents. It was not this, however, but his budget proposals calling for austerity while raising the presidential allocation, which created problems once again between the presidency and the National Assembly. After an announcement that deputies' salaries would be subject to a 10 per cent contribution to the National Investment Fund and that, at the same time, Assembly President Bigmann's salary would be increased, the hand-picked Assembly balked and refused to consider the annual budget at its December, 1963, session. A compromise was arranged and the budget was passed, but Mba blamed much of his difficulty with the Assembly on Aubame and attempted to push through the Assembly a law making Aubame's post as president of the Supreme Court incompatible with that of deputy. The Assembly refused this, but immediately after its session ended Mba issued a decree to the same effect, only to be outwitted by Aubame's resignation on January 10 from the Supreme Court. Mba immediately dismissed a minister considered friendly to Aubame and on January 21 dissolved the National Assembly, claiming that the government's austerity program required a reduction in the number of deputies and calling for new elections on Feburary 23. Opposition groups announced their refusal to nominate national lists of candidates.

At midnight on February 17, military forces and police under the command of junior officers trained at Saint-Cyr seized control of government buildings at Libreville and captured Mba and Bigmann. A committee composed of six young officers announced that the revolution was taking place to prevent disturbances during the elections. After canceling the elections, declaring martial law, and forcing Mba to broadcast a resignation and mea culpa for authoritarian rule, the committee handed political power to a ten-man provisional government headed by Aubame and including Gondjout and several young politicians and administrators. The following evening, however, troops under French command were flown to Libreville from Dakar and

Brazzaville at the request of the French ambassador, who claimed to have received an appeal from Vice-President Paul Yembit for French intervention under a military pact of 1961. After a short military action in which several Gabonese soldiers and a few French were killed, the French took control of the city on the morning of February 19 and restored Mba to office.

Mba immediately promised vengeance on those responsible for the revolution, but in view of continued disturbances at Libreville he was persuaded by the French to move with caution. An investigating commission was set up and the special Court for State Security was revamped to include a number of retired minor political figures, while Aubame and others were arrested and interned. In order to pacify the opposition, Assembly elections were postponed to April 12 and a new electoral law reinstated the old system of regional representation. Several local opposition and independent lists were put forward in addition to those supported by Mba's BDG. Though the opposition won all major cities and the UDSG base in the Woleu-N'Tem, government supporters won several interior regions and official results gave them narrow majorities in three others to provide an Assembly of 31 government and 16 opposition deputies. Shortly after the election Mba replaced a few politicians in his government with young administrators and Georges Damas, another older Mpongwé, replaced Bigmann as Assembly president while Bigmann took Aubame's post at the Supreme Court. The French government had, meanwhile, removed two targets of criticism by recalling its ambassador and insisting on the return to France of Roland Bru. At the same time, several important administrative posts still manned by Frenchmen were Africanized.

Strikes and other disturbances continued at Libreville despite these concessions and all schools were closed early because of student demonstrations, but by July police operations had quelled open manifestations of opposition and late in August the trial of military rebels and provisional government members opened under strict security controls at Lambaréné. Aubame and the other political leaders maintained that they were not aware of the revolution until after its success, and all of them upheld the legitimacy of the provisional government and the illegality of French intervention. The prosecution demanded the death penalty in several instances but the court, probably again under pressure from the French for caution and compromise, issued sentences on September 9 ranging from ten years' imprisonment and ten years' exile for Aubame to exoneration for Gondjout and others. In addition, the government decreed a bill of attainder against those convicted, giving itself the power to withdraw their civil rights and restrict their residence without recourse to the courts.

The second session of the National Assembly in October showed that Mba's police controls were effective in stifling opposition. Of the sixteen deputies elected in oppositon to the government in April, ten had been converted to BDG persuasion, three were in prison, and only three remained in open opposition at the Assembly.

OUBANGUI-CHARI—CENTRAL AFRICAN REPUBLIC

Politics to 1951

Traditional society in Oubangui-Chari, which was severely disrupted during the eras of the slave trade and concessionary regime, was further shattered in the west by repression of the Baya revolt and in the east and center by forced cotton planting. The resulting weakness of tribal structures and the physical structure of the main center, Bangui—whose many small African quarters were pushed out to the periphery of the city—contributed to a relative absence of tribal rivalry and conflict. No large-scale cleavages developed on ethnic or regional grounds, though the small riverine tribes along the Oubangui River had obtained an early lead over those of the savanna in education and hence in promotion within the civil service. In fact, however, very few Oubanguiens had even the beginnings of a secondary education before World War II, and the higher African posts in the civil service were given to Camerounians and others from outside the territory. Hence, the first elite grouping of Oubanguiens at Bangui, the Amicale Oubanguien of 1938–1940, was formed in large measure to raise Oubanguien prestige in the face of the social and economic domination by Africans from other territories.

The leader of the Amicale Oubanguien, Auguste Gandji-koBokassi, the son of a chief near Bangui, had been educated at Brazzaville and Libreville, was active in the early years of the League for the Defense of the Rights of Man, and had established a position as leader of the elite at Bangui. Viewed as troublesome by the administration, Gandji was ruled ineligible for candidacy in the first elections to Paris. In the absence of other candidates of their own, Bangui and other centers on the main routes supported a radical young Gabonese who had been educated in France. A French colonel supported by the Chad and

Oubangui administrations, however, won a contested majority in their combined African constituency, in tandem with René Malbrant, the unopposed candidate for the European seat.

The reputation of Oubangui-Chari for primitive life and proverty did not attract the ablest administrators to the territory, and relations between Europeans and Africans were traditionally worse than in any other territory. Hence, unlike the situation in other territories, there was very little effort by Europeans at Bangui to provide a political education through study groups during 1945–1946, though Malbrant's supporters attempted to capture African support by founding an African branch of their Gaullist association, Combat. One European Socialist did form an African study group which served as the nucleus for a party. In the election of November, 1946, Gandji teamed with this group to support a young Socialist candidate for the French National Assembly. Combat nominated a West Indian civil servant, but his freemason leanings led the Catholic missions to sponsor a candidate of their own: Barthélémy Boganda, the first African priest in the territory and the best-educated Oubanguien. With the benefit of an active campaign by missionaries throughout the territory, Boganda soundly defeated the candidates of both the isolated Bangui elite and the administration. Boganda's supporters then received administration support in defeating Gandji's Socialist candidates for the African seats in the Territorial Assembly.

Boganda's European patrons soon had cause to regret their choice. Though Boganda joined the conservative Catholic MRP in France, he did not hesitate to criticize the record of the colonial administration and the missions in Oubangui, and at Bangui his supporters in the Territorial Assembly quickly outstripped the Socialists in their attacks on European privilege in the territory. Within a year, however, the nascent nationalist movement had been divided. Boganda laid out an ambitious program of economic and social development through regional cooperatives and attempted to initiate a political organization to implement the program against the opposition of both administration and missions. But the territorial councilors, tempted by opportunities for running their own profit-making cooperatives with government credit, disagreed with Boganda's program and, under the leadership of Georges Darlan, broke with him in mid-1948. Boganda, politically isolated, devoted himself to organizing his own cooperative plantation in his home village in the Lobaye and engaged in an increasingly bitter struggle with local administrators.

From 1948 to 1951, several rival political groups developed in the territory. Malbrant's Gaullist RPF, with the support of the administration and almost all private Europeans, set up an African branch around ex-servicemen and docile chiefs. Georges Darlan and the territorial councilors sought to ensure their re-election through the spread of their cooperatives, but lack of experience, widespread embezzlement, and opposition from the administration forestalled them. Darlan's brother Antoine, Boganda's equal in making vitriolic, well-documented attacks on administration abuses, attempted to organize a branch of the RDA, but could not find funds or educated personnel to sustain militant activity outside Bangui. Gandji's Socialists withered for lack of cohesion and power. And Boganda, having quit the MRP after being defrocked, launched his own party, the Mouvement pour l'Evolution Sociale de l'Afrique Noire (MESAN), to continue his war of letters and demagogic circulars against the administration. None of these groups was organized beyond a small nucleus at Bangui, and the interior regions remained almost untouched by political activity.

The Rise of Boganda

The National Assembly elections on June 17, 1951, provided a crucial watershed in Oubangui politics. Each of the political groups in the territory laid plans to present candidates to contest Boganda's seat, and a full year in advance each of the leaders began touring the territory to organize support. Then, in January, 1951, Boganda's long-standing feud with the local administration in the Lobaye led a frustrated administrator to arrest him for endangering the peace. Released after one day of confinement, Boganda succeeded through brilliant propaganda —spread by tracts and by truckdrivers over the excellent road network in the cotton regions—in creating for himself the image of a martyr to the injustice and brutality of the colonial regime. With the tacit support of Antoine Darlan and in the face of discredited rival candidates and a politically weak territorial administration, Boganda won re-election. Seven months later, Boganda's nominees won most African seats in the Territorial Assembly elections, though they were opposed in the Assembly by a majority combining RPF Europeans and a few Africans elected in isolated regions with the support of the administration.

MESAN was an entirely personal organization, with each of its local agents responsible directly to Boganda himself. Having been opposed by the Bangui elite from the start, he distrusted it and relied upon a few mission schoolteachers who had been his students and upon un-educated truckdrivers and others to supply him with information and to spread his commands and advice. After the 1951 election his prestige was so great throughout the territory that he found little need for inter-mediaries, and relatively unknown local candidates were elected to the Territorial Assembly purely on the basis of his sponsorship. Boganda himself had never taken an active role in the National Assembly, and he continued to distrust the RDA and other parties based in French West Africa, insisting that Oubangui-Chari must progress through self-help alone. Hence, he left all affairs at Paris to Antoine Darlan at the Assembly of the French Union and to Hector Rivierez, a lawyer from Guiana whom he chose as MESAN candidate for the Senate. Mean-while Bonganda concentrated his own energies on the development of his plantation and the investigation of alleged cases of administrative abuse.

The administration, faced with Boganda's prestige, attempted to limit its effect but with little success. Governor I. Colombani, who had failed to defeat Boganda in the 1951 election, was removed from his post immediately thereafter, and following another two years of unsuc-cessful attempts to oppose Boganda, Louis Sanmarco was named gov-ernor in 1953 with the express policy of accommodating Boganda and winning his cooperation for administration programs. For the next three years, Boganda was quiet, helping to prevent another Baya revolt after incidents at Berberati and accepting Sanmarco's promises of re-form, while exacting in return the removal of particularly difficult offi-cials and the end of persecution of MESAN agents. Despite the compromise won by Sanmarco, however, Boganda remained the bête noire of the Europeans in the territory.

In January, 1956, the first fair election saw Boganda re-elected easily over nominal opposition from the Bangui elite and remnants of the RPF. At the same time, the announcement of new French reforms abolishing the double electorate and creating elected municipal coun-cils and Councils of Government persuaded a few Europeans to seek political arrangements with MESAN. A number of leading Bangui businessmen supported one of their number, Roger Guerillot, who de-clared support for Boganda in exchange for his promise of European representation in the new institutions. For the first time, MESAN re-ceived European financial support and Boganda was encouraged to revive his attacks on the administration's economic controls and the high cost of its bureaucracy. Thus, the entente with Sanmarco was dropped in favor of an alliance with Bangui business. The Europeans won high places on MESAN lists in the municipal and territorial elections, as well as social peace, in exchange for financial support and social acceptance for Boganda and his French wife. Only minor opposition was thrown up against MESAN in these elections, and the party took almost all the seats in the municipal council and all those in the Territorial Assembly.

With almost unlimited effective political authority, Boganda set up a political machine of three parts: the MESAN executive committee, composed of a small group of confidants, the MESAN group in the Territorial Assembly, and the MESAN-controlled Council of Government. The latter was composed of only six ministers: five young educated Oubanguiens and the increasingly powerful Guerillot. All three groups were directly responsible to Boganda, who decided to refuse a position in the Council of Government in favor of a seat in the Grand Council, where negotiations with the RDA won him the presidency of the council and a position as spokesman for all AEF. From this vantage point he raised to the federal level his attacks on the administration and its failure to begin the process of decolonization.

During 1957 and 1958, Boganda's efforts to capture political leadership throughout AEF brought him into direct conflict with the RDA of Lisette, Youlou, and Mba. He attempted to harass them by creating MESAN branches in Chad and Middle Congo and Lisette replied by financing the re-establishment of a small RDA branch in Oubangui. Boganda, long suspicious that Antoine Darlan and others who opposed the influence of Guerillot were secretly in league with the RDA, seized on this occasion to eliminate them from MESAN. Later in 1958, as his attacks on the administration became increasingly strident, he removed each of his non-African advisers, Guerillot, Rivierez, and even Mme. Boganda, and depended for counsel on his young and inexperienced Oubanguien acolytes in the party and the government.

After November, 1958, the failure of his federal ambitions placed Boganda at the head of a Central African Republic (RCA) whose extent was limited to Oubangui-Chari and, although he continued to work for a wider federation, he was for the first time faced with the responsibility of laying out and executing a positive set of programs for the development of his own territory. On March 29, 1959, however, he died in an airplane crash in the midst of an election campaign for a new National Assembly in RCA. Boganda's regime had been thoroughly autocratic and, having discarded each of his experienced lieutenants, he left behind him neither an heir apparent nor a clear program nor, in effect, a political organization capable of establishing either a succession or a program.

Boganda's Successor

The vacuum of political authority left control over these questions to Mme. Boganda, the French High Commissioner, and the European business community of Bangui. This group supported the candidacy of Boganda's cousin, David Dacko, over his rival in the Council of Government, Abel Goumba. Etienne N'Gounio, MESAN secretary-general and Guerillot's replacement as Boganda's chief confidant, was persuaded to acquiesce in this choice in return for continued leadership of the remnants of the party.

Lacking Boganda's authority, however, the Dacko regime was not easily established in power, and it was rapidly challenged by Goumba and others with alternative claims to Boganda's succession. On October 3, 1959, Goumba and Faustin Maléombho, president of the National Assembly, brought a motion of no confidence which was narrowly averted by use of political pressures and threats of force. The issue divided the deputies of the west, supporting Goumba, Maléombho, and N'Gounio, from those of the east, supporting Dacko and Mme. Boganda, and it opened a regional split in the country which had never appeared under Boganda. Having weathered this test, however, the government took the initiative, and in May, 1960, Michel Adama Tamboux replaced Maléombho as the Assembly president. This substitution provoked the opposition to form a new political party, the Mouvement pour l'Evolution Démocratique en Afrique Centrale (MEDAC). Dacko immediately seized control of MESAN from N'Gounio and called the party's first congress. The two groups, each claiming legitimate descent from Boganda, began the first open political campaigning the country had seen since 1952.

After independence was achieved in August, 1960, Dacko's government pushed through the Assembly a Constitution providing exceptional powers, and with these in hand it was able to restrict the spread of MEDAC and had no problem winning three by-elections in September, 1960. Then, having forced the removal of the French High Commissioner, who had transferred his sympathies too openly to the opposition, and having frightened the French government by threatening to exchange ambassadors with the Soviet bloc, Dacko offered to re-establish friendly relations in exchange for French acquiescence in the suppression of MEDAC. At the end of 1960, despite attempts by the MEDAC leaders to obtain a compromise, their party was banned. Goumba, Maléombho, and other leaders were imprisoned and held until February, 1962, when they were formally sentenced to prison terms for subversive activity. Discontent in the east continued for over a year, but no serious attempt was made to reorganize political opposition. Later in the year the National Assembly declared MESAN the sole authorized political party, banning any further activity by tiny and inactive branches of the RDA and the Mouvement Socialiste Africain.

Having firmly established the power and legitimacy of his government and party, Dacko—and the group of young men around him—turned to the problems of achieving national unity and economic mobilization. Toward these ends ministers and deputies were organized into traveling propaganda teams, and MESAN was revitalized as an active force, with frequent congresses and executive council meetings. At the same time, the government instituted youth labor camps under military direction along Israeli lines and began a program of severe austerity in political and personnel expenditures. To this extent at least, RCA regained the innovating spirit which Boganda had maintained during his campaign for federation. And, as in Boganda's time, this was made possible primarily because of the absence of deep-seated divisions within Central African society. While in each of the other equatorial states increasingly dictatorial regimes met continued resistance and even revolutions during 1963 and 1964, Dacko was able to boast of RCA's calm and stability. The quiet renewal of his regime through presidential elections in January, 1964, and Assembly elections two months later confirmed the absence of open opposition and of important political difficulties.

CHAD

The Politics of Repression, 1946–1952

The territory of Chad straddles the traditional line of conflict between northern Muslims and southern pagans. The Muslims are organized in hierarchic sultanates under traditional rulers preserving much of their precolonial authority. The southerners are grouped in much smaller societies—predominantly those of the Sara tribes—whose traditional local chiefs were generally replaced during the colonial period by French appointees. Reinforcing the traditional division between these groups were the south's higher degree of education and economic development, based on cotton, and the growth of towns such as Fort Lamy and Fort Archambault where Muslims and Sara came into daily contact and rivalry.

In many ways Chad was by 1946 the most retarded of the four territories of AEF. Education, even in the south, had begun very late, and only two groups had received secondary education: a few Muslim chiefs' sons, who had been sent off to Libreville or Senegal in the early years of French occupation and who returned to high positions at Fort Lamy, and the dozen students who had been sent after 1935 to the Ecole Renard in Brazzaville. After 1942, the paternalist regime of Governor Jacques Rogué created semielectoral organizations to replace artificial sultanates in the cities and set up a closely guided cultural center for the educated civil servants and the wealthy Muslim traders who constituted the elite of Fort Lamy.

During the elections to the two constituent assemblies, Rogué and René Malbrant, unopposed candidate for the European seat and unquestioned spokesman of AEF European interests, agreed to support their friend, Colonel Guy de Boissoudy, for the African seat for Chad and Oubangui-Chari. With full administration support, De Boissoudy had no difficulty defeating a young Gabonese who had the backing of the younger elite. During the latter half of 1946, however, Governor-General Bayardelle, who opposed Rogué, arranged for his replacement by a loyal Socialist and assigned to Chad as his personal political agent a young West Indian administrator named Gabriel Lisette. In Rogué's absence, Lisette captured the support of the young elite. By dint of an arduous campaign in the south and through a split in the opposition created by rival European candidacies, he won election to the French National Assembly in November, 1946. A month later his supporters organized the Parti Progressiste du Tchad (PPT) and took a few seats in the Territorial Assembly, but regional administrators sponsored the candidacies of chiefs, sultans, and older civil servants whose votes ensured a conservative majority in the Assembly when combined with those of European councilors.

Rogué's return to the governorship in December, 1946, led to the establishment of the most effective regime of political paternalism and repression in French Africa. The Governor took personal responsibility for organizing the activities of the Territorial Assembly and formed among pro-administration African councilors a Union Démocratique

Tchadienne (UDT), allied with the Gaullist RPF of Malbrant and the Europeans. At the same time he mobilized the systematic recruitment of chiefs and civil servants into the ranks of his party, isolating or removing those who failed to collaborate. Lisette, active in Paris where he took a leading role within the RDA parliamentary group, returned to Chad twice a year for two-month tours, but met increasing difficulty in holding together his supporters and was quickly alienated from the Europeans of the territory, who considered him a threat to continued colonial rule. Within two years, most of his African support had been eliminated from the Muslim north and was restricted to the young elite and laborers in Fort Lamy, Archambault, and Moundou. The survival of the PPT depended almost entirely on the continuing militancy of its two chief organizers, Jules-Pierre Toura Gaba at Fort Lamy and François Tombalbaye at Fort Archambault, both of them Sara graduates of the Ecole Renard.

In 1950, just as the interterritorial RDA broke away from its Communist affiliations in Paris, the French Socialist Party succeeded in its long-term efforts to win the young Fort Lamy Muslim elite away from the PPT and to take from the UDT a popular trader, Ahmed Koulamalla, as leader of a Parti Socialiste Indépendante du Tchad. At the same time the Socialists, through influence in Paris, replaced Rogué's RPF successor as governor with their own nominee and laid optimistic plans for winning at least one of Chad's newly granted two seats in the National Assembly. Rogué and Malbrant, however, had successfully politicized the Chadien administration in favor of the RPF, and in the elections of June, 1951, one of the most obviously rigged elections in the French territories gave both seats by an immense majority to candidates selected by Malbrant—one of them to an illiterate exserviceman. The chicanery in the election, particularly in the north, threw Lisette's PPT and Koulamalla's Socialists into a Front d'Action Civique, which threatened a general strike and withdrew only in the face of mounted machine guns. In the Territorial Assembly elections of March, 1952, the Front, presenting common lists of candidates against the UDT, succeeded in capturing the regions of Fort Lamy and Fort Archambault, though it was overwhelmed by the UDT's administration support elsewhere. In the Logone, the most tightly contested region in the south, the elections led to incidents in one village, Bébalem, where the killing of several dozen people by French-led troops constituted the only important political bloodshed in AEF during the postwar colonial period.

Lisette in Power and Party Instability

The increasingly moderate orientation of the interterritorial RDA in France and West Africa led to a lessening of political pressures against the party by the French administrations throughout Africa, but in Chad Lisette's attempts to win the confidence of the administration were rebuffed. At the end of 1953, however, the return of former Governor Rogué as a politician upset all political forces in the territory and led to a major division and realignment. The administration and Malbrant, fearing that Rogué's personal power would upset their system of political control, fought against his election to the Assembly of the French Union. Rogué, however, won over a sufficient number of his former protégés from the UDT to be elected, and he organized his own party, the Union Démocratique des Indépendants du Tchad (UDIT). Lisette was persuaded to support the administration against Rogué in exchange for concessions toward the PPT, but this action split the Front and permanently estranged Koulamalla and his radical Muslim support.

With his opposition divided, Lisette turned to a policy of seeking the broadest possible entente among all parties in Chad. His responsibilities as a leading officer of the increasingly respectable RDA kept him out of Chad much of the time, but his astute use of pressures from Paris and Brazzaville won ostensible neutrality from the territorial administration by 1955. Although for some time he was unable to pull together the various splinter parties, in January, 1956, with the solid support of the south, he was able to recapture his seat in the National Assembly. Then, in alliance with the UDIT of Rogué and Jean-Baptiste, a Muslim mulatto, the PPT won the Fort Lamy municipal elections in November, 1956. This victory brought the educated Muslims and other splinter groups back into the PPT. The opposition of French Socialists and the local remnants of the RPF kept their African protégés—Koulamalla and the Action Sociale Tchadienne (successor to the UDT)—out of the entente, but in the elections for the Territorial Assembly in March, 1957, Lisette's system of alliances paid off with a clear Assembly majority for his PPT-dominated entente over its two rivals. The PPT successfully invaded the Muslim regions of Kanem and Mayo-Kebbi. Koulamalla, who was feared by the administration as an agent of pan-Arab and Sudanese influences, was entirely shut out of the Assembly.

Lisette's election in May, 1957, as vice-president of the new Council of Government marked the high point of his power. The distribution of posts in the Council of Government, in the Territorial Assembly and Grand Council, and in the reorganized PPT hierarchy gave him an opportunity to balance all conflicting factions within his alliance and to continue in his dual role as African economic spokesman in Paris and RDA boss in Equatorial Africa. An unrelenting campaign of opposition by his long-time European opponents, however, began to weaken the entente. By January, 1958, Jean-Baptiste and the UDIT were in open opposition, aiding Koulamalla's capture of the region of Fort Lamy in a re-election. Increased Muslim defections from the entente during 1958 led to serious instability by the end of the year, though all parties were brought together in favor of De Gaulle's constitution.

In January, 1959, while Lisette was in France, his remaining Muslim allies outside the PPT deserted to the opposition, giving it a narrow majority in the Assembly and overturning Lisette's government. Sahoulba Gontchomé, Sultan of Léré and president of the Assembly, replaced Lisette as president of the Council of Government. The new Muslim coalition, directed by Jean-Baptiste and several Europeans, attempted to set up arrangements for new elections. The purely negative nature of the alliance quickly revealed conflicting ambitions, however, and within three months Lisette had succeeded in winning Koulamalla away from the coalition by offering him the presidency of the Council. This not only outraged Koulamalla's former allies but also frightened the moderate Muslim leaders within the PPT. Koulamalla's government lasted only a week before these groups had agreed to its overthrow and replacement by a broad coalition government headed by François Tombalbaye, leader of the PPT in Fort Archambault.

The PPT had been badly shaken and divided by the fall of Lisette's government in January. Southern assemblymen led by Tombalbaye telegraphed de Gaulle to demand that Chad be split into two republics. Lisette himself was so discouraged by the failure of his efforts that he offered to resign all his posts and return to France where, with Houphouët-Boigny of the Ivory Coast, Senghor of Senegal, and Tisiranana of Madagascar, he was shortly to be named Minister-Counselor in de Gaulle's government. He was persuaded by other PPT leaders to remain, but the Muslims in the party were split on the question of cooperation with Koulamalla, while the southern strength of the party was divided among factions led by Toura Gaba, Tombalbaye, and a group of young radicals from the Logone. The overthrow of the Koulamalla government and the nomination of Tombalbaye were opposed by Lisette, as well as by the radicals of both north and south, and Lisette found that control of the party was no longer exclusively in his hands.

The Tombalbaye Regime

Government instability had given Chad a bad name within the Community. To counteract divisive tendencies the Tombalbaye government, with Lisette as vice-president, quickly pushed through the Assembly a constitution making overthrow of a government more difficult and called for the election of a new National Assembly. Once again Lisette set about arranging a series of electoral alliances. Since the Muslim parties were divided among themselves, he was able to deal with them separately in each region so as to obtain successful local coalitions for the PPT throughout the country. The results of the elections of May 31, 1959, gave the PPT a large majority of its own, ensuring a stable government, and although Jean-Baptiste, Djibrine Kherallah, and other Muslim leaders were brought into the government, Koulamalla was once again completely shut out.

Tombalbaye was re-elected President while Lisette retained the vice-presidency and party presidency, and for several months government and political affairs ran smoothly under their joint direction. At the end of 1959, however, with independence approaching, Tombalbaye began to chafe at Lisette's continued role as spokesman for Chad in its relations with France and the Community, and he demanded full control of all government matters. Then in February, 1960, Tombalbaye was faced with renewed activity by the Muslim parties, which joined together to form the Parti National Africain (PNA) under Koulamalla and Jean-Baptiste. His expulsion of PNA leaders from the Council of Ministers marked Tombalbaye's first personal initiative in internal political affairs. By mid-1960, relations between Lisette and Tombalbaye were strained and there were rumors of plans to remove Tombalbaye. Tombalbaye, however, held the powers of office and had the support of local French representatives. A few days after the declaration of independence in August, 1960, while Lisette was absent from the country, Tombalbaye announced his removal from office and expulsion from Chad.

Thereafter, Tombalbaye's efforts were focused on uniting the party and the country behind him. A week after removing Lisette, he called the PPT into congress at Moundou, denounced Lisette, and took office as president of the party. In December, he pushed through the Assembly a new constitution with strong presidential powers and defeated an effort by Assembly President Allahou Taher to mount a motion of censure against his government. Allahou and Toura Gaba, considered Lisette's leading supporters, were then eliminated from power. Allahou was replaced under the new constitution by another PPT Muslim, and Toura Gaba was first appointed UN representative, then on his return from New York dismissed from the Council. The Logone radicals were successfully isolated by arrest, by the development of loyal rival leaders in their region, and eventually by the division of the Logone into three regions. The Muslim opposition in the PNA was compromised when a few of its leaders accepted ministerial posts. The movement toward unification culminated in April, 1961, in a congress at Abéché at which the PNA accepted alliance with the PPT in a Union pour le Progrès du Tchad.

The tradition of opposition and faction, however, was not this easily overridden. The PNA submitted rival lists of candidates for municipal elections in August, 1961, but Tombalbaye then removed Jean-Baptiste's citizenship and effectively cancelled the Union pour le Progrès du Tchad. Ahmed Kotoko, the new president of the National Assembly, was next to fall, exiled on rumors of a plot against the government. In February, 1962, Tombalbaye decided to impose unity by dissolving all opposition parties and calling for election of a new National Assembly. This time, through a hand-picked single list of candidates, he sought to bring together from all regions a group of men loyal to the government, including a large number untainted by past political activity. At the same time, he cleansed his cabinet of potential opponents and substituted a few educated young men capable of taking an active role in both politics and administration.

In January, 1963, the PPT hierarchy was revised to bring in the first Chadien university graduates, most of whom had until then been treated with considerable reserve and suspicion.

The new men from the south were successfully integrated, but politicians from the Muslim north found continued southern domination increasingly difficult to stomach. The long-term emigration of Muslim students to Khartoum and Cairo increased despite attempts to control the Sudanese frontier and to extend educational facilities in the north. Then in May, discovery of a major plot against the government was announced, entailing the arrest of three Muslim ministers, several other high Muslim officials, and the young man chosen by Tombalbaye to lead loyal Muslim support as president of the National Assembly. At the same time, the young educated Muslim leaders of an outlawed party, the Union Nationale Tchadienne, were arrested on similar but separate charges. The Assembly was dissolved, and during trial by a special court in June the arrested men were accused of having plotted the secession of the north and fusion with the Sudan. Finally in September, 1963, the three outstanding Muslim leaders, Koulamalla, Jean-Baptiste, and Djibrine Kherallah—until then silent or compromised by government subsidies—were arrested after a political meeting at Fort Lamy which erupted in riots upon the arrival of Sara troops, leaving over one hundred dead. At the end of the year, another hand-picked Assembly was elected, and in January, 1964, Tombalbaye made another new start with a completely reshaped Council of Ministers containing several of the educated young administrators and a few new Muslim faces.

The arrests of September, 1963, appeared to have removed the main force of dissident Muslim leadership in Chad, and during the following twelve months the only evidence of continued opposition lay in tracts distributed by an anonymous Comité du Nord du Tchad and in battles between factions of Chadien students at Cairo after Tombalbaye's visit. In April, 1964, Tombalbaye delivered two speeches vehemently attacking Frenchmen, including the president of the Fort Lamy Chamber of Commerce, whom he accused of supporting opposition groups and dividing the north and south. As a result several Frenchmen were deported. Despite an otherwise quiet year, however, it was clear that the traditional rivalry between north and south, sharpened by years of exploitation for political purposes, would remain the overriding political preoccupation of any government in Chad.

COMMON POLITICAL PATTERNS DURING THE COLONIAL PERIOD

Within the political experience of AEF during and since the postwar colonial period can be discerned several patterns common to all four states. The division of African political forces and the weak and inarticulate nature of party organization, which were the outstanding features of the colonial period, continue to shape the political systems of the present independent states.

With the exception of MESAN, none of the political parties which developed in AEF was able to win broad popular support throughout its territory. Strong ethnic rivalries were a leading source of division, and the main line of party conflict was often that which divided Fang from Mpongwé in Gabon, Balali from M'Bochi in the Congo, and

Sara from the Muslims of northern Chad. Another problem was the absence of a well-developed educated elite capable of overriding ethnic rivalries in the name of a broader nationalist or anticolonial cause.

But ethnic rivalries and lack of elitist cohesion were common to almost all African colonial territories. What set AEF apart from most of the others and contributed most to weakening the potential unity of African political forces was the intrusion of Europeans into African political activity. At critical moments, particularly at the end of 1946, when political groups were beginning to take shape, and again in 1956–1957 when realignments and alliances were encouraged by the creation of new institutions, Europeans working for partisan or economic interests effectively prevented African political unity by exploiting personal and ethnic divisions. Administrative officials themselves, often strongly partisan, manipulated employment and patronage, as well as electoral procedures, to prevent the spread of parties which they opposed. Perhaps the most blatant use of European influence and power to divide African political forces were Governor Rogué's creation of the Union Démocratique Tchadienne to oppose Lisette's PPT and the actions of Europeans in the Congo to exacerbate tensions between Opangault and Youlou, in order to spoil any possibility of compromise or alliance between them. Boganda's MESAN was the only party able to override these divisive forces. It did so largely because of the relative absence of clearly defined tribal rivalries in Oubangui-Chari, the impotence and discredit of both traditional and modern elites, and the failure of the territorial administration to mobilize its forces behind a strong candidate in the election of 1951. There was, in effect, a vacuum of political authority in Oubangui-Chari when Boganda began his campaign as martyr and savior.

The divisive forces of tribal rivalry and European intrusion or opposition also affected the structure of political parties in AEF by preventing the development of strongly articulated organization even among the most militant parties. Here, however, institutional arrangements, which were of little importance in dividing political groups, played a significant role in shaping leadership and membership.

The leadership of the first parties in AEF fell almost directly into the hands of the men who were candidates for election to the French National Assembly in November, 1946. These were the first elections held on a territorial scale and the candidates, particularly those who won election, were the men in whose name the first serious attempts at political organization were made. Thus Lisette, Boganda, Félix-Tchicaya,

Opangault, and Aubame each became leader of a party shortly after the election of November, 1946, and the elected deputies—given their parliamentary immunity from arrest, their influence through French parties upon the administration, and their position as sole elected territorial spokesmen—were able either to establish unquestioned authority within their parties or to survive rejection by their party, as in the case of Boganda. Later, Koulamalla and Youlou were able to organize parties largely around their candidacies for the National Assembly, while Gondjout and Antoine Darlan sought to do so after election to the Senate and Assembly of the French Union, positions from which they could assume roles as territorial spokesmen.

What did party leadership mean prior to 1957, when Africans assumed government positions? It could mean leadership of a popular mass movement with direct ties between leader and members, as was the case in MESAN after Boganda's arrest. But it could also mean leadership of a more purely tribal movement, as was true of that of Opangault or of Youlou during his first campaign. Frequently in the early years it meant leadership over an urban elite and a few regional agents, such as that which Tchicaya, Lisette, and Antoine Darlan established with RDA ties. And finally it could mean direction of a group of independently powerful local leaders, as was true of the parties that Gondjout, Aubame, and Georges Darlan formed among territorial councilors. The last situation was similar to that of the elite parties organized by the administration and the RPF among territorial councilors, chiefs, and clients of the administration.

No matter what the organization, party membership tended to be defined in terms of loyalty to the party leader. Though this applied more to MESAN and the PPT than to those parties which depended strongly on local leaders, it was a significant feature of all parties. Only the party leader or his appointed delegate could speak for the party as a whole; his assent was necessary for all important party decisions; normally he was the only arbiter among conflicting groups within the party; and in almost all parties it was he who effectively sanctioned the nomination of candidates for public office. This tended to be true whether, like Boganda, Opangault, or Koulamalla, the party leader sought to retain all initiative and authority in his own hands or whether, like Lisette, or, to some extent, Aubame, Youlou, and Gondjout, he attempted to develop secondary leadership or share authority within the party.

It is significant that no party leader was shorn of his position before

1960, when differences between party leadership and government leadership led to the overthrow of Lisette, Gondjout, and N'Gounio. Prior to that time, prospective challengers to party leadership, such as Tchitchellé within the PPC, were forced to leave the party for rival organizations. The relationship between party and leader was so strong, in fact, that the life of parties depended on the continued exercise of one man's leadership. The Parti Progressiste Congolais, one of the most militant and best-entrenched parties in AEF, disintegrated when Tchicaya's illness and absence prevented him from directing the party's activities, and MESAN became only a nominal organization after Boganda's death.

Behind the party leaders were usually a number of confidants and other close supporters who formed party executive committees. In each party this meant that a group of educated elite living at the territorial capital acted as secretariat, propaganda and tactical directorate, and conveyor of information both to the party leader—especially during his absence in France—and to party members. Frequently the executive committees also included regional leaders from the interior as well as territorial councilors, who attended meetings at the capital when they were there. But there were important differences between the urban militants of the executive committees and the councilors from the interior who generally preferred to take a softer line vis-à-vis the administration and political opponents. In parties affiliated to European parties, particularly the branches of the RPF and SFIO, Europeans maintained a strong advisory or controlling role.

The most difficult aspect of party organization to evaluate is that of party membership and militancy outside the capitals. Parties cooperating with the administration, both those directly sponsored, such as the RPF branches, and those that had administrative favor, such as Aubame's UDSG and the later PPC, seldom tried to recruit electoral support for the party beyond recognized local chiefs and other notables. Parties opposed to the administration, especially MESAN and the early RDA branches, also sought the support of chiefs and other local leaders as a means of capturing the clientele of these men, but their efforts were concentrated upon securing the direct support of villagers and townsmen. In part, these efforts reflected a necessity imposed by the administration's control of chiefs and other local leaders, but the efforts of radical parties to obtain popular support also reflected the belief of their leaders that social, economic, and political reform depended on mass political education and participation. Hence the efforts of Boganda to organize local cooperative societies, and the attempts by RDA branches to develop labor unions and study groups in the cities. Although these efforts had limited local success during their first years, they were effectively discouraged by the administration, and by 1951 mass education had become almost exclusively a matter of electoral propaganda and well-publicized support for local grievances. Thus by 1957, when the first African ministers began to seek popular support for their economic and social programs, their party organizations were of little use in mobilizing popular participation. Party militancy, strong in the days of outright opposition to the administration, had been weakened both by the superior economic and judicial weapons of the administration and by several years of compromise.

Changes in the concept and role of party membership reflected changes in party strategy vis-à-vis the administration even more than they reflected changes in party ideology. Ideology itself was of little serious importance after the early days of radical militant opposition to the administration. The proadministration parties seldom made any pretense of presenting programs for social and economic development, though such moderate leaders as Aubame had well-developed notions of the need for tribal reorganization or for improved facilities in health, education, and communications. Only Boganda, Lisette, Antoine Darlan, and the PPC militants who had been educated in the European-run Groupes d'Etudes Communistes at Brazzaville and Pointe Noire held advanced ideas of social justice and the means for obtaining it. After several years of frustration in fighting the administration, each of these had learned to temper his ideas in favor of a partially effective compromise with official views. In this fashion, improved cotton prices for growers were obtained from the cotton monopolies in exchange for party support of the administration's cultivation programs, and local amenities and even the removal of especially difficult officials were obtained in accordance with the proposals of party leaders.

Thus, by the time the parties were in a position to name ministers to participate in the formulation of territorial programs, there were no programs of revolutionary change ready to be put into effect, and in fact the social and economic systems inherited from the period of full colonial rule were maintained intact. The only groups demanding radical change in the period 1957–1960 were the few labor and youth leaders trained in Europe by Communist-affiliated organizations and the first returning university students. The infinitesimally small numbers of these men and their supporters were shown in the percentages voting in the referendum of September, 1958, against the de Gaulle constitution and participation in the French Community.

Economic and Social Structure

THE ECONOMY

The single most important factor determining the character of the economy of the equatorial states, as well as their political and social structures, is the lack of well-developed resources. The forests, mines, and oil wells of Gabon set it apart, but none of the other states has at present either the capacity to meet its own economic needs or the potential resources which might give it a chance to develop a viable economy. The result is that each state continues to rely heavily on varied French financial assistance and has little chance or incentive to initiate radical changes in the economy. In effect, the economic system inherited from colonial rule remains intact.

Agriculture, herding, forestry, and mining, which produce the staples of the equatorial economy, are determined by geography, ranging from the Sahara to the equatorial coast. Herding by nomads in central Chad provides beef for the markets of Chad and RCA, but exporting the beef by air is too expensive. Cotton is the crop best suited to the savanna belt of southern Chad and central RCA and is the main export of both states. Plantations in the forest area provide a modest production of coffee (southwest RCA) and cocoa (northern Gabon). The southern forests of Gabon and the lower Congo are exploited for their hard woods, especially *okoumé,* which are sought for making plywood. As for mining, small quantities of gold in Gabon and an increasing output of diamonds in RCA have been rapidly surpassed in importance by Gabon's oil, iron, uranium, and manganese deposits, which that country is only beginning to export in quantity.

Industry in the equatorial states is of little economic importance. A few local products are processed, and thus there are abattoirs in Chad, a small textile establishment in RCA, and facilities for meeting some local needs in hydroelectric energy, soap, beer, and palm oil. In addition, a small percentage of the woods exported by Gabon and the Congo are treated first by lumberyards and plywood factories at Port Gentil and Pointe Noire. But opportunities for further industrialization are very limited, though there is important hydroelectric potential in the lower Congo and Gabon.

Because they are weak in production for export and depend on imports for basic commodities, Chad, RCA, and the Congo have serious annual deficits in their balances of trade. The Congo, in particular, with its large urban population and comparatively high percentage of Europeans, has a large excess of imports over exports, which was only partially relieved in 1962 by the development of an important market in diamonds from RCA and Léopoldville. Gabon, on the other hand, has maintained the favorable balance which helped to remedy the annual deficit of the colonial federation, and its increasing mineral and wood exports place it in an enviable position.

France remains by far the most important client and supplier of the Equatorial Customs Union (UDE), taking half of its exports and supplying two-thirds of its imports and thus becoming its major creditor. Since Germany also takes a good share of Gabon's wood and Belgium most of Brazzaville's diamonds, the European Common Market is effectively in command of the UDE economy. This control is further exercised, particularly on the part of France, through several forms of investment and financial assistance. Frenchmen hold majority control of all major forest, mining, and manufacturing companies, and commerce, banking, and transport are almost exclusively in European—primarily French and Belgian—hands. The French government subsidizes each state through technical assistance; all but Gabon receive direct budget subsidies; and the cotton crops of Chad and RCA are protected from world price fluctuation by a stabilization fund which has required French subsidies in each of the past few years. Finally, all government development plans require foreign financial assistance, which is supplied in large measure by France and the Common Market, though the United States, Israel, and the World Bank also make important contributions.

SOCIAL STRUCTURE

Demography and Urbanization

The population density of the four equatorial states is among the lowest in Africa. Neighboring states are well-peopled over most of their area, providing densities of 39 persons per square mile in Nigeria, seven in Cameroun, six in the Congo (Léopoldville), and five in the Sudan. AEF as a whole, however, and each of its four component states, had less than two persons per square mile in 1958. The slow growth rate of the population was a continual preoccupation of the colonial administration, which had difficulty recruiting a labor force adequate for its projects. People are, of course, spread unevenly over the area of each state, and there are heavy concentrations in the relatively prosperous agricultural areas of the Woleu-N'Tem in Gabon, in the area between Brazzaville and Pointe Noire, and in the cotton-growing regions of RCA and southern Chad.

More important than the population density is the extent of urbanization. The four capitals—Fort Lamy, Bangui, Brazzaville, Libreville —and the two major ports—Pointe Noire and Port Gentil—as well as several regional centers, have taken on the aspect of cities, drawing in large numbers of people from distant as well as local tribal groups and developing an economic and social life quite different and apart from that of the surrounding districts. AEF experienced the postwar migration toward cities that was typical of all tropical Africa, but its small population, coupled with the absence of strong traditional social organization to hold it in place, meant that in AEF the migration quickly drained many areas and created cities whose size far outran the capacity of local facilities and availability of employment. This occurred most drastically in the Congo, where 40 per cent of the population is urban and concentrated primarily in Brazzaville and Pointe Noire.

Ethnic Divisions and the Emergence of Social Classes

Identification by ethnic group remains the chief basis of social differentiation in the cities as well as in traditional villages. Traditional ethnic rivalries—both local and those which opposed Muslims to Sara, cultivators of the land to rivermen, and coastal tradesmen to tribes of the interior—remain intact and were in fact reinforced during the colonial period by differences in degrees of urbanization, education, and absorption into the colonial economy. The slow pace of development in AEF has meant that the advantages given to those who adapted themselves earliest to the colonial situation have not been eliminated by the extension of changes to all groups.

In addition, rivalries were reinforced or new ones created by the development of new and larger ethnic groups in the cities. In Brazzaville the tribes of the north, thrown together in the quarter of Poto-Poto, tended to group behind the educated M'Bochi in opposition to the Balali-led southerners in their quarter, Bacongo. In Pointe Noire the native Vili were opposed by northern railroad and port workers from many tribes who were lumped together under a Vili epithet, Landelaïl (followers of the rails). In Libreville the Fang-Mpongwé rivalry had a chance to mature over several decades; in Port Gentil animosity between Gabonese and foreigners, especially Dahomeans and

Togolese, led to bloody riots twice in the 1950's; and in Fort Lamy and Fort Archambault divided Muslim tribes found it necessary to coalesce in the face of the temporary solidarity achieved among Sara tribes. Each of these divisions was heightened by political rivalries which were given full play in the cities, resulting in extreme situations such as the ethno-political riots in Brazzaville in February, 1959.

The division of political forces along ethnic lines during the colonial period prevented a concerted battle against European economic exploitation. Nonetheless, social and economic discrimination against Africans was a potentially explosive issue, particularly in Oubangui-Chari and southern Chad, and it aided the mobilization of radical parties in those areas. The compromise effected in 1956 between African political leaders and Europeans who chose cooperation rather than political elimination muted political demands for radical and economic reforms. Thereafter the new African governments, dependent on European managerial skills and investment, made little effort to change the system inherited from the colonial period. As a result, the development of class consciousness beyond the level of ethnic identification has been limited to urban workers and the unemployed, and even there primarily to Brazzaville and Pointe Noire, where unemployment reaching 40 per cent of the working-age population has been matched by intensive political and trade union activity.

Europeans continue to constitute a social class apart, since they control almost all forms of business enterprise and private employment, monopolize managerial and foreman posts, and even hold many positions at the level of bank clerk and shop assistant. Great divergence in salary scales maintains sharp discrimination between European and African employees, and a large measure of social segregation also remains in effect, particularly in housing and social clubs. Much segregation that is apparently racial is in reality economic, since few Africans except high-ranking officials can afford housing in European residential areas, and most modern housing is actually owned by the government or private companies for occupancy by officials and managers. But even though African officials may reside next door to European managers, there is little social interchange beyond formal receptions, and few Africans, even of the highest rank, have ventured to use their privilege of joining European social and recreation clubs.

No African middle class emerged during the colonial period, for there were few exceptions to the pattern of European control of enterprise. One index of the failure to develop African entrepreneurship was the absence of Africans from the semiofficial chambers of commerce, despite the important powers of recommendation and allocation assigned to these bodies and despite the fact that seats were reserved for Africans. A few African coffee plantations in Oubangui-Chari, several African cocoa plantations in the Woleu-N'Tem, and a very few African forestry ventures in the Congo and Gabon prospered despite discriminatory regulations, but, in general, lack of entrepreneurial talent, of accounting experience, and of credit facilities kept the number of African businessmen severely limited. The only group able to accumulate a certain amount of wealth and with it a modicum of economic power were the Muslim traders and transporters in Chad, almost all from the Sudan, Libya, and Nigeria. This group, whose conservative strength led to its courtship by the administration and by rival European economic interests, is still the only one with any real voice within a chamber of commerce.

Since 1957, when Africans were elevated to high political office, the maintenance of European salary scales within the administration and for parliamentary deputies has created an African middle class. Official positions alone are sufficient to provide the external insignia of middle-class affluence, not merely through salaries, but also through the perquisites of official housing and automobiles or allowances for them. In addition, preference in the allocation of licenses for taxi services, "bar-dancings," and other lucrative businesses tends to give the new political and administrative elite that owns them a monopoly on available sources of revenue and thereby increases the wide gap between them and other Africans. The group that is most conscious of this difference is the one composed of clerks and other lower civil servants, who hold the same educational qualifications as their political and administrative superiors, and who are daily confronted with the continuing, or widening, gap between salaries based on those for the old European and African ranks during the colonial period. In most instances, discontent is channeled into demands for increased civil service pay or into individual political maneuvering aimed at achieving a position within the new elite. There is also widespread, although inchoate, recognition of the lack of social justice in the maintenance of colonial disparities. As a result, it is the new African political and administrative elite, even more than the European managers and bank clerks, who are the object of increasing class resentment.

One group which deserves special mention is the small number of Africans who have received an advanced education in France. Since very few students from AEF were sent to French secondary schools and universities, there were no more than five university graduates among the four states at independence in 1960, and this number had barely tripled by 1963. Most of these students spent from five to ten years in France and were active during that time in student groups affiliated to the radical Fédération des Etudiants de l'Afrique Noire Française. Most have returned with French wives and have found themselves estranged both socially and politically from the controlling politicians who had been their classmates ten years earlier. On the part of the governments there is eagerness to use the talents of educated countrymen but also suspicion that their superior qualifications are matched by political ambitions. Hence, although a few returning graduates have been absorbed into the political systems and given important responsibilities, particularly in Chad and in the revolutionary Congo regime of 1963, most have been placed in technical and administrative posts with no political influence.

Labor Unions

The articulation of economic grievances and class consciousness in AEF was left largely to the trade unions after the effective quieting of the radical nationalist political parties between 1950 and 1952. Yet for lack of political support from local parties or of serious training and financial assistance from French trade unions, labor in AEF remained unorganized and relatively ineffective as an economic bargaining force.

Since the 1937 decrees granting the right in most overseas territories for labor unions to organize were not promulgated in AEF, there was no labor activity until 1946—apart from an Association des Fonctionaires, which had the support of most African civil servants. The Association attempted to organize strikes in 1943 and 1946, but each attempt was easily suppressed by the administration. During 1946, the European Communists and Socialists who organized political study groups also sponsored the first trade unions affiliated to the French Confédération Générale du Travail (CGT), and for several years unions tended to be merely adjuncts of the RDA and Socialist parties, organized by party militants among urban workers primarily for political rather than economic reasons.

The first serious and continuous attempts to organize unions followed the enactment in December, 1952, of a French overseas labor code which granted labor unions broader organizing powers, effective representation on territorial labor commissions, and power to demand trade-wide collective bargaining on salaries and working conditions. At this point, the three French labor federations—CGT (Communist), CGT-Force Ouvrière (Socialist), and CFTC (Catholic)—each of which had sponsored sporadic efforts at local organization in the past, took an active role in recruiting local support in AEF, though they were much more seriously interested in West Africa and Cameroun. The CGT and CFTC trained a few African organizers in Europe, while the Socialist CGT-FO preferred to work through European Socialist party members and tended to be the union most favored by the administration. The Africans who were trained in Europe were chosen primarily from Brazzaville, and although they and a few Cameroun CGT agents attempted to organize union branches in the other territories, the only successful efforts were made in Brazzaville and Pointe Noire, where there were large labor forces and serious unemployment.

One of the strengths of the small band of labor leaders who persisted in each territory was their refusal to commit themselves to political parties and thereby identify themselves with party ethnic backgrounds and with the compromise effected between political leaders and European business interests. The political leaders, however, could not idly allow the formation of independent class interests on their Left, and they made effective attempts either to isolate the small core of labor leadership—as did Boganda in RCA—or to coopt its outstanding members into the party system—as did Lisette and Gondjout in Chad and Gabon. Only in the Congo, where the best-trained organizers had been leading critics of Tchicaya and Opangault as well as of Youlou, was there sufficient militancy and support from organized labor to resist the temptations of political position. It was thus the Congolese CGT and CFTC leaders who in 1957 followed the initiative of West African labor leaders in breaking their formal ties with the French federations and reorganizing as the Confédération Générale Africaine du Travail (CGAT) and the Confédération Africaine des Travailleurs Croyants (CATC). The former group decided to maintain direct relations with the CGT and World Federation of Trade Unions rather than join in the West African-dominated UGTAN, directed by Sékou Touré.

After the creation of the first African governments, party and government leaders began to take a stronger line in limiting the activities of labor unions outside their control. When the moderate Force-Ouvrière was forced to follow the trend to autonomy by sponsoring the creation of a Confédération Africaine des Syndicats Libres affiliated to the International Confederation of Free Trade Unions (ICFTU),

Youlou's government sponsored the formation of a Congolese branch in hopes of weakening the more militant CGAT and CATC, and the other AEF governments made less effective motions in the same direction. In addition, new labor codes have tended to restrict effective union power to organize and bargain, and the more outspoken labor leaders have occasionally been harassed and arrested for open opposition to government policies. This type of action was especially effective in Gabon in throttling organized labor, though it has not eliminated frequent labor disputes and strikes at Libreville and Port Gentil.

In the Congo the long-term independence of labor leaders from political control placed them in a unique position from which to serve as a base for opposition to the Youlou regime. The CGAT, CATC, and civil service union leaders had a tradition of sporadic joint action which facilitated the formation of a Fusion Committee when they were confronted with Youlou's proposal to create a single party. The power of the labor leader at Brazzaville lay not so much in the extent of their organization as in the prestige they had won from their long militancy in favor of improved economic conditions for workers and unemployed and against the obvious abuses of the Youlou government. Even so, Youlou's patience and disposition for compromise and the deterioration of economic conditions were important for the development of mass support for the labor leaders.

The success of the revolution placed the union leaders in positions of political power in the National Revolutionary Council (CNR) and later in the Assembly and Council of Ministers. The CGAT leaders, who had planned a political party as early as 1960, had no qualms about accepting political office but the CATC, which had always been strictly nonpolitical, took office only to keep parity with the CGAT and then insisted that political officials resign their union posts. The creation of a single national union supported by the government was the breaking point between the moderate CATC and the other unions, which formed the Confédération Syndicale Congolaise in May, 1964. During the months that followed, the CATC provided the only moderate critique from within the increasingly radical revolutionary regime and its political isolation almost assured it of an early death.

Repetition of the labor-based Brazzaville revolution in any of the other equatorial states is unlikely in the absence of strong labor leadership and a large proletarian base including large numbers of partially educated, unemployed youth whose economic interests could be mobilized above their ethnic identification. Nonetheless, workers in

Libreville provided strong support for the abortive revolution organized by the military, and in Chad and RCA the single-party governments decided after the overthrow of Youlou to eliminate independent labor unions by imposing labor unity under the national party. In December, 1963, Tombalbaye announced the need to combine Chad's four small labor federations and a month later the Union Nationale des Travailleurs Tchadiens was born, though the local CATC refused to be absorbed in a politically controlled organization. In April, 1964, the biennial MESAN congress in RCA directed the government to unite existing unions in a Union Générale des Travailleurs Centrafricains.

Religion

Except in Chad, the Roman Catholic Church, represented by the Pères du Saint-Esprit (Fathers of the Holy Ghost), has had an influence of primary importance in shaping an African political elite through its schools. Missions and mission schools were established in Gabon, the Congo, and Oubangui-Chari within a few years of the creation of the first administrative posts, and they spread to cover all regions of these three territories. The colonial administration, restrained by its poverty, was unable to set up a large rival school system similar to that in French West Africa. During World War II, the administration offered grants to mission schools on a par with those for government schools. As a result, Gabon and the Congo have higher percentages of Christians and of primary-school pupils than any other former French territories in Africa.

To maintain continued grants against threatened elimination by freemason education officials, the missions entered politics in 1946, sponsoring the candidacies of Abbé Boganda for the French National Assembly and of European priests and African mission-school teachers for the Territorial Assemblies. Then, during the years of radical politics the missions worked actively against the anticolonial tendencies of the RDA and MESAN. The Jesuits arrived in Chad in 1947 to help fight both the RDA and Muslim encroachment on pagan districts. Political opposition backfired most explosively, however, when the missions' open hostility to Boganda in 1951 and Youlou in January, 1956, aided the candidates' efforts to assume martyrs' roles. Since 1956, the missions have withdrawn from open political activity but, aided by the prestige of several leading African clerics, they have used their influence among Catholic politicians during moments of crisis. Thus, Monseigneur Dalmais in Chad has strongly supported Tombalbaye against challenge

by Muslim leaders, and the mission at Brazzaville advised and supported Catholic labor leaders during the weeks before Youlou's overthrow.

Protestant missions, most of them from North America or Sweden,
traditionally provoked the suspicion and hostility of the colonial administration. Local officials were instructed to observe closely the activities
of the missionaries and their disciples; and stiff requirements in French
language instruction removed all but the few French Protestant missions from the field of education. Administration fears were justified in
part by the development of most African syncretist cults among Protestant converts. The later radical nationalist parties, especially the PPT,
and tribal reform movements such as the Fang *alar-ayong* in the
Wolue-N'Tem also developed in strength among them. There is no evidence, however, that Protestant missions engaged in overt anticolonial
or anti-French activity. Today their influence remains confined to the
areas of early penetration: French Protestants in the Woleu-N'Tem
and adjacent Fang districts, Swedish Lutherans and the Salvation
Army in the lower Congo, and American Baptists and others in RCA
and southern Chad. The French administration was particularly zeal-
ous in excluding missionary efforts by Jehovah's Witnesses, who, although they are present in small numbers, have been unable to take on
the importance of the sect in the Congo (Léopoldville).

The presence of Islam in northern Chad dates from the eleventh century, but its penetration to the south is a phenomenon of the past hundred years. The rate of the spread of Islam among animists in central
and southern Chad and northern RCA is difficult to gauge, but it is
based in large measure on the prestige of itinerant Muslim traders who
penetrate as far as Brazzaville. The French colonial administration had
for many years no set policy on religion in Chad but tended to favor
the spread of Islam as a modernizing and moderating influence. After
World War II, however, French suspicion of British ambitions based
on Khartoum and northern Nigeria and of pan-Arab infiltration led
the administration in Chad to canton pagan areas in order to preserve
the close balance between Muslim and non-Muslim peoples within the
territory. At the same time, the administration made continuous efforts
to ensure the loyalty of Chadien Muslims by encouraging the dominant Tijaniyya tarikh against Libyan-based Sanusiyya, Nigerian-based
Qadiriyya, and Sudan-based Mahdiyya, and by intervening in favor of
conservative imams against Cairo-educated younger scholars. Administrative action also helped to align politics in Chad with religion in

order to guard the Muslim north from penetration by Lisette's PPT. The fruit of this policy has been the reinforcement of hostility and distrust between Muslims and non-Muslims in the territory. Although personal differences among Muslim leaders in Chad have prevented the formation of a cohesive Muslim coalition, the tradition of Muslim opposition to a southern government appears to be so well imbedded that no lasting basis for understanding may be possible within the political state enclosed by Chad's present frontiers.

Among the syncretist cults formed in AEF the most significant are those of the lower Congo: Kimbanguism, Kakism, Matsouanism, and the Religion Prophétique Africaine propounded by Zephyrin Lassy of Pointe Noire. The historical importance of the first three as anticolonial movements has been outlived, as has the utility of Matsouanism as a political support for Youlou and of the RPA for Youlou's ally, Tchitchellé. Once an African government had been installed at Brazzaville, the utility of independent movements of any sort was questioned. The reaction to the syncretist cults has depended on their usefulness for political support or their general peaceful influence. Thus the Kimbanguists, whose meetings were proscribed under colonial rule, were given full recognition by Youlou's government, which found them to be a means of attaining influence across the Congo River. On the other hand, the Matsouanist leaders, having reasserted their refusal to collaborate with worldly powers were summarily and systematically beaten and their houses smashed by the roving youths of the UDDIA after their renewed abstention in the 1959 legislative elections. The subsequent deportation of the cult's leaders to posts in the north and Niari probably destroyed their local power, but one of the first acts of the 1963 revolutionary regime was to remove all restrictions imposed on the Matsouanists.

Education

The base of primary education laid by the Pères du Saint-Esprit in Gabon and the Congo during the late nineteenth century was strong enough to survive the wave of secularism that occurred in the first decade of the twentieth century. Despite the influence of freemasons within the colonial administration, and particularly among colonial education officers, the poor financial position of AEF kept it dependent on the missions to provide education, saving their schools from the suppression practiced in West Africa. The parity of mission and government education was ensured by the decision of Governor-General

Eboué during World War II to grant mission schools subsidies equivalent to those for public schools. The expansion of both school systems continued during the postwar period, unhampered by the struggle between the administration and the missions which dominated French West African education until 1951. Oubangui-Chari lagged behind the southern states, and Chad has constantly maintained one of the poorest education records of any African state, despite serious efforts since independence to improve it.

Secondary education, except for the education of priests, was a field forbidden to the missions until after World War II, and the only secondary education offered by the government before 1942 was the three-year course of the Ecole Edouard Renard, founded in 1936 in Brazzaville to train a minimum number of African medical aides, teachers, and administrative clerks and technicians. Lower secondary schools were established in each territory during the war, and these were expanded to full lycées in the early 1950's and began turning out small numbers of African candidates for the first and second baccalauréat in the mid-1950's at Brazzaville and Libreville and in the early 1960's elsewhere. Thus at this level AEF is far behind other French-speaking African states.

University education for AEF was limited during the colonial period to a very small number of students sent to France on scholarships supported by the federal or territorial budgets. By 1957–1958, 221 students from AEF held government scholarships in France but the great majority of these were in secondary schools or professional or technical courses. Of the 221, roughly one-third came from Gabon, one-third from the Congo, and the other third jointly from Oubangui-Chari and Chad. Since then, the number of students in France has increased slightly, though many more are sent for short periods of technical training. In addition, since 1959, a Center for Higher Education has operated at Brazzaville, financed by all four states, and this is gradually growing to full university status with specialized technical faculties located in centers in each of the other three states.

The Press

As elsewhere in French Africa, the press in AEF was never a well-developed independent force. Newspapers representing the views of local French economic interests began to appear in 1929 and during the period after 1943 several attempts, most of them subsidized by the government-general, were made to maintain a federal newspaper at

Brazzaville. The last of these, *France-Equateur,* persisted from 1953 to 1959 and served as the organ of pro-Youlou Europeans from 1956. The territorial governments issued their own daily news bulletins from about 1950, and after 1952 the semiofficial French news agency, Agence-France-Presse (AFP), established correspondents at each of the capitals and replaced the administration bulletins with daily mimeographed bulletins of its own. These continue today under government news agencies as the *Bulletin Quotidien* of the Agence Tchadienne de Presse, *Bangui La So, Gabon d'Aujourd'hui* (succeeding *Effort Gabonais* early in 1964) and *La Voix Africaine* (succeeding the *Bulletin Quotidien d'Information* of Youlou's Agence Congolais d'Information).

In addition, a weekly newspaper, *La Semaine Africaine,* has been published under the auspices of the Roman Catholic mission at Brazzaville since 1952, carrying official news and correspondence from all four states as well as major world and African news and the only political commentary outside government control which appears in any of the states. With a circulation of 10,000 it is the only significant publication issued in the equatorial states, though AFP dispatches from the area are the main source of news about the region for the outside world.

Most political parties issued irregular newspapers and mimeographed tracts at one time or another, especially during election campaigns, but they had difficulty in obtaining financial support for continued publication. A few of the papers had wide circulation and considerable effect, such as Boganda's *Pour Sauver un Peuple* and *Terre Africaine* during 1948–1951 and the RDA's *AEF Nouvelle* during 1948–1949. Between 1956 and 1960, party rivalry extended more often to monthly publications, with the BDG in Gabon and Youlou's UDDIA particularly active in soliciting support and informing supporters through their newspapers. Since independence in 1960, with the effective elimination or limitation of open opposition, party newspapers have tended to become irregular patriotic bulletins issued through the government information services: *Patrie Gabonaise, Unité Tchadienne,* RCA's *Terre Africaine* and Youlou's *L'Homme Nouveau.* The most ambitious of these, *Terre Africaine,* which appeared weekly during 1963, is identified with the RCA governmental attempt to rejuvenate MESAN as an active political force.

Legal freedom of the press was in effect in AEF after 1944 and although the colonial administration frequently used its authority to exclude publications termed "subversive," especially those emanating from eastern Europe and the Arab states, material problems rather than government restrictions were the chief limitation on the life of press enterprises. Since independence, effective censorship has been exercised by each of the four governments to eliminate published criticism and even *La Semaine Africaine,* protected by its link with the missions, restrained its political commentary on the Youlou regime.

The revolution at Brazzaville in 1963 opened the way for at least a temporary revival of press freedom and *Dipanda,* published by two young Moscow-trained Congolese with technical aid from Peking's Hsinhua news agency, has appeared since November, 1963. During 1964, as the new government developed its programs under competing pressures, an issue of *Dipanda* was seized for its attack on a moderate minister and the Abbé Louis Badila, editor of *La Semaine Africaine* and constant critic of the increasingly authoritarian stance of the government and of the irresponsibility of politicized youth groups, became the target of frequent threats of reprisal and of a court action against his criticism of government leaders.

The Political Process

CONSTITUTIONAL ARRANGEMENTS

The first constitutions, drawn up in 1959, were a rough approximation of the constitution of the Fifth French Republic, though the roles of head of the state and head of the government were combined in one person and a unicameral legislature was retained. Under these constitutions the head of the government was elected by an Assembly and was responsible to it since, except in the Congo, he was subject to a motion of censure and possible replacement. Nonetheless he held a dominant position through his power to dissolve the Assembly, through strict limitations on the areas of Assembly competence, and through Assembly procedures which gave priority to government proposals.

The constitutions devised since independence—ignoring the short-lived constitutions adopted during 1960 by Gabon and Chad, and the new postrevolutionary Congo constitution, which is discussed separately below—give to the head of the state and government, now titled President of the Republic, a position almost completely independent of the Assembly. He is elected for seven years by universal suffrage or, in the case of Chad, by an electoral college composed of the National Assembly, municipal and rural councils, and chiefs. He holds exclusive executive power and names the Council of Ministers which serves at his pleasure. In the Congo and Gabon, there is provision for a Vice-President who succeeds the President in case of disability. In Chad the Council of Ministers is empowered to name a temporary successor.

Each Assembly is elected for five years by universal suffrage. Further electoral arrangements are left to law, though in the Congo and Chad the postindependence constitutions specified a single national constituency, with deputies representing the nation as a whole. Each Assembly meets by right in two regular sessions every year; half or two-thirds of its members have the power to convoke short special sessions. Like the parliament of de Gaulle's Fifth Republic, however, the Assembly has a limited area of competence in legislation, with residual subjects left to executive decree. Prescribed Assembly procedures give precedence to government proposals, with limited possibilities for amendment, and the President's veto can be overridden only by a two-thirds majority. In addition, the President is authorized to enact laws by ordinance when the Assembly is not in session. He is also given unlimited emergency powers upon his declaration of a state of siege or urgency, though in all states but Chad these powers are limited to fifteen days. The Assembly must meet and cannot be dissolved during the declared emergency. In Gabon and Chad the President can prorogue the Assembly for up to eighteen months and ultimately, except in the Congo, he can dissolve the Assembly by decree without pretext and call for new elections.

A few constitutional provisions give the Assembly nominal powers over the executive. The Congolese and Gabonese constitutions assure the Assembly of the right to question the government on its policies and actions. In Chad there is even provision for a motion of censure, but in the event of its passage by two-thirds of the Assembly the President has the choice of naming a new Council of Ministers for the Assembly's approval or of dissolving the Assembly and calling elections for a new one. All states but RCA retain the provisions of the French constitution for impeachment of the President for high treason and of members of his government for crimes in office or conspiracy against the state. The Congo and Gabon follow the French procedure, calling for accusation by two-thirds of the Assembly and judgment by a High Court of Justice elected by the Assembly from among its members. Chad varies this procedure by using the Supreme Court as High Court of Justice and creating a jury composed of fifteen members from the presidential electoral college. But, as in other instances, detailed arrangements and procedures are left to determination by laws which have never, in fact, been enacted.

Despite constitutional statements of principle concerning the separation of powers or independence of the judiciary, that branch of government has even fewer effective powers than does the Assembly. In each constitution, the President is specified as guarantor of the independence of the judiciary, aided in this respect by a Council on the Judiciary named by him. The Supreme Court, or in RCA the Constitutional Council, whose organization, composition, and tenure are left to specification by law, has certain limited powers to interpret the constitution. It may advise the President on the constitutionality of laws and other measures, and in the event of disagreement between the President and the Assembly it may be asked to rule on the constitutional domain of laws requiring Assembly approval. In addition, it controls the regularity of elections and, except in RCA, must be consulted on the constitutionality of treaties. But although the Supreme Court must be consulted by the President before he declares a state of emergency giving him special authority, it has no power to prevent such a declaration nor to limit the exercise of that authority, nor is there provision for challenging the constitutionality of ordinary executive actions. The French tradition of considering the judiciary an arm of the administration, particularly in the colonies, has militated against the development of an independent judiciary.

Other institutions mentioned in the constitutions are an advisory Economic and Social Council and regional or local collectivities, but their organization is left to law and they are given no special constitutional protection.

THE PRESIDENCY

The concentration of power in the hands of the President, so clearly evident in the constitutions, is augmented by informal controls that give him almost unassailable authority and a monopoly on leadership within the state. There are variations among the four states imposed by the degree of political unity and stability already achieved and by the character of the President himself, but in each state the power of the presidency keeps other constitutional institutions, the administration, and all informal organizations subservient. With the exception of the Congo from August, 1963, the presidency has developed under one occupant in each state since independence. The position thus reflects in many respects the abilities and idiosyncrasies of the individual as well as the political problems that he faces. It is useful, therefore, to analyze separately the political techniques of each as well as the issues each has confronted.

Youlou

The political education of Fulbert Youlou in the Congo began long before his entry into politics. It consisted of long negotiations with territorial councilors and Grand Council members to ensure the renewal each year of subsidies to mission schools. He had been a shrewd observer of the Matsouanist movement and knew the value of religious leadership among his own people, the Balali. Hence, when he launched his own electoral campaign and his own political party, he was able to combine a charismatic appeal to the Balali with very clever manipulation of alliances with political leaders in other regions to develop a strong coalition under his own leadership.

Once in executive office, Youlou sought continuously to consolidate his regime by incorporating in it representatives of all political tendencies. Although he insisted upon unquestioned leadership at the national level, he found it advisable to leave other leaders in his coalition—especially Tchitchellé and Opangault—in power in their own regions. His skill at negotiating compromise long kept his regime intact, though he occasionally found it necessary to make concessions to other leaders and to the young Balali organizers in his own camp, for instance, by dropping his European advisers from the Council of Ministers in 1961. Youlou's political system depended heavily on large-scale finance to keep flowing the patronage on which it relied for loyalty. Since public funds and French subsidies were barely sufficient to keep the state intact, much less to sustain his broader ambitions, Youlou's foreign and economic policies were based on attracting more funds, and his support was available to the highest bidder. From the beginning of his regime in early 1959, developments in Brazzaville were overshadowed by those across the river in the Congo (Léopoldville), and Brazzaville's greatest importance lay not in its position as focus of French Equatorial Africa's commerce but in its juxtaposition to a much more important economic area. Youlou, ambitious for extended power, used his relation to the Congo (Léopoldville) to advantage by offering Brazzaville as a base of operations for several interested economic and political groups, most of them conservative, European-financed, and able to subsidize Youlou's political budget.

From the beginning of his political career, Youlou accepted the counsel of a small group of European opportunists in Brazzaville, adopting their views on financial and economic policy and their advice on relations with the colonial administration and with other parties and territories. Since no Congolese were sophisticated in the ways of international political and financial intrigue, Youlou leaned heavily on these Europeans, who were given various official or unofficial roles. Among them, Christian Jayle and René Mahé remained particularly close advisers of Youlou, and they were joined later by agents of extreme right-wing groups in France who for a time directed security and information services under the presidency. Youlou also found it desirable to retain as long as possible French administrators both as directors of administrative services and as prefects in the country's regions.

Mba

Léon Mba of Gabon was by far the oldest and most experienced leader among the four presidents in office in 1963. His early years as a modernizing chief of the Fang in Libreville gave him an authoritarian, pragmatic approach to the problems of political leadership. His years of administrative responsibility in exile, followed by long experience as a leading African employee of a commercial house in Libreville, provided him with a solid bourgeois Libreville outlook. Despite this background his intense ambition to hold political power led him into unsuccessful attempts to organize a radical party, to recapture the Fang chieftaincy through the *bwiti* cult, and to win election at every opportunity. From his earliest years as a chief, he was an apostle of ethnic cooperation in Libreville, and it was his ability to win the support of many ethnic groups that gave him political control of the city. By 1957, he had risen far enough above the partisanship of Gondjout and Aubame to receive wide support in both parties for the vice-presidency of the Council of Ministers.

Once in a position of authority, Mba permitted no opposition to his policies within the Council of Ministers, but he continued to leave tribal and party politics to the more ebullient Gondjout and instead built the image of a conservative, responsible chief of his people, available to all who sought his counsel. Only under great pressure from both his European and Fang advisers did he enter into a constitutional dispute with Gondjout and the Assembly in 1960. Only in the light of a pending motion of censure against him did he step in to take full political control by arresting Goudjout, dissolving the Assembly, seizing control of the party, and forcing Aubame to accept a minor role in a coalition. After re-establishing his regime, Mba discouraged political party activity and resumed his paternalist, authoritarian position, leaving party control to Louis Bigmann, Gondjout's successor as Assembly president. Though he approved the removal from the Council of Ministers of Aubame and others who refused to join the BDG, it is probable that this action was initiated by BDG ministers jealous of the prestige and influence of their better-educated rivals. Only when the Assembly rebelled against a budget which invoked austerity but maintained privilege did Mba step in, at first to lecture the deputies on their alleged selfishness, and then to dissolve the Assembly peremptorily to forestall a recrudescence of Aubame's prestige.

Mba's tendency to demand unquestioning loyalty of his collaborators led him gradually away from the coalition of regional political leaders which he inherited from Gondjout and toward a Council of Ministers and Assembly composed of young men whose political position depended on the President himself. His closest advisers, however, remained the former colonial officials who staffed the presidential offices and coordinated both politics and the administration. In addition, he maintained close ties with a few leading French businessmen, particularly Roland Bru who was frequently accused, even by Frenchmen, of dictating the terms of the Gabon budget and government policy on forest concessions. Mba's constant policy of cooperation with France and Western investors unquestionably earned their strong support for his regime and contributed to French willingness to intervene against his overthrow in February, 1964.

The abortive revolution forced Mba to replace his French counselors with cooperative young Gabonese and has led him into a more active political role. At first promising vengeance on the authors of the revolution, then bowing to advice on the need for caution and temporary compromise, he emerged by midsummer with a government propped by French troops to institute a regime of tight police control, arresting all opposition spokesmen and forcibly whittling down the opposition group in the Assembly. His paternalist image as father of the nation was badly tarnished by the revolution, but this merely reinforced his authoritarian stance.

Dacko

David Dacko of RCA is unique among the presidents in having almost no fellow Africans of any political stature with whom to contend for power. Boganda's monopoly of prestige effectively prevented the development of leadership in RCA at any level, and this has worked for Dacko in preventing others from challenging his authority on the basis of organized regional support. But it has also worked against Dacko by providing a specter with which to contend. Dacko is not a demagogue with the enormous self-confidence that enabled Boganda to override all political difficulties, and his years as a schoolteacher scarcely prepared him for ministerial responsibilities, even less for national leadership. Like most members of his generation, he had no political experience during the colonial period and while he served as a minister during 1957–1959 he had no occasion to engage in serious political competition in RCA.

In the political vacuum that followed Boganda's death, Dacko's rise to the presidency was primarily the work of a group of influential Europeans, and during his first months he and the young men around him were no stronger than they had been under Boganda. The challenge of a motion of censure late in 1959, however, forced Dacko to take an active role in politics. He took a series of measures which led from the capture of the Assembly and its presidency to the capture of MESAN, the enactment of a Presidential constitution, the expulsion of the French High Commissioner, and the arrest of the MEDAC leaders. This gave him in 1960 a position of authority not unlike that of the other three presidents of French-speaking equatorial states. The measures also restored, at least formally, the national and party unity that had existed under Boganda.

With political loyalty throughout the country better assured than in the three other states, Dacko has been in a position to experiment with new forms of political, social, and economic organization. With the aid of a few educated and active companions he has set about mobilizing the meager resources of the country. His break with the French High Commissioner in 1960 provided an occasion for Africanizing many high administrative posts, particularly among the prefects, long before any of the other AEF states. He has also pursued a foreign policy slightly more independent of France's wishes than have the others. At home, the development of MESAN as an instrument for national mobilization has led to its implantation in local government councils throughout the country. National congresses are held frequently to promote government programs and advise on social reforms, and an executive committee has been given official initiative to make political changes. Most recently, Dacko has also put the army to use to form cadres for economic mobilization. In all of this, he has shown a spirit of innovation and reform which, though scarcely revolutionary in any aspect, goes well beyond that of the other presidents. He has also made cautious but interesting statements concerning the national ideal of socialism, a term the other presidents have avoided.

Dacko has surrounded himself with a group of young men in their early thirties, most of them his companions from school, former teaching colleagues, or co-workers from various youth groups in Bangui during the mid-1950's. Since he has been responsible in almost all cases for their original nominations to high office—he alone survives from the first Council of Government of 1957—they are personally loyal to him. They also form a better-educated team than those in the other capitals. The only one among them who ranks with Dacko as a national spokesman is the Assembly president, Adama Tamboux, who is also a member of the MESAN executive committee. Along with the Minister of State, Marcel Douzima, Tamboux is a likely successor to Dacko. Dacko's directors of cabinet have moved successively to the posts of Minister of the Interior, head of security services, and assistant secretary-general of the government. His present director is also secretary-general of MESAN. These men, along with a few other ministers and higher administrators form the inner core of the government and party around Dacko. The European business community in Bangui, which still has its representative on the MESAN executive committee, is a force to contend with. Although the government caters to it, the European community no longer participates directly in the formulation of policy.

Tombalbaye

François Tombalbaye of Chad was for many years the prototype of the ardent party militant and organizer. Working without pay, harassed by the administration and dismissed from his teaching post, he was in large measure responsible for the position of Middle Chari as the only safe bastion of PPT support in the elections of 1951 and 1952. Since he was cut off from the policy discussions of the executive committee at Fort Lamy, his primary contact was directly with Lisette, and until 1956 he was Lisette's most loyal and unquestioning lieutenant. As a result, he tended to be disregarded by the more sophisticated party leaders at Fort Lamy, particularly by his archrival Toura Gaba. He

was even omitted from Lisette's first Council of Government and sent
off instead to the Grand Council, and thus began his estrangement
from Lisette.

Tombalbaye was neither a clever political negotiator nor a speaker
capable of competing in the highly charged atmosphere of the Chad
Assembly and the Grand Council. His strength lay instead in the support of the Sara tribes of Middle Chari, which allowed him to claim a
voice as spokesman of the south in both intraparty and interparty feud-
ing. He was thus the obvious alternative to Lisette and Toura Gaba
when the Muslim leaders sought a southern ally to overthrow and replace Koulamalla as president of the Council of Goverment.

Tombalbaye at first lacked the experience and skills to direct a coalition government and to deal as an equal with other leaders of other
states in the executive council of the Community; hence political and
administrative power remained in the hands of Lisette. After several
months, however, Tombalbaye asserted the authority of his office.
Finding himself threatened by a new Muslim coalition, by Lisette, and
by the PPT radicals, he began to develop his own national political
machine through the patronage at his disposal. The daring expulsion of
Lisette was merely the first of a long series of sudden and dramatic
measures by which Tombalbaye systematically eliminated every potential rival leader in Chad and consolidated his control of the government.

In the course of this process of consolidation, Tombalbaye sought at
various times to negotiate for political unity or to impose it by absorption of rival groups into his government and party. Thus he continued
Lisette's policy of offering ministries to minor leaders of the Muslim
opposition and for several years maintained some Muslim support
through Djibrine Kherallah. He also arranged a federation of the PNA
with his PPT in April, 1961, and accepted into the government and
Assembly Toura Gaba and several other men who had opposed him
within the PPT. But in each of these cases, reconciliation broke down
because of objections to the President's policies and actions, and estrangement was followed by elimination on grounds of real or potential
opposition. By the end of 1963, the only new group cooperating with
the President consisted of the young university graduates and administrators who had been coopted into the PPT executive and given high
administrative posts. They were then made ministers in January, 1964.

Because of the traditionally strong divisions in Chadien society and
politics—divisions that are much more clearly defined and deeply

rooted than those in the other states—the position of the President as national leader and symbol of a national community is exceedingly difficult. Lasting conciliation of leaders from the north and south proved to be beyond the capacities of so strong and effective a political negotiator as Lisette, and the task may be impossible for Tombalbaye, a man thoroughly identified with the Sara south, and particularly with his own Sara Madjingaye of Koumra. The long process of weeding out political enemies and potential opposition among even his closest associates has tended to isolate Tombalbaye and to make him distrustful of every man who begins to attract attention as a leader or capable administrator. As a result, like other presidents, he has relied upon Frenchmen and other foreigners who present no political threat as his counselors, and he has placed close relatives and other Sara Madjingaye in key positions as his Director of Cabinet, Minister of the Interior, Army Chief of Staff, Director of Security, and Director of Planning. In addition, he has overthrown the tradition of apportioning cabinet membership and other posts equally between north and south, and has named southerners, generally better educated, to a large proportion of those political and administrative posts with any power attached to them. Finally, the overriding preoccupation with political stability has led to a situation in which all power of decision on even minute details is concentrated in the presidency and in which the ministries have become merely administrative instruments.

THE COUNCIL OF MINISTERS

The Council of Ministers in each state, whose members serve at the pleasure of the President, is a more flexible institution than the Assembly and thus reflects more directly and accurately the directions of political change. Under the earlier parliamentary constitutions, when the Council was subject to the Assembly's approval, there were certain limitations on the power of the Premier to change the composition of his Council, but the frequent alterations that have characterized each of the four councils attest to the ability of the presidents to appoint men, change their ministries, and dismiss them without challenge.

In view of the powers vested in the executive and the common assumption that the Council of Ministers has at least a consultative voice in the formulation of government policy, it is the Council of Ministers, even more than the Assembly, which is the focus for regional and ethnic demands for representation. This is a common phenomenon, especially among federal governments such as those of Canada and Australia, where tradition allots a specific number of ministerial posts to each province or state, according to its importance. The long-standing division of each equatorial state into regions has raised demands from each region for representation close to the seat of effective power, and these demands have usually been met. In Chad, where the Muslim-Sara split divides the country almost evenly, another tradition called for the even division of ministries between Muslims and non-Muslims. The violation of this tradition by Tombalbaye in 1963 led to protests by a delegation of leading Muslims shortly before the arrest of several Muslim ministers on charges of plotting against the state. Such ethnic demands for representation are less easily and less simply satisfied than regional demands, but it has been important for each government to avoid the appearance of domination by the President's ethnic group. Thus Dacko's government in 1960 countered MEDAC charges of Mbaka control with widely publicized lists of ministers showing their varied regional and ethnic backgrounds.

Under the *loi-cadre,* the first councils of ministers tended to be governments drawn from whatever political and administrative talent was available, and both Europeans and nonpolitical younger men were taken into ministerial office. During the period of political instability in each state from 1958 to 1960, ministerial posts were allotted on a basis of political necessity and were used to capture regional and ethnic leaders or representatives and even, in the case of Gabon, to buy essential votes in a narrowly divided Assembly. After the political crises of 1960, however, and after constitutional changes provided much broader presidential prerogatives, the choice of ministers fell more directly under presidential control and each Council reflected fairly clearly the type of regime which its President chose to run within the political necessities of his state. In the Congo and Gabon, where Youlou and Mba attempted to maintain broad-based regimes in states whose politics had broken along regional lines, experienced political leaders of various tendencies were included in the Council. In Chad Tombalbaye attempted for a while to preserve Lisette's policy of bringing together in the Council leaders of all tendencies, but this practice rapidly deteriorated after the creation of the PNA and Lisette's expulsion in 1960. Gradually all experienced leaders were eliminated in favor of minor regional representatives whose personal loyalty to Tombalbaye was unquestioned. Finally, in RCA, where Boganda had never permitted the rise of significant regional leaders, Dacko was able, after eliminating the MEDAC challengers, to choose his men from among the educated members of his own younger generation.

In 1963, the tendency toward single-party regimes drove out of ministries those former opposition leaders in Gabon, Congo, and Chad who refused to join the presidential party. At the same time the further consolidation of executive power freed the presidents from the vestiges of dependence on regional politicians and permitted them to assign ministerial posts to young educated administrators and professional men with little or no political experience, though there was some effort toward maintaining a regional and ethnic balance within the Council of Ministers.

The functions of ministers are nowhere clearly defined in the constitutions or in laws, and ministerial political power and administrative authority depend largely upon informal assignment from the President. Many of the men who have held ministries in the past few years have been neither capable of directing the policy of their ministries nor interested in doing so. In addition, frequent changes in assignment have prevented even educated ministers from obtaining a clear directing influence within a given ministry. As a result, policy direction for the administration tends to come directly from the presidency and the central offices attached to it. Although ministers are called upon to represent the interests of their ministries in the Council, particularly in shaping budgets, there is an increasing tendency to refer all decisions and requests for policy direction to the presidency.

In the absence of clear policy functions within their ministries, ministers have been primarily concerned with more directly political matters, and, in part because they are chosen specifically to give satisfaction to the demands of a region or ethnic group, their most important function has become representation of group interests within the government. Since they are the chief recipients of complaints and requests from their regions, they are given varying amounts of responsibility for the allocation of government patronage within their home areas. They are in effect responsible for seeing that their regions are kept loyal through the efficient apportionment of government resources, especially for roads, schools, and medical facilities. They are also in most cases the government's chief political spokesmen in their home regions and are called upon to direct teams of local deputies in government campaigns, both electoral and economic. Thus in RCA since 1961, ministers and deputies have been assigned to spend several weeks, during the crucial periods of cotton planting and harvesting, touring their regions to ensure that optimum procedures were followed.

THE NATIONAL ASSEMBLY

Since the National Assembly of each state is the most immediately visible and identifiable representative institution, each ethnic group and each region demand representation in it roughly proportional to their numerical importance. This remains true despite the assemblies' loss of real legislative power. In the Assembly elections of 1957 and 1959 nominations were made by a number of leaders in each party but, except for MESAN in RCA, no party was sure enough of success to ignore the advice of local chiefs and elders in preparing its lists. In most elections held since 1959—Gabon, 1961, Chad, 1962 and 1963, and RCA, 1964—the President and his party have been so well entrenched in power that opposition lists have been made impossible, or even illegal in the last two mentioned. With full control over election operations and results, Mba, Tombalbaye, and the MESAN political bureau were able to dictate the composition of national lists of candidates chosen more for their loyalty than for their position as spokesmen of ethnic and regional interests. Nonetheless the government has used the deputies as local spokesmen for its policies and programs and has given them some control over local patronage. Inevitably, too, the deputies have been sought out by the people of their locality and ethnic group to intervene with the government on personal and local matters, and thus after election the deputies have achieved a large measure of genuine representativeness.

Each deputy owes his nomination to a party controlled by the President, and renomination in case of dissolution of the Assembly is in the hands of the President. This gives members of the Assembly little incentive to criticize, much less oppose, the government's legislative program. Thus political sanctions reinforce constitutional limitations on the Assembly's powers. In addition, the power of the government to override the deputies' immunity from prosecution—either by sudden arrest under emergency powers or by dictation of Assembly votes stripping individual deputies of their immunity during sessions—has been demonstrated in each of the four states to the edification of those deputies tempted to excercise their full constitutional rights.

The functions of the current National Assembly in each state are few but still of some importance. Legislation and even constitutional amendments are passed without debate and without dissent, and any local claims pressed by deputies are kept to the earlier legislative stages of administrative drafting, closed Assembly committee, or party caucus. In fact, none of the assemblies appears to have had any appreciable effect upon legislation since 1960. In Chad the Assembly was reduced in 1963 to meeting for one day during the year, and then only to be dissolved.

The chief function of the Assembly, then, is to provide an organized and recognized body of loyal supporters of the regime who can claim to represent a national synthesis of particular interests and who therefore provide both a semblance of parliamentary approval for the policy and program of the regime and practical support as a team of local political agents. Nonetheless, it is clear that the government consults at least certain deputies concerning local opinion, and a few deputies are almost certain to be high in party councils or personally close to the President. The Assembly presidents are usually men of some stature chosen by the President from an ethnic group other than his own to serve as political liaison between the government and the Assembly and also as political spokesmen. The early Assembly presidents, who owed their positions to their own political influence or to that of earlier leaders like Lisette and Boganda, were potential rivals for the presidents of the states, and in the cases of Gondjout, Maléombho, and Allahou Taher they sought to overthrow and replace the presidents. Later Assembly heads chosen by the presidents have occasionally proved to be reluctant collaborators, as was the case with Massamba-Débat in the Congo, and political instability has made the successive Muslim Assembly presidents in Chad almost automatically suspect figures. But Michel Adama Tamboux in RCA, Marcel Ibalico in the Congo, and Louis-Emile Bigmann in Gabon proved to be valuable lieutenants and party spokesmen.

POLITICAL PARTIES

The legal position of political parties in the four states varies considerably despite common lines of development. Since the legalization of political associations in 1946, the colonial administration and successor governments have held the power to deny recognition to any association or to dissolve it, but this power was never formally utilized in the case of political parties before independence. Since then, however, following precedents set in West Africa, each government has taken steps toward the abolition of opposition parties and the erection of a one-party state. In RCA, where MEDAC was dissolved in December, 1960, all other parties were dissolved in November, 1962, and constitutional amendments gave MESAN sole recognition and its Executive Committee important constitutional functions. The government of Chad banned all opposition parties just before the National Assembly elections of March, 1962, but plans put forward by a PPT congress in January, 1963, to give the party official status were delayed until June, 1964, when constitutional amendments similar to those in RCA gave the PPT's national political bureau control over the government and powers of nomination to all important offices. Youlou's failure to create a constitutional one-party state in the Congo is recounted above; his successors, who opposed the imposition of a single party under Youlou, have founded one of their own and given it legal sanction. In Gabon the example of Youlou's failure forced the Mba government to abandon plans to impose the BDG as the only party, but the creation of a single-party state can be expected once the opposition deputies in the 1964 Assembly are converted or eliminated.

At the time the first councils of government were created in 1957, political parties in AEF were primarily electoral organizations used by party leaders and their local allies to win elections and a voice in the control of executive power. Once the 1957 elections took place, however, parties became grouped into Assembly coalitions, each striving to control the Council of Government; once the councils were installed the roles of government party and parliamentary opposition began to develop. Until 1959, the presence of the colonial administration provided a brake on government action designed to restrict political opposition. After the installation of the first constitutional governments, however, the rapid increase of presidential power was accompanied by increasingly stringent limitations that curbed and eventually eliminated opposition parties. At the same time, presidential control of government parties was asserted or consolidated.

It is possible that, if political parties had been well organized on a mass basis as instruments for social and economic change as well as for electoral activity, they would have survived intact as organizations to challenge or direct the executive. But even MESAN, the most successful electoral machine, and small radical parties such as PUNGA of Gabon were in reality mobilized around only local grievances and local leaders and had no force as organizations. The organizers and militants who formed party executive councils were the only men in a position to act purely in the party's name either for or against the government. Organizers and militants of opposition parties were the first to be subjected to government pressures, and most of them were forced into inactivity by 1961. In government parties, the party executives formed potential bases for challenging the government executive, especially where the President was not the effective party leader. When, during 1960, Mba, Tombalbaye, and Dacko seized control of their own parties from rival leaders, the party executives lost their independence and became simply unofficial government agencies.

In the Congo, the one state in which the President was already party leader when he took office, the political authority of the government had been secured by mid-1959, and opposition parties were allowed to remain in existence under leaders who had been coopted into Youlou's Council of Ministers. As a result of the rise of the UDDIA to power with Youlou, its executive council held a certain degree of initiative and sufficient strength to force Youlou to remove Europeans from his cabinet in January, 1961, and to displace a Dahomean serving as executive secretary of the party. The strength of the party as an independent agent, however, arose largely from its domination by Balali tribesmen, whose tradition of cohesive action required the President to compromise with any strong demands.

Since 1961, each President has made an effort to reinvigorate the government party as a means of mobilizing national unity and support for economic and social programs. Party executives, which at first were composed almost exclusively of cabinet ministers and high officials, now include younger men and representatives of traditional chiefs and other groups. Party congresses are called frequently to discuss social and economic programs, and occasionally major political decisions are announced in the name of the party. It is difficult, however, to gauge the extent to which this reinvigoration is genuine and to what extent it represents elaborate window-dressing.

Dacko has probably gone farthest in making his party—MESAN—an agency for political activity. In doing so, he is renewing the tradition, begun by Boganda in 1957, that placed the party executive on a level with, or even above the Council of Ministers. In 1963, constitutional amendments not only specified MESAN as the sole authorized party but also made its executive committee responsible for nominating the president and deputies of the National Assembly. The executive committee, composed of seven members under Dacko's presidency, has attempted to give the party a permanent and active regional and local organization to supplement the government's administrative organization. It meets frequently to discuss political matters and has served as the official sponsor of such important legislation as the constitutional amendment extending the President's term of office. The regional and local organizations have been mobilized for propaganda purposes during crucial periods in the cotton planting and harvesting campaigns. National congresses have been used to assess the tenor of local opinion concerning social and economic reforms and have acted as a spur to party activity. In order to benefit from the experience of other African states with strong party organizations MESAN sent a delegation through West Africa in 1963, in particular to Guinea and Mali, to study methods of mobilizing popular support through the party.

Tombalbaye during 1963 and 1964 also attempted to give new life to the PPT, and the main purpose of constitutional revisions in June, 1964, was to give full nominal control over all branches of the government to the national political bureau of the party. It is difficult to estimate whether this will limit or increase presidential prerogative. Mba began to follow a similar path when a BDG party congress in January, 1963, resolved to bring the Council of Ministers under closer party control, but in fact this appears merely to have provided an excuse for eliminating Aubame and other non-BDG ministers from the government.

Despite the attractions of a well-organized national party as a political instrument of the government, no president now in office is likely to be able to mobilize a strong, active party on purely constructive lines. The absence of an underlying base organized initially in opposition to the colonial regime is almost certain to be fatal to such an effort. On the other hand, a revolutionary movement such as that which captured power in Brazzaville in August, 1963, may provide the impetus for the formation of a continuing revolutionary party organization.

It is difficult to gauge the importance of opposition parties as sources of activity against the existing regimes. In the Congo and Gabon, where parties have remained formally legal, Aubame's UDSG has retained strength in the Woleu-N'Tem and sympathy elsewhere, and Youlou's Balali supporters have undoubtedly kept alive the essence of his UDDIA in Brazzaville and in their home districts. In RCA opposition parties appear to have become extinct, but in Chad the arrest of Muslim leaders during 1963 has not killed off their old parties; the Union Nationale Tchadienne issued the first number of a proposed monthly opposition journal, *Al-Sêhy* (Truth), at the end of the year. The existence or absence of formal opposition parties is not, however, an index of the degree of opposition to the governments, for it is not from parties as such that the most serious recent challenges have issued.

ADMINISTRATION

The administrative system both in the central ministerial offices and in the prefectures is inherited from the French colonial administration and is modeled in many respects on that of France. Hence the staff and the power of decision are heavily concentrated in the capital, and the power of decision is further centralized in the presidency as it had been in the governor's office.

In the central administration the practice in 1957, when ministries were first created, was simply to gather related technical and administrative services under the political responsibility of a ministry and to give each minister a small staff to coordinate the political aspects of the ministry's services. The services, however, obtained a considerable degree of autonomy under their French directors, who tended to deal directly with the governor, and later with the President's office, especially when they were associated with a weak and uneducated minister.

Since independence in 1960, the French members of the ministerial staffs have been replaced by African civil servants with little administrative experience and, since the powers of the presidency have increased, the ministers and their cabinets have tended to be shunted aside altogether while directors of services consult the President's office even on minute details of administration. French directors of services have themselves given way to young educated Africans, especially in the more purely administrative services such as finance, economic affairs, planning, and civil service, though in many instances the African directors are seconded by former colonial officials who have remained as deputy directors.

The tendency to refer all matters, both political and administrative, to the President's office for final decision rather than take responsibility within a service or ministry has resulted in the burgeoning of presidential staffs and a multiplication of special counselors and inspectors in each branch of the administration. In Chad and RCA a secretary-general has considerable powers of administrative coordination delegated to him by the President, and in the Congo and Gabon there are similar though less powerful positions. Since many administrative decisions have political implications, it is also necessary in practice for administrators to consult the President's staff director. The red tape which enmeshes this complex machinery—further complicated by the general refusal to take responsibility without presidential approval—has made the administrative system cumbersome in each of the states. It has erected a major block against effective planning and execution of development programs. Development is also hindered by the commitment of high proportions of each budget to civil service salaries in overstaffed administrative offices. One of the most difficult political tasks faced by each government is that of reducing staff and salary scales inherited from the colonial administration.

Administration in the interior follows the colonial administrative pattern, with only a change in nomemclature from chiefs of regions and districts to prefects and subprefects on the metropolitan French model. Since the prefect is the representative of the national government in his prefecture and possesses broad police and administrative powers, he is in a sense a local governor. The potential political power of the prefects has had different effects on government policy toward Africanization. In RCA African prefects were appointed during 1960–1961 after the Dacko government had broken relations with the French High Commissioner on the issue of his stand in favor of MEDAC. The other states were slower to Africanize their prefects, Chad doing so in 1962, and the Congo and Gabon in 1963, because their governments felt more sure until then of obtaining loyal execution of political orders from Frenchmen than from young Africans. Most African prefects, like many of the young directors of administrative services, have been trained in a two-year administrative course at the Institute for Higher Overseas Studies, the successor to the training school for French colonial administrators at Paris.

In order to obtain ever closer political and administrative control in the interior, and to cater to local prestige, the governments of Chad and the Congo have increased the number of prefectures and subprefectures, and all four states have established many "posts of administrative control" in small centers. On the other hand, the high degree of concentration of administrative and technical staff in the capitals has deprived the interior of much-needed services. One solution attempted in Chad at the end of 1963 was the creation of a small number of superprefects with broad powers for coordinating and directing the activity of branch offices of the technical ministries.

During the colonial period both European administrators and African civil servants were, despite regulations to the contrary, subject to political controls and pressures, and assignments and promotions were more often than not determined on political grounds. One of the first political tasks of the parties controlling the first councils of government was that of winning control over the civil service, and there has been no break in the colonial tradition of tight political control. Appointments and postings are directly under the control of the ministries of Interior and Civil Service, and the civil service commissions which determine promotions are equally under ministerial control.

LOCAL GOVERNMENT

The French colonial tradition of centralization, or indeed the same tradition in France itself, left little room for the maintenance or development of local initiative and responsibility. The rapid decline of traditional local institutions, especially of the authority of chiefs, under French colonial rule meant that despite attempts to institute reforms such as regional councils of notables and regional cooperatives, local rural bodies were certain to fall under the direct authority of regional colonial officials. None of the reforms succeeded in practice despite continual promptings from Brazzaville. On the other hand, in the strongly politicized modern cities the municipal councils elected in November, 1956—the first of a series of new African-controlled political institutions—were given by law a significant degree of authority and drew for a time the attention of all leading politicians.

The development of African governments beginning in 1957 removed rapidly from the new municipal councils the important political position that was at first assigned to them and also removed the energies of the political leaders from the municipal to the national level. Lisette, Boganda, Youlou, and Mba remained titular mayors of their capitals, but their powers were delegated to very secondary political personages who were little more than ceremonial figures, while the actual administration of the cities fell back into the hands of the prefects and subprefects. City budgets are still nominally passed by municipal councils, but the budgets are set by the national administration. There has been a tendency, carried to its full in Fort Lamy and in Congolese cities since the revolution, to appoint urban administrators who are in all respects similar to prefects. From 1957 to 1961, elected municipal councils were established in secondary towns, especially in Chad, Gabon, and RCA, but these have never had adequate resources to balance their own budgets and the positions of mayor and councilman have become simply a minor form of government patronage.

Under the *loi-cadre* of 1956 provision was made for the establishment of rural collectivities with elected councils. In fact, these collectivities were established only in RCA and Gabon in 1960. Although in RCA there was an attempt to give life to the collectivities as local MESAN branches, the refusal of the government and central administration to delegate any significant measure of authority to them makes it doubtful that they are active institutions in either country. This does not necessarily apply to the Mutual Societies for Rural Development (SMDR) sponsored by the prefectoral administration in each state as successors to the unpopular Sociétés Indigènes de Prévoyance. The SMDR are production cooperatives, organizing the sale of local produce and maintaining from the proceeds a fund for the purchase of agricultural machinery and other equipment.

JUDICIARY

The lower echelons of the judicial system inherited from the French colonial regime have remained intact, with the infusion of a few African magistrates. The higher courts of appeal, which have replaced both the federal courts at Brazzaville and the ultimate earlier right of appeal to the Cour de Cassation in France, however, are a marked innovation. Under constitutional provisions each of the governments in 1962 installed a Supreme Court with competence to hear appeals from lower courts on judicial matters and also to judge and advise on constitutional and administrative questions. In RCA, the Congo, and Gabon the Supreme Court was manned largely by French magistrates, with a semipolitical figure as president. For the latter post, RCA recalled Hector Rivierez, the Guiana-born lawyer who had served as senator and president of the Assembly under Boganda; Youlou named his director of cabinet, Joseph Pouabou, a qualified magistrate; and Mba found in the court presidency a useful niche for Aubame, after he had removed him and other former opposition leaders from the Council of Ministers. In Chad, however, Tombalbaye has named a Supreme Court composed entirely of former minor politicians and civil servants, none of them possessing a full secondary education.

A special feature of the judicial system in several African states has been the institution of special courts to try political crimes, and all four states of AEF have legislation authorizing the creation of such special courts. One of President Youlou's last acts was to call into being a security court to try offenses against the state. In Gabon a law of May, 1963, created a court for the security of the state, and Mba named its members under Assembly President Louis Bigmann in November. After the abortive revolution of February, 1964, however, he changed the composition of the court before ordering the trial of those responsible for the revolution. In Chad a special criminal court was created by decree in May, 1963, a few weeks after the arrest of several leading political figures charged with plotting against the government; the court's only activity to date has been to judge and find guilty those arrested at that time. The membership of the court is similar to that of the Supreme Court and its president is procureur-general of the Supreme Court, an ex-politician from Middle Chari. Special procedures provide that charges be brought only by presidential decree, that defendants choose lawyers only from among fellow Chadiens, and that proceedings be secret.

MILITARY FORCES

One new element in the political system of each of the equatorial states is provided by the creation of national armed forces. Up to independence and for some time thereafter the commanding officers of the French military forces stationed in the states were the ultimate arbiters in political crises. It was they who quelled the Brazzaville riots of February, 1959, and it was only with the support of the French commanding officers that Dacko and Tombalbaye broke relations with local French High Commissioners in 1960 and 1961. In 1961, however, the formation of separate national armies to replace that of the Community raised the problem of passing control of significant power to African officers.

The solutions to this problem were similar to those found by the presidents for other political dilemmas. French officers were retained in charge of each of the national armies and the new African officers transferred from the French army were carefully chosen from the President's own tribe and granted promotions, privileges, and considerable prestige. That these solutions have not been entirely successful is evident from the leading role played by the army in the Congolese and Gabonese revolutions, from a minor revolt over pay by Central African troops at Bangui in September, 1963, and from the open welcome accorded by the Chadien and Central African governments to the French military intervention in favor of President Mba in Gabon. During the Congolese and Gabonese revolutions the role of the military seemed to be confined to substituting one civil government for another, and in the Congo the officers who demanded Youlou's resignation quickly retired from the political scene after the creation of the provisional government. It is not clear, however, that the same withdrawal by the army would have taken place in Gabon or would occur elsewhere in the AEF states, especially in the absence of readily available alternative political leadership.

The most important insurance of political stability for the governments after independence lay not so much in the development of local military forces as in the maintenance of French troops in the equatorial states. Among the accords signed at the time independence was granted in 1960 was a military pact between France and the four states creating an Equatorial Defense Council, providing for the continued presence of French troops, most of them African, at bases in Brazzaville, Fort Lamy, and Bouar in RCA. Military intervention in Gabon, following the failure to respond to Youlou's appeal for intervention, placed the French in an embarrassing position which was scarcely aided by French claims of having intervened on several earlier occasions, notably in Chad, nor by resolutions of the national assemblies of Chad and the Congo calling for the withdrawal of French troops. At the end of June, 1964, at a meeting of the Defense Council called by the Congo to discuss its relations with Léopoldville, the French made clear their intention to reduce commitments in Africa; on September 29, the French government announced the reduction of its forces in Africa from 27,800 men to 6,600, the latter to include 1,000 based at Fort Lamy and a detachment at Bangui or Bouar. Promises of additional material and technical assistance for the national armies scarcely compensated for the economic loss and other problems created, especially in Chad, by the closing of bases and accompanying demobilization of large numbers of Africans serving in the French army.

POSTREVOLUTIONARY CONGO

Throughout the discussion in the preceding sections concerning the political systems in the equatorial states, that of the Congo has been described as it existed under President Youlou. Since the revolution of August, 1963, and especially since the passage of the constitution of December, 1963, a political system has begun to develop in the Congo which differs sharply from that of the Youlou regime and from those in the other states. It has been abundantly clear that no president is interested in relinquishing his post voluntarily, and in the light of the development of centralized presidential autocracies, revolution may present the only means of obtaining significant political change.

The new Congolese constitution closely follows that of the original form of the Fifth French Republic and adopts one important feature which has not heretofore been used in AEF. This is the establishment of a government separate from the presidency, which is headed by a premier and responsible to the National Assembly. The President, who is elected indirectly for a five-year term, names the Premier and other ministers and presides over the Council of Ministers, and in an emergency assumes exceptional powers. The Government, on the other hand, is the executive branch responsible for the administration. It is subject to a motion of censure by a two-thirds vote of the Assembly, in which ministers are not allowed to serve as deputies.

In other provisions, the new constitution limits the powers of the presidency and protects those of the Assembly, while ensuring in firm arrangements the independence of the judiciary from both. The President's use of exceptional powers requires convocation of the Assembly, which can by a two-thirds vote terminate the exceptional powers. The Assembly, whose members are paid only during sessions, controls its own procedures, has a certain measure of budgetary initiative, and can be dissolved only after two motions of censure are passed within a period of 18 months. The Supreme Court, sitting as constitutional council, judges conflicts between the government and Assembly, and its decisions are binding upon both. The lower ranks of the judiciary are named and protected by a Superior Council on the Magistracy whose membership must include a judicial majority.

The role of the party is specified in the "transitional dispositions" of the constitution. Article 85 provides that "during the period of consolidation of the Revolution" a National Revolutionary Council (CNR) shall "realize the fundamental objectives of the Revolution, elaborate the general policy of the Nation and inspire the action of the State in accord with the profound aspirations of the masses." The Council was to be presided over by the President of the Republic and ministers were to be members, but other provisions concerning the Council were left to an organic law to be passed by the Assembly. In fact, this transitional arrangement continued the practice which had obtained under the provisional government. The CNR, which grew out of the Fusion Committee of the labor unions, in conjunction with the military leaders, chose the members of the provisional government and later nominated the single list of candidates for the National Assembly. During the period of the provisional government the CNR, whose precise membership was never publicly revealed, attended all sessions of the Council of Ministers. The same practice continued until the new national party, the Mouvement National de la Révolution (MNR), held its first congress at the end of June, 1964, and replaced the CNR with the party's political bureau.

From the constitutional outline above, it is clear that the powers of the presidency—although considerable—are strictly limited and that political power is diffused among the presidency, the Council of Ministers, the National Assembly, and the MNR political bureau, which may in effect be the ultimate source of political decision. Nonetheless, President Massamba-Débat is the single unifying figure in the state and, as secretary-general of the MNR and sole official member of both the party political bureau and the Council of Ministers, he should wield a large measure of influence. In fact, Massamba-Débat's pragmatic, ironic turn of mind and his lack of personal ambition prevent him from taking full advantage of the powers of his office.

A Bacongo from the district of Boko southwest of Brazzaville, Massamba-Débat was one of the brightest products of the federal Ecole Renard in 1940. Teaching at Fort Lamy during the war, he was one of the active founders of Lisette's local RDA branch and so was reassigned by the administration to the Congo, where he spent eleven years as director of several schools in the lower Congo. When Youlou's UDDIA took power at the end of 1958, Massamba-Débat was called in to serve as chief of cabinet for the Minister of Education and in June, 1959, he was elected to the National Assembly from his home district. In order to defeat an ambitious politician from the same district, Youlou arranged the election of Massamba-Débat to the presidency of the Assembly, but found to his regret that Massamba-Débat refused to allow the Assembly to serve as a rubber stamp for the government. He refused the pleas of labor leaders late in 1959 to lead opposition to Youlou by running against him in a national election for the presidency, but his prestige led Youlou to replace him at the Assembly in 1961. Nonetheless, he was too important a figure to leave outside the government and Youlou brought him into his Council as Minister for Plan and Equipment.

His refusal to support Youlou's plans for a single-party regime led to the removal of Massamba-Débat from the government in May, 1963, and made him one of very few political figures dissociated from the regime at the time of the revolution. During negotiations before the crisis leading to the revolution, the labor Fusion Committee proposed that Youlou step up to a de Gaulle-type presidency and name a prime minister with executive authority. The CGAT leaders proposed Matsocota, a young magistrate, while the CATC put forward the name of

Massamba-Débat, a Protestant and neutral. He was adopted by the Fusion Committee but rejected by Youlou. Hence after the revolution Massamba-Débat was a logical choice as leader of the provisional government.

In each instance, Massamba-Débat has not sought office, but has been sought after. His lack of ambition has complemented the delicate position in which he finds himself as nominal leader of a revolutionary government. Rather than assert the full authority of his office, he has attempted to maintain both his own and his government's position by representing the consensus of the day. Acceptable to both the CATC and CGAT at first, he has followed rather than guided the balance of power in the direction of the radicals since the establishment of constitutional government and he has been criticized by the Catholics for failing to stand against the tide and by the youth groups for being more moderate than Lissouba and other leading radicals.

Pascal Lissouba, the Premier, is one of the brightest and most dynamic of the Congolese university graduates. Born at Mossendjo in 1931, he attended secondary school and university in France, was first in his class at the Ecole Supérieure d'Agriculture at Tunis, and married a French member of the Communist Party. Treated with circumspection by the Youlou government on his return to the Congo in 1960, he became Director of Agriculture and was, along with the other university-trained higher administrators, chosen as a minister in the provisional government. There he outshone the other ministers as a politician and became both leader of the radical faction in the government and the most popular of the ministers through his speeches at mass rallies. Since his nomination as Premier at the end of 1963, he has, with Foreign Minister Charles Ganao, taken the initiative in public policy, moving constantly toward the "scientific socialism" and attachment to the Soviet bloc which the Assembly and youth leaders demand, while publicly exerting a brake on their more extreme proposals.

Lissouba has kept close personal contact with the youth leaders, directing weekly discussion groups in his office. The replacement of moderate ministers by young radicals should give him full control within the government. His prestige among the radicals tends to place him in a position increasingly more powerful than that of Massamba-Débat, who may as a result become merely a figurehead.

Since its first session in December, 1963, the National Assembly has proved itself the most markedly radical of the new institutions. Led by its president, Léon Angor, a leader of one of the minor trade unions, it has taken an active role in the shaping of policy by holding frequent extraordinary sessions during its first year. It has embarrassed the government by passing resolutions calling for nationalization, for the prosecution of Youlou and his ministers by popular tribunals, for withdrawal from the UAM, and for closer ties with Communist states. It has also criticized the government for failing to follow a more stringently revolutionary socialist line, and has refused to grant the government power to legislate by temporary ordinance between Assembly sessions.

On the articulation of the new national party, the Mouvement National de la Révolution, little information is available. Its constitutional congress, held from June 29 to July 2, 1964, was organized by the CNR and both the congress itself and its preparatory commission were composed of delegations representing primarily the prefectures and subprefectures, but also the CNR, the National Assembly, the administration, armed forces, labor, youth and other groups. Elections to the political bureau showed a majority of 35 to 28 for radical candidates over Catholic moderates in the preparatory commission, and the congress itself marked the definitive end of collaboration between the two groups. Since the congress most of the harassment of the CATC and moderate political figures has been undertaken in the name of the Jeunesse MNR, the party's youth wing, but by October and November the party itself took the lead in the removal of moderate ministers and the prosecution of CATC leaders and the few moderate deputies.

The provisional government and its successor quickly established a distinctive political style in their announced policies and administrative measures. The ministers retained the houses and automobiles as well as the salaries they had had as civil servants, but motorcycle escorts, large ministerial staffs, and all fanfare were frowned upon as wasteful. An austerity budget and revised development plan, accompanied by an announcement of the size of the deficit left by the Youlou government, were followed by a reduction of the salaries and perquisites of high officials. The administrative structure and its staffing were left largely intact, however, with the exception of key posts already vacated by Youlou's European advisers and closest associates. The Supreme Court was also left intact. The Economic and Social Council, composed of representatives of business, labor, and other interest groups, was dissolved.

One area of innovation has been in local government. In October, 1963, the provisional government created prefectoral and subprefectoral councils, which are to be consulted by the administration on taxation, budget expenditures, development planning, and other economic affairs. These councils have individual and group representation, which indicates an attempt to break down the tradition of ethnic group representation. Up to one-fourth of the membership of subprefectoral councils is composed of chiefs, up to one-fourth is composed of representatives of youth groups and women's groups in equal numbers, and the remainder of the membership is composed of delegates from villages or groups of villages. The prefectoral councils are elected by the subprefectoral councils and have the same apportionment of group representation. These councils were elected and held their first meetings within one month of the issuance of the ordinance creating them. Under the constitution they form part of the presidential electoral college. The municipal councils of Brazzaville, Pointe Noire, and Dolisie, which would normally also form part of the electoral college, were dissolved by the provisional government, and elections to replace them in February, 1964, were annulled when the number of voters proved to be much smaller than expected.

It is worth noting that the same type of group representation was specified in the constitution of the commission that prepared the draft of the national constitution. It was to include members of the provisional government, and several representatives each from labor unions, women's groups, youth groups, student organizations, parents' associations, schoolteacher groups, chambers of commerce, social services, the chieftaincy, and religious bodies, as well as one representative from each prefecture.

External Relations

EQUATORIAL AFRICA AND CAMEROUN

The remnants of colonial federation still link the four equatorial states together. At the time the federation of AEF was dissolved a number of institutions and connecting organizations, primarily economic and administrative, were newly set up or retained from the federation by the four states. The most important of these links survived the failure of attempted refederation in 1960. In economic matters the four states, with Cameroun, have maintained the Central Bank of the Equatorial African States and Cameroun, which issues their common currency. In addition, they have joined in an Equatorial Customs Union (UDE), to which Cameroun has agreed to accede. Most recently, these five states agreed at Fort Lamy on February 11, 1964, to form a Central African Common Market in the future.

Other portions of the colonial federal arrangements that have been kept alive are organized as the Equatorial Posts and Telecommunications Office (OEPT), the Transequatorial Communications Agency (ATEC)—which administers ports, railways, interstate roads, and river transport—and joint stabilization funds between Chad and RCA for cotton and among Gabon, the Congo, and RCA for cocoa. In addition, new forms of cooperation, such as the Center for Higher Studies, with faculties located in each of the four states, and the Equatorial Defense Council, have been established.

All these organizations, in so far as they pertain to Equatorial Africa, come under the direction of the Conference of Chiefs of State, which was organized by a convention dated June 23, 1959. The conference is merely a periodic consultative meeting of the four presidents with no supporting organization beyond a small secretariat in Brazzaville, which maintains records and liaison among the secretariats of the UDE, ATEC, and OEPT. The presidency of the conference rotates among the national presidents, and the site of successive meetings among the capitals; the presidency of the councils of each of the three technical associations rotates among appropriate ministers of the four states. Each organization and its decisions are entirely contractual, and each state has an effective veto.

There has been a tendency for the increasing national independence of each state to lead away from common action. The decision of RCA late in 1963 to drop out of the OEPT and form its own post and telecommunications system may be merely the prelude to similar actions by the other states. Gabon, which is both the most self-sufficient state and least related to the other states and therefore provided the strongest objections to continued federation, has never participated wholeheartedly in the joint organizations. Mba is seldom present at meetings of the Conference of Chiefs of State, and in many respects Gabon has insisted on recognition of its separate interests, particularly in relations with outside states. For instance, Gabon has made it plain to states that wish to maintain diplomatic relations that it does not appreciate receiving ambassadors based at Brazzaville with credentials for all four states. The creation of a common market may, however, forestall the disintegration of all the present forms of association.

Relations among the four states and their presidents are not always cordial. In September, 1962, after a match between Gabonese and Congolese football teams in Brazzaville, garbled reports of a massacre transmitted to Libreville provided an excuse for uncontrolled riots against Congolese residents of that city. Retaliatory riots in Brazzaville and Pointe Noire were aimed not only at the Gabonese but at all foreign African entrepreneurs, especially shop owners who were predominantly Senegalese, Dahomean, Nigerian, and Camerounian. Within a few days large numbers of Congolese were expelled from Gabon, whose government had long resented Youlou's claims to the mineral-rich region of Haut-Ogooué, and where Congolese had provided a high proportion of the working force in the mines. The intervention of neighboring states at a conference at Yaoundé in Cameroun two months later solved immediate problems arising from these events but clearly did not remove the underlying distrust.

Another problem is that of the transport of goods to and from the northern states, Chad and RCA. They had for several years been committed to the plan urged by the government-general for a Bangui-Chad railway to supplement the "federal route" by river to Brazzaville and by railway to the ocean. At the same time, however, Camerounian interests had pushed for the extension of the Douala-Yaoundé line to service the cotton-growing areas by a shorter route. After a premature announcement late in 1961 that financing had been found for the Bangui-Chad line, each government blamed the other for the failure of the project and each began to court Cameroun for an extension of the Transcamerounais from Ngaoundéré to Bangui or to Fort Archambault. After two years of disagreement over this and various minor frontier problems, the governments of Chad and RCA are now reconciled by plans, as yet unfinanced, to extend the Transcamerounais in both directions. The general attitude toward Cameroun is ambiguous. Balanced with recognition of the value of close cooperation with the larger, better-developed state is the popular resentment against those Camerounians who for many years have held a disproportionate number of favored places in government and business establishments in Equatorial Africa, especially in RCA and Chad.

Finally, there is the key importance of personal relations among presidents in states where the president has almost absolute control over foreign policy. The presidents in office between 1959 and 1963 had had no opportunity to work together before that time and no common political experience. No strong friendships developed among them, though Tombalbaye and Youlou worked closely together in the later years of this period. Moreover, cordiality alone has not provided an impetus for frequent meetings, even when common economic interests are at stake. President Ahidjo of Cameroun, however, appears to have won the respect of the others, especially after his mediation of the Congo-Gabon dispute, and his Muslim background has not prevented political cooperation with Tombalbaye.

Until recently, the ideological orientation of the four governments was roughly the same, but the Congolese revolution installed in power a number of people whose views were known to be radically different. The question of recognizing the new government raised problems for each of the other states, as it did for other African governments concerned with the stability of their own regimes. There was a tendency at first to await concerted action by the UAM; then the Malagasy Republic broke the united front of delay; RCA followed with an official visit and *de facto* recognition, and Gabon and Chad gradually accepted the provisional government. A meeting of the Conference of Chiefs of State was postponed, while Dacko and Tombalbaye made special visits to Gabon for consultation. After the passage of the new Congolese constitution and the election of Massamba-Débat as President, however, Congolese delegates were admitted without question to the meetings of the conference and other interstate organs held early in 1964.

RELATIONS WITH OTHER AFRICAN STATES

Broader ties than those that join the equatorial states and, in some instances, Cameroun, have linked the African and Malagasy Union, which was organized in 1961 among most of the former French colonies in Africa. All four equatorial states were charter members of the UAM and participated regularly in its meetings of chiefs of state and of the various technical agencies organized under it. Like the UDE and other equatorial organizations, the UAM grew largely out of the economic association of the member states with France, and one of the features binding the UAM members together has been the variety of benefits they receive through their accords with France and the European Common Market. Each state maintains separate accords with France for technical and financial assistance and membership in the franc zone, but these accords follow one basic pattern. Although association with the European Common Market is a separate choice for each state, the terms of association have been negotiated by them as a group.

In practice the UAM was primarily an economic association and its most active agency was the African and Malagasy Organization for

Economic Cooperation (OAMCE). Nonetheless its members acted as a bloc in African politics at the United Nations and in African meetings. All were present at the Monrovia conference of August, 1961, and became identified with the moderate approach to African unity, as opposed to the proposals for closer political unity made by the Casablanca group. The equatorial states, all heavily dependent on French assistance, were strong supporters of this moderate approach, though they were never leaders or innovators of policy within the UAM. On the whole, they were of little economic and political importance to the other African states and the four presidents, none of whom had served in the French parliament or in the higher councils of the interterritorial parties of the colonial period, tended to be considered "bush" by such leaders as Senghor and Houphouët-Boigny.

The creation of the Organization of African Unity in May, 1963, and the increased tempo of inter-African conferences has allowed the equatorial states to develop their own international personalities apart from their identification with the UAM. Each of them defended the continued existence of the UAM in the form of a purely economic African and Malagasy Union for Economic Cooperation (UAMCE), though RCA failed to attend the initial conference at Nouakchott in April, 1964. But in other respects their policies are beginning to diverge. The Congo has always maintained an independent policy on affairs with Léopoldville, Congo, and the revolutionary government has aligned itself with the activist governments of the former Casablanca group. Dacko attempted for a time to make the most of RCA's central position and political insignificance by declaring it the "Switzerland of Africa" and proposing Bangui as seat for the OAU. Gabon has frequently repeated the objections it made against strong federation in AEF in resisting proposals for increased interstate control over its resources.

Relations with neighboring African states and colonial territories have involved each of the equatorial states in its own particular problems. The most turbulent of these have been relations between the two Congos. Youlou, at the pre-UAM Brazzaville conference of December, 1960, persuaded the states in attendance to attempt arbitration between Kasavubu and Tshombé, but followed his own opportunistic road, first in favor of Kasavubu and a possible larger Bacongo state, then in favor of Tshombé and his ready supply of funds, then in early 1963 in favor of Kasavubu and the central government once Katanga's star was dimmed. The new revolutionary regime, whose leaders opposed Youlou's policies toward Léopoldville, quickly fell into dispute with the Adoula government because of its reception of Youlou's lieutenants who fled across the river. After the Léopoldville government arrested large numbers of its own labor leaders to avoid a repetition of the Brazzaville revolution, Brazzaville itself provided a haven for all groups opposed to Adoula. Relations reached a total impasse in May, 1964, with each side accusing the other of subversion, but the arrival of Tshombé with plans for a national coalition government led to a short détente. The final rupture took place in August when, after Massamba-Débat accused the Tshombé government of smuggling arms to Youlou supporters, Tshombé replied with counteraccusations and began to deport all Congo (Brazzaville) nationals from Léopoldville. Brazzaville's request for an OAU investigation removed some of the danger of open hostilities between the two countries, but no solution is likely without a stable settlement within the Congo (Léopoldville). On another frontier, Youlou's covert cooperation with the Portuguese, which compromised the efforts of Cabindan and Angolan nationalists, has been reversed by his successors who have especially favored Cabindan groups pledged to unite their enclave with the Congo.

Less explosive issues divide other equatorial states from their neighbors. Gabon and Cameroun have both announced their "solidarity" with the people of Spanish Guinea and have indicated their interest in developing closer ties. Cameroun had the advantage of harboring the main nationalist groups from Spanish Guinea, but since the establishment of self-government in 1964 it appears unlikely that the area will go to either of its neighbors for some time. Tombalbaye's government in Chad, surrounded on all sides but its southern one by Muslim-controlled states, has offended both Nigeria and the Sudan by its treatment of their nationals, and it came close to breaking diplomatic relations with the Sudan on charges that the latter had supplied arms to the Muslim leaders arrested in March, 1963, in the hope of annexing northern Chad. Finally, RCA has received large numbers of Christian refugees from the southern Sudan during periods of conflict between the Muslim-controlled government forces and local insurgents, as well as refugees from northern regions of the Congo (Léopoldville), and these migrations have strained RCA's relations with its neighbors.

RELATIONS WITH NON-AFRICAN STATES

Economic and technical dependence on France, coupled with domestic instability, have inclined the equatorial states to follow the lead of France in international affairs outside Africa. Their policy toward France itself is complex because the ties are so many and so detailed. France provides the bulk of their foreign economic and technical assistance and is the major source of their imports and the major destination of their exports, many of which are paid for at subsidized prices above those of world markets. France is also home for most of the business communities in the equatorial states, and French private investment, French trading companies, and French banks are the focus of economic activity. Hence, there is considerable hesitation to offend France, and the personal respect in which de Gaulle is held by equatorial political leaders adds to this hesitation.

On the other hand, the very size of the local French communities and the complexity of French interests create rivalry among Frenchmen which gives each government some room for maneuver. Dacko in 1960 and Tombalbaye in 1961 were able to break relations with their French High Commissioners and to obtain their removal without harming their relations with the French government because they had the support of large segments of the local French communities, both official and unofficial, and could argue cogently in each case that the High Commissioner was harming French interests by dabbling in politics and supporting opposition leaders.

By 1964, though the dependence of the equatorial states on France was still considerable, they varied in the degree to which they had asserted their independence from France and from the local French business community. The new Congolese government, though eager to retain foreign investment, nationalized transport, water, and electricity and demanded control over its treasury. In April, 1964, Tombalbaye of Chad denounced in violent terms the intervention of Frenchmen in the politics of the country and expelled the French president of the Fort Lamy Chamber of Commerce and twelve others, while the National Assembly demanded that French troops be removed. Dacko of RCA followed this with a much milder denunciation of foreign intervention while Mba of Gabon, far behind the others in this respect, attempted to dispel charges of complete dependence on French advisers by beginning to Africanize his higher administrative offices.

French military forces and the French commandants of national armies were for several years looked upon as the ultimate source of power behind each regime's authority, and friendship with the French military commanders was often of greater importance to a president than good relations with the French High Commissioner. As a result, the French officers were frequently consulted before radical changes were announced. The refusal of the French to intervene during the Brazzaville revolution shook each of the other presidents and French intervention to save Mba in Gabon was welcomed by both Tombalbaye and Dacko. Each state began to pay more attention to the development and loyalty of its own army and replaced French commandants with Africans, but de Gaulle's decision to remove most of the French military forces based in Africa came as a rude shock.

Association of former French colonial territories with the European Common Market has come largely as a result of French efforts to maintain close ties with the new nations while sharing the burdens of economic assistance with other European countries. Since all the equatorial states trade extensively with the other members of the Common Market, there is little hesitation on their part to accept the conditions of favorable tariff treatment for imports from the Common Market in exchange for preferential markets in Europe and a share in Common Market overseas development funds.

In broader international affairs, and especially at the United Nations, the equatorial states followed the UAM line in cooperation with France on most non-African issues. Until 1963, this meant that they voted steadily at the UN with NATO against the Soviet bloc, though with other African states they abstained in 1961 on the question of admitting the Chinese People's Republic. At the same time, they accepted the aggressive campaign of Nationalist China for diplomatic recognition and, except for Dacko's short-lived proposal in December, 1960, to allow Soviet representation at Bangui, there were no serious departures from the NATO line. In 1963, however, with the advent of de Gaulle's serious challenge to American policies, leadership in foreign affairs became confused for the equatorial states and different tendencies appeared among them. Gabon, Chad, and Youlou's Congo remained among the staunch conservatives of the UAM in supporting the Western powers. But RCA, always slightly more venturesome, voted alone with France in abstaining on UN support for the Moscow test ban treaty.

The Congo's revolutionary government, inclined toward a radical departure in foreign relations, was the first to follow France in recognizing People's China and Foreign Minister Ganao's tour of Communist nations in March, 1964, led to the establishment of diplomatic ties with most of the Soviet bloc, with Yugoslavia, and later with Cuba. The Chinese tie proved the most fruitful in the first months, with the grant of a 1.2 billion CFA franc credit by Peking, the arrival of technical assistance, and, during Massamba-Débat's trip to Peking in October, the establishment of a whole series of accords and exchanges. Other equatorial states took similar action as RCA dispatched a high-ranking mission to the USSR and China in August and Chad announced the creation of ties with Moscow. Gabon under Mba is unlikely to follow suit in the near future.

Conclusion: The Problem of National Unity

The issues that dominate politics and policy in the equatorial states are national unity and economic and social development. But one of the primary elements of national unity is political stability, which is a precondition both of rational economic and of social development. Political stability and national unity have priority over development plans and projects where these conflict, and often, particularly where a government is insecure, the methods used to obtain stability are those least likely to favor the distribution of resources according to a rational development plan.

The creation of national units within the boundaries of colonial territories is a task common to all African states; the equatorial governments have sought to use a variety of institutions and techniques to develop a sense of national loyalty and national purpose. But even apart from government policies and programs concerning national unity, there are a number of historical and social forces at work to break down traditional tribal allegiance and open the way to wider loyalties. French colonial rule consciously destroyed traditional institutions and cultures and provided a communications system, a common language, and an economic basis for urbanization which permitted tribal interpenetration. More specifically related to each territory were the colonial administrative and political institutions and particularly the development of political leadership at the territorial, or eventually national, level. All these elements have favored the creation of national identity as against tribal identity. At the same time, however, colonial rule ruined the possibilities of basing a national culture on traditional culture and institutions by partially destroying the latter and by helping to create broad intertribal antagonisms.

Government policies on national unity are confused with the chief political concern of each government—the perpetuation of its own power. It becomes difficult to disentangle the two, particularly when the cause of national unity is invoked as a defense for all measures intended to ensure political stability. The degree to which national unity had already been achieved during the colonial period varies widely among the four states, and this changes the nature of preoccupation with national loyalty, or with national mobilization, which presupposes national loyalty. RCA, where traditional institutions were weakest and where political unity was achieved during the colonial period, has despite the MEDAC interlude remained an unusually stable state. Hence, the Dacko regime, faced with no serious degree of tribalism or political opposition, can concentrate on the problem of mobilizing the people in programs of positive action. The other three states, in contrast, where tribal rivalry is fierce and where a long period of political rivalry has created traditions of opposition, are faced with serious problems of national loyalty. They have yet to embark on significant programs of development through mobilization of national resources. For the Congo, however, the revolution may have successfully overridden earlier divisions to create a basis for national loyalty.

National symbols and a national history which glorifies and adds legitimacy to the present regime are standard fare. The presidents not only constitutionally incarnate the nations, but their faces appear on posters and stamps along with the national flags, while official propaganda by radio, newspaper, and public speech makes each president the national hero and logical culmination of deep-seated national historical trends. Dacko is hailed regularly as the "spiritual heir" of Boganda, around whom the national Central African mystique is formed. Mba is the "father of his country." And each of the government parties is given a history appropriate to a grand national movement.

One common policy carried out in the name of national unity has been the elimination of formal opposition through the banning of all political parties except the government party and the imposition of limitations on labor unions and other forms of voluntary association. Another policy has been to give immediate satisfaction to tribal and regional demands for a proportional share of important political and administrative posts and of the national budget, particularly as it pertains to improvements in communications and social facilities. Only the strongest and most stable regimes can afford to disregard these demands and impose a more rational and efficient system of allocating resources. But all governments, while catering to regional and ethnic support, have attempted to reduce its local importance by insisting upon national, nonregional slates of National Assembly candidates and by assigning prefects, subprefects, and civil servants to areas outside their own ethnic regions.

The dangers for national unity are largely intense tribal or religious rivalry and regional disaffection. Secession has been loosely threatened at various times by both north and south in Chad, by eastern RCA, by the northern Congo and by isolated regions of Gabon, such as the politically dissident Woleu-N'Tem or the "forgotten" Nyanga and Haut-Ogooué. This threat can be or has been remedied by improved communications and more evident distributive justice among the regions and the ethnic groups. The only serious and apparently insoluble division remaining is perhaps that between Muslims and Sara in Chad. Beyond these sectional dangers for national unity and, in fact, growing out of the new national sense that is developing in the major cities, there may be a greater danger not for national unity but for the tenure of governments that fail to meet economic and social expectations. The Brazzaville and Libreville revolutions, rising above traditional and sectional loyalties, may point the way to new political systems and new loyalties in Equatorial Africa.

Bibliography

Neglect of French Equatorial Africa in many fields during the colonial period was echoed by the lack of scholarly attention to it. The number of serious works devoted to the region is still very small. The only recent general study is that of Virginia Thompson and Richard Adloff, *The Emerging States of French Equatorial Africa* (Stanford: Stanford University Press, 1960). Although this work suffers from the poverty of the published materials on which it is largely based, and from resultant unevenness and inaccuracies, it is an invaluable compendium of historical, administrative, and economic information up to 1959. Older general works, stronger on history, geography, and ethnography than on politics and administration, are the standard study by Georges Bruel, *La France Equatoriale Africaine* (Paris: Larose, 1935), and a volume in the *Encyclopédie Coloniale et Maritime*, edited by Eugène L. Guernier, *Afrique Equatoriale Française* (Paris: Editions de l'Union Française, 1950), which was brought up to date by the August, 1953, issue of *Encyclopédie Mensuelle d'Outre-Mer*. Shorter works of the same genre are those by Henri Ziéglé, *Afrique Equatoriale Française* (Paris: Berger-Levrault, 1952), and Edouard Trézenem, "Afrique Equatoriale," in his *La France Equatoriale* (Paris: Société d'Editions Géographiques, Maritime et Coloniales, 1950).

No good modern history of the precolonial and colonial periods has appeared, though histories of each territory are currently being prepared

under the general direction of Hubert Deschamps. The French archives for
the period before World War I are beginning to be exploited by Henri
Braunschwig and others. Meanwhile the only studies available are as much
ethnographic as historical, as are Pierre Kalck, *Réalités Oubanguiennes*
(Paris: Berger-Levrault, 1959), Abbé André Raponda Walker *Notes sur
l'Histoire du Gabon* (Brazzaville: Institut d'Etudes Centrafricaines, Mémoire No. 9, 1960), and Hubert Deschamps, *Traditions Orales et Archives au
Gabon* (Paris: Berger-Levrault, 1962). Between the wars the *Bulletin de la
Société de Recherches Congolaises* (1922–1939), sponsored by the Govern-
ment General, published a large number of excellent studies in history and
ethnology. After World War II, the French Office pour la Recherche
Scientifique dans les Territoires d'Outre-Mer (ORSTOM) organized an
Institut d'Etudes Centrafricaines (IEC) for AEF that was located at Brazza-
ville, and the IEC published both a *Bulletin* (1947–1960) and occasional
Mémoires, succeeded in 1963 by the *Bulletin* of the new Institut de
Recherches Scientifiques au Congo. The IEC sponsored very little research
in ethnology and history and, partially as a result, the only three volumes
in the Ethnographic Survey of the International African Institute for which
sufficient fieldwork was available are Pierre Alexandre and Jacques Binet,
Le Groupe dit Pahouin (*Fang-Boulou-Béti*) (Paris: Presses Universitaires
de France, 1958), Annie M.-D. Lebeuf, *Les Populations du Tchad* (*Nord
du 10e Parallèle*) (Paris: Presses Universitaires de France, 1959), and
Marcel Soret, *Les Kongo Nord-Occidentaux* (Paris: Presses Universitaires
de France, 1959).

On the other hand, the IEC sponsored a number of studies in urban
sociology and social change which are of major importance in explaining the
background of political developments. Georges Balandier, in *Sociologie Actuelle de l'Afrique Noire* (Paris: Presses Universitaires de France, 2nd edition, 1963), examines the reactions of the Bacongo and Fang to economic
and social changes introduced by colonial rule and gives particular attention
to political reactions and the messianic religious movements. Balandier and
Jean-Claude Pauvert study the problems of village life in *Les Villages Gabonais: Aspects Démographiques, Economiques et Sociologiques: Projets
de Modernisation* (Brazzaville: Institut d'Etudes Centrafricaines, Mémoire
No. 5, 1952). The most important urban studies are Balandier, *Sociologie
des Brazzavilles Noires* (Paris: Armand Colin, 1955), Marcel Soret, *Dé-
mographie et Problèmes Urbains en Afrique Equatoriale Française: Poto-
Poto—Bacongo—Dolisie* (Brazzaville: Institut d'Etudes Centrafricaines,
Mémoire No. 7, 1954), and Guy Lasserre, *Libreville: La Ville et Sa Région.
Etude de Géographie Humaine* (Paris: Armand Colin, 1958).

Apart from treatment in the general works mentioned above there is no
comprehensive study of the economy of the equatorial federation and its
successor states. During the colonial period the French Equatorial Service

de la Statistique Générale published an *Annuaire Statistique de l'Afrique Equatoriale Française,* covering 1936–1950, and another for 1951–1955, as well as a *Bulletin Mensuel de Statistique de l'Afrique Equatoriale Française,* a monthly *Bulletin d'Informations Economiques et Sociales de l'Afrique Equatoriale Française,* and occasional detailed urban census studies. Each of the states now publishes its own monthly *Bulletin de Statistique,* but most economic and statistical studies are carried out and published by the Service de Coopération of the French Institut National de la Statistique et des Etudes Economiques (INSEE). Other sources of detailed economic information and analyses are the monthly *Etudes et Statistiques* of the Banque Centrale des Etats de l'Afrique Equatoriale et du Cameroun (Paris, monthly), *Marchés Tropicaux* (Paris, weekly), and the monthly bulletins and other publications of the chambers of commerce in each capital.

Political developments in AEF have received very little attention apart from two recent doctoral theses: Brian G. Weinstein, "Building the Gabonese Nation: The Search for a New Order and the Role of the Fang Tribe in This Process" (Harvard University, 1963), and John A. Ballard, "The Development of Political Parties in French Equatorial Africa" (Fletcher School of Law and Diplomacy, 1964). Two recently published French theses, Jacques Le Cornec, *Histore Politique du Tchad de 1900 à 1962,* and J. M. Wagret, *Histoire et Sociologie Politiques du Congo* (both, Paris: Librairie Générale de Droit et de Jurisprudence, 1963), are unfortunately weak in interpretation and frequently inaccurate. Le Cornec is primarily useful in discussing colonial policy toward the chiefs, and Wagret, who covers the period 1956–1960, has detailed information on elections. The best short studies of AEF politics are contained in a few unpublished monographs written by colonial administrators studying at the Institut des Hautes Etudes d'Outre-Mer (IHEOM), formerly the Ecole Nationale de la France d'Outre-Mer, and at the Centre des Hautes Etudes sur l'Afrique et l'Asie Modernes (CHEAM). Among the most useful of these are Alain Mauric, "Le Gabon de la Loi-Cadre au Référendum" (IHEOM, 1959), Charles Schweisguth, "Le Sultanat du Ouaddai: Evolution Politique, Economique et Sociale" (IHEOM, 1957), and J. Duriez, "Etude du Balalisme" (CHEAM, 1952). The last traces in considerable detail the development of Balali resistance to the colonial administration and to participation in politics. Another thesis on the same subject, written by a Balali student, is Martial Sinda, "Le Messianisme Congolais et ses Incidences Politiques depuis son Apparition jusqu'à l'époque de l'indépendance (1921–1961)" (Faculté des Lettres, Université de Paris, 1961).

The evolution of French colonial political institutions has been studied in detail, largely with reference to West African territories, but most of what has been written applies in full to AEF. On colonial politics in Paris and in West Africa, the best study is Ruth Schacter Morgenthau, *The Development of Political Parties in French-Speaking West Africa* (London: Oxford University Press, 1964). Politics in West Africa from 1957 to 1960 is treated with a profederation bias by Gil Dugué in *Vers les Etats-Unis d'Afrique* (Dakar: Editions Africaines, 1960). On institutional and legal aspects the most useful studies are those by Kenneth Robinson, especially "The Public Law of Overseas France since the War," Oxford University Institute of Colonial Studies Reprint Series, No. 1a (n.d.), and "Constitutional Reform in French Tropical Africa," *Political Studies,* VI (Feb., 1958), 45–69. There are also frequent articles on legal and administrative developments in the *Revue Juridique et Politique d'Outre-Mer,* formerly *Revue Juridique et Politique de l'Union Française* (Paris, quarterly), and *Penant: Revue de Droit des Pays d'Afrique,* formerly *Recueil Penant* (Paris, quarterly), which also contain texts of the constitutions of 1959 and after.

The most important official publication concerning political and administrative matters is the *Journal Officiel de l'Afrique Equatoriale Française,* which appeared fortnightly from Brazzaville until June, 1959, and carried the texts of legislation relevant to AEF, as well as the basic content of all significant administrative decisions of the Federation and its territories. Since 1959, each state has published its own fortnightly *Journal Officiel* at Brazzaville. In addition, the *Débats* of the Grand Council (1947–1958) and territorial assemblies were published for each session as well as *Recueils de Délibérations* in certain cases. The assemblies continued to publish their debates until independence in 1960, but some have since been content to mimeograph their debates on a day-to-day basis. The government-general of AEF issued an irregular information bulletin under various titles from 1945 to 1953, and since 1959 the information services of the new states have issued a variety of publications. The most regular and thorough is RCA's weekly *Centrafrique* (1959–1961), RCA's *Bulletin d'Information* (1961–1962), and *Terre Africaine* (since January, 1963). For the postwar colonial period, a new bibliography issued by the U.S. Library of Congress, *Official Publications of French Equatorial Africa, French Cameroons, and Togo; 1946–1958* (1964), is useful.

News of current developments in AEF is exceptionally difficult to obtain. The Agence-France-Presse *Bulletin Quotidien d'Outre-Mer* (Paris, daily) and its *Bulletin d'Afrique Occidentale et Equatoriale* (Paris, fortnightly) contain the important AFP dispatches from the equatorial states. In addition, *Afrique Nouvelle* (Dakar, weekly) and *Jeune Afrique* (Tunis, weekly) both carry frequent articles of considerable interest, such as Adolphe N'Dong M'Bile, "Des Prisonniers 'Français' Devant la Justice Gabonaise," *Afrique Nouvelle* (Sept. 4, 1964), p. 8, and Germain Mba, "Occupé le Gabon Lutte; Humiliée l'Afrique se Tait," *Jeune Afrique,* no. 178 (April 6, 1964), pp. 6–7, which could not possibly have been published at home. Among local newspapers from the equatorial states only *Semaine Africaine* (Brazzaville, weekly) has any significant circulation outside AEF and its news tends to be limited to official communiqués. For 1956–1959, the newspaper *France-Equateur* (Brazzaville, three times weekly) is available on microfilm at the Library of Congress and elsewhere, but because of its strong pro-Youlou bias it must be used with caution. Important equatorial radio news broadcasts are published in the U.S. Government's *Foreign Broadcast Information Service* (Washington, daily). The best summary of events is probably that in *Chronologie Politique Africaine* (Paris, quarterly since 1960).

No full bibliography concerning AEF has been attempted since the publication of Georges Bruel, *Bibliographie de l'Afrique Equatoriale* (Paris: Larose, 1914), though later ethnographic works are covered in P. Sanner, *Bibliographie Ethnographique de l'Afrique Equatoriale Française* (Paris: Imprimerie Nationale, 1949). Kenneth Robinson, "A Survey of the Background Material for the Study of Government in French Tropical Africa," *American Political Science Review*, L (March, 1956), 179–198, is a very useful critical study and the INSEE *Bulletin Bibliographique* (Paris, bimonthly) contains annotated references to French studies on French-speaking Africa.

OTHER BOOKS

Andersson, Efraim. *Messianic Popular Movements in the Lower Congo.* Uppsala: Almqvist and Wiksells, 1958.

Ansprenger, Franz. *Politik im schwarzen Afrika: die modernen politischen bewegungen im Afrika franzosischer pragüng.* Cologne: Westdeutscher Verlag, 1961.

Balandier, Georges. *Afrique Ambiguë.* Paris: Plon, 1957.

Betts, Raymond F. *Assimilation and Association in French Colonial Policy, 1890–1914.* New York: Columbia University Press, 1961.

Blanchet, André. *L'Itinéraire des Partis Africains depuis Bamako.* Paris: Plon, 1958.

Borella, François. *L'Evolution Politique et Juridique de l'Union Française depuis 1946.* Paris: R. Pichon et R. Durand-Auzias, 1958.

Carbou, Henri. *La Région du Tchad et du Ouaddai.* Paris: E. Leroux, 1912.

Chambre de Commerce, d'Agriculture, et d'Industrie du Gabon. *Petit Atlas du Gabon.* Paris: Editions Alain, 1958.

Cureau, Adolphe Louis. *Les Populations Primitives de l'Afrique Equatoriale.* Paris: Armand Colin, 1912.

Denis, Jacques. *Le Phénomène Urbain en Afrique Centrale.* Namur: Secrétariat des Publications, Facultés Universitaires, 1958.

Devèze, Michel. *La France d'Outre-Mer: De l'Empire Colonial à l'Union Française, 1938–1947.* Paris: Hachette, 1948.

Gautier, R. P. *Etude Historique sur les Mpongoués et Tribus Avoisinantes.*

Brazzaville: Institut d'Etudes Centrafricaines, Mémoire No. 3, 1950.

Gide, André. *Retour au Tchad*. Paris: Gallimard, 1928.

————. *Voyage au Congo*. Paris: Gallimard, 1927.

Lebeuf, Jean-Paul. *Bangui (Oubangui-Chari, A.E.F.)*. Paris: Editions de l'Union Française, n.d.

————. *Fort Lamy (Tchad, A.E.F.)*. Paris: Editions de l'Union Française, n.d.

Roberts, Stephen H. *History of French Colonial Policy (1870–1925)*. 2 vols. London: P. S. King, 1929.

Rouget, Fernand. *L'Expansion Coloniale au Congo Français*. 2nd edition. Paris: E. Larose, 1906.

Schnapper, Bernard. *La Politique et le Commerce Français dans le Golfe de Guinée de 1838 à 1871*. Paris: Mouton, 1961.

Teulières, André. *L'Oubangui Face à l'Avenir*. Paris: Editions de l'Union Française, 1953.

Trimingham, J. Spencer. *History of Islam in West Africa*. Oxford: Oxford University Press, 1962.

ARTICLES

Balandier, Georges. "Messianismes et Nationalismes en Afrique Noire," *Cahiers Internationaux de Sociologie*, XIV (1953), 41–65.

Documentation Française. "La République Centrafricaine," *Notes et Etudes Documentaires*, No. 2733 (December 19, 1960).

————. "La République du Congo," *Notes et Etudes Documentaires*, No. 2732 (December 17, 1960).

————. "La République Gabonaise," *Notes et Etudes Documentaires*, No. 2795 (July 10, 1961).

————. "La République du Tchad," *Notes et Etudes Documentaires*, No. 2696 (August 30, 1960).

Dresch, J. "Villes Congolaises: Etude de Géographie Urbaine et Sociale," *Revue de Géographie Humaine et d'Ethnologie*, III (July–September, 1948), 3–24.

Gonidec, P. F. "L'Evolution du Syndicalisme en Afrique Noire," *Penant*, LXXII (1962), 167–192.

Lebeuf, Jean-Paul. "Centres Urbains d'Afrique Equatoriale Française," *Africa*, XXIII (October, 1953), 285–297.

Pauvert, Jean-Claude. "Le Problème des Classes Sociales en Afrique Equatoriale," *Cahiers Internationaux de Sociologie*, XIX (1955), 76–91.

Robinson, Kenneth. "Local Government Reform in French Tropical Africa," *Journal of African Administration*, VIII (October, 1956), 179–185.

Sautter, Gilles. "Les Paysans Noirs du Gabon Septentrional: Essai sur le Peuplement et l'Habitat du Woleu-N'Tem," *Cahiers d'Outre-Mer*, IV (April–June, 1951), 119–159.

Terray, Emmanuel. "Les Révolutions Congolaise et Dahoméenne de 1963: Essai d'Interpretation," *Revue Française de Science Politique* (October, 1964), 917–942.

Wagret, J. M. "L'Ascension Politique de l'UDDIA (Congo) et sa Prise de Pouvoir (1956–1959)," *Revue Juridique et Politique d'Outre-Mer,* XVII (April–June, 1963).

V

UGANDA

By DONALD ROTHCHILD

University of California, Davis

AND MICHAEL ROGIN

University of California, Berkeley

Introduction

"TRIBALISM" is under frontal assault in Africa. It has been denounced by militant pan-Africanists as a divisive force, a tool of the "divide and rule" imperialists. Yet local nationalism remains an essential element of the Uganda scene. Unlike neighboring Tanganyika (now part of Tanzania), for example, where the government has successfully restricted chiefs to traditional functions, Uganda attempts constitutionally to reconcile needs of the central government with the demands of local nationalists by guaranteeing both traditional units and their leaders a place in the life of the nation. For a land as small as Uganda, such a compromise between local and national power is unusual; it gives Uganda a character all its own, which is reflected in its constitutional organization, its party system, and its view of the outside world.

The conflict between local and territorial nationalists has deep roots in the twentieth-century history of Uganda. Separatism and centralism interacted upon each other continuously from 1894, when the powerful kingdom of Buganda became a British protectorate, until 1962, when the entire country (comprising the kingdoms of Buganda, Ankole,

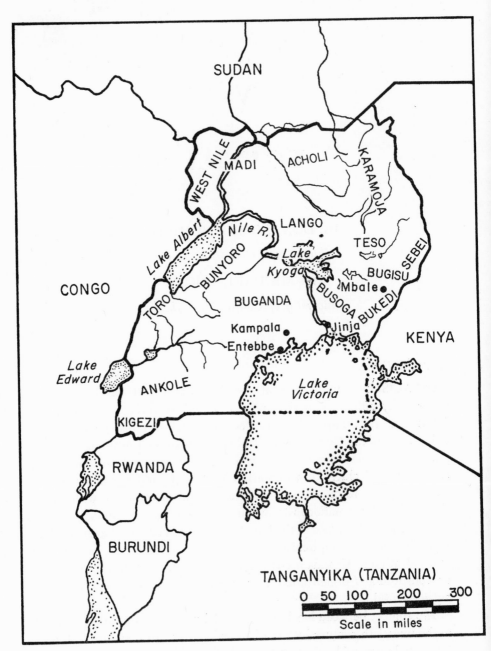

Map 5. Uganda

Bunyoro, and Toro and the territory of Busoga, which are federal states, and the districts of Acholi, Bugisu, Bukedi, Karamoja, Kigezi, Lango, Madi, Sebei, Teso, and West Nile) gained independence. Thus, although central authorities supervised local activities more and more fully in the period after World War I, the expansion of administrative activities that occurred did not go unchallenged by Baganda [1] nationalists and, to a lesser extent, by other local nationalists. Baganda leaders, asserting that the kingdom's relationship with Britain rested squarely on the 1900 Uganda Agreement (which established Buganda's rights within the Protectorate), felt free to act independently of central leadership on various occasions. As a consequence, Uganda centralism tended to be more apparent than real, and Buganda's sense of separateness from the rest of the country was not eradicated. The continuing tensions of this situation are evident in the negotiations establishing Buganda's federal relationship with the center, the rise of a Baganda political party (*Kabaka Yekka*), and the kingdom's determined opposition to integration into an East African federation.

In the face of strong tribal loyalties, then, Uganda has had to make unique political and constitutional adjustments. As a consequence, the country has had broad experience in political engineering. It has known a unitary form of government as well as elements of federalism; both now exist side by side in an uneasy relationship under the same basic law. Although provisions for federalism were included in the constitution in order to accommodate Uganda's ethnic pluralism, it is still an open question whether a strong sense of national unity can flourish in such an environment.

Historical Background

INTRODUCTION

Before the arrival of the British the area from which Uganda was later formed had a continuous history of tribal migrations, warfare, and even diplomatic and commercial relations with other areas. Consequently, the territory came to include many and diverse peoples. In time this pluralism had an important influence upon both the formal constitutional structure and the particular pattern of nationalism which evolved in Uganda. Centralized systems (such as the highly developed

[1] For references to the Baganda and other Bantu tribes of Uganda, we have adopted the Bantu nomenclature: the place is Buganda, the people are the Baganda, one person is a Muganda, the language is Luganda, and the customs are kiganda.

political structure of the Buganda nation) as well as decentralized systems had to be accommodated within the same framework, and each system exerted its influence on the constitutional organization of modern Uganda. Independence came to Uganda only one hundred years after John Hanning Speke's "discovery" of the source of the Nile, but the impact of the past on contemporary politics goes back considerably beyond this limited period of British influence.

The establishment of a British protectorate over Uganda took place by stages. It began with the declaration of protectorate status for the kingdom of Buganda in 1894. This action was preceded by a series of events that began with the explorations of Speke, who arrived in Buganda in 1862 and awakened England's interest in this land. When Captain Frederick D. Lugard (in his capacity as agent of the Imperial British East Africa Company) arrived in Buganda almost thirty years later, he found the kingdom rent by factional strife. The introduction of Christianity in the 1870's had resulted in religious conflict in Buganda. Involving himself in the struggle only a year after his arrival, Lugard helped the Protestants to a military victory over their Catholic rivals, then headed by Kabaka (King) Mwanga. "Lugard's intervention on the Protestant side at the climax of events," notes one historian, "undoubtedly played an important part in ensuring that Uganda became a British Protectorate. . . . Had the Catholic party triumphed under Mwanga's leadership the Company could scarcely have maintained a foothold in Buganda." [2]

Shortly after this episode, Kabaka Mwanga signed a new treaty with Lugard, and Britain, somewhat reluctantly, began to realize that, largely for strategic and missionary reasons, the fate of Buganda had become intertwined with its own. In May, 1893, British Commissioner Sir Gerald Portal signed a treaty with Kabaka Mwanga making Buganda a British protectorate, and the following year Parliament formally agreed to this new extension of British influence in Africa.

Although Buganda's domains were increased during the following period by the incorporation, with British aid, of former Bunyoro lands (now referred to as the "lost counties"), the next formal expansion of British influence occurred in 1896, when the western kingdoms (Bunyoro, Ankole, and Toro) and the territory of Busoga to the east of Buganda were gathered under Her Majesty's protection. In subsequent years, the British spread their authority to the northeast, northwest,

[2] Kenneth Ingham, *The Making of Modern Uganda* (London: Allen & Unwin, 1958), pp. 47–48.

and southwest of the 1896 Protectorate. The Baganda leader Ka-kunguru conquered the area to the northeast in Britain's name, sub-duing such tribes as the Lango and the Iteso. In Buganda itself the situation became stable only after the Protectorate government crushed Kabaka Mwanga's revolt against their authority and deposed him in favor of Daudi Chwa, his infant son. By the turn of the century, condi-tions were sufficiently settled that Britain could sign formal agreements with Buganda (the Uganda Agreement) and Toro in 1900 and Ankole in 1901. Bunyoro, whose relations with the British were far less amica-ble, had to wait for its agreement until 1933.

The special status of Buganda in Uganda was the most important legacy of the colonial era. Buganda's position was specified in the 1900 Uganda Agreement. The Agreement made Buganda a province of the Protectorate and declared, in Article 6, that "the Kabaka of Uganda [Buganda] shall exercise direct rule over the natives of Uganda [Buganda], to whom he shall administer justice through the Lukiko [sic], or native council, and through others of his officers in the manner approved by Her Majesty's Government."

The Agreement brought with it two important consequences. First, a significant alteration of Baganda society took place. Freehold land was introduced, entrenching the power of those chiefs who controlled land at the time of the Agreement. In this and other ways the power of these chiefs was confirmed at the expense of other contenders for polit-ical dominance. Second, British sovereignty over Buganda was now clearly established. The Lukiiko and the Kabaka, before giving effect to their resolutions, were required to consult with "and explicitly follow the advice of Her Majesty's representative." The Baganda rulers were bound not only by their own laws but by those of the Protectorate gov-ernment.

Moreover, it was the interpretation of the Agreement, and not so much its content, that was to prove crucial. The British clearly re-garded the Agreement with Buganda as in a category separate from subsequent agreements with other native kingdoms. As Anthony Low writes: "Since so much apparently came to be based on the Agree-ment, . . . it was natural for the Baganda to consider that their rela-tionship was quasi-diplomatic. Moreover, given the concessions they had secured, the Agreement, equally naturally, appeared to the Baganda as in some sense at least an agreement between equals." [3]

[3] D. Anthony Low and R. Cranford Pratt, *Buganda and British Overrule 1900–1955* (London: Oxford University Press, 1960), p. 154.

The most important concession made to Buganda was the assumption implicit in the Agreement that the British would rule in the kingdom only through the tribal political authorities. Here was a classic case of indirect rule.

Elsewhere in Uganda the situation was different. Appointed chiefs, rather than traditional local chiefs, became the administrative and judicial authorities. Even where the traditional leaders were in fact made chiefs, they operated within a new system of authority foreign, to one degree or another, to that in most of Uganda.[4]

Ultimately, the degree of Buganda's independence from the British depended less on the legal formulas of the Agreement than on the facts of political power. In view of the power of Buganda, with its wealth, size, and unity, and the limited nature of Britain's commitment, the British found that direct colonial control of Buganda's affairs was not feasible. Indeed, there was little British supervision over the internal administration of Buganda during the eighteen years following the Agreement. Such a policy was dictated not by the terms of the Agreement but by reasons of finance and administrative convenience.

In the years following the signing of the Uganda Agreement, it was by no means certain that the Protectorate would not follow Kenya in the direction of white-settler dominance. Sir Harry Johnston, the Special Commissioner sent out in 1899 to organize the administration of the Protectorate, favored introducing large-scale plantation agriculture by Europeans into Uganda, but Sir Hesketh Bell, the Governor from 1907 to 1911, opposed extensive settlement of Europeans. The Colonial Office decided to prohibit the sale of land to non-Africans in 1915, which provoked strong opposition from the many Protectorate officials who still favored Johnston's policy. But despite their opposition, this decision became firm government policy in 1921. Even so, suspicions of settler intentions lingered on.

At the very time when the few existing European plantations were being wiped out by the 1929 depression, African suspicions became aroused by an attempt on the part of the Kenya settlers to unite the three British territories of Kenya, Tanganyika, and Uganda. Why else, they reasoned, did the Europeans of Kenya seek a union with Uganda but to radiate their influence and control over the latter country? As a memorandum from the Basoga to the 1931 Joint Select Committee on Closer Union in East Africa declared: "We fear that if closer union is adopted the white settlers may come into our country and take away our

[4] *Ibid.*, pp. 176–177.

land as they have done in Kenya." [5] Closer union and land problems became inextricably intertwined, precluding any movement toward wider territorial integration at least until African governments came to power in all the East African countries. In any event, the Joint Select Committee's decision not to pursue closer union for the foreseeable future substantially laid the ghost of white settlement to rest.

The fact that colonial officials did not have to contend with an important settler community had little impact at first upon the development of representative institutions. When the first Legislative Council (Legco) met in 1921, no African members took part in the deliberations. Not until after World War II, when concessions were made to African nationalism throughout much of British Africa, did the real development of the Uganda Legco begin. In 1945, three nominated African members joined Legco for the first time. Then in 1950, Legco was expanded to include sixteen official and sixteen unofficial members (of the latter, eight were Africans, four Europeans, and four Asians).

THE ADOPTION OF "FEDERALISM"

By the 1920's, the Protectorate government had begun to intervene directly in Buganda's affairs. More and more it imposed its interpretation of the Agreement on the rulers of the kingdom. Protectorate influence in finance and in the supervision of local administration and personnel increased markedly during this period; by the 1930's, central supervision over traditional authorities had become extensive. In appearance at least, the administration of Buganda was becoming like the administration of the other kingdoms and peoples of Uganda, and the country seemed to be moving steadily toward a unitary system of government.

But as the British increased their control over Buganda, they also provoked Baganda separatism. As early as 1916, the Lukiiko had questioned the Protectorate's authority to issue passports to Baganda, and a decade later a constitutional crisis occurred over the independence of the Buganda *katikkiro* (prime minister) from British control. Moreover, the demonstrations and riots of 1945 and 1949 in Buganda were directed against chiefs who were considered too acquiescent to British control. Then in the 1950's, as the British tried to push direct elections and establish a unitary state in Uganda, their efforts provoked the most serious crisis of the colonial era. Buganda, anxious about its position in

[5] *Joint Committee on Closer Union in East Africa*, III (London: H.M.S.O., 1931), 114–115.

an independent Uganda and refusing to be treated like the other Uganda regions, sought to limit the political involvement of the kingdom with the rest of the country. This assertion of the right to self-determination was an unanticipated consequence of indirect rule. Paradoxically, both Buganda and the British based their positions on the 1900 Agreement, an identity of claims which made a crisis almost inevitable.

By the 1950's, Britain's determination to build a unitary state in Uganda had reached a high point. As independence for Uganda became a serious possibility, practical considerations such as the country's small size and population seemed to militate against launching a federal experiment. The 1953 Wallis report on local government assumed from the outset that a federation of native states was "impracticable" and that the country would be developed along unitary lines. In March, 1953, Governor Sir Andrew Cohen and Kabaka Edward Frederick Mutesa II of Buganda issued a joint memorandum which emphasized Buganda's special position in a unitary Uganda while at the same time devolving powers to provincial authorities in primary and secondary education, rural hospitals, dispensaries and health services, and agricultural and veterinary field services. Moreover, a law enacted in 1955 defined, and thereby limited, the powers of local authorities in the northern, western, and eastern provinces. The purpose of both moves was to assure Uganda's continued evolution as a unitary state. The concessions made in Buganda were considered expedients to this end. Sensitive to criticism that the devolution of additional powers was inconsistent with centralist objectives, Sir Andrew explained later that a failure to work in harmony with tribal loyalties "would have been harmful or at the least unreal, and the view we took was that strengthening the unity of the country would not be furthered by failing to recognise the attachment of the people to the parts." [6]

Sir Andrew's dedication to the goal of a unitary Uganda was put to the test shortly after the joint memorandum was announced. Baganda fears for the future status of the kingdom in a unitary Uganda intensified their general anxiety over a reopening of the question of East African federation. Not only did the Kabaka seek assurances that federation would not be imposed on his people, but he subsequently used the federation crisis to ask for Buganda's separation from the Protectorate as well. His refusal to back down on the question of Buganda's inde-

---

[6] Sir Andrew Cohen, *British Policy in Changing Africa* (Evanston: Northwestern University Press, 1959), p. 58.

pendence, deemed by the British to be a breach of the 1900 Agreement, led Her Majesty's government to withdraw recognition from the Kabaka and to deport him to the United Kingdom. Sir Andrew, who had acted in order to strengthen the unity of the Protectorate, rode through the crisis and saw the 1955 Buganda Agreement restore the Kabaka to his throne as a constitutional monarch and, in effect, recognize Buganda's incorporation in a strongly centralized Uganda.

Sir Andrew's subsequent departure from Uganda had little effect upon the British government's determination to mold a unitary system. A constitutional committee, under the chairmanship of J. V. Wild, made important proposals in 1959 aimed at continuing this general policy. The Wild report recommended direct elections on a common roll basis for representative members to Legco and urged the development of political parties on a national basis—both controversial recommendations in an area where tribal societies place great store in the maintenance of a sense of solidarity. On the establishment of federalism in Uganda the report was unenthusiastic. Certainly support for a unitary form seemed widespread in the eastern, northern, and western provinces at that time. But dissenting views were also in evidence. The Toro *Rukurato* (district council) continued to press for federalism, passing a resolution in May, 1960, which called the federal form of government "the one which guarantees safeguards for the status and dignity of the traditional Rulers." Even so, few can have realized that Uganda was on the eve of a major constitutional experiment.

Separatist Tendencies

As the British pushed centralism in a more determined manner, separatist tendencies came to the fore. Unitary government represented a threat to tribal solidarity, and each advance on its behalf brought about astute and determined opposition. In the final analysis, British policy-makers bent to the forces of local nationalism, seeing a geographical expansion of power as the only realistic means of creating a united, independent country.

The storm center of tribal nationalism is Buganda. Like nationalist movements elsewhere, that in Buganda tends to be exclusive—thereby causing serious strains in a plural community like Uganda. Although not always in evidence, Baganda separatism has been a factor in the politics of Uganda since the signing of the 1900 Agreement. Separatist tendencies have become manifest every time the Protectorate government has asserted more authority or has acted so as to lower Buganda's status as a nation. In 1953, they came into the open over the question of creating an East African federation, and in 1960, a Lukiiko resolution proclaimed Buganda's secession from the Uganda Protectorate.

Early in 1960, signs of an impending crisis became apparent. On February 11, an information officer in the Kabaka's government, placing on record Buganda's intention to secure federal status for itself, spoke ominously of the possibility of secession. The move toward unitary government, he asserted, "was one of the greatest reasons why Buganda desired to go it alone." During the summer months that followed, talks were held between the Colonial Secretary and a delegation from Buganda on constitutional questions affecting the kingdom. These talks broke down in September over such issues as the return of Buganda's sovereignty and the future form of government in Uganda. The Lukiiko thereupon voted overwhelmingly to petition the Queen to secede from the rest of Uganda.[7]

Although all responsible British authorities rejected "any question of any part of the Protectorate seceding from Uganda so long as Her Majesty's Government is the protecting power," [8] there seems little question that the secessionist move did much to force the British to bargain on the nature of Uganda's form of government. Buganda's action, observed the Uganda Relationships Commission, which advised on the future form of government in 1961, "plainly leads towards disaster." Such a conclusion left British authorities with little choice but to rearrange the existing scheme of government to reflect, in a permanent manner, Buganda's power and influence in the affairs of a new Uganda. Thus the trend toward a strong unitary government came to an end.

Reconciling Local Nationalism

The Relationships Commission report marked a major turning point in Uganda's constitutional history. Because a unitary system was no longer practical for political reasons, the commission proposed to incorporate elements of federalism in the constitution. Emphasis was placed throughout the report on reconciling local nationalism and central needs. Uganda's unity was to be secured after independence by accepting and placating particularism.

The commission, under the chairmanship of Lord Munster, denied

[7] For a statement on the plan for an independent Buganda, see *Buganda's Independence* (Mmengo: Information Department of Kabaka's Government, 1960), pp. 32–36.

[8] *Uganda Protectorate, Letter No. EAF 7/6/03 of 2nd December, 1960 From the Secretary of State to His Highness the Kabaka* (Entebbe: Government Printer, 1960), p. 3.

the feasibility of establishing a thoroughgoing federal state in Uganda; there was deemed to be an "absence of a number of more or less self-governing states out of which a completely federal country should be composed." [9] A federal relationship was proposed for Buganda—and for Buganda alone. This violation of the normal equality of the constituent units in a federal system indicated the commission's pragmatic approach: Buganda's administrative experience, size, and wealth justified its special status in the eyes of the commissioners. Perhaps more important, Buganda constituted "a disruptive element" under the arrangement then in force; a federal system (albeit a unique one) seemed a small price to pay to overcome its secessionist rumblings.

The Munster commission also recommended a somewhat novel status for the three kingdoms of Toro, Ankole, and Bunyoro. On the grounds that there are "a large number of possible gradations" between unitary and federal states in their pure forms, it proposed that these kingdoms be given "semifederal" status. This would safeguard local customs, institutions, and languages while preserving central administrative leadership. A federal system, explained the commission, would "be too weak and expensive for these kingdoms. If they were federal states they would have to equip themselves with much more elaborate government machinery than they have now, and they have not the resources, either human or financial, for this task." For the rest of Uganda, the commission favored the continuance of strong unitary government. The remaining districts, lacking hereditary rulers, had not agitated for federal status.

Undoubtedly the Relationships Commission did its utmost to give each political unit the approximate status it insisted upon. The result was a basic law which defies clear-cut classification in its present form. In effect, the commission supported three approaches to constitutionalism—federalism, semifederalism, and a unitary system of government—within the same basic law. Such a pragmatic approach was obviously not ideal because its constitutional asymmetry might lead to conflicts between units of different status, but its justification lay in its ability to ease the pressures of local nationalism.

The Status of Buganda

Although reactions to the Relationships Commission's recommendations seemed generally favorable, strong disagreement was expressed in various quarters. Some referred to the report as part of Britain's

[9] *Uganda Protectorate, Report of the Uganda Relationships Commission 1961* (Entebbe: Government Printer, 1961), p. 40.

"divide and rule" policy and others criticized the extensive concessions made to Buganda. Nevertheless, by providing a basis for discussion, the report did speed independence negotiations.

The thorniest question, that of Buganda's secession, was not decided until the Uganda Constitutional Conference convened in London in the fall of 1961, at which time this crucial matter was settled by the parties concerned. The Uganda People's Congress (UPC) leader, A. Milton Obote, who became Prime Minister in 1962, agreed to Buganda's price for an end to further talk of secession: federal status and indirect Lukiiko election of its representatives to the central legislature. Leaders of the Democratic Party (DP), which formed the government following the 1961 general elections, reacted angrily to Obote's agreement, charging him with "political opportunism" and "conspiracy." Indirect elections prevented the DP from capitalizing on local pockets of dissent in Buganda, and they therefore stood firmly, but futilely, for direct elections.

The agreement according Buganda federal status was a major victory for its politicians. Federal status, as two Baganda writers have recently observed, was sought in order "to safeguard the traditions, Kabakaship, and the customs of Buganda in an independent Uganda." "The nationalists were divided and weak," they asserted, "and thus to hand over political power to these people without safeguarding the integrity of Buganda was to invite trouble." [10] Thus traditionalist leaders, fearful for their position in a centralized Uganda after the granting of *uhuru* (freedom), obstructed the path toward independence until their interests were satisfied. In this they were far more successful than their counterparts in Ghana and Tanganyika had been.

The Status of the Western Kingdoms and Busoga

Buganda's success in securing federal status was bound to affect traditional rulers elsewhere. The rulers of Ankole, Bunyoro, Toro, and Busoga had long sought some form of special recognition. Now they insisted upon being granted full federal status, declaring the guarantees implicit in semifederal status to be "illusory." They claimed to be fully capable of assuming the fiscal responsibilities of federalism, even though their populations were small and their possibilities for economic advancement limited. What all this amounted to, in brief, was a demand to be accorded the same rights and respect as Buganda.

[10] Henry Kyeyune and Apolo Nsibambi, *Buganda, Federal State of Uganda* (Mmengo: Kabaka's Government, 1962), pp. 10, 13.

From the time of the Wild report, Toro took the lead among the kingdoms in pressing for federalism and for a clarification of the position of traditional rulers in Uganda. On August 20, 1960, the katikkiro of Toro cabled the Colonial Secretary, Iain Macleod, making it "emphatically clear" that Toro would not support a unitary system; only a federal system, and nothing less, could properly safeguard its hereditary institutions. The Munster report caused bitter resentment in Toro by providing for no more than semifederal status, and the London conference, by devolving few powers to the kingdoms that were not also assigned to the districts, did little to reduce this grievance. In January, 1962, therefore, the Toro Rukurato went to the length of cabling the new Colonial Secretary, Reginald Maudling, that Toro was not prepared to accept integration with the rest of Uganda unless full federal status were granted. It seemed just possible that a new secession crisis was in the making. Toro leaders even spoke darkly of another "Congo."

Although authorities in London were naturally reluctant to reopen discussions on forms of government only months after the conclusion of the 1961 conference, they were soon forced to take note of the pressures that were rapidly building up. On March 2, 1962, at the ceremony in which he was sworn in as Uganda's first Prime Minister, Benedicto Kiwanuka, spoke of the "anxieties" in the kingdoms and Busoga,[11] as well as of the traditional rulers' legitimate demands. Indicating his intentions of making a fresh approach to British authorities on this matter, he asserted: "I can now see no reason why federal status cannot be granted to the Districts. This will help to allay the fears of the Rulers and their subjects in those kingdoms and the result will be peace and stability of Government." On the following day, UPC leader Obote associated himself fully with these sentiments, while in the National Assembly one of his chief lieutenants, Grace Ibingira (now Minister of State), introduced a motion calling on the Colonial Secretary to negotiate with the kingdoms and Busoga "with a view to granting them appropriate forms of federal status."[12] Because of such pressures, British authorities decided to reappraise the matter.

The immediate reason for re-examining the extension of federal status was the involvement of that issue in the forthcoming 1962 general

[11] Busoga is mentioned in a separate category, because it lacked a single king over the whole tribe and because it had not made the same agreements as the other kingdoms.

[12] Uganda, *National Assembly Debates,* 41st Session, Part IV (March 7, 1962), p. 3431. For official UPC policy, see Uganda People's Congress, *Policy Statement* (Kampala, 1962), pp. 1, 4.

elections. Prime Minister Kiwanuka, faced with the possibility of an election boycott in the kingdoms and Busoga, announced his government's opposition to holding elections in those parts until the Secretary of State consented to their demands. Two ministers of the government then flew to London to explain the reasons for this announcement. Perhaps a chief, although unstated, reason was the DP's hope that in backing the kingdoms' claims it would gain political support in these areas. Meanwhile the leading Uganda opposition parties, UPC and *Kabaka Yekka* (KY), objected strongly to the proposed delays. The spokesmen of the two parties bitterly rejected Kiwanuka's attempt to tie the date of the elections to the issue of broadening the federal relationship.

Kiwanuka's announcement clearly left Britain with three possible choices: to postpone the elections; to hold the elections as planned, despite possible noncooperation; or to grant the kingdoms and Busoga immediate federal status. British officials decided quickly not to postpone the elections; they did not consider the issue at hand relevant to the date of the elections.

Several weeks of rumors and predictions followed. Then two weeks before the general election, after discussions in London with the rulers of the three western kingdoms and Busoga, the Colonial Secretary publicly agreed to grant increased powers and a federal relationship to the western kingdoms. Busoga's request was put off until the June constitutional conference, since it had never made a treaty agreement with Britain. Both the UPC and the DP were elated. They welcomed Maudling's statement and appealed to him to extend the same status to Busoga. When additional guarantees and powers were in fact extended to the kingdoms and Busoga by the 1962 conference, Britain had done much to accommodate the strongest centrifugal pressures in the country.

The grant of federal status to the kingdoms and Busoga raised, in turn, the problem of fragmentation. If federalism was to be based on ethnic units, could the process be stopped short of full federalism, with all its implications in pluralistic and underdeveloped Uganda? In July, 1962, a delegation from the Bugisu District Council met with the Minister of Regional Administrations, Cuthbert Obwangor, to claim federal status. The minister refused to negotiate on Bugisu's claim to federal status, maintaining that the matter had been closed by the recent London conference. The claim went no farther, but it illustrates the difficulty of halting the tendency toward decentralization once it has gained momentum. The emotional appeals of federal status (protection of traditional institutions, power, and prestige) are meaningful to all ethnic groups. It is interesting that many of the tribes which lacked paramount chiefs in the past are now agitating for monarchs. Commenting on Buganda's achievements, A. W. Southall notes: "The other peoples of Uganda, however much they dislike it, have drawn the inexorable conclusion that monarchy pays. . . . Inevitably, the flimsiest evidence is used to build up local monarchs." [13] The Basoga have been given a herditary monarch; the Bakiga and Iteso have demanded one. Here is a recognition that tribes with kings have received greater concessions and have more status generally.

THE RISE AND CHARACTER OF THE NATIONALIST MOVEMENT

In recent times, countries under colonial rule have achieved independence when a growing nationalist movement has been successful both in mobilizing a large section of the population and in extracting concessions from the colonial power. In Uganda, however, it would be more accurate to say that it was not nationalism that produced independence, but that it was the imminence of independence that produced nationalist parties. Independence, rather than representing a goal which unified the various elements behind a nationalist party, was looked upon as a means whereby certain groups (for example, northerners or westerners, Baganda or non-Baganda, Protestants or Catholics, radicals or traditionalists) would become more or less powerful.

Only in 1959 did the coalition that was to lead Uganda to independence begin to take shape. Buganda dominated the political scene in Uganda in that year, as it had done ever since Uganda became a protectorate. The kingdom had refused to participate in the first direct elections to Legco in 1958. The election boycott was used, not to speed independence, but to win concessions for Buganda. A variety of Buganda-based political parties with the more usual nationalist objectives were unable to win popular support in the kingdom. Most of these parties were, in fact, splinters from the Uganda National Congress. The UNC had been formed in 1952 on the organizational foundations of the Federation of Uganda African Farmers. Ignatius Musazi, the leader of this cooperative movement, was its founder. During the years of the Kabaka's exile UNC had become fairly strong in Buganda. But that this was the result of its agitation for the Kabaka's

[13] "Micropolitics in Uganda—Traditional and Modern Politics," in *Proceedings of the EAISR Conference at Dar es Salaam, January 1963* (Kampala: East African Institute of Social Research, 1963), p. 16.

return rather than of its broader political program soon became apparent. With the return of the Kabaka, the issue which had allied UNC with the traditionalists disappeared, and the party largely lost its political significance in Buganda.

But unlike the other Buganda-based parties, the UNC had support outside the kingdom. In the 1958 elections to Legco, the UNC won five of the ten directly elected seats. This victory, however, gave more the appearance than the reality of power. Early in 1959, two UNC Legco members left to form a new political party, the Uganda People's Union. The latter could boast seven Legco members at its formation (some of whom were indirectly elected), reducing the UNC to three. In large part the UPU was formed in an attempt to counter Buganda's political dominance. It was a coalition of several Legco members—a cadre party in the classic sense.

Meanwhile, the UNC underwent a new schism as Musazi led a section of the party away from the larger body. Musazi was the only politician with genuine popular support in Buganda, but his support rested on the exploitation of Baganda traditionalism. With Musazi's exit the UNC was dominated by its younger and better-educated members, as well as Muganda political veteran Joseph Kiwanuka. Its president was A. Milton Obote, member of the Legislative Council from Lango.

These three parties—the UPU and the two UNC's—had different bases of political support. The UPU was exclusively confined to the Bantu tribes of Uganda, with most of its strength coming from the western kingdoms. The Musazi–UNC received most of its support from Buganda, with some from Bukedi and Bugisu, perhaps the two areas after Buganda with the most political activity. The Obote–UNC was a northern party. The geographical distribution of its party officers reflected regional strength. The districts from which twenty-eight officers were elected early in 1959 are identifiable. Of these officers only two were from the west, while nine were northerners, six came from Bukedi and Bugisu, and most of the rest were from Buganda.

The picture of political diversity is completed by a Catholic party, called the Democratic Party, which had also existed in Uganda since 1956. The Democratic Party had been formed on the European Christian Democratic pattern with the encouragement and support of the powerful Catholic missions. But unlike Catholic parties in Europe, the DP did not have Catholic philosophic underpinnings. It arose in Buganda out of the traditional conflict between Catholics and Protestants for control of the province. With Buganda's many Catholics largely excluded from political power, prospects for a Catholic party to challenge Protestant dominance appeared promising. Indeed, the year before the formation of the DP, the Catholic candidate for katikkiro of Buganda had been defeated by only three votes in the Lukiiko. But to the Baganda there was a great difference between a Catholic faction in the tradition of Buganda politics, and a nationwide Catholic political party supporting such progressive policies as independence and direct elections throughout Uganda. Consequently, the DP acquired only limited strength in Buganda. Outside the kingdom, however, the party was strong in such Catholic areas as West Nile.

All the various "nationalist" parties of 1959 were restricted to certain geographical regions, and even in the areas where each was most powerful, party organization was not well developed. They were parties of leaders, not mass-membership nationalist parties.

The Late Development of National Parties

National parties in Uganda did not become a reality until independence was a certainty. How can one account for this late development? Certainly the absence of a settler problem, the tribal diversity, the lack of a *lingua franca,* and the small number of university-educated men (compared to Nigeria or Ghana) must all be taken into account. Perhaps more important than these factors was the absence of large urban concentrations, the most effective agencies for breaking the hold of traditionalism. There were only 75,000 people living in Kampala and its urban environs in 1960. The Baganda lived around this city, but even so, many with urban jobs preferred to dwell on their family farms. Despite their progress in education and their proximity to urban areas and to Europeans, the Baganda failed to act in an orthodox nationalist manner. This failure provides the principal explanation for the late and peculiar development of Uganda nationalism.

Unlike many strongly traditional peoples, the Baganda have shown a striking ability to adapt to Western influences. At the same time, the spread of Christianity, the introduction of cash farming, the impact of British overlordship on the power of the Kabaka, and the changes in internal tribal structure brought about by colonial rule did not undermine the Baganda's strong personal loyalty to the Kabaka. Despite the all-embracing nature of the Baganda consensus, internal conflicts flourished within it. For a number of reasons the advent of British dominance increased the power of the Baganda chiefs, both vis-à-vis the Kabaka and vis-à-vis the *bakopi* (peasants or people). It was the chiefs who adapted Baganda tradition to meet the British challenge, and in the process augmented their own power. The people looked to the Kabaka to redress the balance. They also looked to the *bataka* (clan heads).

The clan heads represented an older tradition, one in which tribal structure had been less hierarchical, society less atomized, and values more pervasively religious. In the eyes of the people, the decline of the power of the bataka and the adaptability of the chiefs to Western influences were destroying the true tribal traditions. The people felt exploited by the chiefs, against whom there have been recurrent popular movements—movements directed less against the ruling class as such as toward the reassertion of an older pattern of tribal cohesion. Between 1926, when the first bataka organization appeared, and 1955, when the Kabaka returned from exile, there were a number of such movements. They varied widely in membership and goals but all had a traditional orientation. Their specific objects of attack were the British and the chiefs; their general target was the kingdom's inclination to adapt to Western influences.

We see here the usual roles reversed. Elsewhere the nationalist movement commonly rejects tribal authority; in Buganda it has made an attempt to reassert an ancient tribal authority which had eroded under the chiefs. Whereas the chiefs in other countries represented tradition against the alien influence of popular movements led by the intellectuals, here the people distrusted the chiefs as alien influences. Like the chiefs, the intellectuals could not be trusted because they were antitraditional and under Western influence. Moreover, these popular movements occurred not against the Kabaka but in his name.[14]

In the 1950's, a significant change occurred. Heretofore the challenges to the Baganda had been social, economic, and cultural, and the chiefs had been able to absorb them. Then the British began to introduce political reforms that threatened the tribal hierarchy itself, the center which had remained stable in the face of all these changes. The chiefs could no longer welcome innovation. The new pattern emerged during the period of the Kabaka's exile. When he returned, the pro-British chiefs lost their power, and the Kabaka's government became dominated by "neotraditionalist" chiefs. Finally the rulers had become as conservative in their outlook as the people. The deportation of the

[14] David E. Apter, *The Political Kingdom in Uganda* (Princeton: Princeton University Press, 1961); D. Anthony Low, "The Advent of Populism in Buganda" (unpublished manuscript, n.d.); Low and Pratt, *op. cit.*

Kabaka had the additional consequence of uniting all the factions within Buganda against the outside threat from the British.

The peculiar nature of Buganda traditionalism thus led to a peculiar form of Buganda nationalism. Here was a pride in traditional institutions, a militant desire to defend the kingdom against any external threats. The very success of Buganda nationalism helps to explain the failure of orthodox nationalism not only in Buganda but in the whole of Uganda as well.

The 1959 Boycott

With this background the events of 1959 fall into perspective. Again the Baganda felt threatened, and they reacted apprehensively to the appointment of the Wild committee. In particular the committee's instructions to consider special safeguards for non-Africans after independence triggered resentment against Asians. On March 9, 1959, the recently formed Uganda National Movement (UNM) declared a boycott of all Asian shops. Although this boycott was effective mainly in Buganda, its consequences dominated Uganda politics until independence. The demands of the UNM were not simply economic. Attacking the Wild committee, it ridiculed Legco as a foreign importation and favored government by the traditional rulers. With this program, supported by the chiefs and the Kabaka's government, the UNM became the first political party in Buganda to attract a mass following.

Baganda politicians, except for those in the DP and Obote–UNC, utilized the boycott to return to favor with the chiefs and the people. The actual organizers and leaders of the boycott were the less-educated. Here was a combination of the urban unemployed and the tradition-minded rural Baganda.

What then were the roles of the chiefs and of the Kabaka's government? Although they had not organized the boycott, they gave it strong covert support. It was a popular movement directed not against them but against foreigners—the Asians economically and the British politically. But if the boycott displayed to the British the unity of the Baganda people and the determination of the Baganda elite, there were lessons also for the Kabaka's government. The boycott continued to flourish even after the Kabaka's government withdrew its support, and political discontent persisted without the chiefs' leadership.

The Emergence of Modern Parties

Only gradually did modern parties emerge. Because the UNM opposed the Wild committee as well as Legco itself, the DP, the Obote-

UNC, and the UPU did not support it. These parties viewed the boycott as a reactionary attempt to delay independence. Indeed, one of the boycott's intentions was to embarrass the political parties in Buganda. At the same time, their apparent disloyalty to the Kabaka during the crisis lost both the UNC and DP what Baganda support they had possessed.

The united opposition of the other three parties to the UNM's position on the boycott continued for a few months. Influenced by the Catholic Church, the DP could not support such a violent and racist movement. But it gradually became clear to Obote that the UNC was forefeiting any chance of obtaining Baganda support. His position on the boycott became ambiguous. In June, 1959, Obote wavered on the boycott for the first time. The British by then had banned the UNM and declared Buganda a disturbed area. UPU Legco members solidly supported British actions, but Obote expressed doubts. In August, the issue of the boycott provided one of the reasons for another split in the UNC. This time the split was between the Baganda section of the party, led by J. Kiwanuka, and the branches of the north and east, which were based more on popular support. In "suspending" Kiwanuka from the UNC, the Obote faction criticized him for supporting the government's suppression of the UNM. Obote blamed Kiwanuka's policies in Buganda for the lack of Baganda support for the UNC. The UNC, which had originated in the kingdom, had now lost all its popular support there.

Throughout the autumn Obote continued to attack the government's handling of the boycott. In October, he even threatened strikes and nonpayment of taxes if the government went ahead with its plan to outlaw boycotts. Soon the UPU also reversed its position and strongly opposed the antiboycott bill. It was anxious to avoid the stigma of supporting oppressive action against African political protest.[15]

At the same time that Obote was attempting to attract Baganda support for the UNC, he also tried to build party strength in the west. In November, 1959, John Kakonge, a Munyoro living in Buganda, became a UNC official. In January, seven new officials were appointed to the UNC, two from the west, and one from Teso, another area of UNC weakness. In March, 1960, the UPU and the UNC merged. The UPU brought with it the western support that the UNC had lacked. The

[15] Obote's change of heart on the boycott can be followed in the *Uganda Argus* (Kampala), 1959; April 6, p. 6; April 11, p. 3; June 15, p. 1; July 24, p. 1; Aug. 14, p. 1; Sept. 5, p. 7; Sept. 19, p. 3.

new party, the Uganda People's Congress, still had no support in Buganda. Only one of its seventeen officers was a Muganda. Before the UPC could become a national party it had to attract Baganda support.

An important question is the degree of continuity between the UPC today and the UPU and UNC. Most of the UPU leaders remain powerful in the UPC, but they brought personal followings, not party organization, to the UPC. Many of those active in the UNC in the middle 1950's are in the UPC today, but they are not among the leaders of the party. Moreover, of thirty-two UNC officers elected early in 1959, only two are in the cabinet today. In the north, however, there is real organizational continuity between the UNC and the UPC.

Throughout 1960, Buganda refused to take part in the deliberations leading to independence itself. Given the intransigence of Baganda leaders, the political parties made a last-ditch attempt to secure support inside the kingdom. Various groups of Baganda intellectuals and politicians merged their tiny parties in an effort to attract support—perhaps even that of the Kabaka's government. These new parties, along with the DP and the UPC, issued statements in support of traditional rulers. But none was willing to go along with the Baganda boycott of elections or the threat of secession.

In the course of 1960, it became clear that the mass of Baganda strongly supported the negative position of the Kabaka's government. The new Baganda parties quietly disappeared. Both the UPC and the DP announced their intention of contesting the 1961 Legislative Council elections in Buganda. The Buganda government urged an election boycott and discouraged registration. Voluntary adherence to the boycott was substantial, although large-scale intimidation occurred. In the elections in March, 1961, less than 2 per cent of the eligible Baganda voted.

In spite of its victory in a majority of Uganda's constituencies, the 1961 election was a defeat for the DP. Even though it won twenty of the twenty-one Legislative Council seats allotted to Buganda, it could command the support of only a tiny fraction of the electorate in Buganda. Most Baganda Catholics would support no party which seemed to be against Buganda and the Kabaka. Moreover, outside Buganda the UPC won a majority of the seats. The Catholic base of the DP brought it sufficient seats in the country to give it a parliamentary majority. The party thus led Uganda to internal self-government, but its victory was a Pyrrhic one indeed. The election was also a defeat for the British. Their hopes of obtaining sufficient Baganda support for independence proved illusory. In a reversal of the normal version of the divide-and-rule strategy, the British were unable to divide Buganda in order to give Uganda independence. They had to take serious account of Baganda demands. Furthermore, the UPC saw that its quest for Baganda support could not succeed against the opposition of the Kabaka's government.

At the same time, the 1961 election boycott hardly provided a solution for Baganda aspirations. The Kabaka's government had shown that Buganda was united. But if the kingdom was to remain part of Uganda it needed some method of electing representatives at the national level. The leaders of Buganda were strongly opposed to political parties, fearing they would divide the kingdom. In June, 1961, a group known as *Kabaka Yekka* (Kabaka Only) appeared. The impetus for the formation of KY came from Masembe-Kabali, a former civil servant of the central government who was not deeply involved in Buganda's factional politics. KY denied that it was a political party; rather it claimed to be a movement which supported the Kabaka and aimed at unity in Buganda. The movement received significant popular support from its inception. Although the chiefs and the Kabaka's government had not created KY, they soon decided to back it.

KY was a practical avenue through which Buganda could enter national politics and yet preserve its own autonomy and unity. Once the chiefs and the Kabaka's government lined up behind the movement, it became difficult for any Muganda to oppose it. Most Catholic chiefs and political leaders worked for KY; some of those who did not, lost their positions. In February, 1962, the first direct elections to the Lukiiko were held. KY won sixty-five of the sixty-eight directly elected seats as the hierarchy of chiefs became the electoral machine for the movement. By presenting the election as a choice between the Kabaka and Benedicto Kiwanuka (Muganda president of the DP), KY took advantage of tribal solidarity. The numerous incidents of violence directed against DP supporters also affected the outcome.

Although KY could not have succeeded without them, the chiefs did not control the movement. It is also a mistake to assume any direct continuity between KY and the UNM. Both were neotraditionalist Baganda movements, not modern nationalist political parties. Many of the same intellectuals appeared in the two organizations. The important names were, however, different. Boycott leader Augustine Kamya was soon to leave KY over its alliance with the UPC. Masembe-Kabali and his colleagues had had no connection with the boycott. Moreover, the outlook of the movements differed. Whereas boycott leaders in-clined toward violence and die-hard traditionalism, KY leaders were more moderate and outward-looking.

In September, 1961, Obote startled the country by concluding a UPC alliance with KY. The two parties seemed to have nothing in com-mon except their desire to defeat the Catholic challenge of the DP. KY agreed to support new elections and independence and to ally itself with the UPC in the National Assembly. For its part, the UPC backed the Baganda demand for indirect elections by the Lukiiko to the Na-tional Assembly. It also agreed to support Buganda's demand for fed-eral status. Having reached an understanding with the UPC, the Kabaka's government was willing to participate in the London consti-tutional conference.

By its alliance with KY, the UPC risked hurting itself outside Buganda. In fact, as the April, 1962, elections showed, the alliance made little impact. The UPC maintained its proportion of the two-party vote (about 53 per cent) and actually gained one or two seats. After two Toro by-elections and the election of nine members by the National Assembly itself, the party balance stood at 43 UPC, 24 KY, and 24 DP.

Problems of KY and UPC

Two themes stand out in the achievement of Uganda's independ-ence. The first is the gradual building of a majority coalition by the UPC. Although the DP was not able to expand beyond its religious base except in limited areas, the UPC welded together a coalition of somewhat disparate elements. The second theme is the ability of the Kabaka's government to withstand all nationalist challenges. It ap-peared to secure a powerful place in independent Uganda. The final ex-tension of the UPC coalition to Buganda seemed at the same time to be an extension of Baganda power outside Buganda.

On October 9, 1962, the jockeying for power that had accompanied independence came temporarily to a halt. The UPC–KY coalition had successfully brought Uganda to independence, but the basic problems that had produced both parties continued to exist. One is reminded of American politics, where political parties are also coalitions, not mass movements, and immediate problems are solved while ultimate ones are avoided. But in the more fluid political situation of a developing country the ultimate problems tend soon to become immediate ones.

The UPC was still little more than a coalition of leaders; it had not succeeded in building a mass organizational base in most districts. Further, the relations between the various semi-independent leaders had not been resolved. Similarly, although KY met Buganda's immediate needs, it raised certain problems. It had virtually no party organization. Internal conflict was always possible between those allied with the chiefs and those opposed to them. There was the danger that KY members of the National Assembly would be seduced away from Buganda by the attractions of national power. One could not predict confidently that the Kabaka's government would be able to control KY; it was even questionable whether the movement would hold together.

The problems of KY and the UPC were not divorced from each other. For any development of the UPC in a more centralized direction was likely to affect its relations with KY. And even apart from organizational questions, could the "unprincipled" alliance endure between a "feudal" political party and one which sympathized with socialism and pan-Africanism?

If Uganda's political parties faced problems in the postindependence period, so too did the country as a whole. How would the ambiguities of federal and semifederal status be resolved in practice? What foreign policy objectives would Obote stress? And what implications would economic development and social stratification have on the politics of Uganda? Events in the years following independence would begin to provide answers to these questions.

Land and People

GEOGRAPHY

Most of the land area of Uganda forms a plateau about 4,000 feet above sea level. Consequently, despite its location in the equatorial zone, its temperatures are generally mild. Rainfall is substantial, averaging more than 30 inches a year in all areas except the northeast. The Republic of Rwanda and the Republic of the Congo (Léopoldville) border Uganda on the west and southwest. Sudan is to the north, Kenya to the east, and Tanganyika to the southeast. The country itself, including open water, is 94,000 square miles in area, considerably smaller than Kenya and less than half the size of Tanganyika. Uganda is 800 miles from Mombasa, Kenya, its ocean outlet. This distance from the nearest available seaport creates significant pressures for joining an East African federation.

The whole of Uganda is in the upper basin of the Nile River, which originates in Lake Victoria in the southeast. The mountain regions in the southwest and northeast are the most densely populated parts of Uganda, much of the two areas containing more than 300 persons to the square mile. In other parts of the country overpopulation is no problem. The area to the north of Lakes Albert and Kyoga is on the whole more sparsely populated and economically more backward than the south.

THE ECONOMY

Uganda's change from a tribal-susbsistence economy to a modern economy is recent and incomplete. Until the twentieth century, modernization was hindered by geographical isolation, tribal strife, and lack of transportation. Uganda exported little save ivory and slaves. But with the extension of the railroad to Lake Victoria in 1901 and the imposition of the *pax Britannica,* the farmers turned to cash crops. Cotton soon became the mainstay of the economy, later to be supplemented by coffee. Tea, sugar, sisal, tobacco, and groundnuts are also raised.

Like other underdeveloped countries, Uganda has a small per capita income—£22 per year including the value of subsistence products. Cash income varies from £19 per capita per year in Buganda to £5 in the western and northern regions. Conditions for food production are generally good, even for Africa, and hunger is not one of Uganda's problems (although the kinds of food consumed have caused widespread malnutrition).

Uganda is essentially an agricultural country. In an adult population of 3.7 million, only 225,000 Africans, 10,000 Asians, and 5,000 Europeans work for wages. The vital positions of cotton and coffee in Uganda's agricultural economy deserve emphasis. These crops alone account for more than 80 per cent of export earnings, which amount annually to just over £40 million. Uganda is thus highly vulnerable to price fluctuations on the world market. When high prices prevailed in the early 1950's, progress was rapid. The marketing boards, government agencies which control the buying and selling of major crops, accumulated surplus funds; the government expanded social services and made such long-term investments as the Owen Falls hydroelectric plant. By the mid-1950's, however, declining prices combined with political uncertainty to create economic difficulties. The volume of exports continued to climb but the income from these exports leveled off. This situation caused the government to fall back on marketing-board surpluses in order to continue necessary development projects. Since income for Uganda's economic development comes largely from export earnings, the stagnation of the economy was almost exclusively a consequence of the sharp and continuing deterioration in terms of trade.

Could industrialization take up the slack? A quasi-governmental organization, the Uganda Development Corporation, has promoted industry with some success. UDC has direct or indirect interests in cement, hotel, textile, and tea enterprises. Copper mining provides Uganda with some £3 million in export revenues. It is in no way detracting from the significance of these activities to note the marginal significance they have on the economy as a whole. "The development potential in Uganda," concluded a mission for the International Bank, "still lies largely in agriculture—there are no easy-to-develop highly profitable minerals and the scope for industrialization is still limited." [16]

This limited scope for Uganda's industrialization can be attributed to such factors as its remoteness, lack of skilled personnel and raw materials, and narrow and vulnerable agricultural economy. Industrialization is difficult to achieve without the presence of a dynamic local market, one which can absorb the locally produced goods on a wide enough basis for profitability. Expansion of the market to include East Africa as a whole goes far to overcome the problem of size, but this wider market is unevenly shared, with major benefits going to Kenya. At present, moreover, interterritorial trade is limited. Uganda's exports to Kenya and Tanganyika in 1961 amounted to £6,856,000; imports were £7,437,000. Such a level hardly indicates that Uganda can anticipate widespread industrialization on the basis of the present market. Therefore, it is possible to conclude not only that most Ugandans are engaged in peasant farming but that the success of agriculture largely determines the rate of government spending as well as the level of consumer purchasing power. Continued and increasing efficiency in agriculture, moreover, is the key to a rising standard of living.

SOCIAL STRUCTURE

Racial Groups and Tribal Divisions

In a total Uganda population of 6.5 million, there are only 11,000 Europeans and 72,000 Asians.[17] For the most part, Europeans are involved in missionary work, the civil service, and business. Although

[16] Mission of the International Bank for Reconstruction and Development, *The Economic Development of Uganda* (Baltimore: Johns Hopkins Press, 1962), pp. 35–36.

[17] Statistics in this section are from Uganda Protectorate, *1960 Statistical Ab-*

some Asians (Indians, Pakistanis, and Goans) have a place in the civil service, they are predominantly in business and trading. Many are also artisans and clerks, doctors and lawyers, and plantation managers.

Nearly all the Asians and Europeans live in the towns. The three largest towns contained more than one-third of the Asians in 1959, and that figure has gone up substantially since the 1959 trade boycott. Tensions exist in Uganda between Europeans and Africans, but these are minimized by the absence of a white settler element. The more important racial conflict is between Africans and Asians.

Uganda's Africans are divided between some thirty tribes, eighteen of which have more than 100,000 members. The million Baganda form the largest tribe, with a population twice that of any other. (See Table 2, and map, p. 338.) It is important to understand the differences in

Table 2. Twelve Largest Uganda Tribes

Tribe	Population	Percentage of African population
Baganda	1,044,878	16.2
Iteso	524,716	8.1
Banyankole	519,283	8.1
Basoga	501,921	7.8
Bakiga	459,616	7.1
Banyaruanda	378,656	5.9
Lango	363,807	5.6
Bagisu	329,257	5.1
Acholi	284,929	4.4
Lugbara	236,270	3.7
Batoro	208,300	3.2
Banyoro	188,374	2.9

tribal structure. A number of Bantu tribes live in southern Uganda. These achieved varying degrees of political centralization before the coming of the British. Only the tribes inhabiting the mountainous regions of Kigezi, Mt. Elgon, and the Ruwenzori lacked a hierarchical political structure. In the present districts of Busoga and Ankole there were several small kingdoms. No king had sovereignty over all Busoga or Ankole. One of the several kings in Ankole was recognized as more powerful than the others, but he did not exercise centralized control throughout the region.

The various kingdoms within Busoga and Ankole, however, were po-

stract (Entebbe: East African Statistical Department); and *Uganda General African Census, 1959* (Entebbe: East African Statistical Department, 1960).

litically centralized. In this they resembled the political structure of the kingdoms of Toro, Bunyoro, and Buganda. There was further variation in the degree of political centralization among the kingdoms. In the Busoga kingdoms the power of the corporate lineage (clan) was strong, and lesser chiefs tended to be hereditary. This limited the power of the paramount chief to control the lesser chiefs. In Buganda, on the other hand, the paramount chief had triumphed over the clans; he had the power to appoint and discharge lesser chiefs.

The kingdoms also varied in their degree of social differentiation. In virtually all of them the ruling family had come down generations ago from the north. Some peoples—Banyoro, Batoro, and particularly Banyankole, though not Baganda and Basoga—had an additional distinction between a hereditary aristocracy and a hereditary peasantry. The aristocracy was composed of cattle-herding intruders from the north. It formed a group separate from the royal clan. In order to grasp the political structure of these tribes, it is useful to adopt the general notion of king, lord, vassal, and serf, although to be sure the details of the relations were very different from those of feudal Europe.

Lakes Albert and Kyoga, and the river between them, divide Bantu Uganda from the Nilotic, nilo-Hamitic, and Sudanic tribes to the north. The only non-Bantu below this geographical line are a scattering of tribes around Mt. Elgon. The distinction among Sudanic, Nilotic, and nilo-Hamitic refers to physical appearance, language, and social organization. For our purposes language is the most important. The languages of one main grouping are unintelligible to members of another group. Thus Nilotic peoples of different tribes can come to understand each other fairly easily, but nilo-Hamitic languages are completely foreign to them.

Even more important than the distinctions among the northern ethnic groups is the contrast between north and south. None of the northern tribes had a hierarchical political structure. There was no recognized individual or group with sovereignty over the tribe as a whole. Authority within the tribes was based on clan segments. Minor segments continually split off to form new foci of political authority. Among the tribes, the degree of decentralization varied. The Alur and Acholi actually had chiefs; their tribal organization was similar to that of the multikingdom state of Busoga, but the power of the chiefs was far more circumscribed. Other tribes had leaders who arose for temporary purposes—particularly war—within a limited area. But the presence of executive authority in the uncentralized societies was only local and occasional. All these tribes lacked the institution of a paramount chief found among most of their Bantu neighbors. In general, social distinctions within these tribes were less developed. Among the northern tribes today, the Karamojong are distinctive in being virtually untouched by either literacy or a cash economy. Other northerners, however, particularly the Iteso, have more money and education than the Bantu tribes of the southwest.

Another important tribal distinction is between the kingdom of Buganda and all the other states. The Baganda are not only the largest tribe; they have also been the most successful in adapting themselves to British rule. This has been in part a cause and in part a consequence of the special treatment they received under the British.

The hierarchical Bantu tribes in Uganda lacked the all-encompassing religious objections to modernity of, for example, the Ashanti of Ghana. Tribal values permitted pragmatic adjustment to new situations more easily than in tribes where power was based more on mystique and less on force. In addition, the hierarchical structures adapted themselves relatively easily to initial British administrative demands. In Buganda the centralization of power under Kabaka Mutesa I in the nineteenth century had diminished the importance of religion even further. This centralization also limited the power of the clan heads, who were a conservative element in the social structure. There was no entrenched aristocracy to resist change. Tribal positions of power were more or less open to talent as the political hierarchy adjusted itself to Western innovations.

When the British arrived, Buganda had become the most powerful state in the area, partly through benefits of the internal tribal structure and partly as a result of the fortunes of war. Since the Baganda cooperated with the British, the advantages of their position increased. They gained sizable territorial accretions, administered some of the other tribes, and kept more control of their own affairs than did the other tribes. With the introduction of cotton and coffee, Buganda became by far the richest area. Moreover, the kingdom had a far greater proportion of the well-educated. These factors helped to make Buganda politically and socially dominant among the tribes.

Religion

Ugandans are divided not only by the great number of tribes in the country; religious affiliation cuts across the tribal distinction. The spread of Christianity throughout Uganda has been remarkable. It arrived in Buganda with the missionaries who followed explorer Stanley toward the end of the nineteenth century. By this time there was nothing in the indigenous religion essential to tribal solidarity. In fact, the decline of traditional religion had left a religious void. The Kabaka had no priestly functions which might have been violated by accepting Christianity.

The missionaries created a patron-client relationship with their followers similar to that running through Buganda society. The Kabaka played off the Catholic, Anglican, and Muslim factions against one another. Unlike traditional factions, however, the missionaries lacked the crucial characteristic of loyalty to the Kabaka. Kabaka Mwanga became fearful of the younger Christian chiefs, over whom he was losing control. In the 1880's, a series of religious persecutions and wars culminated in a successful Protestant–Catholic coalition. Once Christians were in control of the tribal hierarchy, adherence to Christianity became essential to success. Later, owing to British intervention, the Protestants defeated the Catholics. In coalition with a small Muslim minority, they became the rulers of Buganda.

The importance of religion in the politics of Buganda cannot be overemphasized. Freehold land that the 1900 Agreement gave to the chiefs was allocated on the basis of religion. Even today, religion largely determines the distribution of the twenty *ssaza* (county) chieftainships. Catholic and Protestant factions battle for political power. Today Catholics constitute 49 percent of the adult population of Buganda, Protestants 27.5 per cent, Muslims 7.3 per cent and pagans 16.2 per cent.[18]

Once Christianity had been accepted in Buganda, it spread rapidly throughout the rest of Uganda. Today in Uganda 34.5 per cent of the population is Catholic, 28.2 per cent Protestant, 5.6 per cent Muslim, and the remainder pagan. Thus, outside of Buganda there are virtually the same number of Protestants as Catholics, although many tribes are preponderantly of one religion or the other. Muslims are a significant minority in Busoga, West Nile, and parts of Buganda.

Education

Religion and tribe are two important determinants of position in the social structure, and education is a third.[19] Today about 50 per cent of

[18] Cf. D. A. Low, *Religion and Society in Buganda 1875–1900* (Kampala: East African Institute of Social Research, East African Studies No. 8, 1956); Apter, *op. cit.*, pp. 67–82; *Uganda Census of African Population, 1959* (Entebbe: Ministry of Economic Development, 1961).

[19] Cf. unpublished material by Sheldon Weeks of the East African Institute of

the primary-school-age population of over one million attends school. These are usually mission schools; yet most receive grants in aid from local and central government funds. Only a tiny fraction of the children in primary school continue with their education. Since 1960–1961, there has been a great effort to expand the places in senior secondary school. Whereas in 1950 there were less than 600 students in senior secondary school, by 1963 the number had jumped to 8,000. But this is still only 2 per cent of the school-age population. These figures become even more meaningful when one notes that only 278 Ugandans were enrolled in Makerere University College in 1961. Even when one adds the substantial numbers studying overseas, the scarcity of highly educated people becomes obvious. There is in addition a shortage of well-trained teachers. Teachers are not lacking in the primary schools, but many of the older teachers do not have adequate training. Of 248 secondary school teachers in 1961, only 77 were Africans. The bulk of the non-African teachers are missionaries or short-term expatriates supplied by various international programs.

The struggle for education is a difficult and poignant one, in which children, parents, and relatives all participate. Although school fees may be nominal by Western standards (twenty to sixty shillings in primary school), many children must leave school for lack of funds. What of those who leave school after completing primary education? In the past many found jobs as clerks, but now the educational qualifications for clerical jobs are rising. The bulk of Uganda's literate population remains on the farms, vaguely discontented with the rewards of education. Yet for the few who continue through senior secondary school the benefits of education are enormous. These students are the core of Uganda's elite. Often they are bound together by old school ties, particularly by associations at Makerere University College or at such highly esteemed secondary schools as King's College, Budo (Protestant) and St. Mary's, Kisubi (Catholic). Even if many retain tribal loyalties, the range of their experiences creates a certain distance between them and the mass of their fellows.

Urbanization

In the social structure of Uganda, urbanization is far less important than religion, tribe, and education. Urban living does have a real effect

---

Social Research; Mission of the International Bank, *op. cit.*, pp. 343–373; Ruth C. Sloan, "Uganda," in Helen Kitchen, ed., *The Educated African* (New York: Praeger, 1962), pp. 160–179.

on traditional patterns and values. The city provides a faster pace of life and opens up new vistas. Nevertheless, urbanization has had slight impact on the country as a whole. The African population of Kampala, including those living in the densely populated areas on the periphery, numbers only 60,000. Twenty-eight thousand Africans dwell in Jinja and Mbale, the only other towns with more than 10,000 inhabitants. The urban African population is therefore little above 1 per cent of the total African population, but the high rate of turnover among the migrants does increase the significance of this figure. While some migrants remain in the towns for many years, the majority work for only a few years at a time, returning periodically to their farms and families. The Baganda urban workers often live on farms near Kampala, but substantial numbers reside in urban Kampala districts such as Kisenyi and Katwe.

Although it is difficult to find an urban proletariat, one does exist. There is, however, no well-developed urban African middle class, such as one finds in West Africa. There are few African lawyers and other professional people. Moreover, although one should not underestimate the growing number of African traders in the towns, most live in the country and combine trading with farming. In the urban areas a few politicians, civil servants, and businessmen stand somewhat apart from the tribal structure and wield a political influence beyond their numbers. Some of the middle strata, divorced from tribal centers of power, find alternative sustenance in the upper echelons of the UPC. That they do not have complete control of the party is in large part explained by the persistence of tribal groupings and the small progress of urbanization.

Social Classes

Social classes have genuine significance in Uganda, but it is necessary to consider them in a tribal and racial context. Most Europeans are clearly in the upper class, although the composition of this community has changed somewhat with the arrival of white skilled laborers in recent years. Numbers of Asian businessmen as well as African ssaza chiefs, central and regional ministers, company executives, and higher civil servants are also in the upper class, but one should not picture an integrated upper class cutting across racial lines. The Asian community contains a few of the richest and most prominent Ugandans, a number of smaller businessmen, and some relatively poor artisans and marginal traders. The Africans have only recently begun to compete on equal terms with Asian entrepreneurs and tend, in most cases, to hold down the lowest agricultural and industrial positions.

Among the Africans one must not ignore traditional social divisions within the tribes. Even the uncentralized societies had distinctions between royal and commoner clans. Elsewhere social differentiation was more highly developed. With the introduction of education and of a cash economy, the elite began to have experiences which differentiated them further from the mass of tribal members.

The British, desiring to govern through local authorities, largely perpetuated the social distinctions that existed within the tribes. In Buganda there was the possibility of upward social mobility for the peasants, since they could purchase plots of freehold land. British officials did not introduce freehold land in the other Uganda kingdoms, whose upper classes therefore remained more closed. Data from Audrey Richards' *East African Chiefs* documents the existence of an administrative upper class in the Bantu and some of the northern tribes. This class is based on the original families of chiefs and of aristocrats. It perpetuates itself, however, not through the inheritance of chieftainships but through intermarriage, broad kinship ties, and the advantages in education obtained by the relatives of past chiefs. At the same time, British rule often bypassed traditional claims and brought new men to the fore. This was particularly true in the uncentralized societies, such as Lugbara.

Uganda's national elite, the product of educational, hereditary, and economic advantages, is in part simply the sum of tribal elites. But the contrast between the national elite and the mass of Uganda's population is perhaps more important than the tribal differences within the elite. The bulk of the populace is fragmented on tribal and, to a certain extent, religious lines, but socially differentiated in few other significant respects. Uganda is a peasant society, with virtually no urban middle class, only a tiny proletariat, and no important educated strata divorced from political life (in universities, journalism, and so forth). In this society the main social division—tribe apart—is between the relatively homogeneous elite and the mass of individual peasants. Such a social structure, with crucial divisions running horizontally rather than vertically through the society, implies political oligarchy. For the time being at least, tribe and religion form the most impressive bases for a pluralistic society; yet it is by no means clear that the political power of these divisions can survive the national integration of Uganda and the demands of economic development.

The Political Process

FORMAL STRUCTURE

It is not surprising that the British bequeathed Uganda the West-minster model of parliamentary democracy, not in its pure form but modified by features of federalism, a detailed listing of fundamental rights, and a rigid amending procedure. The constitution provided for a Governor-General who theoretically exercised powers on behalf of Her Majesty. He was replaced on October 9, 1963, by the Kabaka, who was elected by the members of the National Assembly. Real executive authority lies with the Prime Minister and the cabinet. Individually the ministers are responsible for the management of their departments; collectively they are responsible for the government's policy. The government remains in office for the duration of parliament, provided that it maintains the confidence of a majority of the members of the National Assembly.

The National Assembly is composed of 82 elected members; only the 21 from Buganda may be elected on an indirect basis. There are in addition up to nine members elected by parliament itself. Parliament has the "power to make laws for the peace, order and good government of Uganda (other than the Federal States) with respect to any matter." In the event of conflicts over an interpretation of the constitution, the High Court of Uganda, and finally Her Majesty in Council, have jurisdiction.

The Division of Powers

The most significant departure from the Westminster model is the way in which elements of federalism were incorporated into the constitution of Uganda. Prior to independence there were a series of concessions to particularist pressures. With the coming of independence the pendulum swung toward central hegemony. The key question was no longer which states were to be regarded as federal but the meaning of federal status itself. How much would the concession of federal status actually imply in practice? Would it significantly alter the distribution of power between the center and the regions?

As the report on the Uganda Independence Conference (1962) observes, the relation of the center to the constituent parts has been "Uganda's most difficult constitutional problem." The intention to provide for central leadership seems clear enough. The basic law seeks to assure the continuance of a strong and effective center. The constitution gives the central legislature exclusive responsibility for the following: external affairs; extradition; immigration and emigration; citizenship; defense; internal security; penal and criminal procedure codes; courts (other than those dealing with Buganda clan cases); the Uganda public service; finance (including currency, loans, banking, foreign exchange, stock and commodity exchanges, and insurance); taxation (concurrently with the Buganda Lukiiko); medical, health, and veterinary services (other than those devolved upon regional units); commerce; aviation; and professional qualifications. It specifically provides that, in the event of conflict between regional and central law, "the law made by Parliament shall prevail and the law of the Federal State shall to the extent of the inconsistency be void." [20]

Substantial local autonomy might still be consistent with central supremacy. In examining the actual degree of power exercised by the federal states, one must distinguish between the western kingdoms and Busoga on one hand and Buganda on the other. Examination of the former makes it difficult to sustain the thesis that they have significant federal powers. In a formal sense they all have equal status with Buganda; yet the constitution does not grant them equivalent governmental powers or functions. Since the powers of these units are so circumscribed, anticipation that their federal status would frustrate the central government hardly seems warranted.

CONSTITUTIONAL STATUS OF THE WESTERN KINGDOMS AND BUSOGA

Throughout the long series of conferences and commissions on the constitution, few participants considered the kingdoms and Busoga prepared to undertake administrative responsibilities as heavy as those transferred to Buganda. The kingdoms and Busoga had limited available revenue, staff, and equipment. Consequently, the Munster commission recommended semifederal status for them. In practice, moreover, the subsequent London conference of 1961 interpreted semifederal status in such a restricted sense that the kingdoms were assigned only those services set aside for the local administrations generally. It clearly stated that central authorities would exercise "ultimate responsibility" for the handling of services.

Even though the 1961 conference upgraded the status of Toro, Ankole, Bunyoro, and Busoga, there seemed little initial impact on

[20] *Uganda (Independence) Order in Council, 1962,* L.N. 251 of 1962, pp. 836–837. Prior to the 1962 London conference, the *Uganda Argus* reported that the Lukiiko sought to have its laws prevail where a matter primarily affecting Buganda was involved. July 20, 1962, p. 3.

their governmental powers or functions. The Hicks/Tress report on fiscal relations had already sounded a note of warning when it concluded: "irrespective of any questions of status, the authorities other than Buganda do not cover a large enough area or possess the administrative range or skill . . . to work a complicated tax structure." The 1962 Uganda Independence Conference provided elaborate guarantees for the rulers and traditional institutions, but was vague as to the powers and functions that accompanied federal status. These were to be determined "by agreement" at a later date. In those areas where it was specific—the local authorities grant structure (the statutory contributions to local authorities), deficiency grants, and grants to meet the cost of salary increments—the federal states, unlike Buganda, were treated in the same way as the districts.

Shortly after independence, authorities in the kingdoms and Busoga were shocked to learn of the central government's interpretation of federal status. The crisis arose in October, 1962, when the government published the original Western Kingdoms and Busoga bill. Controversy became acute because these states felt the bill denied them powers and duties commensurate with a federal position. The status secured at London now seemed hollow.

In fact, the first Western Kingdoms and Busoga bill was modeled closely upon the Local Administrations Ordinance of 1962, which was in the tradition of unitary administration. Whole sections are identical except for the substitution of such words as "government" for "administration," "assembly" for "council," and "speaker" for "chairman." Key parts in both give the Minister of Regional Administrations extensive powers to supervise services, regulate finances, and compel the performance of functions in a proper manner. The lists of permissive functions (control of soil erosion, grazing, vermin, tribal hunting, parks, building in periurban areas, disposal of refuse, trading centers, and so forth) and sources of revenue (graduated tax, rates, rents, market dues, fees and fines, royalties, donations, and so forth) are the same.[21]

When the government presented the Kingdoms bill to parliament, Opposition members attacked it bitterly. Their major criticism was that the bill did not reflect the spirit of federalism. A. K. Balinda (DP, Toro Central), objecting to the concentration of executive powers implicit in the bill, warned at a press conference on November 13, 1962, that "the

[21] See *Uganda Protectorate, Local Administrations Ordinance, 1962* (Entebbe: Government Printer, 1962); and *Special Supplement to the Uganda Gazette*, LV, No. 27 (Oct. 26, 1962).

Government was going to recognise only Buganda as a federal state until the time when it felt strong enough to do the same thing with Buganda."

The rulers of the western kingdoms also acted to head off the proposed legislation. In November, at a meeting with the Prime Minister and Minister of Regional Administrations, C. J. Obwangor, they asked that their assemblies be given an opportunity to examine the bill before it was introduced in parliament. Further talks, between the four chief ministers of Ankole, Bunyoro, Busoga, and Toro and the Minister of Regional Administrations, ended dramatically in December, when the chief ministers announced that Obwangor had "flatly rejected" their proposed amendments to the bill. In particular, the two parties to the dispute clashed over the power of the Minister of Regional Administrations to divest regional authorities of their powers and to approve bills prior to their submission to the regional legislatures. "As it stands," observed the chief ministers, "the Bill does not give us federal status at all. In fact it deprives us of existing powers rather than granting us new ones." [22]

Although the government might have used its parliamentary majority to push the bill through the National Assembly, it chose not to force the issue immediately. With dissatisfaction even in the UPC stronghold of Busoga, such a policy might well have impaired effective administration in the areas involved. Consequently, the government withdrew the bill from parliament's agenda.

In order to gain support for a revised Western Kingdoms and Busoga bill, the central government began a discussion with representatives of the regions involved. Discussions between the Minister of Regional Administrations and the katikkiros produced little compromise. Then, in February, 1963, Prime Minister Obote interceded and startled the country by quickly arriving at what he described as "a complete and amicable settlement."

Even though the original bill was withdrawn, the redrafted version did not depart significantly in spirit or in substance from the original text. Numerous clauses were inserted into the new bill requiring the minister to consult with the regional government involved before exercising his powers. Otherwise the changes mainly included clarifications and modifications. The kingdoms and Busoga, nevertheless, satisfied with their enhanced prestige under the revised bill, placed no further impediments to its passage. After three days of debate the National As-

[22] *Reporter* (Nairobi), Dec. 22, 1962, p. 11.

sembly unanimously endorsed the bill. But not all the members viewed the status of the regions as a truly federal one, since it had now become clear that they lacked the autonomous functions and powers normally associated with federalism. Shortly after the passage of the bill this fact was recognized explicitly for the first time. In April, 1963, UPC Secretary-General John Kakonge stated that Uganda's federalism extended only to Buganda's relation to the rest of the country.

BUGANDA'S CONSTITUTIONAL STATUS

After Buganda's attempted secession, a long series of negotiations took place to determine its powers under the new federal arrangement. Agreements were reached in two areas: traditional rights and institutions, and substantive administrative powers. Buganda secured exclusive authority over traditional institutions: the Kabakaship; the traditional powers, obligations, and duties of the Kabaka and his ministers; the Lukiiko; Buganda holidays and festivals; and traditional and customary matters relating to Buganda alone—all became areas in which only the Lukiiko could legislate. To safeguard the traditional rights and institutions of Buganda, the constitution of Uganda provides for a rigid amending procedure at both the central and regional levels. Two-thirds of all the members of the National Assembly (to which the Lukiiko itself elects the Buganda members) must vote favorably on such amendments. In addition two-thirds of all the members of the Lukiiko must approve the change. Calhoun's principle of "concurrent majorities" has indeed become a reality!

In the second area, Buganda secured many of the substantive powers it sought. The 1961 London conference made important concessions in such fields as health, agricultural and veterinary services, education, African trade development, forests, community development, courts, prisons, police, and finance. But it ignored Buganda's claims to a separate army.

Once the 1961 conference determined the broad lines of policy, the central and Buganda governments began work on the details of the transfer. The constitution is sufficiently ambiguous on the actual powers given Buganda to leave wide scope for negotiation. Certain powers over taxation as well as over agriculture, veterinary services, and education were given to Buganda in due course. The decision on education within Buganda (exclusive of Kampala) is significant. On January 4, 1963, A. K. Mayanja, Minister of Education in the Kabaka's government, announced the transfer of responsibility for secondary schools (except Makerere College School), primary teachers training colleges, housecraft centers and rural trade schools to authorities in Buganda. The central government agreed to provide annual grants of £281,000.

In the vital area of finance the concessions granted by the central government to finance Buganda's governmental services were considerable. The 1962 London conference concluded that Buganda should receive revenues from stamp duties on transfers of *mailo* land, motorcycle licenses, and entertainment taxes. These taxes would be in addition to Buganda's independent sources of revenue (graduated tax, land tax, market dues, education fees, and others) and to the central government's 50 per cent annual contribution toward the cost of running Buganda's services. Buganda agreed, largely for prestige reasons, to be excluded from deficiency or "catching up" grants and from the local authorities grant structure, although it remained eligible for capital grants and loans.

In subsequent discussions between the central government and Buganda, two major disputes arose over financial relations between the governments. First, was the Kabaka's government entitled to personal taxes collected from non-Ugandans? In January, 1964, Nelson Sebugwawo noted in his budget speech to the Lukiiko that the Uganda government had reversed its previous position on these taxes and now regarded them as a new source of revenue for the Kabaka's government. If such a tax were interpreted as a new source of revenue, the central government would be entitled to deduct such revenues (estimated at £240,000) from statutory contributions made to Buganda. The Kabaka's government was still contesting the central government's decision, Sebugwawo said, on the ground that "it is not only a breach of faith but also fundamentally an agreement that has already been concluded." [23]

A second cause of dispute between central authorities and Buganda occurred over the interpretation of the ninth schedule of the Uganda constitution. The central government refused to accept the interpretation Baganda authorities placed upon financial relations between the governments and, in August, 1963, submitted the dispute to the High Court. In the end, the central government's position prevailed. The Uganda High Court, in May, 1964, upheld both the Uganda government's interpretation of its obligations under the ninth schedule and its

[23] *Uganda Argus* (Kampala), Jan. 8, 1964, p. 3.

method of computing grants to the Buganda government. Financial obligations were stabilized under the decision until 1966, when the amount of assistance due Buganda is to be calculated again.

One of the key subjects under dispute between the governments was the disposition of police powers. Buganda's demand, before independence, that the Kabaka's police be given sole responsibility for security matters had been rejected. The constitution gives central authorities great responsibility for the organization and administration of police. Thus the inspector-general of police, on advice of the Prime Minister or appropriate ministers, has the authority "to give directions with respect to the use and operational control of any police force in Uganda not under his command." This ultimate central control raises the crucial question of the degree of immediate regional supervision. Once police powers were transferred, would the inspector-general of police in fact be in a position to direct regional police officials? Certainly, after the transfer, central control would have to be exercised in a more delicate manner than in the past. Would the situation go beyond this and cause central leadership to become dependent on regional good will? Ex-Prime Minister Kiwanuka was asserting central leadership when he rejected claims of the Buganda government to be consulted prior to declaring any part of the kingdom a disturbed area. Would this be as easy to do once Buganda's police force was increased to full strength under its own officers?

Given these dangers, Prime Minister Obote was understandably reluctant to yield to Buganda pressures to transfer existing central authority over the police. Just prior to independence he had successfully resisted pressure from the Kabaka's ministers to effect a rapid transfer. Later, the acting katikkiro, L. N. Basudde, pressed him for the transfer of police posts in the kingdom as well as for grants to meet the costs of maintaining these posts. Subsequently, Basudde publicly reminded the Prime Minister that the latter had promised in London to transfer the police posts. Obote pointedly rejected any obligation of a constitutional nature to make such transfers. The following year, the Uganda High Court upheld Obote's interpretation. The court declared in April, 1964, that there was nothing in the Uganda constitution which required the central government to transfer any police stations or posts to the Kabaka's police force.

Thus a strong central government seemed likely to resolve ambiguities or silences in the constitution in its own favor. In addition the central government had at its disposal certain heretofore unrecognized reservoirs of authority. Its supremacy in juridical matters was dramatically illustrated early in 1963. The Buganda and Uganda governments clashed over the right of Uganda's acting Director of Public Prosecutions (D.P.P.) to discontinue criminal proceedings against Eriabu Lwebuga, leader of the Common Man faction in KY. Lwebuga had been standing trial in the Buganda Principal Court for issuing seditious publications aimed at inciting violence and for seeking to overthrow the Buganda government. Article 82 (2) (c) of the Uganda constitution specifically empowers the D.P.P. (who is to be insulated from political control) with the right "to discontinue at any stage before judgment is delivered any criminal proceedings instituted or undertaken by himself or any other person or authority." The acting D.P.P.'s move caused a storm of protest in Buganda. One minister in the Kabaka's government complained of "unnecessary interference" and called the intervention "unconstitutional and irresponsible." The Kabaka's government presented a bill to the Lukiiko creating for Buganda a D.P.P. who would have control over criminal cases brought before courts in the kingdom. The Lukiiko approved the bill overwhelmingly and the Kabaka immediately gave his royal consent.

The central government acted swiftly to head off any threat to its leading position in juridical matters. The Minister of Justice, Grace Ibingira, declared in parliament that the Lukiiko's law establishing a D.P.P. for Buganda could not alter the constitutional power of Uganda's D.P.P. He also warned that anyone interfering with Uganda's acting D.P.P. by attempting to execute a warrant of arrest on him would be liable to criminal proceedings. The legal proceedings came to an end when Mr. Justice Sheridan of the Uganda High Court released Lwebuga from custody and upheld the original order of Uganda's acting D.P.P. as valid. These events helped to establish the central government's predominance in juridical matters generally and in civil rights cases in particular. The possiblity, however, of future challenges to its superiority cannot be ruled out.

Central hegemony in economic affairs was anticipated before independence, when the constitutional conferences worked out the meaning of Buganda's federal relationship. The constitution gives Buganda such powers in the field of taxation "as may be agreed between the Kabaka's government and the Government of Uganda," and central supremacy is even clearer vis-à-vis the other constituent units. The center controls the aggregate sums to be dispersed, audits accounts, and supervises estimates. Only Buganda seems fiscally strong enough to stand alone, yet even there signs of budgetary strain are evident. (For example, sources in Buganda estimated that the kingdom would have a 1964 budgetary deficit of £117,082, after raising £2,540,454 from local resources and £1,545,733 from a central government block grant and other contributions.) [24] If Buganda cannot obtain sufficient increased funds from internal sources, people in the kingdom may look more and more to the center for welfare aid. In the country at large the center seems likely to play an increasingly important role in economic affairs.[25] Its constitutional position in this field is secure and it makes a vital contribution to development and stability. But will those who have fought for federal status accept a large degree of economic centralization, with all its implications? One thing seems certain: if political decentralization stands in the way of the public welfare, it is likely to give rise to tension.

In view of the traditional rights and institutions guaranteed, the services transferred, and the sources of taxation allocated to Buganda, there seems little question that the kingdom gained power and stature through its years of constitutional deliberations. The central government has not surrendered its crucial position with respect to the security, stability, and well-being of Uganda, but it has decentralized important functions and powers in the case of Buganda. Yet even though the relationship is still evolving, Buganda's autonomy should not be exaggerated. Federalism in Uganda was achieved by bargaining; the greater the power of the constituent unit, the greater the concessions granted. The significance of federalism in Uganda's future will similarly depend less on constitutional mechanics than on the persistence of power and unity in Buganda. The other kingdoms and Busoga, with less power, have already found the promise of federalism largely unfulfilled.

The division of powers between the central and regional governments suggests the conclusion that Uganda has a unique form of center-state relations. In essence it presents a three-tier structure. A different range of powers is assigned to Buganda, to the kingdoms and Busoga,

[24] *Uganda Argus* (Kampala), Jan. 8, 1964, p. 3, and Jan. 16, 1964, p. 3.

[25] Outside Buganda road-building and educational projects can rarely be undertaken without central support. The importance of grants is indicated by the estimated 1961/62 budget of the Bugisu District Administration. Bugisu anticipated receiving £118,951 in government grants out of a total budget of £347,286. The grants included £10,717 for road maintenance, £21,145 for general administration, £2,196 for allowances to appointment board members, and £84,884 for education.

and to the remaining districts. It is very much like a classification of the Austro-Hungarian Empire made by Professor Schücking at the turn of the century. In Uganda's case, Buganda is the *privileged* nation and the kingdoms and Busoga the *mediatized* nations, each having "a sufficiently extended local autonomy." [26] The *privileged* nation gained significantly from the long debates on the constitution. Its traditional institutions are protected, its influence at the federal level is enhanced, and its powers and functions are greatly increased. The *mediatized* nations, while securing considerably fewer concessions than Buganda in the areas of new responsibilities, did gain important guarantees for their traditional institutions. Clearly the constitution did much to accommodate the demands of local nationalists. The vital questions remaining are whether political decentralization can be used to fulfill the aspirations of the country at large, or whether the present arrangements will survive at all.

ELECTIONS: THE SOCIAL BASIS OF UGANDA POLITICS

The influence of Christianity on politics in Uganda is unique in Africa.[27] Although non-Christians still form a large minority of the population, the majority is almost evenly divided between Protestants and Catholics. The vast majority of the educated and influential are Christian.

The political dominance of Protestants, particularly in Buganda, and the political activities of the Catholic missions account for this influence. In modern Buganda religious affiliation quickly took on political importance in the traditional struggle between the factions of chiefs for political power. Protestant hegemony has been firmly established since 1900, although there are twice as many Catholics as Protestants in the kingdom. Thus a series of challenges to the ruling group has come from the Catholics. Indeed, the first president of the DP was a long-time leader of the Catholic faction in Buganda.

In general throughout Uganda, Protestants had the best administrative posts, and in consequence a reservoir of discontent existed among the Catholics. Furthermore, mission schools fed Catholic–Protestant rivalry. Graduates of Protestant schools utilized their school affiliations to political advantage. Their rivalry with former Catholic students was

[26] Oscar Jaszi, *The Dissolution of the Habsburg Monarchy* (Chicago: University of Chicago Press, 1961), p. 109.

[27] We are indebted for much of the material on religion and politics to the unpublished paper of the Rev. F. B. Welbourn, "Catholics and Protestants in Uganda Society."

in part a continuation of school rivalries. Protestant political dominance, as well as religious allegiances produced by the mission schools,
opened the field for a Catholic political party. Moreover, unlike the
Protestant missions, the Catholic Church took an active interest in politics. Catholic missions provided an organizational center for the party
and continue to some extent to do so today.

Protestants dominated the early days of nationalist unrest in
Uganda. In 1952, 70 per cent of the members of the UNC central committee came from the Protestant secondary school at Budo. Of the
branch chairmen 74 per cent were Protestants.[28] In 1956, the DP was
formed in Buganda under Catholic dominance. By 1958, the leadership
of the party had passed from an old-time Muganda politician to Benedicto Kiwanuka, a Catholic lawyer less involved in factional struggles
among the chiefs. Under his leadership the DP spread beyond Buganda.
Consequently, by 1958, the political split along religious lines was created more by the Catholicism of the DP than by the Protestantism of
the other parties.

Evidence of this is provided by the numbers of teachers who stood
as candidates for the major parties in the two general elections. These
teachers came overwhelmingly from mission schools. Whereas 47 per
cent of the DP candidates in 1961 and 1962 were teachers, 33 per cent
of the UPC candidates came from this profession.[29] This suggests that
the DP relied more on the Catholic mission schools than the UPC did
on the Protestant ones.

One can also examine the voting behavior of the populace. Both parties in the 1961 election had a religious base. The greater the percentage of Protestants in a district, the higher the vote for the UPC. The
greater the percentage of Catholics, the higher the vote for the DP. The
relation between the DP and Catholicism, however, was considerably
closer than that between the UPC and Protestantism. Thus the UPC
was considerably more successful in expanding beyond its religious
base.[30]

[28] Apter, *op. cit.,* pp. 317, 321.
[29] *The Uganda Gazette,* LIV (March 6, 1961), 185–304; LV (April 9, 1962),
325–442.
[30] Statistical evidence for these assertions was obtained by computing correlation coefficients between religious affiliation and the party vote. Omitting Karamoja, where there are virtually no Christians, the DP vote correlated .74 with
the percentage of Catholics, the UPC vote .50 with the percentage of Protestants.
In 1962, the correlations were .40 and .14 respectively.
Correlation cofficients vary between +1.00 and −1.00. A high positive correlation means in the present case that the larger the population of Catholics, the

Religion played a less significant role in the 1962 election. In that year the DP lost some Catholic backing and gained support elsewhere. Still it retained a significant Catholic base. The UPC's electoral base, on the other hand, was no longer distinctively Protestant at all.

The influence of religion on Uganda politics has varied with time and place. Among the Kiga, for example, religion is almost the sole issue of political importance. Before the arrival of the British, the Kiga had very little social organization; the British destroyed what little cohesion there was. In this situation feuds between religious factions have replaced the traditional clan and village feuds, and the political activity of these factions at election time is frequently marked by violence. Voters in Kigezi told a politician in 1961 that they were for the Protestant party, although they did not know its name. Stories like this are also reported from other areas. Election returns substantiate the importance of religion in Kiga politics. The two constituencies in Kigezi with the largest number of Catholics have consistently given a higher percentage of their votes to the DP in the two district council elections and the two national elections than have any of the other constituencies in the district.

In some districts religious factionalism is simply the continuation of traditional intratribal conflict under a new label. Elsewhere religious cleavages cut across traditional ones. Often tribalism is important in determining the vote independently of religious allegiances. It is necessary to distinguish between two types of tribalism. In one, the tribe acts as a unit in politics and separatist overtones exist. Buganda is the classic case of this phenomenon. But tribalism can also be a perpetuation of traditional intratribal differences in modern politics. Kigezi district provides an example of this kind of tribalism. The Banyaruanda,

---

larger the percentage of the vote given to DP. A high negative correlation would mean that the larger the population of Catholics, the smaller the percentage of the vote given to the DP. A low correlation would mean that there is no relation between Catholicism and the DP vote.

Buganda is excluded from the present correlations because there were no direct elections there to the National Assembly in 1962. To include Karamoja would also be misleading. It gives correlations of .63 for the DP and −.02 for the UPC in 1961. This understates the relation between Protestantism and the UPC over the country as a whole. The great drop in this relation is explained by the very high UPC vote in Karamoja, which has virtually no Protestants.

For the electoral and religious figures, cf. *Uganda Argus* (Kampala), March 27, 1961; April 27, 1962; April 28, 1962; and Ministry of Economic Development, *Uganda Census of African Population, 1959* (Entebbe: 1961). The religious figures are for those over sixteen years of age. The figures are on a 5 per cent sample of the population.

who inhabit the southern tip of Kigezi, are split between a traditional aristocracy and a traditional peasantry. The tribe began by supporting the DP by a greater majority than its numbers of Catholics would have led one to expect. Under the impact of internal tribal politics, however, the aristocracy largely moved over to the UPC. The shift by the aristocracy gave the UPC a strong majority among the Banyaruanda. In Ankole, on the other hand, although the peasants are politically split along religious lines, the Protestant aristocracy actually supports the DP. In Busoga, the UPC's strongest support is in Bugabula, the most powerful traditional Busoga kingdom—another example of traditional internal tribal politics influencing modern politics.

Perhaps the best way to examine the effects of religion and tribe on Uganda politics is to analyze the relation between the 1961 and 1962 national elections. As Figure 1 shows, there were two types of districts in Uganda. In the majority of districts (those containing the large majority of constituencies), the relation between the 1961 and 1962 elections was extremely close. In the constituencies in these districts the UPC gained slightly from 1961 to 1962, except where it already had a large majority. The influence of religion tended to be strong in these districts in both years.

But the relation between religion and the vote was far lower in 1962 than it had been in 1961, because six districts deviated from the normal pattern. In two of these, West Nile and Madi, the UPC gained strongly. Here the Catholic leader of the West Nile and Madi Cooperative Union brought money and a prominent position to the UPC. In addition the UPC was able to exploit Alur support for a hereditary chief.[31] These factors more than nullified the Catholic preponderance in West Nile and Madi.

In the other four deviant districts the UPC lost votes. Two of these, Bukedi and Bugisu, have long traditions of active, complicated, and violent local politics. Tribal and clan voting are important factors, and elections produce many independent candidates. The UPC lost most seriously in the kingdoms of Toro and Bunyoro. In Bunyoro the UPC alliance with Buganda greatly helped the DP. The vital issue there is the Banyoro claim for the return of its "lost counties" from Buganda. Even the UPC's support of a referendum in the lost counties did not help it in Bunyoro. In Toro the DP gained Batoro votes by supporting the kingdom's claim for federal status more strongly than did the UPC. At the same time it won support from the minority Baamba and

[31] Southall, *op. cit.*, p. 20.

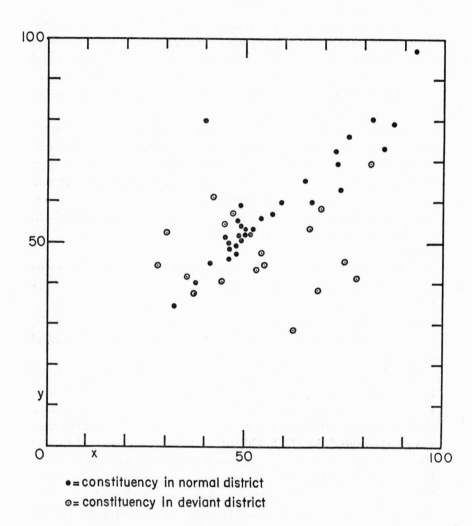

•= constituency in normal district
◉= constituency in deviant district

Fig. 2. UPC vote as percentage of two-party vote: $x = 1961$, $y = 1962$

Bakonjo peoples by exploiting their dissatisfaction with the Toro administration. That the DP's main appeal in Toro was not religious is suggested by the fact that three of its four candidates were Protestants.

Religious and traditional cleavages largely explain the voting behavior of Uganda's population. The selection of candidates also conforms to dominant ethnic and religious patterns. Major party candidates for the National Assembly virtually always come from the main tribe in the constituency. UPC candidates are generally Protestant and DP candidates Catholic, although several prominent Catholics have stood for the UPC. Considerations of clan, tribe, and religion control the selections of district council nominees as well.

Economic and social factors also influence the selection of candidates. Of the 276 candidates who stood for the National Assembly in 1961 and 1962, 37 per cent were teachers. Only nine of the candidates were lawyers, but this is a significant percentage of the legal profession in Uganda. In elections to the district council there are many fewer teacher-candidates; farmers and traders predominate. In local politics one thus finds candidates closer in their orientation to the mass of the people.

Ethnic and religious politics, in sum, dominate Uganda's voting patterns. In 1961, national political divisions were more important than tribal politics, but the national division was one of religion, not political conviction. In 1962, tribalism had increased significance at the polls, which showed that the election was more concerned with local political demands than the previous one had been.

DP strength is concentrated in Catholic strongholds and in tribal areas where the party is able to exploit feelings of separatism and deprivation. It got a majority of the vote in the west in the general election of 1962, and in the country as a whole fell only a few percentage points behind the UPC. Although the latter won several district council elections in 1962, there was no evidence of a widespread popular swing to the UPC. These elections were generally close and conformed to the results of the 1962 general elections. With its defeat in the election to the Ankole *Eishengyero* in June, 1963, however, the DP lost control of its only remaining district council. In addition, although one UPC member of parliament has become an independent, large numbers of DP and KY members have joined the UPC. These defections can only have a demoralizing effect on KY and DP supporters. In any case the future of the opposition will be influenced as much by the actions of political leaders as by the attitudes of the people.

POLITICAL DYNAMICS

Pressure Groups

Although organized pressure groups operate on the fringes of Uganda politics and lack some of the sophistication of their Western counterparts, they still play an important role. Little is known about the operation of pressure groups at the local level. In the National Assembly interest groups are not continuously active as they are in the United States. Their objects are usually either specific and limited or vague in the extreme. Various tribal associations press demands, which vary from a request for governmental action to stop Karamojong cattle-raiding in Teso to a call for the creation of an independent state of Rwenzururu on the Congo border. There are marketing and traders' associations, employers' organizations, trade unions, and cooperatives. In addition to ordinary interest groups, there exists in Uganda pressure on policy from quasi-governmental bodies such as marketing boards and the Uganda Development Corporation, and from Kenya and Tanganyika on issues related to the Commonwealth and East African Common Services Organization.

TRADE UNIONS AND COOPERATIVES

Perhaps the most important interest groups in Uganda are the cooperatives and the trade unions.[32] Cotton- and coffee-marketing cooperatives are politically significant in many areas. In Bugisu factional conflict in the coffee cooperatives greatly influences political preferences. UPC minister Kirya was manager of the Bugisu Cooperative Union. The West Nile and Madi Cooperative Union has played an important role in recent elections there. Its manager, Felix Onama, is now another UPC minister. Nevertheless, there is no integral relation between the cooperative movement and the UPC, such as one finds in Tanganyika between Tanu and the cooperatives.

Late in 1963, Buganda coffee-growers demonstrated the political significance of Uganda's farmers. A government announcement that the price of coffee would be fixed at forty cents a pound for the season then opening precipitated a boycott of coffee sales in Buganda. DP President Kiwanuka, in marked contrast to his parliamentary party, sought to exploit the boycott to embarrass the government. Kiwanuka

[32] Valuable information on Uganda's labor movement is contained in an unpublished manuscript by Roger Scott, "Labor Relations in Uganda." For a discussion of the Buganda coffee boycott, see Cherry Gertzel, "Report from Kampala," *Africa Report,* IX (October, 1964), 4.

dominated a series of large public meetings in Kampala, but soon after the police broke up one gathering and arrested Kiwanuka for holding a meeting without a permit (the charge was later dropped), the coffee boycott ended. A few months later Obote announced that increased coffee quotas for Uganda agreed upon at the London Coffee Conference permitted him to raise the price given coffee-growers. While it would be difficult to attribute the rise in coffee prices to the boycott, it had suggested the explosive potential in the rural areas.

Whereas the cooperatives are the most important rural economic interest group, trade unions have become increasingly important in urban areas. As late as 1958, union membership was insignificant. Since then, there has been a tremendous growth in trade union activity and membership. The following Labor Department figures, although including in 1962 many unionists who existed only on paper, still show the growth in membership: 2,529 in 1956, 7,193 in 1958, 22,000 in 1959, 43,000 in 1961, 90,000 in 1962.

Most of Uganda's trade unions are affiliated with the Trade Union Congress, itself a member of the International Confederation of Free Trade Unions. The ICFTU gives substantial financial and personnel aid to the TUC. Internally the labor movement is divided. The split is primarily on tribal lines, between Kenyan and Baganda leaders. Kenyans, who are only .07 per cent of the population of Uganda, make up 11.4 per cent of the work force in private industry. Kenyans are particularly active in the unions because, remaining in the work force longer than people from other areas, they are more concerned with wages and working conditions. Whereas Kenyan leaders press for immediate benefits for the workers, the Baganda, who dominate the white-collar unions, are more restrained.

Most of the Kenyan leaders belong to the UPC. TUC president Luande, born on the Kenya border, represents the UPC in the National Assembly. His brand of radicalism could not be farther from the radicalism of the UPC left wing in at least one respect: the latter favors government control of the labor movement. The Baganda leaders of the TUC are split between KY and the DP. In the 1962 parliamentary elections, the TUC president at the time, Pulle, ran on a DP ticket against Luande. This action symbolized the absence of a united labor front in politics.

Not only is the labor movement divided politically, but the political affiliations of the leaders have little impact on the party preferences of the rank and file. For these reasons the labor movement has shied away from politics. Politically the leadership is united primarily in opposing a government-controlled labor movement. Unions also agitate for a higher minimum wage and press for a faster pace of Africanization. More important than their specific proposals is their general position as independent centers of power. Thus unions in Uganda are politically important more because of the consequences of their independence than because of their specific political demands.

THE ARMY

Another group making political and economic demands on the leadership is the military. This became apparent during the "pay-packet" mutinies of January, 1964. The crisis, which engulfed all of East Africa, started with a *coup d'état* on Zanzibar and a mutiny by the First Battalion, Tanganyika Rifles, in Dar es Salaam. On January 23, 1964, soldiers of the First Battalion of the Uganda Rifles refused to obey orders and demanded Africanization of posts and increases in pay. When Minister of Internal Affairs Felix Onama arrived at the barracks to hear their demands, he was seized and kept in the guardroom at the Jinja Army Barracks. After Onama's release, the Prime Minister's Office promised that new rates of pay would soon be introduced. That night, seven aircraft carrying 450 British troops landed at Entebbe airport at the request of Prime Minister A. Milton Obote.

The arrival of British troops had a stabilizing effect, for it enabled Obote swiftly to gain control of the situation. The following day, Obote announced sweeping pay revisions. The basic pay of privates, for example, was increased from 105 shillings to 265 shillings a month; that of lance corporals was increased from 200 shillings to 450 shillings. In addition to pay, the men also received a ration allowance of 150 shillings a month. The annual cost of these increases was estimated at £336,000 annually, with an additional £74,000 in ration allowances. In comparison with a minimum wage of 120 shillings a month in much of Uganda and in comparison with army pay rates throughout the world, the Uganda army had indeed become a privileged group.

On January 25, 1964, the Uganda government seized the initiative. Four hundred British soldiers of the Staffordshire Regiment and the Scots Guards staged a surprise, early-morning attack on the Jinja Barracks. On Obote's orders they stormed the barracks with fixed bayonets and submachine guns. No shots were fired and no casualties occurred. Twenty Askaris were placed under arrrest, charged with disorderly conduct and refusal to obey orders. The mutiny was over, but the reasons for its outbreak are still being examined. The fact that no fighting occurred between British and Uganda troops has led some observers to conclude that the mutiny was inspired essentially by desires for Africanization and increased pay. Certainly had the mutineers possessed an ideology and had they been better organized, the consequences might have been much more serious for the regime.

In the aftermath, the gains of the mutiny were preserved, for parliament approved the pay increases in February and two African officers were recommended for immediate appointment to command the two battalions of the Uganda Rifles. But the mutineers themselves received few of the spoils of victory. Obote announced on January 27, 1964, that men of the Headquarters Company and "A" Company of the First Battalion of the Uganda Rifles were dismissed from the army. The ringleaders were kept in custody for later trial on charges of mutiny and incitement to mutiny. By March 9, the situation had returned to normal, and British troops were able to leave for their base in Nairobi.

Obote's over-all assessment of the mutiny is important. "My Government and I and indeed all the people of Uganda," he declared on January 27, 1964, "have been greatly shocked by the action of these disrupting elements in our Army who not only were lacking in Army spirit but also constituted a most serious security threat to our nation. I am sure you will all agree with me that we could not allow the hard-won and well-deserved brilliant record of our Army to be ruined by these irresponsible elements." Obote then concluded: "We cannot be expected to let the people the nation pays to protect us, turn themselves into dangerous elements to terrorise us; nor can we allow our protectors to become our black-mailers."

The army had become a danger to the very community it was expected to protect. Moreover, it had threatened an African government in the years immediately following decolonization, thereby demonstrating the fragility of the government's position to all the world. Although legitimate authorities rallied to meet this particular threat, many observers wonder if circumstances will be as propitious in the event of another such emergency.

Parties

In many African countries political parties challenge the legitimacy of traditional structures. In their desire to become the new sources of legitimacy, such parties usually become centralized and ideological. In

Uganda the power of traditional groups has so far precluded the success of a centralized, ideological mass party. Uganda's political parties have been forced to combine various traditional allegiances rather than try to defeat them. The parties are therefore coalitions. Unable to destroy traditionalism, they assume a generally pragmatic outlook toward traditional structures and do not embrace antitraditional ideologies.

The absence of a systematic ideology manifests itself in party platforms. As coalitions, the parties must appeal to a wide variety of disparate elements, which causes the platforms of different parties to sound similar. All, to use the words of the KY constitution, declare war on "poverty, ignorance, disease and injustice." All call for the protection of hereditary rulers and traditional institutions. Moreover, the UPC and the DP have issued detailed policy statements calling for nonalignment in the cold war, encouragement of private enterprise, increases in the quality and availability of education, improvement of peasant methods of agriculture, and Africanization of the civil service. The DP does not call itself socialist, and conservative forces in the UPC were for a long time strong enough to prevent that party from explicitly endorsing socialism. By 1964, however, Obote began to stress his party's socialist commitment. In January he declared, "We have decided to follow a socialist line of development. Consequently socialist principles must inform, guide, and govern the basis, form, and content of all institutions of our society." [33]

There is some validity to the common assertion that the DP is more conservative than the UPC. Its leadership outside Buganda has perhaps been less anxious to break with traditional patterns of authority. The Catholic background makes it more committed to the West on foreign policy. But the DP's situation as opposition party is more important to its programmatic stance than are any abstract principles. Thus the party obviously opposes centralization of political power and favors the retention of a multiparty system.

THE DEMOCRATIC PARTY

To understand the important differences between the parties one must study party structures and internal forces. The DP is organized into parish, subcounty, constituency, and district branches. The intro-

---

[33] See *Forward to Freedom, being the Manifesto of the Democratic Party* (Kampala: Democratic Party, 1960); and *Policy Statement, Uganda People's Congress* (Kampala: Uganda People's Congress, 1962). On the KY constitution, see *Uganda Argus* (Kampala), Sept. 11, 1962. For Obote's endorsement of socialism, see Gertzel, *op. cit.,* p. 3.

duction of a constituency level in the party hierarchy was caused by the practical need of contesting elections. Formerly the party structure followed the administrative structure and went from the subcounty to the county level. This same change has also occurred in the UPC.

Since 1956, an annual delegates' conference of the DP has chosen a central executive committee and a national executive. The latter includes all district and provincial leaders. Although in theory delegates come from the local branches, in practice a number of people turn up from the various regions (east, north, west, and Buganda). Then, at the conference itself, those from each region choose twenty-five of their number to be official delegates. This mechanism was devised to prevent the region in which the convention is held from dominating the proceedings. Such an expedient indicates the absence of a well-articulated party structure. Party dues are 1 shilling entrance fee and 5 shillings a year. Because annual dues are rarely collected, the DP has no membership figures. Party activity varies greatly from district to district. The DP has been somewhat less active locally since it lost the 1962 general election. It continues, however, to be a functioning opposition in most district councils, has scored victories in some local by-elections, and in February, 1964, swept all six seats to the Jinja municipal council and four of the six seats in Kampala. In Lango and Busoga the party hardly exists. In Bunyoro and Toro it scored electoral victories in 1962 because of the popularity of its stand on local issues; it has little continuing party organization in these kingdoms. In Ankole, Kigezi, and Acholi the party combines active local organizations with considerable electoral success. In Buganda, on the other hand, party militants are active but isolated, as the DP is able to amass only a tiny fraction of the popular vote.

The DP is not a highly centralized party. Although the central party occasionally steps into a local nominating contest, it exercises little overall influence in the selection of candidates. The situation in Buganda is somewhat different. In part because of its proximity to central headquarters, in part because of the peculiar Buganda situation, and in part because many of the central staff are Baganda, the national party is often consulted in the kingdom before candidates are chosen.

The DP members of parliament, although they can be counted upon to vote against the government, show little unity in debate or approach, partly because party president Kiwanuka is excluded from the legislature. This fact, added to the poorly-articulated party structure, has handicapped the DP in presenting a coherent and unified opposition program. Kiwanuka's personality is also a disturbing factor. Although the DP has a reputation for moderation, Kiwanuka made several inflammatory statements while he was leader of the government. These were attributable more to his emotional and unpredictable personality than to any policy of the DP. Since becoming leader of the opposition, Kiwanuka has played the role of agitator, seeking explosive issues—often sectional or religious—which can win popular support for the DP. In addition, Kiwanuka has been fiercely hated in Buganda. By his long opposition to the kingdom's rulers, this Muganda commoner appeared to challenge the status and position of the Kabaka and the entire Buganda hierarchy.

Opposition to Kiwanuka within the DP emerged at the party's annual delegates' conference in December, 1962. Basil Bataringaya, leader of the parliamentary opposition, stood against Kiwanuka for the party presidency. Several issues were involved. Bataringaya felt that Kiwanuka's leadership of the party was vacillating and irresponsible and might lead to the suppression of the DP. Whereas Kiwanuka conceived of the DP as a fighting instrument, Bataringaya saw its role as that of a loyal opposition. In addition, hoping to attract non-Catholic support to the party, Bataringaya desired to play down the influence of the Catholic Church. Finally, Bataringaya hoped for an eventual reconciliation with Buganda's leaders, which seemed impossible as long as Kiwanuka led the party. In spite of contrary predictions, Kiwanuka was easily re-elected. Bataringaya's support came mainly from his home area, the west. After the election several members of the DP continued to campaign for Bataringaya inside the party. As a rift developed between the UPC and Buganda, intraparty opposition to Kiwanuka quieted, impressed by apparent overtures to him from the Kabaka's government. Nevertheless, the contrast in approach between Kiwanuka and the DP parliamentary party ultimately contributed to Bataringaya's decision to join UPC.

The end of the UPC–KY coalition raised the possibility of a KY alliance with the DP. Many of the Baganda DP militants were at first cool, desiring no alliance with a party whose supporters had burned their homes, destroyed their crops, and killed some of their compatriots. Non-Baganda in the DP, lacking this bitter antagonism, were more anxious to form an alliance with KY. More recently Kiwanuka has been the most active proponent of a *rapprochement* with Buganda's leaders; and as both KY and DP became weakened by desertions to the UPC, the two parties began to work more closely together in the National Assembly.

Whereas the DP is a loosely organized party, *Kabaka Yekka* began with little party organization at all. The Kabaka's government was not interested in promoting in KY an alternative organization to that provided by the chiefly hierarchy. It felt that the purposes of KY were only to unite the Baganda behind the Kabaka's government and to give the kingdom representation at the national level. KY had an executive committee but no chairman, no regularized financial machinery, no official local branches, and no provision for an annual delegates' conference. The rulers of Buganda hoped that the necessary party activities would be carried out under the aegis of the *miruka, ggombolola,* and *ssaza* chiefs.

But in fact the chiefly hierarchy did not provide a substitute for political party organization. Local KY branches quickly sprang up. As independence neared, dissatisfaction with the absence of regular party machinery increased. KY activists felt that within Buganda the party was controlled by the chiefs and the Kabaka's ministers, and at the center it was not sufficiently forceful in its dealings with the UPC. In August, 1962, a KY policy committee was appointed; in September, the party adopted its first constitution. The constitution provides for a regular party organization—with a chairman, annual delegates' conference, branches, dues, and the other paraphernalia of a modern party. KY's assertion of independence from the Kabaka's government temporarily faltered when Buganda katikkiro Kintu was imposed in September, 1962, as chairman, allegedly on the personal intervention of the Kabaka. This action provoked a strong undercurrent of protest from KY members.

The KY delegates' conference had met several times before the adoption of the new constitution. In the year after the first meeting in March, 1962, there were approximately eight conferences. These large affairs were attended by one member from each of the sixty-eight Lukiiko constituencies, all the KY Lukiiko elected members, KY members of the National Assembly, and KY ministers in the Kabaka's government. The practice of holding such large and frequent meetings is at variance with that of other parties. It is an attempt to maintain central control over KY and to promote unity in Buganda.

The position of KY members of the National Assembly deserves mention. Many of these men had been critical of the Kabaka's government in the past, and the government may have pushed indirect elections in order to prevent Assembly politicians from developing their own local bases of power. Although local constituencies do not supply independent sources of power enabling Baganda politicians to act independently of the Kabaka's government, the UPC does. The temptations of power and the close association with the UPC create real strains between KY M.P.'s and Buganda's rulers. This was dramatically revealed in June, 1963, when six members of parliament, including two ministers and two parliamentary secretaries, left KY to join the UPC. Since then further desertions have reduced KY to a fraction of its original parliamentary strength.

KY members of the National Assembly are not the only group within the movement with particular interests. KY is a peculiar hybrid of chiefs and peasants, of members moved by economic discontent or traditional loyalties. It contains educated intellectuals of the orthodox nationalist variety; chiefs and other supporters of the Buganda hierarchy; men sympathetic to Buganda tradition but less sympathetic to the chiefs; and semieducated politicians with previous success in arousing popular discontent. The contradictions within KY were the result of its all-inclusive character. This in turn has given KY more success in mobilizing the masses than either of Uganda's other political parties. Nevertheless, the creation of a party organization, by providing an alternative structure to that of the chiefs and the Kabaka's ministers, played up the potential disunity of the various KY components. And in due course the dissension which had created the party organization threatened to destroy it.

The position of the Kabaka has always been the major unifying factor in Buganda politics; ultimately this is what holds KY together. Yet it is difficult to assess the contemporary role of the Kabaka himself. Educated in England, Kabaka Mutesa II slips easily between the roles of a sophisticated, urbane Westerner and the personification of the Baganda people, receiver of his people's homage. But if the Kabaka is at home in the two worlds, he is in some sense removed from both. It is perhaps his qualities of irony and aloofness that prevent him from exercising dynamic political leadership in his kingdom; even so, he is not just a constitutional monarch divorced from politics. Only the insiders at the upper levels of his government know the extent to which the Kabaka is the tool of the chiefs and the extent to which he determines the policies of his ministers. Nevertheless, particularly since his exile in 1953, the Kabaka has retained the personal loyalty of the Baganda masses. Under conditions in which Buganda presents a united front, as it did in the conflict with Bunyoro over the lost counties, he plays a prominent political role. In internal Buganda politics he has avoided taking positions publicly—as indeed he must if he is to remain a symbol of Buganda unity.

UGANDA PEOPLE'S CONGRESS

Unlike KY, the UPC, at least on paper, has always been a well-articulated, democratically controlled mass party. Membership is open to all persons eighteen or over. There is a three-shilling enrollment fee, followed by dues of one shilling a year. The constitution provides for constituency and regional party organizations, and branches in every ggombolola (subcounty) with at least twenty-five party members. Party officials claim a branch in every ggombolola outside Buganda, which would give the party 476 branches. Each branch is supposed to send two representatives to the annual delegates' conference. Between conferences the national council carries out party directives. The central executive committee supervises the national council and carries on the day-to-day work of the party.

One must go beyond the constitution, however, to understand the structure of the UPC. The party is a coalition of several parties. In areas where the old UNC was strong—particularly Acholi and Lango —the UPC comes close to having a mass base. In Acholi there are many more branches than ggombololas, indicating a penetration of the party to the village level not found in most of Uganda.[34] These local parties are not "mass" parties such as one finds in Ghana or Guinea, but they have real support among grass-roots activists. The other extreme is provided in Busoga, an area of UPC strength but little party organization. Iganga, the second largest town in that district, had no party office during the 1962 district council elections. At the village level there was virtually no sign that an election campaign was in progress. Party organization is also weak in the other kingdoms.

The UPC is thus a series of district parties with grass-roots support, district cadre parties, and district parties of an intermediate type. There is little central control of the UPC at the national level. Candidates for the National Assembly have not been chosen by the central

---

[34] For information about the northern UPC and about the party in general we are indebted to Joseph S. Nye for unpublished material.

party organization. Although the national council must formally approve local nominations, it has little actual influence over them. Candidates are thus attuned to constituency needs and dependent for their support on local interests. In the National Assembly the party usually votes as a unit, but there is little discipline in debate. Backbenchers often criticize the government and disagree with one another. Similarly, outside the Assembly it is often difficult to tell when a UPC member speaks for the party and when he speaks only for himself.

Above all, one cannot overestimate the importance of personalities in the fluid internal politics of the UPC. Factions shift and lack internal cohesion. Nevertheless it is possible to discern certain broad and overlapping groupings. The most important groupings are those of northerners, those from the kingdoms and Busoga, party notables, the party machine, and Prime Minister Obote and his entourage.

To begin with, several prominent leaders had brought their own personal followings into the UPC and were not dependent on the central party organization for their power. Virtually all had been members of the UPU rather than the UNC. These men tended to work within the decentralized and pluralistic politics of the UPC. They seemed to form no clear-cut faction; each had his own local fiefdom and interests.

Within this group of parliamentary notables it is necessary to make a further distinction. A man like Teso's Cuthbert Obwangor, now Uganda's Minister of Justice, is clearly a nationalist. Those from the kingdoms tend to have more parochial interests. They are in the tradition of the UPU, which was never a genuine political party, but simply a collection of local men of prominence with personal followings but no party organization. This parochial situation persists in the kingdoms and Busoga. First, there was significant UPC discontent in the affected areas with the Western Kingdoms and Busoga bill. Second, W. W. Nadiope, the elderly and powerful Musoga leader, gave up an important central ministry to become *Kyabazinga* of Busoga. Third, the Toro UPC, ruling party in that kingdom, has strongly opposed the central government's plan to transfer the administration of services in the Baamba and Bakonjo areas of Toro to central government control. The concern with protecting the privileges of the kingdoms creates antagonism between northern and western UPC party members.

The UPC party machine stands at the opposite pole from the party notables. It is made up of men who have risen through the party machinery and whose power rests on it. Unlike the party notables, they have no local bases of support. Their leader is John Kakonge, former

UPC secretary-general. Those who look to Kakonge include the youth league, the appointed party officials, and a tenuous "left wing" in parliament. Members of this group, oriented toward the former Casablanca bloc, desire an ideologically dominated, centralized party giving sole direction to the country. Many of the young UPC "radicals," educated in India, were impressed on trips to China and Russia. Many, particularly in the youth league, attack the Asians in Uganda and are attracted to violence.

Kakonge has often come into conflict with the parliamentary party. In May, 1962, fearing he was to be denied a specially elected seat in parliament, Kakonge left for Tanganyika. Upon receiving assurances of a place in the political life of the country, he returned to his party post but remained out of parliament. Since the UPC is decentralized, the party apparatus is of little value to Kakonge in his power conflict with the party notables. Lacking his own local base of support, he has sought to create one in the youth league.

The youth league assumed real importance after independence, in part as a result of a party vacuum created when party leaders went into the government. Previously the youth league had been active, particularly in the north, but only at election time. The northern youth league retains its preindependence character, but in the east and Kampala the youth league is active between elections as well, issuing statements and calling demonstrations. The growth of this new type of organization within the UPC has not made the party more centralized, but it has shifted the balance of internal power somewhat in a "leftward" direction.

The group around Prime Minister Obote is at the center of the other forces in the UPC. A shrewd politician, Obote has shown ability both in building a grass-roots party organization in Lango and in welding a governing coalition of Uganda's various local political leaders. He seems to have a talent both for political negotiation and for the kind of mass appeals necessary to create a popularly based party organization. Obote's years in Kenya, where he joined Kenyatta's Kenya African Union, contributed to the development of his political skills. He lacks, however, the intellectual sophistication of Tanganyika's Julius Nyerere.

Sincere in his socialism and pan-Africanism, Obote interprets these ideologies with great flexibility. He is a pragmatist, but unlike that of many of the UPC party notables his pragmatism has been put to the service of national power, not of local interests. In order to achieve power in preindependence Uganda, Obote had to act as a broker between the diverse interests in the party. This is still his dominant role. His policy pronouncements take a middle ground between the statements of Kakonge, youth-wing spokesmen, and leaders of the Buganda UPC on the one hand, and the more conservative positions of the party notables on the other.

Nevertheless, Obote is becoming more than a manipulator of UPC factions. He has begun to use ideological appeals to increase his own power and that of the national UPC. Before independence, important elements of the UPC–KY coalition, fearful of losing their power once the British left Uganda, would only have been antagonized by ideological calls for national unity. Ideological appeals would have been dangerous for Obote then; they have become practical now. Obote therefore calls for unity in the name of African solidarity and Uganda nationalism. The desire for power which led him to make use of many diverse interests before independence now leads him to attempt to control a number of them.

Like Obote, several men in the party who achieved power through local prominence now look to expand their authority through increased party discipline and control. Critical of the local parties in the kingdoms, these leaders share with Kakonge and the youth wing an emphasis on discipline. But although the youth wing calls for a disciplined party, the party leaders feel that it is the youth league itself that requires discipline. These feelings were particularly noticeable after the youth league's violence against the French ambassador in 1963.

Efforts to discipline local party officials have met with little success. The 1962 UPC delegates' conference decided to eject from the party all those who had stood against official UPC candidates in the local and national elections. A founder-member of the UPC from Acholi, Erifazi Otema-Alimadi, was thereupon expelled. He refused to recognize the expulsion and, maintaining control of the party organization in Gulu, stood for the Acholi district elections the next month. Ibingira spoke for the national UPC and denied that Alimadi was still a member of the party. He promised an executive committee statement confirming this. Nonetheless, Alimadi was elected to the district council and party officials privately admitted that no further action would be taken.

Attempts by national leaders to discipline the central party organization at first also met with little success. Shortly before independence three UPC officials were fired by Obwangor and John K. Babiiha, the treasurer and chairman of UPC respectively, while Obote and Kakonge were out of the country. Obote felt it necessary, however, to reinstate them. But as 1963 progressed, Kakonge and leaders of the youth wing increased their efforts to play an independent role in Uganda politics. At the annual UPC conference in April–May, 1964, a bitter contest developed for control of the party organization. Minister of Planning A. A. Nekyon attacked what he termed apparent pro-Communist elements in the UPC. Grace Ibingira, a dynamic and thoughtful young minister and party leader who had long been critical of Kakonge, overwhelmingly defeated him for the post of secretary-general. By sanctioning the change of leadership, Obote was acting to curb the independence of the party organization. Obote sought to placate Kakonge by praising him highly, but Kakonge's initial reaction, as when he had been denied a seat in parliament two years earlier, was one of bitterness.

Centripetal Forces

Just as Obote sought to increase the unity of the UPC, he also made efforts to bring events in the country as a whole under greater party control. UPC leaders evidenced increasing dissatisfaction with their inability to direct the course of events. They acted swiftly against the less powerful interests in the country, refusing to negotiate, for example, with the nurses at the central hospital in Kampala who did not want to wear badges with numbers. But their attacks on the more important centers of power—trade unions, the DP, and the Buganda government —were more guarded. In the years immediately following the UPC assumption of power in 1962, it was still too early to say that Uganda politics had changed its pluralistic character.

THE UNIONS

Their economic influence on developmental decisions and their independent organizational base can give trade unions in developing countries an importance that reaches far beyond their membership. In Uganda a wave of strikes in the months preceding independence caused distrust of the labor movement. Two UPC ministers, Felix Onama and Adoko Nekyon, began attacking Kenyan influence in the trade unions. They spoke of "industrial sabotage" by people not loyal to Uganda. Two weeks after independence Onama threatened a ban on strikes if unions pursued their "irresponsible" activities. The ministers' attacks on the labor movement had essentially bureaucratic motives: in their eyes the unions were disturbing stability and national unity. This position was supplemented by ideological criticism. UPC youth leader Raiti Omongin violently attacked the TUC for its connections with the "imperialist" International Confederation of Free Trade Unions.

During the first months of the UPC–TUC conflict Obote kept his own counsel. In March, 1963, the TUC invited him to address its delegates' conference. Obote used this platform to attack the unions for being too independent of the government. His statement provoked UPC administrative secretary Wadada Musani to attack the ICFTU as an "undisguised agent of monopolists, capitalists, imperialists, and neocolonialists." According to Musani, the UPC was considering setting up its own trade-union movement. A month later Obote himself attacked "foreign hands" behind the TUC. Blaming the ICFTU for the strikes in Uganda, the Prime Minister promised legislation to curb the activities of foreigners in the trade-union movement.

THE DEMOCRATIC PARTY

UPC has also threatened the DP's status as an independent center of power. Here a crisis occurred in the month before independence, when the UPC charged that the DP was smuggling arms into Uganda. No evidence for these charges was produced. In the aftermath it became apparent that many UPC leaders tended to confuse legitimate and illegitimate opposition. It was not entirely clear that the DP itself understood that distinction. Both parties spoke of "destroying" the government, without distinguishing between violent and nonviolent means. Explaining why the DP did not deserve to be a legitimate opposition, Minister of Justice Grace Ibingira could only refer to various inconsistencies in its policies. UPC leaders continued to issue "warnings" against the DP from time to time. In February, 1963, Kakonge said that Uganda would have made more progress under one-party government than it actually had since independence. Obote first declared his preference for a one-party state a year later, rejecting the need for an organized opposition as a "capitalist notion." In the furor following Obote's statement, Ibingira explained that the UPC felt the opposition parties would eventually die a natural death. He noted that Obote had mentioned no compulsory steps to outlaw them. At the same time Bataringaya sought to win an institutionalized place for a loyal opposition by developing a restrained political style for the parliamentary DP. But on New Year's Eve, 1964, Bataringaya crossed over to the UPC, taking five DP members with him. Following this, Obote refused to recognize a new official Leader of the Parliamentary Opposition agreed upon by DP and KY.[35]

[35] *Uganda Argus* (Kampala), Feb. 3, 1965, p. 1.

A major factor inhibiting the UPC's ability to suppress other centers of power was the existence of KY in the governing coalition. The presence of KY established some balance of forces. In view of this balance, the split in Baganda unity and the rift between the Kabaka's government and the UPC were extremely significant. The opposition to the Baganda chiefs was exposed in November, 1962. Old-time UNC leader Musazi introduced a resolution in the Lukiiko calling for the chiefs and the Kabaka's ministers to give up the rent from their *mailo* land to the Buganda treasury. This income, in addition to their salaries, is a privilege of their political positions. Musazi's motion was defeated in the Lukiiko by a vote of 45 to 27, but this hardly brought the issue to a close. Supporters of the resolution, including many KY leaders, held mass meetings and attacked the chiefs and the Kabaka's ministers. Several KY members of the National Assembly also spoke against the chiefs.

In January, 1963, a faction known as the Common Man (*Bawejjere*) arose within KY, initiated by its youth-wing leaders. This group demanded the abolition of mailo land benefits and the resignation of traditionalist Michael Kintu from the katikkiroship. By this time there were five or six factions in KY, ranging from total support of the chiefs to outright opposition to them.

Although Common Man drew the backing of many supporters of the 1959 trade boycott, the new movement differed significantly from the old one. The boycott represented the Baganda nation closing ranks against outside threats; supporters of Common Man were class antagonists of the ruling group in Buganda. The 1959 and 1963 movements in Buganda made different demands, displayed different orientations, and had different leaders. Whereas a major strain in the Uganda National Movement was ultratraditionalist, the Common Man movement was opposed by the chiefs in the name of Buganda tradition. The politics of Buganda had come full circle since 1926. In that year the first *bataka* movement represented a traditionalist opposition to the chiefs. Now, reacting to the threats to their power, the chiefs had become the traditionalists.

Nonetheless, it would be a mistake to ignore the traditionalist element in the Common Man movement. Common Man leader Eriabu Lwebuga placed the movement in the tradition of Buganda protest going back to the 1945 and 1949 demonstrations. He had been an important secondary figure in the 1959 boycott, and most of those sympathetic to Common Man were Buganda nationalists. The movement made demands for the preservation of women's traditional rights, and women were active in it. This is usually a sign of a traditionally oriented movement.[36]

One new factor in Buganda politics was the role of the UPC. The UPC's attempt to open branches in Buganda had provoked conflict with KY before the mailo land controversy. Indeed, the terms of the UPC–KY alliance seemed to make Buganda a KY preserve. From its inception, the Buganda UPC was critical of the Kabaka's government; it supported Musazi during the mailo land agitation. In January, 1963, the Buganda UPC announced its intention of contesting the seats in the February by-elections to the Lukiiko. Faced with this threat, the diverse elements within KY temporarily submerged their differences. Leaders who had opposed the chiefs on mailo land now became silent on that issue, and strongly attacked the UPC. Obote did not take sides in the violent conflict that ensued.

In the end UPC contested only one Buganda seat outside Kampala and lost its deposit there. Shortly after the election, however, Obote appeared at a mass meeting called to oppose the chiefs. Adopting the term "common man" as his own, he attacked the Buganda rulers rather openly.

Even this external attack did not immediately unify the kingdom. Musazi and several other members left KY to join the UPC—the first in a series of defections that was to plague the Buganda party. The future of KY seemed clouded, and a KY delegates' conference unanimously chose a committee headed by E. M. K. Mulira to make recommendations about the role of the movement. Mulira recommended that KY become a nationwide party, and KY and Common Man leaders ended their public attacks on the Kabaka's government. But in the words of a Buganda leader, "The conflict is not dying down; it is just resting."

The next shock to Baganda unity came from several KY members of the National Assembly, who recognized that the UPC was no longer dependent on KY to form a government or to make major political decisions. Fearing that the kingdom, and they themselves, would be cut off from "where the national power and authority lies," [37] they urged

---

[36] Cf. Seymour Martin Lipset, *Political Man* (Garden City: Doubleday, 1960), pp. 221, 247, 260.

[37] Dr. S. J. L. Zake and others, *Fresh Political Approach in Buganda—Basis of the M.P.s Recommendations for K.Y.–U.P.C. Merger* (Kampala: 1963), p. 4.

that KY merge with the UPC. On June 17, 1963, six of KY's twenty-one members of the National Assembly, with two leading Democratic Party legislators, joined the UPC. A majority of KY's National Assembly members had rejected the move for a total merger of the parties, and the Lukiiko unanimously condemned, as deserting Buganda, the six who left KY. But the factors that sent these six into the UPC continued to operate. In November, former Buganda Minister of Justice L. N. Basudde, previously closely associated with the Kabaka's government, switched from KY to the UPC. He, too, preferred a party with a national outlook to the party of "Buganda alone." [38] KY's position as the dominant Baganda voice in national politics and the unity of the kingdom itself both seemed in danger.

In the summer of 1964, the alliance between the UPC and KY came to an end. Obote's determination to continue with the referendum in the disputed "lost counties" angered Buganda, and probably precipitated the break. Obote must have had the probability of a split in mind when he decided to hold the referendum as planned. KY bitterly attacked the government both in parliament and in public meetings. The party had, moreover, opposed the UPC candidate in a Busoga by-election. On August 24, Obote abrogated the alliance that had brought Uganda to independence almost two years earlier. Substantial defections from KY continued at both the regional and central levels. By early 1965, the party balance stood at UPC 67, KY 14, and DP 10. Clearly the power of Buganda in Uganda politics, having reached its high point with the adoption of "federalism," seemed now on the wane.

Since the rise of Uganda nationalism in the late 1950's, the central problem has been the locus of political power, both within the parties and within the country as a whole. In the face of the power of traditionalism and the absence of mass political parties, Uganda was brought to independence by a coalition of disparate forces. In his message to the UPC on its third anniversary, Obote referred to the "revolution" initiated by the formation of the party. "However, due to many impediments projected by vested interests," he continued, "we had in the course of our struggle to compromise [with the 'factions'] on the strategy of approach and the speed of the revolution." Here he gave the reasons for the alliance with KY. What of the future? "The time,"

[38] *Uganda Argus* (Kampala), Nov. 2, 1963, p. 3.

he said, "has come for us to pick up the vigour, dynamism and speed of the revolution from where it was left and carry it through to the next phase, namely to afford our people a better and happier life." [39] The compromise with the "vested interests" had been necessary to bring Uganda to independence and the UPC to power; what would happen in "the next phase"?

LOCAL GOVERNMENT

Autonomous units of local government in Uganda include the municipalities of Kampala, Mbale, and Jinja, the kingdom of Buganda, and fourteen districts (the latter including the western kingdoms and Busoga, which have federal status). For Buganda and all the districts except Karamoja the law provides for democratic political control of an administrative bureaucracy. The bureaucracy is composed of trained civil servants in the counties and subcounties and of traditional authorities in the parishes and villages. The local governments have authority over education, medical and health services, water supplies, roads, and means for maintaining law and order.

Since 1959, virtually all the districts in the country have had their first direct elections to the district councils. The district councils, known by such traditional names as *Eishengyero* in Ankole and Lukiiko in Busoga, are the political centers of control. Since the beginning of 1960, all district council elections have been dominated by the national political parties.

The administrative hierarchy is theoretically divorced from politics. At the apex stands a civil servant known in most districts as the secretary-general, although in some he is referred to by a traditional title and has ceremonial functions as well. He is supplemented by the district commissioner, an appointee of the central government. In earlier days the district commissioner ran the district; with the devolution of power to the districts his power and position have become unclear.

The members of the administration below the secretary-general are known as chiefs, although their position is quite different from that of the traditional chief. The structure of the hierarchy of chiefs varies from district to district; most common is a four-tier structure of county, subcounty, parish, and village chiefs. The upper-level chiefs are meant to form an administrative bureaucracy, efficient and nonpartisan. They are appointive and transferable within the district; their income is derived from salaries. Upper-level chiefs are far better educated than the

[39] *Ibid.*, March 9, 1963, p. 4.

local chiefs. The village headmen are an integral part of traditional life rather than of the administrative hierarchy. Many are unpaid; others receive a nominal salary. They are local men of prominence, whose positions are often hereditary and whose effectiveness would be lost if they were transferred. In the kingdoms a hereditary ruler, theoretically a constitutional monarch, caps the entire structure.

In the initial period of British rule, the colonial government was able to utilize much of the traditional apparatus in the tribes that had chiefs. Consequently, at the outset the transition from traditional to modern government was easiest in the kingdoms. British officials accepted the paramount chief, modified the county chieftaincies, and created subcounty chiefs with regular geographic jurisdictions. They attempted to end the king's arbitrary power of appointment. Later they introduced educational qualifications for office and placed chiefs on a salaried basis.

In the uncentralized societies indirect rule was inapplicable, and the imposition of the bureaucratic systems did more immediate violence to traditional ways than it had in the hierarchical tribes. Because there was no structure of chieftainships which the British could utilize, the British-appointed chiefs usually lacked traditional sanctions.

Despite the attempt to create modern systems of government in the districts, the actual administration is a complex product of the imposition of modernity on traditional structures, practices, and attitudes. In traditional societies, for example, political power went with control over a territory and the people living in it. The modern attempt to divorce political power from personal control over territory encounters resistance not only from the chiefs but often from the people. A dual system of legitimacy results. Thus in Bunyoro in 1933, the British substituted salaries for the tribute given by peasants to the chiefs who administered their territories. A chief must, however, still acquire his own estate before the people consider him a real chief. At the same time, those who have estates are considered chiefs even if they are not official chiefs in the bureaucratic system. Accorded traditional rights, they are expected to provide feasts and other traditional services. Consequently, the modern system of appointed bureaucratic chiefs coexists alongside the traditional relation of political power to territorial control.[40]

[40] Audrey Richards, ed., *East African Chiefs* (London: Faber and Faber, 1960), pp. 108–111; John Beattie, "Democratization in Bunyoro," *Civilizations,* XI (1961), 7–11.

Perhaps the most serious over-all problem in affairs of local government is the relationship between political and personal obligations. Traditionally, political relations covered the whole range of personal relations; they were not specific to particular functions (as the doctor-patient relationship is restricted to healing, the buyer-seller relationship to economics, and so forth). With a major exception for performance in war, personal standards of loyalty rather than impersonal standards of competence normally dominated. Gifts and payments were made to people higher up on the scale, who in turn provided services for inferiors. Personal obligations were particularly important in tribes with strong clan and kinship loyalties. The general amalgam of persons and politics is completely foreign to modern bureaucratic norms of efficiency and equality before the law.

Where government is personalized there is no distinction between administration and politics. Today civil servants (chiefs) are supposed to be neutral in politics. In fact the political preferences of most are well known and their political activities only thinly disguised. In Ankole the upper levels of the administrative hierarchy actively sympathize with the DP; in Toro the administration has been pro-UPC. The Acholi secretary-general is known as a UPC supporter; the *agofe/ obimo* (secretary-general) in West Nile is chairman of the UPC regional party there. In Busoga the battle over the election of the Kyabazinga (supposedly a ceremonial official above party politics) was fought openly along party lines.

If political control of administration is likely to continue, to what extent will that control flow directly from the central government? Certainly the legal supremacy of the center over the districts is unquestioned. Under the Local Administrations Ordinance of 1962 the Minister of Regional Administrations is authorized to approve draft laws, to issue written instructions on the management and control of financial matters, to approve the estimates, and to order an inspection into the competency of local administrations. If the minister is not satisfied that a local government body is performing its functions responsibly, he may order reforms. Should local authorities fail to comply with his directions, the minister may then appoint a person or persons to perform the functions properly and, after an inquiry, may even dissolve the council itself. In the kingdoms the minister can only terminate arrangements for administering services upon the advice of a commission of inquiry. Central take-over of services in the Baamba and Bakonjo areas of Toro under this procedure was the first instance of central authorities using their constitutional power to operate services within a district.

Central supremacy also seems implicit in the appointment in 1963 of a Regions Service Commission to supervise standards for the district civil services. The UPC party background of many of the appointees led to speculation about the possible use of this commission as a political weapon.

CENTRAL ADMINISTRATION

As of 1961, there were 2,121 Europeans and 1,950 Asians in the public service. Of these, 731 and 347, respectively, were employed in the central government administration. There were also 93,049 African male employees. This number includes 31,941 (15,791 unskilled) in local government, and 14,162 in central administration. Thus the majority of African government employees are in nonadministrative jobs such as construction, education and medicine, transport and communications, and agriculture, The local figures vary from Mengo's 12,514 to Tororo's 1,412. The significance of public employment as a proportion of total employment is clear when one realizes that 42 per cent of all wage-earning Africans are employed by the public service.[41]

At the lower end of the central service scale is the clerical or technical class. Candidates for entrance into this grade need a school certificate. Clerical personnel can be promoted to the executive and administrative classes on the basis of training, experience, and ability. Similarly, personnel in the technical class move upward through the technician grades to higher technical posts. Direct entry into the executive class normally requires a higher school certificate, a pass degree at Makerere, and a diploma in public administration, or their equivalents. Direct admission into the administrative class normally requires a college honors degree. The shortage of African personnel accounts for some relaxation of these academic qualifications.

The policy of the government is to recruit Ugandans whenever possible. This preference for citizens of Uganda excludes many Asians who have not become citizens. After Ugandans, the government prefers to recruit East Africans on local terms. Expatriates are now employed on a contract basis. There remain, however, many expatriates from the colonial period. These pensionable officers are covered by

[41] *Uganda Protectorate, Enumeration of Employees, June 1961* (Entebbe: Ministry of Economic Development, 1962), *passim.*

costly compensation schemes which increase with promotion. Therefore the government has tended to promote pensionable expatriates only in unusual circumstances. The service also employs, when no local candidate is available, seconded officers from the Crown Agents and other sources in England.

Independence has brought a rapid turnover of civil service personnel. Many officers from the higher level have left or have been relieved of their posts, making the break in continuity particularly noticeable. Thus the Prime Minister's office announced in February, 1963, that 583 out of 1,150 expatriate officials on permanent duty had retired or given notice of their intention to retire by July. Such a heavy exodus seemed bound to be disruptive; thus far, however, the upset caused by this turnover has been kept to a minimum. This is attributable in part to the success of on-the-job training programs and crash courses in public administration and in part to the cooperation of departing expatriates.

A second serious threat to continuity is the diversion of higher level African personnel into other fields. This will become even more of a problem in the future, when the civil service is no longer looked upon as the most attractive career. Increasing competition is in evidence, particularly from quasi-governmental bodies, international oil companies, tobacco companies, and the United Nations. All are eager to appoint Africans, and their ability to pay top salaries places them in an advantageous position to attract key personnel. Perhaps the biggest area of civil service uncertainty lies in the possible loss of talented junior men. These men have not built up vested interests (pension rights, seniority) and are therefore more tempted by opportunities outside the service.

Competition from alternative employers affects not only those presently employed by government but prospective employees as well. It is thus a serious threat to rapid Africanization of the civil service. Africanization of the civil service is essential if Uganda is to be truly independent. No country can rely on the services of expatriates indefinitely, particularly in sensitive areas. Moreover, the cost of inducing qualified people to come to work in Uganda is excessive. In addition, Uganda's leaders must remain responsive to widespread popular demands for Africanization.

Uganda's policy on Africanization is consistent with militant African demands for rapid progress, yet practical and selective in its application. The government aims at the achievement of "complete Ugandanization in the shortest possible time, consistent with the maintenance of acceptable standards." [42] At the same time Prime Minister Obote explicitly disavows any intention either of Africanizing for the sake of Africanization or of Africanizing "at the expense of efficiency or the standards which we consider right for the country's stage of development." [43] In line with this policy, his government declares that it will not act in a way that will undermine the standards of the medical, educational, or police services. Nevertheless, it clearly intends to cut down on costly and top-heavy establishments elsewhere.

The government has made steady progress in Africanizing the civil service. Eighty-six of 259 superscale posts were filled by Ugandans in June, 1963, and officials estimated that by July, 1963, less than six hundred permanent and pensionable expatriate officers would remain in the service. The exodus of more than five hundred officers since March, 1962, has created more vacancies than there are qualified Ugandans for the posts. Thus 3,363 of the 22,560 established posts in the public service were either vacant or filled by temporary staff at the end of 1962.[44] This situation can be rectified only on a long-term basis, as the education system produces qualified graduates to meet Uganda's needs.

The very success of Africanization may bring forth a new problem. The government has already noted dissatisfaction among some central officers seconded to regional and district posts. Such dissatisfaction could become more widespread if the executive and administrative classes were fully Africanized—particularly with less qualified office holders appointed to speed the changeover in the years following independence. Opportunities could then become restricted and capable young candidates left with little chance for promotion or choice of specialty.

What of the relationship between the civil service and politics? Experience at the local level has already shown the difficulty of maintaining impartiality in the civil service. The central administration is less amenable to violations of nonpartisanship as it recruits personnel from all parts of the country and its values and practices are modernist rather than traditional. Nevertheless the elite is small, the traditions of impartiality lacking, ethnic connections close, and the line between po-

[42] *Report of the Commissioners for Africanization 1962* (Entebbe: Government Printer, 1962), p. 3.

[43] *Uganda Argus* (Kampala), May 26, 1962, p. 1.

[44] *Report of the Uganda Civil Service Salaries Commission 1963* (Entebbe: Government Printer, 1963), p. 30.

litical and administrative decisions in a developing country often tenuous.

The constitution clearly intends that the Uganda Public Service Commission minimize direct government political interference in the civil service. Whereas the government sets policy on recruitment and promotion, it is the task of the commission to execute the government's policy. The commission, however, is not fully insulated from political pressures. Members are appointed on the advice of the Prime Minister and their terms expire after four years. Various charges of partiality in the administration of the civil service have already been made. The DP alleges party favoritism in several ministries. The speaker of the Buganda Lukiiko has charged discrimination in recruitment and promotion at the expense of the Baganda. Central government officials have strongly denied these allegations.

THE JUDICIARY

Uganda's judicial system stems from the British policy of recognizing the indigenous legal systems of the countries which they administered. Thus the African courts were originally created to administer customary law. Slowly they were given wider jurisdiction, but they still have important customary functions. To parallel the African judicial system, the British set up magistrates courts to administer the English law which was introduced into Uganda.

In contemporary Uganda the African court system has become the district court system. (The description of the Uganda court system refers to the period prior to mid-1964, when the African courts and magistrates courts were integrated into a single system.) At the lower levels are the district county courts. District African courts (known in Buganda as the Buganda Principal Court) have appellate jurisdiction from district county courts. Their original jurisdiction extends to the more important civil and criminal offenses. Lawyers are not permitted to represent clients in these courts.

Magistrates courts are the subordinate central government courts. Their jurisdiction overlaps that of the district courts, and includes criminal cases other than murder, rape, manslaughter, and so forth, and civil cases where the amount involved does not exceed 4,000 shillings. The Minister of Justice can appoint any "fit and proper" person as a magistrate; no legal training is required.

Appeals are made from the magistrates and district African courts to the High Court of Uganda. Appeals from the district African (or Buganda Principal) courts can be made only with the consent of the judicial adviser for the region. The judicial adviser is an appointee of the central government. His consent is not required on a strictly legal matter. The High Court itself can, on its own initiative, call for records from the lower courts when an important question of law or a substantial miscarriage of justice is involved.

The High Court has sole original jurisdiction in murder, treason, and rape cases, and in the most important civil cases. The court is composed of a chief justice and at least six puisne (associate) judges. The President appoints the former on the advice of the Prime Minister and the latter on the advice of the Judicial Service Commission. Until compulsory retirement, these judges can be removed only for misbehavior or inability to perform the functions of office.

Two postindependence decisions make clear the importance of the High Court. In one, the central government challenged the right of Ankole authorities to appoint an electoral boundaries commission. The court ruled that the Ankole electoral boundaries commission had not completed its work before independence, and therefore its actions were void. It is significant that even Ankole accepted the decision that with independence it had lost the right to determine its own electoral boundaries for the district council election. In another decision, the court ruled that the Busoga Lukiiko was improperly constituted and could not, therefore, legally elect a kyabazinga. In making this judgment the court noted that the situation could be remedied either by the holding of new elections in Busoga or by National Assembly approval of a bill validating the original elections. The following week the government pushed a bill through parliament validating the election of both the Busoga Lukiiko and the kyabazinga. The opposition protested this maneuver and staged a walkout from the National Assembly prior to the bill's second reading. It seems likely that as the legal implications involved in Uganda's complex and often ambiguous "federal" structure become obvious in the years ahead, the court will be extremely active.

Decisions of the High Court of Uganda can be appealed to the Court of Appeal for Eastern Africa, formerly known as the East African Court of Appeal. It hears both civil and criminal appeals. In addition, the Judicial Committee of the Privy Council renders opinions on cases appealed to it from Commonwealth countries still making use of this procedure. Normally the Attorney-General must give permission before cases can go to the Privy Council. Decisions of the High Court of Uganda involving fundamental rights can be appealed, however, as of right.

With regard to the "federal" nature of the state, two points are significant. Except for courts in Buganda, the district courts are under the supervision and administration of the central government. Even though the district administrations exercise a large degree of control, the central government handles appointments, promotions, and other similar matters. It also maintains over-all supervision of all functions performed by the district administrations in relation to the African courts. The only courts which are not largely controlled by the central government are the courts in Buganda. These are fully controlled administratively by the Kabaka's government.

Second, the High Court of Uganda—a central government court—can hear a case on appeal even from a lower court in Buganda. No kingdom or district can insulate its form of justice from that of the central government's judicial system. When the High Court of Uganda sits in Buganda and the western kingdoms, it administers justice in the name of the ruler. Thus in Buganda the court is known as the High Court of Buganda. But the personnel, practice, and procedure of the High Court are the same wherever it sits. Again the federal status connotes prestige but not substance.

Contemporary Problems

NATIONAL UNITY

Indirect rule, by systematizing the compartmentalization of life in Uganda along tribal lines, left the country with a serious problem of national unity. The adoption of a federal-type constitution was an attempt to meet tribal demands within a unified structure. It is important to learn whether the federal approach actually exacerbates rather than mitigates tribal tensions.

Tribalism is a vital factor in Uganda. Its virtue is its capacity to give members a sense of identity and security; its main shortcoming is its tendency to undercut national unity by emphasizing particular over national needs. Where local nationalism fragments the society and inhibits the willingness to compromise, the new state is threatened with separatism, even disruption.

Clearly the federal solution could not satisfy all tribal claims to separate status in Uganda. The various ethnic groups overlap too much to be fitted into an areal pattern of tribal states. Approximately one-third

of Buganda's population consists of non-Baganda peoples—Banyaruanda, Barundi, Banyoro, Banyankole, and others. Bukedi district includes Iteso, Bagwere, Banyole, Jopadhola, Basamia, and Bagwe. A
large percentage of Sebei's population are Bagisu. To try to adapt federalism to such a geographical situation is unthinkable. The result
would be bitterness and economic chaos. To hold back these fissipa-
rous forces, as was inevitably done, means to leave minority ethnic
groups dispersed throughout the country.

The drive to create a federal Uganda has alerted the general public
to growing minority anxieties. Thus, to allay Bagisu fears at the time
Sebei was made a separate district, Minister of Local Government
Bataringaya conditioned the grant of such status in part upon the negotiation of arrangements for the protection of non-Sebei peoples to be
included in the new district. It is a paradox that federalism, which was
sought in order to allay tribal fears, caused them, in some cases, to
come to the surface. Perhaps here the central government will have to
play a larger role in guaranteeing civil rights for all.

Creation of Separate Districts

In addition to heightening fears on the part of those minorities left in
the midst of alien majorities,[45] the struggle to establish a federal
scheme also aggravated disputes over creating new districts and recti-
fying boundaries. The DP government set a precedent for creating new
districts in 1961, when it announced the decision to make Sebei a separate administrative unit. On November 22, 1961, Bataringaya declared
in the National Assembly that the marriage of Sebei and Bugisu was an
unhappy one. He preferred to create two districts rather than continue
an artificial union disturbed by increasing intertribal tensions. His position on the Sebei question was attacked by the opposition, which
considered his policy to be no more than a concession to tribalism.
"The policy of this Government," Felix Onama bluntly told parliament
the following day, "is to fragment that district so as to catch votes."
Such charges no doubt touched a sensitive area. Prior to the passage of
the bill separating the two peoples, most of the prominent Sebei politicians switched from the UPC to the DP.

It is important to note that the central government acted on the
Sebei question without securing the approval of the local councils involved. Prime Minister Kiwanuka based his authority in this matter on

[45] For an analysis of similar pressures in Nigeria, see the section on the Federal
Republic of Nigeria, pp. 7–149 in this volume, and Donald Rothchild, "Safeguarding Nigeria's Minorities," *Duquesne Review,* VIII (Spring, 1963), 35–51.

the provision of the Uganda Order in Council of 1902, which empowered the Governor to divide the country into provinces or districts "as may be convenient for the purpose of administration." [46] Such a sweeping authorization made action relatively simple. When the independence constitution came into effect, however, an elaborate procedure for creating new units was introduced. Now transfers of territory can be effected only if two-thirds of all the members of the regional legislative bodies involved and two-thirds of all the members of the National Assembly concur. Not only did the central government fear further tendencies toward fragmentation, but the leaders of the existing districts did as well.

In spite of the obstacles inherent in this provision, various ethnic groups have sought to follow Sebei's example. The Bahororo of South West Ankole and the Iteso of Bukedi have asked for separate districts. Even more dramatically, the Baamba and Bakonjo secessionist movement in Toro has demanded a "Rwenzururu" district for its peoples. The determination of the proponents of this district can be seen in events before and after independence. Proponents of Rwenzururu walked out of the Toro Rukurato, petitioned the Governor and Prime Minister, burned down a Rukurato hall, assaulted the police, wrecked schools, hospitals, and missions, released prisoners, kidnapped an M.P., and attacked Batoro and damaged their property. Only two months after government authorities lifted an order declaring the Baamba and Bakonjo areas of Toro disturbed areas, police opened fire on armed crowds of Rwenzururu supporters. It emerged that the Rwenzururu leaders had set up their own courts, police, and administrative machinery in the mountains. In February, 1963, the government declared a state of emergency in Bwamba and Busongora counties, proscribed the Rwenzururu Separate District Movement, and sent the Uganda Rifles into the area to restore law and order.

In September, 1962, the Governor appointed a commission under the chairmanship of Dr. F. C. Ssembeguya to inquire into the reasons for the Baamba–Bakonjo disturbances. The commission found that the bitter feelings existing in the area arose from alleged discriminatory treatment in the awarding of places for higher education, in the allocation of schools, in the manner of assessing taxes, in the number of appointments to higher posts, in the use of local languages, and in Batoro arrogance and abuse. The commission acknowledged that many of these complaints were substantiated. In particular the commissioners

[46] See his letter in the *Uganda Argus* (Kampala), Nov. 6, 1961, p. 2.

stressed that the Batoro tendency "to classify the Baamba and Bakonjo as less than humans and as inferior beings . . . still prevails and that it is the underlying cause of the extremely bitter feeling which now exists." [47] The commission called upon the Toro government to end discriminatory practices but, serious as Batoro discrimination has been, for economic and administrative reasons rejected the establishment of a separate district. Perhaps the constitutional difficulties of creating new districts may partly account for this rejection. The government subsequently accepted the recommendation to reject a separate district and endorsed the establishment of county councils with the power to raise rates and taxes.

Continued lawlessness in the Baamba–Bakonjo parts of Toro led the Uganda government to reconsider the means of administering this area. It appointed another commission of inquiry to determine whether Toro authorities were running services efficiently in the disturbed counties. The Lubowa report of March, 1963, found that the *Omukama's* government was no longer able to administer satisfactorily certain of the education, road, prison, and medical services. The central government thereupon assumed responsibility for the administration of these services despite the active opposition of the Batoro. It appointed an administrator for Bwamba and Busongora counties, with responsibility for running the services, collecting taxes, and appointing agents (having the power of chiefs). By this move the central government demonstrated its determination and ability to make use of its extensive constitutional powers to maintain an orderly and united Uganda.

Boundary Questions

Boundary disputes also became acute as independence neared. These conflicts arose as a result of former treaty agreements, poorly demarcated boundaries, and continuous migrations. The line separating Bugisu and Bukedi districts aroused considerable bitterness. Although the town of Mbale lies within Bugisu, it serves as district headquarters for both. Consequently, each local administration claimed it, on the grounds of exclusive tribal ownership as well as administrative necessity. Bukedi also sought substantial concessions of territory in certain *miruka* (parishes) adjoining Mbale. The commission proposed to solve the conflict over ownership by formally recognizing Bugisu's title to the land on which Mbale stands, by adjusting the district boundary

[47] *Uganda Government, Report of the Commission of Inquiry into the Recent Disturbances amongst the Baamba and Bakonjo People of Toro* (Entebbe: Government Printer, 1962), p. 10.

to give Bukedi the miruka where Bakedi predominate (thereby guaranteeing Bakedi free access to the town), and by transferring the Bukedi local administration from Mbale to Bukedi district (attempting thereby to bring an end to the friction caused by housing the two headquarters in the same building). "The vesting of the land of Mbale in the Bugisu District Land Board . . . ," reasoned the commission, "would be construed as an important prestige success for the Bagisu and may be considered as compensating them for the transfer to Bukedi of territory in or about Namabasa and Namunsi." [48] The Bagisu were not tempted by this compensation. Rejecting the proposal to transfer land to Bukedi, the Bugisu *Lukhobo* (district council) asserted in December, 1962, that the report was "unrealistic and mischievous in that in an independent Uganda it asks the Government to prefer tribalism to nationalism." More than two years after the issuance of this report the government had still not published a White Paper on the question.

Another boundary question, that of the "lost counties" in Mubende district, locked Buganda and Bunyoro in a major dispute. Because Anglo–Buganda military cooperation in the late nineteenth century altered the local power balance, Buganda was able to seize a large piece of Bunyoro territory in 1894. This gain was given treaty sanction in the 1900 Agreement.

The inclusion of Bunyoro territory and people—as well as the tombs of the *Omukamas* (kings)—in Buganda soon brought Banyoro irredentism to the fore. Separatist aspirations were also fanned by feelings of alleged discrimination: in administrative appointments, land and language rights, educational opportunities, medical services, and the administration of justice. No doubt some of these claims were exaggerated,[49] but they do show the depth of Banyoro dissatisfaction with Baganda rule.

Irredentist agitation is of long standing. The present Omukama of Bunyoro dates pressure for the return of the lost counties back to 1898. With the establishment of the Mubende-Bunyoro Committee in 1922 to fight for the return of Bunyoro lands, the issue emerged as a major cause of disagreement within Uganda. Succeeding years were marked by petitions and public statements reaffirming Bunyoro's claim to the

[48] *Uganda Protectorate, Report of the Commission appointed to Review the Boundary between the Districts of Bugisu and Bukedi* (Entebbe: Government Printer, 1962), p. 27.

[49] See *Uganda, Report of a Commission of Privy Counsellors on a Dispute between Buganda and Bunyoro,* Cmnd. 1717 (London: H.M.S.O., 1962), p. 14.

disputed counties. Then, as independence approached, Banyoro bitterness and frustration could no longer be contained and political agitation became mixed with violence.

British authorities decided that they could no longer put off dealing
with the issue of the lost counties. Fearing that the dispute might jeop-
ardize future links between Buganda and Bunyoro (perhaps even lead
to civil war), the Relationships Commission recommended that a referendum be held in the three of the six disputed counties where Banyoro
formed a large part of the population. Banyoro leaders insisted that the
referendum be held in all six counties; the Kabaka refused to agree to
the referendum at all.[50] Iain Macleod, the Colonial Secretary, had
reached an impasse and called for another commission of inquiry.
Banyoro leaders, charging bad faith, walked out of the 1961 conference. On October 13, they asserted that Macleod "deliberately shelved
the issue and . . . failed to implement the promises of himself and
those of the Governor." Banyoro disappointment was keen; it did not
prevent them, however, from cooperating with the commission.

The Molson commission opened hearings on the lost counties in January, 1962. The atmosphere was one of considerable tension with no
spirit of compromise. Banyoro spokesmen insisted on the return of the
counties; Baganda leaders flatly opposed border rectification of any
kind [51] and contended that the commission should limit itself to ending possible discrimination toward Banyoro within the Mubende area.
The British government deliberately delayed publication of the Molson
report until after the general elections in Uganda. It thus sought to insulate the lost counties question from partisan wranglings. Inevitably,
however, the two interacted, enabling the DP to capture the two
Bunyoro seats from the UPC.

Because the Molson commission considered a referendum unnecessary, difficult to administer, and likely to stir tribal tensions, it recommended against such a procedure. Instead it came out in favor of
immediate transfer of the two predominantly Banyoro counties of
Buyaga and Bugangazzi to Bunyoro. It proposed to leave the remaining counties with Buganda.

At the 1962 independence conference, Colonial Secretary Maudling,

[50] Cmnd. 1523, p. 28.
[51] Buganda's bitterness on this aspect of the question can be seen in the government's subsequent publication: *Buganda's Position, II: Lord Molson is Wrong*
(Mmengo: Information Department of Kabaka's Government, 1962).

unable to get Bunyoro and Buganda to agree to this or any other formula, imposed one of his own. This provided for central administration of Buyaga and Bugangazzi counties, to be followed by a referendum after two years in these disputed units. Maudling thus returned to the idea of referendum but left responsibility for its implementation squarely in the hands of Ugandans. This was a prudent move to speed independence. It was also interpreted by some as a "pusillanimous surrender, on the grounds of political expediency, to Buganda intransigence." [52] Suspicious British M.P.'s, seeking a commitment that the referendum would be implemented, received assurances from British authorities that Obote would keep the members' views on this matter in mind. Certainly Britain's ability to influence the situation any further had all but passed away.

Although Obote had agreed to administer the two counties in accordance with the terms of the Maudling settlement, his task was complicated from the outset by the sharp and unfavorable reactions to the imposed settlement in both Bunyoro and Buganda. The Baganda rejected any transfer of territory, and the Banyoro, expressing keen disappointment at Maudling's refusal to apply the Molson recommendations, went so far as to talk of Buganda imperialism. After independence, little that was concrete came from the negotiations between the central and Buganda ministers on the interim arrangements in the counties, and the situation in the disputed areas deteriorated badly. Intimidation, crop slashing, arson, and threats of withholding taxes held sway in the counties. To counter the rising tide of lawlessness, the Buganda government banned the irredentist Mubende-Bunyoro Committee. Just as events seemed to be turning for the worst, Obote successfully concluded an interim arrangement with the Kabaka's government. Under this agreement the Uganda government appointed an administrator with responsibility to maintain law and order and with power to reconsider court judgments. Baganda chiefs, nevertheless, held their offices as before and the Kabaka's government continued to be responsible for the general administration of courts, tax collection, and the control of hospitals, roads, and schools. In fact, the interim arrangement took little away from Buganda.

Shortly after the appointment of the administrator, new troubles occurred in the lost counties. In April, 1963, the Kabaka went on an extended hunting trip in the disputed counties, accompanied by 300 ex-

[52] Letter by J. H. M. Beattie to *Times* (London), July 7, 1962, p. 9.

servicemen. Violence broke out anew, and the central government declared Buyaga county a disturbed area. It soon emerged that the Kabaka had business other than hunting. Baganda leaders, describing this sparsely populated area as a promised land, announced plans to settle some 5,000 ex-servicemen in the area. The Banyoro, threatened by this colony in their midst, gathered about 2,000 ex-servicemen at Hoima in Bunyoro proper. Although the Banyoro disavowed any intentions of invading the lost counties, they were clearly girding themselves for a showdown. On the political stage the Banyoro acted to neutralize Buganda's new offensive. A Bunyoro M.P., doubtless reasoning that only the party in power could help his people, switched from the DP to the UPC. His move gave the UPC a working majority with or without the KY alliance. Bunyoro subsequently did receive support from central minister Adoko Nekyon, who stated on June 12, 1963, that "the Kabaka's Government cannot . . . take people into those counties for the purposes of a referendum in which it doesn't believe." Thus the movement of Banyoro into UPC ranks, as with the Baamba–Bakonjo, indicated that the center had become the guardian of their local interests. Ultimately Obote decided on an early referendum in the two counties, and Bunyoro was the overwhelming victor.

The Impact of Federalism on National Unity

Although tribal pressures doubtless played a significant part in causing Ugandans to include elements of federalism in the constitution, it is difficult to determine the extent to which federalism exacerbated existing tribal tensions. Certainly the knowledge that political action won federal status for five states had an impact on less successful peoples. Similarly the tendency to base statehood on a tribal foundation caused the emergence of movements aimed at border rectification. Federalism with a tribal basis seems to possess inherently unstable features, for it cannot possibly be adapted to fit the overlapping pattern of Uganda's ethnic structure. Efforts to build a sense of national unity are especially vital in preventing bitterness, fear, and separatist tendencies from hindering the growth of a strong and viable state. Clearly Obote sets a higher priority on national unity than on tribal claims, reasonable as the latter might seem within their own context. In a speech on March 23, 1963, he declared that the tribe has "served our people as a basic political unit very well in the past. [But now] the problem of people putting the tribe above national consciousness is a problem that we must face, and an issue we must destroy."

THE ASIAN MINORITY

The place of the Asians [53] in contemporary Uganda has become a vital issue for both the African and Asian communities. On the surface all appears to be normal. Asians continue to be active in their business pursuits, to campaign for and win offices, and to make financial contributions to the political parties. Beneath the surface, however, they are nervously listening to the pulse beats of the larger society about them for clues to the role they will be permitted to play in the decades to come. They are trying to decide whether to become citizens of Uganda, and whether to commit their savings fully to the expansion of their business interests in Uganda or to liquidate these interests while there is still time. One M.P. charged in parliament on December 11, 1962, that Asians had transferred more than £22,000,000 to India since 1959. Although this figure may be too high, considerable funds have certainly been sent abroad.

The position of Asians in Uganda is influenced by three main factors: the exclusiveness of the Asian community, its legal position, and its economic situation. Asian exclusiveness has the history of a strict adherence to certain social, religious, and dietary customs. The separateness of this community, concentrated in towns and devoting its main energies to trade and commerce, gives rise to envy and mistrust.

The discriminatory nature of Uganda's laws is the outgrowth of British paternalism. Colonial administrators attempted to reconcile the Asian's bid for equal protection under the laws with the African's demand for economic (as well as political) mastery in his own house. Major areas of discrimination against Asians (as non-Africans) are trade and employment and taxation. Legal discrimination exists elsewhere as well.

In an attempt to adjust the economic imbalance between Asian and African traders, British authorities placed legal restrictions on trading licenses and varied the rates for fees. Thus the law sanctioned discriminatory provisions against Asians in the area of commerce. For example, a non-African is prohibited under the Trading Ordinance from trading outside a municipality, township, or trading center (except in Buganda, provided he holds a valid license issued before July 31, 1950). Moreover, the fees charged for trading licenses differ among the communities. Hawkers' licenses cost non-Africans 150

[53] In Uganda, the term "Asians" refers to the 63,108 Indians, 5,944 Pakistanis, and 2,824 Goans living there.

shillings and Africans 30 shillings; shop licenses outside the townships and trading centers of Buganda cost non-Africans 45 shillings
and Africans 15 shillings. Such restrictive provisions "do not serve
any useful purpose from the point of view of trade," as former
Minister of Commerce and Industry, C. K. Patel, told Legco on December 7, 1961. It must be recognized, however, that the removal of
economic restrictions might well make Asians more prosperous than
ever. This is to be feared if it means heightened African resentment. To
the extent that Asian prosperity is the consequence of deliberate government policy (aimed at increasing the wealth of the country), Africans may be willing to accept such a policy as the price of economic
development.

Discrimination in land ownership has been partly responsible for
limiting the bulk of the Asian population to the crowded municipalities
and more significant townships and for restricting their economic activity in general. In exceptional cases, magistrates have declared Asians to
be legally "Africans" under the Interpretation and General Clauses
Ordinance. Because the majority of Asians must compete for the few
urban leasehold plots available, the costs are high and the attending
risks great. To be sure, some Asian entrepreneurs scale the restrictive
walls to great commercial success, but little is known about the many
who drop by the wayside.

Outstanding among discriminatory laws originally written to protect
the African in Uganda is the Land Transfer Ordinance. Under this ordinance, any land which is registered in the name of an African may
not be sold or given in any form to a non-African without the written
consent of the Governor-General. A special provision, however, permits
non-Africans to occupy land in Buganda provided the plot is less than
two acres, the transaction is made on a yearly basis, and the undertaking has the written consent of the African owner and the ssaza chief of
the county. In practice such provisions make it extremely difficult for
the Asian community to change from its stereotype of an urbanized,
commercially oriented minority which is detached from the cares and
concerns of the average Ugandan. As of this writing, the Land Transfer Ordinance is still in effect; nevertheless, a court test based on the
fundamental rights of the constitution is a possibility.

The major cause of conflict between Africans and Asians is the vital
role the Asian community plays in the economic life of Uganda. In the
past the Asians performed the role of a middle class placed between
the European administrators and specialists on the one hand and the

majority of the African population on the other. As businessmen, traders, clerks, and artisans they have played significant parts in building a modern economy in Uganda, and many have prospered in the process. Despite restrictive laws intended to encourage African enterprise, Asians have gained extensive control over commercial activities in the country. In part their success was a consequence of the African's lack of training and opportunity in the use of modern business techniques, but in part it was the consequence of the Asian's own initiative and willingness to sacrifice.

The result today is a rather unstable situation. The Africans resent the Asians' prosperity because they see it as gained, unscrupulously in many cases, from the sweat of African brows. They feel themselves discriminated against in the world of business, unable, for example, to secure private credit and commercial bank loans as easily as do their Asian rivals. African bitterness burst into the open with full force during the violent non-African trade boycott of 1959 and 1960, which saw many an Asian trader driven from the countryside and smaller trading centers of Buganda to comparatively safe sanctuary in Kampala. Since the coming of independence African pressure has continued. Asians have been advised to "go from the towns in Buganda" and to sell their cotton ginneries or face ruinous competition; they have been told they would be driven out of trade. More and more pressure is being exerted to force Asians to make a place for Africans in the world of business. Although Asians have responded by employing more and more African clerks in their stores, Asian control of business remains fundamentally unchanged.

Asians fear that in the future they will not have an equal opportunity to secure posts in the civil service. The 1962 report on Africanization recommended that in the future "the civil service should fairly represent the proportionate racial composition of the Territory." Considering the high percentage of Asians with advanced training and skills, this proviso might work a hardship on Asian candidates.

Without question the Asian community has, at present, an important part to play. Uganda needs the capital the Asian community has at its disposal. Moreover, Asian merchants, traders, artisans, and professional men constitute a valuable source of energy and ability. Trained Asian personnel (such as clerks and accountants) are willing to accept lower living standards than anyone else of comparable qualifications or abilities—black or white. In an area of vast underdevelopment, their ability can be viewed as complementary to, rather than a displacement of African skill and initiative. This seems particularly true at a time when Africanization of the civil service will drain off most trained Africans into the public sector of the economy. Therefore, since Uganda does not now have adequate capital or personnel available to promote all the necessary projects the general welfare requires, a sizable field is left open to entrepreneurs willing to run the risks of private investment.

The future position of the Asian community in Uganda will be determined finally by the larger community in which it operates. To the extent that the government wishes to use Asian talents, and the Africans are aware of Asian contributions, the Asian community can make a major contribution toward the building of a new Uganda. But Asians can only break the cycle of economic prosperity and resentment by identifying themselves, and being identified as, citizens of Uganda, which means becoming fully integrated in the life of the country. Whether this will happen and whether a fatal time lag will be created before the Africans accept the Asians in their new role are questions that remain crucial to the well-being and security of this community.

ECONOMIC DEVELOPMENT

In order to raise living standards in Uganda, means must be found to expand agricultural incomes, diversify exports, attract capital, and expand consumer purchasing power. As noted before, agriculture is the key to the country's progress. Agricultural incomes must increase if secondary industries are to be developed and the gulf between urban and rural areas is to shrink. This increase can be achieved by bringing new areas under cultivation (as is being done with coffee) and by more intensive farming. Expansion of estate farming accounts for a rising share of sugar, tea, and coffee exports. This type of farming is more adaptable to new techniques, machinery, fertilizers and seeds than is peasant agriculture. The bulk of exports, however, is still accounted for by small-holder cultivation. Investment must therefore be made in this sector in order to increase the peasant farmer's productivity per acre. With this in mind the World Bank mission recommended drawing on the cotton marketing-board funds for technical and capital assistance to cotton farmers.

Although incomes from cotton and, to a lesser extent, coffee seem reasonably secure under present market conditions, sound planning would seem to dictate some diversification, even if it will take time to effect. Uganda is by no means immune to the vicissitudes of price fluctuations. Coffee is vulnerable over the long term, since it is cultivated extensively in Latin America and elsewhere. Other possible mainstays include cocoa, tea, tobacco, sisal, and sugar.

Uganda's leaders must also determine the best means of attracting capital for development—both in agriculture and industry. They speak frequently of the need to encourage foreign and domestic private investment. But large investors are at present hesitant to commit themselves because of the limited size of Uganda's market, the low level of consumer purchasing power, the possible difficulties of transferring funds outside the country, and the general concern about the role the non-African communities are to play. Europeans and Asians cannot expand their estates in the face of racial land barriers, and they are not welcomed in certain industrial and commercial pursuits. There is the danger that the indigenous non-African population will not invest new capital in Uganda; in fact indications of this are already apparent.

Several events have increased Asians' uncertainty about their future in Uganda. On April 2, 1963, for example, the Minister of Agriculture and Cooperatives told parliament that if cotton ginners did not sell their ginneries to the cooperative unions soon, the government would lend the unions money to build new ginneries. Even if this policy is in the national interest, the manner of the announcement was ominous. Clearly grievances against ginnery exploitation are deep and just. Also the government has an obligation to press for Africanization in the private as well as the public sphere. But only if the non-African communities are assured of their future place in the country is a rapid expansion of the economy likely. Ugandans must choose between complete Africanization and the utilization of non-African skills and capital.

Finally, industrial development presupposes a rising consumer purchasing power. Consumer demand is restrained by governmental action in two ways: the taxation of agricultural exports and the retention of surplus profits by marketing boards. Funds from these sources have been spent usefully on roads, railroads, social welfare, and industrial ventures. But their use on these projects is not an unmitigated blessing. The growth of consumer and secondary industries depends upon an expansion of private purchasing power. If the government wishes to encourage consumer and secondary enterprises, it will have to balance its spending on services, infrastructure, and long-term investments against the needs of private capital.

EDUCATION

As in so many countries where education is the key to economic development, efficient administration, and personal advancement, educational policy has not remained insulated from politics in Uganda. Three problems have received particular attention: the proper rate and nature of educational expansion, missionary influence on the school system, and academic content and standards.

It is difficult to see how Uganda can make rapid educational progress at all levels concurrently. The World Bank report recommended concentration on secondary and higher education. Each year thousands of students must terminate their education because there are insufficient places in senior secondary schools.[54] It was felt that the country greatly needed the trained personnel that would be provided by expanding the upper levels of education. Moreover, primary education need not stand still. Mainly through duplication in existing facilities, 90,000 primary-school places were unfilled in 1962. With proper planning these could be utilized with little increased expenditure.

The rejection of the ideal of universal primary education has not sat well with some Ugandans. At the national level discontent with the "conservative" educational policy of the government erupted in November, 1962. Government backbenchers pressed for a greater commitment to primary education. As a result the government appointed a commission which reviewed the country's entire education program. At the district level the Lango branch of the UPC won office with a promise to introduce free universal primary education. It soon found itself in difficulty with the central government, which refused to approve the large budget deficit incurred by the proposed increase in educational expenditure.

Mission influence on the school system provides the second target for critics of the educational system. Mission dominance in education is still apparent. Of those between sixteen and forty-five years of age, 51 per cent of the Christians have been to school compared with only 3 per cent of the pagans. The government assumed control of the schools in December, 1963, influenced, in part, by widespread objections to the amount of religious instruction in the schools; the duplication of facilities at the local level; the refusal to admit qualified candidates of other faiths; the poor academic standards of some mission schools; and, on another level, what is said to be the corruption of the African personality through the instillation of Western values. In addition, it was felt that the division between Protestant and Catholic schools created con-

[54] The Uganda school system has six years primary, two years junior secondary, and four years senior secondary school, two years study for the higher school certificate, and finally university education.

flict. As E. M. K. Mulira declared in a debate on educational policy: "No nation can grow when it is divided at the root of its existence." [55]

There is finally the problem of educational content and standards. Can a country with a desperate need for trained African personnel afford the same standards as the West? Moreover, what kind of education is suitable to a developing country? It is argued that education should be attuned to the needs of an agricultural society and concentrate less on academic subjects. Most Africans see this as second-class education. They are more interested in changing the syllabus at all levels to concentrate less on British materials and more on African subject matter. Many steps in this direction have already been taken. One interesting example is the introduction of an African studies program at Makerere University College.

THE PRESS AND RADIO

The media of communication present two problems: their lack of penetration into the rural areas, and the degree of government control. As of 1963 there were four daily newspapers in Uganda, two in English and two in Luganda. All are published in Kampala and their total circulation was less than 50,000. In addition, a few weekly and monthly newspapers were published in various vernaculars. These were predominantly mission newspapers; of 59,000 people reading the mission press, 56,000 read Catholic newspapers. In a country with a Catholic political party, the mission press would seem likely to help to buttress the DP as other factors work against it.

But more important than the dominance of the Catholic or the Luganda press is the failure of newspapers to reach the mass of the population. This is largely a matter of illiteracy. In the transmission of national political news to the villages, traditional means of oral communication still dominate.

Early in 1963, the government announced that it intended to publish a newspaper in Luganda. In part this was an attempt to meet the need for more newspapers. A more important motivation was the desire to present the UPC point of view in Buganda. The government's decision to publish its own newspaper, although justified in itself, raised the larger question of governmental control of communication.

Thus far government intrusion on the freedom of the press has been limited to the emergency period following the 1964 mutinies. Neverthe-

[55] Uganda, *National Assembly Debates*, Second Series, 1st Session, Part III (Nov. 23, 1962), p. 676.

less, it is important to note that the English-speaking press, run by non-Africans, is often criticized for handling news in a way unfavorable to the government. After one such incident a minister stated that he did not believe in freedom of the press.[56] More common is the warning that the press must play a constructive role. There is a possibility that the ideology of African solidarity may fuse with the administrative heritage of the colonial era, causing increased interference with freedom of speech and of the press.

Unlike the press, radio broadcasting is a government enterprise. Television, which has already been introduced, is, like radio, under the Ministry of Information, Broadcasting, and Tourism. Although supervised by a department of government, these media are meant to be independent of political control. Both the DP and KY have made pointed attacks on political interference in Radio Uganda, particularly concerning treatment of news.[57] It would be a mistake, however, to exaggerate the degree of direct UPC control over the radio.

External Affairs

After independence, the Obote government moved quietly and cautiously in domestic affairs; in external relations its style was more dramatic and its pace swifter. Obote's over-all policy rests on four main pillars: nonalignment, the dismantling of remaining pockets of colonialism in Africa, close relations with neighboring countries, and the advancement of African interests in its dealings with the outside world. Taken as a whole, these policies identify Uganda with "progressive" African opinion generally but not with any African bloc in particular.

The Obote government has consistently called for a policy of nonalignment in the cold war struggle. For example, on March 4, 1963, during his visit to the Sudan, Obote declared: "We in Uganda are against any political blocs in Africa or in the world. We don't believe in a divided Africa or foreign bases. . . . We believe in non-alignment." By "nonalignment" he did not mean strict neutrality. He has made it clear that Uganda must participate in shaping world affairs which affect it, criticizing and supporting whatever the nation sees fit. His government's support for admission of the People's Republic of China to the United Nations is an indication of Uganda's determination to move freely among the world's power groups.

[56] *Uganda Argus* (Kampala), Dec. 19, 1962, p. 4.
[57] *Ibid.*, Dec. 13, 1962, p. 4; *Uganda Nation* (Kampala), Jan. 7, 1963, p. 1; Jan. 8, 1963, p. 1.

Obote has also been quite explicit about ending all traces of colonialism in Africa (under which he includes the entrenchment of white power in South Africa). Because he considered Uganda to be directly concerned with Kenya's political status (as a consequence of their common membership in the East African Common Services Organization), he intervened on Kenya's behalf in its independence movement, with an eye to quickening the pace of its political progress. The significance of this strategy is hard to evaluate, yet it is interesting to note that Duncan Sandys, the Commonwealth Secretary, did hold discussions with Obote in Kampala just prior to returning to Kenya in March, 1963, to announce Kenya's constitutional changes. In addition, the Obote government has firmly supported African nationalist movements in Angola, Mozambique, Southern Rhodesia, and South Africa. Uganda has refused to have diplomatic relations with the governments of these states, and Prime Minister Obote offered his country as an anticolonial training-ground at the African summit conference at Addis Ababa in 1963. Uganda's leaders back UN sanctions against South Africa and demand an effective boycott of South African goods.

To build close relations with neighboring countries is another major goal of Obote's foreign policy. Uganda's relations with the Congo (Léopoldville) and the Sudan are not without their complications. Many refugees from both countries have crossed into Uganda, and during the Rwenzururu emergency in Toro, a number of Ugandans sought safe sanctuary in the Congo. Moreover, when skirmishes occurred between Sudanese and Congolese forces in December, 1962, Ugandan troops were sent to the West Nile as a precautionary move. Obote has acted to clear up any misunderstanding arising from Uganda's activities. After holding extensive talks with Congolese Defense Minister Anany in March, 1962, Obote's office announced plans to set up a Congo export-import agency and to send food worth £10,000 to the Congolese army. Uganda and the Congo also agreed to an exchange of embassies. A week later, Obote visited the Sudan and discussed matters of common interest with President Abboud. The upshot of these consultations was an agreement on educational exchange and a general relaxation of tensions arising from border and refugee problems.

RELATIONS WITH KENYA AND TANGANYIKA

Uganda has had even more intimate relations with its neighbors to the east. The interdependence of Kenya, Tanganyika, and Uganda is becoming more evident each year. In political matters their leaders cooperate in PAFMECSA (Pan-African Freedom Movement of East, Central, Southern Africa). They often present a united diplomatic front, as when they rejected associate status in EEC at the 1962 Commonwealth Prime Ministers Conference. In May, 1963, Uganda and Tanganyika agreed on the need for close coordination of defense matters in East Africa; thenceforth any military attack on one East African land would be viewed as an attack on all. The University of East Africa represents a regional approach to higher education. Economic coordination is implicit in the adoption of common customs, tariffs, and currency. Kenyans purchase cotton piece goods, sugar and low-priced Owen Falls power from Uganda; Ugandans buy Kenya's wheat, dairy products, and manufactured goods and make continuous use of Kenya's harbor facilities.

Moreover, the three territories are gaining in common experience through the East African Common Services Organization (EACSO). As a consequence of vehement opposition to political federation in the past, EACSO is specifically designed as an administrative union concerned with technical, not political, coordination. The emphasis is upon equality of rights and obligations. Each of the contracting governments must consent to all changes in the agreement. The executive, which consists of the principal elected minister in each country, reaches decisions on a unanimous basis. The Central Legislative Assembly is composed of a Speaker, a Secretary-General, and a Legal Secretary; each country sends equal numbers of ministerial and elected members. The Organization administers a wide range of services: the East African Railways and Harbours Administration, the East African Posts and Telecommunications Administration, the Desert Locust Survey, the East African Customs and Excise Department, the East African Research Services, and many others. It is also authorized to enact laws with respect to universities in East Africa, administration of income taxes, civil aviation, merchant shipping, and meteorology. Although these wide-ranging activities are likely to make few headlines, they are nevertheless of great importance to the well-being of East Africa.[58]

The establishment of these interterritorial administrations and authorities stands as concrete evidence of progress toward unity in the region as a whole. But can this structure be held together in its present

[58] For a fuller account see Donald Rothchild, "Uganda and Federation," *Spearhead* (Dar es Salaam), I (Sept., 1962); "East African Federation," *Transition* (Kampala), III (Jan.–Feb., 1964); and *Toward Unity in Africa: A Study of Federalism in British Africa* (Washington, D.C.: Public Affairs Press, 1960), p. 54.

form if it is not backed by greater legislative power? Federation, long regarded apprehensively by Africans in the three lands, is now seen by many as a fulfillment of African aspirations. Official support for federation emerged from the Nairobi summit meeting of June, 1963; at this top-level conference the leaders of Kenya, Uganda, and Tanganyika formally committed themselves, in principle, to the establishment of political federation by the end of the year. "The achievement of truly popular Governments in each country," the leaders jointly declared, "removes fears of minority or settler domination under Federation." They viewed regional federation as a practical step toward the larger goal of pan-African unity. Immediately after this momentous statement was issued, a working party assembled in Dar es Salaam to make proposals for the federation's constitution.

Beneath the surface, however, a number of impediments to regional integration remain. Leaders in East Africa disagree on such issues as industrial location, a unified railway rate structure, the distribution of revenue, the head of state, and the allocation of powers between the center and regions. Perhaps most crucial is whether the countries and their constituent parts will sacrifice hard-earned political power. In Uganda, Buganda has openly expressed reservations. On January 4, 1963, Buganda Legal Officer Fred Mpanga, speaking for the Kabaka's government, cautioned East African leaders against forcing the pace toward federation. That same month the Buganda Lukiiko gave unanimous support to a declaration rejecting federation. After the three national leaders agreed to federation in Nairobi, Buganda's leaders cast about for a policy on federation which would be pan-Africanist and preserve the kingdom's identity at the same time. Pan-African pressures caused some KY members of the National Assembly to shift to the UPC. Pressures for national integrity brought demands for a loose federal structure and appeals for central respect of Buganda's powers under the constitution; thus, L. N. Basudde, the acting katikkiro, stated on June 27, 1963: "Buganda is not going to surrender her powers to the proposed Government of East Africa. It is the Uganda Government that has got to surrender some of its powers." The nature of federation has changed, but the Baganda remain as fearful as ever of being submerged in a wide regional grouping.

Subsequent to Buganda's declaration, the Uganda government displayed hesitancy about plunging into federation. At first the signs were few and irregular. Then, in August, 1963, the head of Uganda's delegation to the Dar es Salaam working-party meeting, Adoko

Nekyon, gave the first official indication of differences at the negotiations; the delegations, he declared, had failed to reach agreement on such matters as the civil service, the organization of the legislature (whether it was to be unicameral or bicameral), and the division of powers between the center and the parts. In reply to claims that Uganda was delaying regional unity, Nekyon asserted on August 21, 1963: "I am not prepared just to throw my nation into darkness, so I must know exactly where we are going and to whom we are surrendering our powers."

During the following month there were more signs of hesitation. Obote's sudden illness in mid-September caused a postponement of the federation summit talks in Nairobi. Meanwhile Nekyon told the Uganda National Assembly that small states like his had "some fears" about an East African Federation. It became progressively clearer that the 1963 date for the implementation of federation was premature. Then, on October 24, 1963, Kenya's Minister of State, Joseph Murumbi, caused a stir by asserting that he did not "know whether we will succeed in bringing about an East African Federation, but I think we will at least bring about a Federation of Tanganyika and Kenya, and Uganda might come in at a later stage." On the following day Prime Minister Obote told a press conference that he wanted an explanation from the Prime Minister of Kenya on the Murumbi statement before he would attend further summit meetings on federation, and he added: "It does no harm to Uganda if she joins now or later, and if they want to go ahead let them do it." Although Kenya's Prime Minister did subsequently dissociate his government from the Murumbi statement, much damage had been done.

In the period from the Obote–Murumbi exchange in October, 1963, until the East African mutinies in January, 1964, the excitement over Kenya's and Zanzibar's independence temporarily diverted some attention from the federation issue. Ugandans spoke of the commitment "in principle" to federation. At the same time, however, they became more insistent upon the need for caution and warned specifically of the necessity to safeguard the interests of small states.

The Zanzibar *coup d'état* and the East African army mutinies brought matters to a head. Since all of East Africa was affected by the crisis, a joint approach to military problems seemed essential—both in this instance and in the future. Yet in the wake of the mutinies it became evident that military insecurity had not been a spur to interterritorial integration. Just as soon as the mutinies were crushed, the sense of common danger disappeared and the push toward East African Federation lost momentum. East Africans were not yet ready to pool their military forces. Dr. Obote gave an indication of a difference of approach on February 6, 1964, when he told Uganda's National Assembly that though the recent incidents in East Africa might speed talks on federation, the answer to the area's military problems really lay in continental African unity. In March, the extent of the divergence on military policy became evident as Tanganyika split with its East African partners by rejecting Britain's offer to train pilots from the three countries at its flying facilities in Kenya. By adopting different training systems, East Africans passed over an important opportunity to coordinate defense arrangements.

Another major crisis in East African unity affected the common market arrangement. Nsilo Swai, Tanganyika's Minister of Development Planning, surprised a secret conference on the coordination of economic planning at Entebbe in March, 1964, when he noted that his government was considering setting up tariffs and import quotas on Kenyan and Ugandan goods as well as establishing a separate currency. His announcement marked the culmination of growing dissatisfaction in Tanganyika both with the delays in negotiations on federation and with the alleged inequalities in the common market arrangement. A conference of East African leaders met in Nairobi in early April to discuss Tanganyika's proposals for limiting trade with her common market partners. At the conclusion of the talks, the conferees issued a statement in which they agreed to appoint an emergency committee to examine trade relations within East Africa. The statement also included assurances by the Tanganyikans that they did not intend to withdraw from the common market.

A Ministerial Emergency Committee, consisting of the three ministers of Finance and the three ministers for Commerce and Industries, held meetings throughout April, 1964, to find ways to ensure a more equitable sharing of benefits in the common market. The committee reached agreement by the end of the month. Trade imbalances among the East African countries were to be redressed by the creation of import quotas and of a new system of industrial licensing. The three East African heads of government accepted these proposals and a serious crisis in interterritorial cooperation was averted. East Africans remained committed "in principle" to federation. Nevertheless, it was becoming increasingly clear that such a goal could not be attained without lengthy negotiations.

During the following months new light was shed on the negotiations for federation. In Kenya and Tanganyika parliamentary backbenchers of both majority parties showed increasing signs of dissatisfaction with the inconclusiveness of the working-party meetings on federation. In April, the backbenchers took matters into their own hands and demanded rapid strides toward unity. By the following month, backbench pressure had become intense, and both Prime Minister Jomo Kenyatta of Kenya and President Julius Nyerere of Tanganyika felt impelled to warn their supporters against any irresponsible action. Nyerere specifically refused to "drag" others into a federation; Kenyatta described backbench efforts to force through a federation as premature. When Kenyatta opposed a motion, sponsored in Kenya's House of Representatives by Kenya African National Union backbenchers, calling upon the government to present instruments of federation for ratification by August 15, 1964, he went down to an unprecedented defeat. Kenyatta subsequently regained his previous control over KANU but not before displaying to all the world the gulf between leaders and backbench M.P.'s on this issue.

Uganda's unwillingness to commit itself at that time to federation also became apparent. It was significant that no Ugandans attended the backbenchers' Nairobi conference in early May. And when the recommendations of this backbenchers' conference were presented to Obote, they met with a firm rebuff. Obote expressed resentment of the general manner with which the backbench M.P.'s approached their task, and he pointedly told their representatives that Kenya and Tanganyika should go ahead with federation if they wished but that Uganda was not prepared to enter the proposed union at that time. He added: "I don't believe that the question of federating Tanganyika and Kenya is as easy as you think."

Then, as the Tanganyika National Assembly debated the backbenchers' call for swift implementation of federation, more information was obtained on Uganda's position. Tanganyika External Affairs Minister Oscar Kambona revealed that Uganda Minister of Internal Affairs Felix Onama had indicated to him on May 30, 1964, at the working-party meeting in Kampala the view of the Uganda delegation: that a political federation was not feasible at present. Uganda's unwillingness to enter a federation for the time being became public knowledge that June. Uganda spokesmen still did not oppose federation, but they sought firm guarantees for their interests as well as more time to work out difficulties. And Adoko Nekyon, now Minister of Planning, indicated that these difficulties were indeed extensive. Ugandans demanded the location of the federal capital in their country, the right of secession from the proposed federation, the authority to conduct their own foreign affairs and to control their labor unions, restrictions on freedom of movement within the federation, continuance of territorial (as opposed to East African) citizenship, and the creation of a senate. As these points indicate, Uganda's stress on safeguarding her position by limiting federal powers was in direct contrast with the stated policies of Kenyan and Tanganyikan leaders. Uganda today supports—even wishes to strengthen—EACSO and the common market; its leaders also remain committed in principle to federation, although it is not possible to predict when or in what form their goal will be put into effect.

RELATIONS WITH NON-AFRICAN STATES

What of Uganda's relations with the outside world? Uganda is an active member of both the Commonwealth and the United Nations. It has concluded agreements for technical and capital assistance with the United Kingdom, Israel, the United States, and other countries, and with the World Bank and the United Nations Special Fund. Its students attend eastern European as well as western universities. Moreover, Uganda welcomes private foreign capital, provided that it complements the development of its economy.

Independent Uganda faces a major foreign policy test in relation to the European Common Market. The growth of an economically dynamic Europe has made EEC a particularly attractive market to the countries of East Africa that produce commodities and raw materials. An increasing proportion of Uganda's trade over the past ten years has been with the Common Market area. Whereas 48.8 per cent of Uganda's imports and 26.4 per cent of its exports were with the United Kingdom in 1950, these percentages had shrunk to 26.2 per cent and 13.9 per cent respectively by 1960. Imports from the Common Market rose from 8.7 per cent to 14 per cent and exports climbed from 6.6 per cent to 15.4 per cent during the same period. It is important to note, however, that exports to Britain picked up considerably in 1961 and 1962.

Britain's failure to enter EEC in 1962 made less urgent Uganda's decision on its future relations with the Common Market. The various possible courses of action themselves remain unchanged, however. Uganda could try to obtain associate status, follow a "go it alone" policy, assist in forming an African common market, seek to build up a Commonwealth market, or negotiate trade agreements.

Like all English-speaking African states, except Sierra Leone, Uganda rejects associate status on principle. The leaders of these countries fear that such a relationship with the Common Market would obligate them politically to the West, inhibit African unity, and relegate African nations permanently to the position of producers of primary products for advanced markets. They are suspicious of the "reciprocity" provisions of the Rome Treaty, which provide for a progressive abolition of customs duties on imports from members and associated states. Leaders in the English-speaking states fear that this arrangement might severely hamper the growth of industries in Africa. They consider that neither the allowances made for the developmental and fiscal needs of the associated states nor the present program of economic assistance would compensate for the advantages given the industrial states. Whether well-founded or not, these apprehensions of "neo-colonialism" are very real.

On his return from London in September, 1962, Prime Minister Obote strongly opposed entering the Common Market. He spoke skeptically of the political implications of associating with Europe at a time when the latter was moving toward federation. He also criticized EEC as a "rich man's club" interested only in Africa's markets and raw materials. But will nonassociation put Uganda's exports to the Common Market at a disadvantage with those of her French-speaking neighbors? If EEC should place a tariff on exports from nonassociated states while admitting duty-free the same items from associated members, Uganda might be put in an awkward position. Roughly half of its goods would still enter duty-free, but the remainder would be seriously affected if the tariffs cause trade patterns to change. Its markets might become uncertain and prices for its products might fluctuate widely. Such a situation would make economic planning difficult unless alternative markets could be found. One Ugandan, seeking to prevent a possible conflict between ideology and national interest in this case, has cautiously written of the need to reappraise associate status if Uganda's justifiable doubts about the scheme were eliminated.[59] This view is unlikely to gain much support as long as other choices remain.

[59] R. J. Mukasa, "E.E.C. and its Meaning for Uganda," *Uganda Argus* (Kampala), October 26, 1962, p. 4. For an excellent discussion of African attitudes toward associate status in the Common Market, see Ali A. Mazrui, "African Attitudes to the European Economic Community," *International Affairs*, XXXIX (Jan., 1963), pp. 24–36.

Of the other possibilities, three have only limited significance for the present. A "go it alone" policy flies in the face of the trend toward regional groupings throughout the world. Such a policy, which would increase Uganda's isolation, seems dangerous. The idea of an African common market, however, has emotional appeal. Its impracticability for the present lies in the low level of trade between the African states as well as in their general lack of complementary economies (that is, many of their exports are identical and they do not produce a wide range of needed goods for one another). Another proposal—a common market embracing the Commonwealth states—might overcome some of the difficulties inherent in a common market based solely on African countries. Nevertheless, present trade trends mark out continental Europe, rather than the Commonwealth allies, as the generally faster growing market.

The last possibility—trade agreements—is the most popular one now. Obote favors this course because such agreements are fully compatible with his country's newly won sovereignty. Consequently, in the spring of 1963, Uganda joined an East African mission which held exploratory talks with Britain and "the Six." It is felt that trade agreements would bring economic advantages without political commitments. Yet nobody knows whether this form of association can guarantee Uganda either permanent markets or equal trade terms. What conditions will President de Gaulle exact in his effort to protect the Eurafrican market he is now painstakingly constructing? At this early stage Ugandans have not clearly determined the implications of trade policy in terms of the country's national interest. Setting these priorities remains a major uncompleted task.

Bibliography

Political science and sociology are relative late-comers to the literature on Uganda. Except for the scholarly efforts of anthropologists during the colonial interlude, our knowledge of Uganda in the years from the signing of the Uganda Agreement in 1900 to the end of World War II, and perhaps even to independence in 1962, is fragmentary and disorganized. Little systematic analysis has been made.

It is striking that most of the research with a wide circulation has been done by non-Ugandans, who in most cases have had limited facility with local languages. Research by political scientists and sociologists, and, in particular, by Ugandans themselves is thus clearly needed. As of late, some effort has been made to close the gap. The East African Institute of Social Research at Makerere University College now includes more political scientists on its staff, and various British publishers have signed contracts with East African scholars to write monographs and textbooks for distribution in Africa and abroad. Even so, it is likely to be some time before the number of studies, especially those by African writers, begins to meet the demand.

Although interviews and official documents—the two main sources for this study—are means of information often not available in Europe and North America, the serious student can expect to find the following materials a helpful starting point for an understanding of modern Uganda. Some of the key works are discussed first, followed by a selected list of readings.

Outstanding among recent studies of the history and character of politics in Buganda are David E. Apter, *The Political Kingdom in Uganda* (Princeton: Princeton University Press, 1961), and D. A. Low and R. Cranford Pratt, *Buganda and British Overrule 1900–1955* (London: Oxford University Press, 1960). By focusing primarily on the Buganda historical and political scene, however, both books leave to other writers the task of preparing a modern political history of the rest of Uganda. Some assistance to this end is given by D. A. Low's short paperback entitled *Political Parties in Uganda 1949–62* (London: University of London Institute of Commonwealth Studies, Commonwealth Studies No. 8, 1962), but much research still remains to be done on this subject.

H. B. Thomas and R. Scott, *Uganda* (London: Oxford University Press, 1935), provides valuable historical material on the colonial period; Raymond Leslie Buell's chapter on Uganda in *The Native Problem in Africa,* Volume I, Section VI (New York: Macmillan, 1928), is also helpful in this respect. Two other useful sources are Kenneth Ingham's books: *The Making of Modern Uganda* (London: George Allen & Unwin, 1958) and *A History of East Africa* (New York: Praeger, 1962), although these suffer somewhat from the tendency to see African developments through European eyes. The new Oxford *History of East Africa* attempts to compensate for this imbalance; yet thus far, only Volume I, edited by Roland Oliver and Gervase Mathew (Oxford: Oxford University Press, 1963), has been published.

Even though comparatively little sociological research has been undertaken to date, any serious student of modern African politics should know the important study of life in two Kampala areas by Aidan W. Southall and P. C. W. Gutkind: *Townsmen in the Making* (Kampala: East African Institute of Social Research, 1957). The East African Institute will shortly publish a number of volumes on similar and related topics.

Other significant, and readily available, materials include the British government's annual reports on Uganda, which cover much of the colonial period; *The Atlas of Uganda* (Kampala: Department of Lands and Surveys, 1962); and the debates of the Uganda Legislative Council and National Assembly, of the British House of Commons and House of Lords, and of the Central Legislative Assembly of the East African Common Services Organization.

SELECTED DOCUMENTS

East African Common Services Organization. *Economic and Statistical Review* (December, 1963). Nairobi: Government Printer, 1964.

East Africa Royal Commission 1953–1955 Report. Cmd. 9475. London: H.M.S.O., 1955.

Uganda Government. *The First Five-Year Development Plan, 1961/62–1965/66.* Entebbe: Government Printer, 1963.

Uganda Government. *Report of the Commissioners for Africanization,* 3 Parts. Entebbe: Government Printer, 1962.

Uganda (Independence) Order in Council, 1962. L.N. 251 of 1962 (October 6, 1962), pp. 777–947.

Uganda Protectorate. *The East African Common Services Organization Ordinance 1961.* Entebbe: Government Printer, 1961.

Uganda Protectorate. *Report of the Uganda Fiscal Commission.* Entebbe: Government Printer, 1962.

Uganda Protectorate. *Report of the Uganda Relationships Commission, 1961.* Entebbe: Government Printer, 1961.

Uganda. *Report of a Commission of Privy Counsellors on a Dispute between Buganda and Bunyoro.* Cmnd. 1717. London: H.M.S.O., 1962.

Uganda. *Report of the Uganda Constitutional Conference, 1961.* Cmnd. 1523. London: H.M.S.O., 1961.

OTHER BOOKS AND PAMPHLETS

Beattie, John. *Bunyoro: An African Kingdom.* New York: Holt, Rinehart, and Winston, 1960.

Burke, Fred G. *Local Government and Politics in Uganda.* Syracuse: Syracuse University Press, 1964.

Cohen, Sir Andrew. *British Policy in Changing Africa.* Evanston: Northwestern University Press, 1959. An interpretation of British policy and administration by a former Governor of Uganda.

Driberg, J. H. *The Lango.* London: T. Fisher Unwin, 1923.

Edel, May Mandelbaum. *The Chiga of Western Uganda.* New York: Oxford University Press, 1957.

Elkan, Walter. *The Economic Development of Uganda.* London: Oxford University Press, 1961. A useful brief treatment.

Elkan, Walter. *Migrants and Proletarians.* London: Oxford University Press, 1960. The character of Uganda's work force.

Fallers, Lloyd A. *Bantu Bureaucracy.* Cambridge: W. Heffer and Sons, 1956. The conflict between traditional and modern methods of government among the Basoga.

Girling, F. K. *The Acholi in Uganda.* London: H.M.S.O., 1960.

Goldthorpe, J. E. *Outlines of East African Society.* Kampala: Makerere University College, 1962. Information on Uganda's social structure.

Hailey, Lord. *Native Administration in the British African Territories,* Part I. London: H.M.S.O., 1950. Analyzes native administration in Uganda.

Haydon, E. S. *Law and Justice in Buganda.* London: Butterworths, 1960. A careful examination of Buganda's legal system.

Hunter, Guy. *The New Societies of Tropical Africa.* London: Oxford University Press, 1962. Good general discussion of African economic problems.

Ingrams, Harold. *Uganda: A Crisis of Nationhood.* London: H.M.S.O., 1960. A broad survey of Uganda society and politics.

Lawrence, J. C. D. *The Iteso.* London: Oxford University Press, 1957.

Low, D. A. *Religion and Society in Buganda 1875–1900.* Kampala: East African Institute of Social Research; East African Studies No. 8, 1956. The acceptance of Christianity in Buganda.

Mair, Lucy. *Primitive Government.* Harmondsworth: Penguin Books, 1962. Includes much useful material on indigenous political systems.

Mission of the International Bank for Reconstruction and Development. *The Economic Development of Uganda.* Baltimore: The Johns Hopkins Press, 1962. The nature of Uganda's economy and recommendations for its development.

Oliver, Roland. *The Missionary Factor in East Africa.* London: Longmans, Green, 1952. Analyzes work and impact of missions in East Africa.

Richards, Audrey I., ed. *East African Chiefs.* London: Faber and Faber, 1960. British impact on tribal government among several Uganda peoples.

Roscoe, John. *The Baganda.* London: Macmillan, 1911. Standard anthropological study on the Baganda.

Rothchild, Donald. *Toward Unity in Africa: A Study of Federalism in British Africa.* Washington, D.C.: Public Affairs Press, 1960. Discusses Uganda's role in East African federation.

Southall, Aidan W. *Alur Society.* Cambridge: W. Heffer and Sons, 1956. A tribal study with theoretical interest.

Sloan, Ruth C. "Uganda," in Helen Kitchen, ed., *The Educated African.* New York: Praeger, 1962.

Welbourn, F. B. *East African Rebels: A Study of Some Independent*

Churches. London: SCM Press, 1961. Discusses, *inter alia*, role of missions in Buganda.

ARTICLES AND PERIODICALS

Beattie, John. "Democratization in Bunyoro," *Civilizations*, XI (1961), 7–18.

East Africa and Rhodesia (London). A conservative weekly magazine with coverage of East African developments.

Ehrlich, Cyril. "Some Social and Economic Implications of Paternalism in Uganda," *Journal of African History*, IV (1963), 275–285.

Engholm, G. F. "The Westminster Model in Uganda," *International Journal*, XVIII (Autumn, 1963), 468–487.

Gertzel, C. J. "New Government in Uganda," *Africa Report*, VII (May, 1962), 7–8, 10.

Ingrams, Harold. "Uganda and Nationhood," *Corona*, XIV (July and August, 1962), 274–278, 300–303.

Low, Anthony. "The British and the Baganda," *International Affairs*, XXXII (July, 1956), 308–317.

Lowenkopf, Martin. "Uganda: Prelude to Independence," *Parliamentary Affairs*, XV (Winter, 1961–62), 74–86.

Makerere Journal (Kampala). A publication of the Faculty of Arts, Makerere University College.

Nye, Joseph S., Jr. "East African Economic Integration," *Journal of Modern African Studies*, I (December, 1963), 475–502.

Pratt, R. Cranford. "East Africa: The Pattern of Political Development," *University of Toronto Quarterly*, XXXI (October, 1961), 110–124.
———. "Nationalism in Uganda," *Political Studies*, IX (June, 1961), 157–178.
———. "A Paradox in Africa," *Listener*, LXIII (April 28, 1960), 739–741.

Proceedings of the East African Institute of Social Research Conference (Kampala). Papers presented to the semiannual conference held by the Institute.

Roberts, A. D. "The Sub-Imperialism of the Baganda," *Journal of African History*, III (1962), 435–450.

Rosberg, Carl G., with Segal, Aaron. "An East African Federation," *International Conciliation*, No. 543 (May, 1963), 1–72.

Rothchild, Donald. "East African Federation," *Transition*, III (January–February, 1964), 39–42.

Uganda Journal (Kampala). Contains much valuable historical material.

NEWSPAPERS AND MAGAZINES

East Africa Journal (Nairobi). Deals with East African problems.
Reporter (Nairobi). Weekly East African news magazine.

Spearhead (Dar es Salaam). A liberal monthly with articles on the East African countries which ceased publication during 1963.

Transition (Kampala). A journal of the arts, culture, and society.

Uganda Argus (Kampala). Oldest Kampala daily newspaper.

VI

ETHIOPIA

By ROBERT L. HESS

University of Illinois at Chicago

Introduction

ETHIOPIA has long exerted a powerful influence on the imagination both of scholars and of laymen. Archaeologists and classicists have attempted to unravel the mysteries of the origin of the ancient kingdom of Axum, its South Arabian connections, and its relationship with the Greek world of the eastern Mediterranean two millennia ago. For medieval and Renaissance Europeans Ethiopia was the land of Prester John, a fit object of both speculation and expeditions by the Portuguese of 450 years ago. For modern Ethiopians it is the land of the Queen of Sheba. Church historians have concerned themselves with the nature of the Ethiopian Christian Church, its long history dating from the fourth century, and the unique aspects of one of the most isolated branches of Christianity. Linguists have found much to study in the Semitic languages spoken in Ethiopia, and much research remains to be done on the other languages of Ethiopia. The historian has the problem of pulling together the pieces of Ethiopian history to make a coherent whole. He is fortunate to have the written records so rare in African historical research, records which date back some two thousand years.

Ethiopia has survived as a political entity since the early days of Axum and has a dynasty which claims to have its origins from about 1000 B.C. This dynasty has been the single most important factor in the

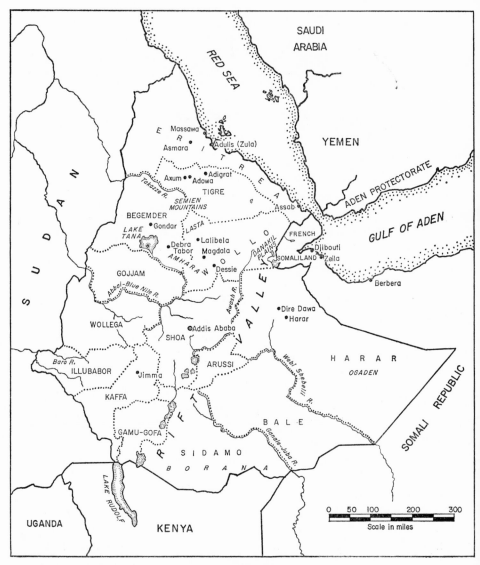

Map 6. Ethiopia

emergence of Ethiopia as a modern state in the past century. Today the center of politics in Ethiopia is held by an Emperor who is venerated by his people and admired for his courageous stand at the League of Nations in 1936. Haile Selassie is almost an anachronism in this present-day world of ever fewer monarchies, and yet he is one of the acknowledged leaders of the movement for African unity.

On the African continent itself Ethiopia is regarded with mixed feelings of admiration as the nation which alone can boast of having successfully fought off European colonialism while other Africans were conquered and of concern over the autocracy of its governmental system and the repression of new ideas or opposition. The future of Ethiopia is no less a subject for speculation than its past.

Historical Background

Ethiopia's long and varied history has left its mark on present developments in the eastern Horn of Africa. Few states can boast of a history that goes back more than two thousand years. Centuries of isolation and encirclement by the Muslim world have given Ethiopia distinct characteristics, including a dynasty that traces its origins to the Old Testament's account of the visit of the Queen of Sheba to Solomon's court in Jerusalem. Out of touch with the Mediterranean and Near Eastern worlds after the rise of Islam, Ethiopian kings constructed an empire that has been reconstituted several times, and which with each reconstitution has come to resemble more closely the Ethiopian Empire of the present.

The Portuguese were the first Europeans to have close relations with the Ethiopians, but although they helped stave off the Muslim threat, they contributed to religious dissension in an empire where regional and ethnic loyalties made the task of political unification difficult. In the aftermath of religious warfare and a series of Galla invasions, Ethiopia disintegrated in the late eighteenth century into a series of petty kingdoms. The task of the emperors since 1855 has been to re-establish and maintain political unity, preserve Ethiopian territorial integrity and independence, and give the state a larger role both in the lives of its subjects and in the field of international diplomacy. No emperor has had a completely free hand, for the past has weighed heavy in Ethiopian affairs.

ROOTS IN ANTIQUITY

Ethiopians are proud of the fact that some sixteen hundred years ago there thrived on the highlands of northern Ethiopia a kingdom, centered in Axum, that had trading connections with the interior, possibly as far as the modern Sudan, with the Red Sea and the kingdoms of southern Arabia, and with Greek-speaking merchants who ranged far from their Mediterranean homelands. It is commonly agreed that emigrants from southern Arabia arrived in what is now Ethiopia more than 2,500 years ago. Tradition claims at least two important immigrant groups, the Ag'azian and the Habeshat; from the latter, some claim, comes the word *Abyssinia.*

These immigrants from Arabia, allegedly the ancestors of the modern Amhara, doubtlessly intermarried with the original inhabitants of the north of Ethiopia, who were most probably a Hamitic people not very different from the surviving Agau of northwest Ethiopia. The South Arabian connection was strongly expressed in language, architecture, and religion. The best-known examples of Axumite architecture, which attests to the high development of early Ethiopia, are obelisks carved to represent doors and windows and crowned with the crescent-sun symbol of the pagan religion apparently common to both South Arabia and Axum.

Not only did the South Arabian religion cross the Red Sea to Axum, but there is some indirect evidence that Judaism and Christianity both may have entered Ethiopia at an early date. Certainly an archaic form of Judaism has survived in the area between Lake Tana and the ancient southern borders of Axum. Like the South Arabian sun-moon cult, Ethiopian Judaism must have come from Yemen, where Judaism at one time flourished among South Arabian tribes. In all probability certain Agau tribes, known as the Falasha, were converted to this form of Judaism some two thousand years ago. Similarly, there are grounds to believe that Christianity may have arrived earlier than the fourth century, as Ethiopian tradition claims.

After its conversion to Christianity Ethiopia was far from isolated from the rest of the Christian world. Not only did Axum have dealings with the Coptic Church of Alexandria but one Ethiopian king concluded an agreement with the Byzantine Emperor Justin I providing for cooperation in war against the persecutors of Christians in southern Arabia in the third decade of the sixth century. To judge from Greek, Syrian, South Arabian, and later Arabic records, the Axumites won a great victory and extended their kingdom to the other side of the Red Sea. Later Justinian the Great proposed an Axumite-Byzantine alliance against the Persians in hopes of expanding the silk trade with India, but nothing seems to have come of this proposal. Persian intervention eventually destroyed Axumite power in southern Arabia and may also have contributed to the decline in Axumite power on the Red Sea.

It is clear, however, that Ethiopia became by extension a part of the ancient Mediterranean and Near Eastern world. Although remote from the main centers of ancient civilization, the distinctive Axumite culture did share much in common with classical antiquity and little with the rest of Africa.

ISLAM AND ISOLATION

The rise of Islam had a tremendous influence on the course of Ethiopian history, and the threat of Muslim encirclement has become one of the permanent factors in Ethiopian history. The Muslims gained control of the Red Sea in the late seventh century and initiated the long period of Ethiopia's isolation from the rest of the civilized Middle East. In the early years of Islam Ethiopia occupied a special position in recognition of the asylum that Axumite kings had given to some of Mohammed's exiled followers. Ethiopia was spared the *jihad* (Islamic holy war) for several hundred years; not until the tenth century did Muslim-Christian rivalry assume fierce proportions. But with trade disrupted first by pirates and later by readjustments in trade routes, Axum slowly declined, and the outside world heard little of Ethiopia for the next five centuries.

Paradoxically, although Axum was declining in commercial prosperity, the kingdom was at the same time expanding, just as the Roman Empire did in its last centuries. The Axumities expanded southward and conquered the northern half of the plateau in the eighth century. Thus, as Ethiopia turned its face from the outside world, the center of gravity of the Christian kingdom in Ethiopia shifted southward across the Takazze River in the conquest of non-Semitic and non-Christian peoples that continued until the end of the nineteenth century.

The expanding Axumite kingdom, now more interested in conquest than trade, gradually experienced an inner transformation. The conquerors imposed their Semitic language and Christian religion on the conquered Agau, who spoke a Hamitic language and practiced a pagan religion. The new people were not readily assimilated into the old culture, which instead absorbed elements of Agau culture. In one respect or another the dominant culture of Ethiopia has ever since been absorbing elements of the culture of its subject peoples.

Southward expansion involved a new threat to Axum from the conquered peoples who maintained their older traditions. This failure to come to terms with the Agau led to the fall of Axum; the dynamics of expansionism proved to be more of a threat than the drying-up of trade in the Red Sea. The first sign of trouble came from the Judaized Agau, the Falasha, who in the tenth century undertook a campaign of destruction, burning churches everywhere and finally devastating the city of Axum itself. Despite their destruction of the power of Axum the Falasha were unable to replace their predecessors with a permanent state, and their power soon evaporated. The Axumites were not able to regain their former power, and a Christianized Agau dynasty, the Zagwe, restored peace and order and for three centuries ruled over the area once covered by the Axumite kingdom.

With the Zagwe era the center of political activity shifted to Lasta, and a new capital was established at Roha, some 160 miles south of old Axum. Claimants to the throne of Axum regarded the Zagwe as usurpers and managed to maintain their independence in Shoa, some one hundred miles farther south.

The Zagwe were not able to gain control of the coastal areas, and, like Axum in its late period and modern Ethiopia before 1951, their kingdom was landlocked. They also found political rivals in a series of Muslim states to the east of the high plateau, where a resurgent Islam had made rapid progress since the tenth century. Muslim principalities like Adal, Ifat, and Dawaro prospered in the lower country east of Shoa and Lasta as well as in the eastern plateau on the other side of the Rift Valley. Beyond Shoa in the south some of the Sidamo peoples also converted to Islam. From the tenth century to the present Ethiopia has been an island of Christianity in a sea of turbulent Islam.

Though ringed by enemies, the Zagwe nevertheless experienced a certain degree of prosperity as evidenced by the remarkable architecture of their capital, where a group of ten monolithic churches were hewn out of the living rock. The Christian kings of Lasta preserved the ancient Ethiopic language and the religion of the Axumites, as well as a connection with the Coptic Church in Egypt. All this indicates that in many respects the Zagwe period was not a break in Ethiopian history but a bridge between the Axumites and the Solomonic monarchs who followed. Additional support of this contention may be inferred from the fact that the Zagwe "usurper," Lalibela (*ca.* 1200), is regarded as a saint by the Ethiopian Orthodox Church, and that Roha, his capital, has ever since been known as the town of Lalibela.

Like the Axumites, the Zagwe were unable to consolidate their holdings into one truly unified kingdom, the accomplishment of which had to wait until the nineteenth and twentieth centuries. Not only was there the constant challenge of those who claimed to be the legitimate descendants of the last of the Axumite rulers, as well as the potential threat of the Muslims to the east, but certain elements of paganism survived among the Agau, cultural distinctions remained, and linguistic differences continued. No doubt in order to give an aura of legitimacy to their rule and to provide some sort of rallying point for unity, the Zagwe rulers put forth the claim that they were descended from Israelite nobility.

Several possible explanations for this claim may be given. The Falasha uprising, with its Judaic elements, may certainly have impressed later Zagwe kings, who surely were aware of the Jewish origins of Christianity. What better way to legitimize their position than to be both Christian and the heirs of the political leaders of the older dispensation. Or, the possibility that some of the early Zagwe kings were Jewish may have provided a belief in a genealogical continuity from a Judaic, hence Israelite source. Alternatively, the Zagwe may have cultivated this tradition of descent as a response to the challenge of the Amhara rulers of Shoa, who traced their origins not only to the old Axumite dynasty but also to the Solomonic dynasty of ancient Israel. The last hypothesis is strengthened by evidence that the Zagwe voluntarily yielded their place to the Solomonic dynasty, for the Zagwe dynasty ended with Lalibela's grandson in 1270.

THE SOLOMONIC DYNASTY: POLITICAL MYTH AND REALITY

Myth has always played a large part in the construction of a national political history, and that of Ethiopia is no exception to this generalization. To understand political realities in Ethiopia it is first necessary to discuss the story of the Queen of Sheba and what is officially described in Ethiopia today as the Solomonic Restoration.

Since the late thirteenth century the history of Ethiopia has in many respects been the history of the Shoan dynasty, which replaced the Zagwe and through which the present Emperor traces his descent. It has not ruled uninterruptedly, nor has it had a sure rule of succession. But by and large the main outlines of the last 650 years of Ethiopian history have corresponded with the fortunes of the dynasty.

Most Europeans and Americans are probably acquainted with the story of the visit of the Queen of Sheba to the court of Solomon as sketchily set down in the Old Testament. It is less well known that the Queen of the South has been the subject of an extensive literature. She figures also in the Koran and in Arabic folklore, in Jewish legend, and in Ethiopian tradition, particularly in the *Kebra Negast* (*Glory of Kings*), one of the most important literary works in the ancient Ethiopic. Ethiopians believe that Sheba, or Saba, was located on their side of the Red Sea within the boundaries of old Axum. To bolster their claim they point to archaeological excavation at Sabea, near the ancient home of the Habeshat or Ag'azian. There is not enough evidence of a conclusive nature to allow positive identification of any one place as Sheba, but this is in some respects irrelevant for an appreciation of the importance of the story for Ethiopian traditions.

According to these traditions, a suitable time after her departure from Jerusalem Makeda, the Queen of Sheba, gave birth to Solomon's son, whom she named Menelik. When the boy matured, his mother sent him to Judea to visit his father, who attempted to persuade Menelik, his first-born, to remain in Jerusalem as heir apparent. Menelik's first loyalty, however, was to his mother and to their Ethiopian homeland. Unable to deter Menelik, Solomon gave him permission to leave. On the eve of his son's departure Solomon dreamed that the glory of Israel departed to another land. As his father slept, Menelik was preparing to return to Ethiopia in the company of a large number of Israelites, the first-born of the priests and nobility, whom Solomon had ordered to accompany his eldest son. Before their departure, however, the son of the high priest absconded with the Ark of the Covenant. Upon his return to his mother's homeland, Menelik became king and the eldest sons of Israel became his councilors and officers.

The importance of this legend for an understanding of Ethiopian history cannot be underestimated. Here we see a host of claims. With Menelik's return Judaism came to Ethiopia; hence the Ethiopians were not pagans before the advent of Christianity. The Ethiopian nobility was descended from the Israelite aristocracy; on this the Zagwe based their claim of legitimacy. The Ark of the Covenant came to Ethiopia with Menelik; hence the Ethiopians are God's chosen people, replacing the sinful Israelites. Lastly, the Ethiopian dynasty to the time of the Zagwe usurpation was descended from Menelik and Solomon, a claim that could not be matched in Christian Ethiopia by any rivals for the throne. By extension and emendation, the house of Menelik was of the root of Jesse. In other words, genealogically, Menelik's descendants were distant cousins of Jesus; all were members of the House of David, a significant factor in the sanctification of kingship in a Christian country surrounded by Muslim rulers who claimed descent from Mohammed.

The chronicles of Ethiopia allege that the Zagwe dynasty freely relinquished the throne to Yekuno Amlak, a descendant of the last of the Axumite kings and of the house of Menelik, through the mediation of the Church. That the Zagwe should voluntarily yield the throne is not easily understood. One possible explanation is that by 1270 the Solomonic genealogy was generally accepted as valid; it is quite possible that the Shoan dynasty successfully used the Menelik story as an ideological weapon. Moreover, there is no conclusive evidence of the existence of the legend before the thirteenth century. A second explanation may lie in the inability of the Zagwe rulers after Lalibela to cope with the encroachments of the Muslim states to the east; there is some evidence that formerly Christian lands had been conquered by these Muslims. Lastly, the role played by the Church suggests that for reasons of its own the Church had thrown its power behind the Solomonic pretenders. Each of these explanations may have a partial validity. Tradition recounts that a treaty between the Zagwe and the Solomonids granted the Zagwe hereditary rule over Wag, north of Lasta—no doubt a secure patrimony contrasted with the endangered empire they had ruled. By this same treaty the Church was allotted one third of the kingdom for its support. Here there are suggestions of an alliance between the Church, which obtained a degree of independence and wealth comparable to that of the feudal church in Europe, and the Emperor, who gained the throne and effectively saw to it that the Church could not become a tool of factions within Ethiopia. The eighteenth-century Scottish traveler, James Bruce, reported that this arrangement continued in his time.

Empire and Emperor

In the course of the fourteenth century two elements of modern Ethiopia emerged and became clearly discernible: ethnic diversity and Christian-Muslim coexistence within the empire. At first the Solomonic kings struck back against their Muslim neighbors, especially to the northeast of Shoa. As they reconquered the once-Christian lands of the escarpment and subdued their enemies, the emperors assigned the new provinces to Muslim governors. At the height of their success against Ifat, Dawaro, and Fatijar, the Christian monarchs of Ethiopia imposed their overlordship on these Muslim states. By 1415, only the Muslim state of Adal remained a potential threat.

Through military conquest the empire once again changed its nature. No longer was Ethiopia a purely Christian kingdom, for large Muslim populations to the east owed their allegiance to the Ethiopian monarchs, and Muslim governors administered both Christian and Muslim lands of the escarpment. In their relation with both the reconquered lands and the defeated sovereign Muslim states, the Ethiopians began to develop a political system of a semifeudal nature with Christian overlords and Muslim and Christian vassals.

By the late fifteenth century Ethiopia reached a new peak in its development. Strong emperors like Zara Yaqob (1434–1468) gave Ethiopia the leadership necessary for the organization of military action against a strong enemy. The empire continued to expand southward and eastward at the expense of pagan and Muslim peoples.

The capital, located at one town or another in Shoa, was the scene of court intrigues. Rivalries within the royal family and between the military nobility and the royal family became the rule rather than the exception. The chronicles indicate that early in the reign of Zara Yaqob there was a genuine resurgence of paganism to the northwest of Shoa. The nobility then spread the rumor that the royal princes were dabbling in paganism, whereupon the Emperor put most of his sons to death and delegated his daughters to govern the provinces. The intermingling of religion and politics also became manifest when a group of governors in the northwest rebelled against the Emperor, converted to Judaism, and briefly posed the threat of a Falasha revival. Yet despite the rivalry of the nobility and the threats of paganism, of the Falasha, and of the Muslims, the emperors enjoyed an immense prestige.

The strength of the royal ruler consisted of several elements. The Solomonic dynasty was firmly entrenched as the only legitimate dynasty; the monarchs styled themselves Kings of Israel. The large bulk of the army, moreover, was loyal to the death; military rank and noble privilege were identical, and both came from the emperor. Thirdly, the Church fully supported the emperor, and Christianity had become a rallying point in an empire beleaguered by Muslims. In short, for all these reasons the monarch had the blessing of God and his person was regarded as sacred. His coronation at Axum was a religious ceremony befitting an Old Testament monarch. For the most part the emperor did not appear in public unless veiled from the gaze of commoners, a practice that the Ethiopians may have borrowed from the Hamitic peoples whom they conquered. The emperor was the main patron of the Church and in every sense the defender of the faith. He assigned all the revenues of Shoa to the famous monastery of Debra Libanos. It was Emperor Zara Yaqob, not the Church, who took the steps necessary to wipe out paganism. By imperial order all Ethiopians were compelled to take an oath and to wear amulets readily identifying them as Christians. The Emperor also decided on purely religious issues and dealt ruthlessly with all opposition. Several religious tracts issued from his pen, and he attempted to reform the faith and purge it of extraneous elements. By order of Zara Yaqob, the Nativity and other feasts were celebrated monthly, a feature unique to the Ethiopian Orthodox Church; both Saturday as the Sabbath and Sunday as the Lord's Day were strictly observed. Religious loyalty and political loyalty became identical for most of his subjects.

The chronicles pay much attention to the complex organization of the empire. It was not completely safe to entrust the rule of outlying provinces to members of the royal family, who might use the office as a means to overthrow the king. Hence surviving members of the royal family were confined to remote mountain areas, and the court too lived in isolation. The empire itself was composed of both hereditary kingdoms and administered provinces, or conquered territories. The most important of the kingdoms, whose rulers were often related to the emperor were Gojjam, Begemder, Tigre, Amhara, and, of course, Shoa. Generally, the emperor was also king of Shoa. The conquered territories, Ifat, Fatigar, Dawaro, and others, were either former Muslim states, occasionally governed by the hereditary Muslim ruler, or reconquered areas, like the Bahr Nagash along the Red Sea. Many of these areas continued to play an important part as recognizable political entities with strong regional interests until fairly recent times.

The Quest for Prester John

Although isolated from major contacts with the world by geography and political circumstances, Ethiopia did have some infrequent contacts beyond the Muslim world. Certainly Christian pilgrims and Crusaders alike must have been aware of the presence of the exotic Ethiopians in Jerusalem after 1187. There is inconclusive evidence that European monks and traders visited Ethiopia as early as the mid-thirteenth century, but scholars dispute whether or not the missionaries were intended for Ethiopia proper, inasmuch as medieval Europeans indiscriminately labeled most of sub-Saharan Africa and southern Asia "Ethiopia." In the reign of Zara Yaqob at least one European missionary reached Ethiopia, for the chronicles describe a theological debate between Ethiopian monks and a European.

By the end of the fifteenth century more than a dozen Europeans, for the most part Italian traders, had reached Ethiopia, only to find that the emperors, who welcomed the technological skills of the foreigners, refused to permit them to leave the realm. Thus Ethiopia came to know of Europe, although Europeans learned little about Ethiopia before the beginning of the sixteenth century. In the meantime, legend once more played an important part. The romantic element of Ethiopian history again appears: to the story of the Queen of Sheba we add that of the fabled Prester John.

Sometime in the twelfth century Western Europe received word of a great defeat suffered by the Muslims at the hands of an unknown ruler to the east of the Muslim world. There was much speculation, and the belief spread that the potential allies of the Crusaders were the descendants of eastern Christians, perhaps of Indians converted by the Apostle Thomas, or Nestorians. Then about 1165, the Byzantine Emperor received a letter from the mysterious Christian king who described himself as ruler over seventy-two kingdoms stretching from Ethiopia to India. The letter, it is obvious, was a forgery. Nevertheless, the story spread of the eastern Christian ruler who was also a priest (*Presbyter*, or *Prester*). European tongues twisted the story sufficiently that by the early fifteenth century the legend of Prester John was fully developed.

The story might have died out if at the same time Europeans had not begun to receive faint word of the existence of Christian Ethiopia. The Crusaders were the first to send the report home, and after the arrival of an Avignon-bound Ethiopian embassy from Jerusalem in 1306 European cartographers began to locate Ethiopia more precisely. That the Ethiopians were also combating the Muslims excited their imaginations, which were further stimulated in 1428 when Yeshaq I proposed a marriage alliance to Alfonso of Aragon. Considering the bad turn of events in Ethiopian-Muslim relations by the end of that century, we must realize it was greatly to Ethiopia's benefit that the Europeans believed the African kingdom to be the land of Prester John. For the first time since the seventh century Ethiopia would again have close relations with another Christian state.

After the death of Henry the Navigator, Portuguese interest in the route to the Indies and in the war with the Muslims merged with the Prester John story. Accordingly, in 1487, João II conceived the idea of a two-pronged expedition to the court of Prester John. From Portugal Bartolomeo Diaz sailed southward to round Africa. Less well known is the other half of the king's plan: Pero da Covilhão was instructed to reach Ethiopia via Egypt and the Red Sea. But the Portuguese never learned the outcome of da Covilhão's mission. After landing at Zeila, he reached the court of the emperor, and like other Europeans then resident in Ethiopia he was compelled to remain in the country.

Meanwhile, Ethiopia's position became increasingly perilous. The Ottoman Turks extended their power down the Red Sea and took nominal possession of the coastal regions. Although the Ethiopians had no argument with the Ottomans, the Turkish presence was ominous for several reasons. Turkish military success had considerably raised Muslim morale, and the Muslim state of Adal prepared for a new round of warfare with Christian Ethiopia. Arabic sources also indicate that there was a religious revival within Muslim Adal; the fervor of Somali converts added to the probability of renewed struggle. Moreover, in the Turks the Muslims of Adal found a valuable ally, who could turn the balance in their favor through the introduction of firearms. Against these new weapons the Ethiopian spear and bow were of greatly reduced effectiveness.

To offset the Adal-Turkish entente, the Empress Eleni, who served as regent until her son Lebna Dengel came of age, contacted the Portuguese in 1509 in hopes of an alliance against the common enemy. The Portuguese were now more concerned with the riches of the Indies, and when the Empress' envoy finally was able to return to Ethiopia in 1520, he was accompanied by an ineffectual Portuguese diplomatic mission. They too joined the ranks of the permanent European community of Ethiopia.

In the meantime the Muslim enemies of Ethiopia, encouraged by the Turkish occupation of Arabia, launched an attack on the Christian kingdom. Lebna Dengel held off the Muslims, and a truce was put into effect. But in 1527, a year after the Emperor agreed to the departure of the Portuguese, the Muslims of Adal, under the dynamic leadership of Ahmed Grañ, decided on all-out warfare. A jihad was proclaimed for the purpose of conquering all Ethiopia. Ahmed Grañ's campaigns inexorably penetrated westward. Lebna Dengel's forces were no match for Turkish cannons and muskets. By 1531, the Muslims occupied Dawaro and Shoa; two years later the historic kingdoms of Amhara and Lasta fell. In 1535, Tigre was vanquished, and Lebna Dengel and those chiefs who had not deserted to the Muslims sought refuge in the mountainous northwest. Totally defeated, Lebna Dengel died in 1540. The chronicles claim that nine-tenths of the population were converted to Islam. Surely this was the blackest hour in Ethiopian history.

Had it not been for the Portuguese, Christian Ethiopia might have disappeared from the map, for in desperation Lebna Dengel had instructed one of the Portuguese who had arrived in 1520 to seek Portuguese aid before it was too late. This time the Portuguese acted decisively, and in 1541, fourteen years after the Muslims had begun their jihad, four hundred Portuguese soldiers, armed with muskets, landed at Massawa. They fought their way into the interior to the camp of the harassed new Emperor, Galawdewos (Claudius), whose few hundred followers welcomed the Portuguese intervention. Soon Tigre and the Bahr Nagash rallied to his cause, and after heavy losses the allies unexpectedly killed Ahmed Grañ in battle early in 1543. With the death of their leader the Muslims retreated eastward, and Galawdewos temporarily reoccupied much of his father's kingdom. The Ethiopians, however, were gravely weakened by the long years of warfare, and had the Muslims been united enough to mount a new offensive a disastrous defeat would have ensued. The Somali allies of Adal had abandoned the cause, and a shattered Ethiopia was safe from an Adali attack for the moment. But weak Ethiopia could not prevent the Turks from occupying Massawa and much of the coastal plain. Ethiopia was preserved, but the Turkish presence ensured Ethopian isolation after this brief period of contact with the outside world.

From time to time other Europeans entered Ethiopia, but through religious rather than political motivation. In 1557, and again in 1603, groups of Jesuits entered the country. Pero Paez, one of the leaders of the second Jesuit group, succeeded in converting Lebna Dengel's grandson, the Emperor Susenyos (1607–1632), to Roman Catholicism. Paez' successor, Alfonso Mendes, decided to press forward and forcibly romanize Ethiopian Christianity. Persecution of monophysite believers became the order of the day at a time when Ethiopia could ill afford the luxury of religious dissension.

Susenyos, who had seized the throne, saw ever diminishing prospects of political unity. His immediate predecessor had been deposed as a result of the religious issue, and Susenyos could not risk a revolt from rivals for the throne who might use the cause of the Ethiopian Orthodox Church for their own purposes. What he feared occurred, and the empire was rent by politico-religious revolts. Finally Susenyos admitted defeat, restored the old faith, and abdicated in favor of his son Fasilidas. The Jesuits were expelled from Ethiopia in 1632, and the good will toward the Europeans who had saved Ethiopia from the Muslims was completely dissipated after a century of contact with later Europeans.

THE ADVENT OF THE GALLA

Ethiopia and Adal had fought themselves to a stalemate, and both sides were weak from the long years of fighting. Unexpectedly, a major threat to Christian and Muslim alike appeared in the mid-sixteenth century. From the south Ethiopia and Adal were faced with a common invader: Galla tribesmen, who rushed into an Ethiopia weakened by two decades of warfare. Within twenty years they had devastated Harar and posed a greater threat to the Muslims than the Christians had ever done. The Hamitic nomads wrested from the Ethiopians control of the fertile provinces along their eastern borders. Soon the Christians found that the pagan Galla were a more persistent problem than the Muslims had ever been.

The Galla swept through the area, occupying much of southern and eastern Shoa, the heartland of Solomonic Ethiopia, as well as areas to the north and west. Galla chiefs helped to place Susenyos on the throne, and in the religious civil wars of the seventeenth century hostile Galla took the opportunity to seize more land. By the end of the century they occupied more than a third of the Empire. The Galla gradually settled down to an agricultural existence and added to the ethnic diversity of Ethiopia, which would never again contain a majority of Amhara. The task of assimilating the Galla has continued to the present. If the Galla had not been so divided among themselves, the history of Ethiopia might otherwise have become the history of a Galla kingdom.

The Rise and Fall of Gondar

In the internecine religious warfare which divided Ethiopia in the early seventeenth century, the power of the monarchy declined. The Portuguese meddling in Ethiopian affairs had encouraged other members of the royal family to make their bid for the throne, and peaceful succession depended on royal strength. The Galla, in constant contact with the Amhara, played their part in Ethiopian politics. Susenyos married a Galla princess, and the blood of the Solomonic line mingled with that of the newcomers. The reign of his son Fasilidas (1632–1667) marked the last period of glory for Ethiopia until the late nineteenth century.

Under Fasilidas a brief revival took place. Since Shoa was greatly subject to Galla influence, the Emperor established his capital to the north of Lake Tana at Gondar. Not since the Solomonic restoration had there been a permanent capital, but Gondar remained the capital for more than a century. To Gondar the new Emperor brought all sorts of craftsmen, some from as far away as Egypt and India, and Gondar became a town dominated by a group of fortress-like castles, monuments to this second renaissance of Ethiopia. Axum was rebuilt, while Gondar became the seat of an Amharic revival; poetry, music, architecture, painting, and literature all thrived at the court of Fasilidas.

After the death of Fasilidas, however, the position of the monarch was slowly undermined. The door to change had been opened through marriage with the Galla, whose influence increased at the capital. Gradually, too, the power of the Amhara and Galla nobles grew at the expense of that of the monarch. As the star of the Galla nobility rose, the old Amhara nobility became increasingly restless. By 1753, the empire was on the verge of distintegration. Galla princesses and advisors tried to outmaneuver Amhara nobles for influence at court. Ten years later Gallinya rather than Amharic was the main language at court, an interesting commentary on the changes that had taken place. Within another ten years the empire was on the verge of civil war not only between the party of the Galla nobles, who had made a puppet of the emperor, and the party of the Amhara nobles, who wished their own puppet on the throne, but among the various nobles of Amhara and Tigre who aspired to the throne themselves.

From 1769 to 1855, central power almost completely disappeared. At one time five men claimed the throne in what was the nadir of imperial fortunes. In the Ethiopian Empire, as in the Holy Roman Empire, power devolved to the nobles. Ethiopia disintegrated into a number of small kingdoms as old local ruling families asserted themselves and appointed governors converted their offices into hereditary positions. Until the mid-nineteenth century the Ethiopian Empire did not exist. It is more accurate to speak of the various kingdoms *in* Ethiopia, for Ethiopia had become a mere geographical expression.

THE RECONSTITUTION OF THE EMPIRE

Since 1855, Ethiopia has had four strong innovating emperors—Theodore II, Yohannes IV, Menelik II, and Haile Selassie I—each of whom has striven to create a national unity that would override earlier religious, ethnic, and regional differences. Theodore and Yohannes did not meet with great success, but they set the pattern for the more successful attempts by Menelik and Haile Selassie. All four did much to affect the destiny of modern Ethiopia.

With the dissolution of law and order in the early nineteenth century, bandit groups, or *shifta,* made their appearance in western Ethiopia. So strong did one of the shifta leaders become that in 1855 he successfully claimed the throne as Theodore II. The new Emperor won his position after defeating the local rulers of Gojjam and Begemder, but he still had to contend with Shoa and Tigre. Military successes eliminated Shoa as an enemy, and Menelik, the young king of Shoa, was taken to Theodore's capital as a prisoner. To legitimize his position Theodore won the Church to his side and claimed to be a descendant of the Solomonic dynasty.

Theodore differed greatly from his predecessors in that he sought to establish the empire on a permanent basis. To do this he hoped to replace local rulers with paid governors loyal to him and not to regional interests and connections. It was an admirable plan for administrative reform, but the circumstances of his time prevented him from implementing it. Modernization of the administrative apparatus had to wait until the time of Menelik and Haile Selassie.

Unable to depend on administrative reform, Theodore relied on military strength to consolidate his empire. For Theodore, as for Haile Selassie and the emperors of the Portuguese era, the presence of foreigners with technological skills was welcome. Soon his capital at Magdala contained a large number of Europeans, including missionaries, who were pressed into the manufacture of armaments. Some of these Europeans became his trusted advisors. Theodore also hoped to import weapons from Europe and departed from Ethiopia's centuries-old diplomatic isolation by proposing a treaty of commerce and friendship with Great Britain. But a series of errors on both sides soon led to a diplomatic embroilment, and a British punitive expedition was dispatched in 1867 to rescue those Europeans who were forcibly detained in Theodore's capital.

The crisis with Great Britain proved to be Theodore's undoing, for a large number of disaffected Ethiopians welcomed the British. The route of march lay through Tigre, and the Tigreans seized the opportunity to help overthrow an unpopular monarch. The Church too did its part, and priests urged all Ethiopians to fight against an emperor who had unjustly seized and not enlarged church lands, for Theodore had rewarded his faithful retainers by giving them shares of confiscated church lands. Lastly, only the Church could release from their vow those who had sworn loyalty to the Emperor. The British action served as a rallying point for the overthrow of the Emperor by all the dissident elements of Ethiopia—the Church, the Tigrean *ras* (prince), and the lesser nobility. As the British approached the capital, Theodore shot himself, whereupon the British easily occupied the capital, freed the captives, and promptly returned to the coast. In the excitement no one noticed the escape of Menelik of Shoa.

The outcome of the British withdrawal was readily predictable. Once again civil warfare rent Ethiopia for a number of years, until in 1872 the ras of Tigre, whose firepower had given him a distinct advantage over all other claimants, was crowned Emperor Yohannes IV. As Emperor, Yohannes continued Theodore's policies of restricting the power of the nobility. But if Yohannes wanted to control the nobility and lay the basis for a state that could be called modern, he was prevented from achieving his goal by complications with regional interests, with Europeans, and with the Muslim world.

The only real rival for Yohannes' throne was Menelik, King of Shoa, who had survived imprisonment by Theodore at Magdala. Menelik's claim to the throne was as good as that of Yohannes: both could claim Solomonic descent and the loyalty of large segments of the population. The regional rivalry of Tigre and Shoa was halted by a truce, however, and peace was sealed by a marriage alliance between Yohannes' son and Menelik's daughter. Moreover, Yohannes recogized the able King of Shoa as his successor to the imperial throne. The price was high, but it was worth it to the Emperor because there was no law of succession. Indeed, one of the basic difficulties of monarchy in Ethiopia has continued to be the lack of a clear-cut order of succession to the throne.

During the course of Yohannes' long reign the Italians established themselves on the Red Sea coast. At first they had only the desolate beachhead at Assab, where an Italian priest had bought land from a local sheik in 1869 as a coaling station for the Rubattino Shipping Company. In 1884, with British support, the Italians occupied the seaport of Massawa, formerly held by Turkish and Egyptian garrisons. Soon they expanded from their coastal beachheads across the uninviting coastal desert to the edge of the escarpment and the very border of Tigre. When they attempted to scale the escarpment and occupy the cool and fertile highlands of the area near Asmara, they were met by the forces of Yohannes and were soundly defeated at the battle of Dogali in 1887, the first major setback received by any European power at the hands of an African army, though only a sample of what was to happen nine years later at Adowa.

Frustrated in their military aims, the Italians resorted to diplomacy and tried to take advantage of Tigrean-Shoan regional rivalry. Knowing full well that Menelik needed arms and munitions, the Italians proposed a treaty of commerce and friendship in hopes of using Menelik against Yohannes. For Menelik the proposal was fortuitous. As long as Tigre was well armed with European rifles and as long as Yohannes' son had hopes of gaining the imperial throne, Menelik was at a disadvantage and could not be certain that he would be the next emperor. Accordingly, Menelik concluded a treaty between Shoa and Italy, an adequate illustration of Shoan regional sovereignty and of the failure of Yohannes to create an Ethiopian state to replace the very loose imperial arrangement.

With Menelik a hostile friend and the Italians encroaching from the north, Yohannes found still another enemy in the Muslims. The Turks and the Egyptians had withdrawn from their garrisons on the coast and to the east in 1884. With British encouragement the Italians took Massawa, while the British, who were about to extend a protectorate over part of the Somalis, took Zeila and Berbera as strategic ports opposite Aden. At the same time, France occupied Tadjoura, Obock, and Djibouti. To Menelik, King of Shoa, fell Harar and most of the eastern highlands. In that one year the territory of Shoa must have doubled, a forewarning of Shoan ascendancy in Ethiopian affairs again. In the west, however, the Turks and Egyptians had been replaced in the Sudan by the Mahdists, whose religious enthusiasm posed a real threat to Christian Ethiopia. Yohannes, of course, also regarded the turmoil in the Sudan as an opportunity to expand his Ethiopian Empire westward into the lowlands, where there were prospects of gold, slaves, and direct access to the navigable Nile. In 1889, deciding to take the initiative, he led his warriors toward the lowlands. There at Metemma, just as the Ethiopians appeared victorious, a Mahdist bullet killed the Emperor and brought Menelik to the throne sooner than might have been anticipated.

The Second Confrontation with Europe

Although the Scottish traveler James Bruce penetrated to the court at Gondar in the 1770's and another British traveler, Henry Salt, visited Tigre in the early years of the last century and was followed by a few Protestant missionaries in the 1830's, not until the 1840's did there begin a thin but continuous and increasing trickle of European visitors to the chiefs, kings, and later emperors of Ethiopia. Ethiopian affairs, always complicated by the problems of regionalism and contacts with Islam, became more complex with the addition of the European factor.

Before the great wave of European imperialism in the late nineteenth century the visitors to Ethiopia were travelers who shared that century's burst of enthusiasm for exploration of unknown parts of the world, missionaries who in their pietistic zeal often naively misunderstood the nature of the country, and envoys hopeful of concluding commercial agreements with local potentates. The first two groups greatly stimulated European interest in Ethiopia, particularly in Tigre and Shoa, and by the end of Theodore's reign there had appeared more than a score of books detailing the geography, ethnology, trade, and religious potential of Ethiopia. All these people, missionaries included, helped to introduce elements of Western technology, especially the technology of firearms, into Ethiopia.

In the last third of the century the number of European visitors greatly increased, and European interest in the area of Ethiopia developed from an investigation of commercial and missionary prospects into a study of colonial potential. To this genesis of colonial interest in Ethiopia, missionaries, travelers, explorers, and merchants of many European nationalities all made their contributions. Most noticeable of all were the Italians.

At first the Ethiopians treated the Europeans as a pawn in their own internal affairs. Thus at the time he became Emperor Menelik solidified his position by immediately concluding with Italy the famous Treaty of Ucciali, whereby he hoped to gain the support of a European ally as a special friend. The Italians, however, interpreted their role as special friend to mean the extension of an Italian protectorate over Ethiopia. Since 1885, they had hoped to obtain from the Sultan of Zanzibar the southern part of Somalia as a means of penetration inland to the rich lands of Kaffa, Sidamo, and Borana, then independent kingdoms lying to the south of Shoa. In 1889, they proclaimed to the rest of the world that the Treaty of Ucciali gave them a legitimate protectorate over Ethiopia. They did not realize at the time that there was a considerable discrepancy between the Italian and the Amharic versions of the treaty.

Meanwhile, in the face of possible European aggression, Menelik's armies imposed his authority over an area much larger than that ruled by any of his predecessors for almost four hundred years. Not only were the traditional kingdoms of Gojjam, Begemder-Amhara, Tigre, and Shoa his, but also the newly won lands to the east around Harar.

His armies scored even greater victories as they occupied the Somali country to within 180 miles of the Indian Ocean. Concurrently other Ethiopian armies marched southward to destroy the ancient kingdoms of Kaffa, Sidamo, and the Galla Borana. Thus by the beginning of this century, Ethiopia, with the exception of Italian Eritrea, had reached its present borders.

Menelik's modernized army, equipped with French weapons, was soon ready to curb the threat of the rival Italian expansionism and to convince the Italians by force that the Treaty of Ucciali did not make Ethiopia an Italian protectorate. The Italians accepted Menelik's interpretation of the treaty only after their disastrous defeat at Adowa on March 1, 1896, perhaps the most famous battle in the annals of imperialism. Ethiopia's independence was secured, Ethiopian prestige was unique on the African continent, and Italy was so shaken by defeat on the battleground that forty years later Italians could still hope to seek revenge for Adowa. Moreover, no other African people could boast of so successful an outcome after a military confrontation with a European power.

MENELIK'S NEW ETHIOPIA

Ethiopia's aloofness from the outside world thus came to an end at precisely the same time that Menelik was consolidating imperial power and authority within an enlarged Ethiopia. From his capital of Addis Ababa, founded only a few short years before he became emperor, he directed the process of converting traditional Ethiopia into a modern polity. Hence the victory at Adowa called to world attention not only Ethiopia's military prowess but also the promise of a new Ethiopia. Europe suddenly became aware of Ethiopia, and in Paris *La Liberté* exuberantly declared, "All European countries will be obliged to make a place for this new brother who steps forth ready to play in the dark continent the role of Japan in the Far East." [1]

Like the rulers of Japan and Thailand, Menelik had learned from his experience with Europeans that if Ethiopia were to maintain its independence in the face of expanding colonialism, it had much to learn from the imposing body of knowledge that is Western technology. Such knowledge would also be of great usefulness in ruling an empire whose size had doubled in a very short time. For these reasons Menelik's European advisors aided him in his attempts to modernize his

[1] Richard K. P. Pankhurst, "How the News was Received in England," *Ethiopia Observer*, I, No. 11 (December, 1957), 366.

army, to introduce modern communications and transportation, and to convert the traditional semifeudal governmental structure into a more modern bureaucratic administration. In the decade after Adowa, Ethiopia took its first steps in this direction, and one European delegation after another made its way to the court at Addis Ababa to help in the process of modernization and to attempt to influence Menelik in his favor. Each of the European powers thought that it could extract from Menelik concessions like those obtained by Europeans throughout the colonial world. Menelik was willing to grant a concession for the construction of a railway from French Djibouti to Addis Ababa, as he was for the introduction of telecommunications, roads, technical assistance, and advisors. Yet this willingness was not a sign of weakness in Menelik. Rather, a strong case can be made that Menelik had an excellent sense of diplomacy and that in this clever ruler all European diplomats, not just those of Italy, met their match. If anything, the Europeans became a pawn in his plans for maintaining the independence and integrity of Ethiopia, for expanding the Empire, and, significantly, for modernizing the state.

For ten years after the victory at Adowa, Menelik had little to fear from European powers. His main concern, rightly, was with rival authorities at home, and by one means or another, Menelik undermined the traditional basis of the Ethiopian State—family and regional connections. Like the emperors of the old Ethiopia he had to deal with regional leaders like Ras Mikael of Wollo and Negus Mikael of Tigre. But Menelik the innovator also had tradition on his side. Only the emperor could create the *neguses* (kings), and here there was ample precedent. Theodore had created neither neguses nor rases. Yohannes IV had created only two neguses (one was Menelik in Shoa, the other Tekla Haymanot in Gojjam); both of these appointments, of course, represented Yohannes' weaknesses vis-à-vis those two regions. Menelik, however, created no new neguses.

By Ethiopian tradition, only the emperor or a negus could create a ras. Menelik created many rases, but whereas formerly appointments of rases had often been an indication of weakness on the part of the emperor, Menelik's appointments signified imperial control over these princes. In particular, he chose to ignore the claims of families who, if not by heredity, at least by tradition, had always filled the office of ras. Instead, he appointed Galla tribesmen to some of the highest positions in the Empire. In this manner he could be sure of loyalty to the Emperor and perhaps to the State. Menelik also employed the traditional marriage connections of the Ethiopian aristocracy: he chose as his fourth wife the Empress Taitu, who was of Galla origin and commanded the loyalty of large sections of the Galla. A cousin was married to one of the most important men of Lasta and thus ensured the loyalty of that province. Another cousin, Ras Makonnen, controlled Harar and the Ogaden. A third cousin, Wolde Giorgis, was particularly influential in the area of Gondar. One of Menelik's daughters married Negus Mikael of Wollo, and so it went.

To replace recalcitrant regional leaders and to complement the ranks of the loyal nobility, Menelik instituted the beginnings of centralized ministerial government, staffed by the forerunners of a modern elite. By 1906, an impartial observer would have noted that he had been largely successful in his attempts to create this new type of government. This success was short-lived, however, for it depended on one man.

In 1906, Menelik suffered the first of several strokes. As the Emperor became physically weaker, there reappeared all the elements of instability that could be found in the old Ethiopia: court intrigues, attempted coups, and rivalries among regional leaders and families for political influence. It seemed as if Menelik's work would be undermined. He himself was too weak to rule; the Empress tried to manipulate factions, but as long as the question of Menelik's successor was undecided, there could be no real stability. Finally, in June, 1908, Menelik's grandson, Lij Iasu, was named his successor. Lij Iasu proved to be an unfortunate choice, for within a matter of a few years it was observed that he dallied with Muslim elements. Perhaps this was his best means of countering the influence of the Tigreans and of obtaining the support of Harar, for Makonnen, who had won the loyalty of the Harari, had died in 1906. Nevertheless, it did not bode well for the future of Menelik's Ethiopia.

THE RISE OF HAILE SELASSIE

After Menelik's death at the end of 1913, Lij Iasu became Emperor. The European powers, contemplating the prospect of the disintegration of Ethiopia, began to vie for influence at the imperial court. The German and Turkish diplomats, in particular, were successful in winning the attention of the young Lij Iasu. Local British consular agents suggested to the Colonial Office that they consider the possibility of extending a protectorate over Ethiopia. The French hoped that their large economic interests would develop into political interests. The

Italian Colonial Minister drew up a grandiose plan for winning allied support for the extension of an Italian protectorate over Ethiopia. Thus, the Italian interests in Ethiopia, more or less moribund since the defeat at Adowa, experienced a rebirth.

While the Europeans were raising high their hopes, Lij Iasu publicly announced his conversion to Islam. Never in the history of Ethiopia had such a startling occurrence taken place, for the official history, so to speak, of Ethiopia was that of a Christian nation, constantly fighting against Muslims and pagans. For many, especially the Amhara and Tigreans, Christianity and Ethiopia had become identical. This action by Lij Iasu was too much for all the traditional elements and many of the modernizing elements of Ethiopia. In 1916, these elements joined to overthrow the Muslim Emperor. The Church, of course, played an important role; the *Abuna* (head of the Church) released all Ethiopians from obligation to respect their oath of loyalty to the Emperor. The nobility, most of whom were Christian Amhara, was also quick to act. The Tigreans, moreover, saw this as an opportunity to extend their power. In the east, the army at Harar, led by Makonnen's young son, Ras Tafari, willingly cooperated with these other elements. Thus the nobility, the Church, and the army joined to overthrow Lij Iasu.

Although the coup was successful, the various groups could not agree on a program for Ethiopia. The nobles would have preferred that power once again be decentralized. But this was no solution; there were too many rivalries among them to permit it. Finally, it was agreed that Menelik's daughter, Zauditu, would reign as Empress, but not rule. The nobility hoped that one of their number could act as regent, and so they chose a man whom they probably regarded as malleable, Ras Tafari of Harar, a distant cousin of Menelik. Habte Giorgis, a noted general popular among the older nobility, remained as War Minister. Thus Ethiopia was ruled by a triumvirate: Ras Tafari as Regent did not have complete powers, Zauditu as Empress commanded great loyalty, and Habte Giorgis was able to control the army in the interests of the nobility.

In the years from 1916 to 1930, the Regent gradually extended his power. Ras Tafari put down several rebellions as he built up his own small military force. After the death of Habte Giorgis in 1926, his task was much simplified. With each unsuccessful rebellion the powers of the Regent increased. Finally, after suppressing an uprising by the Empress' former husband in 1928, the Regent found himself in the position he desired. Zauditu had no alternative to yielding to the wishes of Ras Tafari. Not only did she name him Negus, but she also nominated him heir apparent. In 1930, after the death of Zauditu, Ras Tafari triumphantly ascended the throne of Ethiopia, not without some difficulties, and chose the throne name of Haile Selassie I.

In his years as regent, Haile Selassie demonstrated that he was a man of great political ability and astuteness. He shared many of the characteristics of Menelik. He was not bound by the traditional way of doing things. He also had some characteristics which were not to be found in Menelik. As a boy, he had been educated by French Jesuits in Harar. There he had learned not only French, but also much about Europe and its accomplishments. As regent, he had found it to his advantage—for reasons of state as well as for personal reasons—to continue the process of modernization which had been suspended for more than a decade since the death of Menelik. In his vulnerable position, Ras Tafari realized that if Ethiopia were to develop under his leadership, he must have men whom he could trust. He could not rely on the old nobility: this was a foregone conclusion. Consequently, he established schools and launched a program of sending promising young Ethiopians abroad for study in France, England, the United States, and elsewhere. One corollary of this program of education was the training of reliable military leaders. Significantly, some young Ethiopians were sent to the French military academy at Saint-Cyr.

One of the goals of this program of modernization was the establishment of a new type of political stability. Yet despite the fact that the program may have been aimed at solidifying the position of the Regent, it had repercussions for Ethiopia as a state. In 1923, Ethiopia had become a member of the League of Nations. Subsequently, in 1924, the Regent found it necessary to emancipate all slaves in Ethiopia in order to render Ethiopia less vulnerable in the eyes of world opinion. In that same year, the Regent made his first trip abroad. His tour of England, France, Germany, Italy, Greece, and Egypt gave him added impetus for plans to modernize Ethiopia upon his return. From then on, an increasing number of foreign advisors went to Ethiopia to give assistance in technical matters. After his coronation in 1930, this process speeded up. Certainly Ethiopia was far from modernized, but the Emperor fully realized that the program had become necessary for an additional reason. Not only did modernization aid political stability, not only did it aid the development of the State, but it was also necessary for dealing effectively with European states.

The Ethiopians had good reason to suspect that there would be trouble sooner or later from Fascist Italy and its colonies, Eritrea and Somalia, which bordered Ethiopia. One way to cope with the possibility was to import modern arms, but not until 1930 could this be done with any great degree of success. In 1931, the Emperor made still another departure from tradition, for in that year he granted Ethiopia a constitution providing for a bicameral parliament and a cabinet with responsible ministers. The document was a liberal constitution, but Ethiopia in actuality did not thereby become a constitutional monarchy, in the Western sense. The Emperor was demonstrating to Europeans that the Ethiopian state was worthy of inclusion as an equal in the growing international state system. How far this would have developed in the years that followed is uncertain, for the development was cut short in 1934–1935, after the crisis with Italy at Walwal, which led to the Italian invasion of Ethiopia.

The Italian Occupation

The story of European diplomacy with regard to Fascist aggression in Ethiopia need not be investigated here in detail. Ethiopia had no effective allies. The Italians, with their military supremacy in terms of airplanes and poison gas, overran the country; Adowa was avenged. By early May, 1936, the Emperor was forced to flee the country. Although the Italians occupied Ethiopia, the Emperor won a moral victory at one of his most famous appearances. On June 30, 1936, he gave a remarkable speech before the League of Nations and demanded to know why the principle of collective security had not been applied in the case of Ethiopia. It was an eloquent plea, but it failed and from 1936 to 1940 the Emperor lived in exile in England.

The Italian invasion, like the British punitive expedition of seventy years earlier, was aided by dissident Ethiopians who looked upon the departure of the Emperor as their golden opportunity to re-establish regional family interests. The outstanding example of this tendency was Ras Hailu of Gojjam, whom the Emperor had refused to confirm as Negus. Ras Hailu had been ordered to leave Ethiopia in the Emperor's entourage, but at the last moment he deserted, returned to Gojjam, and by clever negotiations managed to have himself confirmed as King of Gojjam by the Italians.

Although there was some degree of cooperation with the Italians, there was also resistance by guerrilla patriots. The sons of Ras Kassa, a cousin of the Emperor, gave their lives in such resistance. Others attempted in 1937 to assassinate Graziani, the Italian military commander. Their failure caused a reign of terror to be unleashed on Addis Ababa, and in the weeks after the attempt on Graziani's life the Italians deliberately massacred hundreds of Ethiopians, especially many of those who had been educated abroad and those who had participated most devotedly in the modernizing process before 1934. After the incident, however, the Italians imposed the milder administration of the Duke of Aosta. Nevertheless, the countryside was generally unsafe for Italians, and Addis Ababa remained a heavily fortified military garrison throughout the five-year period of the Italian occupation.

After peace and order were restored in late 1937, the Italians embarked upon an extensive campaign to develop their new African empire. Literally millions upon millions of dollars were invested by Fascist Italy for the creation of the basic elements of an infrastructure. At great cost the Italians built a network of superb roads across the rugged Ethiopian terrain, a tribute to their engineering talents. For the first time in Ethiopian history the main urban centers were linked by motor roads. The Italians did more to modernize Ethiopia materially in the five years of their occupation than Haile Selassie, who was always limited by regional resistance and restricted funds, had been able to accomplish in his eighteen years as Regent and Emperor.

Mussolini had great hopes for the economic development of Ethiopia as a granary for Italy, a source of raw materials, and a colony of settlement, but in the years of occupation the Italians became increasingly disillusioned with their conquest. No profits were to be found in this new empire to justify the great expenditure in preparing naval bases, in underwriting the cost of the expensive military campaign, and in building bridges and five thousand miles of roads. Trade had been disrupted; it was impossible to collect revenue from the peasants. After all, even the Emperor had not been able to do this. Foreign capital was not attracted; minerals, especially oil, were not discovered in commercial quantities. Although the basis for long-term development was established, Italy had little to show for it by 1940.

The outside world knew nothing of all this, however, and when Italy declared war on Great Britain in June, 1940, the British feared that the Italians would invade the Sudan from Ethiopia. Fascist propaganda kept the Allies largely unaware of the true situation in Ethiopia until reports finally leaked out that Ethiopia seemed ripe for rebellion. Internal insecurity prevented the Italians from invading the Sudan. But most important, despite Italian claims to the contrary, there was not only a great spirit of resistance in Ethiopia but also great patriotism and loyalty to the exiled Emperor.

On the basis of reports, and after consulting with Daniel Arthur Sandford, who had served as British Consul in Addis Ababa during World War I and then from 1920 to 1936 had settled in Ethiopia as a farmer and advisor to the Ethiopian government, the British developed a plan for the invasion of Ethiopia. At Khartoum they trained a number of Ethiopian refugees, while Sandford made contact with Ethiopian patriots in Gojjam who, although divided among themselves, were still loyal to the Emperor. The plan called for a three-pronged attack on Ethiopia. British forces from Kenya would invade Somalia and then head toward Harar and Addis Ababa. A British Sudanese force would invade Eritrea, and a third force would invade from the Sudan into the area of Gojjam. A small group of English, Sudanese, and Ethiopian troops led by British officers entered Gojjam in January, 1941. The Italians, who were poorly informed of all developments in that isolated part of Ethiopia, assumed that the British and Ethiopians were invading in force and retreated. By the end of March, victories were recorded on all three fronts. Early in May, Haile Selassie re-entered Addis Ababa, and a new era began.

ETHIOPIA SINCE WORLD WAR II

Since the liberation of Ethiopia in 1941, the nation has continued to modernize. The Ethiopian state greatly benefited by the British occupation, which established effective administration over large areas of the Empire hitherto only loosely controlled by Addis Ababa. The rough outlines of change suggested by the actions of Haile Selassie in the years before the Italian invasion have since been filled in. Thus in the postwar era the Ethiopian government has continued to modernize its bureaucratic apparatus, to promote education, and to replace those Western-educated men who had perished during the Italian occupation. Despite regional opposition, as in the serious Tigrean revolt of 1943, continued troubles with the Ogaden Somalis, and other local disturbances, the process has continued apace. The central government has successfully displaced regional rivals, although the historic centrifugal tendencies remain, complicated as always by the polyethnic nature of Ethiopia's population and the heavy hand of the past in conservative Amhara society.

For the Emperor modernization has also served as a means to political stability. His policy has clearly produced a new generation of educated elite. But, whereas the Emperor set the tone for modernization until the mid-1950's, since then the new elements of his own creation have been less easily controlled. The recent university graduates have resented the authority of men who were recruited out of the old nobility to fill the Emperor's ministries. The imperial army, another of the Emperor's creations, disliked the favored treatment received by the haughty Imperial Body Guard, some of whose members harbored ambitions opposed to the goals of Haile Selassie.

In December, 1960, matters came to a head. While the Emperor was on a state visit to Brazil, the Imperial Body Guard staged an abortive coup. In the chaotic December days as the leaders of the coup briefly set up their own government, Addis Ababa reflected the stresses and strains of the changed Ethiopia. Their slogans may have been revolutionary, but their actions reflected the tensions between the old and the new. The Crown Prince was recognized as Head of State, and Haile Selassie's cousin, Ras Imru, was appointed Prime Minister, to the cheers of the small group of university students and graduates. And yet the organization of the coup reflected regional and family divisions such as those found in the old Ethiopia. The coup, which was quickly put down by the army, marked a turning point. Since 1960, observers of the Ethiopian scene have speculated increasingly on the future of the state after the death of the Emperor.

During this postliberation period the size of the Empire grew once more. But whereas Menelik and earlier emperors almost always expanded Ethiopian holdings through military conquest, Haile Selassie I has achieved his greatest successes through diplomacy. At the end of World War II, the Emperor proposed that Ethiopia annex the two former Italian colonies of Eritrea and Somalia, which were then occupied by the British. When Italy renounced all rights to its former colonies in 1947, the issue came to a head and the hotly disputed matter was brought before the United Nations. In 1950, the Ethiopians suffered a diplomatic setback when the United Nations decided to establish a Trust Territory in Somalia under Italian administration for a ten-year period, after which Somalia was to become independent. In the following year, however, they won a major victory: after a great debate and some resistance by Muslim Eritreans, the United Nations approved the creation of a federation of Ethiopia and Eritrea.

The federation of the two areas was established in 1952, and from the beginning it was doomed to failure. Although many Eritreans shared a common language and culture with the Tigreans, they were as reluctant as that province to lose their regional identity. Many Eritreans feared not only subordination to the Empire, but also progressive Ethiopianization of their land. Moreover, the sixty years of contact with Italy had not been wholly unpleasant, and many Eritreans regarded themselves as superior to the Ethiopians. The arrangement was further complicated by the fact that the federation was between Ethiopia as a whole and Eritrea. Within the Ethiopian part of the federation all provinces were strictly subordinate to Addis Ababa, and in practice the Ethiopians treated Eritrea more as a new province than as a federated territory. Although the Eritreans had their own elected assembly, its members were influenced by the Ethiopian government and its prerogatives limited by Ethiopian practices. The federation came to an end by agreement in November, 1962, when the Eritrean Assembly requested that Ethiopia annex Eritrea as its thirteenth province.

After 1941, Ethiopia entered more fully into the realm of international politics. Until 1945, the British presence was strongly felt and resented in Ethiopia. The British, who had not fully informed the Emperor of their invasion plans in 1940 and were slow in recognizing Haile Selassie as an independent sovereign in exile, had at first classified Ethiopia as Occupied Enemy Territory. The proud Ethiopians, however, regarded themselves as a liberated allied country and sought to assert the Emperor's rule and to eliminate British influence as early as possible. By an agreement of January 31, 1942, Britain granted recognition to Ethiopia as a sovereign state, although the British military administration continued to control much of the government. By the end of 1944, a new agreement was negotiated, and the central government at Addis Ababa regained control, with certain limitations, over the administrative apparatus. In the following year Ethiopian sovereignty was completely restored. Since 1945, the Ethiopian government has effectively curbed British influence in the country by turning first to the United States and then to small neutral countries like Yugoslavia.

Not only was the Emperor determined to be free from Italian and British influence, but he also sought to define an international role for Ethiopia. The experience of the Italian invasion reinforced the Emperor's belief in collective security, notwithstanding the failure of the League of Nations to come to Ethiopia's assistance in its hour of defeat. As evidence of this commitment to world politics, the Ethiopian government dispatched a force to serve in Korea in 1951 and in the

Congo in 1960 and since then has expressed a willingness to extend this policy to other troubled areas.

In the past fifteen years the Emperor has made several important state visits to the United States, the Union of Soviet Socialist Republics, India, Yugoslavia, France, and some Arab states. Increasingly, the Ethiopian government has taken an active role in the United Nations, especially at the Disarmament Conference in Geneva. But most striking of all changes has been Ethiopia's new official commitment to Africa, culminating in the summer of 1963 in the selection of Addis Ababa as the seat of the permanent secretariat of the Organization of African Unity. From being one of the most isolated and essentially un-African of the sub-Saharan African states, Ethiopia has made its bid for leadership in the African solidarity movement. Few could have predicted such a startling development.

The Contemporary Setting

Ethiopia is a land of diversity. The varieties of climatic conditions, land forms, ethnic groups, languages, religions, and historical experiences have contributed to the development of regional loyalties, localized economies, and generally weak national bonds. The task of the Emperor and any central government is thus to promote national unity at the expense of regionalism.

THE LAND

Descriptions of the land and people of Ethiopia often read like a catalogue of clichés. Indeed, the nature of the country invites facile generalizations. Few lands can boast of so striking a natural setting as that of Ethiopia, which travelers have often compared to Mexico or Switzerland. The richness of the vegetation in the plateau areas, the haunting loneliness of the stark deserts, the teeming wildlife once found in its lowlands, the contrast between the lofty mountains of the northwest and the Rift Valley which cuts through the center of the country, the tortuous gorge of the Blue Nile as it knifes its way from island-studded Lake Tana to the Sudanese border, all make of Ethiopia a remarkable land.

Just as Ethiopia has historically been isolated from much of the outside world, so internally its regions have been separated from one another. The great gorges which separate one area from another in many parts of the country, together with the unevenly distributed benefits of an otherwise kind Nature, have produced the isolation that in turn has made for regional diversity. Isolation and diversity have permitted Ethiopia to develop regionally and have inhibited the development of national unity.

Modern Ethiopia covers an area of some 432,000 square miles. For convenience, the country may be divided into three broad regions: the western plateau, the Rift Valley, and the eastern plateau.

The best-known part of the country is probably the western plateau, which comprises about 40 per cent of the area of Ethiopia. Within the boundaries of this plateau are to be found some of the highest average altitudes. In fact, the mountains of this plateau are among the highest on the continent. Ras Dashan, the highest peak in Ethiopia, is more than 13,500 feet in altitude. This extensive highland area is sharply divided in many parts by steep valleys. This area—especially its northern half—was the heartland of Christian Ethiopia, the Abyssinia of the Portuguese. It ran from the mountains of Semien in the north just south of the Red Sea as far as Lake Rudolf in the lake area of the south. This western highland may very well be the most fertile portion of East Africa. In some places in Shoa the topsoil is more than fifteen feet thick, despite centuries of erosion.

The eastern plateau, which can also be called Muslim Ethiopia, is part of a larger plateau that extends from Cape Guardafui, the most easterly tip of Africa, in a southwest direction to the mountains of Arussi and Sidamo-Borana. This plateau has many of the characteristics of the western plateau. It is broken and not uniformly elevated, but unlike the western plateau its valleys are not gorges and, for the most part, the area is poorly watered.

The two great plateau regions are divided by the impressive Rift Valley. Not so well known as its more southerly extension in Kenya and Tanganyika, the Rift Valley shares many of the same characteristics. The Valley is well defined and limited by the two plateau areas. The escarpment between plateau and valley is, for the most part, a steep edge frequently broken by smaller valleys. For obvious reasons transportation and communications between these regions have always been difficult.

Because of these varied geographical areas and great variations in altitude, the climate of Ethiopia cannot be easily described. Toward the Somali border and in the Danakil lowlands, there is a hot, dry climate, giving rise to semidesert conditions. On the other hand, the lower basin of the Baro River is hot, swampy, and malarial. In the lower lying deep valleys which cut the plateau conditions also approach those of the tropics. Here one does not find the cool bracing air of the highlands, where, for the most part, the average temperature is between 60 and 80 degrees (F.). Thus although the country lies within the tropics, not too far north of the equator, the elevation of the land more than compensates for this, and the fertile plateau regions enjoy a healthy and vigorous climate, best described as temperate. On the two plateaus the average temperature varies little throughout the year. Between June and September comes the rainy season when the monsoons pour down their heavy burden of water and provide not only for the needs of Ethiopia, but for those of the whole Nile Valley.

The picture thus presented of Ethiopia is of two plateaus—mountain citadels, as it were. Between the plateau country and the Red Sea, the steep escarpment and the desertlike coastal plain make access from the Red Sea difficult. To the west the plains lead into the Sudanese desert. To the east lies the arid steppe country of the Somalis. Furthermore, no navigable river leads into Ethiopia and the highlands from outside. These factors have been significant in maintaining Ethiopia's isolation from the outside world.

THE PEOPLE

Ethiopia today has a population of 22,000,000 or more, far above the estimates made by the Italians in the 1930's.[2] New techniques of demographical research have led to the conclusion that Ethiopia is the third most populous country in Africa, after Nigeria and the United Arab Republic.

Urbanization

The bulk of Ethiopia's people still live in the villages. Urbanization has taken place in Ethiopia to a much lesser extent than in other parts of Africa. Addis Ababa, with its population approaching 500,000, is probably one of the largest cities in Africa between Cairo and Johannesburg, but it is a sprawling collection of villages and modern buildings. Moreover, Addis Ababa's growth has not been phenomenal. The city was founded eighty years ago by Menelik II and had a population of 100,000 by 1910, and a 1952 census indicated that about 400,000 lived in Addis Ababa. In the past decade the growth rate has not been as great as in other African cities.

The second largest city in the country, Asmara, the former capital of

[2] Mesfin W. Mariam, "An Estimate of the Population of Ethiopia," *Ethiopia Observer*, V, No. 2 (1961), 135–141.

Italian Eritrea, was once a prosperous Italian city of more than 100,000 persons, but since 1952 it has slowly declined. In the last five years large numbers of Italians have left Asmara for Italy or for other parts of Ethiopia. The third largest town, Dessie, has a population of approximately 60,000. Harar and Dire Dawa, with 40,000 and 35,000 respectively, rank fourth and fifth. There are approximately only ten other towns in Ethiopia with a population greater than 10,000.[3]

Elements of Diversity

The Ethiopian Empire until its conquest of the southern and eastern provinces seventy years ago was an Amhara-dominated Christian empire with small non-Christian minorities. After Menelik's expansion eastward, large numbers of Muslims came under Ethiopian rule. Significant changes took place, but the Christian Amhara always succeeded in preserving their hegemony.

The population map of Ethiopia displays a bewildering complexity. One may approach an analysis of the Ethiopian population by means of religion, language, or ethnic origin. No one approach is completely satisfactory because the various categories can overlap. The simplest map is probably that of religion. If one were to draw a circle around the western highlands, he would, for the most part, be delimiting the Christian heartland of Ethiopia. Yet even in this area there are significant pockets of non-Christian peoples, including large numbers of Falasha and Muslims north of Lake Tana. In the southwest Islam has also made inroads. The eastern plateau, the Rift Valley and its extension into the Danakil plains, and northwestern Eritrea are Muslim. Along the southern and western borders there are large pagan populations. Since no official census has ever been taken in Ethiopia, it is impossible to tell with any degree of accuracy what proportion of the population is Muslim, Christian, or pagan. Estimates of the Christian population run from 30 to 67 per cent; 35 to 40 per cent is probably the closest approximation.[4] It is quite possible that the Muslim population ranges from 45 to 55 per cent.

The linguistic map of Ethiopia is far more complex.[5] Three major language groups are represented: the Semitic, the Cushitic (or Hamitic), and the Nilotic. By far the most important Semitic language is Amharic, which has become the official national language. Originally

[3] Ethiopia, Ministry of Commerce and Industry, *Economic Handbook* (Addis Ababa: December, 1958), p. S-1.

[4] George A. Lipsky, *et al., Ethiopia* (New Haven: HRAF, 1962), p. 101.

[5] *Ibid.,* pp. 52–61.

derived from one of the languages of ancient Axum, Amharic has absorbed many elements of languages spoken by the Cushitic peoples of the western highlands. The dominant group historically has been the Christian Amhara, who for centuries have extended their control over the other peoples of Ethiopia. All other peoples of Ethiopia have been considered subordinate to this ruling group. The Amhara have planted colonies throughout the country, especially military and administrative settlements in Muslim and pagan areas. Today between 35 and 55 per cent of the people of Ethiopia speak Amharic. This takes us beyond the reaches of the Amhara proper, who probably do not account for more than 25 per cent of the total population. During the last one hundred years, as increasing numbers of non-Amhara have come to speak Amharic, the language has begun to undergo a process of simplification. The Amharic alphabet, written in a script derived from an ancient South Arabian alphabet, has thirty-three different consonants, each of which has seven vowel forms.

The second most important Semitic language is Tigrinya, spoken in Eritrea and the province of Tigre. In many respects Tigrinya is more closely related to ancient Ethiopic, but unlike Amharic Tigrinya has a comparatively poor written literature. Although related languages, Amharic and Tigrinya are not mutually intelligible. The Christian Tigreans have in the past vied with the Amhara for political leadership, but since the death of Yohannes IV they have steadily lost their influence. In their culture the Tigreans are strikingly similar to the Amhara. During the reign of Haile Selassie the Tigreans have from time to time exhibited separatist tendencies. The Tigreans number about 9 per cent of the population. In the lowlands of northwestern Eritrea, Hasi (also called Tigre or lowland Tigrinya) is spoken by related peoples who were probably converts from Christianity to Islam.

To the southwest of Addis Ababa is a large pocket of Semitic-speaking people, surrounded by Cushitic-speaking peoples, who speak Gurage, a language believed to have evolved in a military colony of Tigreans or Amhara planted there several hundred years ago. The Gurage, who number less than 500,000 (2.5 per cent of the population), have maintained their language and separate identity; most, however, are Muslim, not Christian. On the eastern plateau the approximately 35,000 Muslim inhabitants of Harar speak their own language, Adari. Elsewhere in Ethiopia are several other Semitic languages distantly related to Amharic that have been dying out in the last century, of which Argobba is an example.

The Cushitic language group is represented by Galla, Somali, Afar, Sidamo, Agau, Beja, and several lesser languages. The Galla, who are the most numerous element of the population of Ethiopia, number approximately nine million. Ever since they entered Ethiopia in the sixteenth century, the Galla have been divided among themselves. There are three main groups in the west, the south, and the north. Their language seems to be devoid of distinctive dialects and all Galla can understand one another. This linguistic unity, however, has had no counterpart in the political and religious history of the Galla people. Their language has not been studied in any great detail, yet it does have some similarity to Somali and other Cushitic languages. Various authorities state that one-third of the Galla are Christian, one-third Muslim, and one-third loyal to the traditional tribal religion. Those Galla who have converted to Christianity have readily learned Amharic and absorbed elements of Amhara culture. The Muslim Galla are considerably less Amharicized, while the Galla of southern Ethiopia have resisted alien influences and have maintained much of their traditional culture.

The Somali-speaking peoples are located in the eastern quarter of Ethiopia in that area known as the Governorate-General of Harar, including the Ogaden region. They are part of the Somali-speaking peoples of the Eastern Horn of Africa, who are to be found also in Somalia and the Northern Frontier District of Kenya. Estimates of the Somali population have varied from 350,000 to more than 1,000,000.[6] The Somalis, heirs to the Muslim principalities of Ifat and Adal and their centuries-old traditions of struggle against the Christian Amhara, have separatist tendencies which have been reinforced by Somali nationalism emanating from the neighboring Somali Republic.

Another important group of Cushitic languages is that of the Sidamo region of southern Ethiopia, where the kingdom of Kaffa once thrived. People who use Sidamo, many of whom have maintained their traditional religion, were incorporated into the Empire during the reign of Menelik II. The Sidamo areas have been heavily infiltrated by the Galla, and it is difficult to estimate the number of speakers. Among the other Cushitic languages are Afar, spoken by about 70,000 Danakils; Saho, with 50,000 speakers; and Beja, spoken by approximately 60,000. All these language groups are Muslim.

[6] I. M. Lewis, *Peoples of the Horn of Africa* (London: International African Institute, 1955), p. 50; Lipsky, *op. cit.*, p. 45.

The original language of the western Ethiopian plateau was probably Agau. Agau-speaking peoples over the past 3,000 years have been absorbed by the Semitic-speaking conquerors. In the northwest all but 75,000 Agau have been assimilated to the Amhara in language, religion, and way of life. Today there are two major pockets of these Cushitic-speaking peoples left: one to the northeast of Lake Tana, the other to the southwest. Little is known of this language, though it is suspected that upon further investigation important connections may be discovered with the Amharic language, which it probably influenced. The Falasha, who were once more numerous but now number only about 25,000, are known to have spoken an Agau dialect. Many of them, like the Agau and the Galla, have learned Amharic, the first step toward absorption by the dominant group.

Among the Negroid, or Nilotic, populations along the western marches of Ethiopia, one encounters the most bewildering confusion of languages. More than a dozen languages are represented here, many of them having no known relation to other languages. Linguists have much to learn about this neglected group. These Negroid peoples, who probably comprise 3 to 5 per cent of the total population, were among the last peoples to be added to the empire of the Amhara. Least advanced of all the peoples of Ethiopia, they were enslaved in large numbers by the Amhara conquerors in the late nineteenth century. They are generally despised by the highland peoples, who invariably refer to them in derogatory terms, employing a word for black never used in describing a very dark-skinned Amhara. Color prejudice is not unknown in Ethiopia; the Amhara-Tigrean distaste for Negroid peoples is shared by the Somalis and Agau and to a lesser extent by all the other Cushitic peoples. Little is known about the few small enclaves of Bantu Negroids along the Webi Shebelli River in southeastern Ethiopia.

Foreign Residents

Among the significant communities of foreigners resident in Ethiopia are the Italian, American, Greek, Armenian, Indian, and Arab. The largest single foreign community, the Italian, once numbered more than 100,000, but it is doubtful that more than 40,000 remain, many in Eritrea. Although memories of the Italian occupation are bitter, the Italians are well liked, perhaps more so than any other group. Italian influence in Ethiopia has been strong for more than seventy years, and

Italian is heard throughout the country. Many of the remaining Italians are mechanics who keep the 20,000 vehicles in Ethiopia in operating order.

The Americans are for the most part connected with either their communications base outside Asmara or with technical aid missions, such as the Military Assistance Advisory Group, Point Four, the Agricultural College at Alemaya, the Peace Corps, the University, and the Public Health Center at Gondar. The American presence has been felt only since 1948; there may be as many as 5,000 Americans in the country today.

Unlike the Italians, the Greeks and Armenians, who number a few thousands each, are despised as middlemen retailers noted for their avarice and exploitation. Nor are the Indians, fewer in number, particularly highly regarded, except for a small group of secondary-school teachers and military advisors. The Arabs are more widespread than any other foreign group and have traveled with considerable ease about the country for generations. Yemeni Arabs are to be found scattered throughout Christian and Muslim Ethiopia. Never popular among the Amhara-Tigrean people, the Arabs have nevertheless for centuries been the chief merchants, small traders, and importers of foreign objects into northwestern Ethiopia. No figures on the Arab population of Ethiopia are available. Small numbers of Yugoslav, Czech, Russian, Swedish, Norwegian, German, and Israeli technical advisors also are to be found.

RELIGION

Ethiopian Christianity, dating back to the fourth century, is often inaccurately called Coptic. Although the Ethiopian Church established an early connection with the Coptic Church in Alexandria, their relationship through the centuries has been tenous. The two churches share a common theological outlook which sets them off from the Protestant, Roman Catholic, and Greek Orthodox churches. Since the Council of Chalcedon in 451, the Alexandrian and Ethiopian churches have adhered to the doctrine of monophysitism, a belief in the single nature of Christ as opposed to the more common Christian belief in the dual (human and divine) nature of Christ. In addition to this theological unity, the head of the Church in Ethiopia and the only bishop, the *Abuna,* was traditionally an Egyptian monk appointed by the Patriarch of Alexandria. This custom, which dates back to the fourth century, was changed in 1929, when the Regent appointed additional bishops, and came to an end in 1949, when the Emperor chose an Ethiopian abuna. Apart from these two elements, the Ethiopian Orthodox Church, as it is officially called, developed its own Ethiopic liturgy and unique religious practices which clearly distinguish it from all other forms of Christianity.

In the past the Church owned as much as one-third of the lands of Ethiopia and exerted a powerful influence on the local level. Occasionally, as in the coup which deposed Lij Iasu in 1916 and helped to bring Ras Tafari to power, the Church has played a decisive role in Ethiopian politics. In general, the Church has been one of the most conservative forces in Ethiopian society. Like so many other areas of Ethiopian society, the Church has also experienced a change in its relationship to the Emperor and the State. At present the role of the Ethiopian Orthodox Church has greatly diminished. Whereas formerly Christianity was the rallying point for national (Amhara-Tigrean) unity, in modern, pluralist Ethiopia its usefulness has lessened, although several attempts have been made by the Emperor to revitalize the Church.

Islam in Ethiopia was never as well organized as Christianity. Yet in the twentieth century Islam has been more of a vital force than the Ethiopian Orthodox Church, and Islam has spread among the pagans of Ethiopia. Cases of Amhara Christians converting to Islam are not unknown; the Jabarti, or Muslims of northwest Ethiopia, may have originated in this manner. In the east it is difficult to say whether Islam or Somali nationalism is more of a catalyst for hostility to the regime. Certainly in the past two strong Muslim movements, that of Ahmed Grañ in the sixteenth century and of the Mullah Muhammad Abdullah Hassan in the first two decades of the twentieth century, unified large numbers of Somalis in a struggle against Christian Ethiopians. Memories of both men are said to be vivid in the Ogaden today. During the Italian occupation Islam was given special consideration by the Italians, who tried to undermine the strength of the Ethiopian Orthodox Church. The Emperor's policy has been to demand of all Ethiopians, Muslim and Christian, a loyalty to the State and the Emperor that is above religion. Except in the Somali area, religious hostility does not seem to run high.

In the northwest the Falasha practice an archaic form of Judaism, with many borrowings from their Christian Amhara neighbors. The

traditional religion of the border peoples, where Islam has not infiltrated, has changed little, for the Ethiopian Church in the last three
centuries has not been interested in proselytizing.

A number of Christian missionary groups have been active in Ethiopia, but they have not met with great success. In Eritrea the Catholic
Church has made a few tens of thousands of converts, but not many
elsewhere. The government will not permit any foreign Christian
group to proselytize in Ethiopian Orthodox areas, where missionary
work is limited to medical stations and schools. Among the Muslims little headway has been made, either by the Ethiopian Orthodox or the
European and American religious groups. Among the other elements of
Ethiopia, the Sudan Interior Mission, the United Presbyterians' Mission, two Swedish groups, an American Lutheran Mission, and a
Seventh-day Adventist Mission are active.

SOCIAL STRUCTURE

The traditional society of Amhara-dominated Ethiopia was highly
stratified. Until the coronation of Haile Selassie the system had remained unchanged. Since 1930, new elements have emerged, some of
them purposely created by the Emperor.

The Emperor

At the apex of the traditional society stood the emperor, not only a
monarch by the grace of God, but a monarch with quasi-divine attributes. In theory the emperor reigned supreme. He was the commander-
in-chief of the military, the chief executive, the supreme legislator and
magistrate, the source of all land and confirmer of noble titles, and the
ultimate authority in matters of church administration and theological
dogma. He had a mystic bond with the past, represented by his coronation at Axum and his claim to be descended from Solomon and
Sheba. In practice, however, the emperors had to fight for their rights.
The emperor was also limited by the Church, whose head, the Abuna,
consecrated his office. Since early times emperors have acted as a
force against the conservatism of Amhara-Tigrean society, if only to
increase the power of the throne.

The Traditional Nobility

The main control on the power of the emperor was exercised by the
nobility, who were of three types. The royal nobility, also descendants
of Solomon and Sheba, were often regarded as potential usurpers and

thus dangerous. The lack of a law of succession encouraged palace revolutions. In earlier times royal princes were exiled to remote mountain areas. In more modern times a threat to the power of the Emperor came in December, 1960, when the Crown Prince played an ambiguous role in an attempted coup. On the regional level there existed a powerful nobility with a history as ancient as that of the emperor. This nobility, until the time of Menelik, was of military origin, and their titles (*ras, dejazmatch, kegnazmatch, fitawrari,* and so forth) were originally military ranks appointed by the emperor. These nobles became a landed aristocracy, patterning themselves on a smaller scale after the imperial court, and eventually became regional rulers who challenged the authority of the emperor. Such has been the case in Tigre and Gojjam in the past century.

Over the past hundred years, Theodore II, Menelik II, and Haile Selassie I have pursued a policy of curbing and then breaking the power of the old nobility, who exercised almost sovereign rights in the once remote provinces. Theodore initiated the process by attempting to remove control of the armies from the regional chiefs and by appointing new nobles loyal to him. Menelik continued this policy by appointing loyal Galla, as well as Amhara, to high positions; such was the case with Fitawrari Habte Giorgis. Despite their attempts the basic structure did not undergo any major changes, but after Ras Tafari became regent, the decline of the old nobility was accelerated. Opposition flared up from time to time, but the process has been completed. The old nobility has retained prestige and social position, but its political power today is largely nonexistent outside the new framework. The old nobility can now act politically either as agents or as opponents of the Emperor, but it cannot regain its lost regional privileges without plunging Ethiopia into a disastrous civil war.

Although the higher nobility has suffered a diminution of power, the lesser nobility of rich landowners and district judges and chiefs has continued to enjoy its old powers and prestige on the local level. The political changes pressed forward by Haile Selassie have not yet filtered down to the village and district level to have repercussions on their social status, inasmuch as the bulk of the peasantry still consider land ownership and family connections the criteria for commanding respect and wielding power. The Amhara and the Tigreans have remained an intensely conservative group, proud of their Christian ancestry and ancient traditions.

Creation of New Social Groups

Side by side with this older traditional Ethiopia have developed the elements of a new Ethiopian society. The Emperor, though still claiming traditional prerogatives, has been one of the main forces that have reshaped parts of Ethiopian society. Whether intentionally or not, he has greatly influenced the nature of the monarchy, which after Haile Selassie will probably undergo some further important changes. Some members of the old nobility have successfully redefined their roles in Ethiopian society. One means to this end has been marriage with members of the rather large royal family. More often, however, the old nobility has become a court nobility like that of Louis XIV's Versailles. Since 1960, there have been some indications that members of old families may still have some power. The Senate, created as a safe home for old nobles, has shown signs of life and opposition to the Emperor.

The first element of the new society to emerge were the men who were raised to power by the emperors. When Menelik II created the first ministerial departments of the government in 1907, these men made their debut as a new force. Although the development of this group was cut short by the death of Menelik, it was resumed after the accession of Haile Selassie and given fresh impetus. In the past two decades the sixteen ministries of the government, the army, the judiciary, and the diplomatic corps have been staffed by men chosen for their loyalty to the Emperor and for their abilities. This new group of men rose rapidly after 1945, when a revolt in Tigre province, possibly the last gasp of the old nobility, was put down. As the bureaucracy, the military, and the economy expanded they grew rapidly in numbers. Before 1950, most of them were recruited from the old nobility, whose ranks they abandoned for new offices and a new way of life. This new nobility, unchallenged until 1960, developed Western tastes. At the same time the old values of family loyalty, of distaste for business, and of private gain through public office have continued within this new setting. Their position is difficult, for they have been identified by some as the Emperor's men, and a new generation of university students regards them as reactionary, self-centered, immoral, and harmful to the national development.

In contrast with this transitional group, whose members have one foot in the past and one in the future, is the small but growing new elite. The expansion of the economy and bureaucracy has led to the creation of new groups in Ethiopian society: military servicemen, workers, salaried employees, secondary-school and university students, and a large group of Eritreans who had benefited from sixty years of Italian colonialism. These elements have only begun to show some signs of group solidarity. The most dynamic element is the students, who have been exposed to a secular education that has alienated them from many of the values of traditional Ethiopian society. These young men (few women have been educated to date) have come from all groups of the old society, including Galla, Muslims, and Eritreans, but not many Somalis and Negroids. Upon graduation they have been enlisted directly into government service at the middle levels; since 1961, some have started their bureaucratic careers at even higher levels. Others of this group serve as teachers, including a few dozen at the university level, journalists, and professionals. Only a few have pursued business careers. Most are concentrated in Addis Ababa, the one urban center of any importance.

Until a few years ago a distinction could be made between those who had been educated abroad and those who remained in Ethiopia, but by 1963 this distinction seemed to have broken down. Modernization means much to this group, but it is doubtful that they define it in the same terms as the Emperor. Like the youth of many other countries, they speak of their impatience with the older generation—in this case the new nobility who do not appreciate their technical training. They have produced no real leaders so far, although they openly expressed their dissatisfaction with contemporary Ethiopia as early as 1955. This group of young educated Ethiopians also played a part in the 1960 coup, an indication of their attitude toward the Emperor, whom they consider too conservative.

Labor Movement

Until late 1962, it would have been meaningless to talk of an Ethiopian labor movement. Government policy was aimed at maintaining economic production and stability. Strikes were not a legal weapon of the worker, although a number did occur. But a new labor law in that year permitted the formation of labor unions for the first time in Ethiopian history and paved the way for much change by legalizing the status of labor organizations. By mid-1963, forty-two labor unions had been formed, and a Confederation of Ethiopian Labour Unions (CELU) was established.[7] Claiming a membership potential of 70,000 industrial workers, the Confederation has expanded rapidly. Although

[7] *Voice of Labour*, I, No. 1 (July 8, 1963), 2.

the Labour Relations Decree of 1962 does not permit strikes, a number have taken place, with the support of the CELU. At present the labor movement contains hints of a larger, more active role in the years to come.

In July, 1963, the Confederation began to publish a lively little semi-monthly bulletin, *The Voice of Labour,* in Amharic and English. *The Voice of Labour* does not limit itself to discussion of purely economic problems, although that is the primary purpose of the bulletin. In its editorials, which urge workers to unite, *The Voice of Labour* stated, "It has for its task to bring messages of labourers from Ethiopia and the rest of the world to all interested." Thus it intends to broaden the horizons of the small but growing working class beyond the narrow prospects of economic problems.

In its third issue, the labor bulletin began to advocate a new program:

Workers' Education aims to develop in each and every worker a general knowledge which will enable him to assess, understand and evaluate the economic, social and political problems of his own country and the world at large. It enables him to voice his criticism of these problems . . . as a member of a particularly organized big united force—LABOUR.[8]

To lay the groundwork for this program, the Confederation of Ethiopian Labour Unions planned to embark on a three-month literacy campaign in 1964.

The Confederation has thus given signs of becoming more than just a workers' bargaining group. Furthermore, an Ethiopian delegation that included a representative of the CELU attended the 47th conference of the International Labor Organization at Geneva in 1963. The CELU has also joined the International Confederation of Free Trade Unions and has sent delegates to the Fourth African Regional Labor Conference and the 13th Congress of Soviet Trade Unions in Moscow.

It is noteworthy that the main organizers of trade unionism today are not government officials but university students, who have not only instructed labor leaders in their spare time, but also translated trade-union materials from European languages into Amharic. The main contributors to *The Voice of Labour* also seem to be students or ex-students. Thus it may be only a matter of time until the trade-union movement makes its presence felt in Ethiopia, although the economy is still underdeveloped. The implications of this new trend are enormous.

[8] *Voice of Labour,* I, No. 3 (August 11, 1963), 1.

THE ECONOMY

There is little doubt that Ethiopia is one of the most underdeveloped countries on the African continent; the statistics clearly reveal this. Ninety per cent of the population is engaged in subsistence agriculture unrelated to a money economy. Like so many agricultural lands, Ethiopia is for the most part dependent on a traditional agriculture which provides abundant though not excessive harvests for her farmers, in some areas twice or three times a year. The rich soil of the highland regions and the adequate rainfall ensure that few go hungry, although in semi-arid regions local areas can suffer from drought-induced famine, as has been the case in Tigre in recent years. In arid regions what little agriculture there is supplements a nomadic camel economy.

The Traditional Sector

The great variations in soil, altitude, and land formation permit the cultivation of a wide range of tropical and temperate crops. Although it has been estimated that half the land area of the country is arable, the Ethiopians have cultivated only 10 per cent of it. Shifting patterns of cultivation in the past have led to extensive deforestation. By Western standards the Ethiopian farmer uses primitive methods; unlike other Africans, however, he does have knowledge of the plow. By far the most popular crops are cereal grains, including some varieties unknown outside Ethiopia. Barley, wheat, sorghum, and *teff* are widely grown; in 1961, more than 4.5 million metric tons of cereals were produced. Other important crops in the traditional agricultural sector include oilseeds (346,000 metric tons in 1961) and legumes (520,000 metric tons). In recent years vegetable production has increased to 479,000 metric tons (1961, latest available figures).[9] The production of fruit, for which Ethiopia would be well suited, is insignificant largely because of a strong cultural food prejudice. Some subsistence farmers also contribute to the production of coffee, sugar cane, and *chat* for the money sector of the economy. Agricultural experts believe that with improved technology the Ethiopian farmer could make his country the granary of Africa and the Middle East, just as Mussolini envisioned Ethiopia as Italy's breadbasket. The rate of growth in agricultural production in recent years has continued to be greater than the rate of growth of the population.

The traditional Ethiopian farmer also maintains large herds of live-

[9] Imperial Ethiopian Government Central Statistical Office, *Statistical Abstract, 1963* (Addis Ababa: 1963), p. 1.

stock. The traveler through the Ethiopian countryside has always been impressed by the large number of domesticated animals. A 1957 estimate of 65 million cattle, sheep, goats, donkeys, horses, mules, and camels certainly needs upward revising.[10] The pig, forbidden food for both Ethiopian Christians and Muslims, is virtually nonexistent. By far the most important animals are cattle, which number about 25 million, mostly of the short-horned zebu type, although occasionally one comes across cattle with lyre-shaped long horns reminiscent of the original cattle population of northeast Africa. In the drier Muslim lowlands cattle give way to camels. Yet despite the abundance of domestic animals and the potential for exports, meat animals do not find their way into the money economy; the Ethiopian, in common with other Africans, is more concerned with the prestige value than the nutritional value of his cattle. Hides, however, constitute an important export product.

The Modern Sector

In terms of a money economy, Ethiopia is poor when compared to other African countries. United Nations figures [11] for 1958 estimated that the gross national product per capita was $55, much below the $71 of Nigeria, the $89 of the Congo (Léopoldville), the $94 of Kenya, the $204 of Ghana, and the $395 of South Africa, but comparable to Tanganyika's $54 and Uganda's $58. Ethiopian statistics [12] for 1962 indicate some improvement over the earlier figures, but the development has been far from spectacular in absolute terms.

Industry is relatively new to Ethiopia. Until the mid-1930's, the Ethiopian economy had grown at a much slower rate than the economies of colonial Africa. The first great infusion of capital for the development of agricultural and mineral resources occurred during the brief Italian occupation of the country. Only in the past few years has the nonsubsistence sector of the economy, which now produces less than 25 per cent of the gross national product, begun to grow. In 1961, there were only 178 industrial establishments in all Ethiopia (excluding mining, construction, coffee- and grain-cleaning firms), of which 83 were located in Eritrea. These establishments employed approximately 29,000 Ethiopians and 900 foreigners. Seven years earlier there had been 165 establishments in Eritrea and 55 in the rest of the Empire. The de-

[10] Lipsky, *op. cit.,* p. 253.

[11] Groupe d'Assistance pour le développement. *Annexe technique document numéro 5* (Tokyo: July, 1961).

[12] Imperial Ethiopian Government, *Second Five Year Development Plan* (Addis Ababa: Berhanenna Selam, October, 1962), p. 41.

crease in the number of business establishments in Eritrea reflects the gradual withdrawal of Italians from the province. The statistics available for 1957 indicate that there were almost 19,000 Ethiopians and over 700 foreigners gainfully employed in industry. The relative growth of approximately 25 per cent is less impressive when the small growth base is taken into account.[13]

The most significant industries in Ethiopia today are electric power, sugar cultivation and refining, salt, beer, cotton yarn and textiles, and cement. Between 1959 and 1962, the production of electricity, for the most part a government-owned industry, increased from 88.7 million kw-h. to 150.5 million kw-h.[14] The increase over 1961 was 22 per cent, due in large measure to the completion of the Koka Dam project in 1960. Because sugar and cotton figured large in the list of imports into the country, the government has encouraged the growth of cotton and sugar cane in suitable areas of the country and the promotion of the appropriate manufacturing industries. In 1950, a concession was given to a Dutch firm to establish a sugar plantation at Wonji in the Awash River valley; after a refinery came into production in 1957, Ethiopia's importation of sugar came to a halt. Although the consumption of sugar has greatly increased, the country has maintained its self-sufficiency, at great savings in foreign exchange. A similar program is being followed in cotton and textiles. At Tendaho in the Awash valley Mitchell Cotts and Company have a plantation concession; company officials estimate that they will be able to supply Ethiopia's entire cotton needs within a few years. On the basis of this cotton production, industrial production of cotton yarn in 1962 exceeded that of 1961 by 16 per cent, while cotton textile production increased 29 per cent to some 25.2 million square meters. In 1959, cotton textile production had amounted to only 5.7 million square meters.[15]

International Trade

A recent study of Ethiopia declared that the country is only on the threshold of economic development. Ethiopian trade statistics graphically illustrate the truth of this statement. The total value of exports in 1929 was approximately $5.6 million, of which coffee comprised 58 per cent and cattle hides 28 per cent. In 1945, the total value of all exports amounted to $15.2 million; coffee accounted for 45 per cent of this figure. In the following five years exports nearly doubled as Ethiopia exported cereals to the outside world. Since 1950, growth has continued.

[13] *Statistical Abstract, 1963*, pp. 11–12.   [14] *Ibid.*, p. 2.   [15] *Ibid.*

In 1961, the last year for which complete figures are available, Ethiopian exports totaled $75.5 million. Coffee is still by far the major export (45 per cent by value), and Ethiopian trade is unhealthily based upon one crop. In 1961, skins and hides brought in more than $9 million in foreign exchange. Oilseeds and cereals comprise the bulk of the other exports. An additional source of revenue has been the production and export of chat, a mild narcotic held in great favor by Muslims in Yemen and southern Arabia. In 1961, the value of chat exports was more than $1.5 million.[16]

All in all, agricultural goods overwhelmingly dominate the export trade. The principal importers of Ethiopian goods have been, in order of importance, the United States (which purchases most of Ethiopia's coffee), Italy, Saudi Arabia, and Great Britain. Since 1960, Ceylon has surged ahead as a major consumer of Ethiopian goods. Lebanon, Israel, the United Arab Republic, Japan, and Yugoslavia are also important trading partners. Curiously, in the past few years Ethiopian exports to the Somali Republic, with which there has been a continuingly serious border dispute, have doubled.

Until 1961, Italy and the United States were the main suppliers of Ethiopia's imports, followed by the United Kingdom, Japan, West Germany, India, Saudi Arabia, Holland, and a host of smaller nations. Since then Japan has rapidly risen to first place as Ethiopia's chief source of imports, displacing many imports from India (which also suffered from the expansion of the Ethiopian cotton industry) and forcing the United States into fifth place. In the past five years, the pattern of Ethiopian importation has begun to undergo several changes. Sugar importation has greatly declined since the establishment of Wonji. Cotton, which in the immediate postwar world commanded 50 per cent of the value of imports, has diminished its share to about one-fifth. The great increase has been in petroleum products, motor vehicles, machinery, metals and metal goods. Since 1957, machinery imports have more than doubled; metal and metal products have increased by more than 50 per cent.[17]

African nations have held a very small share of the total value of imports and exports. It is worth noting, however, that despite poor transportation facilities Ethiopian trade with the neighboring countries of

[16] Ministry of Commerce, *Economic Progress of Ethiopia* (Addis Ababa: 1955), pp. 88–90; *Statistical Abstract, 1963*, pp. 61–66.

[17] *Statistical Abstract, 1963*, pp. 42–44, 51.

Kenya and the Somali Republic has shown relatively vigorous growth and tripled between 1957 and 1961.

Transportation

The road system of Ethiopia, a major deterrent to both political unity and economic growth, requires much development. The once extensive Italian colonial road system deteriorated to the extent that only the barest traces of the Gondar-Dessie route now remain, and extensive repairs were required in order to make all existing roads passable for motor vehicles. Today a network of roads connects most of the provincial capitals with Addis Ababa, but only a few of these roads are paved, many of them are gravel, and others are passable only in the dry season. The main highway axis runs from Addis Ababa to Asmara and has branches leading from Dessie to Assab, from Asmara to Massawa, and from Adigrat to Gondar and Lake Tana. There are also important routes leading from Addis Ababa south to the coffee regions of Jimma and Sidamo. According to the Imperial Highway Authority there are approximately 5,000 miles of all-weather roads in Ethiopia. The railway line, extremely important for the transportation of export goods, runs from Addis Ababa to Djibouti in French Somaliland, a total of some 470 miles. There is a shorter line running from Massawa to Asmara and on to Adigrat, a total of 184 miles. In recent years the Ethiopian Air Lines has played an important role in connecting distant parts of the country. Today an airplane flight of a few hours accomplishes what formerly took as much as thirty days of travel. But even today less than 10 per cent of the country lies within twenty miles of all-weather roads. In fact, more than half of the country lies more than twenty miles from roads of any sort. The economic development of Ethiopia, as well as its political unity, will depend greatly on the expansion of the present communications and transportation system.

Finance and Development

The Ethiopian state budget greatly expanded in the years after World War II. Statistics, unfortunately, are unavailable for governmental receipts and expenditures in the prewar period. The total government revenue of $11.1 million in fiscal 1942/43 increased to $24.7 million in 1948/49 and $79.8 million in 1961/62. Significantly, the bulk of this income has been derived from ordinary revenues, exclusive of foreign loans and credits. In the same period, government expenditures have risen from $10.7 million in 1942/43 to $27.6 million in

1948/49 and $101.2 million in 1961/62 (i.e., an ordinary budget of $76.1 million, plus an extraordinary budget of $25 million, half of which has been underwritten by foreign loans). The Ethiopian government has not practiced deficit financing to any great extent and has continually sought to maintain a balanced budget. Given the underdeveloped economy of the country, it is possible that the government's conservative fiscal policy has limited the expansion of the economy. Only in 1963 did the government issue its first bonds, perhaps the first step in the direction of increasing public financing of development projects. The breakdown of budgetary expenditures for 1961/62 is as follows: Defense, 20 per cent; Interior, 14 per cent; Public Works, 9 per cent; Education, 8 per cent; Public Health, 4 per cent; Public Debt, 4 per cent; Finance Ministry, 3 per cent; Palace, 2 per cent; Church, 0.2 per cent; and miscellaneous, 10.8 per cent. The remainder of the budget (25 per cent) was destined for extraordinary expenditures in public works and defense.[18]

Since 1950, Ethiopia has received a number of loans and credits from various sources: the International Bank for Rehabilitation and Development ($24 million), West Germany ($26.2 million), Czechoslovakia ($10 million), Yugoslavia ($20 million), the USSR ($100 million, and the United States ($148 million, as of 1960).[19] The Ethiopian government has drawn only partly on its Soviet credits. Of the United States aid, $40 million was earmarked as military aid. For the most part, the government has employed foreign loans and credits for the development of a modern army and for specific developmental projects, including roads and transportation, telecommunications, a development bank, technical surveys, and port facilities. In 1963, a further agreement was reached with the Soviet Union for the construction of an oil refinery on the Red Sea coast at Assab, where the Yugoslavs had completed port works. Italian war reparations amounting to $16 million underwrote the cost of the Koka Dam hydroelectric project and textile plants.

THE PRESS AND OTHER MEDIA OF COMMUNICATION

In Addis Ababa four daily newspapers are published, two in English and two in Amharic. The Ethiopian Patriotic Association, an organization of veterans of the war against the Italians, publishes the *Voice of*

[18] *Economic Progress of Ethiopia*, pp. 103–107; *Statistical Abstract*, 1963, pp. 90–93.

[19] Lipsky, *op. cit.*, pp. 318–319; *Statistical Abstract, 1963*, pp. 90–91.

Ethiopia and *Ya-Ityopya Dems,* its Amharic version. A tabloid, the *Voice* depends on foreign news agencies and official government releases for most of its news. The Ministry of Information publishes the *Ethiopian Herald* and *Addis Zemen* (*New Times*). Each of these newspapers usually consists of four pages of general reporting of world news and feature articles. For the foreigner resident in Ethiopia it is difficult to keep abreast of current affairs because of the superficiality of much of the reporting. The reporting of domestic news is also very inadequate. In recent years the newspapers have printed strong editorials, though never critical of internal affairs. The number of readers for each of these papers is probably not more than 10,000.

The monopoly of newspapers by governmental and paragovernmental offices extends to periodicals. The Patriotic Association publishes in English and Amharic editions a monthly, *Menen,* that gives more or less an official version of certain national and international developments. The Patriotic Association also serves another function. It has occasionally presented morality plays at its clubroom. Comparable to medieval morality plays in their simplicity, the Ethiopian plays try to instill a love of country and Emperor; they meet with a fair degree of success among the older patriots. The Ministry of Education also publishes several official periodicals. One exception to all the official publications is the *Ethiopia Observer,* a monthly which deals with nonpolitical matters. In Eritrea several Italian-language newspapers are published, but these concern themselves mainly with news of Italy, although many Eritreans read them.

Government control is also seen in the censorship of all materials printed in Ethiopia; there are fewer than a dozen printing presses in the country, some of them government-owned, which facilitates this control. Official laws and appointments are printed in the *Negarit Gazeta,* an official journal established in 1942. An attempt is made to control the importation of books into the country. Although no official index of forbidden books exists, it is difficult to find books critical of the country sold publicly. Occasionally the government has also banned foreign periodicals.

Bookshops are few. In Addis Ababa there is only one large bookstore. Significantly, it displays only a few dozen titles dealing with Ethiopia. Publications in Amharic have tended to increase in the past decade, but few works of quality have been produced. Ethiopian intellectuals have not been fully satisfied with a government policy that tends to stifle creativity. The Amharic language, with its ambiguities and opportunities for double and triple meanings, has permitted some writers, however, to circumvent government restrictions.

A National Library was founded in 1944, but its facilities are too limited for a city the size of Addis Ababa. As the University College of Addis Ababa and the Haile Selassie I University both grow, it is believed that their library facilities will also develop. In smaller towns the literate element of the population is completely isolated from any contact with intellectual life.

Radio Addis Ababa does not reach the whole country. Even if it did, most villages would not have the proper receiving equipment. Programs are broadcast in Amharic, English, Swahili, and occasionally Somali, but the schedule of radio programing is never published in the daily newspapers. Like the press, the radio is a useful means of disseminating official information.

The Political Process

When Margery Perham wrote her penetrating analysis, *The Government of Ethiopia,* in 1948, she declared that a definitive study of the Ethiopian government had yet to be written. No such study has appeared. Moreover, much has changed since Miss Perham's time.

The observer of Ethiopian politics is confronted with a confusing mixture of traditional and nontraditional elements, of contradictions and contrasts, and a great gap between theory and practice, for Ethiopia is undergoing a period of transition, entering what may be called a political pre-takeoff period. Diagnosis is difficult; accurate prognosis is impossible. It is the purpose of this section to inquire into the theory and practice of politics in Ethiopia and to examine the traditional and modernizing aspects of the one state in Africa which seems to be farthest removed from the main currents of political development on the continent.

THEORY AND PRACTICE

The formal structure of Ethiopian politics as embodied in the constitution of 1955 gives the appearance of a constitutional monarchy that guarantees the basic human rights so often mentioned in Western liberal constitutions. In reality the constitution provides for a monarchy that has been described by some as medieval or Byzantine, by others as an autocracy or a benevolent despotism; in practice this amounts to a constitutionalized absolutism.

The constitution of 1955 replaced the earlier constitution of 1931, the first in the history of Ethiopia. Neither constitution established a constitutional monarchy in the Western sense of the phrase, for Article 26 of the more recent constitution states that "the Sovereignty of the Empire is vested in the Emperor and the supreme authority over all the affairs of the Empire is exercised by Him as Head of State."

The constitution assigns to the Emperor his traditional privileges, that is, the right to determine the organization, powers, and duties of all executive and administrative offices. Full powers over the armed forces belong to the Emperor, including the right to declare martial law or a national emergency. "Supreme direction of the foreign relations of the Empire" also belongs to the Emperor, who alone can ratify international treaties. Only the Emperor can confer and withdraw titles and honors. He can initiate legislation; his is the sole right to maintain justice. Thus, limitations on the powers of the Emperor are few and not well spelled out. The role of the Emperor is defined in modern terms; his real power, however, is not different in kind from that of emperors who had never heard of the concept of limited monarchy.

The constitution freely borrows from European models to guarantee basic freedoms and human rights. Within the limits of the law, never clearly defined, the constitution provides for freedom of religion, speech, assembly, and the press, and speaks of the due process of law and the basic rights of life, liberty, and property. In accordance with ancient tradition, Article 63 states that all have the right to present petitions to the Emperor. It would be difficult to find a more liberal statement of the rights and duties of the people. It would be even more difficult to demonstrate that the peasant or nomadic population is aware of the existence of the constitution, let alone of the meaning of these rights. Moreover, there is evidence that the government itself does not always respect the paper rights set forth in the constitution.

A Cabinet, whose members are chosen and dismissed at the Emperor's will, is also mentioned in the basic law. Membership in the Cabinet is not permitted the Crown Prince and the children of foreigners. Because the Cabinet ministers are individually responsible to the Emperor and the State rather than to the Parliament, this arrangement has in practice tended to stifle individual initiative. Yet the Emperor, who always has the final word, has repeatedly encouraged his ministers to take the initiative.

The administration of government business is conducted by the following ministries: Pen (i.e., Keeper of the Privy Seal, who coordinates all administration), Foreign Affairs, Defense, Interior, Education, Justice, Finance, Public Health, Mines and State Domains, Agriculture, Public Works and Communications, Commerce and Industry, Posts and Telecommunication, Information, Community Development, Pensions, and Stores and Supplies. The Emperor, who formerly held several ministries personally, now holds only the portfolio of Education, which is his special interest. The Cabinet can present legislative proposals to Parliament only with the approval of the Emperor. Ministers are required to answer before Parliament questions concerning their particular offices, and they are forbidden by law to have a conflict of interest between public and private affairs. In addition to the ministerial Cabinet, the constitution provides for a Crown Council consisting of the Abuna, princes, ministers, the president of the Senate, and dignitaries selected by the Emperor. In the final analysis, the Emperor directs and controls the whole decision-making process.

Article 76 of the constitution calls for a salaried bicameral Parliament consisting of a Chamber of Deputies and a Senate and convening annually. Legislative initiative, however, may come only from the Emperor or from a group of ten or more members of either chamber. In budgetary matters, all proposals must first be presented to the Chamber of Deputies. Deputies, elected for a four-year term by universal suffrage, must be Ethiopian, at least 25 years old, and owners of property in their home constituency. Senators, appointed by the Emperor for a six-year term, must be at least 35 years old, and a prince or other dignitary, or a former high government official. The senators are to number no more than half the total number of deputies.

At present the Chamber of Deputies numbers 251, and there are approximately 125 senators. For a bill to become law, both chambers must approve it. In the event that the two chambers disagree a joint session takes place. The senators, appointed by the Emperor, can then tip the balance in favor of the regime. Moreover, the president and two vice-presidents of the Senate are appointed by the Emperor, although the same officers in the Chamber of Deputies are elected by members of the Chamber from among their number. Elections were last held in 1959. They were characterized by a lack of political parties, little campaigning, nomination of "government" candidates, and the election of men who had strong local influence based on traditional regional interests. To date the Parliament has not functioned as an element in a system of checks and balances. In 1963, it began to exhibit some tendencies to act independently of the Emperor, who has effectively limited its real power. More often than not, however, opposition to the

Emperor within Parliament has reflected petty traditional regional cleavages and family rivalries rather than the nucleus of a true political opposition.

The constitution provides for a Supreme Imperial Court and other courts as authorized or established by law. All judges are appointed by the Emperor. Except in cases endangering public order or affecting public morals, courts must hold public sessions. On the local level, justice is actually in the hands of traditional local leaders, especially Amhara landlords. Occasionally public executions take place for the punishment of such crimes as murder.

In addition to articles establishing Addis Ababa as the capital of the Empire and Amharic as the official language, there are articles defining the Ethiopian Orthodox Church as the Established Church of the Empire, supported by the State. The Emperor, who must always be an adherent of that confession, has the right to legislate in all Church matters except monastic regulations and "other spiritual administrations."

Subsoil natural resources are declared State Domain, as is— significantly—"all property not held and possessed in the name of any person, natural or juridical, including all land in escheat, and all abandoned property, whether real or personal, as well as all products of the subsoil, all forests and all grazing lands, watercourses, lakes, and territorial waters."

ADMINISTRATIVE DIVISIONS

The main task of provincial administration to the present has been to ensure that the process of centralization of authority continues and that the provinces remain loyal to the Emperor. Ethiopia is divided into fourteen provinces, some of them roughly corresponding to older regional divisions. Gojjam is clearly delimited by the gorge of the Blue Nile, and Eritrea has the boundaries of the former Italian colony. The other provinces are Arussi, once the seat of a powerful sultanate; Bale, recently separated from the province of Harar; Begemder, an Amhara region of which Gondar is the capital; Gamu-Gofa; Harar, the largest province in the Empire; Illubabor, with its Negroid population; Kaffa, a province thought to have given its name to coffee; Shoa, the center of political activity; Sidamo, rich in coffee lands; Tigre, the traditional northern rival of Shoa; Wollega, inhabited mostly by Galla; and Wollo, once an influential Galla area, but not with its redrawn borders a deliberate mixture of Amhara, Galla, and Danakil peoples.

All provinces are ruled in the Emperor's name by governor-generals, some of whom spend their time in Addis Ababa and not in the provincial capitals. The affairs of the province are usually managed by younger men asigned to the provinces by the Ministry of the Interior. The borders of the provinces have been shifted about in the past fifty years in a conscious attempt to destroy the cohesion of older political entities. Thus the region of Amhara, which loomed large in Ethiopian history, has been divided between Begemder and Wollo. In making such changes, the Emperor has pursued a policy of undermining the power of regional leaders and replacing them with bureaucrats loyal to the State.

As a consequence of this policy, two forms of government, the modern state and the traditional local government, exist in Ethiopia. The regional governments have yielded to governmental pressure from the center, but modernization of the state apparatus has yet to percolate down to the local level. The provinces are subdivided into subprovinces, which are again divided into districts and subdistricts. The subprovincial and district governors are often appointed by the Emperor from among the ranks of young educated men. More often than not, however, these men may derive from the traditional ruling clan of a given area.

The farther one is removed from the central government the more the traditional political pattern comes into play. Thus Amhara and Galla village chiefs and Galla clan chiefs today hold their office by virtue of local tradition. On this local level, where frequently neither taxes nor land dues are collected, the older pattern prevails. In the past ten years the government has made some efforts to use the traditional local headmen to enforce government policies, but the degree of success is debatable. Among the Somali, the Danakil, and the Negroid tribes, the Ethiopian government deals with the people only indirectly through their traditional tribal chiefs. It remains to be seen whether in time of crisis the central government will exert effective authority down to the village level.

POLITICAL DYNAMICS

The government of Ethiopia is essentially that of the Emperor Haile Selassie I, King of Kings, Elect of God, Conquering Lion of Judah, and, in the words of the constitution of 1955, descendant "without interruption from the dynasty of Menelik I, son of the Queen of Ethiopia, the Queen of Sheba, and King Solomon of Jerusalem." Here traces of divine kingship still survive: "By virtue of His Imperial Blood, as well as by the anointing He has received, the person of the Emperor is sacred, His dignity is inviolable and His power indisputable."

Haile Selassie is remarkable in that he has held power longer than any other political figure in the contemporary world. After coming to power in 1916 as Regent at the age of 24, he successfully prepared the way for his coronation as Emperor in 1930. During his fourteen years as Regent he demonstrated his political shrewdness in undercutting power of all potential rivals to the throne and his political astuteness in pursuing a policy of modernization that saw Ethiopia join the League of Nations, abolish the slave trade, and lay the basis for increased effectiveness of his authority.

The role of the Emperor has expanded immensely in the third of a century since his coronation. Haile Selassie still depends to a great extent, however, on traditional politics. In his early years his power was based on regional strength; he had assumed his father's place as Governor of Harar in 1909. He has strengthened his position through matrimonial alliances, typical of Menelik and earlier monarchs. He has been more successful than any other ruler of Ethiopia in playing the game of palace intrigue; his enemies even accuse him of poisoning plots in the best Italian Renaissance tradition. He has maintained himself in power through appeal to the baser instincts of ambitious and talented men of humble origins; he has appealed to the awe of the peasant for the sacred person of the king. There is strong evidence that the quasi-divine kingship is the one institution that successfully binds Ethiopia together.

The Role of Traditional Elements

Haile Selassie has successfully curbed the powers of the three traditional conservative elements: Church, regional nobility, and military. He has done more than any other Ethiopian emperor to prepare the way for modernization and national unity through the changes which have made his reign noteworthy.

Through a series of measures the Emperor has controlled the conservative power of the clergy for state purposes. As Regent in 1929, he took the first step in securing the independence of the Ethiopian Orthodox Church from Alexandria by obtaining the right to invest five Ethiopian bishops who, like the Abuna, had the power to ordain priests. For the first time in Ethiopian history there was to be more than one bishop. In 1950, the Emperor successfully arranged for the installation of the first Ethiopian Abuna, a move opposed by some members of the

Ethiopian clergy. Finally, in 1958, the Ethiopian Church became completely independent of Alexandria. Fourteen bishops, one for each province, were appointed, with an Abuna elected from their own numbers but confirmed in office by the Emperor, and the hierarchy of the Church was reorganized.

Independence from Alexandria, however, has meant dependence on the State. The new organization of the Church corresponds to the provincial administration of the State. Moreover, the constitution of 1955 defined the clergy as subordinate to the power of the Emperor, who is not only Head of State but also Defender of the Faith and Head of the Ethiopian Orthodox Church.

During his reign the Emperor has completed the task of weakening the Church's control over his subjects. In this he was aided by events of the Italian occupation. The Fascist policy aimed at destruction of the power of the Church; monks were massacred, and the famous monastery of Debra Libanos destroyed. Although the Abuna went into exile and two bishops were martyred, the other two Ethiopian bishops collaborated with the Italians. Upon his return from exile the Emperor had good reason to deal strongly with the Church, whose loyalty he suspected. In 1942, the Church lost both its right of exemption from land taxes and all temporal jurisdiction over Ethiopians. In practice the Church continued to levy fines and to conscript labor, but all revenues from Church lands went to a central treasury administered for the Church by the government. Lastly, the Church's monopoly of education has ended, and the prestige of Church schools has fallen. To modernize the Church along lines of his own choosing, the Emperor has encouraged the use of Amharic in place of ancient Ethiopic; the Theological College in Addis Ababa is intended to produce a loyal but more progressive group of leaders for the Church. Thus the Church has been divested of much of its influence in national affairs. But although the Emperor has tamed the Church, its influence is still great on the local level because of its large landholdings.

The Emperor has also broken the power of the old nobility, although to do so took almost forty years. As Regent, Haile Selassie built up his own local forces and revenues in Harar until he was in a position to take command of the imperial army and bring his own forces into Addis Ababa in 1926. In that same year he angered the provincial rulers of Gojjam, Amhara, Tigre, and Shoa by suggesting that the provinces be administered by paid officials appointed by the Imperial Government. After his accession to the throne he faced a series of revolts by the nobility of Tigre and Gojjam, some of whom threw in their lot with the Italians in 1935 in order to preserve their traditional privileges.

Only after his restoration in 1941 did the Emperor find himself in an opportune position to check the nobility. In the aftermath of reconquest, the imperial forces, directly under the control of the Emperor, became stronger than the regional armies, which had been weakened by their opposition to or collaboration with the Italians. Since then the army has become an instrument of the State, and the nobility has lost its original character as a military aristocracy. To train a new group of military elite, Haile Selassie instituted the Imperial Body Guard.

The second blow to the nobility after the loss of military power came in 1942 with the centralization of tax collection. The Ministry of Finance by law became the sole collector of taxes. Shortly thereafter the Ministry of the Interior redrew provincial boundaries and assigned new governors to the new provinces. Thus the nobility lost a major source of wealth and has since been limited to the small rents and income in kind from their own estates. With these reforms the nobility was deprived of its traditional role as independent local agents for the central government. Because of the Emperor's new position of power, greatly helped by the presence of British occupation forces, the old nobility had to submit. In some cases it was bought off by titles or assignments to diplomatic posts. In other cases nobles were raised to the powerless rank of Senator and compelled to remain in Addis Ababa under the watchful vigilance of the government and far from their regional backers. In still other cases the Emperor has won the cooperation of nobles who have made the best of a bad situation.

The men who hold the highest offices and titles in the Empire today are either members of the old nobility, relatives of the Emperor, or men who have risen on the basis of talent and loyalty. The old nobility, stripped of its former power, still survives in significant ways. To control them the Emperor has given them offices, titles, and wives in the royal family.

Some of the members of the old nobility were themselves in the royal line. The late Ras Seyum of Tigre was a grandson of Yohannes IV. Ras Imru and Ras Kassa, as cousins of the Emperor, both had valid claims to the throne. Their relatives today are influential in Ethiopia. Asrate Kassa, a fourth cousin of the Emperor and sole surviving son of Ras Kassa, holds the high office of president of the Senate; his extensive landholdings give him a large income and local influence. A nephew, Amaha Aberra Kassa, has served as ambassador to Yugoslavia and Governor-General of the important province of Begemder. Mangasha Seyum, son of Ras Seyum, is popular among those elements hostile to the regime. He was active in the Tigrean revolt of 1943, but because of his position in that key province and his noble origins, he was appointed Minister of Public Works in 1958 and now is Governor-General of Tigre, where he has won a reputation for his energetic policies. Zawde Gabre Selassie, a grandson of Ras Seyum, has served as mayor of Addis Ababa, ambassador to the Somali Republic, and Minister of Justice. Ras Imru served as Governor-General of Gojjam and of Begemder and then, in turn, ambassador to Washington, New Delhi, and Moscow. It should not be overlooked that in the 1960 coup the rebels nominated him as their apparently unwilling choice for Prime Minister. A personal friend of the Emperor, Makonnen Endalkatchew, has served as mayor of Addis Ababa, Governor-General of Illubabor, Minister of the Interior, Prime Minister from 1945 to 1957, and Senate president from 1957 to 1961. He has been awarded the title of Ras-Bitwoded, the highest title ever granted outside the royal family. His son, Endalkatchew Makonnen, also served as Senate president, at one time was representative to the Bandung Conference and later ambassador to Great Britain, and more recently has been Minister of Commerce, Industry, and Development. Still another noble family is represented by Andargatchew Massai, Ethiopia's representative to the League of Nations in 1923, one-time Governor-General of Begemder, former viceroy in Eritrea, and now Minister of the Interior and Governor-General of Sidamo.

Many of these men are tied to the royal family by bonds of matrimony; all were loyal during the 1960 coup. Asrate Kassa is married to a granddaughter of the late Empress Menen. Mangasha Seyum is married to the Emperor's granddaughter Aida; his sister was the first wife of the Crown Prince. Andargatchew Massai is a son-in-law of the Emperor. These families have also intermarried among themselves: Amaha Aberra Kassa is a brother-in-law of Endalkatchew Makonnen.

The Rise of New Elements

The Emperor has also taken men of humble and often non-Amharic origins and raised them to high positions. These men have become dependent on the Emperor for their positions and have exhibited a strong loyalty. They have been rewarded by office, rank, wealth, and marriage. General Merid Mangasha, whose efforts were largely responsible for the suppression of the 1960 coup, was discovered by the Emperor in exile; by 1959 he had risen from aide-de-camp to Chief of Staff of the Army. Brigadier-General Abeye Abeba, of fairly modest background, has served as Governor-General of Wollega, Minister of War, ambassador to Paris, and Minister of Justice. In 1942, he married the Emperor's daughter, Tsahai, shortly before her death. Aklilou Habte Wold also belongs to this aristocracy of loyal talent; through his competence he rose to become Minister of Commerce, Foreign Minister in 1949, Minister of Pen in 1960, and Prime Minister in 1961. Similarly, Ketema Yifru, Acting Foreign Minister, was discovered by General Merid Mangasha and brought to the Emperor's attention. Lastly, there is Assafa Ayene, about whom little is known before his promotion to Commander-in-Chief of the Air Force. These are the men of the new nobility who have been disliked by the other new elements of Ethiopian society.

There has been much speculation about the nature of the newer elements in Ethiopian society. The products of postwar attempts at modernization, these include the youthful civil servants, bureaucrats, and university students who comprise a small but growing intelligentsia, labor leaders, and members of the military, as well as Eritrean separatists.

Little evidence exists to indicate the positive aspirations of the first group. In informal discussions they exhibit a general distaste for the *status quo* and often a sharp criticism of the distribution of political power in the hands of the Emperor, the old families, and the aristocracy of privilege and loyal talent. Occasionally the landholding system is the object of their complaints. From time to time they also attack the judicial and administrative systems for inefficiency and corruption. For them too much of Ethiopia is too far from modernization.

These impatient young men talk of having a greater share in policy-making on the national level. Whether or not their impatience is a function of their age group or an indication of real disaffection, they regard Ethiopia as being behind the times. Those who studied abroad are painfully aware of Ethiopian backwardness. For the most part, however, these young men cannot be labeled ardent nationalists or pan-Africanists. They are the generation caught between the dream of the future and the reality of the present. For them talk has been an adequate substitute for action. Significantly, they played no major part in the 1960 coup, although many of their leaders voiced sympathy for the aspirations of the rebels. Moreover, many of these young men are still tied to Ethiopia's past by family connections. In government service they rise with initial rapidity. Many of them have been recruited into the ranks of the new aristocracy, and it remains to be seen how they would behave during the uncertainty of a possible future crisis.

The Role of the Military

The second element to consider in any discussion of potentially active groups is the military. Estimates of the size of the Ethiopian army range upward from 25,000. The spectrum spreads from jet pilots to spear-throwing infantrymen, and of this number the majority of rank-and-file soldiers display poor abilities and training. The army and the air force, however, contain a cadre of officers who have received the equivalent of a university education in officer-training school. Several thousand men have been exposed to American influence through training in Ethiopia and in the United States. Many of these men were the pick of secondary-school graduates who had been arbitrarily assigned by the government to the army and the air force.

Originally the army was developed by the Emperor as a counter-weight to the regional armies of the rases. After the liberation of the country the Emperor promoted an Imperial Body Guard as an elite corps. The events of December, 1960, reveal that the Emperor had misplaced his faith in the Imperial Body Guard. At that time the army remained loyal and was the principal instrument for the suppression of the coup. It is worth noting, however, that after the coup the army demanded and received an increase in pay and for the first time asserted itself. Since 1960, the Emperor has encouraged the organization of the militialike territorial army as a balance to the army.

The course of these events has led some observers to infer that there may be some restlessness in the army. Certainly army officers have family connections, regional ties, and common school experiences with the civilian intelligentsia. The army is still an unknown factor, however, and appears to have less political consciousness than in other underdeveloped countries where a pattern of military coups has established itself. The American training of army officers has been technical in nature and largely devoid of political content. If a political interest has developed in the officer corps, it has been through contact with other elements of Ethiopian society. Older officers, as loyal to the Emperor as members of the new aristocracy, still have considerable power. It may be that restlessness will first become apparent among the younger officer group. It is also quite possible that the air force as an elite branch of the military may very well bear watching as a future political nucleus. Whatever happens, the army and the air force are the only two groups in Ethiopia today with organized strength sufficient to determine the outcome of a future crisis. One informed observer has expressed the opinion that the military could almost be classified as a party.

Eritrean Separatism

The third new element in the political process is in many respects a latter-day incarnation of the traditional problem of regional separatism. The Federation of Ethiopia and Eritrea in 1952 added to the Empire a group of people politically more sophisticated, with a history of activity by more than a half-dozen political parties dating from 1947.

The federal arrangement pleased neither the Ethiopians nor the Eritreans. Ethiopian administrative officials of the area consciously pressured the Eritrean Assembly to make changes in Eritrea's federal status. Ethiopian laws and administration were deliberately applied to the territory in an attempt to Ethiopianize the country. In general, Ethiopians referred to Eritrea as their lost province. Some Eritreans, including urban Ethiopian Orthodox Christians, a group of Muslim traditionalists, and some terrorists, favored annexation by Ethiopia, but they amounted to less than half the population. Another group, recalling the precolonial past of the Tigrean-speaking territory, favored the creation of an Eritrean-Tigrean state, while a Muslim party advocated the creation of an independent Muslim state embracing Eritrea, the Danakil region, and parts of the Sudan. Only a small group wanted the Italians to return. Finally, in 1962, after the Eritrean Assembly, which some observers regarded as packed by the Ethiopians, went through the necessary parliamentary motions, Ethiopia willingly agreed to the Eritrean request for annexation.

In the last decade Eritrea has been less prosperous, and there has been some dissatisfaction among Christian and Muslim elements alike. Political parties no longer exist, and political groupings are weak. Tigrean-speaking Christians resent the spread of the Amharic language and Amharic influence. Muslim elements have formed a coalition Eritrean Democratic Front, but its headquarters is in Cairo, not Asmara. Although the Front is mostly Muslim, one of its three principal leaders is Woldeab Wolde Mariam, an Eritrean Christian. The Eritrean Democratic Front, no doubt with the tacit support of the

United Arab Republic, has addressed several petitions to the United Nations and to the members of the diplomatic corps in Cairo. Ethiopia has firm control over Eritrea today and values its two ports at Massawa and Assab. The Eritrean Democratic Front in exile, however, is symptomatic of the tendencies toward regionalism in the Empire. It is ironic that just as the older problems of regionalism have been controlled by the central government, the annexation of Eritrea has again given the government a problem. Eritrean separatism in times of trouble could easily trigger renewed separatist feelings in Tigre. This new element in Ethiopian politics must also be an unwelcome one from the point of view of foreign policy, inasmuch as educated Ethiopians today are strongly suspicious of the motives of the United Arab Republic in Yemen and the Somali Republic, as well as in Muslim areas of Ethiopia.

THE NO-PARTY STATE

With the suppression of Eritrean political parties, Ethiopia has maintained its purity as a state without political parties. In a continent that has seen a proliferation of political movements, the absence of this modern means of political organization is striking.

No provision is made in the constitution for political parties, though there is no outright ban on such organizations. Imperial appointment has prevented the Senate from becoming a nucleus of party activity. Similarly, in the elections of 1957—the first in Ethiopian history— candidates for the Chamber of Deputies were carefully screened and generally were not interested in running on party tickets.

Nor is the Cabinet tied to any system of parliamentary or party responsibility. Behind the scenes of parliamentary politics there has developed some tension over the question of cabinet responsibility. The Emperor has publicly voiced his desire for true cabinet responsibility and initiative, while his opponents claim that he does not really care to delegate any of his power to such a group. In 1963, in answer to the annual speech from the throne, members of Parliament demanded full ministerial responsibility. Because of the Emperor's apparent indecision on the matter, the Cabinet has remained in suspension between real and nominal responsibility. At present the Cabinet cannot be said to represent any party interests in the broader sense of the word.

The lack of modern political sophistication on the part of the peasant masses means that the proper environment for a mass party is yet to be created. Both traditional and new elements of Ethiopian society are remarkable for their political astuteness in everyday situations, and traditional Ethiopian politics could almost be called overdeveloped. Yet these two groups have not cared to depart from the traditional basis of operation: personalism and factionalism. Not only the Emperor but also the aristocracy have strong tendencies toward personal rule. This is true on the local level as well as on the regional and national levels. The tendency to factionalism, which has precluded the development of a political party, has led to a splintering of political groupings to the point of petty intrigue or ineffectiveness. In such an environment Haile Selassie has proved himself a master of political manipulation. He has been able to outmaneuver rivals by their own methods. To this he has added a generous amount of paternalism and personal interest in the few thousands who comprise the Ethiopian elites. An extensive information-gathering service both for palace and government enables him to remain closely informed about the activities of all potential political activists.

The Ethiopian political scene is singularly devoid of political slogans. No external threat exists to unite the country in one political movement. The colonial experience was too brief to produce the nationalism found elsewhere in Africa. Thus one observes a great deal of political intriguing but little of the political activity characteristic of other African states. The sole rallying point of the state has become the person of the Emperor. The army, although it hesitantly took a position in the 1960 coup, has remained apolitical, and other than the Emperor there is no basis for unified political action on a national scale.

In maintaining Ethiopia as a no-party state, the Emperor has walked a tightrope between traditionalism and modernism, stability and change, direct and indirect controls. We have seen how he has undermined much of Ethiopian traditionalism. At the same time he has often declared that change must be firmly rooted in the traditional values of Ethiopian culture—as he defines it. Undeniably, the modernization that has taken place in Ethiopia has served to strengthen the ancient institution of the monarchy. In modernizing, however, new elements making for change have been created. How well they can continue to be controlled remains to be seen.

Lastly, the *status quo* within Ethiopia received the official approval of the Heads of the African States in assembly at Addis Ababa in May, 1963, by their acknowledgment of Ethiopian leadership on the African continent. Had an important African state chosen to criticize Ethiopia for the absence of those institutions considered characteristic of most

African countries, then the authority of the Emperor at home would have been shaken. Perhaps because the Emperor's position in Ethiopia, though without benefit of a mass movement, nevertheless has some analogies to that of leaders of one-party states where the government is clearly dominant over any political movement, he has been welcomed into the fold of African unity.

The 1960 Coup

The one serious challenge to the Emperor's authority in recent years occurred in December, 1960, while he was on a state visit to Brazil.

On the evening of December 13, 1960, numerous ministers and other important people received telephone calls urging them to come to the royal palace as quickly as possible. The appeal was made in the name of the Crown Prince, Asfa Wossen. Those who went to the palace found themselves prisoners of a group of conspirators. Others, especially several high-ranking army officers, were suspicious about the whole affair. Soon the army was alerted, as were tank and air units outside the capital. The following morning key army positions in Addis Ababa were surrounded by units of the Imperial Body Guard. In the confusion that followed there took place the first real attempt at revolution in Ethiopian history. Hitherto there had been a number of court intrigues, palace coups reminiscent of fifteenth- and sixteenth-century Italy, and regional disturbances, as in the Tigrean uprisings of 1943 and 1952 or the defection of Ras Hailu of Gojjam to the Italians in 1936. The purpose of the leaders of the coup was different, however, and marks a major turning point in modern Ethiopian history.

In the early hours of December 14, it was uncertain whether the army or the Imperial Body Guard had initiated the coup. Officers of the Body Guard claimed that the army had revolted, while the army stated that the Body Guard had begun the disturbances. On that day the Crown Prince declared in a radio broadcast that the old regime had come to an end; no more would it oppress the people of Ethiopia, who "have lived by words and promises which have never been fulfilled." The radio speech referred to Ethiopia's lag behind the former African colonies in economic, social, and political development and attributed it to "repeated corruption in the government" and "selfish people with unquenchable thirsts." Furthermore, the broadcast stated that the army, the police force, and the young educated class all supported the new regime.

On December 15, a series of announcements was made on the rebel-controlled radio station. All air service was suspended, supposedly by order of the army. Yet the Crown Prince a half-hour later declared the army leaders enemies of the people. In the same princely declaration all soldiers were given an immediate raise of $20 per month. By mid-morning Radio Addis Ababa announced the appointment of Ras Imru as Prime Minister. Shortly thereafter a statement by students of the University College of Addis Ababa was read: "The new government is doing all in its power to free you from all oppression, giving you freedom of speech, press, and political parties." That afternoon, after thirty-six hours of mounting tension, fighting broke out between the army and the Body Guard. After several days of sharp fighting the back of the revolt was broken by December 19, although mopping-up operations continued for several days. In one last act of desperation the rebels shot their ministerial and other hostages, killing fifteen of the more than twenty important Ethiopians whom they had kept prisoner throughout the coup.

In the aftermath of the coup the government sought to identify the main conspirators. What they discovered must have been disturbing. The two chief leaders, without a doubt, were the brothers Mengistu and Girmame Neway. Mengistu had served as deputy commander of the Imperial Body Guard for ten years and then for five years as commander; Girmame had been governor of the Jigjiga subprovince east of Harar. With them was a cousin, Girmame Wondefrash, governor of Ulat Awlalo in Tigre. All three were members of the powerful Moja clan of Shoa. Brigadier-General Tsigue Dibou, Commissioner of Police, and Lieutenant-Colonel Workeneh Gebeyehu, Chief of Security, also figured in the organization of the conspiracy. Involved in the events were various second-rank officials, some of whom were also of the Moja clan.

Although family ties are significant here as in traditional Ethiopian politics, additional motives came into play, some of them personal, others symptomatic of the changes that had taken place in Ethiopia. Mengistu Neway was known as an able man of unquestionable loyalty to the Emperor, to whose attention he had come at Khartoum in 1940. In 1951, he was active in the suppression of a plot against the Emperor. Afterward he served with distinction as commander of the Kagnew batallion in Korea. In 1955, Mengistu was made commander of the Imperial Body Guard and welded it into a real force again after a period of deterioration. In Addis Ababa it was rumored that Mengistu had ambitions to marry one of the Emperor's granddaughters; his rejection as a suitor in mid-1960 allegedly was the cause of his disaffection. He was known as a man without ideas, other than a basic distrust of all foreigners which he shared with many Ethiopians of the same background. Mengistu's home was the scene of a weekly luncheon for a group of frustrated men who soon came under the influence not of Mengistu, but of his brother Girmame. It would seem that as late as the first week of December Mengistu still knew little of the projected coup.

Girmame Neway was admired by many for his education, which included several years of training in the United States, where he had an outstanding record. In Ethiopia as governor of a district in Sidamo he won a reputation for progressiveness and antagonism toward the old landed nobility and the missionaries. Girmame was responsible for the establishment of several schools financed by "voluntary" contributions from the landed aristocracy and for his attempts to get increased government services in his area. Foreign missionaries in Sidamo distrusted Girmame for his Marxist bookshelf; Girmame, it would seem, enjoyed distressing them but was little more than the clever young man trying to shock his conservative elders. Among his several remarkable accomplishments was winning the affection of local Somalis by digging wells and storing grain for them.

Outraged by his treatment of them, the local aristocracy succeeded in having Girmame appointed titular governor of Jigjiga. Thus Girmame was brought to Addis Ababa, where in his idleness he conspired to change things. It is he who assumed leadership at his brother's luncheons and gave the gathering a political direction. Within the first twenty-four hours of the coup Girmame was directing everything. His reputation for forcefulness accounts for some of the ruthlessness of the rebels during the coup.

In November, 1960, Workeneh Gebeyehu, Chief of Security, discovered the plot. Rather than report their activities, he joined the plotters, for reasons not known. Tsigue Dibou, the Commissioner of Police, was a close friend of Workeneh, but it is unknown at what point he joined the conspiracy. Curiously, neither man brought with him any of his followers in the security police or the general police force. Later events revealed that the police, who were neutral during the coup, were not an effective fighting unit.

For several months before the coup the Body Guard had been building up a number of grievances against the Emperor. Some of the officers of that elite corps, as well as Girmame Neway, had taken extension courses at the University College of Addis Ababa, where they had some contact with the students and faculty. These men took courses in constitutional history, European history, and economics, in which there was discussion of political and economic matters. In the general interaction between officers and students there developed a keen awareness of Ethiopia's backwardness. The blame for this state of affairs was placed partly on the Emperor, who, it was thought, had not proceeded with modernization at a fast enough pace, but mostly on members of the old and new aristocracies who opposed modernizing changes. Clearly, some of the conspirators were young idealists; a few of them have been reinstated by the Emperor after a two- or three-year period of probation.

It is also apparent that a large number of men in the Imperial Body Guard did not understand the nature of the coup. Cooperation with the army was rendered difficult by the Body Guards' tendency to look down on the army, which was jealous of that elite group. It would also seem that the Body Guard feared the air force and the navy as rivals for the Emperor's favor. In this confused welter of events and attitudes, certain rebels were involved in the coup because of their desire to continue their privileges or to pursue traditional selfish interests. Others, however, were idealistic, if inexperienced, and the idea of a People's Government of Ethiopia, as suggested by Girmame Neway, appealed to them in a vague sort of a way; this accounts for the students' reaction and inaction.

The elements of idealism and revolution for progress are also seen in several documents discovered in the possession of Girmame Neway. According to official government sources, Girmame advocated the nationalization of all land, especially that of the Church, and the disestablishment of the Ethiopian Orthodox Church. As a means to achieve his goal of a new Ethiopia, there is evidence that he was willing to assassinate ruthlessly all government officials from the level of governor-general to the subdistrict governors, ministers, judges, notables, and tribal leaders; in other words, the whole of both traditional and new aristocracies. If the government's allegations can be believed, Girmame Neway would have ordered the execution of all commissioned army officers, all higher officers in the police force, and all private soldiers within the armed forces and the police force above the age of forty. This ruthlessness, which is not out of keeping with Girmame's character, would have been the Terror that could have irrevocably destroyed the Old Regime.

As their final desperate and perhaps irrational act the rebels ordered the execution of the hostages held in the imperial palace. Their victims had in common only the fact that they were important men; they were executed regardless of their attitude toward the old regime. Some of the victims went unmourned. Such were Ras Abebe Aragaye, pretentious Minister of National Defense, who had a bad reputation with the educated group; Makonnen Habte Wold, brother of the present Prime Minister, hated as a colleague of Ras Abebe, Minister of Commerce, Industry and Planning, and one of the men most distasteful to the young progressive element; Tadesse Negash, Minister of State in the Ministry of Justice, who had personal enemies among the rebels; Abba Hanna Jimma, a priest and chaplain to the royal family, despised for his venality; and Lemma Wolde Gabriel, Vice-Minister of Mines and the State Domain, a protégé of Makonnen Habte Wold. Others had been assembled only because of the office they held; this was true of Ayale Gabre and Letibelou Gabre, senators of little consequence; Ishete Geda, who occupied the office of *Afa Negus* (Chief Justice); Dawit Ogbagzy, a Minister of State in the Foreign Ministry, who had no known enemies; Amde Mikael Dessalegne, who although he had once collaborated with the Italians held the important position of Acting Minister of Information; Gabrewold Ingedaworq, a minister in the Ministry of Pen; Abdullahi Mumie, a vice-minister of Finance; and Kebrete Astakkie, assistant minister in the Ministry of the Interior. But what was most shocking to many educated and politically experienced Ethiopians was the death of the well-known Ras Seyum, Governor of Tigre, who could by no stretch of the imagination be considered a supporter of the Emperor, and Major-General Mulugeta Bulli, Minister of National Community Development, a national hero for his role in the liberation of Ethiopia and one of the most popular men in the country.

There were other elements of confusion about the events. By some accident six other men escaped the rebels' bullets, including the universally respected Ras Imru, and the Emperor's son-in-law, Ras Andargatchew Massai, who was high on the list of those whom the rebels disliked. During the early hours of the coup Major-General Mulugeta Bulli was appointed rebel Chief of Staff of the Armed Forces without his knowledge, and Ras Imru, who never agreed to an appointment, was nominated Prime Minister. Both actions were apparently an attempt by the rebels to win badly needed popular support, for outside Addis Ababa the provinces remained loyal to the Emperor. Abroad only the chargé d'affaires in Sweden declared for the rebels. The am-

bassador to the Congo (Léopoldville), suspected of sympathizing with the rebel cause, later denied any such sentiment. All this points to poor planning on the part of the rebels, among whom there was no consistency of action. When casualty lists were compiled, it was found that 174 Body Guards, 29 soldiers, and 120 civilians had been killed, and 300 Body Guards, 43 soldiers, and 442 civilians wounded. Official sources also indicated that approximately 2,000 members of the Imperial Body Guard had been captured, of whom 1,000 were subsequently released. The government claimed that no more than twenty University College students had supported the coup, although there is evidence that as many as one hundred had.

In a press conference for foreign journalists shortly after his return to Ethiopia from Brazil, the Emperor avowed that "the force which motivated these men was clearly personal ambition and lust for power." The Emperor made a point of referring to the rebel program as "only a copy of existing programs." Since their program was the program of the Imperial Ethiopian Government, the Emperor reasoned, it was obvious that these men had acted only to improve their own personal positions. But the Emperor also recognized the difficulties of his own program; in a special editorial of the *Ethiopian Herald* on December 19, 1960, Haile Selassie I with great insight stated, "Trees that are planted do not always bear the desired fruit."

Events Since the Coup

In the aftermath of the coup, the Neway brothers fled southward. Early in January, 1961, the army cornered the two men at Mojo, some fifty miles from the capital. Girmame, who was shot in the ensuing encounter, died while resisting capture. Seriously wounded, Mengistu was taken to Addis Ababa to stand trial in a special court. Although the trial was supposedly open to the public, the spectators consisted mostly of members of the families of the victims of the coup. At the end of the trial Mengistu gave a stirring speech to the court and predicted ultimate success for the coup. The sentence of death by hanging was carried out at the end of March.

On the day of Mengistu's execution, the Emperor announced several appointments which were interpreted as the beginning of liberalization of the regime. It was thought that great changes were in the offing. In April, the army successfully demonstrated for a raise in pay, which was granted at the expense of civil servants who received an equivalent cut. Because the army, the mainstay of the regime, acted in such a disrespectful way and because younger men were appointed to the Cabinet, it was popularly believed that the Emperor might be trying to avert a second coup.

By August, 1961, however, the government had consolidated its position. Only one of the new appointments remained in office after August. At that time Aklilou Habte Wold, brother of the dead Makonnen Habte Wold and more or less an enlightened conservative, became Foreign Minister, marking a return to the earlier practice of appointing loyalist men of talent. The Emperor also took steps to lessen his dependence on the army; a territorial army, or militia, was formed to replace the older balance between army and Imperial Body Guard.

What went on during the trials of the lesser leaders of the coup is unknown. Many of them had been killed in the fighting. Ethiopia is short of educated and talented men, and the execution or imprisonment of many of the men involved in the coup would have supplied more fuel for the fires of criticism. Moreover, the Emperor has frequently demonstrated a willingness to restore to office men who have purged themselves of disloyalty. Such was the case of the regional leaders, many of whom have been more useful alive than dead, and such was the case with some of the rebels. Thus Getachew Bekele, who had been Acting Minister of Marine, was made Governor of Bahr Dar in November, 1961, barely eleven months after the coup. In February, 1963, he was placed in foreign exile as Ethiopian ambassador to Haiti. Ras Imru, who was publicly cleared by the Emperor of complicity in the coup, was appointed ambassador to India. Lastly, Lemma Frewehot, former executive secretary of the National Coffee Board, whose name appeared in the published list of conspirators in the *Ethiopian Herald* in December, 1960, has quietly been reinstated in his position.

Although the threat of a new coup has subsided, evidence of unrest among the young men of talent persists. The students, often looked to as a source of action, in the year following the coup finally organized a student union, which the government refused to recognize. In May, 1962, at Student Day ceremonies a group of students read poems containing ambiguous references to politics, and the government took steps to restrain the students, who were warned by college authorities to steer clear of politics. No Ethiopian student was allowed boarding privileges at the University College. Some students were suspended from the institution. Nevertheless, a National Union of Ethiopian Students was reconstituted and bears watching for future developments.

By the time of the African Heads of State Conference in Addis Ababa in May, 1963, the Emperor had regained full control of the situation. His achievements in the field of African diplomacy have been most useful in demonstrating the vitality of Ethiopian leadership in Africa and have effectively stunned much of the criticism of the regime. But the coup has had its impact, and the Emperor is in some respects compelled to move faster than he cares to. The Emperor now follows rather than directs the tide of modernization, it would seem. The Emperor is still respected for his power, but that power is no longer surrounded with a near-religious awe in the eyes of students, army officers, labor leaders, and young officials. The coup suggested for the first time in Ethiopian history that change was possible and has further aggravated the impatience of youth with government inactivity. Some observers claim that Ethiopian fatalism and patience and tolerance of an unpopular system may have come to an end.

One question, however, still looms large: what will happen to the Empire after the death of the man who has ruled Ethiopia since 1916? Although the Emperor has many times displayed a preference for his other sons, Asfa Wossen is the sole male heir to the throne in his generation. Moreover, the Emperor has publicly stated that the Crown Prince did not act of his own will in the coup, but that he had been forced to act as he did. Ethiopia needs a monarch to hold the diverse elements of the Empire together, but the Crown Prince has been known as an indecisive man who might be dangerous or difficult in the role of constitutional monarch. Other observers feel that the army or the air force will play a decisive part, as they have elsewhere in Africa and in Asia, the Middle East, and Latin America. At present Ethiopia is enjoying a period of political stability that might come to an end with the death of the Emperor. How the army, the air force, the young intelligentsia, the old and new aristocracies, the new labor movement, and members of the royal family will act remains to be seen. For the foreseeable future Ethiopia will remain a no-party state.

Contemporary Issues

Of the many problems facing traditional states that pursue a policy of deliberate modernization, three problems have received particular emphasis in Ethiopia: education, economic development, and the creation of a national awareness. All three may be viewed as aspects of the central problem of strengthening national unity at the expense of regionalism. Education as a means to achieving national goals has been given special recognition by the Emperor, who has always held the portfolio of Minister of Education. Ever since his early years as Regent, Haile Selassie has been deeply concerned with the development of an educational system that would serve state purposes. Similarly, the apparatus of the modern state cannot grow beyond the limits imposed upon it by the nature of the economy. Hence, the Emperor, whose wealth traditionally consisted of land and service, has had to promote a money economy in order to give Ethiopia the economic viability that must underlie political unity. Here too economic development may be regarded as still another means to further the development of Ethiopia as a nation-state, rather than as a dynastic state or a loose federation of diverse regions.

EDUCATION

Paradoxically, although Ethiopia has been the one sub-Saharan land where a literate culture has thrived for some two thousand years, today it has the lowest literacy rate in the whole continent. A recent United Nations survey of African education [20] reveals that the continent as a whole has a literacy rate of approximately 15 per cent. The highest rate, that of Madagascar, was between 30 and 35 per cent; southern and central Africa had rates above 20 per cent; that of northern Africa was slightly above the continental average; while East Africa's rate of 9 to 14 per cent was still considerably higher than that of Ethiopia, where less than 5 per cent of the population is literate. As the third most populous country in Africa, Ethiopia faces a tremendous task of educating its millions.

In the traditional society of premodern Ethiopia, education in reading and writing was the province of the religious schools. In the Muslim eastern half of the country, Koranic schools have long given a minimum education in liturgical Arabic. Few Muslims became fully literate in Arabic. Only in the city of Harar did there develop a creative literature, written in the Arabic script, but in the Adari language. No more than a few thousand Hararis can have been literate. In the Christian Amhara and Tigrean country the schools of the Ethiopian Orthodox Church were the mainstay of the literate culture. The church schools had their limitations in terms of modern pedagogy and utility, for not Amharic but ancient Ethiopic was the main language of rote study. Nevertheless since Amharic is written in an expanded form of

[20] Personal communication from Richard Jolly, United Nations Economic Commission for Africa, Addis Ababa, August 1, 1963.

the Ethiopic syllabary, the religious school also indirectly promoted secular studies.

In recent years the administrative organization of the Church has come increasingly under the control of the Imperial Government, but the resources of the Church as an educational institution have not been fully employed because of the conservative resistance of many of the clergy to reforms accompanying modernization. Many clergymen bitterly resented the early educational reforms of the 1920's as a threat to their monopoly of education. Only in the past few years have some of the church schools accepted the educational curriculum established by the Ministry of Education. The number of church schools in Ethiopia is unknown. Traditionally, every church is supposed to instruct the young in the fundamentals of the Ge'ez liturgy. Estimates of the number of students in all church schools have run from 100,000 to 600,000.[21]

Government schools are the main means of effective education today. The first modern school was established by Menelik II in Addis Ababa in 1908. Shortly before he became Emperor, Haile Selassie founded the Tafari Makonnen School in 1929, but Ethiopia's embryonic educational system did not grow rapidly. The Italian invasion was a major setback, and it was not until after the war that a serious attempt was made to improve education. Only slowly did a system of elementary education develop. By 1955, there were no more than 70,000 students enrolled. Since then in relative terms the system has greatly expanded and in 1961/62 embraced more than 180,000 students. There is much to be done, however, for even after this expansion only 4 per cent of the students of primary-school age are now enrolled in school. Since 1953, the government has increased its budgetary expenditures on education from $4.9 million to $8.2 million (1961/62). The rate of expansion of the school system has also been stepped up.[22]

In 1961/62, the Ethiopian government claimed that there were 184,890 students enrolled in 635 government schools, with a faculty of 4,642 Ethiopian and 355 foreign teachers. In addition, 185 mission schools taught 27,096 students; the missions employed 790 Ethiopians and 284 foreigners as teachers. Private schools, originally established for the children of the aristocracy and of foreigners, but now ostensibly open to all, numbered 138. The 19,570 students of the private schools were instructed by 319 Ethiopian and 426 foreign teachers. The 130

[21] Lipsky, *op. cit.*, p. 89; Imperial Ethiopian Government, *Second Five Year Development Plan*, p. 260.
[22] *Statistical Abstract, 1963*, p. 93.

church schools following the government curriculum had an enrollment of 14,705 and a faculty of 306 Ethiopians. A recent development,
the community school that is jointly financed by local private interests
and the local administration, has grown rapidly to number 143 schools,
with a staff of 408 Ethiopians teaching 17,869 students. Mission schools
are limited to those areas where they are not in competition with the
Ethiopian Orthodox Church.[23]

Whereas the number of elementary-school children has increased
annually, the percentage of primary-school students who complete
eight years of education is small. Only 5.3 per cent of primary students
have continued their education. Elsewhere in Africa the record is
slightly better or slightly worse, for the continental average of 8.6 per
cent is greatly inflated by northern Africa's enviable figure of 17.2 per
cent. In the continent as a whole, the United Nations Economic Commission for Africa reports that in 1961 5.5 per cent of those of
secondary-school age were in school; for Ethiopia the figure is 0.5 per
cent, considerably below that of any other area in Africa. But although
the last figure is small, more than 20 per cent of those completing secondary school continue their education on the university or technical
college level, and Ethiopia has been training at home and abroad more
than 1,800 advanced students annually in recent years.

Until a few years ago large numbers of Ethiopian students were sent
abroad to study. In 1961, almost one thousand Ethiopians were studying in the United States (211), Italy (143), Germany (111), the
United Arab Republic (100), Lebanon (84), the United Kingdom
(81), Israel (49), France (48), and nineteen other countries.[24]
Czechoslovakia (17) and Yugoslavia (21) at that time were the only
representatives of the Eastern bloc. The basic pattern has remained
unchanged, but since the opening of the Haile Selassie I University in
1959 the number of those studying abroad has declined slightly. At
present Ethiopia has fewer than two dozen trained physicians. Other
technicians are also in great demand. More than one thousand foreigners have been teaching in schools in Ethiopia and in 1962 comprised 16
per cent of the total number of teachers at all levels. The secondary system benefited greatly from the arrival in 1962 of some 350 Peace Corps
volunteers. In that one year the number of students in the secondary
schools was doubled. In addition to American teachers, Frenchmen,
Britons, Indians, and various Europeans have been employed by the
government and private schools.

[23] *Ibid.*, pp. 103–106.   [24] *Ibid.*, p. 109.

Besides the University College of Addis Ababa, founded only in 1950, and the Haile Selassie I University, advanced training is given at the Public Health College in Gondar, the Agricultural College at Alemaya, the Ethio-Swedish Building College in Addis Ababa, the recently opened (1963) Law School of the University, and the Theological College. Total enrollment in these institutions of higher learning in 1962/63 amounted to 978. The Second Five Year Development Plan for 1963–1967 envisages an increase to 1,560 students by the end of the planning period. It is questionable whether by 1967 Ethiopia will have trained the 160 mechanical engineers, 107 electrical engineers, 129 chemical engineers, 156 civil engineers, 470 economists, 35 veterinarians, 175 agricultural engineers, 20 mining engineers, 8 forestry engineers, 100 physicians, and 473 other graduates that the plan calls for. In the meantime, as in all Africa, there will continue to be a serious shortage of trained personnel.

Ethiopia has a long and difficult road to travel, for in 1963 less than 1 per cent of the population had completed a primary education and not more than 10,000 Ethiopians had completed their secondary or higher education. Yet the Emperor regards education not only as the means to economic development but also as one of the keys to greater political unity. In recent years, therefore, there has been a tendency to promote the teaching of Amharic in all schools as an instrument of national unity. In 1963, the government required that all schools in all areas henceforth employ Amharic, not the local vernacular, as the means of instruction at the primary level. The difficulties of multilingual education will soon become apparent in Ethiopia. Much has been demanded of its small but growing educational system.

ECONOMIC DEVELOPMENT

For the economic future of Ethiopia, the long-range prospects are good. Ethiopian agriculture has a great untapped potential. Until a complete geologic survey of the country is completed, it is impossible to ascertain the mineral potential of the country. German and American firms are hopeful about the prospects for discovering oil along the Red Sea and in the Ogaden. Large salt deposits and perhaps the richest potassium deposits in the world make the barren hinterland of Assab attractive. Consumer-goods industries like textiles, soap, beer, and canned goods are developing apace.

In contrast, however, almost all trade has been in the hands of the foreign communities. In comparison with the rest of Africa, and by the criteria of Ethiopia's own five-year plans, an enormous task lies ahead. Subsistence agriculture will not provide exportable crops until the level of technology is improved. An inadequate transportation system presents the challenge of building some of the world's most expensive highways through difficult terrain. Education takes time. The short-range prospects of the economy give rise to pessimism.

Although Ethiopian economic development compares unfavorably with that of most other African countries, Ethiopia has taken some steps in advance of them. Ethiopia was the first country on the continent to attempt to coordinate economic growth. In 1957, shortly before the Emperor made state visits to nations where experiments in planning were taking place, a First Five Year Plan was inaugurated. The Ethiopians recognize that the first plan was a failure in that it did not achieve many of its goals. Nevertheless, it marked the first attempt at a rational development of the nation's economic resources.

Foreign capital has not moved freely into Ethiopia; domestic capital has been reluctant to invest other than in land. Consequently, the government has had to take the initiative in promoting development. With the aid of Yugoslav advisors, a Second Five Year Plan (1963–1967) has been drawn up. Some Ethiopian officials have privately expressed their doubts about the assumptions made by the planners. The second plan is a document worth studying, however, for it has outlined for every phase of the economy a multitude of projects that are remarkable in their ambitions. The plan calls for a 68 per cent increase in exports and a 79 per cent increase in imports. Hopefully, the plan envisions a sevenfold increase in industrial production, a fivefold increase in mining, and a 29 per cent increase in agricultural production. The success of the plan may very well depend on the extent to which Ethiopia overcomes very serious problems of transportation, education, and financing.

Both critics and advocates of the plan recognize that Ethiopia will remain an agricultural country, and that if its economic position is to be improved, great emphasis must be placed on diversified agricultural production. The danger of coffee monoculture is obvious. But the greatest drawback to increased production, it has been claimed, is the land tenure system. In Ethiopia today land reform has been bruited about by foreign advisors, foreign visitors, Western-educated Ethiopians, and from time to time the government. Too often it is made to appear a panacea for Ethiopia's social, economic, and political problems.

The land tenure system in Ethiopia, the product of centuries of historical development, is one of the most complicated in the world. It is doubtful that any non-Ethiopian has completely mastered all the complexities of the landholding system. Some lands are the hereditary property of individuals; some belong to villages in which the individual has a right to share in the inalienable collective land. It is unknown, however, how much of the land is owned in this fashion; there has never been a complete land ownership survey. Generally, this hereditary type of ownership, individual or collective, is found in the Amhara lands of the northwest.

A second type of landholding is that which was granted by the emperor to his civil servants or military leaders before the advent of a salaried bureaucracy. This system, like that of early medieval Europe, gave the official the right to collect taxes from his benefice. Here the line between rents and taxes was blurred. In general, the official did not have the right to dispose of such land; at his death full title reverted to the emperor, who often invested this right in a member of the same family. In this manner Menelik secured the loyalty of his nobility. Similarly, after the conquest of Galla lands in the south in the last century, land was distributed to soldiers who were obligated to quarter horses or donkeys of the imperial army on such land. In certain areas local officials were given the right to collect taxes in lieu of pay from the central government. Still another form of land tenure, often given to churches and monasteries, was a permanent right to collect and use taxes on certain landed properties. Upon the death of the landlord, his heir could be confirmed in this right after payment of a fee, usually a mule. In Muslim areas, variants of Muslim and pre-Islamic customary law determined land tenure. These are but the most important types of land tenure and give an indication of the complexity of the system.

Because of the many varying types of land tenure and the complicated history of local tenure rights, there has been much property litigation in local courts. In Ethiopia, it has been said, land is wealth and an indication of status. Less than a tenth of the land is owned by small farmers. Church holdings, in some provinces 40 per cent of the land, may include one-quarter to one-third of the land of the nation, possibly an indication of continuity from thirteenth-century practices. Most of the rest of the land is the property of the imperial family, the nobility, and kinship groups. In Menelik's time whole conquered provinces became the property of individual officials. Further complicating the matter is the lack of a clear distinction between state property and that of the imperial family, a situation reminiscent of premodern Europe.

It has been argued that land reform would increase agricultural production. With present Ethiopian agricultural techniques, there is no guarantee, however, that the farmer would have adequate incentive to use increased landholdings for production purposes. Moreover, cash crop agriculture is developing on large private estates, not on small holdings. Ethiopia is relatively sparsely populated, and there is little pressure on the land, as in other parts of the world. The farmer has little political consciousness today, and it is difficult to determine what the political consequences of land reform might be. Lastly, there has been no demand for land reform from those whom it might benefit most directly. The Ethiopian peasant is politically an unknown factor.

That there is, nonetheless, a demand for land reform may be partially explained by the fact that Western-educated officials are aware of land reform schemes elsewhere in the world and, without examining the matter further, believe that it would accomplish the same results in Ethiopia as in India, the Middle East, or Latin America. More likely an explanation is the desire to appear favorable to reform in the eyes of those nations that have been sponsoring reform elsewhere in the world. To date no one has sponsored land reform as a means to increase the political awareness of the peasantry, as was the case in Mexico earlier in this century. It is quite possible that the political effects of land reform eventually may overshadow economic goals. This is reinforced by the Emperor's most recent policy statements which declare that every Ethiopian has the right to own land. It is much too soon, however, to make predictions.

NATION-BUILDING IN NORTHEAST AFRICA

It is only since 1855 that Ethiopia has been reconstituted as a state. In the past one hundred years the Ethiopian concept of the state has developed from that of a loose federation of kingdoms within a near-dynastic empire to a modern political state. The main innovating force in this process has been the monarch. In some respects Haile Selassie may seem an exception to this trend, for the constitutions of 1931 and 1955 proclaim his line to be the sole legitimate heirs to the throne, but he too may be counted among those who, like Theodore, Yohannes, and Menelik, have favored the creation of a modern state.

Under Haile Selassie I, in fact, this development has progressed farthest. In his years as Regent and Emperor he steadily undermined the power of traditional forces within Ethiopia and promoted the authority and bureaucratic apparatus of the central government. His enemies accuse the Emperor of extending the authority of the state in order to expand his own personal power, and certainly Haile Selassie enjoys more power than any previous emperor of Ethiopia. Until December, 1960, it could be pointed out that modernization was intended to increase the stability of the regime. But even if this be the case, there are other factors at work which may serve to make the imperial power–state authority argument irrelevant.

In his pronouncements and actions Haile Selassie I has demonstrated that he has been less deeply attached than most Ethiopians to the *status quo*. This is borne out by an examination of his behavior as Regent and in the early years of his reign. Since World War II he has given further evidence of a willingness to innovate. Although he came to power in 1916, at a time when the Christian Amhara had rallied against Lij Iasu, he has continually demonstrated his intention to act outside the limiting framework of a purely Christian Amhara Ethiopia.

A devout man who believes in the revitalization of the Ethiopian Orthodox Church, the Emperor does not view the Church as the binding force for national unity. The Church may have once been a rallying point, but in mid-twentieth-century Ethiopia its conservatism has operated against modernization and its particularism has been a divisive force. The abandonment of the Church as a pillar of political unity marks a major change in the operation of the state. Not only in his words, but also in his deeds has the Emperor expressed the opinion that political unity may be achieved in the midst of religious pluralism. The age-old struggle between Christianity and Islam in Ethiopia has officially come to a halt. Few Muslims hold high positions in the government today, but the door has been opened to them. In the name of national unity, the Emperor has declared that Christian or Muslim, all are Ethiopians.

In questions of regional traditions a similar policy has been enforced, but perhaps with less success. Shoan Amhara are still largely resented throughout the Empire for their favored position, but officially the government makes no mention of Gojjami, or Shoans, or Eritreans, but consciously refers to Ethiopians. Muslim Eritreans, Tigreans, and Somalis also have displayed separatist tendencies, but only the Somalis still pose a serious threat to national unity.

Although the traditional role of Amhara culture has been played down by the government, in the area of language the Amhara may always maintain their dominance. In describing the linguistic complexities of Ethiopia, some authors have been discouraged by the implications of such diversity for national unity. It is true that if one were to list the languages of the Empire he would have an appalling array of tongues. Yet the fact remains that Amharic has become the language of almost half of Ethiopia, that Amharic has been learned through trade, through the army, and through government, and that even in remote Dankalia a bit of Amharic is spoken. In other words, in recent years Amharic has made tremendous strides in developing as the language of national unity. It may be only a matter of time before Amharic displaces the other Semitic languages and many of the Cushitic languages. It is open to conjecture whether the Somalis will yield to this pressure, but the more numerous Galla, who have been most willing to accept elements of Amhara culture, have readily learned Amharic. Here one finds an interesting process taking place, for those peoples of the western plateau who have learned Amharic and have been converted to Christianity have often taken Christian Amharic names and have come to consider themselves Amhara. Thus, as the Galla and other peoples are assimilated to the Amhara, there will probably develop an Amhara people that is no longer purely Amhara. All this may facilitate the process of unification.

Under Haile Selassie I, then, a new departure in Ethiopian history has taken place. Within the boundaries of this religiously pluralistic, ethnically and linguistically diverse political entity that is called Ethiopia, the government has been deliberately pursuing a policy of creating an Ethiopian national identification, a higher loyalty than that to religion or ethnic group. Ethiopian emperors historically have sought various solutions for the problems of ruling a heterogeneous empire. The imposition of Christian Amhara culture worked in some areas but failed in dealings with the Muslims. Zara Yaqob in the fifteenth century, Menelik in the nineteenth, and Haile Selassie in the twentieth have each cultivated among the diverse ethnic elements a personal loyalty to the monarch. Yet at the same time that Haile Selassie has continued in this tradition and has enjoyed being a living myth, a modern incarnation of the traditional African divine king, he has deliberately cultivated the idea of an Ethiopian identity. In this age of growing nationalism it remains to be seen whether or not an Ethiopian nationalism can be forged out of the various elements that constitute the Empire. The new government emphasis on Ethiopians as Africans may also be interpreted as an attempt to foster the idea of an overriding unity. For Ethiopia, whose diverse elements are held together by the slender threads of history and the sinewy will of the present Emperor, the future may well depend on the success with which new bonds of unity are developed.

External Relations

Ethiopian foreign policy today rests on the foundations established by Theodore and Menelik in the nineteenth century. Theodore, intent on securing modern arms for his military forces, invited European artisans to Ethiopia for the express purpose of applying their techniques. Anticipating modern practices, he insisted that at all times foreign technicians remain subservient to the will of his government, not interfere in the affairs of the state, but provide the needed technology. His one failing was not to promote the training of Ethiopians in these skills. Menelik continued this practice and expanded Ethiopian contacts to deal with the diplomats, as well as the artisans, of European states. The skill with which Menelik balanced off the aims of Italy, France, and Great Britain is noteworthy and clearly foreshadowed the policies of contemporary nonalignment. It may very well be that the pursuit of such policies by Theodore and Menelik ensured the continued independence of Ethiopia during the period of greatest European expansion into Africa.

Haile Selassie I has continued these traditional policies and has added two policies of his own: support of supranational organizations and leadership on the African continent. To implement these policies modernization has been necessary. These policies in turn have obtained for the Emperor international recognition and, perhaps, have given him added prestige in his own country. Ethiopia's isolation from the rest of the world has ended, while modernization, state-building, and African leadership have interacted to preserve a modernizing autocracy.

RELATIONS WITH OTHER AFRICAN STATES

Historically, Ethiopia has been isolated from contact with much of Africa. When attention has not been focused on purely Ethiopian affairs, it has been turned only to its immediate neighbors or across the Red Sea. In the precolonial period Ethiopia was concerned with invasions by Muslims from the Sudan and from the east, from what is now the Somali Republic. As late as the 1880's, Sudanese dervishes raided across the border to threaten Gondar. Somali tribesmen have posed a continual threat to security in the Ogaden ever since its conquest during the reign of Menelik II.

Relations with the Sudanese Republic today are good, and there is no reason for them not to continue so. A branch of the State Bank of Ethiopia has been opened in Khartoum, and both governments have made efforts to increase trade between the two countries. There is no outstanding dispute between the two states, and there is some evidence that they have been drawn together by a common apprehension of the expanding influence of Nasser's United Arab Republic. The Ethiopians have been concerned about the extension of Egyptian influence down the Red Sea and into war-torn Yemen, a land that has always had close relations with the Horn of Africa. Moreover, it is no secret that the Egyptians have openly encouraged the Somali Republic in its territorial claims on Ethiopia's easternmost province. Ethiopian distrust of Egypt has revived some talk of fear of Muslim encirclement, and for this reason perhaps the Ethiopians have gingerly increased their contacts with Israel. Ethiopia's recent emergence as a leader in the African solidarity movement may in part be attributed to a desire to undercut the influence of Nasser in the affairs of northeast Africa.

Somali Border Dispute

Relations with the Somali Republic, in sharp contrast to those with the Sudanese Republic, have deteriorated in recent years. Somali nationalism has come into direct conflict with Ethiopian state-building policies, and perennial border skirmishes have often attained the proportions of minor battles along the 1,100-mile common border.

The Somali border dispute is the most serious diplomatic problem that faces Ethiopia today. Somali claims to the Ogaden region, if recognized, would lead to the disruption of the polyethnic empire. The government cannot afford to establish a precedent. The eastern borders of Ethiopia are a result of negotiations with Great Britain and Italy more than a half-century ago. Menelik had expanded Ethiopia's territory into the tribal lands of the Somalis after the conquest of Harar, at the same time that the Italians made their first tentative efforts in Somaliland. Ethiopian military units at one time penetrated to within less than fifty miles of the Indian Ocean. In 1897, the Italian government concluded an agreement with Menelik declaring the boundary to run parallel to the coast 180 miles inland; no relevant documents seem to have survived in the Italian archives. The border, not realistic in terms of the distribution of watering holes in the arid steppe country, was never delimited. In 1908, the matter was renegotiated on the uncertain basis of the earlier treaty and, to the satisfaction of neither party, a provisional line was agreed upon. By this date the Somali tribes had been partitioned among the French (Côte des Somalis), the British (Somaliland Protectorate and Kenya), the Italians (Somalia), and the Ethiopians (the Ogaden region).

Throughout the colonial period the border was an unhappy area of tribal raids between the various Somali groups. Somalis from the British protectorate were guaranteed winter grazing rights in Ethiopia by an 1897 agreement. During the Italian occupation, Italian Somalia and the Somali areas of Ethiopia were joined under one provincial administration. In the course of the British military occupation that followed, the Italian administrative divisions were continued by the British, much to the dislike of the Ethiopians. In fact, the Ogaden was not returned to Ethiopian administration until 1948 and the borderland Haud Reserved Area not until 1955. In the meantime Somali nationalism had grown and its leaders appealed to all Somalis to join in a struggle for the creation of a Greater Somalia that would include all lands occupied by Somalis. No final border agreement was ever reached by the European colonial governments and the Ethiopian government. When former Italian Somalia and British Somaliland became independent and amalgamated in 1960, the Ethiopians repudiated the Haud grazing agreement and the new Somali Republic inherited the border problem.

In the past fifteen years border incidents have continued and occasionally have become intensified. The Ethiopians keep a large part of their army on permanent maneuvers in the Ogaden to counter any possible threat from the Somali Republic and to maintain peace among the Somali tribes. Travel is often restricted into the Somali areas of Ethiopia and little is known about the feelings of the Ogaden Somalis. It is difficult to gather evidence of Somali nationalism in the region. Many Somali chiefs in the Ogaden apparently owe their offices and allegiance to the Ethiopian government. On the other hand, not many Somalis have been absorbed into the national life. Memories of Mohammed Grañ, the Mullah, and past victories of Islam can easily stir the Somali tribes to action. It is debatable whether this represents *Somalia irredenta* or the centrifugal forces of an Ethiopian minority group. Even if Somali nationalism has taken root in the Ogaden, the

Somali tribes on either side of the present frontier remain mutually hostile over watering and grazing rights. The age-old pattern of nomadic life has not been altered by political change.

The Ethiopians are content with the *status quo,* it would seem. From time to time, to counter Somali claims, Ethiopian official statements refer to Somalia as anciently a part of the Solomonic dominions, but there is no historical basis for such an allegation. On more than one occasion, the Emperor has proposed a federation of the Somali Republic and Ethiopia. This unlikely proposal rings hollow in the ears of Muslims who remember the fate of the Eritrean federation. More recently, there was some talk of resolving the problem through an East African Federation that would include not only Kenya, Uganda, Tanganyika, and Zanzibar, but also Ethiopia and Somalia. The Somalis, however, remain adamant in their demands for a Greater Somalia.

The Somali-Ethiopian border dispute came to a head in May, 1963, at the Addis Ababa Conference of the Heads of State of 32 African nations. The ground had been carefully planned for discussion of African unity, and the Somali President, Aden Abdulla Osman, disrupted the atmosphere of solidarity by accusing the Ethiopian government of expansionism and demanding application of the principle of self-determination to all Somalis outside the Somali Republic. The Somali leader argued that the problem was unique in Africa. The Somali case could not have been presented at a more inappropriate time, however, and Ethiopian Prime Minister Aklilou Habte Wold, in answering the "unthinkable accusation," accused the Somalis themselves of seeking territorial aggrandizement. The sentiments of the other African leaders present were clearly with the Ethiopian Prime Minister when he declared, "It is in the interest of all Africans now to respect the frontiers drawn on the maps, whether they are good or bad, by the former colonizers, and that is the interest of Somalia, too, because if we are going to move in this direction, then we, too, the Ethiopians will have claims to make." [25]

Although the Ethiopians won a great moral victory over the Somali Republic at the Addis Ababa Conference, the matter is far from a happy conclusion, and the Somalis darkly threaten that they will abandon their pastoral democracy for a military regime that will better be able to achieve the goals of Somali nationalism.

Not only did the Ethiopians receive tacit support for the mainte-

[25] *Proceedings of the Summit Conference of Independent African States* (Addis Ababa: 1963), CIAS/GEN/INF/43.

nance of their control over the Ogaden, but Kenya, whose Northern Frontier District is also coveted by the Somali Republic, has strongly condemned the Somali stand. In northeast African affairs Ethiopia and the Kenyan African Government were drawn closer together. Tribal clashes have frequently occurred along the borders between the two states, but the two parties have chosen to ignore these skirmishes in the interest of East African amity.

Pan-Africanism

Ethiopia's increased involvement in African affairs, as exemplified by its relations with its immediate neighbors, is but symptomatic of the end of Ethiopian isolation, for in the past five years Ethiopia has awakened to the necessity of acting a major role as an African country.

Ethiopia's emergence has been rapid, but it should not have been entirely unexpected. Haile Selassie has been openly admired by Jomo Kenyatta, President of Kenya, as a great figure in modern African history. Kwame Nkrumah of Ghana too mentions in his autobiography the great respect he had for the last independent nation in Africa, as Ethiopia was often called in the 1930's. Nnamdi Azikiwe, President of Nigeria, and others in their writings poured out their grief at the Italian invasion of 1935, and Ethiopia became a symbol of Africa's struggle for independence. In the postwar years Ethiopia has skillfully played on the sentiments of other Africans and maintained its prestige, despite its aloofness to the cause of African nationalism and anticolonialism. Nevertheless, until 1955, Ethiopia was isolated from African affairs and did not participate forcefully at the Bandung Conference of Asian and African states. The revolutionary aspect of much of pan-Africanism disturbed the Emperor, who held back from actively supporting the movement.

Only gradually did Ethiopian policy change. In 1958, the Ethiopian government accepted an invitation to attend the first Conference of Independent African States at Accra, capital of Ghana, and Haile Selassie began to end Ethiopia's isolation from the rest of Africa. That same year the Emperor proposed the establishment of an African Development Bank, marking one of the earliest attempts to shift the focus of African independence from the realm of revolutionary politics to realistic economic planning. By the end of that year the United Nations Economic Commission for Africa had been formed, and the awakened Ethiopian interest was rewarded by the location of the Commission's permanent headquarters in Addis Ababa. Further recognition of the emergence of Ethiopia in African affairs came in 1960 after the meeting of the Conference of Independent African States, still less than a dozen in number, was held in the Ethiopian capital. From this time too the Emperor made available a number of scholarships for African students to study at the University College. There is also evidence that the Emperor privately supports African political refugees from South Africa and colonial Africa.

After 1960, as the number of independent African states increased rapidly, the Ethiopians quietly stepped up their activities. The Ethiopian delegation to the United Nations strongly supported the condemnation of South African apartheid, the investigation of conditions in South-West Africa, the limitation of French nuclear tests in the Sahara, and the cause of the Algerian nationalists. Late in 1962, Haile Selassie finally took the initiative and invited the heads of state of all independent African countries to Addis Ababa for a conference on the subject of African unity. No African leader could refuse such an invitation. What Nasser or Nkrumah or the Casablanca or Monrovia or Brazzaville grouping could not do, Haile Selassie accomplished with little difficulty. Radio Addis Ababa prepared its audience for Ethiopia's new role by urging all Ethiopians not to refer to their African brothers with the same derogatory epithets they ordinarily applied to the Negroid populations of the southern and western borderlands of the Empire.

Much to the surprise of many observers, the Conference was a complete success. The Emperor presented his guests with a well-organized and uncontroversial agenda, and the one African state that had operated free of regional or ideological alignments achieved practical results. In May, 1963, the Emperor served as an honorary president of the conference, an Ethiopian became provisional secretary-general, and by midsummer Addis Ababa was chosen as the capital of the newly formed Organization of African Unity.

The Conference had several significant results in relation to Ethiopian affairs. Firstly, Haile Selassie effectively eclipsed the less moderate leaders of Africa and gave the pan-African movement a new and more moderate direction. Secondly, Ethiopia committed itself to Africa, thus completing the termination of its traditional isolation; contacts with Africa had come only after increased contact with the Middle East, Europe, the United States, and Asia. Thirdly, the Ethiopian government has become an important spokesman for Africa not only in the United Nations, but also in diplomatic exchanges with the United States and other countries. There is no indication that Ethiopia's role will diminish in the near future. On the contrary, the creation in Khartoum in August, 1963, of an African Development Bank, a pet project of the Emperor, and the extension of Ethiopian Air Lines service to West Africa are evidence of increasing leadership. These developments are all the more impressive when one considers the history of Ethiopia, the national detachment from African affairs, and the cultural prejudice against Negroid peoples.

Equally important is the impact of the African "Summit Conference" of May, 1963, on Ethiopia. It enabled the Emperor effectively to undercut the opposition from those modernizing elements which had criticized him for not being in the mainstream of continental developments. The new emphasis on African unity also serves to broaden the horizons of loyalty of Ethiopians, who are asked to think of themselves as Africans and Ethiopians, not as Shoans, Tigreans, Eritreans, or Amhara. Admittedly, this propaganda does not reach the peasant masses, but it does affect the educated elite and the nobility. The Emperor has acquired new prestige in the view of many who would once have condemned him, and his role as a leader of his people and of the continent, now recognized by all Africa, has enabled him to strengthen his own position in Ethiopia. Lastly, as Ethiopia becomes more involved in African matters and as other Africans come to know the country better, pressures will mount for the government to come to grips with the immense problems of education and economic development. It is a source of embarrassment to some young Ethiopians that their country, the symbol of independent Africa, is one of the most backward countries on the continent. Once again a step in the direction of modernization has led in the short run to increased stability of the imperial regime, but it has also thrown a spotlight on Ethiopia in such a way that sharper criticism of the regime may result and the rate of change may accelerate.

RELATIONS WITH NON-AFRICAN STATES

Although the Ethiopian government has recently pursued a more energetic policy in Africa, it has carefully continued its older cautious approach to relations with non-African states. Basically, the Ethiopian policy is one of furthering Ethiopian national interests, such as technical assistance and territorial integrity. The experience with the British military occupation rapidly disillusioned the Emperor about the motives of Great Britain in coming to his aid. The British at one time briefly toyed with the idea of encouraging Galla separatism, cultivated the Greater Somalia movement, treated Ethiopia as enemy occupied territory, continued to occupy the Haud and the Ogaden long after the war ended, insisted that the Emperor have British advisers, resisted Ethiopian ambitions in Eritrea, and in general caused the Ethiopians to suspect them of duplicity.

Even before the restoration of full Ethiopian sovereignty in 1945 the Emperor sought to counter British influence. In 1944, he welcomed an economic mission and lendlease aid from the United States and appointed American and Swedish technical advisers. In February, 1945, Haile Selassie had a meeting with President Roosevelt, and the beginnings of an Ethiopian-American entente were made. The Ethiopians turned to the Americans to counter British influence and from 1948 welcomed increased American aid. It was recalled that the United States had never extended recognition to the Italian conquest of Ethiopia. When the United States supported the federation of Eritrea and Ethiopia in the United Nations in 1951, the friendship deepened; Ethiopia supported the American initiative in the Korean crisis in return. In 1953, the United States began to supply Ethiopia with modern weapons and military training, and a communications base at Kagnew near Asmara expanded its installations. In 1956, the Emperor made his first visit to the United States, and seven years later returned in even greater triumph.

It would be a mistake, however, to think of Ethiopia as dependent on the United States. Ethiopian relations with the United States are closer than the Imperial Government will admit, but considerably less close than the United States would like to believe. Although the Ethiopian government has depended on the United States for technical assistance and financial aid, the Emperor does not wish to become an American satellite. To counter the excessive influence of any one state, Ethiopia has encouraged relations with a dozen small nations, many of which can supply technicians and aid. The United States probably has not a stronger friend in Africa at present than Ethiopia. But the Ethiopian government has maintained its freedom of action throughout the relationship. Symptomatic of this was the complete repayment of lend-lease aid. This independence of action became evident in 1959, when the Emperor made trips to Czechoslovakia, Yugoslavia, and the Soviet Union. When Ethiopia concluded aid agreements with those nations, some American newspapers hastily jumped to the improbable conclusion that Ethiopia had moved to the left. Moreover, the American policy of aid to the Somali Republic including some military assistance, has not been welcomed by the Emperor. Thus, although Ethiopia has many and varied ties with the United States, the Emperor has been able to follow a foreign policy of nonentanglement similar to that of Menelik.

The Emperor has further demonstrated his intention to have an independent foreign policy by strengthening Ethiopian contacts with nonaligned states like Yugoslavia, India, and the United Arab Republic. From time to time the government has attempted to improve relations with the Arab states. A first effort during the Suez crisis of 1956 did not bring the desired results, but since 1959, in a sharp break with historical tradition, state visits have been exchanged with the United Arab Republic, Saudi Arabia, and Jordan. Radio Cairo has reduced the intensity of its attacks on Ethiopia, although it still encourages the Somali Republic.

Relations with other states are conducted with the same eye to Ethiopian advantage and independence. French influence in Ethiopia, strong for the past seventy years, was weakened by the Italian invasion. The second language of the Emperor and all high officials was French, and the Djibouti-Addis Ababa railway shipped the goods which once bound France and Ethiopia in a close commercial relationship. Today French influence is minimal. In November, 1959, the Ethiopian government demanded and was accorded a half interest in the Franco-Ethiopian Railway Company. To dramatize this move the company was converted into an Ethiopian corporation; its headquarters was moved from Paris to Addis Ababa. At present it seems likely that in the event the French should pull out of their Somaliland territory, the Ethiopians would be given control of the valuable port of Djibouti, thereby further complicating Ethiopian-Somali relations, but assuring Ethiopia of possession of the most valuable outlet for her trade.

A deep suspicion of Italy has persisted in Ethiopia, even though individual Italians are well received in the country. Nevertheless, Italy has probably had the greatest cultural influence on Ethiopia, for Italians had close contacts with Ethiopia long before the time of Mussolini. Ethiopia found distasteful the presence of Italy in Somalia as Trust Territory Administrator, and strong distrust of Italy's motives in aiding the Somali Republic remains. Bad feelings were partly assuaged by the payment of a large sum as reparations in 1957. Only in 1963, however, did the Ethiopian and Italian governments begin to discuss expansion of contacts between the two states.

Soviet Russian influence in Ethiopia is minimal. The Ethiopian government has not forgotten Russia's postwar hostility, and relations between the two countries are formal. The Russians support a hospital established by the Tsarist regime and are nearing completion of a technical secondary school at Bahr Dar. If the Russians intend to increase their influence in Ethiopia, they will discover, as the Italians, French, British, and Americans have, that Ethiopia still intends to limit the influence of all other countries in the Horn of Africa. The purpose of all external relations is to strengthen the state and the regime.

RELATIONS WITH THE UNITED NATIONS

Although Ethiopia became a charter member of the United Nations Organization on July 28, 1942, the Emperor has not relied unduly on the international organization. Time and again, as at the session of the United Nations in New York in October, 1963, he has called attention to the failure of the League of Nations to act when Italy invaded Ethiopia in 1935 and warned the United Nations of the necessity to apply the principle of collective security. For this purpose in April, 1951, the Ethiopian government gave its backing to United Nations policy by dispatching troops of the Imperial Body Guard to Korea. Between 1951 and 1954, approximately 5,000 Ethiopians saw service in that strife-torn country. Again in 1960, when the United Nations faced a serious crisis in the Congo (Léopoldville), 1,800 Ethiopians were sent by the government, aboard Ethiopian Air Lines planes, to demonstrate both Ethiopian support of the United Nations action and the newly acquired modern arms and techniques of the Ethiopian army. In 1964, the Emperor also indicated a willingness to send troops to any East African state to help maintain internal stability.

For Ethiopia the United Nations has also been a means to the attainment of political goals. In this area Ethiopia achieved both a notable victory and a noteworthy setback. In November, 1949, the General Assembly appointed a Commission for Eritrea to report back with suggestions for the future of the former Italian colony, then under British administration. Late in 1950, the United Nations adopted a resolution favoring the federation of Eritrea and Ethiopia under the Ethiopian crown. By peaceful diplomacy Ethiopia took the first step; in 1962, the last step was taken when the territory was annexed, as originally desired by Ethiopia twenty years earlier. Although successful in its Eritrean policy, Ethiopia failed in a similar approach to the former Italian Somaliland. Neither federation nor Ethiopian annexation was seriously considered by the United Nations, and the Ethiopian government uneasily watched first the return of Italy to East Africa as Trust Administrator and then the creation of a hostile, independent Somali Republic.

For the most part Ethiopia's relations with the United Nations have been in the field of technical assistance. The list of projects in Ethiopia sponsored by United Nations agencies is long and impressive. Some of these projects are joint endeavors of the Ethiopian government, the United States, and the United Nations. UNESCO in 1954 made contributions to a ten-year project for controlled expansion of the Ethiopian educational system and to a training program for teachers in the new community schools. In addition to a milk distribution project in Addis Ababa, UNICEF has sponsored sanitation projects in northwestern Ethiopia and a program for leprosy control. WHO has helped set up malaria eradication projects, tuberculosis control demonstration centers, eye disease clinics, and the promising Public Health College and Training Center at Gondar. The crowning achievement was the location of the United Nations Economic Commission for Africa in Addis Ababa. But even in its dealings with the United Nations, the Ethiopian government has maintained the same cautious attitude that it exhibits toward foreign states. Africa Hall, built as the home of the ECA, has remained the property of the Ethiopian government, and United Nations officials in Ethiopia report occasional instances of harassment by lesser Ethiopian officials.

Since the Addis Ababa Conference of 1963 the likelihood has increased that Ethiopia will pursue a more active role of leadership in African affairs in the United Nations. Here too Ethiopia enjoys a political advantage, well stated by the Secretary-General in 1954, when he described the Emperor as "a symbolic landmark, a prophetic figure in the path of man's struggle to achieve international peace through international action." It is ironic that his image abroad is so different from that presented at home.

Bibliography

The bibliographical materials dealing with contemporary Ethiopia are highly limited and vary considerably in quality. A definitive up-to-date study of the country has yet to be written.

In recent years several studies of a general nature have appeared, of which George A. Lipsky, *et al., Ethiopia, Its People, Its Society, Its Culture* (New Haven: Human Relations Area File, 1962), is probably the best. This useful compendium of information on all aspects of contemporary

Ethiopia is based on a limited-circulation intelligence report for the Pentagon. Dependent as it is on secondary sources for the most part, the book adds little new knowledge to the field, nor is it entirely free of factual errors. Ernest W. Luther, *Ethiopia Today* (Stanford University Press, 1958), written by a man who spent several years in Ethiopia as a financial adviser to the government, is disappointing and strongly biased against the Ethiopians. E. Sylvia Pankhurst, *Ethiopia: A Cultural History* (Woodford Green, Essex: Lalibela House, 1955), is a staunch apologia for Ethiopia. Unfortunately, the quality of the work does not match Miss Pankhurst's enthusiasm and ardor for things Ethiopian. Much more useful is Richard K. P. Pankhurst, *An Introduction to the Economic History of Ethiopia* (London: Lalibela House, 1961); although Mr. Pankhurst does not deal with the nineteenth and twentieth centuries, much of what he says is applicable to traditional rural Ethiopia today. For a work by an expatriate West Indian, strong supporter of the imperial regime, and frequent contributor to the *Ethiopian Herald,* see David A. Talbot, *Contemporary Ethiopia* (New York: Philosophical Library, 1952). Edward Ullendorff, *The Ethiopians: An Introduction to Country and People* (London: Oxford University Press, 1960), is an excellent historiographical description of the literature on Ethiopia by a distinguished linguist. In a popular vein, David Buxton, *Travels in Ethiopia* (London: Lindsay Drummond, 1949), is an excellent introduction to little known areas of the country, while Jane and Jean Ouannou, *L'Ethiopie: Pilote de l'Afrique* (Paris: Maisonneuve et Larose, 1962), is superficial.

The best historical studies of Ethiopia are A. H. M. Jones and Elizabeth Monroe, *A History of Ethiopia* (Oxford: Clarendon Press, 1960), and David Mathew, *Ethiopia: The Study of a Polity, 1450–1935* (London: Eyre and Spottiswoode, 1946). The former is the standard history of Ethiopia, despite the shortcomings of its original publication date (1935) and the fact that the most recent scholarship was not incorporated into the book when it was reissued. The latter is a highly detailed political history of Ethiopia prior to the Italian invasion. The early origins of Ethiopia are dealt with in Sabatino Moscati, *Le Antiche Civiltà Semitiche* (Bari: Laterza, 1958), while various volumes of the Hakluyt series deal with what might be called the medieval period of Ethiopian history. Luca Dei Sabelli, *Storia di Abissinia,* 4 vols. (Livorno and Florence: Edizioni Roma, 1936–1938), is a useful study by an Italian scholar, Luca Pietromarchi, who preferred to write under a pseudonym. For the Italian invasion, G. L. Steer, *Caesar in Abyssinia* (London: Hodder and Stoughton, 1936), is a journalist's excellent account of that time of troubles. Ernest Work, *Ethiopia, A Pawn in European Diplomacy* (New York: Macmillan, 1935), was at one time the standard study of European diplomacy relating to Ethiopia.

In recent years Ethiopian authors have begun to make some contribution to an understanding of their country. Two short histories are particularly useful: Aleqa Taye, *Ya-Ityopya Hizb Tarik* (A History of the Ethiopian people, in Amharic) (Addis Ababa: Commercial Printing Press, 1963), and Tekle Sadiq Makuria, *Ya-Ityopya Tarik* (A History of Ethiopia), 2 vols. (Addis Ababa: Artistic Printing Press, 1953–1954).

The most outstanding analysis of Ethiopian politics is Margery Perham, *The Government of Ethiopia* (London: Faber and Faber, 1948). This classic is noteworthy for its completeness and is useful not only for the Ethiopia of eighteen years ago but also for contemporary insights. In Nathan Marein, *The Ethiopian Empire: Federation and Laws* (Rotterdam: Royal Netherlands Printing and Lithographing Co., 1955), the reader will find an excellent introduction to the modern legal system of Ethiopia by an expert on matters of jurisprudence. Christine Sandford, *The Lion of Judah Hath Prevailed, being the biography of His Imperial Majesty Haile Selassie I* (London: Dent, 1955), is a revised edition of *Ethiopia Under Haile Selassie* (1946). Although the book falls far short of being a definitive biography, the author, an Englishwoman long resident in Ethiopia and an admirer of the Emperor, does present some useful information. A recent biography, Leonard Mosley, *Haile Selassie: The Conquering Lion* (Englewood Cliffs, N.J.: Prentice-Hall, 1965), tends to emphasize the more sensationalistic aspects of recent Ethiopian history. Recent events are better handled in Richard Greenfield, *Ethiopia, A New Political History* (New York: Praeger, 1965).

Frederick J. Simoons, *Northwest Ethiopia, Peoples and Economy* (Madison: University of Wisconsin Press, 1960), a useful regional study of one of Ethiopia's most important provinces, would have been of greater value had it contained more historical and political materials. Simon D. Messing, "The Highland-Plateau Amhara of Ethiopia" (unpublished Ph.D. dissertation, University of Pennsylvania, 1957), one of the few studies of the Amhara ever made, is a study of the dominant group in Ethiopia and contains some information pertinent to an understanding of contemporary Ethiopian society. Far more helpful is Donald Levine, *Wax and Gold* (University of Chicago Press, 1965). J. Spencer Trimingham, *Islam in Ethiopia* (London: Oxford University Press, 1952), complements these works as a scholarly investigation of an aspect of Ethiopian life that is often considered apart from the history of Christian Ethiopia.

The following list is meant as a supplement to this introduction to the bibliography of Ethiopia.

GOVERNMENT PUBLICATIONS

1. Ethiopia

Chamber of Commerce. *Guide Book of Ethiopia.* Addis Ababa: Berhanenna Selam Printing Press, 1954.

Ministry of Commerce. *Economic Handbook*. Addis Ababa: Berhanenna Selam Printing Press, 1958.

Ministry of Commerce and Industry. *Economic Progress of Ethiopia*. Addis Ababa: East African Standard, for the Ministry, 1955.

Ministry of Finance. *Annual Import and Export Trade Statistics, 1962*. Addis Ababa: Customs Head Office Statistics Department, 1963.

Ministry of Finance. Central Statistical Office. *Statistical Abstract, 1963*. Addis Ababa: Commercial Printing Press, 1963.

Ministry of Foreign Affairs. *Proceedings of the Summit Conference of Independent African States*. Addis Ababa: Ministry of Foreign Affairs, 1963.

Ministry of Information. *The African Summit Conference*. Addis Ababa: Berhanenna Selam Printing Press, 1963.

Ministry of Pen. *Negarit Gazeta* (Official Gazette).

Planning Board. *Second Five Year Development Plan, 1963–1967*. Addis Ababa: Berhanenna Selam Printing Press, 1962.

2. Italy

Ministero degli Affari Esteri. Comitato per la Documentazione del Lavoro d'Italia in Africa. *L'Italia in Africa*. Rome: Istituto Poligrafico dello Stato, 1955–.

3. Somali Republic

Information Services of the Somali Government. *The Somali Peninsula. A New Light on Imperial Motives*. London: Staples Printers for the Somali Government, 1962.

Ministry of Information. *The Somali Republic and African Unity*. Somali Government Official Publication 20681/22962. Mogadishu: Stationery Office, 1962.

4. United Nations

United Nations. *Compendium of Social Statistics: 1963*.
———. *World Statistical Yearbook*.

UNESCO. *Report of Meeting of African Ministers of Education*, Paris, 1962.
———. *La Situation actuelle de l'éducation en Afrique*. UNESCO/EDAF/S/4.
———. *World Illiteracy at Mid-Century*.
———. *World Survey of Education*, Volume III, 1961.

BOOKS

Beckingham, C. F., and Huntingford, G. B. (trans. and ed.), *The Prester John of the Indies, A True Relation of the Lands of the Prester John, being the narrative of the Portuguese Embassy to Ethiopia in 1520* written by Father Francisco Alvares. 2 vols. Cambridge: Hakluyt Society, 1961.

——. *Some Records of Ethiopia, 1593–1646, being Extracts from the History of High Ethiopia or Abassia by Manoel de Almeida, together with Bahrey's History of the Galla.* London: Hakluyt Society, 1954.

Crawford, O. G. S. *Ethiopian Itineraries circa 1400–1524.* Cambridge: Hakluyt Society, 1958.

Doresse, Jean. *Ethiopia.* London: Elek, 1959.

Ewert, Kurt. *Aethiopien.* Bonn: Deutsche Afrika-Gesellschaft, 1959.

Howard, William E. H. *Public Administration in Ethiopia: A Study in Retrospect and Prospect.* Groningen: Wolters, 1955.

Lewis, Ian Myrrdin. *Peoples of the Horn of Africa.* London: International African Institute, 1955.

Longrigg, Stephen A. *A Short History of Eritrea.* Oxford: Clarendon Press, 1945.

Matthews, Daniel G. *A Current Bibliography on Ethiopian Affairs: A Select Bibliography from 1950–1964.* Washington: African Bibliographic Center, 1965.

Nicolas, Archbishop of Aksum. *Church's Revival: Emancipation from 1600 Years Guardianship: Free Church in Free State achieved by His Majesty Haile Selassie Ist, Emperor of Ethiopia.* Cairo: Costa Tsouma & Co., 1955.

Perruchon, Jules (trans.). *Les Chroniques de Zar'a Ya'eqob et de Ba'eda Maryam, Rois d'Éthiopie de 1434 à 1478.* Paris: Bouillon, 1893.

Rennell of Rodd, Lord. *British Military Administration of Occupied Territories in Africa during the Years 1941–1947.* London: H.M.S.O., 1948.

Sykes, Christopher. *Orde Wingate.* London: Collins, 1959.

Trevaskis, G. K. N. *Eritrea, A Colony in Transition: 1941–52.* London: Oxford University Press, 1960.

NEWSPAPERS

Addis Zemen (New Times, in Amharic)
Ethiopian Herald
Giornale dell'Eritrea
Il Mattino del Lunedì
Il Quotidiano Eritreo
Voice of Ethiopia
Ya-Ityopya Dems (Amharic edition of the *Voice of Ethiopia*)

PERIODICALS

Ethiopia Information Bulletin
Ethiopia Observer
Ethiopian Trade Journal

Éthiopie d'Aujourd'hui
Ethnological Society Bulletin (University College of Addis Ababa)
JESAME, Journal of the Ethiopian Students Association in the Middle East
Journal of African History
Journal of Ethiopian Studies
Menen
University College Journal
University College Review
Voice of Labour

VII

CONCLUSION

By GWENDOLEN M. CARTER
AND ROBERT L. HESS

THE eight states considered in this volume provide abundant material on the diverse ways in which nations of such varied sizes, backgrounds, and ethnic compositions have attempted in either their first years of independence or, in the case of Ethiopia, in what might be called its pan-African period, to pursue their three major objectives: to build or strengthen national unity, further social reconstruction, and advance rapid economic growth. These three objectives are intimately related in the minds of most African leaders, although the advantages for economic growth of supranational entities have not been overlooked. So far, however, African leaders have concentrated upon organizing both economically and politically the areas encompassed by the boundaries defined when independence was achieved. Thus they have failed to respond, even in East Africa, to the economic argument for closer union with other states, which would reduce the importance of the national unity that is the base of their own political power.

Distinction between National Unity and Nationalism

In an evaluation of the factors making for national unity in these and other African states, it is important to differentiate between national unity, involving only the continued cohesiveness under a national administration of those groups and that area enclosed within defined frontiers, and nationalism, a sentiment that reflects a dominant loyalty to a political entity. With the exception of Ethiopia, where there is a traditional form of nationalism, and of Somalia, the African states are not infused with a spirit of nationalism like that of nineteenth-century Europe, where the way to independence had often been paved by cultural nationalism. Nigerian or Ghanaian nationalism was a concept developed by a small group of leaders who, at given moments, were able to mobilize mass support behind them. There is little evidence, however, that the mass following of these leaders understood or had much feeling for concepts of nationalism.

There is good reason why the present African experience differs fundamentally from that of Europe in the previous century. The classic nineteenth-century European model of nationalism was based on qualities of nationality and hence could produce an ethnic national unity. But African leaders are not interested in creating ethnic nations, even if it were in their power to do so. In the contemporary African context are to be found both the more or less ethnological definition of groups, which accents a possibly divisive tribalism; and the more modern political ideological definition that recognizes the broadest possible group, that of Africans. African leaders tend to go beyond common national, ethnic, and racial definitions to accept as African all who acknowledge that continent as their home and who reject any notion of racial discrimination. They are empirical, however, about feasible means of holding their own people together within their own territory. The immediate goal of most African leaders, therefore, is the creation of a unified state rather than a unified nation.

At the same time, to strengthen state unity African leaders accentuate their concept of "Nigerian" or "Nigérien" or "Chadien," so that a new sense of identity may be created within the framework of what may be colonialism's most enduring legacy to Africa, existing state boundaries. While this sense of national identity is not yet readily observable within African countries, Africans abroad identify themselves in such terms. Contacts with non-Africans both within and outside Africa increasingly foster this attitude. Thus identity with a state may well be established as a by-product of external relations, as much as or even more than as a result of internal efforts.

In some countries, an external threat, such as the earlier Canadian fear of attack or absorption by the United States, aided the growth of a sense of common nationality transcending group differences. External danger, real or imagined, has also been an important stimulus to European nationalism. In Africa, fortunately, there is at present no serious danger of attack by one state against another or of invasion from abroad. This does not mean that there is no tension among states in Africa. But with the exception of the Somali Republic, no African state has deliberately developed this tension to strengthen national unity. The closest approach to exploiting an outside threat is probably to be found in accusations of neocolonialism leveled against the United States and the former colonial powers, but this appears to be sporadic and not deliberately aimed at increasing internal unity.

Cultural nationalism as another base for state unity has not been greatly in evidence in tropical Africa. The Somali Republic, where a religious revival laid the basis for a form of cultural nationalism at the end of the nineteenth century, is probably the sole instance, and is for that reason closer to the European or the Arab and Middle Eastern patterns. But although there is little cultural nationalism in the new states of Africa, appeals for African nationalism have often incorporated a cultural element in traditionalism that either recalls ancient days of glory or artistic achievements or emphasizes concepts of *négritude* and the African personality. It remains to be seen whether a new cultural syncretism is developing that relates these concepts to the empirical use of ideas and experiences from outside Africa, and, in turn, whether this effort strengthens state unity.

Effect of Internal Divisions

To evaluate against this background the chances of continued unity in the states considered in this volume, we must first analyze those forces that might seem to make for division and possible separatism and then the policies through which unity is being strengthened. The forces that are possibly divisive include intranational and supranational regionalism and religious separatism. The experience of these eight states seems to suggest that none of these factors works exclusively in the direction of division, but on the contrary sometimes act to strengthen state unity. This apparent paradox needs to be spelled out in more detail.

Intranational regionalism is clearly a problem for most African states. The counterdemands of regional loyalty and national loyalty may easily lead to an instable political situation. In Nigeria, where an uneasy balance had been achieved among three large internal regions, subregionalism continues to pose problems. The creation of a fourth, the Midwestern Region, seems to effect only a partial solution to the

problem. Moreover, if the creation of the new region becomes a precedent for future subdivisions, the danger of internal Balkanization
might further threaten national unity and political stability. The new
linguistic federalism in India—constitutional divisions based on language groups (not unlike the older, somewhat comparable Swiss and
even Belgian situations)—has tended to accentuate the sense of separate identity of the local units and thus works against national cohesion.

On the other hand, in a country as large as Nigeria, with a population of more than 50 million people, it might well be useful from the
administrative point of view to have a large number of federal divisions to decentralize decision-making, to relieve an overburdened and
correspondingly slow central administration, and to provide more local
opportunities for administrative and political experience. If the divisions do not follow ethnic lines too closely and thus intensify the
importance of ethnic groupings, the result of further subdivisions
might be the broadening of political party alignments, with national
issues cutting across regional interests. There is evidence that this latter
process is already at work in Uganda.

The Role of Tribalism

The cause of most of the regionalism within African states is ethnic,
linguistic, or cultural diversity. But diversity can also contribute indirectly to state unity. "Tribalism" in some of the states under consideration has been important as a staging ground for leadership. The
"tribal" base of key leaders like Haile Selassie and Prime Minister
Obote has been made abundantly clear. Yet the particularistic base of
these leaders and their closest associates has not oriented them solely to
their own groups. Some leaders who have risen from sectional groups
have developed theories of national unity to override internal divisions.

Ethnic, linguistic, and cultural pluralism in these eight African states
has led for the most part to the establishment of a pragmatic balance
of internal elements. Even where one group has been traditionally able
to dominate, as have the Hausa-Fulani in Northern Nigeria or the Amhara in Ethiopia, there is a growing demand that national leaders
who are derived from these major ethnic groups should subdue their
tribal affiliations and interests and associate themselves with larger and,
in this sense, more influential groupings.

In Nigeria, Ethiopia, and the four equatorial states, this pragmatic
approach reinforces a pluralism in which the bulk of the population,

still tribally oriented, remains politically unchanged. The component parts of this pluralism have been balanced to achieve a political entity, though not necessarily national unity. Therefore one might say that although the internal divisions of African states attest to the importance of tribalism, tribalism does not, despite its obvious influence, dominate African politics. Indeed, pragmatic African politics are leading to major efforts to channel Amhara, Baganda, Sara, Fang, Bakongo, Balali, Yoruba, Ibo, and Hausa-Fulani tribal nationalisms into the main stream of movements for state unity, rather than separatism.

The Role of Religion

Following the model of their tradition of secular nationalism, Western political scientists and historians have tended to regard movements for national unity in most African states as being largely secular. The studies of eight African states in this volume indicate, however, that religion should not be underestimated either as a force for unity or as a cause of division.

In many African states religious groups have joined the political opposition to the government, and religious divisions have been related to claims for particular political rights. Muslim opposition has been a continuing difficulty in Chad, Ethiopia, and Niger. The potential threat to national unity in such states is increased by the affinities of their Muslim populations for Muslims of neighboring states. Nor has Christianity succeeded as a unifying force. Among those states considered here, there are only two major Christian groups, the Amhara and the Baganda. Yet by Haile Selassie's own admission Ethiopia cannot be a Christian state; it must be a secular state. In Uganda, Protestant-Catholic rivalry long contributed to disunity among all Christian tribes.

A far more serious threat to national unity than these has been the syncretist cults, such as Bwiti, Kimbanguism, Matswa-ism and Kitawala. All these cults have reinforced factions that are not interested in the goals of the secular state and have handicapped secular leaders in their efforts to establish state unity.

Although in these cases religion has been a divisive factor, it has in others promoted unity through a leader with religious sanction. Particularly important is the cult figure, who uses or has used the syncretist cult as a springboard for his development. Men like Mba and Youlou in his heyday have been able to use their membership in syncretist cults as well as their tribal background to catapult themselves into national politics. Haile Selasse finds useful the idea of the divine right of the ruler, which is traditional among the Christians, Muslims, and pagans of Ethiopia, and has transformed traditional religious reverence into a religious aura about his person.

If there is to be any national unity, all these elements have to be reconciled; they cannot be dismissed, ignored, or overridden. To override them in Ethiopia would cause a Muslim insurrection. To ignore them in Uganda might conceivably incite a Catholic uprising. The very nature of Nigerian federalism takes into account the strongly Muslim north. In Gabon and the Congo (Brazzaville) the present political regimes face the same problems and sometimes use the same methods in dealing with cultists as the French and the Belgians did in the past. But if, as seems to be the case, reconciliation is the only alternative to repression, then this fact cannot help but strengthen what tendencies exist for politics by coalition, by consensus formation, and by manipulation. In effect, religious factionalism demands the same response as political factionalism.

The Political Process and Modernization

The continuing strength of regional and tribal factors in African politics raises the question of how deeply the modern nation- or state-building political process penetrates African society. In the case of Nigeria it extends down to the village level through the political parties; the same would appear true of the activities of dominant parties in Ghana and Guinea. Yet the sectional basis of the Nigerian political parties limits their effectiveness in promoting national unity. Even in Mali, for all the talk about mobilizing the masses, the extent to which party activity affects the local level is not clear; the same is true in Guinea. In Uganda, not only are Buganda, Toro, and Bunyoro politicized, but so also are the less highly organized traditional areas. In Toro and Bunyoro, however, politicization is a function less of traditional organization than of intertribal conflict. In Niger, the nomads are completely unpoliticized, and it is doubtful that the remote villages of the equatorial states participate at all in the political process. In Ethiopia, where there is a modernizing autocracy, the political process is confined to the Emperor and his elite, which is smaller than that of other states.

African states have modernized generally at the top of the political order, and the process of modernization has filtered or is slowly filtering down. This process and its direction may be more characteristic, however, of West Africa, and particularly of Nigeria, with its historical urban centers, and strong penchant for modern urbanization, than of East Africa, which is oriented more toward village units, from which have sprung much of what nationalist fervor they have displayed. Both areas in any case have been strongly affected by the modernization of the administrative framework of the government. In comparison with this administrative influence, that exercised since independence on behalf of political modernization through party politics, mass movements, and the like appears less significant.

Educational and economic advancement and fear of domination by other ethnic groups give impetus to the desire for political and administrative modernization. The Ibo and Yoruba of Nigeria are good examples of modernizing groups that have advanced educationally and economically. The need to meet them on even terms has given modernizing impetus to the strongly traditional Northern Region. Educational programs, aided from outside but encouraged by the Northern Region, may soon produce enough secondary-school students to outnumber the graduates of the Koranic schools. In general, however, the pressures for modernization through education still come from above. Advanced academic and technical education still remains the prerogative of a relatively small group, though most political leaders view the expansion of education as a major way to strengthen state unity and to aid material progress. Indeed, the proportion of state budgets devoted to education is far too high to permit any other interpretation.

To a greater or lesser extent, the eight African states studied in this volume must be characterized as economically underdeveloped. All have noticeable economic deficiencies. Nigeria alone appears to stand a good chance of developing an advanced economy, but even that country has very serious problems of capital formation. Most African states have drawn up economic development plans aimed to promote their material prosperity in such a way as to transcend traditional subsistence economies and to establish a more integrated national economy. The development of an infrastructure of communications and transportation is essential if the political bonds of state unity are to be underpinned with new economic ties.

The relatively large area of many African states and the lack of thoroughgoing political mobilization down to the village level—except to some degree in the formerly British territories of East Africa—emphasize the importance of rapid economic growth for political as well as for nonpolitical purposes. Yet though supranational regional economic cooperation would seem to be a more fruitful means in East

Africa to achieve economic growth, Kenya, Uganda, and thus necessarily Tanzania have prepared their five-year plans with *national* economic development primarily in mind. Thus the supranational regionalism that economics would seem to dictate is being sacrificed to the interests of the state unity of each of the three countries.

Now that the political problems of attaining independence have for the most part been overcome, African concern to build state unity and to foster nationally oriented economic development produces sensitivities that give rise to the accusations of neocolonialism that have been leveled against the former colonial powers and the United States. It must be realized that there is often a genuine fear that economic dependence on external interests in internationally organized firms will compromise the political gains of the last decade. Moreover, some African states are also concerned lest the present structure of production and trade work against the organization of political unity within their existing boundaries. As with East African federation, however, it is all too easily possible to sacrifice economic advantage on the altar of state unity.

Economic underdevelopment in Africa means prolonging a situation in which there is lack of political sophistication among all except the small elites. The almost complete absence in most African states of what might be called a general public opinion stems not only from the hesitance of some governments to promote a force they might not be able to control, but also from the common lack of independent communications media and of universal education. Both of these defects can be remedied through economic growth and educational advance, if a government is not committed to prevent the rise of an independent public opinion. The tendency toward state control of communications is strong in most African states, however, and news media are often used to control the thinking of the rank and file, and to reduce regional and other differences rather than stimulate diverse and possibly opposing trends in public opinion. At the same time, despite censorship and controlled news media, it appears that villagers learn a good deal about current events by means of transistors, the vernacular press, and word of mouth. For a more accurate view of African opinion, greater attention should be directed toward a study of the characteristics and interests of people at the village level as a balance to the present concentration on analyses of urbanized groups and elite structures.

The elites of the African states are represented by the white-collar members of the administrative hierarchy as well as by the ruling executives and their top-level assistants. Since independence a progressive Africanization of the administrative personnel has taken place in most African states. It tends to promote national unity by identifying state interest with personal commitment and harnessing the energies of what might otherwise become a disgruntled elite. At the same time, Africanization tends to run counter to supranational regional tendencies by promoting restricted recruitment programs, heavily weighted in favor of—if not limited to—nationals (or citizens) as, for example, in the Uganda and Nigerian civil services. It is quite possible also that Africanization of the administrative hierarchy can strengthen the forces of intranational regionalism, as it has through the efforts of the leaders in Nigeria's Northern Region to increase greatly the proportion in their administrative staffs of ethnic groups from that area.

As Africanization progresses, the relation between administration and political leaderships tends to change. Increasingly there is an integration of politics and administration. In many African states today there is no longer a clear distinction between the politicians and the administrators. Before independence the African politician pitted himself against the colonial administration which was regarded as the major obstacle to rapid achievement of independence. With independence, the administration has become the chief instrument of the African leaders in their efforts to organize their unevenly distributed and developed people and to press modernization and economic growth. The African one-party state is but the most distinctive example of this integrative tendency to identify as one the purposes of the party, the government, and the bureaucracy.

A second phase may be one in which the administration becomes virtually indistinguishable from the executive and/or the party, depending on which of the latter is making the political decisions. Scarcity of personnel may result in the same person doubling in administrative and party roles, as in regional offices. In Ethiopia, the imperial government attempts to monopolize all political functions and to maintain constant awareness and ultimate control of all decisions. The same centralizing and controlling role is sought by most African leaders. Initially they may find opposition from members of the civil service which, under the colonial regime, was relatively autonomous, but as the party that carried the country to independence finds itself involved in administration rather than agitation either its vigor fades or it absorbs the administration. In either case the process is one of establishing close, if not identical, objectives and patterns of action.

Nonetheless, although the political process is largely in the hands of an elite, that elite is not always of one mind. In many African states there is tension between older and new elites, between senior new elites and junior new elites, and between new elites as a whole and nonelites and/or traditional elements. The older elite that has been exposed to Western thought but still maintains a strong footing in the traditional area is an impressive group in its own right. It has included leaders like the Sardauna of Sokoto, the Kabaka, Emperor Haile Selassie, and Mba. The traditional elites which they represent have retained a high degree of political influence, especially through their use of patronage. In some cases, the persistence of nepotism has built up frustrations among new elites of detribalized men who could not have risen in traditional society but are indispensable for meeting the new administrative and economic responsibilities of the African state. This new elite was often created unintentionally by the old colonial regimes and may now be stimulated by the modernizing tendencies of the old elites.

Dissatisfaction of the new elites with their position has led to a certain amount of instability. In Ethiopia, their dissatisfaction contributed to or perhaps motivated the coup in December, 1960; the rebels and their supporters were in all cases members of the new elite. This seems also to have been the case in the attempted coup in Niger in October, 1964, when the instigators of rebellion were detribalized opposition leaders.

Without a tradition of loyal opposition, any overt challenge to the government tends to take on the aspect of treason. From the other side, those opposed to the government in power, or eager to share in its exercise of authority may see revolution as the only means of obtaining significant change of policies and/or personnel. Yet if revolution becomes the means to secure all changes, constitutional government will be at an end. Moreover, the purpose of such a revolution—i.e., to force change —may be nullified by the uncertainties produced and the possible encouragement to repetition. Continued instability in the Sudan after the anti-army coup in September, 1964, reflects this danger.

Although elements frustrated in their ambitions may challenge the prospects for stability, they are commonly committed to modernization in the name of national unity and material progress. When the tension between state unity and regionalism, the exacerbation of tensions among the elites, the rivalry of ambitious individuals and local discontent create instability as in the Sudan in the late 1950's, in the Congo

(Léopoldville) since 1960, and in Equatorial and West Africa in late 1965 and January 1966, the military may act. To some degree their intervention (if strong enough and by disciplined units, aspects not present in the Congo situation) may strengthen state unity because the army commonly strives for the same goals as the modernizing elements and the new elites. Nonetheless, in the Sudan repression of the south increased regional divisiveness, and it has yet to be proved that the stability initially established by army leaders can lead to a more cohesive regime under civilian control.

Despite external concern about future instability in African states, the prospect of further political disintegration is not great. The likely alternative to disorder like that affecting the Congo (Léopoldville) is the replacement of an existing government by modernizing elements which use force or bureaucratic techniques or attempt to operate through a charismatic leader if they can find one. The latter process tends to strengthen the inclination toward politics by coalition or absorption (as in Kenya) or by consensus formation. In any case in states that have such diverse and distinct elements as Nigeria and Uganda have, political leaders must work to obtain for government policies the approval of a broad range of interest and ethnic groups in order to foster state unity. To do so, the government or the ruling party or parties must either modify policies in order to encourage the necessary consensus or include other groups in a party or government coalition. The penalties in division and repression for not doing so can be high, as the disruptive tension in Nigeria's Western Region demonstrated.

Some African leaders have chosen to maximize the power of the chief executive in order to cope with their political problems. In Niger and in the equatorial states power is increasingly concentrated in one individual, the president, who is both head of state and head of government. In Nigeria, in contrast, the power of the Federal Prime Minister, Sir Abubakar Tafawa Balewa, was checked and balanced by the powers of regional premiers, particularly those who were also leaders of the major political formations, Premier M. I. Okpara, the leader of the United Progressive Grand Alliance, and Premier Ahmadu Bello, the Sardauna of Sokoto, the leader of the Nigerian National Alliance. In addition, influence of Dr. Nnamdi Azikiwe, the first president of the Republic, and Nigeria's earliest nationalist leader, figured in Nigeria's political equation despite the largely formal nature of his office.

Nigeria's election crisis of 1964–1965 demonstrated the necessity for cooperation between Azikiwe and Balewa. In Uganda the balance between the president, the Kabaka, who is also a regional leader, and Prime Minister Obote leans heavily toward the latter. Admittedly these situations are more complex than those in Niger and the equatorial states, but such counterpulls may lead in the long run to a more genuine stability than does total centralization of power.

External factors may also operate to strengthen the position of the accepted head of state. This has been particularly noticeable since the formation of the Organization of African Unity. The effect of personality was obvious at the Addis Ababa meetings in May, 1963, and at its subsequent sessions, and effective international roles have helped to strengthen national ones.

Traditional Base of Modernizing Elements

The importance of personal loyalty to the leader is an obvious characteristic of African political systems. Most other political systems have at one time or another also passed through this patron stage. In some respects the African system is similar to the politics of eighteenth-century England, with the element of personal loyalty reinforced by traditional loyalties. Of the strength of this combination, the Kabaka, Haile Selassie, and the Sardauna are well aware.

Although these African leaders have a traditional base of personal loyalty, their goals are often far from conservative. Mba, the Bugandan and Ethiopian monarchs, and some Nigerian leaders have espoused the nonconservative goal—in the African context—of promoting a national unity that overrides tribalism. Yet attempted coups such as those in Ethiopia, Gabon, and Niger have only reinforced the determination of existing leaders to maintain the *status quo* of the present power distribution. The means used to do so are partially traditional, partially modern. Thus African leadership must be examined in relation to its total base.

The contributors to this volume have suggested that charisma plays an important part in buttressing loyalty to leaders. This quality is, of course, more than simple personal appeal. In the case of leaders like the Kabaka, the Sardauna, and Haile Selassie it is, or was, an ascriptive charisma automatically attributed to them by tradition. But often these men have been able to add to this traditional appeal that of a modernizing charisma, such as possessed by Nkrumah. This combination contributed to the success of Boganda in the Central African Republic and of Mba among the Fang of Gabon. Such a charisma is apparently shared by men like Azikiwe, Kenyatta, and Nyerere. On the other hand, Sir Abubakar Tafawa Balewa and Prime Minister Obote, despite their high reputations and skillful leadership, do, or did, not appear to possess a charismatic appeal.

Traditional charisma makes some African leaders religio-political figures. The function of such a figure is not limited to societies where traditional tribal religion is widespread. Its values have been metamorphosed to reappear syncretistically elsewhere. Thus Fulbert Youlou gained great strength in his period of power from his connections with both traditional religion and Roman Catholicism. Even though defrocked, he insisted on wearing his vestments for political purposes. The Sardauna was not only the outstanding Hausa-Fulani leader but also a great Muslim figure.

Personal leadership may be the most effective means in this period to override regionalism within African countries and to promote national unity. Yet the Latin American experience of *personalismo* is suggestive in considering the limitations of such leadership, for the Latin American *caudillo* or *líder* who rules only through personal charisma can do little to change an underdeveloped society. What is needed for stability and growth, in African countries as in those of Latin America, is a network of personal loyalties of bureaucrats, party men, and nonbureaucratic followings that can operate for the proper political purposes. Implicit in this argument is that the leader can trust his aides, another dimension of political-administrative integration.

Yet the rivalries that contribute to instability can also arise from personal groupings around individual leaders. In some cases the party is the rallying point for a collection of factions attracted to the same leader. Basically, the pattern of personalism then reasserts itself on a lower level. Yet this factionalism, with its base in tradition, may also serve as a force to temper the policies of the leaders of the state. The presence of factionalism necessitates political manipulation at every level. The number of political parties involved in the process may thus be irrelevant. In the end the stability of an African state will depend on the ability of its leaders to conciliate their differences among themselves, whether within a single party or between parties.

In addition to the significance of the personal element, the ability of particular individuals to play one group against another is a striking aspect of contemporary African leadership. Like their tribal predecessors, African leaders are eminently expert at political juggling; they know how to deal with complex personal loyalties, regional rivalries, and the like. The comparison with traditional politics may be more apt than generally suspected.

National Unity and Regionalism

A common means to achieve national unity is through political centralization. Such an approach has necessarily been rejected in Nigeria, embraced in Ethiopia, and toyed with in other of the eight states under consideration. Excessive centralization tends to alienate regional, tribal, or particular groups and to require a stronger political party base than any of these states yet possess. Ethiopia has known another approach to centralization through the predominance of one ethnic group, the Amhara; this situation is changing, however, because the conservative Amhara provide no modernizing impulse. In the preindependence period the Baganda achieved a predominant measure of influence within Uganda but political power is now shared much more evenly throughout that country. Although the Hausa-Fulani have not yet aspired to a similar role of dominance in Nigeria, their predominance in the Northern Region and that area's numerical superiority in the Federation make it virtually impossible to exclude them from a share, possibly a decisive share, in national political power.

Still another approach to national unity, as we have seen, is federalism. The Nigerian federal constitution has had moderate success in balancing varied interests, but the prospects of the quasi-federalism of Uganda are uncertain, less because of conflict between regions than of growing integration within the state unit. The Federal Cameroun Republic holds together two units with diverse colonial backgrounds but with ethnic and cultural links. The only other examples of federal arrangements in Africa have ended in disruption, as in the cases of the ill-fated Central African Federation of the Rhodesias and Nyasaland and the Mali Federation, or in annexation, as in the case of Ethiopia's absorption of Eritrea. Despite the experience of Nigeria and the Cameroun Republic, the trend seems, therefore, toward states within which intranational regionalism lacks constitutional reinforcement.

The second, or supranational, type of regionalism in Africa points to the creation of larger federations. In recent years the push for regional unity has taken place under the aegis of pan-Africanism, although the idea antedates African independence. Regional federalism can serve several purposes. The colonial powers, notably France and Great Britain, viewed federation as a means of coping with the financial and economic problems of administering vast territories. The federations of French Equatorial Africa and French West Africa were the two most obvious efforts in this direction, and neither survived the French transition to the Fifth Republic. British and subsequent local attempts in East Africa and the federation in the Rhodesias and Nyasaland, endorsed by the British and the white settlers, have proved unsuccessful. Yet vestiges of the older policy remain very much alive in equatorial Africa. Chad, the Central African Republic, the Congo (Brazzaville), and Gabon have gone their separate ways in most matters, but they still cherish a sentimental attachment to the older larger unit, and find some association with one another very useful. Other states, like Ethiopia, view supranational regionalism as a means to a quite different end—to furthering national interests. Thus the Emperor has proposed that the Somali Republic and Ethiopia submerge their differences in an extended East African Federation. This proposal is considerably beyond the scope of the arrangement endorsed—although not carried through—by Kenyatta, Nyerere, and Obote, but it has had the desired effect of casting the once aloof Ethiopian monarch in the role of pan-African leader.

Practicality and response to obviously useful cooperative ventures are likely to be the best stimuli to formal international arrangements. A promising example is the convention signed in May, 1964, by Nigeria, Niger, Chad, and the Federal Cameroun Republic to develop the basin of Lake Chad—an area as large as Nigeria itself—as a single economic region. Another imaginative and complementary plan is to build a paved highway across the Sahara, linking Algeria via Tamanrasset to the Mali road system in the west and via Agadès to the Nigerian road system in the south. Such functional rather than political schemes of bridging division seem the most likely to succeed.

At the same time, for ideological reasons, African leaders cannot ignore appeals for pan-African unity, although they can and do interpret its implications in their own ways. Nor can pan-Africanism be ignored for its practical contribution as a counterbalance to both tribalism and internal regional divisions. Many African leaders can seek to disguise or subdue the internal divisions of their states by an appeal to the "African" feelings of their citizens. What is strange here is that pan-Africanism, which is always over the horizon, has been proposed as an antidote to internal divisions, as well as a functional solution to economic problems, but with little consideration of how this sentiment could promote the unity of any given African state.

Given the manipulative aspect of African politics and the element of personalism, the danger to national unity does not seem to come from regionalism *per se*. Intranational regional interests have been kept fairly well under control. Although the influence of pan-Africanist sentiment is such that no African leader wants to leave himself open to the charge of Balkanization, supranational regionalism is supported only insofar as it poses no threat to the existing state system. The chief threat to national unity comes from the continuing possibility of political instability.* Insofar as each African state manages to find a *modus operandi,* if not ultimate solution, for dealing with its regional and internal divisions, factionalism disguised as regionalism, rather than regionalism itself, may constitute the chief danger to national unity.

African leaders confront major problems in operating independent states. The evidence in this book points to their difficulties and the efforts they are making. Even dealing with regionalism does not in itself create national unity. The neutralization of regionalism as a divisive force is only the first step to a stable national unity.

None of these eight African states and few, if any, of the other African states, have yet been able to inculcate the sense of national patriotism that citizens of many older states possess. But the absence of a positive and even vigorous sense of national identity, as compared to mere political identity and vague nationality, is not of necessity a detriment to African stability and growth. Exclusivist nationalism in the European setting has been in the past a cause of continued conflict between countries, and such a form of nationalism might well tend to disrupt the peace that generally prevails along the borders of the new African states. In an era when internationalism and supranationalism are supposedly recognized as the goals of the member-states of the world community it may well be to the general advantage that there is so little state-wide sense of nationalism in Africa.

It is still possible, however, that nationalist sentiments may develop within one or more of the polyethnic states of tropical Africa. If it should, it remains to be seen whether that state, or states, will preserve the internal divisions of a Switzerland or a Belgium or whether this sentiment will create, as in the United States, new national identities that command a greater loyalty than that now felt toward the tribal or

* A few modifications have been made in the text of the Conclusion following the army take-over in Nigeria in January, 1966, but no essential changes.

kinship group, the linguistic or religious group, or the regional entity, and which will thereby strengthen the political unity of the state. If so, or even if current types of relationship continue, perhaps the economic returns from larger groupings may develop bonds of communication and association among contiguous African states that sufficiently bridge political divisions to stimulate economic growth and thereby combine it with national unity within existing boundaries.

INDEX

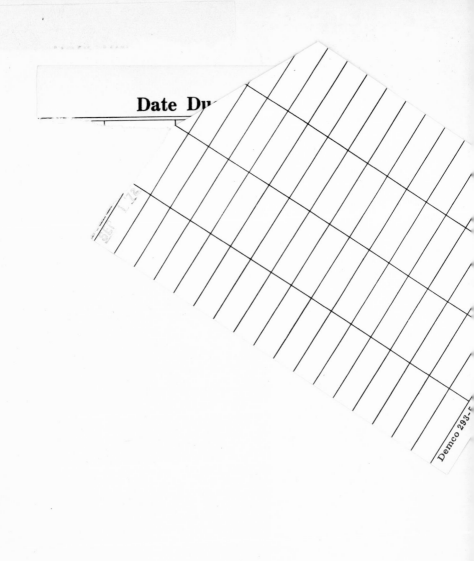

Date Due